SHIMMERING SHADOWS

Shimmering Shadows

The Music and Life of Ran Blake

by Janet McFadden

Leo McFadden
contributing editor

BlackBag Books

Copyright © 2022 Janet McFadden

First published 2022 (limited edition).
First general edition published 2025 by
BlackBag Books, Brisbane, Australia.
contact@blackbagbooks.com

Cover design by Inkahoots – inkahoots.com.au
Back cover photo by Baojun Tan
Photo restoration by Peter Cooney
Edited and typeset by Leo McFadden

We thank you for buying an authorized edition of this publication and for complying with copyright laws by not reproducing or distributing any part of it without prior written permission from the copyright holder.
Every effort has been made to contact the copyright holders of the material reproduced in this book. If any have been inadvertently overlooked, the publisher will be pleased to make acknowledgement on future editions if notified.

ISBN: 978-0-6456046-1-0

Contents

Acknowledgments	xi
The Beginnings of a Biography	xix
Author's Note	xxvii
A Note on the Conversations	xxix
Preface	xxxi
Introduction	xxxiii

I. The Early Years

1.	That Spiral Staircase Boy	39
2.	Springfield, Mass.	46
3.	Spellbound—The Power of Story	59
4.	A Little Drama	63
5.	Radio	67
6.	The Dream World	72
7.	Church—Its Heart and Soul	82
8.	Celebration—A Perspective on Joy	91
9.	A World of Wonder—The Lady of the Lake	99
10.	Suffield, Connecticut—A New Start	106
11.	Early Teachers and Strange Chords	125
12.	The Church on Russell Street	134
13.	Jazz Clubs of Hartford, Connecticut	144
14.	Records, Records, Records	150
15.	Civil Rights and Eleanor Roosevelt	157
16.	Bard College	162
17.	Jeanne Lee	176
18.	Those Summers at Lenox	183

| 19. | Atlantic Records | 190 |

II. NEW YORK

1.	Miss Amelia Lehrfeld	199
2.	New Jobs, New Friends, New York	210
3.	Sweet Daddy Grace's Church	217
4.	Jazz Clubs of New York	225
5.	Nica de Koenigswarter	231
6.	Mostly Monk	239
7.	Teachers	248
8.	George Russell	259
9.	The Apollo	268
10.	First European Tour	273
11.	Florence de Lannoy	285
12.	Ready, Willing . . . Waiting	293
13.	A Cat Called Ludwig	300
14.	1967—Athens Coup	307
15.	Aftermath	314

III. BOSTON

1.	Crossroads—The Move to Boston	335
2.	Gunther—A Personal Look	346
3.	Mentors and Father Figures	357
4.	D.C.W—Mentor, Patron, and True Friend	363
5.	Community Services	385
6.	The Third-Stream	398

IV. MAN, MUSICIAN, EDUCATOR: A DISTILLATION

| 1. | Mainly Music | 407 |
| 2. | More Music—Essence and Process | 414 |

3.	Performance	426
4.	Pluperfect Flashbacks	432
5.	A Catalog of Dreams	436
6.	Film Noir	441
7.	The Golden Art	453
8.	A Sense of Wonder	460
9.	Food and Music—"The Master of Spice"	468
10.	Brookline—The Hub	478
11.	*Spiral* Revisited	483
12.	Postscript	487

V. APPENDICES

1.	Discography	490
2.	Dorothy Wallace's Creamed Spinach	504
3.	Gardiner Hartmann's Baking Powder Biscuits	505
4.	Ten Favorite DVDs	506
5.	Ten Favorite Pieces	509
6.	Ran: The Master Weaver of Friendships	511
7.	Four Perspectives on "the Rhythms of Ran"	516

VI. ENDNOTES

1.	The Early Years	523
2.	New York —"The Happy Period"	563
3.	Boston	589
4.	Man, Musician, Educator—A Distillation	608
5.	Index	621

*Based on the conversations of Ran Blake and Leo McFadden
2007–2019*

Acknowledgments

This book would not have been possible without Leo McFadden (contributing editor, musical advisor, and typesetting). His vision and enthusiasm ensured its beginning; his drive saw it through to its end.

I also acknowledge with thanks Clare McFadden for her financial assistance and common-sense approach to procedure.

I thank my husband, Peter, for his energy, support, and readiness to consult on anything and everything. As well, I thank Teresa McFadden and Gerard McFadden, who have lived and breathed this book with us, willingly acting as sounding boards and offering encouragement, inspired suggestions, and helpful advice.

Together, we fondly remember the project supervisors Miss Polly and Dek-Tor.

Many people have contributed to this book; all have done so with a ready enthusiasm and a conviction of the worth of the project. My heartfelt thanks goes to them. While it is impossible to acknowledge everyone by name, some deserve special mention:

I thank Ran's family, whose anecdotes and childhood photos have been of enormous assistance in setting the scene for "the early years": Michael Koleda and family (especially Jen Hoenscheid and Joan Kade); Ran's sister, Marte Koleda (October 6, 1940–January 11, 2014); and Ran's cousins, Jerry Powers, Joanna Carpenter, Wende Reynolds, Susan Alima Friar, and Andy Clapp.

I thank all of my extended Australian family and friends, especially Tomas O'Malley, Frances Cooney, Chris Hartigan, Angela Scarfe, and Judith Hamilton.

I thank Ran's many friends who have come forward with such fabulous stories. From Ran's early years, I remember Gil Ahrens (June 24, 1938–June 21, 2017) and sincerely thank his son (also Gil Ahrens), Judy Grisamore, Dan Carlinsky, Ricardo Gautreau, Ernie Wilson, Wilma Srob Odell, Don Strange, Maro and Greg Avakian, Sally Ann Bolhower (great-niece of Amelia Lehrfeld), John D'Agostino, and— remembering his father—John E. D'Agostino.

I send thanks to Europe: Ricky Ford; Guy Ducornet; Catherine Ballé and family; Shaun Koenigswarter and family; and Constance, Rose, Minthia, and Hermine de Lannoy.

I thank the extended community of the New England Conservatory in Boston—faculty, staff, friends, and alumni—who have helped and encouraged us all along the way. Especially (and in no particular order) I wish to thank: Hankus Netsky, Sara Serpa, John Campopiano, David (Knife) Fabris, Anne Elvins Grace, Aaron Hartley, Gardiner Hartmann, Eileen Murphy, Alice Russell, George Schuller, Maxine Dolle, Blair Dutra, Matt Delligatti, Lukas Papenfusscline, Claire Ritter, Fred Harris, Andrew Hurlbut, Maryalice Perrin-Mohr, and remembering Jean Morrow (1944–May 15, 2022).

Leo and I wish to acknowledge the following people whose talents have contributed so much to the visual presentation of this book: Jason Grant and Jordan McGuire for their striking cover design as well as their encouragement and support; Peter Cooney for his patience and expertise in restoring and preparing the photos for printing—the images look fantastic and really enhance the telling of this story.

For Ran:
Thank you for your belief in us and commitment to this project;
for the delightful spontaneity and quirkiness of your conversations
with Leo;
for your patience;
but most of all, thank you for your friendship.

"How would you describe your music to an amateur?" I asked Ran.
He thought for a moment before he said,
I think that my music…

[*a pause*]

I would say…

[*another pause—then, decisively*]

mystery, anger, outrage, calm meditation, sleep… some people might say it makes them sleepy—that might be a put-down.
For me, personally, sometimes it's boring—I'd rather hear singers.

[*His voice lifts on a tremor of excitement before he continues in a monotone.*]

And it's very dark, and sad, and disillusioned—always thinking of the past.

[*a pause; a new start*]

How would I describe it to an amateur?

[*another pause—considering, and then the answer comes—resigned*]

A really dark solitude.

What is the use of a book without pictures and conversation?

LEWIS CARROLL, *ALICE'S ADVENTURES IN WONDERLAND*

The Beginnings of a Biography

Reflections on a Process

The idea to write a biography on Ran Blake came to me in 2006. I was then a first-year master's student at New England Conservatory (or NEC as it's widely known), majoring in what's now called Contemporary Musical Arts—a department that Gunther Schuller and Ran Blake had founded in 1972. In the years prior to my coming to NEC, the name Ran Blake had become something of legend for me, and so after applying for, and being accepted to his studio for lessons, I was excited at the chance to know him better.

I spent a year studying with Ran; I was certainly not his best student. Looking back, I can see he was giving me exactly what I needed in order to move forward, but I wasn't ready to acknowledge it at that stage. This is one of the inevitable truths about learning—we don't know what we don't know. Ran did not give up on me though, and through the fall semester, we made considerable inroads. Although it would take years for me to even begin to grasp the importance of the lessons I took from Ran, by the spring semester of 2006, I could recognize the progress I was making. Perhaps Ran, aware of this, relaxed the format of lessons to include the odd anecdote, here and there. (Up to this point, his sole preoccupation had been that I complete the tasks he set.) One day Ran told me how, back in 1961, he'd lined up a lesson for himself with Thelonious Monk. The lesson never took place due to a most dramatic turn of events; however, what did happen would bring Ran closer to the Monk family than he could have ever otherwise imagined. The event also brought the young Ran Blake more into contact with other (now legendary) figures in Monk's orbit, such as Baroness "Nica" de Koenigswater, with whom Ran would remain in correspondence until her death in 1988. I won't divulge any further details of what happened here, as you can read all about it in the book. Perhaps, though, your interest has now been piqued, as mine was during that 2006 lesson: "You've *got* to write the stories of your life down," I'd said to Ran.

"I haven't got time for that—with my classes and teaching, and then there's a recording I'm preparing for and a tour to Europe..." Ran listed the reasons why it would not be possible for him to undertake such a task before adding: "Besides, nobody cares; who's going to read it?"

"I care; I'll write it!" I replied.

"You don't even have time to do the work I set you," retorted Ran. "How are you possibly going to find the time for this also?"

For the moment, that was that; however, I wasn't going to give up so easily. In the weeks that followed, I pestered Ran about letting me write his biography until, finally, he relented.

I'd never written anything before, and, with the bravado of youth, the thought of what such an undertaking might actually entail never entered my mind. To quote Lionel Trilling, I "felt the charm of the beginning of things when intention is still innocent and uncorrupted by effort."[i] The timeframe I would require to complete my book was also the pure fancy of my imagination; though I had no clear end date in mind, "a year or two" seemed more than generous. Perhaps the only sensible idea I had pertained to method. I'd long used audio recordings to document my studio lessons. Their capacity for documentation goes far beyond a mere reproduction of the words said or music played at a given place and point in time. Unlike Walter Benjamin,[ii] I do not believe these mechanical reproductions separate us from the essence of something, present at the moment of its happening. On the contrary, I continue to be amazed at recorded media's almost "magical" capacity to transport the listener back to the moment of its making. This is especially true when the listener was present at that moment. When I listen to any of the many interviews I made with Ran for this book, I am transported back—not only to a time and a place but to the tastes, opinions, and aspirations I espoused at the time. I cringe momentarily

---

i   Lionel Trilling, "Of This Time Of That Place," in *The Experience of Literature: A Reader With Commentaries,* ed. Lionel Trilling (New York: Holt; Rinehart and Winston, 1967), 335.
ii   Walter Benjamin, *The Work of Art in the Age of Mechanical Reproduction* (London: Penguin, 2008).

at my ignorance, but it's also hard to suppress a smile on hearing a student so self-assured, blissfully unaware of the shakiness of the ground upon which he and his arguments stand. And then there's Ran. Though he will be impatient with me at times, fundamentally he is unchanging. He has seen countless students like me, and countless more will follow. To all of us, he offers the priceless acquisitions of his life's work; a life devoted to and driven by the touchstones that have accompanied him along his own life journey. It's for this reason that I doubt whether *any* student has been "ready" for what Ran Blake has to teach them. This, of course, is not the point, or perhaps it's exactly the point—you don't know what you don't know.

Our interviews fell into a regular rhythm. When it came time to graduate, I followed what has become something of a rite of passage for New England Conservatory Jazz and Contemporary Musical Arts majors—I moved to New York City. There was no question, however, of stopping the interviews; while internet video calling certainly existed then, it was not nearly as developed (or entrenched) as it is today. Moreover, the inspirational theory professor, Lyle Davidson, gave me another reason to commute to Boston—a *partimento* harmony class, begun as something of an informal offshoot of his legendary 16th-century-counterpoint classes.[iii] And so a new phase of interviews commenced. I would take the Greyhound bus from New York arriving in time to attend Lyle's class at NEC before continuing on to Ran's Brookline apartment for more interviews.

It was around this time that my mother agreed to take on the task of writing the book. At some point, I must have realized the enormity of the project; to see it through would require a collaborative effort.

---

iii   Lyle Davidson held the class each weekend for interested students, past and present. Sometimes he'd invite people—professors from other universities, interested lay-people, etc. with whom he'd crossed paths—to visit the class, too. Such was the nature of these sessions. The regular semestral cycles of the academic year had minimal impact upon his teaching—as long as there were students willing to learn, he was eager to teach them. I realise to mention Lyle Davison's class in this forward constitutes something of a parenthesis; however, doing so bears witness to the dynamic, groundbreaking learning environment that I was privileged to encounter at NEC—an environment that of course befits Ran Blake and his unique teaching methodology as well. I was saddened to learn of Lyle's passing in 2021. He will be remembered by the generations of students whose lives were touched by his transformative approach to music and to learning in general.

Working from Australia, my mother painstakingly transcribed the hundreds of hours of interviews that Ran and I had made. Like a dogged detective in one of Ran's beloved noir films, she set about establishing the relationships between each person, place, or thing mentioned. Working out these details left her with questions of her own, which she would send me to ask Ran at our following interview. She began to understand Ran's life. I myself would need the help of her initial manuscripts (still some years off at that time) to fully understand how the elements fitted together, so I breezed along during our interviews, asking the "sensible" questions that my mother had written, interspersed with my own tangential, off the cuff questions about elements of Ran's responses that particularly interested me.

I know Ran will not mind my saying that he was at times exasperated with my failing to keep up, or indeed, recognize the significance in his life of the events, places, and people he mentioned. (Some of these moments—at once humorous and poignant—are captured in the conversations.) However the blame, I believe, is not entirely mine. Anyone who knows Ran will be aware that his approach to conversation, not unlike his music, is beguilingly unconventional. Past, present, and future are often traversed in a single statement laden with intertextual meaning in which he somehow manages to weave something or someone from his life with that of his present collocutor. It's a deft sleight of conversational hand that, like Ran's playing, is of such intricate complexity it perhaps lies beyond his own conscious experience. Upon adequate reflection, connections begin to reveal themselves; however, on the surface these are sometimes so obscure that even Ran must abandon them for that moment, trailing off mid-sentence on a few seemingly unrelated words. They are *never* unrelated. My mother realized this; her insight, talent, and tenacity made the telling of this great story possible.

The Beginnings of a Biography xxiii

SOME REFLECTIONS ON THE CONTENT

During the editing process, Ran expressed a persistent desire to bring things back to the music. However, our interviews had offered him ample opportunity to talk about his music,[iv] and he had not done so. A complicated relationship between a musician and their music is nothing new. In D.A. Pennebaker's 1967 documentary *Dont Look Back*, a young Bob Dylan is backstage in a pre-concert interview with a reporter for *Time* magazine. After ascertaining that the reporter will be attending his concert for that evening, Dylan tells him:

> It's gonna happen fast, and you're not gonna get it all, and you might even hear the wrong words, you know, and then afterwards…see I won't be able to talk to you afterwards; I got nothing to say about these things I write; I mean I just write 'em; I got nothin' to say about them; I don't write them for any reason; there's no great message.[v]

Talk about music is just that: talk. It is *not* the music, but rather a commentary on it. In this way, it is a form of *analysis*. All analysis is *reductive* since no single analysis could consider all constitutive elements of a musical object.[vi] Where music analysis looks inward, music itself projects outward. While the former must necessarily define the limits of a musical object *prior* to any examination of it, the latter is free to evolve in the minds of those who encounter it. Consequently, a great deal of meaning can be packed into a very small amount of music. This is especially true of an artist of Ran Blake's caliber, and as Duncan Heining observes:

> Listening to any one of Blake's solo recordings, there are moments when it seems that a single chord echoes the music of a continent.[vii]

---

iv   This was especially true of the initial stages of the project, where our interviews followed the flow of Ran's thoughts.
v   *Dont Look Back*. Leacock-Pennebaker, Inc., 1967.
vi   My comments concerning music analysis and, more broadly, criticism are in no-way intended as a slight upon these disciplines. Indeed, my own work, a doctoral thesis (in progress) on the music of Ran Blake is concerned primarily with analysis. It is a subject about which I am passionate. My observations here reflect the limits of analysis as I have perceived them in my analytical work thus far.
vii   Duncan Heining, "The Very Singular Mr. Ran Blake," All About Jazz, January 23, 2020, https://www.allaboutjazz.com/the-very-singular-mr-ran-blake-ran-blake.

Such a chord might conceivably keep an analyst busy for the rest of their life.[viii] Analysis is the work of stratified abstraction, which, removed as it is from the act of musical creation, is often best done by those apart from the creative process. While examples of musicians providing good musical criticism of their own work exist (Schoenberg comes to mind), these are the exception rather than the norm. To return to Bob Dylan, he has long disappointed—and perhaps tantalized—those hoping to understand how he considers his music. In an interview on the occasion of the songwriter's 80th birthday, Dylan scholar Sean Latham remarked:

> Artists don't really care that much; they can't really tell you the questions [sic] you might want to know: where did that song come from? What does this line or this word mean? They made the thing; it's up to us to decide how we use it, how it lives in our lives, and how we find ourselves living within it.[ix]

The music that Ran has given the world throughout an illustrious recording career spanning more than sixty years offers us as listeners the chance to relate to Ran Blake. The man and his music are one dynamic life force, constantly in motion yet at the same time unchanging, eternal even.

If the music, then, is all that is needed, why this book? The answer, I believe, lies in the fact that music is *communal.* Social elements are strongly interwoven with many of our musical experiences—attending concerts, getting into a taxi to discover that your driver's a fellow fan of Albert Ayler or Pee Wee Russell, and, of course, introducing someone to something: "you *have* to check this out," you'll say to the neophyte. And often their first encounter with this music is more important to *you* than it is to them—at least at that moment—because musical experience is transformative. It can reach beyond the present moment... into the future, but also the past! In introducing others to something that we love, we revisit the time, place, people, and atmosphere that accompanied that music, or perhaps, rather, that that music accompanied. The point of view we take is irrelevant in the end; what we are actually doing is connecting with a reality that is greater than

---

viii   Such a statement is not without precedent when one considers the amount of critical commentary written about Wagner's famous "Tristan" chord.
ix   Latham and Pollard, Bob Dylan turns 80.

ourselves, one which manifests itself to us as music. For an ephemeral and perfect moment, the music becomes a part of us and we a part of it.

Such an experience is beautifully portrayed in Luke 24: 31-32. Initially, when Jesus joins the disciples on the road to Emmaus, they do not recognize him. When they finally realize, the moment has already passed:

> And their eyes were opened and they recognized him; but he had vanished from their sight.[x]

Although the experience itself may be fleeting, it is nonetheless transformative. And, like the disciples, those who live the experience with us are vital access points to something that exists most fully in a communal consciousness:

> Then they said to each other, "Did not our hearts burn within us as he talked to us on the road and explained the scriptures to us?"[xi]

Ran Blake's music extends beyond Ran himself. The present biography provides an opportunity to get more acquainted with the people, places, sounds, films, and flavors that have accompanied Ran on his life's journey. Above all, though, it *is* a book about his music. For if someone asked me to summarize Ran's music in a sentence, with the benefit of having worked on this book, I would describe it as a rich sonic tapestry that is at once abstract and warmly familiar.

My heartfelt thanks go to my mother, Janet, for seeing this project through so consummately, and to Ran, for giving us all the privilege to know him and his music better through the pages of this book.

Leo McFadden, Paris, September 2022

---

[x] Lk 24: 31 JB
[xi] Lk 24: 32

Author's Note

This biography draws heavily upon extensive interviews and conversations between Ran Blake (pianist, composer, educator) and his one-time student, Leo McFadden. They took place, initially at Ran's Brookline apartment during 2007 and 2008, and, later, online. These conversations are the backbone of this book. They give an insight into Ran that would not be possible with a strictly third-person approach.

Writing this book has taken me on an incredible journey—every moment has been a new discovery. The best part has been getting to know Ran. Initially, I had to listen to the taped conversations over and over and over again—struggling with the accent, the speed of delivery (much faster than "the Australian" I was used to), the phrasing, the mercurial flow of ideas, the unfinished sentences, the beguiling lift of humor, wonder, and excitement. And my repeated listening enabled me to discover threads of meaning that were not immediately obvious. I didn't realize it then, but I had stumbled upon one of the central ideas in Ran's approach to teaching music (outlined in his book *Primacy of the Ear*), the importance of repeated listening to gain familiarity with a style or piece. As I became familiar with Ran's speech patterns, I began to know him through his voice. I don't remember when I moved from familiarity with the form of these interviews to a more detailed understanding of their construction, where I knew how pieces fitted together, where I understood that, with Ran, there simply are NOT any abandoned themes or incomplete thoughts.

Recurring themes, dreams, and memories have colored the factual foundation. Ran's music is very much a part of him. And his life, with all its experiences, is very much a part of his music. It has been my challenge to set the focus and highlight those features that would give a general audience some insight into this interconnectedness.

Janet McFadden, Brisbane, September 2022

A Note on the Conversations

The indented quotations in this book are taken verbatim from the interviews done with Ran. Occasionally, for clarity, words or phrases that Ran has left unsaid are "guessed at" and included in brackets.

Ellipses are used liberally throughout. They indicate, primarily, a trailing off—an unfinished sentence or a pause or a break in the train of thought. To distinguish these ellipses from those that, following convention, indicate text omitted from a citation, the latter type are placed in brackets.

The use of italics indicates stressed words or phrases. However, when the emphasis has been so strong as to be called a "cry" or a "shout," I have opted for capitals.

Any phrases in quote marks embedded in the text without reference belong to Ran—given in the context of interviews for this book.

All other quoted text (including that from interviews with Ran conducted by other people) has been referenced accordingly, with the exception of those citations that have been sourced from a few documents in Ran Blake's personal archive. Although these documents often lack adequate referencing information, they were obviously considered important enough by Ran to be filed away (and then packed into a large mailing box and sent to Australia to assist me in my research for this book). In such cases, all available information has been given, though this often constitutes little more than a month of a given year, added as an afterthought to the top of an untitled document.

Preface

It is quite true what philosophy says: that life must be understood backwards. But then, one forgets the other principle: that it must be lived forwards. Which principle, the more one thinks it through, ends exactly with the thought that temporal life can never properly be understood precisely because I can at no instant find complete rest in which to adopt a position: backwards.

Soren Kierkegaard, Journals IV A 164 (1843)

Ran Blake will readily volunteer the "eight or ten" pivotal events of his life. (He has them written down "somewhere.") And though the sequence may vary with each re-telling, the essential chapters are *Spiral Staircase*,[i] the Gospel Churches, meeting Sr. Tee at Sweet Daddy Grace's[ii] church on 124th[iii] and St. Nick, the first day at (Lenox) school with Ornette Coleman, meeting Jeanne Lee in Bard Hall, working for Atlantic Records

---

[i] In this book, the film "The Spiral Staircase" is generally referred to in a "familiar" way as "Spiral Staircase" or "Spiral." Such contractions were privileged by Ran in the many interviews he gave for this book. In employing these shortened versions myself, I hope to convey something of Ran's relationship to the work. For him, it is more than a film—almost like a friend or a character in itself.

[ii] "United House of Prayer for All People." The church's founding bishop, Marcelino Manuel da Graça (Sweet Daddy Grace), died in 1960—just prior to Ran's moving to New York. Nevertheless, Ran always refers to the church as "Sweet Daddy Grace's."

[iii] Ran's shortening of street names throughout refers to the streets of New York.

with the Ertegun brothers, first appearance at the Apollo Theatre on 125th, first night in Paris in 1963, Greece in 1967, meeting Gunther…

Then, there is meeting Chris Connor, Thelonious Monk, and Belkis ("the Ertegun cousin") on 57th Street. But with these, Ran confesses, he is improvising—they are not on the written list—and he muses, "Perhaps there should be a secondary one."

Whatever the sequence of the list, with each re-telling, *Spiral Staircase* is always there. It wound itself persistently around the axes of my questions, insinuating itself into each fresh approach.

"What was your most exciting childhood memory?" I'd asked. The reply was prompt, "*The Spiral Staircase*—there was nothing like it in the world."

In the course of researching this book, I asked Ran the following question, based on Kierkegaard's famous quote: "Is there a vantage place in your life—a point from which you can look back on your childhood, but also look forward to what has happened since, and say, 'Ah yes, it all makes sense now—that moment was the catalyst?'"

Ran was captivated: "But this is such a wonderful question! I think that it's going to be a great assignment for me. So, have I learned anything from my four trips to Greece? Have I learned anything about Gunther's nurture and care for me? Do I put that [which I've learned] to my students?" He breaks off and adds philosophically, "and some don't want it… What are the pivotal points? I certainly look back at my life and look at things that don't make sense. I see childhood, walking through the cemetery—that became the precursor for *Spiral Staircase*, film noir…"

There it is again, *Spiral Staircase*. Ran is a man whose touchstones haven't changed over time. Seeing *Spiral Staircase* was a life-changing event for him at the age of eleven. It remains a significant event for the man in his eighties. At age eighty-seven in 2022, Ran Blake sees his life from a unique perspective in which these touchstones are the structure upon which his ideas, insights, and creative interpretations crystalize. And at the bottom of that structure is the leveler—the foundation which gave Ran the courage to express himself, free from the dark shadowland that can often haunt and immobilize a sensitive child. *Spiral Staircase* and the whole film noir genre were the outlet Ran needed. Through them, he was able to accept and accommodate the flawed nature of being human and at the same time celebrate a great creative talent.

Introduction

A Lifetime of Achievement

I desire no future that will break the ties of the past.

George Eliot, *The Mill on the Floss* (1860)

In late October 2012, friends of Ran Blake gathered at New England Conservatory, Boston, for the presentation of his Lifetime Achievement Award. They were celebrating a life devoted to music, education, and friendship. They were also recognizing forty years at the Conservatory where, in 1972, he had co-founded the Department of Third-Stream Studies [i] (Later known as Contemporary Improvisation and now as Contemporary Musical Arts).

The year 2012 also marked, for Ran, fifty years as a professional recording artist—an outstanding achievement in itself. Fifty years prior, he and Jeanne Lee had released their groundbreaking album *The Newest Sound Around* (RCA Victor), which had taken out the 1979 "Prix Billie

---

i   Also known as the "Third-Stream Department." In creating the core syllabus for the department, Blake and his colleagues developed a unique pedagogy that sought to identify the student's key musical influences and then combine these into an organic synthesis in their own music. This synthesis represented the first step towards the development of the student's unique musical style.

Holiday" of l'Académie du jazz (France).[ii] At the time of receiving the Lifetime Achievement Award,[iii] Ran Blake had recorded around fifty albums on some of the world's best labels; he was still fully engaged in teaching, recording, touring, and writing.

THOUGH PRIMARILY CELEBRATING past accomplishments, a lifetime achievement award also carries connotations of closure or, at least, of a slowing down. Introducing the awards event at Williams Hall, Steve Schwartz (the longtime WGBH radio jazz host) indicated that discussion would indeed cover some of Ran's *past* accomplishments, before adding, "and some of the things that he still wants to accomplish, if I know Ran." A ripple of appreciative laughter greeted his words. The audience knew that time—lifespans—were irrelevant. In Ran's case, there would be no slowing down; there was still much to explore, much to arouse his curiosity, and thus much to achieve.

Several of the speakers at the Awards ceremony spoke of Ran's curiosity. It is something that he himself admits has sustained him over forty years of teaching:

> I think really my curiosity in seeing people grow and seeing people gain some of the craft and confidence—I think that's what nourishes me.

Ran sees curiosity as the number one characteristic of a good musician. Just as his teacher and mentor Gunther Schuller encouraged him to seek out his passions, he encourages students to be curious about past experiences so as to discover themselves—and the music within themselves. Curiosity has driven him—right from boyhood. Curiosity about different cultures, different ways of worship, different music, different food… and film, and

---

ii   The date of this award is often misreported as being for the year 1980. The website of the *Acadamie du jazz* lists comprehensive details relating to all awards given. This particular award was announced on December 9, 1979, and was indeed for the year 1979, as confirmed to Leo McFadden by Francis Capeau of the *Académie* in an email (February 3, 2021).

iii   In the decades preceding, there had been many awards, including fellowships from the Guggenheim Foundation, the National Endowment for the Arts, and the Massachusetts Artists Foundation—all in 1982. In 1988, he won a MacArthur Fellowship. (Sometimes called the "Genius Grant.")

books, and people! Ran savors and explores every moment. It is an approach to life that has kept him vital right into his eighties.

At the awards presentation, Dave "Knife" Fabris[iv] (friend, collaborator, and former student) spoke of Ran's "deep love and curiosity of the essence of the person he is with at the moment."

Ran loves people; above anything else, he loves introducing people. Every aspect of the meeting is cherished—integrated into the story of his life. The people he's known; the places he's seen; the music he's heard and played—this is where Ran Blake can be discovered. The story is open-ended—there are no boundaries or restrictions. Because, for Ran, there is no real distinction between the present, the past, the future, the imagined. Experiences meld into one crystalline revelation, which becomes the moment of departure for his creative process. Jeanne Lee once observed that Ran Blake could see the pattern where all the disciplines meet.[v] As Leo McFadden puts it:

> Whenever he plays music, it is more than music—it is something atmospheric to transport the listener to another dimension. Time and dimensions are flexible. He is not concerned as to whether something is physically possible—that is a dimension he can cross in his mind. His dream world allows him to meet with people from 'Hotel Heaven,' and he savors the miracle of this.[vi]

RAN BLAKE'S LIFETIME Achievement Award celebrates the multi-dimensional seamlessness of his music and his teaching. On a personal level, it is a vantage point from which to view how others see him, to think, to dream, to re-visit the past.

---

iv   Dave Fabris was given the nickname "Knife" by Ran while the former was still an NEC student. Fabris recounts how Ran had asked his class to view the film *My Name is Julia Ross* and then write a musical piece based on it. The film, according to Fabris, was "tediously melodramatic," and he found himself parodying this by playing his guitar with a knife, staring at it "longingly"—just as the actor had done in the film. As Fabris explains: "Ran was tickled by the performance and started calling me 'the Knife' exclusively (and also to distinguish me from the two other 'Daves' in the class). To this day, there are still people in his [Ran's] circle that don't know my real name."

v   Christine Sandvik, *Streaming* (USA, 1991). (Extract shown at commencement of Lifetime Achievement Award.)

vi   Leo McFadden

In the years since the award, Ran has maintained his curiosity about people, places, films, food, and music. And the award, as Steve Schwartz suggested, has not marked any slowing down of achievements on the part of Ran Blake. Since 2012, he has released at least sixteen new albums; he has performed regularly on America's east coast and undertaken several European tours. He has maintained his commitment to students and to his friends. He has made new friends. It is therefore not altogether surprising that, in 2022, ten years after receiving the Lifetime Achievement Award from NEC, Ran was honored with another prestigious accolade—The Louis Armstrong SATCHMO award, honoring "living jazz artists, who have a history of sharing their love of music through a lifetime of performance and jazz education."[vii]

There is certainly a lot to celebrate when looking back at the life of Ran Blake; the man behind the achievements is sometimes elusive.

This is his story.

[vii] "Louis Armstrong SATCHMO™ Award," Louis Armstrong Educational Foundation, accessed October 17, 2025, https://louisarmstrongfoundation.org/programs/louis-armstrong-satchmo-award/.

Part I

The Early Years

1

THAT SPIRAL STAIRCASE BOY

*Spiral Staircase changed my life when I watched
it for the first time at age eleven.*

RAN BLAKE

When the Robert Siodmak Gothic thriller[1] *The Spiral Staircase* commenced its season at the Capitol Theatre[2] in Springfield, Massachusetts, in early 1946, there was a lot of local interest. Anything coming to the Capitol[3] was of interest—it was Springfield's showcase (RKO & Warner Bros.) first release theater. It was the theater where you'd see the top tier movies with all the big stars, as well as the lower budget, RKO Radio Pictures (for which film noir had become something of a house style).

The Capitol (1362 Main Street), with its striking neo-classical facade and marble entrance, was a landmark building. It was capable of accommodating over 1700 people—the majority in its large, curved balcony. Beyond this, a beautiful proscenium arch framed the curtained screen, and to the right of the stage was a pipe organ that had played during the silent movie days.[4]

First opened in 1857 as Gilmore's Opera House, the Capitol had, over the years, assumed the comfortable familiarity of an old friend. In the dimly lit interior, where the smell of popcorn pervaded, each new audience could settle down with a collective sigh of pleasure—and anticipation.

And Siodmak's new movie *had* been eagerly anticipated in Springfield. Posters that had been on display in the theater's foyer for some weeks were compelling. They showed an apprehensive-looking Dorothy McGuire checking over her left shoulder. Something had alarmed her. Just what had this beautiful girl seen?[5] Bosley Crowther—journalist, author and film critic—writing in his regular *New York Times* column "The Screen in Review," had given the movie (which he called a "creepy melodrama" and "a shocker, plain and simple") a largely positive review. Indeed, he awarded it his "New York Times Critics' Pick." Writing on February 7, 1946 (the day after it opened at The Palace, in New York City), he observed that Siodmak had used "the rumble and cracking of thunder, the flickering candlelight, the creaking door and the gusts of wind from out of nowhere to startling advantage," and concluded that "the film is likely to scare the daylights out of most of its audiences."[6]

In addition to such tantalizing snippets, word-of-mouth recommendations from family and friends in New York City, one hundred and fifty miles away, had made *The Spiral Staircase* the talk of the town. The war was over; there was general optimism. Though money was still short, Springfield was determined to see this new movie. After all, anything with Ethel Barrymore in it was bound to be good![7]

On the first matinee screening (a Wednesday), people queued outside the theater as they waited for tickets. The crowd was good-humored, anticipating an afternoon's entertainment and diversion—as well as the "cold chills," "goose pimples," and "spasms of nervous giggling" that Crowther had promised. As they filed into the dim theater, one small boy, eleven years old, slipped in unaccompanied. No one took much notice as he found a single vacant seat towards the back of the theater and slid into it. The lights faded, the excited chatter hushed, and the small boy melted into the darkness.

Over the next eighty-odd minutes, the patrons at the Capitol Theatre sat transfixed as thunder rolled and the suspense built. They gasped in horror as the camera focused on a malevolent eye, watching from behind clothes in a closet. They held their breath as the heroine, caught in a raging storm, searched for a dropped key—they'd noted the figure of a man lurking in the shadows close-by. From the depths of the audience, someone choked on a squeal; one elderly couple fumbled and stumbled from their seats to escape into the reassuring sunlight on Main Street.

But the young boy didn't move. He was captivated by the sheer spectacle—the shapes, the shadows, the music, the candlelight. The plight of the heroine, "Helen,"[8] played by Dorothy McGuire, reached out to him and drew him into her world. Indeed, it had become so real that when Mrs. Warren (played by Ethel Barrymore) appeared on screen, he blurted out, "Grandmother?" (for her "big brown eyes" looked so much like his grandmother's that he could not be completely sure they were not). And even though he registered the few people who turned around to look at him, he remained mesmerized. He was paralyzed with fear as the killer, in pursuit of this most innocent of victims, confronted her on the spiral staircase. And the relief, when the killer was stopped in his tracks, was overwhelming. Indeed, for this young boy, the whole experience was so significant that it would prove to be the catalyst for an abiding passion for movies (particularly the film noir style)—a passion that would shape his future. That young boy was Ran Blake.

Ran "didn't want to go home that night." Trembling and overawed, he'd remained in his seat, through the late afternoon session, till the ushers came with flashlights and asked him to leave. (It was theater policy that there could be no unaccompanied children after six. Had that not been the case, he would have stayed for the next session as well.) He had wonderful dreams that night, and the very next day, he was back at the Capitol:

> I asked my grandparents for money, and on the fourth or fifth day, the manager said, 'Why don't you bring your bed here?'

Anything to do with the movie was of interest. Ran followed all the press coverage and still remembers that it was Louise Mace, a distant friend of his parents, who wrote the review in the *Springfield Union Republican*.

While not strictly film noir, *Spiral Staircase* was the first film with noir references to captivate him. He had been taken by his parents (as a birthday treat with friends) to see *Murder my Sweet* in 1944.[9] (Ran remembers this movie as "a boring crime," though admits it did have a good dream scene, which he must have ignored at the time.) He'd also seen *Shadow of a Doubt*[10] and *The Thirty-Nine Steps*[11] with his grandparents. But no other movie had affected him as *Spiral Staircase* had:

> R: The films were under control till 1946; then *Spiral* came, and I got hooked. They [my parents] had to call the theaters, 'Don't permit Ran Blake… [to enter.]'
> L: [*interrupting*] Why do you think the movie had this effect on you?
> R: [*His tone is hushed in wonder.*] I don't know to this day. *Frankenstein* didn't; *The Wolfman* didn't; *Dracula* didn't; *The Big City* and *The Public Enemy* with James Cagney didn't.[12] I saw *Murder My Sweet,* a real film noir, two years earlier. It didn't affect me.
> Every night, I played *Spiral Staircase* on the piano. People—my aunt and uncle—said, 'I used to like the way Ran played years ago, but since that *Spiral Staircase* stuff, his piano doesn't sound so good.' They felt I was making a lot of mistakes.

Ran saw *Spiral Staircase* twelve times during its first season at the Capitol Theatre in downtown Springfield. He got there by whatever means he could:

> I was taking money out of the piggy bank. I hear I stole money from my parents' drawer. I hate to say it—I borrowed five dollars from Mary Garvey's shelf.[13] I had to see it. I was missing birthday parties of relatives...

He realized he had become a bit of a curiosity with the management and staff and dreamt up schemes to get himself into the theater unnoticed. He even entertained the possibility of painting a beard on his face: "At eleven!" (He says it with a self-deprecating chuckle.) On one occasion, he was caught trying to get in through a back door:

> [...] and the manager said, 'Well, you've come in here five times to pay, [so] I'll let you go, sonny.' He held my shirt up... [*Ran demonstrates, grasping a good wad of shirt at his right shoulder.*] 'But don't tell anyone.' And he took me through a dark hallway that led to the back of the theater and said I should never tell a soul.... [*He pauses for a moment, then adds sincerely*] I think I can tell you [now]. This happened in 1947, so I've kept that secret!

Towards the end of the *Spiral Staircase* run in Springfield, Ran called the theater: "Could it play till Friday? I've got to... [see it again.]"

To this request, there was a cutting response, "Who do you think you are, you pipsqueak? We can't arrange our schedule around your life."

Ran was at a loss when *Spiral's* season finished. But the Art Theatre on the corner of Main and Bridge Streets did re-runs of movies that had been successful at the Capitol, and he began to ring the management, pestering them to show it. Nothing could dampen his enthusiasm, for the movie itself had become part of a total experience that was both daring and compelling. Looking back, Ran can conjure up the skittish thrill—the terror even—of walking home down those dark, early-evening Springfield streets when, his head filled with the sounds and images of the movie, he perceived shadows lurking at every corner and heard in each small sound something suspicious—something frightening. And so he can dismiss the horror element of the movie itself because:

> Much more scary were the routes home from *Spiral Staircase*.

After all the intervening years, the thrill is still there in the tone of his delivery. And even though he knew a back road,[14] the whole journey was an agony of wondering—wondering whether he had been spotted, whether people were following. And all the while, he needed to be planning his excuses:

> I had to remember other movies that were in town, so I'd... [have a response when] they'd say, 'Were you at a movie?'

So the family meal was an added suspense: waiting, dreading, wondering if he would be found out:

> I remember Mary[15] and the mashed potatoes coming in. I said, 'Could I be excused?' I would rather go without dinner than to have that stuff. And I was so afraid they would ask, 'Have you seen *Spiral*?'

Though people may not have been following him on that back-route home from the theater, some were certainly watching. People did find out. The school principal called Ran to the office and said, "What is this addiction you have? Do you go to this movie every day?"

Her questions were pointless, as disapproval could not touch him. He had experienced something so profound that, even now, when over seventy years have passed, his voice will rise in excitement when asked about the movie:

> I can tell you everything that happens.

The upward inflection, the excited tone, make such a re-telling superfluous. And then, unexpectedly, he adds:

> And my friend Carlton was in it. He's there to protect Helen. Do you know Carlton?

And it is possible, at once, to see things from a different perspective, to see the many layers of appeal—the mix of innocence, horror, and suspense—that this movie held for him as the young boy he was then, for Carlton was a dog.

A dog was something that an eleven-year-old could relate to—and depend on. Pet dogs (and cats) were part of everyday life. Ran had his own pets. He regarded his Siamese cats Ping and Pong as "brothers." Throughout his life, there have been a whole series of cats and dogs to love. Carlton would have had instant appeal, and Ran was keen to know more of him—to claim him as a friend. Indeed, he wanted to cement friendships with all the cast and set his heart on writing to each of them:

> R: I wrote Mrs. Warren—that's Ethel Barrymore; Blanche, the secretary; Dorothy McGuire; George Brent; Elsa Lancaster—I had to write her in England. (She was married to Charles Laughton.) Sara Allgood, who played Nurse Barker, was from Trinity Theatre in Dublin. My grandmother thought, 'Will we let Ran Blake make a trans... a long-distance call?' So my parents said I had to eat potatoes and peas. [*His hands flutter to erase the thought.*] I think I'm exaggerating; I don't know.
> But they wouldn't answer my letters. [*It's said on a rising note of incredulity.*] Of course, Carlton sent a paw print.[16]
> L: [*interrupting*] Hey Ran, how did you get the addresses?
> R: Well, it was mostly RKO. I wrote the theater again, or I went down, and the usher took me in to see the manager. She said, 'It's that *Spiral Staircase* boy again—he's been here every day.' The manager said, 'What do you want this time?' And I said, 'I want the address for RKO,' and then, it was three or four years later that I knew enough to write Dublin—this [fixation] had been going on for years.

It had indeed been going on for years. When the family moved to Suffield, *Spiral Staircase* continued to influence Ran's choices, but by then, of course, there were other distractions:

> Maybe I just saw how beautiful girls were. [And though] I didn't like to play sports, I saw people [playing them]. And I think I did a few good things on the piano.

Nevertheless, Ran saw every movie that had anyone from *Spiral Staircase* in the cast and, at intervals, would approach theater managers with the same earnest plea: "Bring back *Spiral*."

The movie had had a profound effect—igniting a life-long dedication to the noir style:

> The visual characteristics of this film haunted my day and night dreams for years. Mirrors, staircases—each one had its own personality—shadows, lighting, tracking shots, stark black and white. There were post World War II musical nuances that, if occasionally banal and as clichéd as yesterday's soap operas, were so often eerie, haunting, and unforgettable to my ears.[17]

Spiral Staircase had a huge impact on Ran when he first saw it in 1946, and he has continued to watch it on a regular basis ever since. In his film noir class at New England Conservatory, there's always a reason to include a reference to "*Spiral*."[18] Four DVD copies of the film take pride of place on the bookshelf in his Brookline apartment. (Ran explains that three of them have already "worn out" due to constant playing.) The fascination felt as an eleven-year-old boy has never really diminished.

It was not surprising that the young Ran Blake was captivated by this film style. He'd been primed for it. Film crystallized a formation in story, dramatic representation, and musical expression that had been part of his life from his earliest years. And for a clever and sensitive boy (whose priorities were different to most other boys his age), the shadowland of film noir must have been a welcome counterbalance—a means of giving expression to the ghosts that had loomed at the edges of his early experience and had flitted across the stage of his childhood games and imagined scenarios.

2

Springfield, Mass.

> *There is a great deal of unmapped country within us which would have to be taken into account in an explanation of our gusts and storms.*
>
> George Eliot, *Daniel Deronda*

To begin to understand the young Ran Blake and the intensity of his fascination with the film *Spiral Staircase*, it is necessary to return to Springfield, Massachusetts, the city of his birth. Despite widespread economic gloom, Springfield in the mid-1930s had an air of quiet confidence. Its citizens were resilient and resourceful. They'd taken on recent hardship and natural disaster with a mixture of sanguine practicality and stoic tenacity—and had survived. Their strengths, particularly those in the commercial sphere, had been secured by a combination of hard work and creative thinking. Throughout the 19th and early 20th centuries, Springfield had earned a reputation as "The City of Progress."[1] This was a city that got things done. During three hundred years of commercial trade, rock-solid assets had been accumulated. Springfield was better placed than many other cities to ride out the economic storms.

The Springfield Armory was of paramount importance to the city's industrial strength. It was the primary center for the manufacture of small arms for the U.S. military from 1794 to 1968.[2] The employment it provided was central to Springfield's prosperity and growth.

Another great source of economic stability was the railway. Springfield was 89 miles southwest of Boston, 25 miles from Hartford, Connecticut, and 134 miles from New York City. The major north-south and east-west rail links crossed through the region. It was ideally situated to be a rail center and, as such, the logical place for the production of the iron goods and rolling stock to support such a center. The railway was also a reliable outlet for manufactured goods, thus ensuring diversity of enterprise.

The Civil War brought an economic boom to Springfield, which resulted in rapid growth downtown. Four to six-story office buildings sprung up along Main Street, along with stores and theaters.[3] These buildings were buff or red brick, relieved only by the stone detailing around windows. Shoulder to shoulder, they managed to exude an air of gravitas, which fitted well with the aspirations of the burgeoning merchant/manufacturing class.

With a sound and conventional business front established, the residential sector had the freedom—and funds—to experiment. Domestic structures borrowed from the architecture of the Victorian era and included an eclectic mix of styles: Italianate, Stick style, Queen Anne style (particularly the Painted Ladies), as well as turn-of-the-century apartment blocks of Georgian and Neo-classical design.[4] They were tasteful and well maintained; due to their heterogeneous character, the city became known as the "City of Homes."[5] This was the domestic face of Springfield: a progressive and cultured city with diverse interests (notably the arts, education, and sport) and an overriding charm.

When the Civil War came to an end (April 1865), this combination of industrial know-how[6] and charm allowed Springfield to transition easily from the manufacture of arms and ammunition. It accelerated its already diverse manufacturing industries and introduced "genteel" leisure-time goods such as parlor games, photo albums, gold chains, and boxed stationery.[7] This transition brought with it new opportunities in the business sector—opportunities that were recognized by Lewis J. Powers, Ran's great grandfather.

BORN IN SPRINGFIELD in 1837, Lewis Powers[8] started his working life—aged eight years— delivering *The Springfield Weekly Sentinel*. He was later joined by his twin brother, Lucius,[9] and the two boys soon had a monopoly on sales at the railway station. Lewis's "unusual energy and activity in the prosecution of his business"[10] caught the attention of Mr. Marshall Bessey, a newsman with a bookstore under the Massasoit House Hotel,[11] near the railway depot. Before long, Mr. Bessey had offered him the position of "newsboy" on the Worcester to Pittsfield train route. Here, Lewis worked from "early morn till dewy eve" for $2.50 a week.[12] After two or three years on the trains, he took a position in the store. Here, on his own initiative, he introduced small stationery samples and made his first sale of these to a gentleman named Williams of Huntington. It was the seed of a business which would grow steadily,[13] expanding to include "blank-books, paper, envelopes, paperies," with Lewis showing the same "energy, indomitable will, and keen business foresight" he displayed as a young boy.[14]

Lewis's enthusiastic approach to life was not confined to his business dealings. He was also passionately committed to his local community and, during his twenties, served as a member of the Springfield Council on three separate occasions. Further, he was an alderman in 1874 and 1875. In 1879, he was elected mayor by a "handsome majority."[15] It was an office he held for two terms.

As well as his public life, Lewis had family commitments. On December 25, 1855, aged eighteen, Lewis had married Martha E. Bangs. Martha, also eighteen, belonged to a pioneering New England family (with leanings towards the military and the clergy) who could trace their lineage back to the *Mayflower* and the *Anne*.[16] Lewis and Martha had four sons,[17] the second youngest of whom, Philip Carson Powers, was Ran's grandfather. All the boys were involved in the management of the family business—Powers Paper Company. The eldest son, Frank, had "unusual musical talent" and, after being instructed by "capable" teachers at home, "went abroad and for three years studied under music masters in Leipsic" [sic].[18] It was only his father's ill health that brought him back—to take on the role of vice president of Powers Paper. Philip and Walter—the younger members of the family—attended Massachusetts Institute of Technology[19] before returning to work in the family company, which continued to do well under their stewardship.[20]

The Powers family could be regarded as doyens of Springfield society. At home, Lewis and Martha entertained many visiting dignitaries: colonels, generals, governors, as well as President William Taft. There were also visitors from overseas: Charles Stewart Parnell, the Irish nationalist; Hiram Powers, the sculptor (and kinsman) who was visiting from Florence, Italy; Sir Henry Irving, the English stage actor; and Charles Dickens (on his second visit to Springfield in 1868).[21] Lewis would have been an interested—and interesting—host. By all accounts, he was very well-read. He was a member of the Connecticut Valley Historical Society as well as being the only Springfield member of the American Bibliophile Society.[22] He was a very public man, and the respect and admiration that the Springfield community had for him is well documented. After his death in 1915, Edwin Hill wrote the following vignette:

> His personality, his social nature, his hospitality, his cordial greeting, would have made for him a host of friends everywhere. But it was the quality, the character, of his friendship which was so exceptional. In the midst of a very busy life there was no exertion too great to make for a friend. His great delight was to give pleasure. It might be to send a flower or a book or a line of sympathy in their sorrow or joy. His many acts of kindness will never be forgotten in the hearts and lives of those who received them. He possessed that rare combination of simple virtues and signal achievements which marks the great citizen.[23]

The words could well describe Ran Blake.

LEWIS'S SONS SEEM to have led comparatively more private lives. Frank, having had to abandon his music studies, displayed "inventive genius" in constructing new machinery for the paper plant, which would "bring about a revolution in manufacturing certain lines."[24] And it would seem that his musical ear was offended by the "clickety-clacking" of typewriters. In 1917 he took out a patent for a "silent type-writing mechanism."[25] Lewis Jr. and Walter both married. (Sadly, at least two of Lewis's children died in infancy.) Philip married Marion Burbank, and they had three daughters: Frances; Martha, known by her second name of Alison; and Josephine.[26] The marriage ended in divorce in 1913, and the girls were "motherless for twelve years"[27] until Philip married Jessie M. Arnold on January 26, 1925. According to Ran, while his grandfather was busy building up his paper company in Brightwood, Jessie "my grandmother" stayed at home and "was wonderful to her three stepdaughters—my mother and her two sisters." She provided for them a home-base where they could return, bring their own families,[28] and feel cherished.[29]

Alison Powers, Ran's mother, was "warm, loving and charming,"[30] with a great sense of fun. She loved to laugh, and chat, and entertain.[31] She was also very creative and "loved to paint small watercolors" (mainly "cute little animals") and do "lovely crewelwork."[32] As a young woman, she'd worked as a teacher in New York, as well as traveling extensively in Europe and "the East." She loved books. (Ran has emphasized that his grandfather, P.C. Powers, was *not* a "book man" though his great-grandfather, Lewis, certainly was.) This love of books was shared by Ran's father, Philip Blake.

Philip had a lively mind and artistic appreciation. As second youngest of eight siblings,[33] he was "outgoing and pleasant" with a "good sense of humor."[34] He was a young man with a quest for knowledge, a fascination with the world, and a robust spirit of adventure. After college (he was a scholar and sportsman at Williams), he'd traveled on a freighter through Latin America. He'd studied at the Sorbonne. (He loved the French language and all things French.) He'd also studied at Columbia University and become a teacher—he taught at Deerfield Academy. Born at the turn of the century, he embodied the open-minded progressivism[35] of the age as well as maintaining links to a gracious old-world Eurocentric period when a man of letters—a teacher—was revered.

Philip and Alison had much in common: the love of teaching (something they passed on to their son, Ran); a love of literature and travel. They made a striking pair, with Philip's good looks, athletic prowess, and composed manner and Alison's beauty, warmth, and vivacious charm. They were adventurous and well-educated. They came from what would have been described at the time as "good" families.[36] It was an ideal and enduring match. As Ran recalls, "They remained great friends for life."

They were married on May 19, 1934, in Manhattan and lived in New York for a period until moving to Springfield in time to welcome their first baby. Here Philip got a position teaching at the Deerfield Academy, thirty-five miles to the north, and Alison worked locally at Miss Rude's Nursery School in Longmeadow. It was a time of limited means. The Wall Street crash of October 1929 had ushered in a decade of uncertainty, high unemployment, and deflated opportunity. Initially, the Blake family shared a house near Walnut Street[37] with "two or three families." But they were keen to make their own way in the world, and so for extra money, Alison would work extra hours. This continued after Ran was born. (A lady in the neighborhood would babysit two or three children, including Ran.)

But the family would have been aware that they had back-up support, if needed, as, in contrast to the Blake's situation, the Powers' circumstances were quite comfortable:

> I know that my mother would say that her father, P.C. Powers, 'had money.' They could afford [to have] a person come once a week to cook French food, and my parents loved to be invited there.

Springfield Childhood

While yet a boy I sought for ghosts, and sped
Through many a listening chamber, cave and ruin,
And starlight wood, with fearful steps pursuing
Hopes of high talk with the departed dead.

P.B. Shelley, Hymn to Intellectual Beauty

L: Tell me about when you were born.
R: [*He is irritated by the question but obliges after a moment or two of grumbling.*] On both Easter and Adolf Hitler's birthday, in the year of Our Lord[38] 1935—on April 20th... [*He pauses to consider this collision of events before continuing easily*] and I decree, as of a year ago,[39] that my birthday is now August 20. I no longer celebrate it [in April] because everybody [*there is careless exaggeration*] does graduation concerts at that time, and I missed thirteen parties of Dorothy Wallace, the great patron, as they had to be always on that day.
L: Why August 20th?
R: Well, because 20th is easiest to remember. If you have another suggestion for the date? [*there's a flash of impatience*] Maybe I'll change it to the 25th? Why don't we? This is such an important topic of world-wide import.
[*Leo laughs easily, and Ran, equilibrium readily restored, continues.*]
R: I forget the date of Charlie Parker's birthday?
L: 29th. I was just about to say...
R: Of what month?
L: Of August. So, you know, I thought you were trying to get closer...
R: [*interrupts, shocked*] That would be a little pretentious as I'm one-tenth of his league or one-thirtieth...

Ran Blake was born in the glimmer of light between the Great Depression and the recession of 1937. America had suffered greatly, but Franklin Roosevelt's New Deal seemed to be making an impression on the number of jobless. Spirits were lifting; hopes were high. There was no better way to signify a hopeful future than a new baby, and the whole extended family shared Philip and Alison's joy.

Then, in 1936, the Connecticut River flooded and inundated the city at its south and north ends. Damage was two hundred million in 1936 dollars.[40] Much of Brightwood, where the Powers Paper factory was located, was destroyed. Undaunted, the people of Springfield set about restoring order; indeed, the clean-up operation provided much-needed employment.

Though a return to the prosperous days of the 1920s was not to be, Springfield had other advantages. The community was tight-knit—there was solidarity both in bearing present difficulties and in expectation for a better future. Personal achievement was valued. The city was big enough to stimulate and challenge but small enough to be friendly and supportive. In the period of time up to the end of World War II, Springfield, Massachusetts, had all the ingredients to inspire a young boy with an enquiring mind and huge untapped talent.

For a child growing up in Springfield, the war in Europe was a long way away. Even while the Fox Movietone newsreels told, in bracing tones, of bombings on foreign battlefields; even while the newspaper headlines shouted of "grave peril" and "threats" to freedom and democracy; even while the dreaded telegrams kept coming; and despite regular blackouts;[41] a boy in Springfield—reassured by the calm beating of his city's heart—could feel secure. The young Ran Blake had the opportunity to explore without too much restriction, to meet people beyond his own family's social set, and to spend time alone with his thoughts. Springfield was safe, without being restrictive, and there were nice people—decent people—who lived all around and shared similar values. The Blakes were friends with their neighbors: the Wallaces,[42] the Maynards, the Studleys. As Ran's sister, Martha, recalled, "We had a nice life. There was a lot of bicycle riding and climbing trees. It was a very nice place to grow up… we would go from backyard to backyard." There were few limitations on the time or the place for these wide-ranging games. Martha could not remember Ran being involved (but of course, he was five years older). Ran had his own agenda. He was always on a mission: to see *Spiral Staircase*; to catch the singing at the Hancock Street Gospel Church; to visit the Mulberry Street cemetery, where he liked to go to be alone.

Perhaps, for the Blake children, the most important thing about Springfield was that they were surrounded by family:

> When I was in Second Grade, we moved to a very, very nice house—our own house.[43] There was an attic where the au pair lived, and we each had our own rooms, and [there were] two bathrooms and a living room. I would say that it was very, very middle class. It had a little front porch with three upright pianos.

Circumstances had improved for the Blakes. Sometime in the '30s, Philip Blake had joined the family paper factory. It was a move that improved the Blake's financial situation but came at a cost to Philip:

> He was *very* unhappy. It soured him. My mother said his whole personality changed. He was terribly, terribly unhappy there—he *loved* being on the faculty at Deerfield.

Ran's cousin Jerry Powers[44] concurs:

> Ran's father, my father, and Duncan Clapp worked together running the Powers Paper Company in Springfield. My impression is that they were three nice guys who wouldn't necessarily have chosen that particular line of work if it hadn't been for the Depression. I know that my father had gotten married early in 1929, planning to become a stockbroker... I don't recall ever seeing my father, and Ran's father, and Duncan Clapp together when they weren't all wearing suits. Sometime in my teens, my family hoped I might become a lawyer, but I came to the conclusion that I didn't want to be a 'suit.' I guess on some level, Ran had already independently come to a similar conclusion. I understand that in retirement, Phil Blake took up sculpture with great passion and considerable success. I wonder if he too would have preferred being an artist if he'd had the option at a younger age...

THE BEST THING about this new house on Union Street was that Alison's parents, Philip and Jessie Powers, lived a two-minute walk away at 42 Ridgewood Place. From a very young age, Ran made the journey on his own, and the two houses formed the boundary of an extended home territory—a place where a young boy could roam with complete freedom. Often, on his way home, he would continue around the block and slip into the cemetery on Mulberry Street. There it was dark and still—the tombstones ghostly with reflected light from the streetlamp on the corner of Ridgewood Terrace. Ran would slip into the shadows near the tombstone of his "friend" Albert Bruff[45] (Ran has said, "a lot of the graves were my friends") and sit quietly—his back resting against the cold stone. This was a powerful and emotive place; a place of mystery and deep solitude; a place where dreams were dreamt:

> There I could hear all kinds of music. Some was in my imagination—hymns, mystery soundtracks—but in reality, there was the wind and night sounds… In early Fall, there was a fog, and near the entrance, I would hear a radio as I walked away.

As well as having his grandparents close-by, Ran had aunts, uncles, and cousins. Alison's sister Josephine; her husband, Duncan Clapp (Uncle Dunc); and their four children Joey, Wende, Andy, and Susie were all part of the extended family circle.[46] They always had Christmas and Thanksgiving together. There was also Lew[47] and Betty Powers and their son, Jerry, who lived "right 'round the block." The Powers had strong family ties:

> I guess I knew my mother's side of the family better. We had a very delightful person called Aunt Joe and then Aunt Frances Powers who, I guess like me, had never married. She was an alumna at Smith College and a house mother at Wellesley College. She went to school with Madame Chiang Kai-Shek, from China.[48]
> L: It sounds like your mother's family was reasonably well-off?
> R: I don't know… we had a little money in the fifties. We were not nearly as hard up as…

The sentence drifts away. For uncomplicated souls, there can be such a thing as a carefree childhood, but sensitivity does not come cheaply, and for a child like Ran, worry was a burden. He was contemplative, solitary, and did not seem to fit in. Luckily, his beloved grandmother, Jessie Powers, was close-by, able to soothe any concerns. She was very important to Ran: the heart and soul of his childhood experiences. She was, he says, "one of the most caring people alive."

The Powers home at Ridgewood Place was a sanctuary—a place where the young Ran felt valued, being exactly who he was. Jessie was the keeper of his secrets, the nurturer of his dreams. Ran recalls that his grandparents were "fantastic":

> R: My grandfather was P.C. Powers—Philip Carson Powers. He could be ornery until four-thirty or five at night, and then I was the bartender. I'm told I made a nice gin drink before I could drink them. It was implied that he might have been Catholic at one time [*thoughtful pause*], and then he pretended to be Protestant. I think he walked me to Sunday School. We'd go out, and he'd start saying, 'My foot hurts,' [so] he'd never have to go to church. He played cards, and he used bad language—the word "damn" was heard… maybe other things. There would be bridge parties; I think he liked poker and chips. He loved his rowdy men friends and would tell *racy*—my

grandmother used the word *racy*—stories that she said 'a gentlewoman like me wouldn't know.'
He said [that] I played piano like nobody...
L: He liked it?
R: Yes! or so he said. But he was a very ruthless, rough man at the paper lumber factory. He would talk about his opponents like it was a chess game. He was endearing to me and my cousins and would be very paternal to my mother. She called him Pop. I guess I called him Grandpa.
I would get an occasional hug, and he was very civil to my father.... [*There's a pause as he considers this, before adding*] I remember him saying, 'Phil, why did you let this order get away from you?' [It was] almost like 'Off with his head!' like the Red Queen says in *Alice in Wonderland*... I mean, I'm exaggerating a little—I mean, I saw the side... [the gentle side.] These grandparents were very important to me.

Ran would visit them at night—alone. It was his escape. There, he could step into a different world—a world where he played a different role and enjoyed different relationships, where he was pampered by his grandmother and treated with robust affection by his grandfather. The atmosphere of coming in from the dark and being greeted warmly, then wandering from room to room, relishing the familiarity and the strangeness of each—noting any changes, entertaining possibilities—is captured in his rapidly sketched description:

> There was a front parlor, and my grandfather had a den with a spittoon. [*The detail is given nonchalantly.*] Upstairs, there was a beautiful room that my grandmother used—a suite. I found an attic; I found a back room, and I remember thinking, 'Oh, I love this!' and I began staying out at night and my parents called... Sometimes [*he adds it thoughtfully*], I stayed in the cemetery. There was a secret entrance—maybe that's a little exaggerated—and I would go there, but then my parents got wise to it, and when I ran away from home, they'd find me there. Oh, did I get a few wallops in life when I was at the cemetery![49]

The house at Ridgewood Place was the center for many memorable dinner parties—wonderful gatherings when all the family, including Aunty Jeanne, Ran's "foster aunt,"[50] would come. Until they were "ten or twelve" (as Ran's cousin, Joanna— "Joey"—remembers), "the children had to sit in a small room adjacent to the main dining room, monitored by probably our Aunt Fran."[51]

Wende, Joanna's sister, agrees, "We actually ate dinner with the adults very rarely." She recalls an occasion when her grandfather was sneezing at the dinner table. She and the other children proclaimed that the number of sneezes was equal to the number of martinis he had consumed.[52] (Any diversion was welcome.) Joanna, for her part, remembers "shuffling off to the movies after a large, boring, holiday dinner."[53]

A French chef, Simone, cooked for these occasions. "I think she and her Scottish husband had rent there," Ran muses. Simone would cook casseroles with "different herbs," but as far as Ran was concerned, the highpoint of the evening was the cocktail hour:

> My grandparents made a big thing of the cocktail hour. They served all kinds of smelly cheeses... and *Liederkranz*—I don't think you can get it anymore. They had little baby plates with all kinds of relishes and pickles, sharp cheeses, olives, and they'd have very good food at a dinner later, but then my grandfather may have been half-soused by the time he got to dine. I don't remember wine being served (at dinner) except on a holiday, but the cocktail party was more than... [generously supplied.] The elaborate hors d'oeuvres were wheeled in by my grandmother. What do you call that thing? It's laden with stuff, and you wheeled it in—with little salads and the celeries and all the kinds of olives—and just to [have to] go back to a potato and a cooked carrot [after that]. I mean, I just remember gorging on the cheeses...

The sharp cheeses and all the other delicacies were in stark contrast to the bland carrot and potatoes of day-to-day life. They signified that some days were special—part of a deeper social experience to be celebrated and remembered. Even a trip downtown to the department store Forbes and Wallace[54] was treasured:

> We don't know who the Forbes were, but my parents knew the Wallaces—no relationship with Dorothy Wallace [*he hastens to clarify*]. I would go to the top floor[55]—I guess I was not so afraid of heights then. I was only seven. And when I was a messenger at the Union Trust Bank on Main Street, once in a while, I could have lunch [on another floor], and I thought it was so great to have a thing called Waldorf Salad and a little iced tea in the summer.
> L: What age were you a messenger at the Union Trust Bank?
> R: Oh my God, fourteen or fifteen? I don't know. That was the summer vacation. I think it would be around my 10th or 11th grade because there [at Classical High School] I met Annette Stefopoulos—who later changed her name to Annette Stevens—and George Russell

> produced an album of Annette and myself—Annette was singing.[56] We can't find the recording—it never came out—but that would be my first record before the *Newest Sound Around*.
> L: Maybe George Russell has it; maybe he took it with him... to the next world.
> R: Yes, it's probably in heaven with George Russell. [*With scarcely a pause, he continues.*] My father took me once to a new little place for sandwiches called Friendly, and it was at East Longmeadow, I believe, and they had a milkshake called the Awful Awful. It was very big and thick, and they would serve the cheeseburger on a toasted... [bun.] You could get peppermint stick ice cream.[57]

Ran savored each experience and, having sampled some of the variety of tastes on offer, could tolerate no restrictions:

> There was a Grandmother Blake, who said, 'Never put cinnamon on apples!' And so, when I was told not to do [something], I did it!

This compulsion to follow his own instincts was characteristic of Ran. Without it, he may never have discovered the Gospel Church or film noir. It certainly assisted him in developing his own unique talent.

His independence of spirit showed up initially in his determination to attend the church services of his choice:[58]

> That's why I became a good secondary Catholic—because Mother said, 'Why go to that church? We think it's better you stay home and read,' and then I said, 'I'm definitely going. I can't WAIT to go.'

It also compelled him to frequent movie-theaters and listen to radio programs, despite his father's entreaties to "join the real world." It was not so much obstinacy as a will to survive, to honor his dreams, and to follow leads—first encountered in the dream world—into the "real" world, dominated by adults.

It was this spirit—this determination—that meant that he forged ahead with his first overseas tour, despite few bookings. It would get him into trouble later, when he told Jeanne Lee, "I'm definitely going" (to Greece), on the eve of the 1967 coup. At New England Conservatory in Boston, it allowed him to initiate a prison support group; it was the hidden strength that enabled him to establish himself as a leading educator in his field.

It was a spirit that was encouraged by his parents, who were keen for their only son to be capable, well-rounded, resilient; it was a spirit influenced by his grandfather, who lived nearby and wanted robustness in his grandson.

But it was only part of the boy. There was a contemplative side—the solitary child who spent time alone, dreaming, in the Mulberry Street cemetery.

∼

RAN, BY HIS own admission, had a "rich fantasy life." He "knew hiding places to go to" when he wanted to dream, or simply when he was upset:

> I think I felt everybody's [moods]. One time, when it was too cold to go to the cemetery, I got into the garage at 42 Ridgewood Place and hid under the car. My grandparents had a garage where they parked the car—it looked like the one in *Sunset Boulevard*. The car was very old, and they brought it out once a week. There was a driver with a cap...
> So I hid there one time, and my father and mother gave me a licking.

For a boy who was sensitive to the moods of others, who felt the little injustices of childhood, there would always be time spent in worry and brooding. A time in which he struggled to understand himself—and the world. Life was not straightforward. There were shadows and mystery:

> I certainly look back at my life and look at things that don't make sense. I see childhood, walking through the cemetery... then that becomes the precursor for *Spiral Staircase*, film noir.

Ran's determination and spirit, initially evidenced in the "gusts and storms" of childhood, grew, nourished by contemplation and dreams, into a deep-seated commitment to, and perseverance with, the music which was to become his life's work.

3

Spellbound—The Power of Story

> *"No, no! The adventures first," said the Gryphon in an impatient tone: "explanations take such a dreadful time."*
>
> Lewis Carroll, *Alice's Adventures in Wonderland*

Ran Blake's fascination with mystery, darkness, and ominous shadows, which would manifest itself in his lifelong devotion to film noir, became evident at a very early age. It had its roots in story—the allure of the unknown, dreams of the possible and the impossible. The essence of a good story was part of his early experience.

Ran's parents were educated and articulate.[1] They were great readers *and* great storytellers. As Ran recalls, his parents had separate sitting rooms where they would go to read. Alison would also pursue her creative pastimes of painting, knitting, and crewelwork. They would then get together for their "little knit"—which was what they called the cocktail hour—to discuss the books they'd been reading. It was not difficult for the very young Ran to sneak downstairs and allow himself to become immersed in the patterns of their discussions—the re-telling of stories and plots—and in the warm, family atmosphere that generated them. These stories, at first only partially understood, inevitably percolated into the deep recesses of memory and subconscious. They were Ran's first experience of structure, rhythm, and form.

Later, Philip Blake read to his son from the books he loved himself. Having studied at the Sorbonne, Philip had a preference for French writers—Flaubert's *Madame Bovary* and Victor Hugo's *The Hunchback of Notre Dame* and *Les Miserables*.[2] His favorite writer was Guy de Maupassant, the master of the short story. (Ran particularly recalls *The Necklace*. This classic tale had intrigue, suspense, and a surprise ending.)[3] Philip also introduced Ran to Thackeray's *Vanity Fair* and its ambitious, clever, and manipulative protagonist, Becky Sharp—a glimpse of the darker side of human nature and society.

His mother loved Pearl Buck.

> R: Do you know her? [*He asks it with sudden interest.*] She wrote about China.

As a young woman, Alison had been invited to chaperone the young heiress Julia Donahue (a former pupil) on her overseas travels.[4] At the time, it was fashionable for wealthy young ladies to travel in this way, and, in all probability, Julia's family would have spared no expense ensuring the expedition had glamour and excitement. Ran admits that he never met Julia Donahue:

> [...] but I've heard these stories often through childhood. That [world tour] must have been in the late '20s—before I came on earth—and my father, I believe, was teaching at Deerfield Academy. But I don't really know—I probably yawned when I heard the story.

Yawning or not, Ran has very fond memories of sitting at the dining table and hearing his grandmother draw out his mother on many topics, including her overseas travels with Julia Donahue.

Their travels took them to Japan, China, India, and Kashmir, and they certainly had their fair share of excitement. They were robbed in Japan and actually confronted by bandits in India, but neither incident dampened their enthusiasm. Alison's favorite place, by far, was Kashmir. This "paradise" was known for its breathtakingly beautiful scenery: snow-capped mountains and high pastures, dotted with delicate alpine blooms; crystal clear lakes and streams; valleys where colorful flowers grew and where apricots, apples, pears, plums, cherries, and mulberries were produced in abundance. The pristine beauty made a lasting impression on Alison.

In addition to Pearl Buck, Alison would also read her young son favorite stories from her own girlhood—books like *Alice in Wonderland*, which, portraying as it does a world of strange and marvelous dreams, still holds a fascination for Ran; and Frances Hodgson Burnett's 1904 novel *A Little Princess*. Ran still remembers vividly the main character of this book:

[…] a young lady, Miss Crewe, who grows up in India and goes to school in England… and there was a monkey which brought secret food through the window, so she doesn't starve.

Ran tolerated—and probably enjoyed—his parents' choices of books for him (even if, looking back, he felt they could have made better ones) because he loved having them read to him. As he puts it:

> So even though they would not choose [a story of] a dark house like *Spiral Staircase* or that kind of stuff, [at least] my parents would be reading.[5]

Stories read and stories told, each with their own fascinating rhythms and exotic plots, were the sustenance of his imagination in those early years, and with both parents teachers, it is probable that the exposure he received was more a planned banquet than a haphazard feast. Young Ran was guided through these texts by skilled interpreters who helped him to discover other worlds and times, far removed from the 1930s America of his birth. Among these was the Victorian England described by Charles Dickens; Ran heard the story of how his great grandfather, Lewis J. Powers, entertained Dickens when he visited Springfield on his second trip to America in 1867–68.[6] He also heard how the great writer had arrived by rail amid a "raging snowstorm" and dazzled his audience with his personality and performance.[7]

Such accounts—unstructured and told around the dinner table—added another dimension to Ran's appreciation of story:

> My grandmother Jessie loved to tell stories—she loved books. I don't know [whether] she was as erudite a reader as my father. She would bring out my mother[8] a lot at dinner parties [asking her questions] about her trips to Asia. She was extremely warm: my mother probably could be too, but she [Jessie] was demonstrative and probably the warmest member of my family. I could tell her about the ghosts—she would believe me… all the stories and fantasies—I could tell her so much stuff.

Through story, Ran was able to express—and process—some of the fears, insecurities, and shadowy, unexplained places that can intrude into a young child's world. From a young age, Ran realized the importance of story as a means of establishing connection with family, friends, and later, the wider music community.

Ran's cousin Susan can trace the seeds of her life-long friendship with Ran back to his storytelling:

My memories of Ran are particularly during Christmas when we had meals with aunts, uncles, and cousins.

I fondly remember sitting with Ran under a piano as he read *Mary Poppins* to me. That laid the groundwork for a sweet friendship. The picture I remember in my mind is when I was about five, and Ran had to be fifteen that year.[9]

4

A LITTLE DRAMA

Come, sit down, every mother's son, and rehearse your parts.

WILLIAM SHAKESPEARE, *A MIDSUMMER NIGHT'S DREAM*

When Ran was five and a half, his sister, Martha, was born. Ran was, as Martha attested, a "wonderful big brother," but those early months must have been challenging as, up till then, he had enjoyed the undivided attention of his parents and grandparents. And the baby was not the only addition to the family. While Martha was still very young, the Blakes took a young Irish girl—Mary Garvey—into their household. Her primary role was to care for Martha during the day so that Alison was free to return to Miss Rude's Nursery School. Ran, being of a suitable age, was able to attend the school with his mother:

> I was told I was there one year. I have no memory [of it]. I once told Miss Rude she was rude, and I got the first slap in my life on my lips.[1]

After school, Ran was in Mary Garvey's care; she made a big impression. Right from the start, he loved her. She was warm and cheerful, with a certain earthy robustness that he found exciting. He loved her accent and how it turned mundane utterances into song; he loved her sense of fun. Yet, there were contradictions, and her carefree nature was tempered by the demands of her religion, which she fulfilled with child-like faith. Sometimes, it seemed she was not much more than a child herself. (Ran can remember his mother guiding the young Mary, just as she would a daughter; he remembers personal hygiene being discussed.) Mary loved movies and movie magazines. She had her crucifix side by side with a picture of Marlon Brando.² She loved Betty Grable and Rita Hayworth:

> She once wore her hair that way [like Rita Hayworth's] and told my mother she wanted to dye it red, and my mother said, 'I'd advise against it, but you're a free agent.'

If naive in some ways, Mary was worldly in others. She'd left her home and family to travel across the Atlantic to the "land of opportunity." Along with her cheerfulness, her accent, and her sudden superstitions, there was a whiff of distant shores and a whisper of adventure.

Mary was a great storyteller. As her young charge lay in bed at night, she'd tell him stories of the "old country." She talked of "spirited little fairies that would come out of plants"; she talked of "ghosts and creaking steps in crumbling castles, where floors gave way as you walked." Her whispered words kept Ran spellbound. She often acted-out her stories with basic costumes. On one occasion, a story was getting a little boisterous, and Ran's parents were heard on the stairs. Mary discarded her ghost costume and hurried from the room, leaving Ran to deal with their questions. (He remembers explaining that he'd wanted the sheet because he was cold.)

Mary altered stories to suit her own purpose. She changed Mary Poppins into an orphan girl from Northern Ireland and peppered her tale with political comments and darkly muttered references to the British. She told of "knights and plunder"³ and an "evil man who had a castle," and there was mention of a "magical drink which made you dream."⁴ She wove her own adventures into the stories too and told how late at night in the country, she'd be out collecting moonstones and suddenly have to hide from pirates.⁵ She would add scary sound effects, and then, when Ran was at a fever pitch of excitement, she'd finish abruptly with: "You'll find out tomorrow what happens." And Ran remembers:

> I'd call out, 'Mary!' [*His tone has both protest and pleading.*] But it made no difference. She was better than some of the radio shows. [*He adds this with a hint of awe.*]

Inspired by her tales, Ran went to the piano to re-live them. He called one of the pieces he composed "The Ghost Shamrock." Mary's stories contributed to Ran's preoccupation with shadows, darkness, and mystery.

With Alison teaching extra hours, Mary's responsibilities were significant. She was also expected to do some light house duties, and she usually cooked an early meal for the children. Cooking may not have been her strong point—Ran still remembers, with horror, her mashed potatoes and carrots:

> She would serve me an early supper with cooked carrots and mashed potatoes, and overcooked liver. So I *beg* [*he forms the word with dramatic emphasis*], if I come to your house in Australia, please don't serve… [*The dreaded 'mashed potato and carrots' is left unsaid as he continues*] Everybody says, 'Well now, try *my* potato, try *my* carrots,' and it is better than the way Mary Garvey cooked it. But why not give me wild rice or pasta that's not cooked [too much]. Mary Garvey cooked everything *so much.*

If Mary's carrots and potatoes have left a lasting, negative impression, Ran is much more enthusiastic about the "seaweed" that her family sent out from Ireland on a regular basis—and which she allowed him to taste:

> When I was good, I had seaweed, and I *loved* that. I don't like… Irish food would not be my ideal… but the seaweed! [*He finishes on an upward rapturous note.*]

It tasted of the sea—that same sea woven into Mary's hair-raising tales of pirates and shipwrecks. It was foreign and exotic, and Ran's love of it was evidence of a developing adventurous palate that craved "a little bit of spice."

Mary's cooking may have been bland, but Ran found her religion anything but. She was a devout Catholic, attending Mass three mornings a week, as well as weekly Confession and Benediction on Friday evenings. For whatever reason, young Ran sometimes accompanied her in the evening. It was here, at the Cathedral of St. Michael on State Street, that he was introduced to the rudiments of drama. The dim lighting and deep still, the red lamp that winked from the altar, the murmured chant drifting out of the darkness, the heavy confessional curtain behind which Mary would briefly disappear—all these aspects fascinated him. Best of all was when, at the sound of a bell, an altar boy, not much older than himself, entered with a taper on a long brass rod and proceeded to light banks of candles. And as he did, the darkness was banished, and the church filled with glowing light. It was magical—the soaring notes of hymns in the unfamiliar yet beautiful Latin, the strong, sweet smell of incense, the rising spiral of smoke—and everything was shot with candlelight.

Benediction aroused Ran's sense of the mystical and, with it, an appreciation of ritual and theater. There, he found all the elements that would continue to intrigue him throughout his life: darkness, shadows, mystery, and candlelight.

5

RADIO

It was the biggest thing in my life.

RAN BLAKE

If Mary Garvey's devotion to her church introduced Ran to the richness of liturgy and ritual, it was her devotion to radio, and more specifically, the radio serial, that led Ran into the realm of dreams and mystery, dark drama, and intrigue.

Radio was *big* in American homes of the 1940s. In the decade before Ran's birth, radio consoles had become generally available, and despite the economic hardships of this time, by 1935, two out of three homes had radio. There were four national networks and twenty regional networks providing programs throughout the United States—all day, every day.[1]

The programs that came to fascinate Ran were first broadcast during the 1930s. *Jack Armstrong, the All-American Boy* and the *Lone Ranger* (with its distinctive theme music from Rossini's *William Tell* overture) debuted in 1933. *Tarzan* followed in 1934 and then *Mr. Keen, Tracer of Lost Persons*, in 1937. *Sherlock Holmes* aired from 1939 to 1947, while *The Adventures of Mr. and Mrs. North* made a debut in 1941 and then ran continuously from 1942 to 1955. (The domestic setting for these mysteries, and the couple's light-hearted conversation, aimed to make the program less terrifying than its subject matter of murder and mystery might imply.) The infinitely scarier *Inner Sanctum* went to air in January 1941. First known as *The Squeaky Door* because of the opening sound effect, the series dealt in death, murder, and things macabre. It was introduced by the sardonic host with the sinister voice—Raymond Johnson.[2]

Nineteen forty-one, though, was the high point for radio, with thirteen million sets manufactured. It was in this year that radio's emerging role—as a source of information (particularly regarding the war in Europe) and also as a means of communication—became obvious.[3] At this time, radios were still troubled by static, and poor reception required the listener to sit close-by. Ran clearly remembers the big console radio near which his family gathered:

> [...] in the front parlor—we called it the parlor—the console was there with the phonograph.

Console radios were floor models and were a highly prized piece of furniture. The cabinets were fashioned in beautiful timber and often cost more than the radio itself. In addition to this radio, Ran had a little radio near his bed:

> [...] and I would secretly put it on after I'd been checked.

For Ran, this little radio was the entrance to another world: an escape into the realms of the imagination. It became for him:

> [...] the biggest thing in my life. [*He reflects in wonder at the memory.*]

Mary Garvey had her own escape from the monotony of her domestic duties. She was obsessed with the radio program *Stella Dallas*—a serialized soap opera based on the novel by Olive Higgins Prouty.[4] It told the story of a beautiful young woman from a poor background who had married above her station in life. It drew big audiences for its fifteen-minute weekday afternoon spot. The program first appeared in 1937 (following the highly successful movie of the same name, starring Barbara Stanwyck) and ran till 1955.

Presumably to keep young Ran quiet and occupied as she listened, Mary inveigled him into taking an interest in her show. She would hurry him inside with a promise of a ginger cookie if he would sit still and listen. As Ran recalls:

> She was a fanatic of a show called *Stella Dallas*—about a young lady that became pregnant—and in order for me to hear *Sherlock Holmes* and *Jack Armstrong*, I had to hear this women's soap opera [first].

Ran's recount, to this stage, has been "matter-of-fact"; then, the tone brightens as he adds:

[...] and then, after, came the mysteries, and so I got addicted to *Jack Armstrong*![5] And then came *Mr. and Mrs. North*—which was pure mystery. But then there was *Inner Sanctum,* and that really affected me. [Mary] told my parents that she saw my hands... [trembling.]

These stories were a new and exciting approach to the age-old tradition of storytelling that had been so faithfully upheld by his parents. They came with dramatic voices, music, and sound effects:

I don't think, at six years old, I read those [stories], so in other words, it was the oral tradition... and that spooky music. And in those days, the radio could not afford an orchestra, so there would be an organ. And I mean, if I heard it now, I would burst out, 'Hammy,' like I remember I did as a child when I...

Abruptly, Ran gets up from his chair and rushes to the piano. He plays briefly before returning to explain:

R: Dup-pra-up-pup-up-pra-up-pup-pa—that's the *Lone Ranger*—that's from Rossini's *William Tell*. But that's... [nothing.] Pretty well every kid could play that.
L: So you would sometimes play along with the radio?
R: Yup. But then I would try to retain it.

There was nothing that could keep Ran from *Mr. and Mrs. North* or from the scary *Inner Sanctum*, and by the time he was seven or eight, he had learned to control the trembles and was able to listen without drawing unwanted attention.

Darkness added to the experience. (Ran has said that *"Inner Sanctum* was my favorite because it took place at night.") The darkness, the stories—read with vivid sound effects—stimulated his imagination. The habit of visualization, begun with the stories read to him by his parents and Mary Garvey, was becoming more entrenched and was now associated with the soundtrack that radio could provide.

For Ran, radio had become a great companion *and* educator. It was compelling and addictive—jostling with his formal education until school became an interruption to be endured:

I couldn't wait to get home and get in the dream world. That was my school.

This lack of interest in his classes must have worried his parents, but Ran—imaginative and highly intelligent—would have been bored to the point of stupor by the daily grind of school life. And though his parents saw to it that he had "fairly good attendance," his mind was elsewhere:

> I think it was deliberately 'out there.' School wasn't as interesting as the North family. I did get A-minus for a paper when they said one day, 'Do what you want,' and I talked lots about *Mr. and Mrs. North*, the radio show, and Miss Henriquez called up my parents and said, 'I got the most remarkable paper from your son. It was hard to read the handwriting...'
> L: [*interrupting*] Nothing's changed!
> R: [*ignoring this*] 'but he read it out loud,' she said, 'and I could not get over it—the retention of this mystery show—and she said, 'If your son could pay *half* as good attention in class... but he finds the North family much more important than the classes.'

If Miss Henriquez was left wondering as to how she might engage her young pupil, Ran's classmates also found him remote:

> I ignored the students. Some might have wanted to be... [friends], but I withdrew. I couldn't wait to get home. I *ran* [*he emphasizes the word*] so I could get there for the radio show. One guy asked me over to his house—Bobby Timmon. Oh, but when I knew that *Mr. Keen* and *Mr. and Mrs. North* were going to be on and that they were going to reveal the murderer. It was a rival. We didn't have a tape-recorder, and the radio program was my life—not [being] with friends.
> L: So, were you friends with Bobby?
> R: Oh, he was nice. He sort of stuck up for me and said, 'Come another time,' and my parents were furious [with me] because some of the class were going—some of the other boys.

Ran's aloofness challenged the boys in his class. There was a lot about him that they did not understand:

> I remember they were staring at this Mary Garvey [and wondering] how she had given me *Forever Amber*[6] to read—it was a risqué novel...

Ran's classmates would certainly have been shocked by this choice. The 1944 book by Kathleen Winsor had been banned in fourteen US states. (Despite this, it was the best-selling US novel of the 1940s!) It was also condemned by the Catholic Church—for indecency. But this only seems to have made it more popular. Mary had her own philosophy: "I'm from a good family, but you can't read the Bible all the time."

So that was okay, for young men can learn about sex and love, and brotherhood and knighthood, but how could I get hooked on these radio shows? [*The puzzled tone indicates that even Mary found this unusual.*]

All afternoon, from straight after school until four-thirty, Ran listened to his shows, and then, later, there was *Inner Sanctum*:

And my parents kept saying, 'Play outside!' They wanted me outside—walking, doing things, and not just living in the world of radio. 'Why don't you [tell us] what happened in school?' they'd say. But obviously, A-B-C, *Dick and Jean Went up the Hill,* two and two is four... argh... There are three kinds of sciences we study in school—elementary biology, chemistry, physics—was that more interesting? Or was finding out why Mr. and Mrs. North were not allowed to leave the room... and that there's a sadistic killer out there and Mr. and Mrs. North are talking about their happy life, and then, they keep hearing this knock at the door.... That was much more interesting. I knew that there was Louis Armstrong and his big band, but what about the North family! They were locked in their house; they couldn't get out, and a murderer was around there! I had to wait! [*His tone demonstrates how agonizing that wait was.*] My grandparents came to visit. I said, 'I'm sorry,' I had to... [be excused.] It was the biggest thing in my life. [*His tone rises in wonder.*]

The radio story had taken charge, and though his father lamented that his son spent so much time devoted to his serials, he probably did not consider that he himself had been partially responsible for stirring such an intense interest. As Ran says, recalling his very young years:

My father was quite a storyteller and [so was] my mother, so that [their storytelling] was *live* radio... but not quite as scary.

Absorbed in these stories, fascinated by their plots, it wasn't a very big step to enter into a world where story was often incomprehensible and unreal—terrifying at times. The world of dreams.

6

THE DREAM WORLD

Though, I did know reality from dreamworld.

RAN BLAKE

Inner Sanctum took "story" to a whole new level. It was so compelling, perplexing, and frightening that it blurred the boundaries between reality and dreams. It was undoubtedly, the precursor of Ran's passion for film noir. More than any other show, *Inner Sanctum* had the power to transport him to this place of dreams—or perhaps, nightmares—a world inhabited by ghosts and shrouded in mystery, a place where he began living in his own stories—his *own* mysteries. Ran, himself, speaks of *Inner Sanctum* as being "part of the dream world." It was a world that was becoming more and more a part of his life. He listened to *Inner Sanctum* at night on the little radio next to his bed. There is no doubt that Mary Garvey knew he was listening but chose to turn a blind eye... until:

> She came in one night when my parents were out, and she saw me sobbing on the floor. [*He pauses and adds sotto voce*] *Inner Sanctum* still haunts me.

Inner Sanctum, created for radio, relies on the ear. The reader's tone, cadence, pauses, and silences—along with sound effects and dramatic, evocative accompanying music are orchestrated to achieve a significant shiver down the spine.[1] The young Ran was instantly attuned to the impact this had. For him, it was a new dimension of story—much closer to performance than Mary Garvey's best renditions of her pirate and ghost stories. Story and music were now woven into one creative expression.

The Dream World

Radio plays influenced Ran to create "mystery stories," which he performed with his own musical accompaniment.² He had a sure instinct for structure and progression, gleaned from the stories his parents had read him. Mary Garvey had added the visual interest of simple costuming. She also had introduced programming, requiring Ran to wait in suspense—overnight—for a conclusion. By the time he was listening to radio serials, Ran would have had a highly developed imagination, readily able to supply alternative story-lines and, most importantly, that element of a radio program that only the imagination can supply—the visual element. Thus, the radio programs became very real—their impact dramatic, and at times, even disturbing.

RAN'S CHILDHOOD HOME on Union Street provided every opportunity for creative expression. The family, as mentioned, had three pianos—uprights—that were in a little, enclosed porch at the front of the house. One was in bad condition and rarely used; Ran believes an uncle may then have given them another, and his parents had bought the third after they had seen him, as a persistent two-or-three-year-old, drawn over and over again to the front parlor, desperate to play the pianos. This small piano room also had a radio, and Ran remembers that he liked to sit there, near the pianos, listening to his favorite programs; the pianos were open and ready should he wish to accompany one of the radio stories.

Very quickly, Ran learned how to achieve maximum impact for his compositions. He performed with dramatic effect, translating each radio program into a visual storyboard in his head, which then directed his playing. These early performances had a mixed reception:

> My Aunt Frances Powers³ screamed. She said, 'What's gotten into…'
> She called me a 'little monster.' She used to love…
> [*Ran breaks off to demonstrate—at the piano—the more traditional music she used to love.*]
> L: [*laughing*] Nice trills, Ran.
> R: [*ignoring the interruption*] but then I did that Haydn '*Surprise' Symphony* and something crashes…
> [*He crashes on the keys, and it is easy to imagine the front room in Union Street and Aunt Frances's disapproving glare.*]

Then one night, when Philip and Alison were out, Ran was listening to *Inner Sanctum* on his own little radio. When it was over, Ran recalls that:

> I crept down to the piano, barefoot, and I played something, and I gather Mary was in the kitchen, talking on the phone or something, and she heard this crash, and music—and I hear she screamed. [*The tone is incredulous, and Ran pauses for a moment on the upward inflection before continuing more matter-of-factly.*] Now nobody's a witness 'cause Martha, and my parents are in heaven, but I guess… she said I had a black mask on when she came in, and she had to call a friend. She didn't want to be alone with me in the house. This was 'when I got in these moods,' she told my parents.

This account of Mary's may, quite possibly, have been convenient for her. She had already told Ran of the boy she "half-dated," confiding in Ran how she would "let her boyfriend kiss her once a year." Romance in general, and this young man in particular, were obviously on her mind. This *may* have been a good excuse to see more of her boyfriend—if *he* was the friend she called.

Ran's memory of the event is that it was not so dramatic as to necessitate the calling of a friend:

> You know, I don't think I ever went [crazy] like that.

Despite these initial reactions, Ran continued to use his new skill to entertain, and perhaps even shock, local children. Usually, they came in groups, and at first, they tended to mock the performance, egging each other on: "Oh, I'm so scared," they'd say. When Ran introduced the story of the "Jolly Ginkie Dream Ghost"—one of his favorites—they'd burst out laughing, so Ran would have to tweak the story a little and have the dream ghost wearing a number eight football jersey, and that would interest them. On one memorable occasion, a boy who habitually taunted Ran at school came over on his own. Ran took him to the piano room and, with lights off and window shades drawn, began to play:

> [This boy] suddenly had to leave—he ran out—and my parents said, 'What the… what's happening now?'
> And maybe there wasn't a phone call to my mother; maybe the two people met on the street? [But] his mother complained that I'd frightened her son, and my mother said, 'It's about time… but I do sympathize.'
> I guess my mother maybe had [spoken to] someone else. I didn't like to tell people when I was bullied, but I guess it got out. I really don't know how old I was when I scared this taunter, but I just remember he looked very big… and I don't think he burst out in tears—I think that's a little exaggerated—but BOY [*there's heavy emphasis*], WAS

I treated well for the rest of the year by this kid! And he wouldn't go back to the chamber of horror; my father was rather proud that he never taunted me anymore.

For Ran, the incident demonstrated the power of story combined with music:

> When I played the piano alone... [*He breaks off his account to make a snoring noise.*] boredom! 'Do we *have* to hear Ran Blake play?' If I told the story in the recess or gym [they'd say], 'We don't want to hear about *Mr. and Mrs. North*! Come and play ball with us.'
> I said, 'What about *Jack Armstrong, the all-American boy...* or the *Lone Ranger* with the horse?'
> 'Ah, we've heard that.' [*He mimics their dismissive tone.*]

Then, he would produce his *pièce de résistance* and murmur enticingly, 'But *Inner Sanctum*?' (Even the re-telling is chilling. The words are left suspended, trembling with mysterious possibility.) But it was all to no avail. There was only one way to interest them, and Ran knew it:

> When I got to the piano and spoke—that was the way to go.

The dream world, accessed through radio programs and played out on the piano, captivated Ran. It was a world of the imagination where he explored the whole scope of another reality. Radio shows were merely a starting point from which he could insert himself into stories—recreating, re-interpreting and re-shaping the storyboard, composing a soundtrack, and, finally, giving it life through performance.

His mind teemed with scenarios. He was so absorbed by them that once, coming home and hearing his mother talking in the kitchen, he thought *she* was on the radio:

> I can see this graveyard.[4] I remember that better than the houses... and walking [home] in the fog. I remember coming in and hearing my mother on the phone saying. 'It seems unhealthy to have such an obsession,' and for a minute, as I walked in the door, I thought my mother was on the radio—an actress in a radio show called *Inner Sanctum*. But then, I think in reality, she must have been talking about me.

For Ran had indeed become obsessed with his radio programs—particularly the scary ones that came on at night. He lived for the night. In winter, darkness came early. This was the time he needed to be indoors, ready to tune in to his programs. It meant he shunned engagements with family and friends. It confined him to his room. It even, on occasion, led him to the point of rudeness and obstinacy so that his father was at a loss as to how to handle the situation:

> And my father would say [*Ran claps once, loudly*] 'Come on [*more claps*], into reality. [*more claps*] Wake up, and we'll get your bed made.'

Compared to his radio programs, everything else was dull. The radio and the dream world had joined forces to create for Ran a rich interior life.

The world he discovered—the unconscious—was a place of limitless possibilities, and Ran's reluctance to return to "reality" is understandable. But Philip Blake's attitude to his son's compulsion is equally understandable. He was seeking balance between the two worlds—an equilibrium that would allow his son to participate more fully in the day-to-day life of Springfield, Massachusetts.

THE SHIFTING BORDER BETWEEN DREAMS AND REALITY

He is a dreamer; let us leave him: pass.

WILLIAM SHAKESPEARE, *JULIUS CAESAR*

THE DAY-TO-DAY LIFE of Springfield, Massachusetts—as in any other American city or town of the early 1940s—was haunted by a shadowy presence. It was a time when the war, raging from Europe to the Pacific, had impacted America directly—first, with the bombing of Pearl Harbor at the end of 1941 and then, with the sinking of American ships in their east coast ports early in 1942. America was involved. Newsreels, radio news, and newspapers were full of it. Hushed adult conversations whispered of it. Telegram boys brought dreaded news to ordinary homes in Springfield streets. Children would have been aware of this shadow, would have picked up on the fear. For Ran, there was a direct connection in that his father was an air raid warden. He had probably discussed the reasons for this work with his son. It was no wonder that Ran sought another reality—the world of dreams—where the only entry requirement was a fertile imagination.

> [...] Do you know the movie *Dream Child* about *Alice in Wonderland*? If you have a minute, if it ever warms up here... [go to see it.]

> It shows the imagination of the radio—all these sounds. I can't tell you how important the radio was.

The movie *Dream Child* offers a behind-the-scenes look into the work of the radio "sound effects operator," whose highly inventive methods were instrumental in painting a vivid, visual picture through the means of an auditory medium. An umbrella, open and shut rapidly, is used to evoke the sound of a vulture flying away; coconut shells clapped together mimic hoofbeats.

This movie, however, would have also interested Ran in the way it depicts the dream world—through blurring of tenses and the constant shifts between present and past.

The reference to this movie had come up in the middle of a conversation between Ran and Leo on a morning in early February 2007. It was cozy in Ran's Brookline flat—they were bunkered down against the cold, but winter was loitering outside, and Ran was tired of it:

> Even here, I'm freezing—your blood gets thin when you get old.

Nevertheless, it was a good time for telling stories, and the conversation ranged from the Depression years to Springfield, Suffield, and Sunapee, and back to Springfield. They were discussing Ran's school years in Springfield. Leo was having difficulty following:

> L: Sorry for not understanding this, but did you go to the Classical High School for a little bit before you moved to Suffield?
> R: [*obligingly*] Oh yes, I went to the junior high school there. I think I told you I was twelve... no, I would have been nearer fourteen/fifteen. Yeah, the years are sketchy, but it's coming back. It's just like the movie *Dream Child* about *Alice in Wonderland*. She's reading about being the real Alice—in Wonderland—and all this stuff comes back, and she dreams about when she's a child, and it's the present tense.

And it was at this point, with the subject of dreams introduced, that the fragment of a dream flashed unexpectedly into Ran's consciousness, and he is compelled to whisper in awe:

> My parents just nodded at you in a dream.

The dream had occurred the previous night after he'd returned from a gig he'd been attending. Ran was worried that he had not been giving enough support to his students because of the cold weather and had ventured out to this one, even though the night was bitter.

> I should keep up with people, but it's so, so cold. Last night at tai chi,[5] it was freezing. I only heard twenty minutes of it [the gig]. It was wonderful, but my mind wandered, and I knew you'd be here [today], and then, I came home and dreamed, and you were in Suffield.... Your face walked in, your body walked in, and my parents were saying, 'Why have you turned white?' They said, 'Oh...' but then they started staring at me, and I'm over by this bureau. [*He indicates the bureau in his bedroom—one inherited from his parents and now cluttered with books, CDs, DVDs, a bottle of asthma medication, and other items.*] 'Oh, it's a mess, it's a mess, but the quadratic algebra takes a lot of time.'
> [*Without warning, he returns to the dream.*]
> I said, 'There's something wrong here,' and my father said, 'Is this the way you treat a guest?' And I think I may have introduced you as 'English' seeing as they detected an accent... and I said, 'But Leo's not to enter my life for thirty-five years!'
> It's like some days you say, 'Someone walked over my grave.' It was like: what tense am I in? But this was the dream, last night, in this house. It was the most amazing dream, and it was s-s-so s-s-scary. [*The words shiver with sibilants.*] I woke up at two o'clock, but it is so interesting.

Dreams can sometimes be very real, especially on a winter's night when it's deeply dark and cold outside and the mood is melancholic. It is certain Ran dreamed often as a child:

> I think I did have worlds of ghosts and dreaming and screaming in the night.

But the dreams of this childhood world, with all its imaginings—the fears, terrors, and indeed, the hopes—could never foreshadow the world that would be revealed to him as an adult.

Ran has often said that it is "sad" going back to childhood; indeed, he's had dreams about this. It's a complicated emotion, tinged with nostalgia for a simpler time—a time of innocence:

> [It's a time of] being safe in a house, having the indulgence of grandparents, and not worrying about the horrors of world famine and war. [It's a time of] thinking that the world might have the 'Jolly Ginkie Ghost'—the dream ghost—but not realizing there was starvation; lack of democracy in Greece....

> It was a safer world. I don't want to make it seem naive—like a delicate childhood with *Mary Poppins* and *Peter Pan*—no, not that, [but] life was simpler. [There was] stability of parents, sister, cousins, schoolteacher. [But there was also] the evil of the night—the dreams; walking in one's sleep. There's the cemetery, the dead....
> You knew [as a child] that at some time there might be some people without food, [that] people get old and die. But you don't know about political revolution; you don't know the evils of child labor.
> And [it's] almost like more of a primitive understanding—if you sin, you get a black mark and go to the fire instead of upstairs to heaven directly, but it's an easier... [time], and yet one could feel strangled there....

There was *something* just out of reach. It was only with experience that the innocence of childhood could be understood. The realization that evil exists in the world is frightening and, to those with innocent hearts, bewildering and inexplicable. It was the dream world that helped the adult Ran to reframe and restructure—to make sense of—the world in which he found himself.

Soon after Ran arrived in Boston in 1967, Dorothy Wallace encouraged him to keep a dream diary in which, on waking, he wrote his dreams. (She realized that he was still traumatized after being caught up in the Greek military coup.) She would ring him at a prearranged time and question him about what he'd been dreaming. This dream diary, which helped Ran to cope with the persisting nightmares as well as the everyday challenges of his new life in Boston, has unfortunately been lost. Since this time, however, Ran has been very aware of his dreams and interested in their messages:

> So, the dreams that I'm having... I think they started with a lot of our interviews. Last night I spent the evening with Chris Connor in my dreams. I was about twenty-five. She had just made two medium hit records, and she couldn't give me the time of day. We happened to be at a hotel in New York, and I was a porter. Now, I never was a porter in a New York hotel, and she never was a guest at a hotel [I was at], but [in the dream] she said, 'Yes, I've heard you; you're Ran Blake.' And she was almost sort of saying, 'I have many other fans—hold back buster.'

Dreams that deal with fears can often seem prophetic—worryingly so.

This morning I dreamt that August 14th[6] would not be the celebration for Chris Connor but a memorial. This horrible thing of foretelling the future—Gunther's death and Abbey Lincoln's.
L: Have you been accurate in the past?
R: Yes. [*It's said in a small, almost scared voice.*] But I haven't had a second dream about Chris Connor [and August 14th, 2007, being a memorial for her]. I've had dreams of her a lot this week where she's at the seashore. [*There's a contemplative pause.*]
I also thought that the world would end on January 20, 1953, and I had three dreams in the late forties about that—and obviously, it didn't—so I've been sixty to seventy percent pretty good, but not eighty or ninety percent.

Dreams, by their nature, are cryptic and illusionary. The fragment of a dream that lingers at the edge of the conscious mind on waking can be maddeningly elusive—and can easily be misunderstood. But dreams do reflect an ability to imagine. They are in sharp contrast to another dimension of Ran's dream world—the flashback. These involuntary memories are real, immediate, and demanding, often summoned by a sound or smell, and though Ran's words tumble out quickly, they can barely keep pace with the vividness of his recollections:

Alright, I just got a flashback, Janet—you asked for more memories—do I just skip all over?
L: Yeah, you can.
R: Right! Today, I'm with the beautiful young attaché of Andrew Fenlon, Svetlana—and Svetlana is the name of Stalin's daughter. [*This is thrown in inconsequentially.*]
[Andrew's] Svetlana makes cold borscht soups and goes to the Russian temple in Brighton. I walked into this church with TV cameras. There was an organist, two keyboard players, then a grand piano, an electric bass player, a drummer, and a superb guitar player.
In a flamboyant shirt and Italian coat with dungarees was Alonzo Harris from south of Atlanta. The first few minutes was reggae. I thought, 'Why is everything amplified?'
Then, I was back thirty-five to forty years, and I was at Bishop I.L. Jefferson's church… and I was eighteen, nineteen, seventeen years old. So, this is this morning! And I remember in that church I accidentally pulled the pigtail of the girl in front of me; Mother Carter was there—by the way, you may want to discuss the photographs in the hallway?[7]
Then the vision left me, and I'm right next to Svetlana and Andrew. He seemed to be snoozing, and he had on a shirt, tie, vest, and dun-

garees—that's the mode of young people these days—you can be sure. Boy, this congregation! Alonzo was a little [more] dressed than the white boy playing the organ, but boy, these people—they know how to dress! It's not NEC Huntington Avenue dress; I can tell you: colors! [*The tone is full of admiration.*] And now the sermon... I'm back in present tense, Janet—when I went to Alonzo's concert at the church in Roxbury—these AMAZING tenses! And here I have grey hair, losing [it]. Janet, will this do? I feel like I'm talking to you like Special Agent Cooper does to Dianne in *Twin Peaks*. Are these enough secondaries for you, Janet—and um, of course, it rains in Seattle, and it did in Bergen, Norway, so okay, but let's go on, Leo.[8]

These flashbacks revisit all sorts of memories and are fascinating in their intensity. They are a means of ordering past experiences and are of particular interest to Ran in that flashback is such an important technique in film noir of the '40s and '50s.

But while the dream world is an important part of Ran's life, he is anxious that it is kept in perspective:

> You could add a few more dreams, but I do hope people know I played the piano and used to run a department and [did] not just sit on my bed with dreams.

In an interview, Jose Antonio Luera[9] asked Ran what epitaph he would like, and Ran replied, "I believe I would put simply this: here lies the man who likes to dream."

On reading this chapter, Ran is anxious to add a postscript:

> I hope we say somewhere in the book that I LOVED my parents. It's my own problem that I got in a dream; it's like a drug. Other people are on Jack Daniel's every day and single malt whisky... [for me] it's the dream world—you can't break that.

7

CHURCH—ITS HEART AND SOUL

> *I don't judge a church by its buildings. It is the soul that's important—the flavor, the kindness, the tolerance of the congregation.*
>
> RAN BLAKE

The mystery world of murder, intrigue, and solitude that had been revealed through the allure of radio had a counterbalance primed and ready. Ran's fascination with different religions and cultures drew him out of the shadows and led him, with certain steps, to one of the great influences of his life: the Gospel Church and gospel music.

Springfield was a city of churches. Its citizens were God-fearing, and, for many, this meant attendance at church every Sunday. In the immediate neighborhood of Ran's home on Union Street, there were at least half a dozen churches.

One of these churches was the Blake family church—the South Congregational Church on Maple Street,[1] a couple of blocks from State Street. It does, however, seem to have been the family church in name only; Ran admits his parents were not "deeply religious."

Philip Blake was nominally Episcopalian. It was Alison who was the Congregationalist.[2] Ran remembers going "two or three times in life" with each of his parents to their respective churches. The Congregational Church on Maple Street was, however, the one chosen by the Blakes for their children's Sunday school education. Even the building—a beautiful Gothic-style construction in two-toned stone with a tower, deeply recessed tympanums, and a spectacular rose window facing High Street—spoke of history, tradition, and respectability. It dominated a street that Ran remembers as "elegant." He is excited at the clarity of his mental picture: "I can see it. It was a couple of blocks from State Street." For Ran, this church epitomized "pomp and ceremony."

The minister at the Maple Street Congregational Church was the Rev. Dr. Gordon Gilkey: [3]

> R: My grandparents knew him slightly. He had a son by that name who was the preacher at the Riverside Church in New York, right near the International [House]. He just resigned now—five or ten years ago.[4]
> L: What did he look like?
> R: Oh my gosh—no memory. He might have been balding; he might have been five/nine. I don't think he was thin. I do remember he wasn't shy... maybe a pomposity in his voice? He was very well-read. He was very worried about the war.[5]

There it was again—that shadow hanging over the Springfield of Ran's boyhood. Worry about the war would have been uppermost in the minds of most adults in America at that time. In Springfield, the gnawing concern about casualties and the uncertainty that shrouded "censored engagements" overseas were given ominous authenticity by the very real presence of the Springfield Armory, where production peaked during WWII. During this time, due to the large numbers of young men away fighting, forty percent of workers at the Armory were female.[6]

Dr. Gilkey was, according to Ran, well informed politically:

> L: Conservative or liberal?
> R: [*Dismissing this quickly, his tone incredulous*] This is at seven or eight years old! [*He pauses before continuing.*] But he had brilliant rhetoric. I remember seeing people taking notes at his sermon; I can see him on a pulpit. I think one time, his wife helped me get a dime—or was it nickel—outside of my nose. [*The coin had been intended for the collection, and how it became stuck in the young Ran's nose is left to the imagination, for he continues without elaboration.*] I'd love to know his wife's name—it wasn't quite Mabel... or Melba—it was so unusual. She'd been at Wellesley College.[7] She was very gregarious.... And then, we would leave—quite often either before the sermon or directly afterward—[for] Sunday School [which] must have been downstairs.
> L: And you had to go to that as well?
> R: Yeah, they took attendance. [*The tone is practical, in contrast to the outburst that follows.*]

> But oh, those awful hymns! Standing up... 'We gather together for the thanksgiving hymn.' Ah, I used to have the book... those Protestant hymns—no modulation. 'Onward Christian Soldiers' [*He sings a few bars as evidence.*] They had a 'I—IV—V' progression and vibrato.
> L: [*surprised*] There was vibrato?
> R: Oh yes! [*He shouts out a strangled Ahhh note to demonstrate.*]
> L: What type was it? Was it organ and choir?
> R: Yeah, so it was very...
> L: But they'd sing in harmony, the choir?
> R: To me, they were trained. I liked it when I'd been to white churches where it was less trained, and there'd be little mistakes that created dissonance. But we pl-od-ded [*The pace is mimicked in the delivery of the word.*] and that sluggish... [*he starts slow clapping*] and there'd be the mashed potato roll derby. Once or twice a year, [after Sunday school] they had a lunch—of potatoes and carrots and peas mixed together—that had been boiled à l'anglaise for hours and hours, and they said, 'Wouldn't you like that with liver?' And that could have been cooked for a...
> L: For a year, yeah.
> R: And I put a little pepper on, and they said, 'We're trying to hide the devils from you.'

For a child introduced at an early age to his grandfather's hors d'oeuvres and Mary Garvey's seaweed, the food was as stodgy as the bible lessons had been. Immensely preferable were those times after church, when the Blakes took the family to the Colony Club, where the Powers had membership. This very exclusive club (membership was invitation only) was situated directly opposite the church on Maple Street. There, in what was left of the morning, Ran and his young sister Martha ordered peppermint stick ice-cream and macaroons (Ran sometimes had a little iced tea), while their mother with her coffee and their father with a glass of rye smiled indulgently, perfectly relaxed in the elegant surrounds.[8] This, for Ran, was the highlight of the day. It made the interminable mornings of plodding hymns and Sunday school lessons bearable. But it was a fleeting experience, for while Ran's parents approved of the notion of a Sunday School education for their children:

> They were not so committed to regular Sunday attendance themselves.... Will you forgive me, Mother and Father? [*He delivers the question theatrically, and then adds in explanation*] They're upstairs listening to me.

So, Ran was expected to attend Sunday School at the Maple Street church, regardless of his parents' attendance. They happily entrusted their children's religious formation to this "legal" church (Ran's descriptor), unaware that their son was already looking elsewhere, developing a broader fascination with churches in general—their music, their drama, their culture, their people.

During Ran's lifetime, there were "twelve to fifteen churches" with which he had some degree of connection. One of the earliest of these was with the Catholic Cathedral of St Michael on State Street—Mary Garvey's church,[9] where she took him for Friday night Benediction. Many things about Mary's church impressed Ran, but the best thing was the candlelight and the fact that "it was night."

> I don't think Mary would have dared take me on a Sunday morning when I was supposed to be at Congregational.

Ran loved the night! It thrilled him to be kneeling in that dimly lit church where shadows played in the corners and darkness was kept at bay by banks of votive candles. It thrilled him to see the altar boys, dressed in cassock and surplice, who needed to stand on tiptoe to light the tall altar candles with their flaming tapers. It thrilled him to see them ring the bells, with two-handed enthusiasm, and wildly swing the incense burner till a curl of smoke rose to permeate the church and tease the nostrils with its strange, sweet tang.

Ran could identify with these boys—he remembers them distinctly:

> [...] and you know what really took me back, did you see the Alfred Hitchcock film *I Confess*? I'll tell you, seeing those old vestments... that flashed me back.

The vestments added to the drama, but it was the Latin hymns that captivated him. They were, he says, "wonderful." Later, he would allow that the music lacked the "horseradish spices" of the Gospel Church. But he could never forget the Latin chants. They remain, echoing on the edge of understanding—a sound memory woven through the whole fabric of the experience. And so, when asked his impression of it now, Ran answers in a hushed tone, "Beautiful," and the word is wrapped in reverence.[10]

But the beauty was tinged with awe. The priest at St Michael's was somewhat frightening with his vivid descriptions of the suffering in hell. Ran still recalls this with a touch of dread:

> R: Sometimes, the priest actually spoke directly to you, or I thought it was to me. Had he found out that my grandparents had given me a hamburger one Friday? He said I was to suffer the condemnation. Maybe there were four or five of us that had and…
> L: [*interrupting enthusiastically*] Me too, so we're in it together!
> R: Oh my gosh, so I'll see you in hell, Leo. May the fire not be too warm…
> L: Well, you like the heat up.
> R: I know I do.
> L: Okay, but did you ever confess to the priest?
> R: I might have once or twice—how did he know I had meat? [*He pauses, remembering that peccadillo.*]
> L: And what did he say?
> R: He said, 'You belong to another faith. We're going to tolerate you here.' And then, he said, 'Our beloved Mary lives with your family, does she?' and *I* think, 'Does *he* think that that book *Forever Amber* came from my parents and that they were trying to delude her?'

Mary had a simple faith that believed in salvation, the glories of heaven, and life eternal. But the other side of the coin—the dark side—was the loss of that salvation: the damnation of eternal punishment in the fires of hell. Intriguingly, Mary seemed to have the ability to live with this dichotomy, bending the rules to accommodate her interests—particularly her love of risqué romantic stories—and absolving herself of perceived "sins," even before they were committed. To this end, she created her own little prayer space in her attic bedroom. Here, she had Ran kneel down quietly while she said the rosary.[11] To the young Ran, this "church in the attic" was captivating. When comparing the churches of Springfield, he can still say, "the real church was in Mary Garvey's attic!" His recollections are shrouded in mystery:

> Did it really have a candle?' [*he asks himself*] or was it only a light that looked… [like a candle.] It was very strangely lit. But it was the *real* church. [for me] And to think Mary Garvey had the x-rated book under her bed. She had to confess it every week. 'I read *Forever Amber*,' she said, 'God will you forgive me, but I have to read a chapter more to see what happens to the girl who's pregnant without the husband,' and she said, 'Forgive me, Jesus Christ.'

Mary had no hesitation in involving Ran in her attic church. She also had her own particular slant on taking him to St Michael's. Ran remembers the gist of what she told him:

She said that my parents still wanted me to go to the Congregational Church, but they did approve of me going to the Catholic Church. They said, 'We just want to know where he goes.' They said they wouldn't mind if I became Catholic. They said not to tell my grandparents, but they approved... though they still wanted me to go to their Church.
They knew I had gone to [Mary's] church because once, when they took me to an Episcopal church, I said, 'Oh, this is close to Mary's church,' and my father said, 'What is this? You're leaving your own church?'
But of course, [*Ran murmurs it philosophically.*] I had [already] left to go to the Pentecostal church.

Ran can't remember how he first came upon the Pentecostal church—the church on Hancock Street. It was certainly quite a walk from his home:

I must have walked by it sometime—how else would I have discovered it? It was quite a walk from one church to another; I must have gone into that neighborhood because there was a comic book about a murder mystery coming out... and then, I heard the most wonderful singer, with a drummer, and so then... this is a downbeat; this is a lick now; this is like the Charlie Parker... [*He is intrigued by the pattern of the story and the way it is unfolding.*] I began asking... They couldn't get over how often I wanted to go to church. They only wanted me to go once a month, and I was going every week. I think Mary began to catch on where I went Sunday morning.

Mary, of all people—with her stories of pirates, and shipwrecks, and spirited little fairies— would have understood the lure of the drummer from the church on Hancock Street.

THE FIRST DAY Ran attended the Pentecostal service, he felt he'd been encouraged to do so by his "brother" Pong. He remembers this moment of encouragement as one of the happy moments in his life:

My favorite brother, Pong; he was my 'fair cat.'[12] This young man was terrific. He would sit near my lap and meow. I remember getting up early Sunday morning, and I told my parents I was going early to the Congregational Church where Dr. Gilkey preached. I started to walk down Union Street, and then I circled back. This memory was very intense because I felt my brother [Pong] was endorsing the trip when he'd got up on the sofa.

> I could see my parents saying, 'It's time for Sunday school.' Each Sunday, they got up later and later—they pretended to like Jesus Christ, but really, they weren't much of churchgoers. But this wonderful Pong would nod to me, and it was like saying, 'Get lost—get out of here,' and I would go out the door, pretending to go down to Ridgewood Place and then cross over and up again—never going to Maple Street where the family church was—and then going further up, and I remember one young black gentleman saying, 'Is there something... [you want?] What are you doing here?' And I had hairs from my brother Pong on my coat.

Every week after this initial encouragement, Ran, dressed in his Sunday best, embarked on the elaborate subterfuge that surrounded his church attendance. He needed to make it seem that he was going to the Congregational Church on Maple Street as usual, but then, as soon as he felt he was not being observed, he had to backtrack:

> I knew the back way to go to the church on Hancock Street. I would leave the Congregational Church [on Maple] and walk up High Street so nobody could see me; I then walked up there on that back street to Union, turning left onto Union, then crossed over Walnut. I went further east, and there was a bar called Jinxey,[13] but I didn't know about those liquids then. I turned right onto Hancock Street. I think it was a few streets more, and the church was a little to the left on the Chase Estate, Hancock Street.[14] Now later, I could walk directly home, down Union, but when I felt I was being observed, I would walk down High.
> L: That's amazing that you can remember the actual directions, but do you think it was the illicit nature of it that made it more enticing?
> R: Oh yes [*definite*]. But then, of course, much more scary were the routes home from *Spiral Staircase*.

Ran's visits to this church were certainly associated with a degree of anxiety. In the first place, he was aware that he was playing truant from Sunday school, and his parents would be disappointed. Secondly, he was aware that Sunday school took a roll, and it was only a matter of time before his absences would be discovered. The third factor was the amount of time it took him to walk from one church to the other and back again. Because of this, he was never able to embrace the experience fully. For no sooner had he arrived than he felt a dreadful need to return to where he should be:

> I think there were several of the times that I went to that church that I didn't get inside [at all] 'cause I'd suddenly [need to] walk back to the other church to get home from the other direction.
> It was quite a walk from one church to the other—much longer than from here to Dalia's.[15] But I wonder if I went there as much as I... [thought] because I can remember Gilkey, and I can't remember this preacher. So, I don't know. In any case, it didn't compare to the North Hartford church.[16]
> L: So, you were going to hear this music? What was it like?
> R: I think it was spiritual as opposed to gospel. At this church, you still had the flavor of... strange chords.

Ran's memory is that he attended the various churches in Springfield from when he was eight years old till when he was eleven:

> Then I moved to Suffield at fourteen or fifteen years old, so I bet for years I didn't go to church at all.

However, it does seem that his attendance at the church on Hancock Street continued right up to when he left for Suffield. By then, he was fifteen years old and had no real urge to be elsewhere. He was able to join in freely and recalls that one day the pianist was ill and he had to substitute—it was a great thrill.

The church on Hancock Street was plain, poor, and unpretentious. Ran's regular attendance was an important stage in his development—a stepping-stone to his involvement, later, at the North Hartford Church.

Ran heard about the Pentecostal Church, North Hartford, from Eunice Bell.[17] (Eunice helped-out occasionally at the Blake's new home in Suffield; Ran loved her delicious "pecan southern pie with custard on top.")

> I remember her saying, 'Son, you've seen and heard nothing yet. You don't go [back] to that Springfield Temple anymore honey-child' (or however she called me). 'You're going to go down to Hartford.'
> I went with her and heard Edith Powell sing—what a contralto voice she had! It was Eunice's son-in-law, Nathanial Wilson, who drove us the first time, and I just remember walking in; I don't know if it was 1950 or '51—the years blur—but it was just... [*He holds his head to contain the momentous nature of the experience.*] I flipped. I just couldn't get over it. And I remember Edith Powell's son, Hubert Powell—he had knee pants; he must have been eleven or twelve at the time as he was two or three years younger than me—playing organ. Oh, it was so exciting! And to have the bible read with that punctuation... and the screams and the frenzy. So, to have the morning there,

and then, the night with *Spiral Staircase*—oh God, [*fervently*] what moments! And the Powell family and Bishop Jefferson and Mother Carter have been my surrogate family ever since.

Ran spent "hours and hours" at the Pentecostal Church of North Hartford, immersing himself in the gospel music that was to become a distinctive feature of his own. For if at the heart of Ran's unique style there is a narrative inspired by film noir, gospel is its soul.

8

CELEBRATION—A PERSPECTIVE ON JOY

*No matter what the celebration, sadness, the
other side of the coin, is not far away.*

RAN BLAKE

Ran's involvement in celebrations at the Pentecostal Church on Hancock Street (and later, at North Hartford) was unreservedly joyful. He was less able to respond with joy at family celebrations. The reasons for this were complex and most likely stemmed from the nature of the participation required. The church took him to a different dimension of experience—one that was out of the ordinary, one in which he could cease to be himself and become part of something bigger. In this respect, it was not unlike his experience in the darkened Capitol Theatre, viewing *Spiral Staircase*. There too, he was able to forget himself and be drawn into another world that was bigger and more compelling than his own—a world where the emotions he experienced were involuntary.

Family gatherings, however, required very personal attendance—and personal responsibility for enjoyment. Despite all manner of preparation (Ran's cousin Joanna recalls that for one birthday party, a magician was hired to amuse the children) and despite happy anticipation by all, the events were rarely able to fulfill Ran's vision for them. Primed by the ability of Mary Garvey to turn her nightly bedtime stories into thrilling productions,[1] his expectations were always high. He wanted mystery—he wanted ghosts and candles. It was impossible for family gatherings to reach standards that, for him, were still only half-imagined hopes and possibilities. His reluctance to attend, his propensity to disappear into his room to read and to dream, reflected a desire to avoid disappointment.

Family gatherings at the Blakes' and the Powers' followed the tried-and-true recipe of good company, good food and drink, and good conversation. Mary Garvey had hinted there were other ways of celebrating. She had told her charge that his parents were "proper," adding that they were not like her parents. The merest hint of dissociation implied in her words cast a small shadow. Added to this, Ran's radio hour had become an important daily ritual; any other proposals to fill the late afternoon/early evening time slot were regarded with varying degrees of coolness, depending on how greatly they interfered with these broadcasts.

This was not always the case:

> I'm sure the first six or seven years I loved birthdays—what child wouldn't? Presents were very important to me at the time. I was self-centered—*I* got presents! I remember enjoying my sister's October 6th birthday; you know, I hear that I liked cake, but I was fascinated by candles—and not just blowing them out. I would try to grab them out of the cake! I loved the flames and the dark. My parents would turn the lights off, and I would say, 'Can we keep it dark for a few minutes longer?' and people would sigh. [But] I had my way—I had whatever I wanted on my birthday. And then, there was always a candle kept in the kitchen in case the lights went out, and of course, candlelight's very important in *Spiral Staircase*.

Birthdays were big occasions, celebrated with all the family, including grandparents, aunts, uncles, and cousins. At the end of the meal, Mary Garvey would bring in the birthday cake, alight with candles:

> I remember Mary coming in—isn't there a scene in Brian de Palma's film *Sisters*[2] where the sisters are bringing some candlelight—a candle on a birthday cake—when a knife comes out to kill somebody? [*The digression*[3] *is fleeting and does not disturb the story's flow*] But what I wanted when I was seven, eight, or nine was a ghost for a present. I wanted a live ghost with a sheet!
> One birthday, they let me invite children to a movie called *Home Sweet Homicide*,[4] and that was my favorite thing to do on my birthday—my father would pay for all the children.... We took about five or six children—friends my age and Martha's—and my father said, 'You and your sister looked so cool.' I don't think he used that word, but Martha was fanning her face and wasn't very scared, and I... [*He makes a nonchalant face.*] Of course, [it was] a soap opera mystery,

but the other children were transfixed, and my father said, 'You and Martha—you both were so blasé.'
But we were experienced. I had taken Martha to the real stuff! So, two or three children—and I *do* like Dean Stockwell as a child actor—but two or three children helping their mother solve a mystery while she has romantic pressures. [*His tone implies that this was humdrum.*] Martha and I would dig into our popcorn while the other children were going like... [*He demonstrates a fearful face.*] And that was at the theater on State Street in whatever year it came out. It was *Mary Poppins* meets *Nancy Drew*. There was no spice! It was better than cooked carrots but... [*He shakes his head regretfully before becoming suddenly impatient with the line of questioning.*]
Have Aaron[5] make us three cocktails and put me to sleep here. I mean, this book is... [*Good manners prevent his finishing the sentence.*] But I guess it's going to keep our friendship alive, Leo—if you're going back [as far as childhood birthdays], but really... it's the birthday... it's really the one in Greece.

Ran was in Greece for his birthday in 1967. It was the day before the Coup d'état,[6] and because he was a foreigner, Ran was stopped and questioned by police. He found the experience frightening, and from that day, birthdays were always associated with this event.

Greece was pivotal—a moment in time that changed everything. It cast its dark shadow back onto happy times and memories, robbing childhood of its innocence and fantasy. It consumed the present and with brooding persistence, tainted perceptions of the future.

Leo avoids Greece[7] at this stage. Instead, he asks easily:

L: Okay, tell us about Thanksgiving.
R: Well, that's not a memory! We had turkey and that dreadful dish called mashed potato ...turnips. My grandparents one day made an exception—they served me mango chutney with shrimp. They said there's a thing called the pepper mill, and years later, Dorothy[8] gave me a portable one for my pocket. You ask about Thanksgiving? [*It's said with a challenge.*] It was with the family: the Clapp family—Joanna, Wende, Andy, Susan—Aunt Frannie, Grandmother Jessie, the dogs.[9] What more? There was no *Spiral Staircase*.
L: You never enjoyed Thanksgiving?
R: It's alright—do you like mashed potato?
L: [*laughs*]
R: I mean, it's not *Spiral* or...
L: Was it a big thing in your family?

R: Well, I guess so. Martinis were served. I don't know. What a prosaic question; you're studying with Lyle and Frank Carlberg![10] That's an awfully mundane question. I don't think it's anything to write home about—Thanksgiving... what about it? When did you get your last haircut? What about Thanksgiving?

Christmas fared no better:

R: What about it? [*the tone is truculent*][11] I got up Christmas and looked to see if there was a package for me, and I remember that the food was similar to the food of Thanksgiving. There was a man down the street who had come from Mexico, and I thought that was much more elegant because they had a thing called avocado and a hot red sauce. Carols were sung on the corner of Union and Main Street. [*He considers this for a moment before continuing.*] Union and Main don't intersect, so whether it was Maple and Main or Union and Maple, but you could say between Union and Main.... What about them? They didn't change key!
L: Right, ah, you're in a very cynical mood.[12]
R: Well, I mean, these are... There was no murder.
L: [*laughs*] So this was a disappointment?
R: No, you know, I don't want my family members murdered, but I kept looking... [for something exciting.] Everything was sort of normal. People wore ties and coats and rather stiff dresses. My Dad would like a little nip on holiday noons—he was allowed one at one o'clock—what about it? [*His voice rises, the tone is challenging.*] There was no detective! I remember my cousin, Joey, mentioning a detective called Nancy Drew. My father had me read *The Hardy Boys* but not *Nancy Drew,* and so I read this "girls'" novel, and there was much more threat of danger, and I thought maybe somebody was going to be killed, so it was a little better. I remember running into a bedroom one Christmas and reading *Nancy Drew*, and then, better yet, was Edgar Allen Poe *The Pit and Pendulum*.[13] And I was told later I was interrupted reading, and they said why didn't I go back to the table, and this was not very good behavior—not acceptable—and I said this was more interesting, and they grabbed me and said, 'Your life is here at this table!' Now I don't know, Janet, if that's Thanksgiving or Christmas, [but] it happened at a holiday celebration.

IF THE MEMORIES of childhood birthdays, Thanksgiving, and Christmas have blended together— stored in association with mashed potato, turnips, and routine haircuts, and wrapped in the shadow of Greece—Halloween has fared better:

> Sitting 'round having turkey at Thanksgiving was a... [bore] while there was Halloween.... [*His voice lifts in a tremor of remembered excitement.*]
> All the houses would be dark in Springfield. My first memories [were that] my father was the superintendent of our block for the blackouts during World War II. Now, when the war was over, I was ten years old, so I remember walking out.... At Halloween, there'd be people with candles, but I think I'm over-glamorizing—I bet that happened one Halloween—but going out at night.... There was no curfew [anymore]. There'd be moans at night, and I hear my mother moaned one time trying to get me... [back to reality.] They [my parents] wanted to control the mystery... and violence. There would be people with sheets over their heads as ghosts, and I hear I took over that [practice] and scared my sister to death as the 'Jolly Ginkie Ghost.'

The fever pitch of excitement that Ran felt at Halloween is palpable in the re-telling. It is no wonder his mother "moaned." The excitement was so great that it extended into dreams; and it is plausible that Ran's parents devised schemes to dampen it somewhat:

> One Halloween [in Suffield], I took a walk going north and walking home with candlelight, I ran into a witch-lady with her cheek debarred [*sic*] with red paint.... Now, later, I was told that she was a neighbor, Doris Leete.

Whether or not Ran recognized his neighbor is immaterial. He was determined to recapture some of the intrigue and mystery of the Halloweens of his childhood, and finding Mrs. Leete, an adult neighbor, right in the spirit of the feast, encouraged Ran to enter into the drama also:

> I was fourteen or fifteen then, but I *wanted* to be scared. It got harder and harder to be scared at Halloween. I had to read Poe [because] it—the Halloween pumpkin and all that—got to be babyish.
> But I didn't recognize Mrs. Leete at the time. She said I could not go any further and that she had broken into a neighbor's house [Mrs. Leete's]. We went down steps to the cellar, and I was put in a room. I was locked in. I think my parents felt that I should have some experience in real life, not just live vicariously through the characters in *Spiral Staircase*, and I remember screaming to get out. I think I was there five minutes locked in, but it seemed like an hour. I did get scared.

L: So, did someone... why did they?

R: Oh, it was a trick. I don't know. I think they... And then I read that Alfred Hitchcock, once as a child...[14] [*He does not continue, but the story of the lesson Hitchcock's father arranged for him can be read in the footnote.*] Anyway, then I was let out ...going up some stairs— but they weren't spiral—and she [the witch] said, 'Mrs. Leete's in bed, but you can come in,' and we had apples with cinnamon; dark, strong, root beer... and she said, 'Do you want pepper in it?' and I said, 'Oh, that's carrying it too far.' She said her name was Ghost Nadine.... There was candlelight. Part of this doesn't make sense; I KNOW [*with emphasis*] I'm exaggerating this story. I wasn't there for long, but I think, in my dreams, I was there in that room overnight.

Halloween was the stuff of dreams ...of nightmares. It was also the inspiration for shadowy movie scripts to play out in a young boy's imagination. The dream world, conjured through imagination, was the place Ran preferred. So, though the Blakes and the Powers went to a great deal of trouble to celebrate birthdays and other seasonal feasts, these offered Ran little pleasure. He preferred solitude, and he found this in the cemetery on Mulberry Street— so close to his grandparents' home on Ridgewood Place and his own home on Union Street.

MULBERRY STREET RUNS alongside the old Union Street Methodist Society burial grounds. These grounds were merged with the larger Springfield Cemetery in 1844, thus giving access to a vast tract of beautiful countryside with gently sloping hills and hollows deep in shadow, with wide, sunny spaces and thickly treed inclines—a natural sanctuary for birds.[15] Along Mulberry Street, the cemetery is bounded by a red-brick and wrought-iron fence with wide gateways; the eye is immediately drawn through the fence and onto the open space beyond. That space would have been extremely inviting, and the fact that a young child could easily slip through the upright iron bars made it very accessible.

Martha Blake, five years Ran's junior, always spent a lot of time (along with her big group of friends) in the cemetery. She thought it was a 'beautiful place to walk' and recalls she was 'skinny enough to get through the bars.' But for Ran, it was more than a beautiful, open space. For Ran, it was an essential escape from the repetitive dreariness of life in a small, sleepy city in 1940s America. For Ran, this space was a blank storyboard, a movie set waiting for a director. Tall trees cast dark shadows, and white tombstones rose up out of the gloom. For him, it was not the place to walk with friends, for him, it was a place of solitude—for thinking, for dreaming, for acting out large-scale productions:

> Well, you should know that at nine, ten, eleven, when I was in Massachusetts, I visited the cemetery very often—so a lot of the graves were my friends, like Albert Bruff; he was the husband of my grandmother's sister, and I don't remember him. I knew his wife Clara—Clara B-R-U-F-F. And Clara and Albert lived in Boston before I knew them, and then, Albert died. Isn't that funny—I've been trying to think of his first name, and it is Albert. So, then the sister, Clara, moved to 42 Ridgewood Place after her husband died—so maybe [that was why] he was buried in Springfield... Was I in a dream when I was talking to you, Leo?
> L: I don't know—sometimes you were.
> R: But it was on Mulberry Street, and there was a secret entrance.
> L: Can you describe the secret entrance?
> R: No. [*very definite*]
> L: Yeah you can.
> R: [*without a moment's hesitation*] I can see me walking down Mulberry... I'm on the left, and it just starts... It's perpendicular to Union, and then, it starts going parallel to Union, and there's a gate there—maybe 'semi-secret' is a better word because Martha would have gone there. A mile or two away would have been a more major entrance, or maybe I knew a way-in at night that was secret. I would think that maybe they closed it at nine or ten at night. I know that my parents once... I seem to think they had a car, but why would a car go in there? [But] they knew a rock where... maybe Martha knew where I would meditate—but not in the yoga sense of the word—and showed them. Towards the end, when I ran off, they knew I'd be in that cemetery, but I don't know if it was open all night. You know, I haven't been there since '52/'53. And I would go there, and then my parents got wise to it, and when I ran away from home, they'd find me [there]. And you know Hitchcock's last movie was *The Family Plot*?

The Hitchcock reference is unexpected, but the cemetery on Mulberry Street, with its peace, solitude, and dark shadows, was a place that evoked the moods of film noir. Later, after the family moved to Suffield, Ran admitted going back to the cemetery "a few times."

> R: It felt sad going back to the past and seeing the houses.
> L: Why did you start going down to the graveyard in the first place?
> R: Because that's what the mystery said.

Ran craved solitude and mystery. But there was one event that did capture his imagination. It had none of the nightmarish thrill of Halloween; rather, it had a gentle magic, almost like a fairytale. It took place in summer, at Sunapee, and though the little ritual was repeated year after year, its power to enchant never diminished:

> In the summer, a lady dressed in white would come out of the lake. She was called the Lady in White or the Lady of the Lake—and I was fourteen or fifteen before I realized it was a real relative. This was where the joy was!

9

A World of Wonder—The Lady of the Lake

> *Anon, to sudden silence won,*
> *In fancy they pursue*
> *The dream-child moving through a land*
> *Of wonders wild and new,*
> *In friendly chat with bird or beast-*
> *And half believe it true.*
>
> Lewis Carroll, All in the Golden Afternoon

Shadows may have blurred many of Ran's childhood memories, but Lake Sunapee was always drenched in sunlight. It was a place where the young Ran experienced moments of magic, mystery, joyful exhilaration, and deep, abiding peace.

Lake Sunapee, located in Sullivan and Merrimack Counties, New Hampshire, was the summer holiday destination of the Blakes. P.C. Powers had purchased a big, rambling house—Ran remembers a "dilapidated mansion" that the children liked to think was haunted—on the north-eastern shores of the lake at Herrick Cove, quite near to New London. (Diagonally opposite, across the water, you could see Georges Mills.) Here the Powers would retreat each summer—arriving at the end of May and staying till mid-September. (There was no heating, so they did not stay longer.) It was an idyllic spot—a place where, relaxed and free from business concerns, P.C. liked to gather his family and friends around him for a summer of swimming, sailing, reading, and resting.

Lake Sunapee is a magnificent and ancient expanse of water—crystal clear and often cold, with depths that dream of a glacial past. The water, being fed from bedrock aquifers, is exceptionally pure. The lake itself is flanked by rocky hills, with the imposing Mt. Sunapee at its southern reaches and Mt. Kearsarge to the east. For thousands of years, it had remained a gathering place for tribes of the indigenous Algonquian culture—a place which they called *Soo-nipi* or "wild goose waters" because of the migrating wild geese that came to feed there. It was a place of incredible beauty, abundantly blessed with native flora and fauna.[1]

Mercifully, this environment was not marred by early industry (such as tanneries and sawmills) along the Sugar River. The importance of preserving the area's breathtaking beauty for a vital tourist trade had become apparent soon after the Civil War. Indeed, holidaymakers had begun arriving as early as 1849, when the railway was extended to Newbury Harbor. By the time P.C. Powers moved there, the shores of the lake were dotted with small communities, which had been mostly established by professional and business-folk who brought with them the sense of stability, respectability, and tradition they enjoyed in their hometowns. The holiday homes they constructed reflected this in their preference for traditional styles—English and Dutch Colonial with an occasional hint of Tudor. Some were simple cottages sheltering behind picturesque—and occasionally, grand—boat sheds, some were imposing two and three-story wooden structures, some had elaborate entrance porticos with columns, others had gables and attic windows. Together they created a picture-perfect holiday village of timeless appeal.

Sunapee was a drive of a little over a hundred miles north from Springfield—a drive that, in the 1940s, would have taken three hours or more. For a young child, it seemed interminable, and Ran's mother would encourage him to look out for familiar landmarks to help pass the time:

> I remember, outside of Newport, I would see a big fuel pipe on the side of the road, and it was the longest pipe—it seemed to be about a mile long—and I would always wait for that pipe. [*He shakes his head in wonder, remembering.*]

For when he saw the pipe, he knew they were on the home stretch of their journey—in ten minutes, they'd be in "Sunapee." Before long, there'd be a view of the lake. Any discomfort experienced on the drive was forgotten at the first glimpse of the lake and the thought of Philip and Jessie Powers and possibly a houseful of other guests—aunts, uncles, cousins—waiting to welcome them. The first glimpse of the house never failed to delight.

It was all very luxurious. Part of the house might have been a little bit decayed, but we thought it was grand. There were palatial grounds and dark woods at night. There was a lot of room to wander and to walk. We lived near the icehouse, but we also had our own... [icehouse.] It was a room bigger than this room. It was locked, and it had cubes of ice this big [*He stretches arms wide.*], mixed with sawdust. My grandparents had somebody who would help them cut the ice up—it supplied the whole family. People liked a nip in the evening, and the ice would go... [in the drink.] They liked to put ice on fish to keep it fresh, and I liked to have ginger ale with plenty of ice and then iced tea, iced coffee—so ice was very popular. And then we had a thing that LOOKED like a refrigerator, but you couldn't... it didn't make ice. And I think we had that in Springfield, but in Sunapee, ice would be chopped. You could keep butter and water cold, but the ice would melt about a day later.
L: How did they chop it?
R: There was an ax. I tried to take the ax away one day, and they said, 'No, no, no!' I felt very vengeful.
L: Oh, Ran!
[*Ran smiles mischievously.*]

Sunapee was crammed with happy memories:

> To get a couple of quarters was great when you were ten years old in summer. And you could get soda pop, as they called it, and special chocolate with pistachio ice cream.

Ran's cousin Joanna recalls:

> [...] driving on Sunday mornings to the Gray House [the ice cream parlor] in New London with Grampa to get a five-gallon container of mint ice cream for lunch. I think he took all the grandkids.[2]

There was also a general store with an old-fashioned soda fountain at Blodgett's Landing, three or four miles south from Herrick Cove,[3] where they served the "Awful Awful," but Ran remembers going to Mr. Lovely's drugstore.

> Mr. Lovely[4] ran the drugstore in New London. We would go there, and you could buy—for two dollars—a rose, and it would turn blue if the weather was nice and green and yellow if there was to be a storm. Oh, I loved that!
> And then there was a tree where I would give sermons on Sunday morning, and my cat Pong came, and other animals... and I would tell ghost stories! Late at night, the atmosphere was scary and won-

derful for ghost stories. I liked the night. People would come over [to the tree] to hear my ghost stories, but then they'd say, 'Oh, we can't hear them again.' They got very tired! But it was a magic tree, and Alice in Wonderland had dug a hole there.

It is not surprising that Alice—who began her journey to Wonderland on a "golden afternoon" on the river in July 1862[5]—came to Ran's mind when he, as a young boy, was enjoying summer days on the shores of Lake Sunapee. His parents had often read the book to him when he was six or seven years old. And there was something very magical about the golden afternoons of long summer vacations when the sun shone warmly:

> And those goldenrods—those tall yellow weeds—goldenrods. It was like a weed, and it would be two feet [high], and they would be mown down.[6] There would be a lot of dirt roads, so to get to the main highway, my grandparents and another neighbor, Grayce Poor,[7] collected the money, and they made a dirt road, and there'd still be the flowers—the goldenrods—on either side. I can just see them. The mosquitos were not too kind, but the days stretched on and on, and the whole family was benign and relaxed.

Lake Sunapee in the summer was a special place for P.C. Powers and his extended family. Away from the routine and rituals of daily life in the city, adults and children alike could relax; there was plenty of time to indulge the children's delight in imaginary worlds and, for the adults, to recapture some of the pleasures of childhood themselves.

Jessie Powers (the children called her "Ga Ga") was one of those special people who still knew her way back to the "wonderland" of childhood, and every summer, she delighted the grandchildren with her appearance as the Lady of the Lake.

> I remember evenings at the lake… and then [*his voice rises in excitement*] suddenly a lady in white would walk out from the water. She was wearing big gauzes—a veil—so we could not see her face. We really didn't know, for two or three years, who she was, and when we did, there were younger cousins and the children next door, so… [we didn't tell.] It got to be quite a legend. And when she came from the water, there were these fingers of phosphorescence streaming from her hands. And she carried bags of coins, and in the waters of the lake were quarters, fifty cents or silver dollars—they'd be cast out at my sister and me and all the children. Different people from New Hampshire would be there—and the cousins…. We thought she was wonderful. She couldn't speak—this lady in white…. I haven't

thought of this in years. [*There's joy in his voice.*] For years I kept asking... ['who is she?'] and I'd graduated from Junior High School when I remember my aunt and uncle said, 'You don't believe in Santa, do you?'

'Of course not,' [*He adopts a scoffing tone.*] 'that's for kids! I know there's nobody.'

'But you do believe in the Lady of the Lake, and you know her very well,' they said.

And then I began to have a year when I half-believed and half-didn't, but she brought SUCH GOOD LUCK. There were spices at the table that night—after she came—and fresh things... and [*added quickly*] NO cooked carrots and mashed potato! And I said I wanted it to go on for all my life—the Lady of the Lake.

Her real name was Jessie Arnold: A-R-N-O-L-D.

L: Who was she [*Leo is entranced. This was an early interview, and we had not come upon her name before.*]

R: My grandmother, disguised as the Lady of the Lake. She would surreptitiously disappear around dark; my grandfather wanted more than two martinis, and he'd let me—with my fingers in the olive juice—make them for him, and my grandmother would... [slip away], and I'd hear her voice booming while she was probably changing her gown to go into the lake.

[Then] I would hear a moan, and we'd walk right out and from here to there [*He gestures, his arms wide—his tone is uplifted.*] was the lake, and then [*with excitement*] suddenly a lady in white would walk out from the water! And then, we wanted to see her leave, and my parents would say, 'Hush, you can't see her leave.'

So, we children were taken back to the house—we could never see. She probably scrambled in, circled around, went through the kitchen door while my grandfather said, 'I want a drinkie—another drink.'

And so, I remember one time I thought I saw her with water on her face as she came in—she looked awfully refreshed, my Grandmother Jessie. Her hair seemed wet at dinner that night. OH JESSIE! And she looked like Mrs. Warren in *Spiral Staircase* with those [big brown] eyes, so that's a memory....

L: That's a good memory.

FOR RAN, HIS sister, and his cousins, the comforting routine at their grandparents' grand, old house consolidated childhood memories. The day-to-day rhythm of life at Sunapee (as well as its magic, mystery, and natural beauty) has been preserved in great detail:

> I just got a vision—my grandparents—they spoke to me from heaven. My grandfather LOVED his room with a deck overlooking the lake, and he had then a front room where he could see any cars coming up the road. He had a little telescope, and my grandmother had the room OVER the lake at the back or front of the house—whichever way you think it. And I should say that the main rooms where we entertained, and the kitchen were not dilapidated—they were well kept up. They had a service tray with cocktails, and cheeses, [and] devilled eggs. There were luxurious sofas, good light; then, you'd go right outside, and if you didn't watch, you'd go down a big hole (and I know somebody broke a leg).... So there were things that would fly apart— the ice part: the roof fell off; there was a small fire one night in one wing, but the front room was ELEGANT. They had that reconstructed. And you know, we didn't need to be inside—there would be special steps to the [*He pauses—back there for a moment—before continuing.*] the WATER was as close to us as I am to the kitchen in my apartment now!
>
> There were so many people there; people would drop in to eat—the staff was big. A man would bring his wife and three kids to stay for a week or two, and they'd prepare meals. They'd have a chance to do a party once every ten days, and my grandparents would be there as guests. And liquor flowed....

Ran's cousins recall holidays at Lake Sunapee with equal fondness. Joanna remembers the icehouse (off the kitchen and laundry area) where:

> Wende and I would go on a hot day and scratch around for the ice covered in sawdust. We also liked to walk on the roof and look down at whatever and whomever. [*She hastens to add that it must have been the lower roof area over the kitchen, which was only one story high.*][8]

Wende recalls cocktail hour on the screened porch:

> [...] where we children, all spiffed up, were allowed one hors d'oeuvre after greeting the guests, then waited to see whether Grampa would toss his martini contents through the screen, yelling at Jess to make another.[9]

Wende also recalls that Ran would play the grand piano there,[10] frequently favoring loud, crashing sounds, imitating thunder and lightning.

The lake was not without its challenges. It was a wild and exciting place, and Wende remembers:

[...] the fenced yard where we [children] were banished until old enough to survive the potential perils of a big lake and deep woods.[11]

Ran was also aware of the dangers:

> And oh, I just thought of something else…. I have been told that many people have drowned in that lake—late at night—and that I didn't know the people. But I decided to swim [anyway]. We had three rocks. [One was] A little rock, and that got me swimming more. And so, I know that the lake had mystery, and it tried to eat other people, but then, the lake would be nice and let other people go back home safely! So, it was a very special lake with a personality. And often, in winter, I would dream about Lake Sunapee.

It is little wonder that Lake Sunapee featured in Ran's dreams. Here there was the time, the space, and the freedom he needed to engage with his creative self. Here, free from the tyranny of the school-day routine and his compulsion to get indoors in time to hear his radio programs, he was able to truly relax. At Sunapee, the Blake children were out after dark to witness the arrival of the Lady of the Lake, to tell ghost stories under the special tree, to explore the wild woods. There was a happy balance of exercise and rest, of storytelling, reading, and dreaming. There was plenty of opportunity for Ran to play with his cousins and other children staying nearby. Sunapee became a celebrated childhood memory.

10

SUFFIELD, CONNECTICUT—A NEW START

The place where I grew up.

RAN BLAKE

When Ran was fifteen years old, the family moved from Springfield, Massachusetts, to Suffield, Connecticut. It was a move that made no sense to Ran. From his perspective, Springfield had much more to offer. He knew the neighborhood and relished the mix of cultures; he had finally been "accepted" there, and he had freedom, especially regarding his choice of church. As he recalls, "By then, my parents didn't give a damn if I went to church or not." Suffield was a step into the unknown.

Suffield, as the crow flies, was approximately ten miles south-west of Springfield. By car, through Longmeadow and Thompsonville, the journey took around thirty minutes. It was, then, a small town—just under five thousand people.[1] It had wide, tree-lined streets and established homes, dating back to the late 18th century. Philip Blake had inherited a little money after his father's death, and he and Alison had decided it would be nice to get their family out of the city and into a more relaxed environment.

> They wanted to get out of the 'horrible'— they used that word [*Ran is amazed at their choice of adjective*]—mystery jungle of the city. They had to get me away from the grave, from radio, but particularly from the cinema.

They had seen a beautiful 19th century home for sale on the corner of Main Street and Marbern Drive— "a really elegant house" with plenty of room and spacious grounds where Alison could indulge her passion for gardening.

> My mother was such a well-known gardener; people would come from miles around to look at her garden. It was a gorgeous garden. She was always outside, gardening. She grew blue flowers.

The Blakes had no doubt hoped that by moving into the country, they could encourage Ran to spend more time outdoors engaged in healthy, physical activity. Indeed, his mother was successful, when the spring came, in getting him involved with her garden, as he did a lot of the digging required in setting it up. He also did "lawn duties" and brought in the wood. These tasks were done willingly enough, but unlike his mother, who was captivated and inspired by the peace and beauty of the countryside,[2] Ran felt he was "in the provinces." Even having his own little wing in the new house (with a bedroom, a small bathroom with shower, and a room that he could use as his record room) could not compensate:

> Suddenly, I had this privacy—instead of a small, cramped room. My father would still inspect my room—I wish he would today. [*It's said in a wry aside.*] Oh, *is* there clutter here today! How unappreciative I was [back then] when I had a place for all my records, and I had twice the space to dream. Right in front of the house was a big highway leading to Hamilton Standard[3] and to the airport—which is now the Bradley International Airport—and to the headlock of the Windsor Locks canal.

Such positive aspects of the move would not be apparent till later. For when the Blakes arrived at their new home in January or February of 1951, Suffield was still in the grip of winter, and "Boy was it cold!" Ran desperately missed the little world he had carved out for himself in Springfield—with its solitary walks in the cemetery, its radio programs, its movies—as well as all the memories tied up in the Union Street house, for he was not only leaving his childhood haunts but his beloved grandparents as well. He felt isolated and lonely. For him, the move was "a big, big shock."

Occasionally, in those early Suffield days, Martha would join her brother in his suite. To entertain her, Ran would put on a record of Rachmaninoff's second piano concerto, and they would get down "on all fours, pretending to be animals of the forest or ghosts." These were those poignant moments when siblings, straddling two different stages of development, could come together fleetingly in the world of imagination. But most of the time, Ran was left alone with his own thoughts and dreams, the peace and solitude of the tranquil surroundings going unnoticed.

Ran's room was at the back of the house, protected from the noise of any traffic on Main Street. The view from his window was, he eventually realized, "spectacular." It scanned the little houses that seemed to go "on and on" down Marberg Drive and on into the valley below:

> I would look down, and there would be tobacco farms, maybe large hills—I don't think they were mountains—gorgeous color in the spring, snow, and mystery at night. And I had a little door in the back which would lead to the roof of the garage where I would sit in summer... but ah, [*suddenly realizing*] I don't have a view here in the [Brookline] basement.
> L: I like your view in the basement, Ran. I always found it so magical when I was there as a student, studying from you, to see the feet of people going past; I liked that.
> R: Yes, I do too, and it reminds me of *The Lodger* by Alfred Hitchcock.
> L: I love those little windows that you have. I'd love to have a place in a basement.
> R: [*smiling broadly*] Would you now, would you now? And, of course, compared to the view of Sunapee, Suffield was nothing, but did I care about it? My parents said, 'Look, you're one of the luckiest boys—you've got these two small rooms; you're in a gorgeous house...' Ah, [*mournful tone*] there was no theater! Somebody would have to drive me five miles to Thompsonville. What could I do? I could sneak out of the house [but] where was there to go? Football and baseball were popular, but I would do everything [to get away]. My grandparents were alive for years, and I would do all I could so I could go back to Springfield to see them ...and go to the movies.
> L: So, did you ever go back to that graveyard when you were living at Suffield?
> R: A few times, but... it felt sad going back to the past and seeing the houses, the people...

Growing Pains

Some day you will be old enough to start reading fairy tales again.

C.S. Lewis, Letter to Lucy Barfield[4]

Ran's parents had wanted a new start for their son. They had worried about his "obsession" with the graveyard, with cinema and radio. Suffield had no cinema, and, it seems, radio was also restricted at the Blake house:

> When we moved to Suffield, [I noticed] one or two radios were broken, and I mentioned that at dinner, and my father tried to suppress a laugh, and my sister, Martha, winked at my mother.[5]

Perhaps it was simply a reflection of the times. Things were changing, and radio's days as a dominant presence in many homes were numbered. Public television broadcasting, along with all sales of television sets, had been halted during the war,[6] but this situation was reversed post-war, and by 1949, sales of black and white sets had skyrocketed.[7]

The Blakes moved from a city "jungle" with all its diversions and mysteries to what they thought would be the more wholesome atmosphere of a small country town. But elements of the "jungle" were poised to encroach right into people's living rooms; the Blakes arrived in Suffield just prior to the invasion of television. By 1950, one in every eleven houses in America owned a TV set.[8] By mid-1952, the Springfield Broadcasting Corporation was formed, and on March 1, 1953, WWLP TV transmitted the first television signal in that area.[9] Television sets continued to become more affordable, and by 1954, over 50% of US homes owned a black and white television.[10] The Blakes' search for a relaxed life with congenial society coincided with one of the biggest social changes in American lifestyle in living memory, and though they still could know the postman by name (Thomas Kennedy), though they shared a party telephone line with five other families, and though the one general store just down the street was the source of all their supplies, each evening the whole town disappeared into the privacy of their living rooms to watch whatever programs were on offer. *I Love Lucy*, which starred the madcap Lucille Ball and her then-husband Desi Arnaz, was extremely popular, as was the *Ed Sullivan Show*[11] and the wholesome family show, *Father Knows Best*, starring Robert Young.

Television, however, didn't enthrall Ran as radio had done:

> Things weren't scary enough. There was *Perry Mason,* but, you know, it was sort of static.[12]

The whole rigmarole associated with family viewing in those early days of television would have been anathema to Ran's sense of the theatrical. This was the same boy who, at a very young age, had staged performances of his own ghost stories complete with drawn curtains, dimmed lighting, and menacing, clashing chords.

Ran's parents insisted that the evening meal be cleared away with the dishes done before the family could retire to the den in time to watch the television news and whatever other programs were on offer. At first, it seemed exciting to gather in the den; it was something out of the ordinary:

> My father's little bar was there, the French library, a couple of prints. Pong, the cat, and Buffy—and all the delightful dogs—would be there, and we would stay there for the evening to watch *Perry Mason* and *Della Street*[13] and something about a woman called Lucy, with Lucille Ball. *Perry Mason* was on a Sunday night, and later, when I would have to return to Bard College [after the weekend], I would stay and see *Perry Mason* first. It's a wonder the car didn't break down on a dark road—I often thought it might. But *Perry Mason* wasn't nearly as scary as *Inner Sanctum,* and we weren't particularly addicted—I think only the news [program] at night... [was obligatory viewing.]

In many ways, watching television in the den ended up being a chore rather than a pleasure. The nature of the den had been changed by the intrusion. In the past, this room, where there were "no pianos allowed," was his father's domain. It was "just for contemplation, reading, and good whiskey." The television seemed to be a vulgar addition. And the screen was small! For a boy who loved the "big screen" movies, this small box in the den was no substitute. Television was too small, too contained, too one-dimensional, and "the music was too diatonic!" Ran preferred to go to his own room and listen to records or read a mystery.

It was not till many years later, when he was sick in Boston, that television entered his life in any way at all. At this time, he became fascinated with *Twilight Zone*:

> *Twilight Zone* WAS scary. You'd be in an airplane, and you'd see a hand coming out—it was before *Twin Peaks*; it was scary. It had

strange music. Some [episodes] were on Mars and Jupiter, but some would take place right on earth. The guy who produced it did two or three other series but nothing like this one. But that hadn't started by the mid-fifties—or, if it had, I didn't know about it [14]

SCHOOL—SQUARE PEGS AND ROUND HOLES

"If there is no meaning in it," said the King, "that saves a world of trouble, you know, as we needn't try to find any. And yet I don't know."

LEWIS CARROLL, *ALICE IN WONDERLAND*

BUT IT WASN'T just the world that was changing—Ran was changing too. He was no longer a child. The move to Suffield had coincided with a new stage in his life. Ran was growing up. He was becoming social and had started to identify with the cosmopolitan atmosphere at Classical High:[15]

> My Italian—a lot of Italians—Greek, black friends, and white friends, they gave diversity. Women and men were both teaching. 'Classical' was so diverse—different accents. A nice German girl's father and mother ran a German deli; they had been ostracized after World War II, but then people knew that they hated Nazism and they would go [to their deli]. Anthony Fulkalora, from the Italian north-end, became a friend, and there was a very nice guy from Mexico. And it was so great being with these people.

Ran suddenly had friends. And he was taking a vital interest in school subjects as well: "A wonderful journalism course with Miss O'Grady" and an "excellent literature course." Though the algebra teacher had to be "very patient" with him, the music department valued his input. For the school's performance of *The Mikado*, he helped with the set and worked as a "runner"; he wrote music for *Arsenic and Old Lace*. He also played piano for school assembly each week.

> Marjorie Goodhines, the music teacher, was so encouraging. She sent my music to a state convention. Her belief was so tremendous.

Ran was also nominated as vice president of his class:[16]

> I was so overjoyed to be nominated as vice president of the student body at Springfield, [then] I was shunned in Suffield. Once my family left to relocate to Suffield, I became a recluse.

And though he was not sports-minded, he had, at Springfield:

> joined Sidney Burr in the track club—I knew him. They were very proud—the guys—that I tried out, and I wasn't good at sports. It was a really good environment.

Ran was suddenly at the center of school activities and his parents began to wonder if they were doing the right thing, taking him away. But the move was organized; plans were in place. Anxious to lessen the upheaval for their son, Philip and Alison decided to let him continue at Springfield Classical High school to complete his tenth grade. As it turned out, he stayed for "one year and one month" after the move. He even got a job as a messenger at the Union Trust Bank on Main Street, Springfield. Ran remembers this happened in the summer vacation, around 10th or 11th grade at "Classical." Ran commuted to school with his father. Philip Blake had to travel to Brightwood for work each day. It was a twenty to thirty-minute drive. The arrangement had its difficulties:

> My father had to get up an hour early—at five-thirty or quarter to six—so that we could leave the house at six-thirty or seven, and he dropped me near the school and then continued to Brightwood. And then, in the afternoon, I couldn't do all the [after-school] activities. I finally had friends, and I couldn't [stay]. Even if, once or twice in a great while, my father would drive me home as a treat, mostly I was expected to find my own way home.

The relatively short car journey between Springfield and Suffield became quite an undertaking when using public transport. Ran had to keep to a strict timetable after school. He needed to walk downtown—or, if it was cold, take a bus—to catch a connection to Thompsonville, Enfield.[17] From Thompsonville, he could catch another bus to Suffield, which would get him home at six-thirty or seven at night. It was a long day (beginning and ending in darkness in the winter months):

> I liked to stay at school with guys till four-thirty or five, and then, there was the madhouse [rush] of going down Worthington Street to... where was that bus?[18] It was a real drag going on the bus. The bus only ran once an hour to Thompsonville from Springfield. If I waited very long, there'd be a bus to Hartford, which I could get off

a few blocks from my house. It was a real drag—I didn't have any place to wait. I loved my chocolate peppermint milkshakes and coffee—I had discovered coffee—and coffee ice-cream was good too. But there was no place.... Later, I knew there was a movie house there—I would have liked to wait in the movie house—but that would have got me in at eight-thirty or nine.

Thompsonville, as the urban center of Enfield, did have its own diversions... and temptations. The Strand movie theatre (overlooking Freshwater Pond at 11 North Main Street) and Gatto Music Center and Appliances on Pearl Street were to become favorite haunts. Ran didn't visit them initially, but one night the temptation was too much, and he was enticed into the Strand, where he became engrossed in the movie that was playing:

> My father had beat me [home] by an hour. They couldn't find me, and my father was very angry. When I got home, I didn't get a treat. They gave me some supper, but I could tell.... When he was angry, my father would turn red in the face [*Ran draws a small circle high up on his cheekbone to illustrate*], and his fingers would go like that [rubbing his fingers against his thumb], and my mother's nose would get a little bit bigger, and she'd say, 'How are you?' with a little kiss, but I knew something was bothering her. And my sister said, 'I know where you were—in a theater.'
> They'd called my grandparents; they couldn't find me. And then, somebody with a flashlight went in the theater and found me.
> L: Was that embarrassing—being pulled out of the theater?
> R: No, it was MUCH more embarrassing at *Spiral Staircase* when I was in sixth or seventh grade, and the manager said, 'Oh, that kid again!'

This incident at the Strand may have been a catalyst; Ran's schooling arrangement was becoming untenable for the Blake family. Ran sensed that it was "a drag" for his father to have to get up early enough to drop him at Classical High. He also knew that the early mornings in the cold air were playing havoc with his allergies. "I had such allergies," he recalls, "They called me foghorn." In addition, the evening meal was often disrupted, and, with all the bus travel, it was very hard for him to complete his homework, so his marks were going down:

> because I couldn't do homework till eight o'clock, and my mind [was occupied with] how am I going to get a ride Friday because there's a movie by Hitchcock showing in Thompsonville; I've got to go there—'Yes, I did my homework,' I'd wink to my parents—and the

grades went down and down, and they said, 'You need more discipline.' This was when they thought of Suffield.

Something had to change. Suffield High School was discussed—but it had no college preparation course. Suffield Academy appealed to Philip Blake. He knew the headmaster as well as some of the teachers. The school had a college preparation year, and though fees were expensive (at the time, it cost two to three hundred dollars a year for a day student), it was a saving on the costs involved in keeping Ran at Classical High:

> And now they'd turn-over [in their graves] to hear I did take taxis [from Thompsonville] a few times...
> So, my parents urged me to go to Suffield Academy. My father said, 'Don't you dread another winter, having to wait in the cold?' And I think they said, 'Oh, you can go to the Thompsonville movies; we'll drive you there.'
> But of course, they showed adventure movies there and didn't have the mysteries of Springfield. [*It's added in a thoughtful aside.*] My parents did everything they could to make Suffield Academy [attractive]: 'Oh, you can sleep another hour, and you can get into a great college.'
> But boy, that's the worst mistake I made...

At the time, his parents seemed to be putting forward a convincing argument, and Ran, caught up in "the whole joy" of having friends and being "more accepted," had no reason to suspect that this acceptance might not carry over to a new school.

Suffield Academy, however, was quite different from Classical High and Ran had to find his way all over again. He had to make new friends and deal with those who found him "different." At that time, Suffield Academy was all-male (and this included staff). The students were "white and privileged." To be a boarder cost a couple of thousand a year, but Ran lived several doors down the street, so he was a day student:

> When I first left Classical, I thought it was for the best—to go down the street, to get home at four o'clock in the afternoon. So, I could do piano then, and I [also] started with Ray Cassarino, and I had a few lessons... Other times I would dream—I had a lot more time.

Despite the extra hours in the day for study, Ran's marks showed no sign of improving:

> There was no competition at Suffield at that time, so I would be doing a really bad job. And as bad a student as I was, some [of the others] were dreadful—They didn't do the homework. I was terrible at French—they [my parents] gave me private lessons—it embarrassed my father. I flunked algebra, geometry... I was not an "A" student at Classical. I should say my best subject was Latin: it's the only thing I ever got A's in. I could write murder mysteries, and I didn't have to speak it; I could just do the homework in Latin. But as for the irregular... [verbs] oh, I forget them all—my ears were always picking up music.

Ran's parents hit upon a plan of giving him pocket money for records if his marks improved. They gave him $50 a month to spend at Gatto's Music store—if certain conditions were kept:

> I had to stack wood, mow the lawns, keep my grades up, do what I was told to—be home on time.
> L: How much would a record cost then?
> R: Four, five, six dollars—they gave me a great discount. The store was run by Helen and Chick Gatto. Chick was a drummer. I got to be a record addict, and that's where all my money went. In one way, they [my parents] liked it better than [my] going to movies.
> And of course, in Suffield, I was known for my punctuality. I didn't want to hang with those guys at school. So, they found me idle in the living room—in my dream world. It [my dream world] had come back! It had gone away while I was at Classical. But occasionally, I would get a good mark, so I could get my records. Looking back, I didn't know how sad I was.

Imperceptibly, though, things were changing. Ran was beginning to fit into Suffield, and his sadness was tempered by new friendships. There were neighbors with boys his age, and he was beginning to connect with the things that interested them. He began to pay attention to sporting heroes:

> They didn't mean much to me, but I knew who Jackie Robinson[19] was; I knew Joe Louis,[20] so I had something to talk about to other people.

And he did notice "how beautiful girls were":

> Of course, I didn't know what it meant to sleep with people then. People said, 'I slept with this person or that...' Were they having night parties?

His lifetime interest in record collecting had also begun. He now had money to spend on records—an interest encouraged by a young neighbor who Ran would later refer to as:

My best living, live friend—but I didn't know that then.[21]

FRIENDSHIP

There is nothing on this earth more to be prized than true friendship

THOMAS AQUINAS

GIL AHRENS WAS two years younger than Ran; he lived just down the road. Ran first noticed him mowing the lawn next door, on Marbern Drive:[22]

> At Marbern Drive—and it was right next to me—I saw a young man mowing a lawn, and he became my oldest friend in Suffield. I've known him since 1951. His father owned the lot next door. (There was no house there, but he would go and mow the lawn.) Martha's babysitter said, 'He's cute.' She would go out with a pitcher of iced tea and lemonade, and Gil didn't seem too interested; he just waved. I was playing music high on my stereo—because my parents were out—and he came to the door and said, 'Would you like to come and see my collection?' And he lived between me and Suffield Academy, just down the road.

Gil was a drummer, and like Ran, he was passionate about music. His parents supported him in his interest. (It intrigued Ran that he had his drum kit set up in the parlor of the family home.) Gil was the youngest of four boys, and Ran found that the Ahrens' home was a lively place: "It became a house that I liked a lot." Gil introduced Ran to his friends: "It was through him I met Jimmy De Preist,[23] nephew of Marian Anderson." It was Gil, also, who introduced Ran to the music of Chris Connor:

> He brought home [a record of] a lady, a singer. He said, 'You're going to like her; her name is Chris Connor.' [*Ran is thoughtful for a moment.*] It's either Gil or Helen Gatto [who introduced me to her] because I don't remember knowing much about Chris Connor at Classical—why would I? She came out 53/54, and her breakthrough years

were 55/56. Gil certainly introduced me to regular jazz, bebop, Benny Goodman (who I liked a little bit), Sidney Bechet.[24] I knew gospel, and I knew the right-hand side of the early black culture and religion, and I knew the white noir Kenton jazz,[25] but I certainly didn't know the small group jazz, so we taught each other, and I *do* think he might have introduced me to Chris Connor. And Helen Gatto said: 'We have a new Chris Connor—it's a blue album.[26] I don't know what direction she's going.' So, at that point, I became a fanatic.

Because of their shared love of music, Ran spent a lot of time at Gil's place:

He had a 'Birdland' drum set.[27] First, he had a regular set, and then he got this great set. And I remember Gil and I did get a band [together] with Eddie Young, a rock and roll saxophonist from Windsor Locks, and there was somebody called Robert Brett, a guitar player. But I did duos with Gil mostly, and his mother loved our music—and the dad. And there was an older brother called Loomis who became quite a fan. He was twenty-five/twenty-four, and it made us feel great that they liked our music.

Gil's son has recounted the following snippet from the family history as it was told to him:

They used to jam in my grandmother's parlor with other local jazz musicians. I'm told it was quite a scene and that my grandmother, despite the likely hue and cry from her socialite friends, was doubtless silently giddy that she was hosting such rebellious young men in her stately home.[28]

Gil's parents were from old, established Suffield families. They liked to entertain and have parties, and as Ran recalls:

Things—good things—[happened]. The best New Year's Eve I ever had was at the Ahrens' house. I had one of my first drinks there. I don't know whether my *first* drink was at the Jinxey Club in Springfield or the Elks Club in Hartford. I do remember my first drink was a rum and coke.
But Mary Ahrens was the model of sobriety. I know some New Year's Eve her voice got thick, and though she was very shy, she said, 'You're playing divinely.' I'd never heard the word 'divine' [used this way], and she said, 'I'm going to have a couple of drops more of this dark liquid; why don't you try it?' And it was delicious. And probably she put [together] ginger ale and whiskey (which I would hate now), but I know we played better then, and even the brother, Leavitt, said,

'Gee, you're playing well tonight,' because he lived right behind my mother and father in a house where they could hear my piano. And I couldn't get over the friendliness of people—with this ginger ale—and I knew something was up; I wasn't *that* naive.

And we DID NOT over-drink. They put in lots of ice, and they kept adding [ice], and I thought, 'Wow, eating at nine-thirty or ten at night' these hard-boiled eggs... there's a word for it—hard-boiled eggs where you take the yolk out and put pepper and celery.... And they had these different cheeses, and at one o'clock, somebody walked me home.

Gil Ahrens has written in detail about this time, confirming that they met soon after Ran moved to Suffield from Springfield:

> Ran was experimenting in jazz using big block chords but still had a classical background. I was just getting jazz at that time, and I introduced him to Benny Goodman's music, which didn't thrill him. I had just started playing drums, and we started playing together as my family had a large Steinway piano in our parlor. Ran was a big Stan Kenton fan, and Stan greatly influenced his playing at that time.
>
> I can't describe the jazz scene in the 1950's—it was simply beyond belief. If you were in New York City, you could catch Stan Kenton at one club, and it was just a short walk to catch Count Basie or Duke Ellington. All the greats were there: Stan Getz, Miles, Diz, and, of course, the Modern Jazz Quartet. This great music didn't cost a fortune to enjoy. I can remember paying two dollars to get into Birdland and sitting in the "Bull Pen" two feet away from Count Basie when Joe Williams was just starting.
>
> Stan Kenton was a major influence on Ran initially, and I will never forget when Ran played for Stan for the first time. I think it was at a dance at Lake Compounce. After the band was finished for the night, Ran met Stan, and a small group of us went back to the bandstand. Ran started playing, and Stan's jaw nearly dropped to the floor. Ran had been writing to Stan for some time, but I don't think that Kenton ever expected anything like that.
>
> Shortly after that, we were making many quick trips into New York to hear Thelonious Monk, who became the major influence on Ran. After his cabaret card was restored, Monk had a six-month stint at the Five Spot Cafe in New York in 1957.
>
> Locally we were continuing to visit and sit in at Jinxey's in Springfield and the gospel church on Russell Street in Hartford's north end. Ran was well known in the church, and gospel music had a major influence on Ran.

Ran and I would always introduce new musicians to each other. I can remember one time around 1958 when Ran was running a jazz festival at Bard College, and I came up from Philadelphia with another jazz drummer to meet Ran. I was studying at the University of Pennsylvania and was highly involved with the Mask & Wig Club. Our shows toured the country, and our band was led by a very talented young drummer by the name of James DePreist. I didn't know that Jimmy's aunt was the great contralto Marian Anderson or that Jimmy had written a symphony before entering Penn. I just knew him as a great guy and a great drummer. He and Ran hit it off and were friends for many years. Jimmy went on to become a world-famous conductor.

Among my best memories of Ran were the jam sessions we had. These were usually on a Sunday in the summer and lasted two or three hours. I think that we started them around 1954 or 1955. I just got a new set of Gretsch Birdland drums. We both lived in large homes on the Main Street in Suffield, and Ran's house was four houses away from mine. Ran knew a lot of musicians in the area. What started off as a casual sort of thing just grew and grew. We would completely open our houses up to jazz lovers on Sundays for a session that lasted around three hours. We would alternate homes. Ran would do it one week, and I would do it the next time. It was nothing fancy. No alcohol was served, just sodas and snacks—like popcorn or peanuts. We usually had between fifteen and twenty at each session. People brought their own instruments. You didn't have to play to attend; you just had to love jazz. My home had a large parlor, which had a Steinway concert-like piano and enough room for my drums and could seat up to fifteen people with ease. Ran had his piano in a room near the living room, and the spill-over could move into the living room. Since it was usually hot during the summer, we opened the windows and doors for the whole town to hear.

The quality of the music varied but was usually quite good, and many went on to play professionally. I can remember that I met Houston Person at Ran's house. Anyway, it must have made quite a scene in little old conservative Suffield in the 1950s: Two young kids throwing what seemed like wild parties every week; black musicians and their friends came from Springfield and Hartford. We never had any complaints from neighbors, and things were always under control.

In hindsight, I think that both Ran and I should have thanked our parents, Mary and Bernie Ahrens, and Phil and Allie Blake, for putting up with these seemingly wild scenes in their homes. I didn't realize it at the time, but I think that these old conservative New England parents were setting the pace for future generations to follow. Ran and I were doing just what seemed natural."[29]

Ran's version of the meeting with Stan Kenton is not as positive as Gil's:

> In the summer in the early '60s—I can't remember... it could have been anywhere from '57 to '61,[30] Kay Fisk[31] drove me to hear Stan Kenton. He was playing in Connecticut, and there was a piano there, and Kenton said, 'Play something for me; I know you want me to hear you.' And then [he said], 'Play another piece. Is this all you can say? There's something wrong. You've a very limited perspective on life. I'm sorry, I don't think there's an audience for your music.' [*Ran nods his head and gestures into his heart, saying*] 'Well that's true,' [*before going back to Kenton's words*] 'I wish you luck though, and I'm glad you like my music.'
> I still love the period 1949 to '54. That's the highlight—not the '40s— *Innovations in Modern Music,* and *Sketches* [*on Standards*], and *Portraits on Standards*, and *City of Glass*. After *Cuban Fire*, it went way down.
> L: What did Kenton's dismissal of you do for you? How did you take it when one of your heroes...?
> R: Well, I was very depressed. I went home and said, 'I don't know if I want to look much more ahead.' I didn't eat for a week. I got in a big funk.

Ran's account of the meeting with Kenton illustrates how deeply the perceived criticism from someone he respected could hurt. Earlier, at Suffield Academy, Ran had no trouble defending himself against criticism from his music teacher, Raymond Lindstrom:

> Let's see. There was a Mr. Raymond Lindstrom. [*Ran's tone is lightened by amazement as this teacher's name, long suppressed, re-surfaces.*] He loved diatonic mashed potato. He came to my parent's house one day. He said, 'I told your son to play hymns, and he's going out of the key' ['deliberately']. And I remember he slammed at the table. [*Ran bangs the table to demonstrate.*] But I could hear the jazz coming, this blue note [coming] when I was playing S*ilent Night.*
> [*he pauses, reflecting for a moment before adding*] And I don't know for certain if Mr. Lindstrom banged on the table, but let's have one inaccuracy in the book.

Ran and his teacher Mr. Lindstrom continued to clash over the matter. At one stage, Mr. Lindstrom escorted Ran to the Principals' office, and

Suffield, Connecticut—A New Start

while both Principals supported their staff member, they were not unsupportive of Ran.[32] Classmates, witnessing the clashes, sided with Ran, which earned him some friends. Philip and Alison Blake advised their son that he should be "a little politer." It was later, with the experience of many years' teaching behind him, that Ran was able to say:

> I was insufferable. I really hated being there.[33]

DESPITE NEW FRIENDSHIPS, Ran did not fit well into day-to-day life at Suffield Academy. He liked the Latin teacher, Mr. Osnick, "and *there* I did excel." But, in general, he maintained his detachment:

> I once endowed a chair to Mrs. Seaverns and said she was the only one who understood my music, and nobody agreed or disagreed. And to this day, I've never been asked there to play. Suffield Academy was a very sorry chapter in my life.

Thus, Ran retreated into his music and books:

> Conan Doyle came in[to] my life, and there were thrillers by Edgar Allan Poe, and I was hearing Bartok—those crazy chords—Stan Kenton's *Innovations*, Bill Russo's writing... so many things. Then, I heard of a guy called Gunther Schuller. Somebody told me about him, but I don't think I got records at the time—I don't know if there were any. It brought a little more fervor to my piano playing. But did I do anything new? Did I join the football team or do anything? No! But my sister had a babysitter with an automobile, and if I went to this young woman's romantic love dramas and teenage comedy, she would take me to a murder mystery.

The move to Suffield did not diminish Ran's love of film. In fact, because of the difficulty in getting to a theater, it probably intensified it. Ran soon found parents of friends who would drive him into Thompsonville to see a movie; if the movie seemed unsuitable, his own parents would ring Chuck Stewart, the manager of the theater, to clarify its rating:

> [My parents] called up to ask if there was violence or mystery. I didn't want comedy or love. Westerns were alright, and then, of course, at sixteen, you get your automobile license, and then I began not to have to be so dependent.

By the time Ran was seventeen or eighteen, he was driving an English Squire station wagon. It was "One of the cheapest cars you could get."

IN SUFFIELD, RAN had a lot of freedom in what he did and where he went. This was evident in his continued interest in churches and church music. Suffield was, according to Ran, "quite a church town," and he readily admits:

> I was very promiscuous with Suffield churches. There was a very conservative black church, like a storefront, in east Suffield—it didn't have the music of Hartford, Connecticut, but it and the Polish-Catholic church were my two favorites. There was also a prosperous Catholic Church which I also liked better than the white Protestant Churches. There was a Baptist church on Main Street, and on the other side of Main Street was a white Protestant. Later, there was an Episcopalian church, and my father said he liked that church and that it was the best white church in Suffield. But I remember the Baptist church because that's where we had the assemblies [for Suffield Academy], and Mr. Lindstrom was Director of Music there and Rev. Pryor—P-R-Y-O-R; he's probably dead now—who was a friend of Gil Ahrens' father, had evidently heard from Raymond Lindstrom that maybe the devil had gotten into me, but this is my word—he didn't use the word 'devil.'
> So Rev. Pryor, for the first ten minutes [he] would be like Gordon Gilkey, and you'd think, 'Oh, he's well-read, why don't I sit back... [and listen].' And then he looks at you [*Ran's tone turns low and menacing as he leans forward in his chair*], and I thought he was looking at me! And he says, 'You may think you can do good, but if you don't come here on Sundays...' And those teeth!
> And he looked, and he said, 'It's one thing if you're five minutes late once a year—you will be forgiven,' and I got so... [*Ran holds his head, remembering the worry.*] I had never met anyone quite like that. And of course, he repeated himself, so he wasn't like Gordon Gilkey, who was a great speaker.
> I did go to the new Episcopal church. When churches are new, and people are giving furniture, there's a wonderful feeling of building, and brotherhood and sisterhood. They were a little more progressive—younger; they didn't go ga-ga at my music.[34]
> It was later that I started going to North Hartford [to hear] Bishop Jefferson.
> I really got away with murder in Suffield.

But this was Suffield, where everyone knew everyone else, and freedom happened under the protective and watchful eye of the whole community. So if Ran, no longer able to retreat to the Mulberry Street cemetery, sought out other places to walk and to dream, he could be certain that his parents would get a phone call, "What's Ran doing out at night, walking down Marbern Drive?"

Ran accepted this philosophically—"In one way, they looked after you."— but he was very much aware that it was "not the same as Springfield."

> So, I had friends in Suffield, but only two or three school friends, and that was my fault too. I kept up with a few boys from Springfield, but it was too hard to get there. They once drove to Suffield, but after a year or two, it was like I was never in Classical—and when I went back, the school was gone; how I miss that [school]. Really, it changed my life.
>
> So *Spiral*, the Gospel church, and now… I've never [before] called this an event of life—leaving Classical High School, and then moving to New York …and Greece—but leaving Classical made me much more introverted. It's like tenth grade never happened.
>
> Later, in New York, I had friends— some were five years older; some were five years younger. But in tenth grade in Classical, I had friends my own age.

The stab of nostalgia for this period, with all its happy, personal associations, gives rise to a new reflection: Suffield did have its own happy memories and a community that was warmly supportive. Gradually, Ran "got to like Suffield" and "mentioned to people, 'I am from Suffield.'"

This period of his life serves as inspiration for the album *Suffield Gothic*.[35]

Looking back, Ran can say:

> I have a pride in that town. Later, I could walk down a few blocks and see Joe Hardin, who was on the cover of *Suffield Gothic*. He came to Jordan Hall to sing 'Old Man River' I remember the shoe [incident]. He did 'Satin Doll' and do you remember the bridge—'switch-e-rooney?' In the rehearsal concert, he'd got to that part [*Ran sings and imitates a few dance steps… 'dah dah dah dah… switch-e-rooney'*], and his shoe fell on Marjorie Schuller's lap and oh, he… [*Ran holds his face, remembering the embarrassment.*]
>
> He got to love retsina when I came back from Greece, but all that came later.

[When at Bard] I would go home on weekends, if I could [...] I remember, though, when bringing Jeanne Lee there in '56, my parents got a complaint at the office that I had negroes at my house, so in '56 [*His tone is incredulous*] that was unheard of.

[But] all that changed, and ten years [later], it was Suffield where the people came hugging me when I came back from Greece, and there was such a feeling of fellowship. There were very beautiful things [said and done].

Suffield was the bridge. A leisurely move from early adolescence (with a foot still in the Springfield of childhood) to the young man finding friends and passions and treading that delicate place between innocence and awareness. It was a gradual awakening until, at last, Ran could claim Suffield as "home."[36]

11

EARLY TEACHERS AND STRANGE CHORDS

*Teaching is a very important thing—it's a golden
art.*

RAN BLAKE

During his childhood, Ran studied with a number of different teachers, who guided his early formation in music. He has an enormous respect for teachers and their "golden art" and asserts that his own teaching can be more important to him than performance, and at the very least, that it is the balance that actually refreshes performance. Ran has teaching in his blood—both his parents were teachers:

> They were much better teachers than I was. People RAVED [about them]. Mother had people [asking], 'Can we have a class NOW? I have to hear what happened in China and Japan.'

From childhood, he would have been aware of the unspoken *esprit de corps* of teachers—a mutual esteem grown out of an understanding that imparting knowledge is both a calling and a challenge and that anyone who participates in it is worthy of respect. This respect is wedded to a keen discernment that allows each teacher to realistically evaluate another—a discernment that would have been exercised by Philip and Alison Blake in seeking a music teacher for their young son.

Ran's musical formation started at a very young age. For as long as he could remember, he had had free access to the three upright pianos in the small front room. At some stage in the house's history, this room had been part of an open porch. Closed in, it was a secure space that looked out over Union Street "like a summer room." And while pleasant in summer, it could be quite chilly in winter, being only partially heated. It was certainly not soundproof, and family and neighbors were all treated to Ran's experimentations and "concerts." Philip and Alison Blake could not explain the intensity of their young son's interest in these pianos. Neither of them played, and Ran cannot remember any musical evenings at home.

Music, however, was playing an increasingly significant role in American society. The twenties and thirties had witnessed the "golden age" of Broadway musicals. Added to this, the thirties on-screen sweethearts such as MGM's Jeanette MacDonald and Nelson Eddy; and RKO's Fred Astaire and Ginger Rodgers had captured public hearts. There was brisk trade in the sheet music of songs made popular in theater and film. Cole Porter, Irving Berlin, Jerome Kern, George Gershwin, Richard Rodgers, and Lorenz Hart were household names, and the love songs they'd created gave people, battered by the Depression (and later, the war), something to hope for. By the time Ran Blake came into the world, America's hopes were embedded in song.

Ran's parents were not swayed by this new wave of performers and "preferred Dickens," though Ran admits:

> I think my father once saw Ethel Merman in New York—the lady with the loud voice who sang "I Get a Kick out of You." But they wanted other (more serious) theater, and my mother liked movies a little bit, but nobody liked movies like me.

The American public's fascination with musicals continued throughout the forties; in 1946, two in three people went to the movies at least once a week.[1] During this time (with advances made in sound, lighting, and color), film musicals became more realistic and modern-looking. Characters were believable and plot, often exploring serious themes, became an important element. A new type of performer was emerging—Judy Garland, Gene Kelly, and Kathryn Grayson to name a few. Ordinary folk were delighted to be able to enjoy and share this music. Mary Garvey greatly admired Rita Hayworth, and Betty Grable, box office favorites whose dancing prowess meant that they starred in many of the popular musicals of the 1940s; she would certainly have been humming the songs from these movies. And Ran's first music teacher, Janet Wallace, had a sister-in-law, Sara, who would let Ran borrow some of her favorites:

> [She loved] *South Pacific*,[2] and there were two or three other show tunes that she liked [from] *Annie Get Your Gun*[3] [for example]. So,

they were lent to me to play on my Victrola.[4] You had to crank it up. [*He demonstrates winding a handle.*] So, I heard some of those tunes.

FROM A VERY early age, it was apparent to Ran's parents that he had a unique talent. ("I was told I always played—I don't remember.") Ran can't remember whether he had a favorite among the family's three pianos either. He recalls that he "liked to sit between them." The respective differences in their timbre, but more importantly, their tuning, allowed Ran to explore sounds that, for the most part, were largely unknown to western music.

> Well, remember George Ives[5] did that with his son Charles with two bands in the woods.[6] I loved it when one [piano] was more out of tune than the other—and I don't know whether I knew about the Joe Maneri[7] microtonals, but I loved that. And they were almost around in a circle, and before my first dog, Duke, died, he would sit on one piano and play [*he demonstrates—fists banging up and down like paws*], and I would play the other two, and then [there would be] these great tone clusters, and I said, 'What is that?' and I looked right at Duke and said, 'What IS that?' just like I might to you Dek-Tor. [*He turns to pat the cat, which is lying stretched out on its back— paws in the air— on the couch.*]
> So, I loved it, and then, one time, the pianos were all tuned the same day, and my parents... [*He breaks off, trying to verbalize his parents' motives*] thought that they'd now have some good music... with the shock at the cost involved—seventy-five dollars [*incredulous tone*]— for three to be tuned, and the guy stayed for five hours. And [after that], it was a little more bland. I decided not to stretch my hands [between two pianos]. When all were out of key, it was not so good, but when one was out of key... [*He lingers on the phrase*] and the others were regular—what FUN it was!
> L: So, what would you do? Give us an example. Would you play the same note on the one in the regular key and the one in the...
> R: [*nods*] And then, I'd do a couple of ghost chords. But I didn't do it methodically—I didn't know what 'microtone' meant, or 'semitone'—I just... I LOVED that weirdness.

Family and neighbors, who had at first been enchanted with Ran's playing, were less so as he grew older and began to experiment with elements that would become building blocks of his own style.

> At four, my parents called me a genius; at eight, I was considered a disaster. They liked me until I started seeing too many mysteries. [When I was younger,] I tried to do the *Grieg Piano Concerto*, and my hands would go fairly fast, and they came in and said, 'Oh, don't stop. In the summer, you can play as late as you want.' But that changed in 1946 after *Spiral Staircase,* and my father got a... [*He makes a knocking sound on the table.*]
> 'Who is it?' [*He puts uncertainty into his tone.*]
> 'What is that awful noise? It can't be your talented son!' [said the caller.]
> And his name was Mr. Neale, and he lived on the side nearer Walnut Street. There was an Irish couple and a Jewish couple. They said, 'WHAT is going on in this house?'
> L: So, you're not making this up?
> R: [*shaking his head emphatically*] NO, and my mother said to the neighbors, 'I couldn't agree with you more!' And she could be feisty and defensive.
> And my father said, 'We'll have to speak to him.'
> And my sister didn't like it, and the relatives said, 'Would you stop! It's hideous.'
> One uncle, Duncan, was tolerant, and my grandfather...

His grandfather's reaction to the music is left unsaid, though it is possible he was also tolerant because, as Ran continues:

> He liked the martinis [I made him] with my hands in the olives and the gin. [He said,] 'Pour gin; sanctify...' He didn't use the word sanctify—that's too religious— 'Bathe your hand in the gin.' My grandmother was too sweet to say anything, but she would shake her head sadly.

Ran's favorite time to play was after he had heard a murder mystery in the afternoon. Then, still gripped by this dark, heart-stopping experience, he would go down, shut himself in the lobby and recreate the mood, the mystery, the thrill. And this time, it was Ran who was the master storyteller. When Mary Garvey—startled by the dramatic sounds coming from the front room—complained, Philip Blake became concerned that things were getting out of hand:

> He said it was jarring to the ears of my mother. They [my mother and father] said I played better at five than I did at eight or nine and that I had been 'corrupted' by the communications system; I guess [they meant] radio.

Philip Blake was very perplexed at this turn of events. 'You used to be so talented,' he said, and, in desperation, he went to see Ran's piano teacher.

For the past two years, Ran had been taking lessons from Janet Wallace, a piano teacher just around the corner in Mulberry Street. He had been making good progress, working through scales and various fundamentals of technique. But then came *Spiral Staircase* and the completely original musical approach that it elicited from him. Philip went to see Miss Wallace with a simple and heartfelt plea: "What is going on? Would you try to temper my son?" But Miss Wallace could not explain the departure from what was seen as "normal and healthy." She could only reply, "I'm innocent!"

Ran believes he might have been about six or seven when he started lessons with Janet Wallace. There was a hole in the back fence; he would go through this and across a neighboring garden onto Mulberry Street. He knew all the people along that street[8] and remembers that he would knock on his teacher's door, feeling very important, and say, "Hello Janet Wallace."

Ran's memory of Janet Wallace is sketchy, but he remembers the formal lessons—the scales and then, when Janet deemed him ready, the classical pieces. Prominent in his memory is the Grieg Piano Concerto. Ran, challenged by reading musical scores, endeavored to learn each piece by heart. Indeed, Martha's earliest memories of her brother were of him at the piano playing classical music. She said that this was how she picked up classical music herself.

Janet Wallace could see that reading music was a problem for Ran:

> She got me to read a little bit but knew I wasn't top at it. I had to do scales, she said.

Janet Wallace was strict about scales, but she also gave her young charge "interesting things to do, like Bach's children's pieces." She was pleased that Ran was up to this challenge: "I am so glad you are doing A flat and A and E and D. You seem bored by C major." Ran was later to describe C major as "worse than F," which he had already described as being "like mashed potato" (in other words, "boring"). And it was true—Ran was bored with the simple little exercises for beginners. He recalls one lesson when he had to play a study in C major:

> I went to other keys, and my fingers slipped, and I made a mistake, and she went like that. [*He demonstrates with a quick click of the fingers and a point in the right direction*].

But Janet Wallace had seen where her pupil was going. That night, she called his parents. She was so amazed at what she had witnessed:

> She gave me a compliment. [*Ran's tone is humble.*] She said I took a little longer than other students to learn a piece, and yet I could do all these interchanging keys.

The Blakes, due to budgeting concerns (and probably also to Ran's struggles with the set pieces), had been planning to stop his lessons, but because of the phone call, they decided to let him continue. The call also vindicated their choice of teacher in Janet Wallace—she had seen past the difficulties to the talent beyond.

Janet Wallace began to encourage Ran to improvise. She also introduced a little Russian music, and it was soon after this, according to Ran, that she "married a Russian man." Looking back, Ran credits Janet Wallace with teaching him modulation.

After Miss Wallace married, a new teacher had to be found. Mr. Lloyd Stoneman was chosen.

> His wife was a psychiatrist [*sic*] at a department store, and he had looooong hair.... [*With a minimum of words and a stretched-out vowel, he manages to conjure a mental image of this young piano teacher of the 1940s.*]

Lloyd Stoneman came weekly to the Blake house at 359 Union Street. And though Ran's parents thought that the six dollars an hour he asked for a lesson was "the height of extravagance,"[9] Mr. Stoneman obviously put a lot of thought into his lessons. Each week he would set a homework piece to be played the following week, and once a month, he would write a review.[10]

While Ran cannot remember the pieces he learned, he does remember his teacher's tolerance and encouragement; Lloyd Stoneman allowed Ran to give a regular "concert" of his own compositions and improvisations; he would then comment on these in his report.

> We used to have these reports in the attic of Gunther's house—the *Union Street Concert Series*—but then, they got moved, and now they are lost.

Lloyd Stoneman was a very observant teacher. He knew that Ran got frustrated trying to play pieces from sheet music, yet Ran would always be ready to play his homework piece perfectly. Unbeknownst to Stoneman,

Ran had devised a method to learn each set piece by ear. He would locate a recorded version of the work and then, through repeated listening, work out the piece on the piano, ready for the moment when Stoneman said, "I hope you've learned this. I told you we'd do it today." One day, just as Ran was about to play the set-piece, Stoneman strolled casually to the other end of the piano where the record was partially visible—peeping out from under a newspaper—and said, "What have we got here?" To Ran's dismay, he extracted it from its hiding place.

Later in life, Ran called on his old teacher, Lloyd Stoneman, "to see how he was."

> His wife answered the door, 'Well, we remember you, Ran Blake, but Lloyd died five years ago. I can't talk to you now; my house is being sold in five minutes. I'm moving to a nursing home—the city's moving me—I can't… Why did you never call?'

AFTER THE MOVE to Suffield, there was a brief period when Ran was without a teacher. But as his passion for the piano had in no way diminished, Lloyd Stoneman volunteered to continue lessons at Suffield. It was a long drive from Springfield; after two or three lessons, the arrangement was discontinued. Ran then worked on his own. There was a room in the Suffield house where the doors could be closed, and he could play the piano as much as he wanted without disturbing his family or neighbors. And while he did continue with the technical exercises he had been taught, the isolation of the room allowed him freedom to experiment:

> I would storyboard, though I didn't know that word [at the time]. I would be hearing the *Scythian Suite* by Prokofiev—one of his best pieces. I would play 78 records over and over again, and ah… it was gospel and classical, or some type of church music, and there was jazz. I was using the system of the old jazz musicians. I got these themes in my head. But I really affronted them [my family] in the way I played—the strange chords.

Philip and Alison, possibly as a reaction to these "strange chords," encouraged their son to enroll for lessons with Ray Cassarino from Wethersfield (some twenty-four miles from Suffield and six miles south of Hartford). Ray Cassarino was a professional keyboard player—a respected jazz musician who had just returned from touring with Woody Herman. Ran was around fifteen or sixteen at the time, and to have a young male with considerable performance experience as his teacher seemed ideal. He commenced having Saturday lessons, which continued over a period of four years. At first, his parents drove him to Wethersfield, but as soon as Ran was able, he drove there himself "under strict conditions." (Ran recalls he was only allowed to take certain routes):

> There had been a policeman in Suffield called Roger Waterman, and he saw me make a right-hand turn on a red light, and I had trouble parking, and he gave me a ticket, and my father went to see him, and he said, 'We think your son's a hell of a pianist. Let's give him less liberty. Let's map out where he can go with the car.'
> One place I could go was Ray Cassarino's.

Ray Cassarino admired Ran's harmonic ideas and melodic quirks, though he felt certain rhythms could be improved and wondered whether he was the best person to help with this. He suggested that Ran try to extend chords and encouraged him to continue listening to records.

> L: What type of pianist was he?
> R: Elegant cocktail—one of the most ferocious velocity techniques. And he got to hate it. He said, 'It's my curse, all these patterns.' He was the rage at the Adajian's Armenian restaurant, off Farmington Avenue, in Hartford.[11] I would go there a great deal to hear him—nice chords. He later said I began to do things a little more avant-garde than he. He could play quite well fast—he said that he loved that he could dazzle people, but he said he kept telling the same story to the same people.
> Anyway, that's Ray Cassarino. He was VERY patient. We went through the chord systems. I found that I could get a lot more freedom if I did what I was supposed to for thirty or forty minutes, [then] he allowed me to do my own stuff. [So] I cultivated more scales and things, which I frankly didn't like because I'd begun getting into singers. I think I lost touch with him when he was fifty-five or sixty; maybe he's in heaven now.[12]

Cassarino assessed his own musicianship with honesty and confided in Ran about his own perceived limitations. He insisted that comparisons should be avoided: "Comparisons are odious," he said. "Why do that?" This approach suited Ran, and he began examining his own musical direction with growing confidence. Ray Cassarino's influence in these formative years should not be underestimated. Though his own style may have been quite different from that which Ran would continue to develop, Cassarino's tuition provided a thorough foundation in jazz piano—an essential element in Ran's mature style. Moreover, Cassarino guided his young pupil through the dreams of adolescence and into the more disciplined life of an aspiring professional musician.

Ran has made a list that includes many other people he remembers were "teachers" in his life.[13] Some of these were teachers in the traditional sense, like those he encountered at Bard, Lenox, and New York; others were his colleagues—both at New England Conservatory and Berklee; and some were his friends, such as Jeanne Lee.

12

THE CHURCH ON RUSSELL STREET

The church I grew up with.

RAN BLAKE

Suffield was an important stage in Ran's "growing up." Here he made the transition from school to college; here, he began his lifetime passion for collecting records (and found employment to sustain the practice); here, he made his first real friend; and here, he commenced frequenting jazz clubs in Hartford. It was from Suffield that he moved out of home to take up residence in New York City. It was also from Suffield that he found his way to the Pentecostal Church of North Hartford—the church that figured so greatly in these growing up years—the Holy Trinity Church of God in Christ:[1]

> This was the church I grew up with. It was in North Hartford—but it's moved now to East Hartford—and it's called the Latter Rain Christian Fellowship, and Jackie and Hubert Powell are still there, should you want to go there on your way to New York. It's Pentecostal. It's where I really went—hours and hours—and I wish I recorded more thoughts. It was on Russell Street—on the corner of one of the great big streets; thus, on my album with Jeanne Lee it says, 'Church on Russell Street.' And you know, right near it, there was a street called Blake Street and one called Lee Street, and we thought... Jeanne Lee thought...
> [*The significance of this coincidence is left unclear.*]
> Then the church moved to the corner of Pavilion and Wooster Streets, and right next door was the Elks Club where I had my first rum and

Coke. And I was afraid Mother Carter would see me because choir rehearsal was in the evening. It was later that the church moved to East Hartford; well, it's still North Hartford. Actually, the old building is still in North Hartford, but the congregation has moved to East Hartford, and it's called the Latter Rain.

He'd gone to the North Hartford church the first time to hear Edith Powell sing. He had been encouraged to go there by Eunice Bell—the lady who provided occasional home-help for the Blake household... and made delicious pecan pie.

It was through her that I got learning about the Gospel churches in Hartford. She told me about the Hartford Church of God in Christ, but I don't think she went [there] with me. She was more of a respectable Baptist if she *did* go to church. She kept fully abreast of Oscar Peterson's rhythm section—she got autographs. She loved Ray Brown, and [later] she told Jeanne Lee, 'You'd better get to a more earthy music!' She was a very sophisticated woman. She lived on Kent Avenue, which was the heartbeat of the Harlem of Suffield, and she knew things that I didn't know.

It was Eunice's son-in-law, Nathanial Wilson,[2] who drove Ran to Hartford, where he was immediately captivated by the Powells, by the presiding bishop—Bishop I.L. Jefferson, and by Mother Carter.[3] He felt compelled to return to this church, week after week. He was usually able to get a ride, but if not, he would hitchhike, and then, someone would drive him home:

I think my parents knew I was going. [*It's said confidentially, in a lowered tone.*] There must have been various groups of people that drove me to the church 'cause I didn't have a license for a long while. And then they [my parents] worried I went to the church so much— when at one time they complained that I didn't go [enough].

Bishop I.L. Jefferson made a big impression on Ran. Indeed, Ran considers him one of his four "father figures."[4] He had, as Ran remembers:

a special relationship with God. He was found on a river—I'm really sure I'm right [about that]. He never brought it up much. I loved his wife.[5]

Ran readily recalls the "brimstone lectures," though he hastens to add they were "not nearly as fearful as Rev. Pryor's, of the Baptist Church in Suffield." He goes on to state that, of all the preachers he has known:

> I.L. Jefferson was probably the MOST electrifying because the first five minutes he might talk about something like how hard it is in Switzerland for people that make clocks, and then, suddenly [*he interrupts the telling with a loud, unexpected shout*], OH, there would be fire and brimstone! Only once or twice would he talk about hell—it was not the whole guilt thing. He would LEAP out of the pulpit, and OH! [*covering his eyes with his hands*] I thought, 'My God!'
> I begged my sister to go. I gave her money from my… She went once, and then, she wanted to go again and again. My parents said, 'What are you doing? It's one thing for you [to go], but this is your younger sister! We think it's good she's no longer hearing your ghost stories, but now you're taking her to this temple! What is going to happen next?'

But brimstone notwithstanding, when asked what it was about Bishop Jefferson that appealed to him, Ran answers without hesitation: "his love of people." He still remembers the "wonderful hug at the door" that was Bishop Jefferson's greeting. He felt at home in that church, and there is no doubt that Bishop Jefferson kept a "fatherly" eye on him, even though he was probably a little disappointed that Ran had not become a church member. There was one major thing that stood between Ran and the church—his love of movies. It was something the church would not tolerate, and the one thing that Ran could not forgo:

> I didn't gamble. I never made drinking a… [habit.] I would have given up quickly. But I HAD to go to movies.

Member or not, Ran's memories of the years he spent at this church and the people he met there—Bishop Jefferson, Mother Carter, Edith Powell, and Eunice Glover—are treasured ones.[6] Edith Powell's son, Hubert (who wrote "There's Been a Change"), stood out.[7] Ran would have been a little older than Hubert, but he was obviously impressed with the boy's playing:

> He must have been ten or eleven at the time playing organ. Hubert Powell—an incredible composer who George Russell championed as well as other members of the Powell family, Pinky and Jackie. While at Bard, I was able to arrange a concert service for not just the choir but also four busloads of the key members of the congregation to sing at Bard. And we had a special three-course dinner, with creole rice and salads, when they came. Later, Hubert came up to Jordan Hall with two busloads.[8] They came twice to Jordan Hall—once under Gunther Schuller—and I remember we went 'all out,' and Gunther ordered a Lobster Newberg dinner, and they were very pleased—so

were our students. They said the dormitory food had never been better. So, Jordan Hall BECAME the Gospel Church [that day]—we had it sanctified—and they were screaming; the nurse was there. Oh my gosh!

As good as Hubert was, it was his mother, Edith Powell, who people came to hear at the church on Russell Street. Born in Hartford, she was a long-term member of the church and was actively involved in its music program as both a choir member and soloist. Sometime in the sixties or seventies, Ran jotted down his impressions of her prayerful singing and "rich contralto" voice:[9]

> Dressed in stark white with her long, black hair in a bun and with her son accompanying her on the drums, she stands, prayer book in her hands; with closed eyes, she states the melody of a particular composition. At this point, there is nothing extraordinary happening other than the fact that you are hearing a classic singer—one of the elite. Usually, a second chorus is sung, and she begins to embellish with unexpected silences, occasionally using a glissando no less dramatic than Albert Ayler.[10] By now, the prayer book has dropped from her hand, and she is no longer standing. The chorus enters—clapping, tambourines beat, and gradually dancing commences; this happens elsewhere without Sister Powell. Her voice glides overall, her majestic tones crying, even screaming at times. The rhythms become jagged, unpredictable—her voice an exotic horn.[11]

Ran also wrote down some thoughts about church member and composer Sr. Eunice Glover, whom he considered an "even more rare phenomenon" than Sr. Powell. Examining her compositional style, he noted some "startling differences" from established models. It was "spare and avoided the harmonic cliches of the Anglo hymns." Such signal traits are nowhere more evident than in her composition "Looking for a Home," which was, according to Ran Blake, "no longer a song, but a composed piece of choral music, carefully thought out (if not written) with rhythmical breaks that creep up unexpectedly.[12]

Edith Powell's and Eunice Glover's reputations as singers and composers had enticed Ran to the Church of God in Christ, Hartford. While he formed close friendships with many of the people he met there, none were so important as the one he shared with his mentor, Mother Carter. Ran has a clear memory of their first meeting—that day when Nathanial Wilson dropped him at the church, and he walked in alone. Mother Carter greeted him at the door, asking "with a wry smile" whether he was lost.

It was "1952 or '53 on a bright, sunny day," and right from that moment, there was a special bond between Ran and Mother Carter. She was kind. She could see he felt uncomfortable:

> I felt, 'Boy, will they kick me out? I'm the wrong color…' and Mother Carter said, 'Come on in.' I really didn't feel discrimination. And then Mother Carter said, 'You like it here? You want to come back tomorrow night and Tuesday and Wednesday? We'll feed you Thursday.'
> I said, 'I think I better come back Sunday.' And she said, 'Where are you from?' and I said, 'Suffield.' And she blinked and said, 'I think I understand.' Because that was mainly… Joe Hardin[13] did live there, but it was mainly pretty much 'supper club.'

Ran soon recognized that Mother Carter "reigned supreme" at the Holy Trinity Church of God in Christ. She was an active lifetime member; she was larger than life. She took Ran under her wing—she guided him, encouraged him, and strove to protect him from the temptations of the outside world. She did not hesitate to chastise him if she felt it necessary:[14]

> I remember Mother Carter kept looking at me, and if I yawned once, there would be a recrimination. Oh boy, was there ever! [*He hides his face in his hands at the memory.*] Just verbal, or Shhhh! [*He lets out a long shooshing sound.*] from the back row. I think once something like a piece of chalk… I felt something in my hair, and I turned around, and she was like this [*He demonstrates an open-armed, wide-eyed, 'What? It wasn't me,' gesture.*], and I KNEW it was her. I could tell. But she looked innocent as a babe. She said, 'Ran, this is the age when your life [could be] destroyed, and we've got to keep a good eye on you. Now you be here, well dressed and groomed on Sunday morning.' (She one time said I was a little untidy—my tie.)
> Mother Carter was not maybe as important as Dorothy Wallace, but she would play the spiritual trumpet. She was kind, and she was pleasantly plump. She was a devoted woman to that church.
> And there she is on the bottom of my stairway. [*It is added in a tone of happy wonder—probably at the notion that she is still there, 'keeping an eye' on him.*][15]

Mother Carter was the choral director at the church on Russell Street. In addition to overseeing the choral program, she was actively involved in the day-to-day running of the individual choirs—the Gospel Chorus, the Lighted Path Choir, as well as the church's "third choir." Each of these choirs met three times a week, and Ran has attributed the musical success of the church to their "highly motivated drive" and "church-oriented devotion." He states that: "The musical growth of the Church of God in Christ might have been impossible without Mother Carter, who served as a catalyst in a way similar to Duke [Ellington] in the forties."[16] According to Ran, it was not merely rehearsing that gave these ensembles such a fantastic sense of musicianship; the intensity of the practice schedule also left little time for exposure to commercialism via television, movies, and the like. The church, at that time, was very much self-reliant, offering "child training and discipline, gardening programs, finance, and serving of the meal after the sermon."[17]

> The Pentecostals went all day. Oh boy, they knew how to make cold pork! The biscuits—those baking powder biscuits, I love… [them.] And those dishes on the side with corn, and the flavor, the pepper, the spices… OH!!

Ran was warmly invited to these church suppers:

> And I didn't have the money, and they said, 'Next time, when we ask for eight donations, just make your first donation twenty-five cents, and when we say twenty-five cents, we mean it!' [*He pauses to explain quickly*] Because you march up there again and again [for various donations]. There was the women's fund, the men's fund, the athletic fund, the church for poor people, the fund for the minister…

Holidays at the Church of God in Christ were cause for modest celebrations:

> when they had sweet potato pie in the basement and the best lemonade and cold tea… hot beverages for those who like it.
> If I got there ten o'clock, I would go to the Sunday School. I wanted to get there early because the choir marched down [*He makes a forward motion with his arms rising and falling from the elbows*], and if I got there at eleven o'clock, I missed the procession. So, I would get there early!
> And two o'clock I wanted to leave—and she [Mother Carter] usually said, 'Leaving early again?' [*It's said with a downward inflection and a disapproving tone.*] And she usually added, 'There's sweet potato pie if you stay longer.' And, of course, there were ham hocks, collard greens—the soul food, but my God, if you went to Sunday School, that's ten to four! And meanwhile, there'd be movies starting at three-thirty, and my parents wanted me home. And then, academically, I started slipping. I couldn't speak French; I told that to Mother

Carter, and she said, 'But you're beginning to speak the Gospel! Now just leave the French. Your rhythm of speaking the Gospel... [is more important.]' And she would wink at me. [*He demonstrates a VERY broad wink.*]

The Church of God in Christ blended music, drama, fellowship, and the promise of salvation in a mix that was intoxicating. It was a church:

where people would get in trances. There were two trained nurses there in case people... [fainted.] Have you been to a church like that? You should go. We have maps [to get there]. Knife[18] goes to that church. Alonzo[19] went with us; he sang there, and he brought the congregation swooning. And now they only have one nurse because people are less excitable. But there were so many nurses there [in the past], and I think that one time, my parents couldn't understand why this nurse was calling from Hartford [to say] that I had seen the Lord. Now maybe they look just like nurses—they could be spiritual healers in nurses' uniforms, but I did call them nurses.

For Ran, the overwhelming attraction of the church was its music. The Church on Russell Street was alive with music. According to Gil Ahrens, there was "a full sit-in band," and "Ran would sit in as well." From the first time he attended, the music made a huge impression,[20] but Ran felt "alien—at least temporarily—from this rich musical world."

This choir, with Eunice Glover (and Hubert Powell Jr. as the organist), I've never... [heard anything like it.] The VOICES were so alive. And there are very good voices now, but I heard the greatness!
The music of Eunice Glover and Edith Powell was to create a lasting impression and was to lead me to Mahalia Jackson, Ray Charles, Marion Williams, Claude Jeter, and C.L. Franklin and his teenage daughter, Aretha.
Now there are drummers, but [in those days] it was all acoustical; the clapping: Blessed Je-he-sus—bah-bah-bah-bah-two-three [*clapping in time*]. We'd stand up and sing. And the dancing and the joy!
So that and *Spiral* were my world. The endorsement of I.L. Jefferson, Mother Carter, the Powell and the Hodges families, and Sr. Eunice Glover... the rejoicing! What Sundays I had! I couldn't wait—the church in the morning, and the mystery movies at night! I couldn't wait! It was the most alive I have ever been. And I didn't give school a chance, but how could I with Mother Carter and I.L. Jefferson, and Dorothy McGuire from *The Spiral Staircase*? And then there was the movie *The Red House* and Ingrid Bergman in *Gaslight* and *Spellbound*. I didn't want to hear [from the boys at Suffield Academy]

> some story about some girl who had dandruff, or some move on the baseball field, or [about] somebody got divorced: who needs it!
> But I couldn't stop the day-dreams—I would sleep through [lessons]. And I got to know the letter 'D.' 'D' and 'D-plus,' and 'C-minus.' [*He smiles—he's kidding us.*] And tonight, I just had a lesson—Robert Sealy came here to do it—on 'Inequalities in the Matrix System.' I was SO alive tonight! I wish my father could see me, and [*he continues on the same breath*] Mother Carter would say, 'Do your studies.' [*He wags his finger to demonstrate.*] 'I hear you're not doing them. You wouldn't be at a movie, would you?'

Movies and music preoccupied him, and Ran could not get enough of the music at the Pentecostal church.

> By constantly attending services and choir rehearsals, one could absorb 12/8 time, melisma, and dynamics that I never heard in Suffield, Connecticut—my sleepy New England home. This music was both earthy and sanctified.[21]

On a couple of occasions, Ran played for Mother Carter:

> I only played there once or twice, and she said, 'Once a year is quite enough.' She said, 'We'd have you play again; that was a nice solo, and you have a nice beat, but I can't stand… there's something funny going on.' She looked at me, 'You haven't been drinking, have you?' And ah, you know, what could I say? I'd had a little nip the night before, at the Elks Club, right down on the corner from the church.

For the music on offer in Hartford was not confined to the church; Ran had very quickly discovered the Elks Clubs, which were drawing big crowds for live jazz. Thursday, Friday, and Saturday nights were big nights for the jazz clubs in Hartford.[22]

> Often, when the club got out at one o'clock, I would try to stay [in Hartford] Saturday night. Would somebody put me up—that neither was a drinker, nor a church-man or woman—so that I could go to my beloved church?

For Ran understood full well that while he could embrace the clubs and the church with equal enthusiasm, there were others who could not:

> One time I was leaving the church and one of the sidemen of the Elks Club saw me and his mouth opened—I thought his teeth would fall out—and I said… like that [*he gestures with a finger to his lips, begging not to be greeted or recognized*]. And Mother Carter came

up and said, 'What are you doing?' and I said, 'I have an itch here…'
What if the church saw me going to the Elks Club? [*It's added with a
flicker of remembered trepidation.*]

The thought of discovery tormented him:

> I'd have nightmares, and [in the nightmare] it was either the *Spiral
> Staircase*[23] or Mother Carter finding me. And then when they mixed
> together, and Mother Carter had a larger eye like this…. [*He demon-
> strates with his fingers, and Leo laughs.*]

But Mother Carter's all-seeing eye had a warmth and benevolence that was in stark contrast to any nightmare or any of the threatening shadows portrayed in film noir. In Ran's papers, he sums her up thus: "Mother Sarah Carter, known far and wide for her ribs, collard greens, black-eyed peas, soul rice, sharp talk, humility, and warmth."

For many years, the students of the Third-Stream Department made a field trip to the Holy Trinity Church of God in Christ in North Hartford. Among Ran's papers is a memo to students proposing a trip for October 18, 1987, leaving Jordan Hall at 7 am and stopping in Sturbridge, Massachusetts, for breakfast at the Publik House.[24] The memo requested students to "Please bring $9.50 for breakfast; $8.00 for travel expenses (gas and tolls), and a small contribution for the church."

In a "P.P.S.," the students are also asked to: "Please dress appropriately for a Sunday service." However, Ran was disappointed with the students' attempts in this regard:

> They didn't know how to… [*He interrupts himself suddenly*], and
> we should say, a great deal of this was arranged by Scott Sandvik.[25]
> He said, "Ran, this is part of their education to go," so he arranged
> transport. But the students didn't know how to dress—one with a torn
> shirt and one with long, blond hair—seemed as if there was no bath-
> tub or shower… and he said he would be made clean by the church.
> [*The sense of hurt Ran felt in the face of such levity is still palpable.*]
> And the air wasn't very good in the van that we rented. And I was
> really embarrassed [because] the people at the church, [they were] the
> height of great fashion—very religious—the men in suits, the women
> in long… to the ankle… distinguished white gloves… beautifully…
> But even the best students couldn't do it. Some wore designer jeans,
> but really… And my clothes were badly fitted, but at least I put some
> kind of a shirt and tie on, tried to brush my hair. I know Dorothy
> Wallace was thrilled.

In subsequent years, after Third-Stream Department became Contemporary Improvisation, there were other excursions in which it was Sr. Natalie Arthur who greeted Ran at the door with a hug. But all this would happen later. For the young Ran, the church in Hartford was merely a glimpse of what was to come: its music a tantalizing prelude—a baptism in gospel music that sowed the seed for a lifelong devotion to the form.

Hartford in the 1950s, however, had other attractions to claim the attention of the young Ran Blake. The "hours and hours" he spent at the church—whether it be at its Russell Street address or, later, at Wooster Street—melded with those spent at the jazz clubs into one happy memory, woven through with music and impervious to the restrictions of time and place.

The words of I.L. Jefferson—their wisdom and kindness— had been imprinted on Ran's heart, and in 2016, when his dear friend Sandi Peaslee died, Ran wrote to the pastor, Rev. Wendy von Courter,[26] to thank her for her "elegance and personal feeling and prayers" on this occasion. The service, he said, reminded him of the funerals of Thelonious Monk and Abbey Lincoln, and he added: "I've never heard such golden words in New England since my childhood attendance at the Church of God in Christ in North Hartford."

13

Jazz Clubs of Hartford, Connecticut

> *Ran was in the formative stages of his career, absorbing the different aspects of music in general, while developing his own style specifically.*
>
> Ernie Wilson

The camaraderie, the music—"both earthy and sanctified"— and the shared sweet potato pie, lemonade, and cold tea available at the Church of God in Christ, was only a block away from the entertainment at the Canton Street Elks Club where, Ran says, "I heard my first live jazz."

Hartford, at the time, was still enjoying its "Golden Age" of jazz.[1] There was an enthusiastic following for the music and lots of local talent. The North End was "alive with jazz clubs."[2] The Elks Clubs (one on Canton Street and the other on Bellevue Street) also hosted live music.[3] When the church moved to Wooster Street, it moved into the heart of the north-end jazz scene. (Bellevue Street ran parallel to Wooster with a short-cut across Belleview Square Park between them, while Canton connected the two.)[4]

Windsor Street, one back from Bellevue (going towards the railway), was where the famous Club Sundown was located.[5] This was the club that brought in the big-name players from New York and Boston. And it was here, it is said, that Stan Getz discovered Horace Silver.

> The Sundown was another black club. I can't remember [going to see] a big name there.[6] I wanted to support local people, though I did go to big names too.

Across the street from the Sundown, the Cotton Club also drew big crowds. And a mile or so downtown on Wells Street was the Heublein Hotel.

Judy Grisamore, a college student who met Ran in 1959 when they were both working in the Hartford record and bookstore, Witkowers,[7] remembers Ran taking her and a group of friends to this "wonderful jazz bar in Hartford."[8] As Judy recalls, the jazz bar was "operated by the Heublein Liquor distributor, and it was a sophisticated nightclub."[9] Cozy and dimly lit, the jazz bar was set up in the lounge of the Heublein Hotel.

The Heublein "brought a steady parade of talent to Hartford, including Coleman Hawkins, Dizzy Gillespie, Teddy Wilson, and Cannonball Adderley,"[10] and Hartford residents could enjoy "the pleasures of a Manhattan jazz club in downtown Hartford," until the grand old building was torn down in 1965 to make way for Bushnell Towers.[11]

Another of the venues that Ran frequented (also since demolished) was the Adajian Restaurant at 297 Asylum Street. The "wood-paneled restaurant, whose carpeted steps led to a smoky, cave-like lounge,"[12] was where Ray Cassarino played for up to six weeks every year. It was well known for its Art-Deco-style murals, which were considered "racy" at the time. Ran remembers the piano, the food, and the music:

> There was a beautiful grand piano, and you would have shish kebob, but it was Armenian-American. They had Armenian food, but it wasn't... I mean, they'd sell alcohol. Oh, but they made Armenian brandy. I would take crowds of people to hear Ray Cassarino. I would bring my sister, and Sandi Fisk, Barbara Hanson[13]— all these people to hear him play these great standards. Ray was a traditionalist; he loved John Lewis; he was not a big fan of Monk, but he did like Chris Connor.

There was a certain elegance about these clubs and their patrons:

> There would be beautiful young ladies in their thirties and GORGEOUS dresses... impeccably groomed, and I [around the home] wore a tee-shirt and old trousers, but you can be sure I'd be dressed to the hilt... [to go to church or the clubs.] My parents couldn't get over my wardrobe between church and the club—they sort of knew... [I went to the Elks Club]. My father noticed a little buzz in my breath, one night coming home.[14] My mother didn't! But they couldn't get over... My father was a great dresser [*it's said in a quick aside*], and I still was sloppy. But I took such care... [when going to the Elks Club]. I might wear a crew neck sweater with a nice shirt and a coat.

And with Mother Carter and the church, I put on a white shirt, tie… My parents thought I looked so immaculate on Sundays, and they once took my photo. They said I was handsome for once.

Jazz was the music of choice for young people at this time, and age restrictions on club entry did not seem to be enforced. Marte remembered going to nightclubs with Ran when she was fourteen or fifteen. At the Heublein Hotel lounge, if dressed appropriately (jacket and tie), you could be served drinks, even if you were still not twenty-one. Ran remembers that it was the Elks Club where he had *his* first drink.[15]

> I was quite young to be there when I started going, and I think I did spy a preacher from the Church of God in Christ there, and he… Oh! [*there is a sudden exclamation as the memory crystallizes and he claps a hand over his mouth*] [The preacher] hid his face, and I think I ran out saying, 'I hope you enjoyed your Coca Cola,' and he said, 'Don't come by—I don't want you to smell my mouth.'
> Maybe there was rum in it? [*He contemplates this possibility for a moment.*] But I never told Mother Carter, and he never told on me…

The Elks Club on Canton Street was Ran's home from home. He would go Thursday and Saturday. It was here that he heard Norman Macklin on piano and Ernie Wilson on bass, as well as saxophonist Houston Person:

> Houston Person, he played four tracks on *Suffield Gothic*. We appeared together in Vancouver. I knew that guy since he was fifteen, and he used to bring a beautiful young lady with him called Fern—she was a fixture at the Elks Club—the beautiful Fern… Oh, it's all coming back; it just seems like yesterday. [*He opens his arms wide as if to embrace a tangible presence before continuing.*] Ever heard of 'Sister Sadie,' Horace Silver's piece? Moe Cloud was married to Sadie. Moe [Maurice] Cloud would sit in for Ernie Wilson. And there was Norman Macklin, and Bunny Mills was the drummer. Cliff Gunn… oh and Fred Tinsley would be a wonderful African American bass player that played at my graduation concert at Bard; he came from Hartford. So, it was a bustling place, Elks Club. It was THE place to be.

According to Ernie Wilson, "The Elks Club was a magnet for musical talent and hosted many established as well as up and coming jazz musicians."[16] Wilson was part of the regular trio there, along with Norman Macklin and Bunny Mills. He recalls:

> The job at the Elks Club was three nights a week, Monday, Thursday, and Saturday, which seemed rather odd for a three-nights-a-week gig rather than a more normal Thursday through Saturday. However, it worked out well for the club as it had good crowds on a Monday (when most clubs were closed). On one of the Saturdays, Ran and several of his friends occupied one of the tables. During a break, I went over and greeted them and asked them if they were enjoying the music, to which they said yes. I was not aware that Ran was a pianist at the time; however, I learned from other members of their party that he was. I learned that he was attending one of the Gospel Churches in Hartford as well […] Although I did not have the opportunity to play with Ran during that period, we did perform together for the Hartford Jazz Society in late 1962 at a place called The Tobacco Valley Inn.[17]

One of the first pieces Ran heard at the Elks Club was a piece called "Trio," composed by Erroll Garner,[18] who Ran remembers as a "wonderful pianist."

> "Trio" was a very easy, catchy piece. I can go to the piano and play you a couple of bars. I can do it right now! [*He does!*] The last part was my re-harmonization [*he explains, coming back to the webcam*]. A very famous piece was "Satin Doll," and I can't wait to hear Janet do it sometime… [*He smiles mischievously*].

BUT PLAYING THE piece has brought back memories and, sitting there in his Brookline apartment, Ran is suddenly transported back sixty-odd years to Hartford CT, and he cries out in wonder and joy:

> I can just see it—the Elks Club—walking down that lot.[19] I don't even know if the Elks Club is there anymore. That wonderful moose would be sitting there at the door, and there would be another one inside.
> I can barely remember The Heublein—I'm glad Judy [Grisamore] told you about it. I DO know I went to Jazz at the Philharmonic, and that was my only meeting with Ella Fitzgerald, in the backstage… [area]. And I don't know what I was doing backstage at that big concert hall in Hartford.[20] That was the Bushnell—B-U-S-H-N-E-L-L.

> And the Headmaster at Suffield Academy—the second year—was Appleton BUSHNELL [*said with emphasis*] Seaverns.

Coming from close-knit Suffield (where everyone knew you—and your background), it must have seemed surreal for Ran to be meeting Ella Fitzgerald, one of the jazz greats he admired so much. The jazz scene in Hartford and the Church of God in Christ had opened up his world and was changing the course of his life forever.

Later, during his first year at Bard, Ran, along with his friend Gil Ahrens, started going to Jinxey's in Springfield:

> once a week on Sunday [when Gil was not away at school]. And that was on Hancock Street, where the spiritual church was. Jinxey's was run by Frankie Jones and his aunt; Frankie was the bartender.
> To my knowledge, Jinxey's was the first jazz club that my father went to. He and Sandi Fisk's father went there, and they never got over that experience—they saw Martha running up and talking to all the group. She had her hair all in a ring; they couldn't get over her poise.
> Jinxey's was THE place to be. They would serve a thing called 'Champagne Ale'—a poor man's champagne, mixed with light beer. But both clubs were very civilized (compared to the way people dress now), and we wanted to look rather sharp.
> J: How did it come about that your father went there?
> R: Well, he didn't want me taking my sister. And Sandi's father... [evidently didn't want me taking Sandi either.] They didn't want me to drive. They said, 'Have a drink at home, don't drive.' So, they went, and my father talked about it for days afterward—what a wonderful place!

Through the jazz clubs he frequented and the people he met there, Ran was able to get a rhythm section together, which played at Vassar[21] a couple of times. Houston Person joined this combo after relocating to Hartford in 1958. (He had enrolled in an advanced course at the Hartt College of Music.) Ran was at Bard, and they would meet up at weekends.

Later, they were to collaborate on Suffield Gothic.[22] The album cover features a whole crowd of people carefully chosen by Ran to represent certain aspects of his life in Suffield. Even his neighbor Mrs. Leete is there. (She's the lady with white hair.)

But it wasn't just jazz and gospel music as the soundtrack to Ran's social life in those Suffield days. He also joined Eddie Young's rock and roll band in Windsor Locks:

I had to do Fats Domino; this was happening at the same time as the Elks Club, but it would have been at a little high school auditorium or a little bar. Oh, and they did "Night Train" [*hums a bit*], and then, I had to do "Hound Dog"—there was some singer called Presley. Now, the English invasion—The Beatles—they hadn't come yet.

Sometimes, Ran played jazz gigs. He had a bass player called Wil ("one 'l'") De Sola, who later played with Jeanne Lee and Ran at the Apollo Theater amateur night. Wil was a student at Trinity.[23]

But the gigs were not enough to support Ran's great passion for LPs and live music. There were expenses involved in the frequent club attendance, and always determined to pay his way, Ran was ever-alert to opportunities to earn the money he needed.

14

Records, Records, Records

Such sweet compulsion doth in music lie

John Milton, Arcades

Ran was still at school when he first heard Hubert Powell play at the Church of God in Christ in Hartford. The music there and the movies at the Thompsonville and Hartford theaters preoccupied him. But it was difficult to get there from Suffield, and in the "long while" before he got his license, he had to rely on the goodwill of friends and neighbors. When he was unable to find a ride, he had his record collection to occupy him. Ran began collecting records at a young age—the first steps along a musical journey that would map out his life.

> I became quite interested, you know [in collecting records], and I was a great friend of Jimmy and Helen Gatto, G-A-T-T-O, in Thompsonville, Connecticut. So, I would be fifteen, sixteen, seventeen, eighteen, nineteen, working at [record] stores and *flipping*—just so excited to, you know, get records at half price and try to promote them. It was a very, very exciting time.

Ran found a job at the Belmont Record Store[1] in Hartford. For him, it was the perfect job, as a small salary was supplemented by ten albums of his choice.

> I knew I'd build up my record collection. Later, I could get these Prestige[2] records that sold for nine or ten [dollars]—I could get them for two dollars by saying, 'I'm writing for the *Dutchess County Jour-*

nal,' and so I had ways... But I loved... records, records, records. Charlie Parker to Bartok to Charles Ives... Ohhh!
[*The cry of delight is followed by a nostalgic pause...*]
L: I'm glad I got in on the end of CD stores.
R: [*shakes his head sadly at their passing, before suddenly exclaiming*] Oh, have you seen *Strangers on a Train* by Alfred Hitchcock? Tennis player Farley Granger is visiting his ex-wife in a record store, a big store, like Belmont.

The thought triggers a vision of the store on the corner of Park and Washington Streets, a mile or so from downtown Hartford and a block from the Hartford Hospital. A drive-thru Walgreens Pharmacy now occupies the spot, but remnants of the flat-profiled, stoic red-brick district Ran knew remain. It is easy to imagine the old-style record store:

> There'd be four or five private rooms. You'd go in, and there'd be a couch, a little water, paper cups... And you'd sit, and they'd let you play the record. There would be a store copy—you couldn't open... [a new one.] And they'd play Duke Ellington and Rosemary Clooney. One day I remember some lady saying, 'Ran Blake, come into the room, they're playing the new Duke Ellington record, and I hope my cigarette doesn't bother you.'
> [There were] these very nice chairs.... And of course, every now and then, the store hoped you'd buy the record.
> And there'd be two or three other people because it got to be THE thing—to go to the Belmont lounge... and I think I hear the door?
> [*He does! It's Stephanie—one of Ran's young assistants. She has come to prepare a meal for Ran to serve to the guest expected that night:* 'Goat cheese fritters with a salad and Israeli couscous with caramelized fennel and a walnut tart—he's lucky, right?' *Stephanie announces with a grin.*]

WHETHER HE WAS at home, in Suffield—in his own little suite looking out over the tobacco fields—or relaxing in those "very nice chairs" at the Belmont Music Store, Ran was listening to a lot of records. He particularly remembers those of Mahalia Jackson and also Stan Kenton's *Innovations Orchestra*.

> Monk I discovered—but more like '54/'55. And people like Dizzy Gillespie, Charlie Parker—that was a lot later. So, I loved Bartok, some Debussy, Stravinsky, and I didn't like that much jazz—unless

it was gospel. But Kenton, in that one period, was noir jazz. And the June Christy/Chris Connor school were good, and of course, Sarah and Ella... but Mahalia... and Sr. Eunice Glover from the Pentecostal.

So music really... I got to know my record collection. THANK GOD, there were no videos then, and so I had a choice: do you want a movie on Sunday or go to the Gospel church?

But could we just make a note of the Kenton *Innovations*. Just so we know that [particular] music's in my life.

Buying records and getting to church—and, later, to clubs—necessitated that Ran thought beyond the domestic boundaries of Suffield. He needed money, but he also needed transport:

R: The only thing was getting in; then, I had a car...
L: [*interrupting*] You drove?
R: Oh, I did indeed. [*He's amused at Leo's amazement.*]
L: Wow, I never imagined that!
R: I got an English Squire, and it was the cheapest thing—one of the cheapest cars you could get.
L: Wow, this was when you were about eighteen years old?
R: Seventeen or Eighteen...

Having a car not only solved the problem of getting to Hartford and Thompsonville but also provided an opportunity to earn extra money delivering newspapers in Suffield and surrounds:

Suffield was quite extended. When we think of Suffield Academy and the town, it's all on one street, with four central stores and five or six churches, but to go to West Suffield would be further than to go from my house [in Brookline] to the Conservatory.[3] So I would go to West Suffield, three or four miles away. It was quite different. It was all tobacco [farms], and of course, I would pick up the papers in Thompsonville to deliver, and I might go down to Windsor Locks, to the south, but it was primarily Suffield. I had the Squire, and I would deliver [the newspaper]—every Thursday afternoon—and I got two dollars.

I got to know all the people on Marbern Drive—everyone on that drive wanted the Thompsonville press. I got to know Danny Sullivan from Suffield High, who was very good at sports. Once somebody called my parents. Their paper had come, but they complained to my mother: 'I didn't appreciate Ran's appearance.' It was somebody that knew my parents... I really got to know Suffield through the newspaper route.

In recent years, Ran has had some unexpected correspondence—from a man who lived, as a child, on Marbern Drive. This man fondly remembered the Thursday afternoons when Ran's car would drive by, with music playing out from the car radio. He told Ran he was eight years old at the time, but Ran always greeted him by name and said, "How are you doing?"

While owning a car brought Ran freedom, it also generated expenses. Furthermore, Ran had taken over responsibility for his continuing piano lessons with Ray Cassarino in Wethersfield. And all the while, he was adding to his growing record collection.

It was necessary to take on whatever employment he could find. One of these jobs was that of a cheese cutter, working at the S.S. Pierce and Co. store in West Hartford. S.S. Pierce prided itself on the variety of its products, which included a large selection of cheeses.[4] It soon became apparent that Ran was entirely unsuited to the job. Ran recalls his time there with some irony:

> R: The blood! [*said dramatically*] The people said, 'Why are we having red…'
> L: [*laughing*] 'Red-vein cheese!' They didn't like it?
> R: Yeah, and I had Mr. Callanan, who was the boss, and he said, 'I have some news for you: there's too many [customers] complaining. We just think…' He'd never heard me play, but he said, 'We hear you're very talented, and we think you should not be here anymore as a cheese cutter.'
> L: How long did you stay cutting cheese?
> R: Oh, about a year, I guess.
> L: [*still laughing*] So how many times did you cut yourself?
> R: Oh, twice a week… Friday was a busy day, so maybe once a week. And the things wouldn't heal, and all the paper we wrapped the cheese in—there'd be these red stains. A nurse was there one day, and she said, 'This is not for you.' But she took the cheese eventually. She spoke [to me] afterward. She said, 'I think one of the reasons you lost your job is me, but you'll thank me someday,' and she handed me thirty or forty dollars. She said, 'This will ease it.' I ran into her a year or two after that at a Hartford movie theater—that will surprise you. [*He laughs, enjoying the ironic quip.*] I was well known in movie theaters, and I went to a lot of clubs and church services too.
> When I went home [after losing the job], my parents were so embarrassed. They said, 'You can't even cut cheese at our favorite store?'

It was also around this time that Ran wrote a column for the *Thompsonville Press*. It was called "Here and There in Suffield."

> L: What was the column about?
> R: [*dismisses it with a downward thumb*] Just little things—pretty lightweight. I can't believe that I wrote... [stuff like that.] I went to the office and asked could I work there, and they said, 'We don't have a columnist for Suffield.'
> There were two or three good columns, but really, it was mainly Mr. and Mrs. 'Joe' are bringing their son home from college, or 'Joe Schmo' got a promotion. Once I printed, 'Mr. and Mrs. Ahrens are going to be in Bermuda,' and Mr. Ahrens said, 'Ran, don't ever tell people where we are because we don't want to be robbed.' The paper went out of print years ago... I threw a bunch of them out.

Ran was obviously alert to what was happening around the town. If his brief at the *Thompsonville Press* had allowed it, he would have certainly explored more serious issues:

> And it was about that time [when writing for the *Thompsonville Press*], and with me going to church [in Hartford] and thinking on these things, that I wrote to Eleanor Roosevelt at United Nations[5] for advice on something. I just said, 'What can I do because there's not enough integration here?'
> I never thought I'd have an appointment with her. But she wrote back, asking me to visit her in Hyde Park.[6]

The invitation caused quite a stir. Eleanor Roosevelt had remained actively involved in public life after leaving the white house. Furthermore, she was well-known and loved by millions of Americans through her syndicated newspaper column "My Day," which had been published six days a week since its inception in 1935. She approached social and political issues in a personal, conversational way, and her writing style was warm and inclusive: the whole of America was her family. She was well aware that a newspaper column was a powerful means of connection and communication.

Ran was also aware of the role of journalism. He honed his skills at the Thompsonville Press, and while a student at Bard, he wrote for the *Dutchess County Journal*—a weekly publication based in Red Hook, near the College:

> This was better writing. My first review for The *Dutchess County* was Oscar Peterson, and Mr. Clair Leonard helped edit it. But that was four years later. But it *is* good to mention that I DID write newspapers, and I later wrote for the *Bay State Banner* when I moved to Boston. And then I could go to Newport Jazz Festival free and do

all these places because I was a newspaper columnist. My boss was Kay Bourne.[7] I did a review of Anthony Braxton and then a review of Chris Connor at Newport.

The columns were a means of reaching out and sharing the wondrous discoveries he was making in the world of music. But at this time, his greatest joy was playing records. It was not surprising, then, that he chose to spend his first "field period" at Bard College in a music store:[8]

The store was a branch of the old Hartford bookstore, Witkowers, which had traded at 77 Asylum Street in downtown Hartford. The new West Hartford branch on Farmington Avenue included a record section; Ran remembers the sheer joy of flipping records there as a paying job:

> I was just so excited to, you know, get records at half price; to try to promote them. It was a very exciting time.

Judy Grisamore remembers Ran's enthusiastic approach to his job at Witkowers: "He very much wanted me to learn about jazz, and so he played all kinds of music in the shop." He was "always pleasant with customers," which she concluded was because "He was— and probably still is—interested in people and what they like and how they think."[9]

Judy and Ran became good friends: "not in any romantic way at all," Judy explains. She was invited to the Blake home for dinner on a couple of occasions and "attended a party or two." She remembers Ran's mother as "a lovely woman" and remembers their home, also, as "lovely—very New England-y." It was a contrast to her own home—above an ethnic grocery store in Bristol, Connecticut. As a child of immigrant parents, she saw the Blake's Suffield home as "very much upper class!" However, with hindsight, she sees it as "a pleasant home—not large—and in a nice neighborhood."[10] Judy further reports:

> Ran was definitely not a 'snob,' and he was interested in all sorts of people, irregardless of their race, level of education, or finances. That's one of the things I have always loved about him! We always had a good time, and I cherish the memories and the wonderful experiences at that store.[11]

Though Ran may not have realized it then, the time he spent in Suffield (and Hartford)—after he had finished school and before he left for college—shaped his character in a way that a smoother transition from school to college might not have.[12] Ran's strong connection with Hartford's jazz clubs and the Pentecostal church, and his passion for listening to—and buying—records provided a focus, but he needed an income to support his lifestyle. (Marte recounted with a sense of pride that she was always amazed at the assortment of "crazy jobs" that her brother had.) Ran, however, has a different memory of this time. He recalls that he was "very depressed and lounged around the house. I think I felt very sad."

It is challenging for any young person to leave school, with its predictable certainty, and find themselves in a vast emptiness with no immediate prospects. But the idea that he "lounged around the house" is something of an overstatement. During this period, Ran devoted what spare time he had to his music, and what might have seemed a fallow period was, in fact, a time spent preparing for his future.

15

CIVIL RIGHTS AND ELEANOR ROOSEVELT

> *Back then in that pre-Civil Rights Movement era, there was little socializing between blacks and whites in Hartford. Racism was an evil, oppressive force not just in the South, where it was enshrined in the legal system, but also, if less overtly yet still perniciously, in Northern cities as well.*
>
> OWEN MCNALLY [1]

While the rhythm of life in Suffield continued at its own sweet and tranquil pace, the struggle that was central to the American Civil Rights Movement was reaching boiling point in the South. 1954 saw the Supreme Court rule against segregation in public schools,[2] and in 1955, first Claudette Colvin[3] and then Rosa Parks each made a courageous stand by refusing to give up their seats to white bus passengers. This gave rise to the bus boycott in Montgomery, Alabama, in 1956,[4] which resulted in buses being desegregated by December 21, 1956.

Three months earlier, Ran had commenced his studies at Bard College. As he began his sophomore year, nine black students were blocked from entering the all-white Central High School in Little Rock, Arkansas. These events were the beginning of a long, hard-fought struggle in the Civil Rights Movement's aim to eliminate segregation.

Ran was painfully aware that the town where he lived, and the clubs and the church he attended, had distinct racial demographics. Suffield was predominantly white with a black area, "the Harlem of Suffield" (as Ran called it), in the east, around Kent Avenue, where Eunice Bell lived. The Church of God in Christ was black, just as the churches on Main Street, Suffield were white.

The lack of integration was something that worried Ran. He had been warmly received at the Church of God in Christ, and his mentor, Mother Carter, and father figure, Bishop I.L. Jefferson, had given him generous support. He'd been to the clubs of New York and witnessed first-hand that the appreciation of jazz had no racial boundaries. In Hartford, the black clubs in the North End welcomed any white jazz fans who ventured "from the then lily-white burbs."[5] Jazz, the musical heritage of an enslaved people, had a deep understanding of the nature of racial intolerance. And black jazz musicians—irrespective of their stature —were frequently subjected to racism in their professional lives: overlooked for awards and accolades or prime-time TV slots in favor of their white counterparts and offered second-class travel and accommodation options where they toured. Their music echoed widespread cries for freedom and foreshadowed a groundswell of demand that would reach a defining moment in the 1963 march on Washington.[6]

But this moment of truth was yet to come. While Ran was working in Suffield and Hartford, preparing for college and attending jazz clubs, the musicians' union "still maintained separate memberships for white and black."[7] The Elks Club was a club where whites didn't go, and Ran was: "one of the few blue-eyed guys there."[8]

The situation worried Ran. He wrote to Eleanor Roosevelt, voicing his concern about the lack of racial integration. He didn't expect a reply, but Eleanor Roosevelt—who had always had a vital interest in youth and their opinions—was very approachable.

> I know I wrote one letter and she said, 'Keep trying,' and then, I wrote a second letter saying that I had followed 'some thoughts of yours and I still don't like the way people are being treated.' And then the second letter got the lunch invitation.[9]

The Blake family was shocked and surprised when Ran received an invitation to lunch. The very personal and breezy letter—posted in early October—proposed a lunch meeting at 1 pm on November 21. It stated, "I am in the process of changing my address, so I cannot now tell you where we will have our meal together," and requested Ran to ring closer to the date. He was then told he should come to her cottage, Val-kill.[10]

> I don't remember it being a cottage—that sounds like a one-bedroom shack—perhaps a cottage compared to the White House, but it wasn't shabby. I remember the dining room on the right and the parlor with the piano on the left.
> L: Was it a grand?
> R: I don't know. I think so. It's such an important day in history, the day Ran Blake came at Val-kill in Hyde Park, just north of Poughkeepsie. [*It's said with heavy irony.*]

It was, however, an important day for the people of Suffield. News quickly spread, and neighbors were full of praise for Ran, as his mother proudly showed them the letter with its large type and scrawling signature.

> This was in the Year of Our Lord 1959, and I'm in Suffield, Connecticut. THEN [*it's said with droll emphasis*] did the neighbors love me. They told my parents they always felt I was incredible, and my mother showed the letter... Oh, my relatives were so impressed! They couldn't get over it! There were times when I disappointed them and [got] the bad review at Town Hall [*He doesn't elaborate, continuing without a pause*], but [this time] they were gaga—my grandmother's name. [*He acknowledges the verbal coincidence matter-of-factly.*] I know my aunt and uncle had a special dinner for me before I went. They gave me a course on how great Franklin was. I don't think everyone in the Connecticut town knew (but it was in the newspapers) that I was going down there. Even people who didn't like my music came up to congratulate me.

Nothing was overlooked in preparation for the occasion. There was speculation as to what might be on the menu and who else might be present:

> My parents thought that there'd be steaks. They said, 'We'll just give you this much breakfast; you'll have a big lunch. And I'm sure it was one o'clock, not twelve. It was about a two-and-a-half-hour trip from Suffield—maybe it was three. I can't believe I was allowed to take the family car alone... [*He considers this for a moment.*] Now, if my parents were here to say that they drove me to Bard and they went out shopping and were to meet me in Poughkeepsie, or that they were to take a cab to the Roosevelt house...I don't think that happened, but I wouldn't deny it.

By then, Ran, having completed three years at college, would have been an experienced driver; his little English Squire (with a top speed of 35mph) could have been considered inappropriate, or perhaps too unreliable, for the occasion. The family car seems a distinct possibility, fitting in with the careful preparations for the event.

> I got a special shirt to wear—they had it all pressed. And there were maps: I had to rehearse the map of how to get to Hyde Park. And they said, 'Don't be late!' So I arrived early and sat out in the street because I was told not to be early [either] but to be acceptably two minutes late. The family was so afraid I'd crack up.

They need not have worried. Ran, and the other young people there, were in excellent hands:

> Wow! She was SO NICE! I was there for lunch—was it in January, February, March, April 1956—could have been 55/56?[11] There were six other people there. I know we were in a drawing-room; there was a table, and we stayed at the table. We had scrambled eggs. I talked about the slowness of civil rights. I know I spoke about the Elks Club in Hartford and that the whites didn't go there. I spoke of the rudeness [to Jeanne Lee] in Suffield, Connecticut. There were things that I was very concerned about. I remember I was asked to play a number. She was very gracious, and I didn't see anybody laughing at my playing, and I know somebody said that I could 'get around the piano well...'
> L: What did you play?
> R: I forget. And you could ask me at ten in the morning or four in the afternoon—I would have no idea.
> And then, after I played a second [number], she said, 'That will be quite enough. That was quite an interesting experience, but you have that long ride back to Connecticut.' And she was standing up, and I knew my parents had said, 'Don't overstay.' And I saw a breath of relief.[12] I know there were two or three "stiff" guests there and one of them said my performance was very interesting.... I saw that steely look.
> L: [laughs]
> R: I think I acquitted myself fairly well at lunch, though—answered questions—civil rights—and she did say I was full of very good intentions. I didn't hear again. I wrote her, of course, a thank you letter, but I'm sure I was very naive. And you can be sure twelve relatives called me up to ask if I'd thanked her.... I never got another invitation—why should I?

AFTER THE EXCITEMENT of the visit died down, Suffield returned to its sleepy self where nothing seemed to change.

> Somebody from Suffield, Ruth Barkley—whose sister, Doris Leete,[13] had played the witch— did a radio show on me, and someone told my parents at the market, 'Your son's not bad,' because Ruth Barkley played Ran Blake on a little Hartford radio show.[14]

But things were changing. 1960 dawned on a restless world. Africa, having seen the success of Mahatma Gandhi's non-violent resistance to colonial rule in India, wanted freedom also. Ghana became independent in 1957, but 1960 was the year when Africa really shook off colonialism; seventeen African nations gained independence. And these changes in India and Africa influenced the civil rights movement in America. Martin Luther King Jr.,[15] along with his wife, Coretta Scott King, had been present at Ghana's independence ceremony in 1957. Dr. King was moved by the ceremony and saw it as giving "new hope [...] in the struggle for freedom."[16] The Kings also visited India in early 1959.[17] King was committed to non-violent protest. On February 1, 1960, the non-violent "sit-in" by black college students at a "Whites-Only" lunch-counter at Woolworths in Greensboro, North Carolina, took place.[18]

Then in March, in South Africa, police opened fire on an unarmed crowd who were demonstrating against apartheid, and sixty-nine people, including women and children, were killed.[19]

This was the climate in which Ran completed his final semester at Bard: the semester in which he and Jeanne Lee revived a partnership begun in their first year there—a collaboration that would give birth to a highly original musical sound. And during that long summer of the last year of his Suffield boyhood, Ran knew he was on the threshold of a whole new and exciting phase of life. By the end of the year, he would be living in New York City—working at the Jazz Gallery. There, he would see Max Roach and Abbey Lincoln, adding to the growing cry for justice with their *We Insist Freedom Now Suite*.[20]

16

BARD COLLEGE

I think Bard is the place for Ran.

FRANCES POWERS

There was never any doubt in the Blake household that Ran would pursue a college education after high school. Philip Blake had been keen for his son to attend his old school, Williams, and while Ran did, at least, make the waiting list, he readily admits that his father would probably have liked a more definite offer. The fact that he didn't receive one did not seem to worry Ran, however, who detected in the school a "whiff of elitism."

Ran also made the waiting list for Juilliard, perhaps a more appropriate placement considering his passion for music. His application was assessed on the basis of his classical playing as Juilliard had no jazz program at that time:

> My reading wasn't good enough, but they liked my touch. I didn't have repertoire. I remember Martha Hill—who (later) ran the dance department, where the Manhattan School [is]—she voted for me, but she did not have an equal vote—she was not senior. Some faculty DID NOT [*the emphasis is strong*] like me—they felt it would be a struggle—and it was controversial. Somebody said, 'Yes, you have to get this Ran Blake. He'll be something.' Others… [were not so complimentary.]
>
> L: Do you remember what you did for your audition at Juilliard?
> R: Probably "Take the A Train." And maybe I did the Chopin *A major Prelude*—pah pah pa pa pa [*he sings a snatch*]. And I may have done

my own interpretation of the *7th symphony* [of] Beethoven; I can play it on the piano. Let me play it for you now. [*He gets up eagerly and rushes to the piano to play.*]

After deliberation and in the absence of any firm offer, Philip and Alison came to the conclusion that Ran was not quite ready for college. They encouraged him to continue with the extra "college preparation" year at Suffield Academy. His grades needed improvement—Ran was still spending a lot of his time going to movies, which the Blakes felt had a direct influence on this. They also worried he went to church so much.

In all, they felt there was "a lot of growing up... [to be done.]" Ran seemed young for his age, and while he did have friends (mostly younger than him), he was basically a loner:

> There's some isolation I have, and... there are just certain acts of maturity, and I guess I didn't have them in high school. So, I stayed another year [at Suffield Academy], getting nice high C marks and low Bs and no honor work. I think I felt very sad; I was bored.

According to Ran, for the two years that followed, he "was very depressed" and "lounged around the house." But this dismissive summary fails to recognize time spent storing up experiences that would serve as the foundation for his life as a musician. When he set out for college in September of 1956, he was twenty-one years old and showing definite maturity:

> Finally, I liked Suffield. I had discovered Bishop Jefferson, Sister Eunice Glover, Mother Carter, and Edith Powell—whose son wrote "There's been a Change." As well, during this extended period in Suffield, movies—particularly film noir—had become part of my whole psyche.

While Ran was focusing on movies, his parents were researching college options. Bard College at Annandale-on-Hudson, New York State, had a good reputation and no waiting list. Despite its lack of history when compared to Williams,[1] despite the fact that it did not have the musical pedigree of Juilliard, and despite the fact that it cost $5000 a year ("my mother and father called that 'highway robbery'"),[2] it gradually became attractive to Ran and his parents:

> It was really my aunt Frances Powers who wrote the letter to Richard (Buz) Gummere,[3] who was Director of Admissions. She said, 'I think Bard is the place for Ran.'

As a small institution dedicated to the promotion of liberal arts, Bard College offered a broadly-based education built on literature, languages, philosophy, and history. Its program would have dovetailed with Philip and Alison's own educational experiences and preferences.

Buz Gummere, interviewed in 1957,[4] said that increasingly, laymen were seeing Bard as "strong and successful academically," though he did believe that this was somewhat canceled out by the further perception of Bard as "a large-scale Black Mountain,"[5] with a "social freedom" that was not desirable. This, however, would not have worried the Blakes. They knew their son and his dedication to his music. Besides, he was a little older and used to freedom—freedom to attend the churches, movies, and clubs of his choice. The Blakes would have been more interested in Gummere's recognition of Bard students as "articulate, imaginative, intellectually curious," if "over critical and uncooperative." (Gummere saw this as "not a bad combination judged in relation to American undergraduates generally.")[6]

Other more practical considerations would have also held appeal for Ran's parents. The college was small; its class sizes ensured that a new student, away from family support, was not overwhelmed or lost in the crowd. Also, being situated on the east bank of the Hudson River, Bard was only a two-hour car trip west from Suffield. The sprawling rural campus, with its spectacular views of the river and the Catskill Mountains and meandering walks through pristine woodland, had the feel of a tranquil holiday destination. It promised personal enrichment for their son.

Bard (originally St. Stephen's) had been set up by the Episcopal Church of New York City with the aim of providing a classical education for young men destined to enter their seminaries.[7] But by the early 20th century, it was moving toward a more secular vision. In 1928 it became an undergraduate school of Columbia University, and in 1934 the name was changed from St. Stephen's to Bard—to honor the founder, John Bard. The church connection did continue, however, and this may have had some influence on the direction the college took.

During the 1930s, unlike other colleges at the time, Bard put strong academic emphasis on fine arts and performing arts. Its aim, as stated in the College catalog of 1943, was to preserve liberal arts education in America as "an important value." It felt that education was, like life itself, a "continuous process of growth and effort." Students needed specific instruction that would enable them to facilitate their own growth and direct their own efforts. Because of this emphasis, the school was seen as progressive and attracted intellectual refugees, including scientists, artists, teachers, and writers fleeing the war in Europe.

The choice of college was to be an important one for Ran. Bard was different in its approach from that of many other colleges, and with the influx of professors from Europe, this difference became even more pronounced. Bishop I.L. Jefferson went so far as to voice objections to the choice on these grounds, fearing it was a college dominated by "yesterday's intelligentsia." (No doubt his comments reflected the anxiety he, a "father figure," felt as the boy he had nurtured in the Pentecostal community at Hartford ventured out into the secular world.) But Bard could offer Ran independence—freedom to make his own way in a place where individual differences and talents were acknowledged. At Bard, he encountered three important teachers: Kate Wolff, Clair Leonard, and Ralph Ellison, to guide him on this journey.

ONE OF BARD's "intellectual refugees" was the noted psychologist Werner Wolff, who was teaching psychology during Ran's first year there.[8] But it was Werner's wife, Kate Wolff—Ran's piano teacher at Bard—who he remembers as one of his great teachers. Kate Wolff, he claims, taught him touch.

In the 1930s, Kate Wolff had been a concert pianist in Europe, giving recitals across that continent and playing as a soloist with such world-renowned ensembles as the Berlin Philharmonic Orchestra.[9] When she fell in love with the psychologist Werner Wolff there was no question—they could not remain in Germany. By the mid-1940s, they had fled to America and were both teaching at Bard College. A graduate of *Stern'sches Konservatorium* in Berlin, Kate Wolff was a great believer in practice. She would tell her students that their music "would only work with practice."[10]

Ran remembers her insistence on this:

> She said I could do scales my own way but do them I must. I was a very slow... [reader.] She pushed me into sight-reading, though she never put a ruler on my hands. But she was tough on the position of the hands, on clarity, on whether to use the pedals or not to use the pedals. She gave me various expressions because she'd say, 'Listen to the violinists—you get this sound, and you love singers... what about the terminal vibrato of Miss Connor, as opposed to the gorgeous color of Sarah...?'
> She really didn't—you know, she's in heaven now—but if I was to bring up people like Monk, she would barely know who I was talking about. I mean, she got to know the names through me, but she could

seize characteristics, and she said, 'Gosh, Monk is a terrible pianist, but what exciting music; how he attacks the piano is everything!' And she barely could pronounce the word Thelonious. [*This is added in a tone of wonder.*] So, Kate Wolff [*He thinks for a moment before effecting a character summation in bold, brief strokes*]: steely discipline with kindness—she was never cruel.

There is something of this kindness evident as he continues:

I noticed that once in a while, I'd get a cold Coke in the middle of a lesson, and it was very important [for her] to have Coca-Cola with a lot of ice and a lot of lemon—lemon juice, no sugar. She felt that gave caffeine but not as strong as coffee or tea. And then, when you got tired again at the end, you'd take a piece of lemon again in your mouth, and she'd say, 'Wake up.' [*He pats his hands on either side of his cheeks.*] 'Let's get back to using your eyes!' [*He makes little goggles with his fingers 'round his eyes.*] Just having to read and do things that were not so natural [for me] meant that after thirty minutes I could be exhausted, and she could see that, so I'd get a cold CocaCola and lemon in the middle. She was WONDERFUL... wonderful.

Kate Wolff devoted herself to her students at Bard, and when, in 1957, her husband died, the Bard family closed around her:

I remember they'd gone to New York, to a Hotel called The Baltimore, and I remember that somebody—Mr. Leonard—wrote me a note: Would I come over to see him? And they told me—I think it was during March or April—that Mr. Wolff had had a heart attack and died and that we should do all we could to comfort Kate Wolff and welcome her back. And she lived at Bard—I think [they] gave her two rooms. And when she retired, they took one room away, and all her stuff [went] into the larger room, and she ended up there for life.

Bard became Kate Wolff's life. It was where she lived out her last years. A tribute to her which appeared in *The Bard Observer*[11] in 1984, captures something of the energy that challenged and encouraged so many students during the 1940s and '50s. Even though, at eighty-four (at the time of this tribute), she had slowed down to a "shuffle," there was still a vibrancy that allowed her to quip, "I'd rather have my mind work than my feet." A familiar figure around the college, she was well known to the students who "warmly" called her Kate.[12]

Christina Griffiths description of her as she made her way to the faculty dining room each day for her lunch is charming:

She wears a coat of gold and clutches a wooden cane from Mexico, and always, she is smiling. For a moment, she pauses and simply looks around her. 'Oh, how lovely,' she says, pointing at a tree ablaze in crimson. 'Fall is my favorite. I love the colors of the leaves... how lovely.'[13]

In 1985 Kate received the Bard Medal, the alumni association's highest honor, for having "significantly advanced the welfare of the college."[14] After an eventful life, with its difficulties, dangers, and sorrows, she provided an example of good humor, endurance, and a positive outlook, which could not help but inspire those around her.

On January 31, 1986, Ran wrote to Kate:

Dear Kate,
I want to say how often I think of you during the years. Also, how I hope you enjoyed your trip to Tennessee. I'll never forget my lessons with you. Coca-Cola has never tasted so good as it did in the middle of a lesson with my five-and-a-half-minute siesta. I do hope to be up in May and see you, the Gummere's, and the Walsh family.
My love to you, Kate
Happy New Year,
Ran

Ran followed up on his promise to visit, and on May 8, 1986, he wrote:

Dear Kate,
How wonderful to see you. Thank you so much for lunch in the faculty room. Please tell Curt Crane[15] that I was so pleased to see her. Have a wonderful summer.

Another of Ran's special teachers at Bard was Clair Leonard—Professor Leonard was chairman of the Art, Music, Drama and Dance Division and was Bard's organist and choirmaster. He had studied with Nadia Boulanger[16] and was a great friend of Walter Piston.[17] Leonard was an organist/composer in the mold of the European Kapellmeister—he led the services in Bard's chapel each Sunday and composed many works for its chorus. He also wrote instrumental works.[18]

Clair Leonard valued each student for who they were and was at pains to encourage them to respect themselves and to respect others as well as to maintain a positive attitude to life and a healthy sense of humor—"because out of this attitude can develop a true and natural growth toward concrete, tangible ideals within the reach of us all."[19]

His advice had a fatherly concern as well as down-to-earth commonsense. It is no wonder that to Ran, he seemed "a really awfully wonderful guy."

> He really pushed me through the college—getting my piano sonata ready—so it was really composition [that he taught], some piano, a little tutorial, and wonderful things on organ. He had a great organ at the Bard Fellows Chapel [*sic*]. He loved Paul Hindemith.[20] He loved the perfect 4th. He said, 'Emulate Paul Hindemith. Germany didn't like the tritone 150 years ago, and I'd like to forbid you to use it.' About my improvisations, he was semi-moderately impressed, but he could take it or leave it.

The thing that pleased Clair Leonard the most about Ran was his study of organ:

> Learning the stops…I even got my feet working. I did a piece called 'Glaciation'—the first piece on my senior recital. The Gummeres took people to the chapel [for it], and then, we went to Bard Hall where we had concerts.

THE THIRD TEACHER of note at Bard was Ralph Ellison, who taught American literature and was well known for his book *Invisible Man*,[21] which looked at social, intellectual, and political issues affecting African Americans in the early 20th century. Ran remembers well the conversations he had with Ralph Ellison. Despite an abiding passion for jazz, Ran was, at that time, mostly unaware of the complex interrelationship between jazz as music and jazz as an expression of culture, the latter having far-reaching social, racial, and political implications. Ralph Ellison, it seems, was able to "meet Ran where he was at," taking the time to talk with his student, answer his questions, and introduce him to some of the issues surrounding the music, along with some important characters of whom he had been hitherto unaware.

> We would talk about Monk. He [Ellison] was also quite a writer of jazz. I got from him a sense of history—how to take a kernel of an earlier idea and develop it. I NEVER [*with dramatic emphasis*] could get my writing up to it, but I would try it on the piano—we didn't know the word 'storyboarding.'

> He talked about an amazing lady—the Baroness Pannonica de Koenigswarter. [She] lived at 63 Kingswood Avenue at Newark in New Jersey, and she was the sister of Lord Rothschild of London [Victor Rothschild, 3rd Baron Rothschild]. You know, those are the banking family of Europe—the Rothschilds. Jazz Baroness, she was called. Well, she and Ralph were friends. I only really went to Nica's house three or two times in life, but she became... I was her waiter.
> But back to Ralph. He was a wee bit rigid. His novel had come out in 52/53—*Invisible Man*. It's not an easy book to read. There's quite a bit there to it. I don't think I put it down. I think I asked a lot of awkward questions—I hope I didn't do it in an insulting way. I just was beginning to feel... There were two... three periods of my life—and this was the first one—where I felt guilt. And this is not new. Other white people have felt this; it is not unique.

Having Ralph Ellison as a teacher gave Ran insight into the injustices and inequality that were becoming more and more a matter of knowledge, and yes, guilt, among a growing number of Americans at the time.

When the US Supreme Court ruled on desegregation in public schools in May 1954,[22] there had been immediate retaliatory action and an upsurge in violence against blacks in some parts of the country, particularly Mississippi; this was reported in the black press. But the horrific murder, in August 1955, of young Emmett Till[23] and the subsequent acquittal of the perpetrators was reported with grief and anger worldwide. The trial had awakened the nation's conscience; there is no doubt that Ran would have discussed the guilt he felt with his teacher. And the feelings stirred by these discussions, along with resolutions reached, were all part of his Bard experience.

THE MUSIC DEPARTMENT at Bard was less structured and less academically rigorous than the introductory humanities subjects. The school seemed genuinely willing to accommodate Ran's passion for jazz:

> I don't think the music department had stars [as compared with the 'intellectual lights' in the academic streams], and, for me, with both my creative talents, but also maybe undeveloped academic skills, it was the perfect place because I did learn some things in orchestration. I mean, I had to work hard, and then, I remember flunking music history in the first month. I'd just creep by, but once it had got up to the 20th century, there was so much I knew.

This realization put college studies into perspective. Suddenly it was obvious that this was the period of music that vitally interested him—the period he knew so much about. He finally persuaded the college to allow him to complete a jazz major, even though there was no precedent.[24] To achieve this, he continued to work with "classical people" and had individual advisers such as Janice Watson, John Hammond,[25] John Esperence, and Albert McCarthy ("the London critic" as Ran describes him)[26] to assign him jazz reading. "They served as some kind of board." John Hammond agreed to do Ran's senior project—as his examiner. By his senior year, however, Ran had begun to realize that what he was playing was not jazz.

> I did not feel comfortable playing in trios. I really am solo piano, picking up Messiaen, Bartok, and Monk and some gospel and noir. I remember Mr. Ellison saying that I had some skill at the piano. But did it REALLY have a black sound? [*He asks himself.*] I think that I surprised them when I did a Gospel [piece]—you know, he might have heard me all of three times. Some of the classrooms had pianos; I was playing one night [when he passed], and he said, 'It does sound like you've been to church,' and then he winked at me and said, 'but it's still a bit of a mess, isn't it?'
> L: that's not too nice.
> R: Yeah, but I don't think it's too bad either.

But there was more to Bard College than the teachers, the courses, and the study. Bard was a time of substantial personal development. It was exhilarating and liberating, as well as confronting. Ran embraced his opportunity for education, and on the surface, life was busy and exciting. He was in control, it seemed—meeting the trustees, arranging his own jazz major, introducing a jazz festival, bringing in groups, conversing with faculty. However, beneath the surface was loneliness:

> I lived in the same room for four years—isolated. I had few friends.

During lonely times, Ran recalls that he "lived to go back to the Gospel Church" (and the warm support of his family, including his grandmother). At Bard, he spent a lot of time in the practice rooms—alone. He also frequented the Red Hook[27] movie theatre:

> Well, you know *Vertigo* came out [in] 1958.[28] I would have been a sophomore junior at Bard College. So that explains why I began flunking in class—I went to Red Hook movie theatre a lot. It was all Hitchcock's fault!

There were also times that brought him to tears. Throughout it all, the letters from his grandmother, Jessie, were a constant—a strong link with family and their love for him:

> I remember at Bard College going through [hard] times, and this and that—and her nice letters... [*He drops his head into his hands, remembering this very dear grandmother.*]

It was not surprising that Ran was lonely. It was the first time he had been away from home, and he missed his family. They missed him too and, as he had no classes on Friday, encouraged him to return to Suffield each Thursday evening for a long weekend there.

But despite the lonely times, there *were* friends—and good friendships built over time. There were a small number of students: Kip Walsh and his sisters; Carroll Moshier; and Henri de Seynes—"a French guy," who Ran was to stay with on his second and third trips to Europe:

> And Henri later married Karin, and I lived with them in Paris, and I took care of their child, Ludwig L-U-D- [*trails off*], and this cat gained seven or eight pounds in the three weeks...
> L: Under your care?
> R: Under my care—and Ludwig appears on the cover of my Madrid concert [program]. So, I was always kept as a friend but told I should stay out of the kitchen! And we served French fries to this cat and a special goat curry.

And then, of course, there was Jeanne Lee.

Another Frenchman, Guy Ducornet, who came to Bard as a freshman when Ran was completing his senior year, has described an encounter that beautifully captures the young man that Ran was and his very special friendship with Jeanne Lee. Guy Ducornet remembers meeting Ran after enquiring about jazz groups on campus. He was told that Ran could be found in a certain practice room:

> I remember going there one day and a lean, pale-blond "New Englander"—who looked as if he had just debarked from the *Mayflower*—was sitting at the piano and throwing in the air strange 'sheets of notes'—something which reminded me of a mixture of Eric Satie and Thelonious Monk—and he was intently listening to them die in the air and, after long meditative silences, he would launch another salvo. Jeanne Lee was there, sitting on a table in the yoga position, fervently listening to each flight of semiquavers, and she smiled at me, obviously thrilled. When Ran stopped with a final complex, re-

sounding, and dissonant two-handed block chord, he turned to me to say, 'Hi,' and asked me if I played anything. For some strange reason, there was an alto saxophone on a chair. I had my Selmer mouthpiece in my pocket... I stuck it on the instrument, and without a word, Ran struck the first chords of a mid-tempo blues in B-flat, and I jumped in—happy not to have too many 'sharps and flats' for my alto sax in E-flat, for this was my first jazz playing in months.

What I remember most clearly about Ran Blake, that short year, was how poised and intense he was, as if he carried with himself the solemnity of a music revisited and extended to other limits—new creative areas—with episodes of sudden violence, explosions of sudden wrath followed by periods of Zen quiescence... and his restrained and friendly discourse made his music more mysterious still.[29]

There were faculty members, also, whose friendship and support meant a great deal to Ran. Among these was the Director of Admissions, Buz Gummere, whom Ran regards as a mentor and father figure. During his time at Bard, Ran was welcomed warmly by the Gummere family, with Buz, his wife, Peg, and children—Duff, Lish, John, and Christine—creating a home from home for him. It was Buz Gummere who comforted Ran after a disagreement with Bard's Chairman of Music, Paul Nordoff—a man who Ran found "intimidating":

> He was scary. He couldn't stand me, and I was even told to take a semester off—because he was going to flunk [me]. I think I did take some months off—things are hazy. You know, I have such a good memory for some things...

This incident, recalled more fully in the chapter on father figures, gives some insight into a young man, away from home, trying to understand the world and his place in it— trying to express, artistically, something within him that he himself did not yet fully understand.

Nevertheless, Ran did not allow such setbacks to dampen his spirit. He approached everybody, whether they be students, faculty, or trustees, with the same honest, earnest enthusiasm. He had endless energy—working to promote his great love, jazz, at a school that paid it modest homage. He established the Bard Jazz Lab—his first-ever jazz group—with Lish Gummere, Kip Walsh and his sisters, and several other students.[30] There was also a dog that lived at school; Ran adopted him as a mascot and called him Count Basie:

> That was my first group at Bard College. The number [in the group] ranged from seven to eleven, including the dog, and the dog played a little bit of drums, and I hear the dog was older than I was.

When it was official that he could become Bard's first jazz major,[31] Ran organized to bring the gospel choir from Hartford to the school:

> I remember that, when I brought the choir, many people who had left religion [behind them] stopped drinking for a few days, and a lot of things happened.

Ran also organized and presented an annual Bard Jazz Festival.[32] Programs featuring musicians such as Tony Scott,[33] Jimmy DePreist, and Paul Bley were supported by students from the college, including Ran Blake, Jeanne Lee, and alumnus Jonathan Tunick. Alex Bradford's Men of Song, a gospel quartet, brought "the house down" in 1959. This was also the year that Jeanne Lee gave her first public performance.

Panel discussion groups were an important part of Bard jazz festivals, and there was a large number of people to facilitate these: Nesuhi Ertegun from Atlantic Records; Martin Williams, jazz critic and founder of the *Jazz Review*; George Russell, pianist, composer, and theorist; and Gunther Schuller, composer, conductor and jazz musician—who was to become Ran's great mentor and friend. Philip and Stephanie Barber from the Lenox School of Jazz were also there as guests.

Martha remembered attending the Bard Jazz Festival with friends and feeling proud and excited that it had been organized by her brother. Buz Gummere, who welcomed visitors to the 1958 Festival, acknowledged the "greatest credit" due to Ran Blake, who "had been instrumental in introducing jazz to Bard College." He went on to say that while no formal courses were offered in jazz at the time, "Ran has received recognition from the music faculty of his desire to do a senior project in that field." Buz Gummere could see the implications for the future (indeed, Bard College maintains its commitment to jazz education today, proudly celebrating the "uniqueness" of the self-expression of its jazz students), and he concluded his address by saying that the jazz festival "did much to arouse outside interest and knowledge about Bard."[34]

Ran organized the third Bard Jazz Festival in his senior year (1959), but by this time, his focus was elsewhere. Bard represented a period of transition—a bridge between home and the outside world. With each year, Ran's confidence in his position in this wider world strengthened. There were only so many possibilities that could be explored at Bard; Ran was eager to explore the world of jazz that existed beyond the college:

> I began gravitating towards New York City and up to the Lenox School of Jazz.

In the summer break of 1960—apart from his annual attendance at Lenox—Ran enjoyed a quiet period at home in Suffield, where he concentrated on composition as he prepared for the next big step in his life—New York City.

In this period of reflection and re-grouping, away from the formal course structures and commitments, Ran was able to immerse himself in the diversity of the musical influences that were to play a crucial role in the development of his own style. This was his unofficial education; the long summer break gave him the time and space he needed to seek out and follow his musical instincts.

WHEN PHILIP AND Alison Blake chose Bard College for their son's further education, their hope would have been that it equip him with the knowledge and skills and the values, ethics, and sense of civic engagement that are the benchmark of a liberal arts education. (And whether or not the school can claim credit, the mature Ran manifested all of these attributes.)

> *At this point in the reading, Ran protests. He actually attempts to push the words away with his hands.*
> L: Take a compliment, Ran!
> R: [*still protesting*] I have some bad moments.
> J: Well, I'll include your bad moments.
> R: Smiles and nods at the assurance.

Bard's approach (as stated in the college catalog) of facilitating the student's growth by encouraging individual efforts would have been particularly suitable for someone of Ran's energy and commitment, and the Blakes must have felt very satisfied with the level of their son's response. Ran threw himself wholeheartedly into college education. For him, the courses, the people, the music, the friends he made, and even the loneliness he felt were part of the Bard College experience—all contributing to his future growth.

And yet, while acknowledging all this, there was one stand-out influence—one particular friend who was to make a huge impact on both his life and his career. That person was Jeanne Lee, and her impact was so profound that Ran can still, in an unguarded moment, say simply: "Bard College *was* Jeanne Lee."

17

JEANNE LEE

> *Jeanne Lee is the greatest musician I have ever played with. I taught her a few things, but she taught me much more—about love, death, passion, Billie Holiday repertoire, and mint juleps.*
>
> RAN BLAKE

There is no doubt about the impact Jeanne Lee had on the life of Ran Blake—as a friend, an artistic collaborator, musical soulmate, and as someone especially dear. When asked directly about their relationship, Ran is firm:

> It's too personal. [*Then, almost immediately, he relents*] But let's say I loved her more than I did a… [admit? *The word is cut short, but the implication is clear.*]

Ran and Jeanne met at Bard. Jeanne was there to study psychology and dance as a double major. She also studied literature, which was a key element of a Bard education. Though he was nearly four years older, Ran feels she was in his year at Bard and that they shared some classes. (She graduated in 1961.) His memory of their meeting is recorded by Bill Coss in a 1962 *Downbeat* interview:

> 'We met September 26, 1956, at 3.45 pm. I remember because the lecture on the Humanities began in 15 minutes. I didn't sit next to her in that class during those days because I was in my anti-social stage at the time.'

> 'He was playing the piano,' Miss Lee added, 'and he wasn't flattered when I told him he sounded like Art Tatum.'[1]

There are differing accounts of Ran's reaction to Jeanne's comparison, ranging from "What could make a beautiful girl like that make such an idiotic statement—nothing could be further from the truth."[2] to the milder, "what an interesting comment," with Jeanne Lee's pert response, "I am considered somewhat interesting by some."[3] Looking back after more than fifty years, Ran remembers it (and the date) this way:

> I met Jeanne September 22, 23, or 24 in Bard Hall. She said, 'What a pianist you are—you sound like Art Tatum.' Nobody ever said that to me, before or after. It was a dark afternoon; the evenings started early. I was very sleepy at Bard. I missed... Finally, I liked Suffield.

Ran missed his home in Suffield. He missed the life he had there; he missed being able to go into North Hartford to attend the Pentecostal church; he missed his family. Loneliness may have robbed him of some of his energy, but no matter how sleepy he felt, nothing would have kept him from his piano. On that afternoon, he was playing in Bard Hall.

Bard Hall was the college's original academic building, dating from 1852—even before the college was founded. The wood-frame cottage originally served as a parish school for local children and doubled as a chapel on weekends. Its style reflects this dual purpose. It is situated centrally within the college grounds, just back from the Chapel of the Holy Innocents. It was (and is) considered community space but was used extensively by the music program. On that dark and drizzly afternoon, as music flowed out into the surrounding space, the atmosphere was alluring.

Though Jeanne was captivated by the music, the friendship was slower to blossom. However, soon after meeting, they did hire a recording studio in Springfield to record "Jeepers Creepers" and other audition pieces. For this, they paid something between $25 and $100, depending on your source.[4] Ran has no idea what happened to this "homemade LP."[5] He does, however, remember taking Jeanne Lee home to Suffield, and just when he was beginning to like the town— to be proud of it—he was embarrassed and let down:

> I remember when bringing Jeanne Lee there in '56, my parents got a complaint that I had negroes at my house, so in '56... [*His tone is one of utter disbelief.*]

There does not seem to have been an immediate follow-up to this visit. "We both found different friends after a year."[6] Perhaps, as Ran admits himself:

> I think I kept people at a distance. Jeanne Lee and I communicated less our sophomore and junior years. I was very jealous of her new pianist, Jonathan Tunick, who became a Broadway pianist. Then, Jeanne and I began our performing again in our senior year.

During their senior year, the partnership, begun earlier, was reignited. By then, there was a particular practice room that Ran used. Jeanne would go there to listen. It was here that Guy Ducornet caught up with them. Ran—pale, blond, and intense; Jeanne, enraptured and sitting cross-legged on a table.

Ran's playing was impressive. He had already set the pattern of intensity and engagement that would characterize his professional life. He had broken out of the confines of college life and was mixing more and more in the outside world—first at the Lenox School of Jazz and Atlantic Records, but then further afield. He was active politically and professionally. He had played at the NAACP benefit at Poughkeepsie,[7] and in March 1960, he was the only solo pianist selected for the Notre Dame University (Indiana) Jazz Festival. (The festival featured more than thirty college combos and big bands, which had been selected from tape recordings submitted from universities all over America. The story was first-page news in *The Bardian* at the time.)[8]

Jeanne was Ran's greatest musical supporter. She came regularly to the practice rooms to hear him; after college, when they were both living in New York, they would meet on weekends:

> I got to long for her visits, and we would work on repertoire development, on ear training, and she taught me Billie Holiday. I would have seen her every day of the week if I could have.

Indeed, Jeanne Lee had become "one of the most important people" in Ran's life. Ran also got to know and love her parents. The Lees lived in the Bronx, on the corner of Freeman Street and Prospect Avenue, just near the subway (and close to Nellie Monk's sister, Skippy). Ran was made very welcome:

> It was exciting getting lost there. I loved her parents. Her father was a postman, Alonzo—a very dignified guy. He was a great friend of Brock Peters, who was in *The Pawnbroker* and *To Kill a Mocking-*

bird. He [Alonzo] was a well-known concert and church singer in New York City. He said working with mail was an honorable position. Little did I know that this would be my first job at New England Conservatory of Music when I arrived from Greece in 1967.

Her mother, Madeline, was quite a dancer. She appeared in a group called 'Over 70.' Madeline, who had such a long life—I thought Jeanne and I would grow old together. [*It's added wistfully, remembering Jeanne's struggle with cancer.*]

Ran felt very much a part of Jeanne's family. "Her parents adopted me," he says. It was during this period that he and Jeanne worked on *The Newest Sound Around*, which they recorded in late November/early December of 1961[9] for release in 1962.

Jeanne was living on Bank Street, in the heart of Greenwich Village—a center for American bohemian culture in the early and mid-twentieth century. It was the home of writers[10] and playwrights, actors, artists, and musicians. There was a cutting-edge cabaret and music scene.[11] The Village Vanguard, The Five Spot, the Half Note, and Slug's Saloon were all in easy walking distance of Jeanne's apartment. Bank Street itself had old-world charm—a cobble-stoned, narrow street of three to five-story red brick buildings, with their quintessential iron fire escapes. Jeanne's neighbors were Bill Dixon and George Russell:

> There were three addresses: 119, 121, and one other. Bill Dixon[12] lived at one, Jeanne Lee at one, and George Russell the third, and we called it the 'Jazz Row' or the 'Aristocrat Row.' Well, you know, getting to know Jeanne—those years—was great.

It was less than thirty minutes on the subway from Ran's lodgings at Miss Lehrfeld's apartment on West 113th Street. Ran and Jeanne traversed the distance frequently:

> When I went to see Jeanne Lee and George Russell on Bank Street—George lived at 121 Bank Street—well, I loved the journey. Usually, if I got on at 116th Street, I would get a chair [*sic*]. The *New York Times* was too big to read, so I would read *The Post* or the *Daily News*, but then, I liked to people-watch. One of the great movies [advertised] on the subways [was] *Pawnbroker*.
> And Jeanne Lee would come [to Miss Lehrfeld's] every Sunday morning at 11.30, and we rehearsed. And it was like she was part of my body—her playing music—and I think there were times I was in love with her—if I was in love—a lot of people I loved were movie

stars. And I think maybe that's all it [was]—like Kim Novak and James Stewart…

It may have been a role they were playing, but as performers, they made a compelling duo.

COMPELLING OR NOT, the club scene in New York City seemed impossible to break into, even despite a degree of welcome—if unexpected—success at the Apollo in 1961.[13] Bill Coss, writing in *Downbeat* in September 1962, said, "Jeanne Lee and Ran Blake are two youngsters in New York City with high hopes and low pretensions." He goes on to say they were an unlikely combination to have won an amateur night contest at the Apollo, then adds, "but they did."[14]

In retrospect, they were very much one of the upcoming acts to watch. By the end of 1961, they had had success at the Apollo, signed with George Avakian, and recorded *The Newest Sound Around*. In April of 1962,[15] they appeared at the Collegiate Jazz Festival at Notre Dame University, where Jeanne went on to win the individual award for "Outstanding Vocalist." For this, she received a VM model 722 Stereo Tape Recorder and Model 166 matching amplifier speaker from Voice of Music Corp., Benton Harbor, Michigan.[16] George Avakian wrote to Jimmy Lyons (Monterey Jazz Festival founder) in April of 1962 to suggest he book them as a supporting act at the Festival in September of that year. There were also a "few" concerts and local TV appearances scheduled. It was enough to excite and inspire the two young artists. As Coss reported:

> Both say they are convinced that they are only beginning to explore all the music available to their talents, singly and in combination. They feel the possibilities are unlimited.

Coss continues, quoting Jeanne:

> 'Ran's sound, his sense of harmonies, is our sound. It used to scare me. When I was seventeen, I couldn't really do it. Now it jells. I have a whole new sense of hearing.'[17]

Then, in April of 1963, with the prospect of one firm booking in Baden-Baden, the pair embarked on their first European tour. It was a heady time, buoyed by their mutual enthusiasm. There were some big successes, such as their reception at the Golden Circle in Stockholm, and there were some performances that were less well-received.

In Palermo, Italy, Jeanne Lee was hailed as the successor to Billie Holiday. (In fact, *The Newest Sound Around* won the Billie Holiday award of the *Académie du jazz* in 1979, a success which Ran is quick to attribute to Jeanne's interpretations.)

Despite their success in Europe, the duo received very little recognition on their return to America. As Ran recounts in his 2009 interview with Byron Coley for *The Wire*:

> Max Gordon said we weren't ready for the Vanguard; that I wasn't very relaxed. And I probably was awkward as hell at the audition. I really was not a swinger.[18]

Jeanne fared better:

> I know Trude Heller on Sixth Avenue in New York City once suggested to Jeanne Lee that she drop me. Jeanne, of course, appeared with so many musicians, but at that time, she said, 'I won't drop Ran.'[19]

And so, on their return to the States, they continued as they had begun—rehearsing, working at part-time jobs, and doing the occasional gig. But priorities, for Jeanne, were changing. She had become interested in a multi-disciplinary approach to art. Ran had introduced her to sound poet David Hazelton when they were at the Monterey Jazz Festival in September 1962. Romance blossomed, and in 1964, not long after the European tour, Jeanne moved to Berkeley, California, and married Hazelton. During this period, Jeanne was active in the Californian art scene. She also sang at the Jazz Workshop and composed music for a number of sound poets. Jeanne and David's daughter, Naima, was born in 1964.

> R: That [moving to Berkeley] probably didn't help our music—but I still think, if she hadn't met David and we had been in New York—I'm not sure the clubs would have hired us.
> L: No! I think you probably would have been famous. I mean, not that it matters—what's fame? But you had such a lot of momentum coming out of that trip…
> R: And of course, I was the one that introduced Jeanne to David Hazelton because he was the lifeguard for people at the Lenox School of Jazz.
> L: [*jumping in gleefully*] Ah, so you've got yourself to blame!
> R: [*philosophically*] Yeah. I do introduce people. [*He hides a small smile behind his hand.*]

Jeanne and Ran would work together again,[20] and there would be another European tour in 1966/67. The friendship they shared would continue, but the nature of their friendship had, of necessity, changed.

> So, I think, really, I'd rather not say too much more about Jeanne. Certain relationships I keep quiet; I mean, there was so much of it in the dream world... And I wouldn't have... [even] if she had accepted more, but I don't think I was ready for it—I *would* walk away that night in Stockholm. I retreat... so...
>
> And ah, [later], she was very much in love with a man called David Hazelton, and so, you get on... some things are sad, but I hope you like the music that we did...
>
> I'll let the music tell more about the relationship.

18

THOSE SUMMERS AT LENOX

It was such an important time in my life—those summers at Lenox.

RAN BLAKE

The period that Ran remembers as the highlight of his youth, which "helped shape my life," occurred over four summers from 1957 to 1960. This was the time of the Lenox School of Jazz which, despite the short span of its existence, had a profound and far-reaching influence. Apart from being a new and visionary approach to jazz music and education, it took an important step towards racial integration and harmony in a climate of uncertainty and distrust.

1950s America might have seemed tranquil—on the surface, at least. But underneath it was a bubbling mass of contradictions and conflict. The Great Depression, which began with the stock market crash of 1929, brought with it years of disastrous economic hardship. World War II, which followed, necessitated expanded industrial production. Combined with widespread conscription from 1942, it was enough to reverse the Depression unemployment levels. But war replaced economic hardship with social disruption and, for many, tragic losses to be endured. This was compounded by the Cold War, with its attendant crises,[1] which instilled fear and strengthened conformity. However, the fifties had brought an upswing in the economy and, with it, general personal optimism. In an increasingly consumeristic society, Americans sought bigger houses, equipped with all the labor-saving devices that were coming onto the market. Their homes were their castles—secure, comfortable, and able to supply their every need, even entertainment. It was a decade that saw the coming-of-age of television: a conforming influence in itself but also, perversely, opening eyes to other lifestyles—other experiences.

Rosa Parks' 1955 decision to remain seated on that crowded bus in Montgomery, Alabama, was well documented and televised, along with Martin Luther King Jr.'s support of the subsequent bus boycott. The Brown v. the Board of Education ruling in 1954 had opened up the way to achieving integration in schools, and while smoldering resistance to such integration continued to make the news, the Civil Rights Movement was gaining momentum. So, in a period when mainstream America might have clung doggedly to the perception that a decent society was white, suburban, hard-working, and middle class, they could not completely ignore the rumblings of dissatisfaction and rebellion.

It was against this background that the story of the Lenox School of Jazz played out. The Lenox School of Jazz was an experiment in jazz education—an opportunity for promising young students to be taught by (and have the chance to play with) some of the world's greatest jazz musicians. It was history-making in that it presented jazz as an art form in its own right—an art form with a background, a history, and its own pedagogy. For many young enthusiasts, jazz seemed to be an escape from conformity. At Lenox, they could immerse themselves in this music in a way that, in itself, flew in the face of convention. They relished the chance to mix freely with a racially integrated faculty—something viewed as very unusual at the time. To participants and teachers alike, the school must have seemed like a beacon of hope, illuminating a new way forward and giving a brief glimpse of the possible.

The idea for the school grew out of seminars and discussions that had been going on since 1950 at Philip and Stephanie Barber's Music Inn[2] at Lenox in the Berkshires, Massachusetts. These discussions, dubbed the "Folk and Jazz Roundtable" and centering on the origin and development of jazz and its place in American culture, had been established by Marshall Stearns[3] and had proved to be highly successful. The school, with the Modern Jazz Quartet's John Lewis as the Director,[4] was an offshoot of these discussions and of discussions between Lewis, Gunther Schuller, and the Barbers in late 1956, in which the actual form the school should take was decided.[5] It was "an effort to ensure the continuing development of jazz within its own traditions and conceptions."[6]

The Barbers had bought their property—the outbuildings, along with one hundred of the surrounding acres, of the "Berkshire cottage," Wheatleigh—in 1950. The outbuildings included a barn, a carriage house and icehouse, the potting shed and greenhouse, as well as stables. The Barbers had plans to provide accommodation and relaxation for holidaymakers; they also wanted to focus on music, particularly jazz and folk. They arranged a music forum at their "Inn" as early as the summer of 1950; discussions were led by Marshall Sterns.[7] Interest in the whole concept continued, and the Barbers converted the barn into an indoor/outdoor space (The Music Barn) which would eventually seat nine hundred. This capacity attracted performing musicians who might have found smaller venues limiting. On July 2, 1955, for the first concert in this new space, the Coleman Hawkins Quartet had an audience of five hundred,[8] while Louis Armstrong, opening the 1956 season (July 1, 1956), played to over one thousand.[9]

The Wheatleigh mansion itself, an impressive building in buff-colored brick and inspired by the 16th-century palazzos of Florence,[10] had been in the hands of the Boston Symphony Orchestra since 1947 when it was bought as accommodation for Tanglewood[11] students. The Barbers bought Wheatleigh from the BSO in 1957, so it too became part of the Lenox experience.

The spirit of Lenox stemmed from the live-in nature of the school. Faculty, students, and participants were able to step outside the everyday world and immerse themselves in the music they loved in a setting of exceptional peace and beauty. While the quality of the music ensured that the program was stimulating, the salubrious surroundings and the un-rushed timeframe created the perfect space for creative endeavor. Having such a large number of exceptional musicians gathered together, with no pressing duties other than to share their knowledge and experience, was beyond the wildest dreams of the young Ran Blake.

He was thrilled to personally meet (and play with) people whom he had so long admired and whose records he had collected.[12] For him, the highlight of that first year, 1957, was:

> an appearance by the king of the New York underground, George Russell. John Lewis stood up, greeted the audience, and said we were about to hear a special guest who has a unique design for the future of tomorrow's music. Immaculately groomed in an Italian suit, George Russell stood up, made one of his customary bows to the audience, smiled, and proceeded to tell us about the Lydian Chromatic Concept of Tonal Organization.[13]

There was something exceptional about the Lenox School of Jazz. The concept was presented in such a way that new and exciting experiences could be discovered within the reassuring homeliness of a predictable daily routine.

A typical day at Lenox consisted of ensembles, private lessons,[14] a history course (taught the first year by Marshall Stearns[15] with Willis Lawrence James and subsequently taught by Gunther Schuller). There were also theory and composition/arranging classes taught by Bill Russo and George Russell.[16]

After a busy day, students had the choice of a variety of evening lectures. Among those offered in 1957 were talks by Lennie Tristano and Bill Russo on "Jazz Frontiers,"[17] while Willis James spoke on the "Primitive Beginnings of Jazz." Ran remembers taking long walks on the Housatonic River with James, where they'd discuss the lectures and where James would often sing field cries. Ran later dedicated his composition "Field Cry" to his teacher and friend:

> Dr. James and I would walk around the Housatonic River. One day he literally broke into a field cry, and the birds seemed to answer. I wish Messiaen had been present.[18]

Concerts were an essential part of the school's curriculum. Jazz performed in concert-like venues was still a new idea in '50s America.[19] In the summer of 1955, the Barbers had created a concert space, with seating for seven hundred and fifty, in the barn on their property. It caused a stir at the time, with people questioning its presence so close to the classical heart of Tanglewood—a twenty-minute stroll away. But when the Lenox school commenced, the venue proved to be popular with Tanglewood's classical musicians as well,[20] and many set out along the peaceful country road that separated the two centers to enjoy the jazz concerts on offer.

The Lenox school's concerts usually took place on Thursday nights, Saturday afternoons, and Sunday nights (so as not to clash with Tanglewood's concerts).[21] Here students had the opportunity to play alongside top-tier professional musicians—an invaluable experience. The appearance of Mahalia Jackson (1957)[22] and Chris Connor (1958) were highlights for Ran. In 1957, the Sunday night (August 25) concert featured the Oscar Peterson Trio, Dizzy Gillespie, and Max Roach.[23] In the final concert of 1957 (August 29, starting at 8.40 pm), Ran played his composition, "Wende," as part of a small ensemble directed by Ray Brown. This concert was very long, requiring two intermissions.[24] In the 1959 concert, Ran played "Vanguard" as reported in the *Berkshire Eagle*:

> Best individual performances of the evening were turned in by pianist Ran Blake and alto saxophonist Ornette Coleman. Young Blake has tremendous talent both as a composer and a player, and his rendition of his own "Vanguard" had wonderful feeling and expressiveness… The twenty-nine-year-old Coleman created quite a stir at the school this season with his unique style and theories, and the short hearing Saturday night was a revelation both as to style and creativity. Three of his originals were played by the small ensemble, and they were quite interesting.[25] This west coast musician is obviously about to embark on the crucial voyage of his career.[26]

For the first year, 1957, Ran was a paying student; he had auditioned to gain a place.[27] But the experience had had such a profound effect on him he resolved to return the following year:

> I attended the school the summers of 1957–'60. My parents paid for the first summer, and I said, 'Mr. and Mrs. Barber, I want to come every year!' and they said, 'You'll have to work.' So, every year I got it free after the first year. I was the only one there for four years. I worked there all summer as a waiter.

Ran worked in the Potting Shed, where he served drinks and coffee. At the same time, he was able to hear the "fabulous jam sessions" there. The Barber family treated him very well, and before long, they had him help them with their special dinners for guests. As well, he did odd jobs like mowing the lawns and some driving. Ran remembers driving Stephanie to the Pittsfield Hospital, seven or eight miles away, "just before the birth of Hilary or his brother."[28] In the program notes for his *Cat People* concert,[29] Ran's description of Stephanie Barber was that "she was tough, she was charming, and she glittered." These qualities, he goes on to say, were balanced by "her deeper emotions" that he was to witness in the following summers. One such "emotion" was her care—evident in her willingness to promote Ran and find opportunities for him. She arranged for him to have "one or two lessons" with jazz pianist Randy Weston[30] (a friend of hers) at his piano residency at Avaloch Inn,[31] near Tanglewood. Ran recalls that "He was very kind to me."

One of Ran's main jobs at Lenox was as the after-hours switchboard operator:

> I had to answer the phone at night. So, at the bottom of Wheatleigh, there was a basement, and they had a switchboard there. I was there the night Abbey Lincoln called up Max Roach—a lot of people would call the Giuffre family—it was a very busy switchboard. My hours

> were eleven at night till eight in the morning, and they put a bed right there, but I had to have the bed right up near the switchboard. I was allowed one drink at night, and then, at 2.30 or so, the night guard brought me an iced tea or an iced coffee and a little cheese sandwich or something, and I did that for about two summers.
> I don't think I even had a night off, except for once when they let me out to the Newport Festival.[32] I slept right there in this dank basement—there was sort of a door, but anyone could walk right through; it's a wonder I wasn't stabbed.
> L: That would have been too noir!
> R: [*ignoring him*] It was dark; there were wine cellars; sometimes I saw a lady, late at night, called Emma Oates, who was searching for brandy—do you remember her Leo?
> L: No, no, I don't.
> R: You don't remember Mrs. Oates? [*incredulous*] She was in *Spiral Staircase*; she was...
> L: Oh yeah, I remember her—she was the mother or...
> R: She was the cook.

Lenox was a testing ground. It allowed the student to present their ideas and compositions in front of very experienced professionals. Sometimes this was exhilarating:

> Mingus was so nice to me at Lenox and got me up to play and asked me to join him, but then, when I moved to New York, he never brought that up again... and [anyhow] my parents didn't want me to leave Bard.

Sometimes it could be daunting (For Ran, the memory of Stan Kenton's "dismissal" was still raw),[33] but on the other hand, there were pleasant surprises, like the endorsement from Oscar Peterson,[34] who Ran had expected to be more critical:

> [He] said that I was one of the most talented people at Lenox [even though] John Lewis did NOT have that feeling of me... or Ray Brown...
> Gunther defended me.

Gunther Schuller certainly believed in Ran. He invited Ran to take his courses at Lenox in the summers of '59 and '60. Schuller was taking composition classes and giving evening lectures on the relationship between jazz and contemporary (classical) music. In addition, he taught jazz history. His 1960 course, The Analytical History of Jazz, approached the subject from a stylistic perspective rather than taking a purely historical approach.[35] Ran also studied with John Lewis, Oscar Peterson, Bill Russo, and many others on faculty. At the same time, he began working in earnest on his own style.

By now, however, the days for the Lenox School were numbered. In 1960 the Barbers sold the Music Inn's surrounding buildings and grounds; only the Wheatleigh mansion was kept—to accommodate students, faculty, and staff. Financial problems caused the 1961 school to be canceled, though Gunther Schuller did feel the reason for closure was more that the concept and mission of the school—teaching and training in jazz—was too far ahead of its time; the world wasn't ready for it.[36] Luckily for Ran, the school's brief and shining moment-in-time coincided with his most formative years. It was a significant period—one he remembers very fondly:

> L: I'm curious because I suppose with me when I went to NEC—that whole time—meeting people who had been my heroes—was very special.
> R: I bet.
> L: And I just wonder for you—when you went to Lenox School—I know you had been at Bard, so maybe it wasn't quite the same?
> R: [*breaks in excitedly*] Oh, I FLIPPED. I FLIPPED! There is my… Oh, that's Max Roach! And there goes… that's Dizzy Gillespie! I couldn't get over it! Bill Russo, Stan Kenton! Why there's Chris Connor—she came for a weekend. And then, there's Mahalia! It was so exciting! It was such an important time in my life, those summers—and those first years in New York—those summers at Lenox!

19

ATLANTIC RECORDS

> *I had the whole run of the place. Ahmet would say, 'What are you doing here?' when I was listening to records—looking through a stack—I had the life of Riley.*
>
> RAN BLAKE

It was during the first summer at the Lenox School of Jazz (1957) that Ran secured the promise of a six-week work-experience position at Atlantic Records—a groundbreaking independent label founded by Ahmet Ertegun and Herb and Miriam Abramson. For Ran, this brief stint at Atlantic was to prove pivotal, for it was here that he would first meet Gunther Schuller, the man who would become his great friend and mentor.

That year at Lenox, Nesuhi Ertegun[1] gave a talk (with Jack Tracy) entitled "Problems in Jazz Recording."[2] The topic would have been very real for him. At that time, Atlantic was recording sessions on the top floor of a 1910 red brick building located at 234 West 56th Street.[3] There, sound engineer Tommy Dowd[4] did the best he could, recording by night (to reduce unwanted background noise) in a space that served as the office by day. For recording, the furniture had to be pushed back against the wall. It was not ideal. The floor was old and sagging, and there was a skylight in the sloping ceiling. Despite all this, Dowd claimed the room on 56th street had everything required for great recording. The room had amazing acoustics over a wide dynamic range—in Dowd's own words, "It was like magic."[5]

Ahmet and his Atlantic partner, Jerry Wexler,[6] were "sticklers for a clean, crisp sound"; Tom Dowd was determined to give them this.[7] At Dowd's insistence, Atlantic was looking to upgrade to eight-track capability—one of the first, if not *the* first label to do so—and, as with all new systems, there was skepticism to be overcome.[8] Around this time, there was a lot of new equipment coming onto the market which needed to be assessed, and for Atlantic, a move to a studio specifically designed for them by Dowd was imminent. No doubt, these challenges were touched on during Nesuhi's talk, and Ran Blake, in the audience that night, was fascinated. It was another side of the jazz scene, one that was not so familiar to him.

Nesuhi Ertegun had joined his brother at Atlantic in 1955. Although the label was still small at the time, Jerry Wexler believed it was very much in their interest to promote black artists. Trying to engage the broad American public in black artists was a bold move, particularly in the prevailing political and racial climate, but Ahmet Ertegun and Jerry Wexler were both good businessmen with discerning musical taste. The move instantly expanded their territory, secured some outstanding artists, and also started breaking down barriers in the music industry. When Nesuhi joined, he broadened the jazz interest and was instrumental in bringing Charles Mingus, John Coltrane, The Modern Jazz Quartet, and many other great musicians to the label.

When Nesuhi spoke to the Lenox students that year, he more than likely would have mentioned some of the artists Atlantic had on their books at the time: the Milt Jackson Sextet; Chris Connor; LaVern Baker with the Quincy Jones Orchestra; Willis Jackson and his Band; Charles Mingus Quintet; Clyde McPhatter; John Lewis Trio; The Modern Jazz Quartet; Art Blakey and the Jazz Messengers with Thelonious Monk; Ray Charles and Jimmy Giuffre, to name but a few.[9] Ran also recalls that he "told a small group of us: 'We will be recording Ornette Coleman.'"[10] The thought of being "near the music" of these artists was thrilling. After the lecture, Ran approached Nesuhi, who agreed to let him carry out six weeks' work experience (as encouraged by Bard College) at Atlantic Records.

When Ran walked into Atlantic Records' office at 157 W 57th Street in January 1958, his excitement levels were high. Atlantic was, at that time, the second-largest independent jazz label in America, and its address, it seemed to Ran, was just as it should be: West 57th Street was a center of artistic activity. The street was wide; the buildings were tall yet gracious and stylish—mellow brick, bay windows, and cast iron. The elegant Carnegie Hall was just across the street, and the beautiful Art Students' League building[11] was two hundred yards away. For the boy from Suffield, Connecticut, this was certainly the epitome of a big city address. Ran was eager and ready to begin, but when he arrived that Monday in January, nobody was expecting him. Nesuhi was out of the office, and Ran had to report to Ahmet. Though not yet thirty-five, Ahmet—suave and assured, in business-shirt-and-tie and sporting a neatly clipped goatee—appeared much older. He was quite bald, and his eyes, when he glanced up briefly from behind tortoise-shell-framed glasses, were heavy-lidded, tired-looking... remote. (Though, as Ran discovered later, when they engaged, they were direct and compelling.) Ran greeted him enthusiastically, "Oh, Mr. Ertegun, I'm so happy to be here!"

Ahmet's reply was sobering, delivered in a gravelly voice, which was cosmopolitan with a dash of jazz: "Who the hell are you?"[12]

Ran spent the rest of that morning making coffee:

> Ahmet Ertegun would want coffee one way, Jerry Wexler another.[13]

At that stage, Ran was not yet aware of Ahmet's humor nor his sense of fairness, his respect for musicians, his charisma. So, this first encounter would have been confusing, if not challenging:

> I do recall how much both brothers were admired by the musicians, the fellow employees, and the 57th Street community. They were also known for their exquisite, tasteful hospitality and for their dapper dress. But when I walked into Ahmet Ertegun's office on my first day and said, 'Here's your coffee Mr. Ertegun,' he said, 'Please knock. Call me Ahmet; you call this coffee!'

To Ran's relief, Nesuhi returned in the afternoon. But even then, there were some anxious moments. "Ah yeah, Ran Blake. You were going to work here a few days?" Ran, however, was not going to be deterred and responded promptly, "Six weeks, Mr. Ertegun." Nesuhi sent him over to the West 56th building, where it was Ran's job to deliver the coffee and do a bit of filing:

> There were all these alternate tapes of Chris Connor, Mingus, Ray Charles, and they all got burned later.[14] They'd said, in a few years, they'd send me copies. I tried to get the tapes in order... till Tom Dowd said, 'Oh Ran, whatever you do, please don't touch the tapes! You're trying to be so kind but go out to an Italian lunch [instead].'

Ran recalls the incident with wry humor. It did not deflate his enthusiasm, though. He was overjoyed just being there:

> To see these people walk in was absolutely incredible. Willie 'The Lion' Smith[15] would drop by—I don't think he was recorded. I recall

Ahmet saying to either George Avakian or John Hammond or Gunther—when speaking about a young Detroit singer whose father was a famous clergyman—'We could do wonders with Aretha.' And in 1967, they did!
My real boss was Nesuhi... and Tom Dowd. Oscar Petersen came and gave me three lessons. I went to Long Island and had a lesson with Tristano. I was at LaVern Baker's [recording session].[16] She said, 'I want a drink.' I bought her a Coke. She said, 'Buddy, you may be white and from Connecticut, but when I say I want a... [*Ran's tone has risen in shrill imitation, and he breaks off, slapping the table, before continuing*] don't bring me this stuff!' And she threw it—the bottle of Coca-Cola. And that was LaVern Baker recording Bessie Smith, and that happened on West 56th Street. Chris Connor was away those three weeks.
L: What did you bring her after that—some Jack [Daniel's]?
R: I don't know what. They sent me out [for something].

The interview with Byron Coley sheds more light on this period:

> To absolutely see people I'd heard about, and to have my ears extended—to the Platters [...] MJQ, John Lewis, Percy Heath, Connie Kay, Milt Jackson...they would be dropping by, and sometimes some of them would say, 'Ran, do you want to join us for coffee?' But I knew that I was just there [to sweep the floor].[17]

It was exhilarating and sobering at the same time. Ran began comparing himself with these artists, with the result that he felt dissatisfied with his own music.

But of all the people Ran met at Atlantic, there was one that was to have a profound impact on his future: Gunther Schuller. Ran was sweeping the floor when Gunther walked in, and for one moment, there was a spark of connection. As Gunther reports in his autobiography, Ran "looked at me, almost as if he recognized me."[18] For his part, Gunther felt compelled to ask Nesuhi, "who's the kid out there sweeping the floor?" because, as he saw it, "there had to be something special about someone who was willing to spend his entire school vacation cleaning and sweeping floors just so he could be around jazz musicians and soak up the atmosphere of a major record company."[19] For Ran, the chance meeting with Gunther Schuller in the corridor was simply part of a whole series of encounters set against the exciting backdrop of New York City during his extended stay there:

> Although I had visited New York to hear Thelonious Monk and Chris Connor, I had never really stayed for more than two days.[20]

During his time at Atlantic, Ran stayed at the King's Crown Hotel at 420 West 116th Street—near the Columbia University Campus. (Later, when he came to New York to live, he would get a job as a desk clerk at this hotel.) It was three and a half miles from King's Crown to Atlantic:

> I took the IRT subway every morning and night between 116th and 57th. My hours were 9.30 am until mid-evening, with extremely generous lunch breaks.
> Just to BE there and to go to the studio in the evening at 56th Street. I was stunned. I was hypnotized. I thought, my God, these people are ALIVE... this is [after coming] from a small town with a party-line, and now I'm in New York seeing all these people!

In his time off, Ran got further acquainted with New York City, discovering the places that would become his haunts when he moved there after Bard:

> I would walk to the Apollo theater. I was so excited to be at the Apollo. There was a big aisle in the middle. I never felt unsafe—I would be there till eleven at night. I can still see myself going out at eleven o'clock (I left early as I knew I had to get up early), walking a block east, crossing at 8th Avenue near St. Nic, then walking to Amsterdam. I loved Amsterdam Avenue. There'd be a few housing projects—18-floor apartments. I remember waving to people coming back. I might have been moving like this. [*He starts swinging his arms like a band conductor.*] I was SO alive, and it was SO exciting. I was so trapped in Suffield, Connecticut, with the mashed potato mentality. To be there in New York City—the sounds, the aromas, the kebobs on the street... I could hear people laughing, and I could imagine they had been at the Apollo. Or I could go to Joe Wells' and the Count Basie Club on 136th and 7th Avenue, and I could subway to the Village Vanguard, Five Spot, Carnegie Recital Hall, and the Greek district. And they were talking about a new man that was coming in the news called Kennedy. I remember somebody saying, 'Let's get rid of Ike.' I could be now walking on 118th Street—I'm almost home.
> I don't particularly remember special drinks—a year or two later, I would go for Ballantine Ale, which was cheap and white and delicious. But [along the way] I would stop, and the Vietnamese restaurant would be closing. I didn't like coffee till later—I didn't know about espresso then—and there might be some kind of a rich donut that I could have before going to bed. Then, taking the elevator; waving to the desk clerk—you had to leave your key at the desk like the old European hotels—taking the elevator up, putting my light on,

looking through the rear window, and seeing the lights in the other apartments, and sometimes I'd wave to somebody.

I met a girl called Eileen Beach. I was on the 5th or 6th floor, and I could see her room two floors above me. We would go to New Jersey to see Alex Bradford at the Abyssinian Baptist Church[21] and hear Sister Tee at Sweet Daddy Grace's church.[22]

And I don't even know if there was TV in the room—what did I care! I had so much music in my head. And then they would wake me up at 7.30, and I would go to work. They served weak coffee in the lobby and a roll, but if I had the money, I would go to the Vietnamese [restaurant].

RAN'S SIX-WEEK STINT at the Atlantic had far-reaching implications. It was here that Ran got a behind-the-scenes look at how some of the best musicians in the business worked. He saw their skills and their foibles and was able to compare his own position (and abilities) with theirs. The extended stay in New York gave him a chance to explore the city and to feel at home there. It was a perfect initiation into metropolitan living, and his family, knowing his ambition to move to New York after Bard, probably saw it as a valuable "trial run." Some fleeting moments at Atlantic inspired future compositions.[23] But most of all, the job at Atlantic was an opportunity to meet people; Ran's meeting with Gunther Schuller was the beginning of their lifelong friendship.[24]

The time at Atlantic was a golden time for Ran Blake. Though there was still one year of college to finish, he had already, in spirit, begun to embrace the next stage of his life. His sights were now firmly set on New York City and his place there—as a musician.

Part II

New York
"The Happy Period"

1

MISS AMELIA LEHRFELD

Your whole life's shaped differently once you've met Ran.

LEO MCFADDEN[1]

In the early Fall of 1960, after completing his fourth and final summer at the Lenox School of Jazz, Ran moved to New York City. He found accommodation boarding with eighty-nine-year-old Miss Amelia Lehrfeld in her apartment at 507 West 113th Street.[2] This apartment was to be his home for the next seven years.

It was an interesting time to be living in this part of Manhattan's Upper West Side. The area (which pre-1930 was a desirable address, largely populated by the "respectable classes") had been in decline since the Depression. During the thirties and forties, elegant and spacious apartment buildings, which had gone up with the advent of the IRT subway line, were subdivided and sublet and inevitably neglected by absentee landlords. Throughout World War II, the area—bordered by Amsterdam Avenue, West 113th Street, Broadway, and West 110th Street—had a reputation as a "red-light district."[3]

After the war, when the middle classes were moving into the suburbs, waves of immigrants from Eastern Europe and the Caribbean began surging into the area.[4] They joined the elderly and the poor who'd been stranded there and created a vibrant cultural mix in a neighborhood that was becoming increasingly overcrowded and dilapidated.

> I lived in a block that was somewhat—maybe sixty percent—white, but I only had to walk four blocks, and then I'd be in Lower Harlem and then, some blocks further, was the Apollo and Sweet Daddy....

The area's proximity to the jazz clubs of Harlem and to the Pentecostal church—Sweet Daddy Grace's—made it a very desirable one for Ran.

Amelia Lehrfeld's apartment was diagonally opposite the fire station on 113th Street, just off Amsterdam. One Hundred and Thirteenth Street appeared narrow when turning into it from the broad thoroughfare of Amsterdam Avenue. Six and seven-story brownstone apartment buildings seemed to bank in from both sides, conspiring to cast deep shadows and channel the wind. On a clear day, when shafts of sunlight picked out their limestone trims and the carved features of their window balconies, they had their own beauty. They assumed a mellow warmth—the dark of their brick facades softening. But with the Fall chill descending, they could appear cold, drab, and forbidding. Ran's walks along 113th Street were often by night—when families and the elderly were already asleep and the shadowy figures of the hapless haunted deep doorways and narrow lanes. The decorative iron fences and solid pipe bollards and rails that marked the property line were icy to the touch. From below, soft yellow light glowed in basement windows, and often, a concoction of stale cooking smells and "all kinds of smoke" hung about listlessly:

> It was really run-down between 100 and 105th Street in the '60s, but it had got a little bit safer where I was because of Columbia University.

Ran's new home was typical of many apartments available at the time—a little tired and shabby, but with the enduring good lines of a more elegant past.[5] Other apartments in the area had not fared so well. The district had been in decline for decades; less than half a dozen blocks away, there were brownstones that were empty—boarded-up and graffitied—their dark stoops a shelter for drunks and vagrants. Despite this, the immediate neighborhood was robust and earthy. Even if some spots were deserted and seedy and 113th Street was narrow and dark, Amsterdam Avenue, just yards away, throbbed with life. The emergency entrance for St Luke's Hospital on the opposite corner of Amsterdam ensured twenty-four-hour activity. Ran was on a great adventure—bustling thoroughfares and narrow city streets with dark shadows were all part of the heady mix for this new phase of his life. Like so many young men in his position, experiencing independence for the first time and envisaging infinite possibilities, Ran found New York absolutely alluring. It is a period that he has often referred to as "the happy period."

Ran met Amelia Lehrfeld through "a friend of a friend" at Bard. (This friend's grandmother was a neighbor of Miss Lehrfeld's.) As things worked out, the meeting was fortuitous on both sides. Ran was aware that Miss Lehrfeld usually rented to "people who were kosher—Jewish people who would observe the Friday holy night," but she made an exception for Ran, who recalls:

> I paid my thirty or thirty-five dollars rent for a small room, a little piano, Friday night supper, a small breakfast, and use of her telephone, and life moved on.

He says it with the familiar upward lift of his voice that cannot be easily defined: a beguiling mix of 'matter of fact' and 'wonder'—because, for Ran, there is always wonder. Those who come into his orbit are touched by it; this was certainly the case for Miss Lehrfeld. This "solitary lady" of eighty-nine was swept up by the young Ran's enthusiasm for life and for music, and to her joy, the last few years of her life were dramatically transformed.

Ran's own description of Miss Lehrfeld begins laconically enough:

> Miss Amelia Lehrfeld... [*He pauses, gathering his thoughts*] lived on Upper West Side most of her life. She moved there in her early twenties. She had relatives earlier on from Vilna, Lithuania.

But the memory of Miss Lehrfeld is a vibrant one, and he cannot leave it there:

> And she lived there in that apartment [on 113th Street] for years and years. And before that [she] had lived on Claremont Avenue, near where Juilliard was, so she knew the upper west side. She said, 'I AM the upper west side—I know everything in the neighborhood.'[6]
> But [*he is pensive*] she didn't know where the bars were, and she wasn't up on her pizza and Vietnamese food.
> Except for Jeanne Lee, not many people dropped by because it was much more formal at the beginning. I would call her Miss Lehrfeld. She was very reserved—everybody would bow[7] to her, 'Good morning,' they'd say.
> She'd worked in the garment industry. She knew people in that big fire.[8] She used a cane, but she would not when out.

It took Ran years to persuade her to come out with him:

> When I first took her to a jazz club,⁹ she said, 'Am I going to a den of sin? That's not water they're drinking; that's not ginger ale!'
> We took her to the Gospel Church; we took her home to Suffield, Connecticut; she met my whole family. She said, 'It's swell to be here in Connecticut.' She [always] used the word swell.
> She served a gefilte fish dinner on Friday night. Curfew was at sundown. George Russell brought (instead of Welsh's grape juice) a Bordeaux wine. She said, 'This is glorious,' and from then on, Bordeaux wine was served at her house. Her nephew and niece thanked me forever—they went out and bought all of George's records. [*There is a pause before he adds succinctly.*] She was some lady—Amelia Lehrfeld!

In another discussion, Ran adds a few more brush strokes to the picture of his landlady. He volunteers that she came from "a strait-laced background" but is quick to add, "she certainly didn't have the usual Connecticut prejudices."¹⁰ Her fairness and open-mindedness had impressed Ran from the start—hence the surprise in his tone when he adds, "But she didn't have very many close friends…"¹¹

> She was a really solitary person; she never married. And she would sit and read… listen to music, though not too much radio.

Often on a Friday evening, when the curfew was strict and the nights were long, Ran would listen while his landlady talked till late about her "life and memories."¹² She told him about when she was young, riding the A train to the Upper West Side ballrooms. (There was a young man called Eugene "who was a swell dresser," and who "took her to Harlem on the A train and gave her a music box.")¹³

She showed Ran her scrapbook with photos of her family and the fashionable gowns she'd worn in her youth:

> I saw her photos from the '20s and '30s. She was BEAUTIFUL—absolutely gorgeous in 1925—and she wore a long white gown, and she was so excited to be on the A train…

Then she told of the time—in the middle of a bright evening at a dance—when she was brought news of the death of a family member, and she collapsed. For death had visited too often, and amid her "beautiful" memories, with their "essence of deep nostalgia," were the sudden, sad thoughts of relatives "who were caught in the Holocaust."¹⁴

Ran's interpretation of "Lush Life" is his homage to Miss Lehrfeld; here, he revisits those evenings when she told stories about her life. While soft rain fell outside and "the lonely dalmatian" remained at his post, Ran was transported to another world, the only sound to break the spell the "occasional murmurs" of pedestrians as they made their way home from St John the Divine or St Luke's Hospital.[15]

> And I played that ["Lush Life"] as one of my repertoire pieces because she would look at her old scrapbook and re-live the memories.

And as she turned the faded pages, bright memories from her youth lit up her face and lightened her voice, eclipsing—at least for a moment—the sad times, the lonely times, and the struggles that she'd faced.

> She was extremely frugal. She would have a slice of bread—she would make a meal out of that. In other words, you would not go to her for great food, as she lived on hardly anything! She must have lived on seven or eight dollars a week. I mean, she walked everywhere. She would walk to Broadway because onion and cabbage was cheaper there than on Amsterdam Avenue.
> One time, she took a subway to 23rd Street near the Leo House Hotel and walked all the way to the East because she forgot to get a transfer. She walked all the way to First or Second Avenue, to a doctor—every penny counted. I had to pay twenty cents a phone call, and I DID make some. [*The degree of emphasis suggests he made quite a few!*]

But if Miss Lehrfeld was frugal, she was not mean. She had a generous and kind heart—caring for Ran if he were sick, encouraging him, welcoming his friends even though, as her niece once admitted to Ran, she felt he had "an unusual group of friends." She kept the apartment spotlessly clean so that it was a pleasant place to stay. She offered more than lodging—she offered security and a place where Ran could begin to fulfill his potential. As he states simply, "She provided a home for me in New York."

Miss Lehrfeld, eighty-nine years old, had taken upon herself the role of caregiver, and with this came an emotional investment. She was anxious for Ran, especially when he went out at night, and advised him to "stay around Columbia and our neighborhood." For her, it was safe and familiar, and she didn't want him venturing beyond it into Harlem (in the north). She was also worried about 105th Street to the south:

> [...] where there were red light [areas] and gambling, and [it was] quite wild. Coming from the country of Connecticut—or Bard College—it was very earthy. It was quite a shock.
> One-Hundred-Thirteenth Street was faded gentility. There were beatnik students, older people on an income, and then you could walk

to Harlem, and that was safer than 105th. It was dangerous south of Columbia—below 110th Street—she just didn't want me out.

It was probably her own anxiety. She had retreated to her own little bolthole between Harlem and Columbia after the Triangle factory fire. Before the fire, the lower East Side was a familiar haunt, and she knew what it was like in the tenement buildings—she had had aunts and uncles there. But the fire had shocked her deeply. She had known many of the people who had died, trapped so tragically behind locked doors.

> Of course, after a while, I did take her to the local Irish bar. She was something. I wish you had met her, Janet.

But, with all of the New York jazz scene at his doorstep, Ran was never going to be confined, and Miss Lehrfeld—who Ran once referred to as "a wise woman"—realized it. When Ran became a waiter at the Jazz Gallery, soon after moving to New York, he was required to be out till four or five in the morning. Miss Lehrfeld found the positive in this, stating that four-thirty or five was a better time to take a subway than twelve o'clock [midnight].

> R: I got out of the Jazz Gallery at 3.55/4.05 in the morning and would take the IRT back to Columbia. I would often take that subway. I would walk across to the West Side, and you had to wait and wait and wait, and I would meet all [sorts of] people—they were falling off the banisters—I remember having to keep my wallet in my front pocket. Many people were paranoid; of course, the real crime wave had not come to New York yet. And I could hear the chug-chug of the train—and it was not that clean!
> L: Did you just go to Jazz Gallery and ask for a job, Ran?
> R: Yes, about three weeks after [arriving in New York]. The owner, Joe Termini, said he would never hire me because he thought I would listen to music too much, but he was away, so his sister gave me a job. On my first night, I met Leo, the bartender, and Gil Evans was playing there ...and Max Roach.

When Ran moved to New York, he was twenty-five years old and well and truly ready. Having spent six weeks at the King's Crown Hotel on West 116th Street while working for Atlantic Records, he felt comfortable about the move. Also, prior to that—though he had never stayed in New York for a prolonged period—he had taken many trips there to see some of the club acts. Martha, his sister, had memories from her high school days when Ran would take her to New York to see Thelonious Monk at the Five Spot, or Charles Mingus at the Half Note, and then, Chris Connor at the Village Vanguard. She was fourteen at the time and would later reflect:

> I don't know what my parents were thinking.

But Ran was a "very good big brother" and looked after his little sister well. Martha grew to love the music and the club scene that Ran loved and was content to sit and listen. The only drawback for her was the thick cloud of cigarette smoke that made her eyes stream.

When Ran came to stay with Miss Lehrfeld, he was in familiar territory. His life soon settled into a pattern of lessons by day (the gospel church on Sunday) and live jazz by night—with a variety of jobs to help pay the bills.

> I went to Mr. Russo—Bill Russo—in Riverdale twice a week. And then, I went down to Gunther Schuller on 92nd Street, and Miss Lehrfeld again said, 'Don't walk 105th,' but it was daytime, so I would go. Then I would go to Harlem to work with Brother Porter—Hugh Porter—playing gospel piano and then later, Mal Waldron. And, of course, Mary Lou Williams… We would pray, then do blues, then pray, then have fried chicken and a little glass of scotch whiskey. And don't forget, my second year, I worked at King's Crown as a desk clerk.

Ran relished every new experience. New York fascinated him. His appetite for it was insatiable—its diversity, its anonymity, its vibrancy, its lazy eddies and electric currents. He took it in and loved it all. Part of his fascination was with the people. Coming from a small town, the sheer mass of humanity was mesmerizing. As a whole or as individuals, here were people very different from those he was familiar with in Suffield, Connecticut, and he wasted no time in getting to know them.

Soon after Martha graduated from college and moved to the West Side of New York, Ran arranged to meet her. He was enthusiastic about sharing his New York experience—and friends—with her. He promised her, "We'll get together, and we'll all go out."[16] Martha readily agreed:

> I was thinking, 'This will be nice; it might be a small group,' and he arrived with twenty people at my apartment! We'd then all go to Harlem, to Small's Paradise, and have food there—eat chicken. It was wonderful.[17]

Wherever Ran went—whatever he was doing—he made friends. The young boy from Springfield who'd worried his parents because he seemed such a loner had grown into a young man with a talent for meeting people—and then introducing them to each other. It was only natural that Ran wanted to bring his new friends to meet his landlady, even though Miss Lehrfeld's apartment was probably not ideal for having guests. It had, as Ran recalls:

> [...] her bedroom, my bedroom, a living room, a kitchenette, and a very large foyer. When she went to heaven,[18] her room either became a guest room or... more the study. And then there was the front 'parlor,' [as] she called it. She used to separate the two when she lived there, so I had the better room, and I used to have several mattresses on my bed, so I could look across at a firehouse on 113th Street and see a dalmatian dog, and that would be the first thing I'd see in the morning. I always had a very high bed.
> L: I wonder why that was?
> R: I wonder—it's too long ago, and I don't think it affected my music. [*with a cheeky grin*]

Miss Lehrfeld nevertheless welcomed Ran's friends into her home, and her life was the richer for it:

> My friends were wild about her. Jeanne Lee would be popping around, and Jeanne would make some warm, brown bread in the oven, and Amelia would say, 'Oh, you're such a darling,' and every Sunday morning, Jeanne Lee came at 11.30, and we rehearsed, and Miss Lehrfeld would be [*he claps out a beat*] at the door with her cane, tapping.

Another of Ran's friends to visit at 113th Street was George Russell. Ran had built on this friendship—begun at Lenox in 1957—after moving to New York. (He had had a few lessons with George at his Bank Street apartment.) Subsequently, George visited Ran at Miss Lehrfeld's. When Ran first arrived in New York, Miss Lehrfeld had had her rules: "It's required that you have the Friday night curfew," and "We don't want any of the devil's liquid." But with the arrival of Ran's friends, these rules began to be broken.

One such relaxation was when Miss Lehrfeld finally allowed Ran to have a party at the 113th Street address:

> I know it was not on a Friday because Friday was matzah ball soup and gefilte fish—so I think she had something [else prepared], and I had a few friends up.
> And George Russell said, 'Madame, it's so wonderful to meet you,' and kissed her hand [*Ran demonstrates kissing his own hand*], and

she said, 'Ohhhh!' And at that time, a murder mystery novel came out about old New York, and the killer was a man called 'George Russell,' and she said, 'My George wouldn't do that!' She had this cane and... [*Ran cuts short his explanation and demonstrates by tapping his cane.*]
L: [*immediately sidetracked*] Yeah, why do you have that cane?
R: I'm not walking so well—my back hurts, but we don't have to talk about the ailment of the week. [*It's said impatiently... tetchily, and Leo knows better than to pursue it.*]

The second relaxation concerned the so-called "devil's liquid." Miss Lehrfeld had a liking for Welch's Grape Juice,[19] and George Russell knew her preference. But one evening, he chanced his luck and brought along some regular wine. Miss Lehrfeld examined the label. "It's not Welsh's," she said, and "Oh, it says 'Bordeaux'... are they in the grape business?"

The next day she confided in Ran, admitting it was not sweet enough for her, but that she'd slept soooo well—could he tell her what drugstore they'd bought it at, or what market; soon after that:

> She came up with her cane [*he makes a knocking noise*], and I said, 'Yes, Miss Lehrfeld?'—when she was ninety, I could call her Amelia—I said, 'Yes, Miss Lehrfeld?'
> She said, 'Could you get some of that grape juice? And be sure to hide it.' Steve, her nephew, found it, and he said,
> 'Oh, Ran Blake, this is the best news!'

It was the beginning of a new era at 113th Street:

> George Russell used to bring beer once 'liquids' were allowed. DID she enjoy these bottles of red liquid that were NOT called 'Welch's'! She said that Jack Daniels was a little strong, but we had a bar there [in the house], and George Russell could come at any time. Her transformation was amazing.
> We gave her white wine on weekends, and suddenly one night, there was a little curry in the gefilte fish and the matzah ball soup. And dah, da-bah... [*he sings*] There was a Friday night song—I almost can remember it.

Miss Lehrfeld's love for Ran allowed her to deviate from the rules she'd lived by for many, many years. It also led to the re-shaping of her whole musical taste. At the start, her tastes were fixed, and Ran recalls:

> I think she said that really, even though she did NOT [*he stresses it*] go to the synagogue, the music there was 'the good music.'

But, under the influence of Ran and his friends, "suddenly she began loving all kinds of music." (Ran recalls it with an amazed upward-lifted tone.) She particularly liked The Modern Jazz Quartet—she said that was "proper jazz" for a "young lady like me." She also developed a taste for Thelonious Monk's music:

> So, when Miss Lehrfeld came ninety/ninety-one, she started having T.S. Monk and Barbara Monk over for afternoon ice-cream, and the Monk kids were sliding down the banister at her building.

Miss Lehrfeld and the welcoming home she provided for Ran and his friends remain at the center of Ran's memories of this period in New York City—his "happy period."

> When Miss Lehrfeld became a patient at St. Luke's hospital (which was just up the street), I would go up every day to see her. She regained her memory after the operation but then jaundice set in—her skin... [*He breaks off before recommencing.*] She survived the operation about eight or nine months, but it was a very sad time and Myra, a niece from Yonkers, came to look after her. She [Miss Lehrfeld] had a sister she'd lived with who'd died ten years earlier. Her descendants felt I'd given her [Miss Lehrfeld] a new lease on life and that she'd lived longer because of it.
> She died in '63 or '64—it's hard to remember exactly. She might have died before my first trip to Europe with Jeanne. I wonder if we could find an obituary, but I don't think she got one. A paragraph in *The Times*, perhaps?

His voice is hopeful, but Amelia Lehrfeld's death was not newsworthy. After she died, Ran inherited the rental of the apartment for one hundred and ten dollars a month:

> I mean, it could have been sold for one hundred and twenty; instead, I got it for one hundred and ten. My parents thought it was 'highway robbery'—that was their word. But it never went up one penny till my father HAD to force me to move when Gunther offered me the job after I got back from Greece.

It would have been hard for Ran to leave 113th Street. Miss Lehrfeld's kindness, and love, and indomitable spirit pervaded. And the memory of her stories—her whole life had been captured in those stories—was vivid. The friends that had gathered there had left warmth and love behind, and then, there was the music—with Miss Lehrfeld tapping out the beat with her cane. That whole apartment echoed with music![20]

2

NEW JOBS, NEW FRIENDS, NEW YORK

It was the happiest time of my life—I was very excited to be in New York.

RAN BLAKE

New York in the sixties was a place of opening horizons. There was a thirst for freedom, and 1950's society, with its staid expectations and well-tried mores, was slipping away. A new generation had come of age and was flooding the universities. They wanted freedom in all things. They already enjoyed a degree of prosperity, free time, and access to a robust media, through which they had become aware of injustices facing minority groups on a day-to-day basis. Inequality that was not necessarily in some far-removed corner of the world but in the very cities and towns they called home; they wanted change. Ran lived and worked on the edge of Columbia University campus. By the mid-1960s, Columbia was becoming a hub of political activity, with the student protest movement agitating for social reform. The energy was unmistakable. The city seemed poised on the threshold of a new era of social and cultural history.

In such a climate, possibilities seemed limitless. For Ran, the once impenetrable bounds of his Suffield adolescence were fast disappearing. But in order to become part of New York, to be absorbed into its frenetic energy, he would need a job. Not only this, he would need enough employment to ensure he was able to take full advantage of what was on offer in the form of lessons and club attendance—the cultural riches so vital for his musical development.

My stint at Atlantic enabled me to return to New York in 1960, where I lived near Columbia University and the Apollo Theater and where I would hear Ornette, Monk, etc., at the Five Spot and become a waiter at its sister club on St Marks Place. I also held many day jobs. I became a pin pricker[1] for a traffic engineering firm (Wilbur Smith), a desk clerk at the King's Crown Hotel (my work at Lenox got me that position); I also did an occasional job at Morningside Heights.[2]

Ran was no stranger to work. He'd had casual jobs from an early age. Like his great-grandfather, he'd delivered newspapers—he also was a bank messenger and freight elevator operator. While at Bard, he had always worked during holiday breaks. He was, as noted earlier, able to fund his attendance at the Lenox School of Jazz for the years 1958, 1959, and 1960 by working on the switchboard, waiting on tables, and carrying out other general duties at the school's Berkshire venue. This experience at Lenox (particularly as switchboard operator) got him a position as desk clerk at the King's Crown Hotel at 420 West 116th Street.

THE KING'S CROWN was postcard pretty—a narrow, nine-story building in the Beaux-Arts style.[3] It had been affiliated with Columbia University since the 1930s. (Whenever there was a shortage of student housing, two or three floors of the hotel were allocated for that purpose.) Short-term guests were often "relatives and guests of members of the university community"[4] who, because of their connection with the university, were accommodated at reasonable rates. (Ran remembers a figure of $35 a week for a single room.) As a result, the hotel often seemed like home to a large—if somewhat disparate—family, with students cheerfully mingling with long-term residents.

Dan Carlinsky lived at the King's Crown while studying at Columbia.[5] He shared the penthouse with four roommates, and he and Ran soon formed a friendship which was to last a lifetime. Dan remembers some of the long-term residents:

> An elderly lady named Regina Hughes, a dapper gentleman we called 'the Colonel,' and Mae Skidmore, an older woman who wore her hair braided and in a bun.[6]

Ran takes this memory further:

> And it was Colonel Parker. He had lived on the 5th or 6th floor for years and years. He carried a cane. There was also a blond woman called Ella,[7] who had hair down to her knees. A beautiful cat would sit outside the hotel—this was at 116th Street and Morningside Drive. One time, Nahid Mahdavi came from Tehran, and she had an apartment there with a couple of friends and would serve sumptuous dinners.

Ran continued to lodge with Miss Lehrfeld at West 113th Street during the eighteen months he worked at the King's Crown. He worked part-time, doing the day and early evening shift at the front desk. As well as welcoming guests, assisting with the check-ins and check-outs, and responding to queries, Ran was required to operate the switchboard. And while his experience at Lenox may have secured him the job, his genuine interest in people and his friendly and energetic manner would have delighted his manager, who was "typically around during the day."[8]

> I outlived several managers, but then they had to cut down staff. Adolf Meyer (as in Meyers Lemon Juice) from Deutschland was the first manager; then Phil Stewart [Stew][9] from Atlanta; Judith Gallante, and then, I'd heard through the grapevine I'd to be let go [sic] on a Saturday afternoon, and I was all prepared, and I was only there a week with the new manager, Judith Gallante. Isn't that funny? I can remember all these names of authority figures and not the student who was in a class two years ago.

Ran shared the desk clerk duties with the overnight clerk, Ed Browning, who worked every Friday night from midnight to eight o'clock and had, as Ran remembers, "an interest in songwriting... he would sometimes sing of the cornfields of Kansas." The other desk clerk was "Herr Eck, from Germany. He was Swiss/Deutsch—very proper, very organized, and had very good posture. He did the late shifts on weekends."[10]

The two porters, Arthur Horsey ("he had a marvelous gold tooth") and William Hinton, were elderly African Americans: "Arthur Horsey was probably about eighty at the time and still working."[11] They brought experience and dignity to their roles, overlooking any boisterous behavior and treating the students who lived there with the utmost respect. Dan Carlinsky notes that William Hinton used to call everyone "Mr." and yet was called "William" in return. However, as he adds, "Ran, of course, called him 'Mr. Hinton.'"[12]

The job at the King's Crown led to another opportunity for Ran. Dan Carlinsky had heard of a part-time job operating the switchboard at a residential hotel at 150 West 58th Street. As he couldn't operate a switchboard, he sought help from Ran and got a "crash course in switchboards."[13] Once Dan had the job (he even remembers how he was instructed to answer the phone: "6373, good morning!"), he got Ran part-time work doing the overnight shift. As Dan recalls, the accommodation was for permanent guests only, and the job involved "running the switchboard, announcing guests, and accepting packages—serving as a seated doorman, essentially."[14] It was an intriguing place. Many of the people who lived there were musicians as it was just a block from Carnegie Hall.

> Most memorable was Russian composer Sasha Votichenko. He lived in apartment 14B. He had a standing order for a wake-up call every day at something like 10.45 am.
> [There was a masseuse whose studio] was directly across the hall from the small switchboard room. We sat to the right as you entered the building; the masseuse was to the left. [Straight ahead, towards the rear of the building, was what was called the Round Room] which was a nightclub of sorts—I don't remember music… it was a place for drinks and socializing.[15]

A matchbook cover from the time describes the Round Room as a place for "intimate rendezvous," which seems to fit with Ran's memory as a place where, as he puts it:

> Aging beautiful women could have gentlemen callers, like in Tennessee Williams.[16] They made silver daiquiris in big goblets, and they made them rather mild because they didn't want people to get tipsy. My first boss was Mr. Bruce,[17] and then there was a man that whistled and got cabs for people outside. I was a switchboard operator, and they told me every Friday night I could have people in. They told me to go easy on the booze but never fall asleep and never so much as walk one inch out of the hotel—never, never, on the cost of my job! So this was on West 58th Street near 6th Avenue, every Friday night from midnight till 8 am [Saturday morning]. I was allowed six drinks a night, and supper was served 2.30 to 4 am. I had a room a little bigger than my living room here. I was running a big switchboard. People still remember coming to see me at that hotel; they brought thermoses. A lot of the traffic engineers from Wilbur Smith came, and people from Jazz Gallery, and Jeanne Lee would drop by, and Ann Noriega,[18] and Edythe Dimond, and a lot of students from Kings Crown Hotel.[19]

Ran also recalls the massage artist, Shirley, who he remembers sent him trays of food. Though he was aware of the comings and goings at her studio, it was not in his nature to question:

> She said, most of the time, she was holding hands and hearing confessions about business deals and husbands and wives fighting. She said she might as well have a medical degree and that she was hardly a woman of ill repute. She saw herself more as a counselor.

Ran had been told he could never sleep on the job. This was not difficult. There were regular visits from friends, and he could also rely on his dream world to keep him awake—his head was always full of movies and imaginings. If all else failed, he had Thelonious, a black leather bag that he had commissioned from "a wonderful shoe man" and in which he collected all sorts of things—notes from lessons with Gunther and Mary Lou Williams, manuscripts, records. He took it wherever he went, and at the hotel, he began to be known as "the Black Bag." It became a symbol of the whole mixed bag of his musical experience—a trademark image that featured, along with Jeanne Lee's shawl, on the cover of *The Newest Sound Around*.

If staying awake on the job was not a problem, the second stipulation of his employment—that he should never leave the hotel—was to be Ran's undoing:

> R: One time, I crossed the street to help someone—a girl. I got fired the next morning!
> L: Wait, Ran! [*Leo interrupts urgently.*] Who was the girl, and why did she need help?
> R: Oh, I don't think I knew. It could have been a woman or a girl; I don't know. Maybe somebody was yelling. I just had to run out into the street, but [it was] the wrong moment! Somebody noticed me from the window! So anyway, I lost the job. But I forget who the person was. You want me to make up a story and say it was a lady from *Spiral Staircase*?

There were other jobs to replace this one—Ran worked as a waiter at the Jazz Gallery and at Joe Wells' Supper Club. He also worked counting traffic through intersections for Wilbur Smith's traffic engineering firm:

> L: Why did you have to count traffic at traffic lights?
> R: Because I couldn't make a living as a pianist!
> L: But what…
> R: They were doing a whole re-design of the traffic in New York City. I just had an $80 a week job.

One of Ran's friends from this period, Wilma Srob Odell, recalls:

> There was a time—probably around 1963 or '64—that Ran applied to be a policeman. He wanted a job (he needed money), and we were so worried that he would pass the test. Oh my gosh, Ran with a gun... I don't think so! Anyone could take it from him in a second—he's such a gentle person.[20]

Ran had a large group of friends in New York. Dan Carlinsky recalls the "little address book with contact information about dozens and dozens of people he knew to varying degrees." His friends reflected his life—and the times—in New York and included teachers and the musicians he met at clubs, as well as people whom he met through his various jobs and his study at Columbia University.[21] Ran was proud of the fact that people entrusted him with their keys; he soon had a large collection:

> Cevira Rose—who became Mrs. Allen—was a person I met at Lenox. I would go to her apartment on 1220 Park Avenue, and she had a beautiful Steinway. She'd be going out to dinners with her friends, and I would practice there. I also had a key to the apartment of Lloyd Delaney, which was one block further north to that of Cevira Rose. He was an African American psychiatrist who was on the faculty at Queens. He was gregarious. We had discussions about art. He had me for a bourbon in his apartment.

Another of Ran's friends at this time was poet Bob Marius. He was a conscientious objector who served time on Riker's Island for his stand on Vietnam. His poem "Ran Blake" appears as part of the liner notes for the 1965 ESP-Disk recording, *Ran Blake Plays Solo Piano*.[22] Ran enjoyed meeting all these people and getting to know them better. They were part of the 1960s New York he was discovering. In a place where people were coming and going, Ran was not the only newcomer; some of his new friends were far from home. Nahid Mahdavi says she met Ran in New York in 1962 when she was "completely alone and friendless" and living "at a hotel on Columbia University campus."[23] He asked her to introduce a concert at the university, saying her accent would "delight the students." (As a child, Nahid had attended a boarding school on the outskirts of Paris.) Her first impression of Ran was a "thin, white, blond-haired young man with the black portfolio—an appendage—called Thelonious." Ran became Nahid's friend and guide, and through him she got to know a New York that most visitors would never get to see. He took her to the Wednesday service at Sweet Daddy Grace's church in Harlem and poetry readings by

James Baldwin and other young black poets in the Village. He also took her to Hartford to hear Edith Powell sing. Nahid helped Ran and Jeanne Lee when they put on parties for an "improbable" mix of people—musicians, students, and "the guys at the Wilbur S. Smith organization." (Ricardo Gautreau would come over with "the best iced-coffee—South American coffee, Dominican Republic.") Wilma Srob Odell recalls that Marte and her roommate, Linda Abrams Glass, put on a party for Ran in August of 1962 in an apartment in Manhattan. There was, she recalled, a lot of southern food and weed, and the police came because of the noise.

And no matter how many friends Ran was seeing, he always had time for family. Ran's cousin Susan remembers coming to New York City after having finished junior college:

> After an extra academic year in Paris, I moved to NYC. Ran was there and had many friends and a connection at Columbia University. He invited me to come see a computer there. The computer took up the whole room, and Ran had created music on that computer. It was amazing. During that year, he introduced me to friends from the Caribbean and took me to Daddy Grace's Church in Harlem. What an awesome experience. The music was rich and loud, and there were people called 'Holy Rollers' in a trance state. After the 'service,' Ran took me out for dinner—to enjoy some Harlem Soul Food—Fried Chicken and Waffles. Yum!

Ran embraced a new life in the city and took his family and friends along for the adventure. As Wilma Srob Odell puts it:

> For Ran, there are no boundaries; no horizon is too far. He expanded our musical interests; he introduced us to the Apollo. That was his thing, opening horizons.

3

SWEET DADDY GRACE'S CHURCH

*I was on my way up to hear Ray Charles at the
Apollo, and I heard the most exciting noises.*

RAN BLAKE

From a very young age, sneaking out to listen to the music at the church on Hancock Street, Ran had been captivated by Gospel music. This fascination continued in New York. One of the first churches he attended in New York was the Abyssinian Baptist Church[1]:

> There were two in the New York area: one in Harlem, where Adam Clayton Powell[2] gave those wonderful salty cocktail sermons in the fifties, and one in Newark, New Jersey, where Alex Bradford sang.[3] For several Sundays, I attended services and was impressed by Alex Bradford and by the excellent, if uninspired, professionalism of the choir. Later this choir cut an album for Columbia, and Alex Bradford and the wonderful Princess Stewart traveled through Europe as part of the Black Nativity Troupe.[4]

But by late 1962, Ran had discovered a Gospel church that was to be an important part of his New York experience—the church of "Sweet Daddy" Grace[5] on 8th Avenue in Harlem, between 124th and 125th. (It was diagonally across from the Apollo.)

Ran was already fairly familiar with the area from trips he had made to Manhattan while still at Bard; during his stint at Atlantic Records, he'd had the opportunity to explore much of the neighborhood that was close to his base at 116th Street. The crisscross of streets and avenues is still imprinted in his mind:

> Now, if you go from near the river, you have the Riverside [Drive]. Then comes the street that the old Juilliard was on; it became the Manhattan School of Music; there's a little name for that street [Claremont Avenue]; then comes Broadway; then comes Amsterdam, which I would have walked on, and then comes St Nick,[6] and then 8th Avenue. Then, what was called 7th Avenue has... maybe it's the Powell Avenue,[7] and then Lenox Avenue, and that has a new name now.[8] So... 132nd Street and the original 7th Avenue was where the Joe Wells' Club was, and right next door was Count Basie's. [*There is an upward inflection to his voice, and the implication is: 'Isn't that wonderful?'*]

On the night he discovered Sweet Daddy's, Ran was on his way to hear Ray Charles at the Apollo (mid-way between 7th and 8th Avenues on 125th Street). He was early but didn't want to watch the movie the Apollo was showing prior to the live act. Wandering around the block as he considered whether he should go home, he heard "the most exciting noises near a subway on the 8th Avenue line."[9] He set out to investigate the source of this music, which he later described as "more vivid" than Hancock Street, Springfield, but possibly lacking "some of the sonorities of the Hartford church." He remembers the experience vividly:

> There was a modest storefront with what seemed like two flights of stairs: there may have been an anteroom. There were people in the street saying, 'Come, come, we're going to be saved.' I walked up the steps, and there were people on the second floor. I went through the auditorium, and a lady... with bright gold teeth [*Ran adds this detail with wonder*] said, 'What are you doing here?'
> And I said, 'I heard the music.'
> She said, 'Sit over there.' Then, before I could move: 'Where were you going?'
> And I said, 'The Apollo,' and she frowned.
> [*Ran mulls over this frown, still trying to pinpoint a reason for it before deciding*] I guess there were comedians there [at the Apollo] that maybe told jokes that were not sanitary, and I got a little frown...

Ran took the back-row seat she'd indicated, just as the choir walked in and the hat was passed around for money.

> Suddenly a group of young men and a girl, who were sitting in the right-front, picked up their instruments and began to play. It was an electric shock—eight trombonists, a couple of trumpets, a French horn! One trombonist was called Jesus, and his sister Maria played bongos. This was a perfect unity between gospel music and unaffected New Orleans jazz. The drummer was a bit heavy, and there were musical faults, but they were creating—not re-creating.

There were a lot of young men in the congregation, unlike the Hartford church, where it was mostly young women. The woman with the gold teeth walked near the beginning of the procession. She was an imposing figure, and Ran was transfixed:

> The way the light from the window reflected and the smile, the color from the teeth and these bright glasses. She was wearing a white gown, and maybe she told me she could not play anymore, but I had visions that on my first trip, she played some kind of horn. She was very tall with big, big hair; it might have been greying. The musicians followed her: there was one sax, a clarinet, and different brass, brass, brass: three or four trumpets; one or two trombones; horns, but they didn't seem like common horns—maybe some kind of euphonium… I don't think I knew what it was. I DO remember a tuba. And was it eight trombones or two? Sometimes it was a smaller brass group. I believe the choir marched in front of the brass. The choir was good, but the brass… [*He pauses in admiration*] was great—with harmony or primitive chords, but the beat… [*He doesn't finish. There is a sense of awe.*] There was a piano up the front [of the church], and drums…

Ran couldn't help it—he kept returning to the church. As he got to know it better, he ventured further up the front, though he never participated. There was a window looking out toward 125th Street and the Apollo. One day Sr. Tee (the lady with the gold teeth)[10] caught him looking at the "place of hell." The descriptor is offered nonchalantly as if the term were entirely appropriate. Then, unexpectedly, he lowers his voice and forms each word singly and chillingly, "Did - you - come - here - for - THAT - purpose?" Even the re-telling has an unsettling undertone. She spoke with a Southern accent, but there was something about the accusation that took Ran back to Mary Garvey and her private "confessional" in the attic. Like Mary Garvey, however, there was a soft side to Sister Tee, a kindness that recognized human imperfection and was reluctant to judge. While she felt compelled to spread the gospel, she was keen to avoid burdening people with her message:

> In Harlem, she would run a cart, giving out Bibles and things... and didn't one large Bible have an indent, and there was some Gordon gin or something in it? [*He asks himself.*] And then people would get their [ration] of gin, but then they'd have to say a prayer; I think she might have had a little nip once in a while herself. She ran the choir at Sweet Daddy Grace's, and she was young; I probably thought she was old; she was forty-five. She was very stingy on the gin. When I met her years later, she denied that she had that, but it was like Mary Poppins putting the spoonful in the mouth. She was less tough than Sarah Carter—a little more tolerant. She knew I liked movies. She came from Newport News, Virginia—she said she grew up with great music there. She always said, 'When I go, will you remember that I came from Newport News, Virginia?' She is on the ESP record that got re-released.[11]

Sister Tee had an all-abiding love of music which was to influence her relationship with Ran. Before long, she began expressing an interest in 20th-century music, and Ran invited her to his apartment where he could play some records for her and demonstrate some harmonies:

> She heard me do "Swing Low Sweet Chariot," and she said, 'We should have this harmony.' And then, somehow, she... somehow the church said, 'No.'

Whether the church allowed her to use the harmonies or not, Sister Tee enjoyed the lessons. In return, she would teach Ran Gospel clapping.

> She got me in the feeling of 12/8. It was not clear whether Sister Tee gave me a lesson or I gave her one. She did the *Rite of Spring* but thought it was out of key. She liked the Montreux LP version. We danced to it, and Miss Lehrfeld... [*he makes a tapping noise to substitute for words*] with her cane. Miss Lehrfeld said, 'You're wild!' Sister Tee thought Miss Lehrfeld was glorious, and Miss Lehrfeld loved her.

Sister Tee became a frequent visitor, and Miss Lehrfeld was happy to have it that way. When she heard that Sister Tee had not tried gefilte fish, she insisted that she should come for the Sabbath meal:

> She would come over to the house. We knew her enough for her to have a key. We'd hear her coming in: 'Hi,' [*He lightens his voice and gives the impression that she is calling from afar.*] 'Brother Ran, Sister Amelia...' and her voice would ring out, and we never would know when she would come. She had never had gefilte fish

and matzah ball soup, so Miss Lehrfeld… [invited her]. I think she hadn't been seduced by George Russell yet with the pseudo wine [*sic*]. I know that she was rather surprised when Sister Tee put some hot Louisiana sauce in her matzah ball soup. She said, 'It's a little flat, isn't it, Miss Lehrfeld?'
Sister Tee made wonderful little chicken and porgy[12] dishes, and she served collard greens and black-eyed beans and baking powder biscuits. She preferred them to gefilte fish; she said matzah ball soup was okay for Miss Lehrfeld, but she liked her other vittles. I felt I was between two cultures, and I was right squeezed in the middle. We had the smallest little kitchen. I just felt I was hearing history.

He was. And the stories of two women of very different cultures, their experiences of poverty, alienation, and struggle in the country they called home, made a lasting impression. They spoke of hard times—the Depression, war, intolerance—but they spoke of good times as well. Sister Tee talked of her childhood in Newport News, Virginia. Miss Lehrfeld spoke of New York in the early 20th century. Ran was fascinated. While they talked, he deliberately pulled the shades up at one window. The setting sun slanted in, alighting on the two women, and their faces, a study in chiaroscuro, were etched into his memory.[13]

Such evenings cemented a warm understanding and friendship between Miss Lehrfeld and Sister Tee, who brought something of her own religion to the Sabbath observance:

One Friday night—I'll never forget it—the two meetings… and there was a guy called Steve who was the nephew of Miss Lehrfeld, and he said, 'What have we got here: a revival meeting?' And I know that we weren't supposed to answer the phone that night. Somehow the lights were on, or Sister Tee had candles. Sister Tee believed the Spirit of God would be right in the room, and she would ask Him to come into my arms so that I could… I didn't own the tambourine; I think she gave me one, but I had to toss it and then go to the piano. And occasionally, Miss Lehrfeld would join in with her cane—it was more of a three-four time. She did awfully well for her age when we consider that she liked Viennese waltzes at the beginning of her life. And then we had Eugene, who was the concierge of the house—of the apartment—and he would come up.
L: Was he black or white?
R: Black—Mr. Coleby was the white man, the superintendent. And so, the two of them would dress up Friday nights and come up to the service, and after it was allowed, Mr. Coleby brought in liquor, and Sister Tee said, 'If we have to drink this kind of spirit… DO

IT! HALLELUJAH!' [*He shouts it out.*] And there was a word for Hallelujah in Yiddish, and Miss Lehrfeld would say it more mildly, with her cane tapping.

BUT OUTSIDE—ON THE street—things were changing. By the mid-1960s, there was dissatisfaction among some groups with the civil rights movement. Young blacks, in particular, were frustrated by the apparent lack of progress. New energy was being invested in change; the call "Black Power" was its rallying cry.[14] However, this was not without problems as quite a number of whites, as well as some blacks, saw Black Power as a separatist movement. This was the atmosphere. It was a time of change, and it occurred during a period when Ran was—because of commitments to a second European tour and the cutting of his second album[15]—less able to visit the church on 8th Avenue and West 124th Street. When he *could* get there, he noticed a change:

> Outside was like a marketplace—people debating the value of Heinz soup and Campbell's soup. I think it was outside. I wonder if I might have dreamed this. It might have been one incident.

It was not a dream. Various counterculture groups of the 1960s were focusing on the power of food to transform society. Some of the young participants from the "summer of love" (San Francisco, 1967) had, in fact, continued their search for an alternative society, establishing rural communes which sought to reclaim simple, home-grown food and reject the canned and frozen food industry. But in the city, food gave activists from the Black Power movement a way to express their identity—to promote soul food and resist the food of the dominant American culture. Soup kitchens sprung up to attract the poor and underprivileged, with the activists and those inviting salvation competing for attention. Ran felt uneasy when he returned to the church at this time, though he did notice that once past the throng outside, things were more as he remembered:

> I went back and didn't feel it was cool. Downstairs, in the street, I felt it was not-very-comfortable [*He spaces the words out, saying them carefully.*] outside the church. I'd always felt welcome upstairs, though not warmly welcome. As the years went by, nobody remembered me... there would be a smile: impersonal.
> L: Why was that?

R: I think it was that a lot of curious whites came in. These spectators would laugh at people having what they called 'fits.' A lot of people got very excited. They made them dress starkly in white, but if you really... [wanted to be saved], they'd come over and put their hands on your head. I know one or two times I got an excited cough, and maybe there was a bit of a laugh, but it was a nervous laugh, not a laugh at... [them]. And then I saw people really laughing at what some young black people did. I remember wanting to stay away from them. I knew that I wasn't really a blood member, but I had paid dues in Hartford, and I didn't want to be part of those coming in with the long beards. And there might have been a soup car below... [which attracted this crowd]. I don't know. I just... [*A new breath and a fresh start*] Sweet Daddy's had a little bit of theater and, by the way, I just flashed back... It was Sweet Daddy's where I was told to hear Sr. Ernestine Washington,[16] and that was my first trip to Brooklyn... and you're living in Brooklyn or Queens?
L: Brooklyn.
R: [*Pleased*] Brooklyn.

Wilma Srob Odell also remembers these times:

Ran assembled a large group of seven or ten people to go to Sweet Daddy Grace McCullough[17] on 125th Street. The music—unbelievably wonderful gospel. Many instruments. Everyone was asked to dance up to Sweet Daddy Grace and give a donation. We were welcomed in the church, but a few years later, that would not be the case.[18]

Ran attended Sweet Daddy Grace's church "fifteen to twenty times," and Sister Tee was very much part of his life in New York between 1960 and 1964. Even after Miss Lehrfeld died, Sister Tee continued to come for a time to help him clean the apartment. And after Ran moved to Boston, Sister Tee was still looking out for him. She introduced him to her friend Ouida.[19] She said, "There's somebody that will look after you," and Ouida (who, Ran says, was a "taskmaster") did look after him when he was living on St. Stephen Street in Boston. At this time, just back from Greece, he was certainly in need of moral support. Sister Tee's kindness in contacting her friend was typical of the care she had always shown toward Ran. He treasures a memory of Sister Tee—with her big smile and gold teeth—marching down the church aisle:

and if you've heard the album, I go right into what happened on the street.

When discussing his compositions on another occasion, Ran mentions this track, first recorded on *Ran Blake Plays Solo Piano* in 1965:

> "Sister Tee"—that's dedicated to Sister Eliza Lowery. She was called Sister Tee, and I knew her from 1960 to 1964. She came from Newport News, Virginia.
> L: I never knew that was her name. I just thought she was Sister Tee.
> R: She was to me and to George Russell.
> L: Why was she called that?
> R: I think… I don't know if she drank tea? I don't know. I guess that became the name of my composition, and then I called her that. But I DO realize how important Sister Tee was to me—and you know… she always liked the key A major.[20]
> L: Really… I don't mind 'A'—It's a nice solid key.
> R: Beautiful key! [*It's said in a hushed tone of great appreciation.*]

4

JAZZ CLUBS OF NEW YORK

When at Bard College, I would go every weekend to hear jazz... into New York or Connecticut.

RAN BLAKE

A vital part of Ran's New York experience centered around its jazz clubs. Ran began attending New York clubs while still a student at Bard.

> My parents paid for me to take the train back some weekends to Suffield, but other weekends I went to New York. [Then] my father gifted me with an English Squire car—like a station wagon. My first trip on my own took place, I believe, in 1957. I was to meet someone at the Celebrity Club in Harlem to hear Buddy Tate, but somehow, I got lost. I ended up at The Five Spot. The street was dark; I'm [maybe] exaggerating. Bodies of drunk men sprawled on the sidewalk. They were so kind [*sic*]. They would slowly get up, begging. Their skin was sallow, the breath stench unpleasant, but [they were] honest. One or two would offer me a sip of the bottle.

It was thrilling, walking into the Five Spot bar:

> As soon as you walked in, the bar was on the right-hand side. Now, I bet there were eighteen or twenty chairs—it seemed to me only twelve. There would be tables on the left and one or two behind the bar. If I recall, the bandstand would be straight ahead. It was run by Iggy Termini. I think Monk[1] was the reason I came, but there were others.

At that time, Monk was playing six nights a week with four sets each night, which gave Ran ample opportunity to get in from Bard. Monk's band was made up of John Coltrane on tenor saxophone, Ahmed Abdul-Malik (who had replaced Wilbur Ware) on double bass, and Shadow Wilson on drums.

> I loved the atmosphere [there]. Even if I had to stand up, the evening was magical—even when there were a couple of tourists who attempted to speak [through Monk's set]. Compared to trendy nightclubs, there were moments of sustained silence, but beer bottle requests COULD break spells.
> I heard Trane. (At first, I resented long solos—not because I was bored, but I wanted longer Thelonious.)
> What bothered me was the smoke. I would gasp and run to the street [for air]. One time I was refused second entry; this was the Bowery. Ahmed Abdul-Malik found me on the street; he was so kind to me. I was aware of Nica [being present] but wasn't watching her, nor did I attempt to speak to any musician except Abdul-Malik.

On at least one occasion, Ran brought his sister, Martha, who was still at high school at the time. (She loved the atmosphere and the music, but she also remarked on the smoke—which made her eyes stream.)

Ran was at the Five Spot when Ornette Coleman made his New York debut:

> I was there the night that Leonard Bernstein was there. I can be precise—that would have been the fall of 1959.[2] Ornette had moved to New York. He had been a student at the School of Jazz in Lenox, where I used to stay up all night running the switchboard and connecting calls between Abbey Lincoln and Max Roach.

Nothing now remains of the old Five Spot. In 1962, the Terminis were forced to move a few blocks further up 3rd Avenue (and around the corner) to 2 St. Mark's Place, where they could increase their fire-risk capacity (and thus, decrease the need for regular police headcounts!). In other respects, the club was reassuringly familiar with its walls painted warm-red and covered with flyers and posters. There were, however, those who felt the club's "golden years" were behind it.

On June 14, 1960, the Terminis booked Monk to play at their second— and larger—club, the Jazz Gallery,[3] on a double-bill with John Coltrane, who was leading his own newly-formed quartet. The crowds thronged in. It was an exciting time for Ran—being able to attend the gigs of his heroes.

Soon after this, he moved to New York, and one of his many jobs in that city was as a waiter at the Jazz Gallery.

> The Jazz Gallery[4] was a little bit bigger and a little more plush, and that was on St. Marks—between 2nd and 3rd. One night, we ran out of ice, and I had to go… Joe Termini sent me over [to the Five Spot] to his brother Iggy:
> 'Would I get some ice back?' [he asked]. So, I could really walk without having to cross a big avenue. I lived and breathed and loved the times I was waiting on tables there—what a golden opportunity.

Ran had come to New York City to "study with Bill Russo, Gunther Schuller, and most of all, to experience the city itself." He set about absorbing all the city had to offer, and a lot of that was the opportunity to hear his favorite musicians live. Working at the Jazz Gallery was a bonus, but Ran frequented all the clubs in the vicinity of his lodgings at 113th Street.

The Joe Wells' Supper club, on 7th Avenue (now Adam Clayton Powell Boulevard), between 132nd and 133rd Streets, was a much-cherished part of Ran's New York. Indeed, the aura which surrounds it is so great, even Ran's journey to the club (from his lodgings at Miss Lehrfeld's apartment) has been vividly etched in his memory:

> How well I remember leaving Miss Lehrfeld's apartment, walking east of Columbia University on Amsterdam Avenue to the Sweet Daddy Grace Church (where I would walk up to the 2nd floor and hear Sister Tee leading a brass choir), then crossing 125th Street to the Apollo and walking up to what was then called 7th Avenue—crossing that street and walking up to 132nd Street on the East Side. There would be all kinds of music coming from apartments and a couple of clubs. I could detect some of the Latin sounds from East Harlem. […] I used to compose and memorize all various types of music on my walk to Joe Wells' club. There were all kinds of smoke in the air. I would often look in at the Count Basie Club on 136th and 7th Avenue, and, of course, one could subway to the Village Vanguard, Five Spot, Carnegie Recital Hall, or the Greek district. I loved Joe Wells' Supper Club. There, I saw Gunther—Gunther and Margie Schuller would often go—and I occasionally saw George Russell there. Sheila Gordon [would be there, and] Leila White, Don Ellis, Abby Lincoln, Mary Lou Williams—ALL these people. There were limousines there—the elegance!

The club covered two levels:

> Mr. Wells would seat you, and there was a room for people who wanted to talk and [one upstairs for] people who wanted to listen. So I'd [go upstairs] to the very svelte second floor, which held about twelve tables that were very low; it had dark lighting—terribly chic—and there, one would hear great jazz. The room would hold thirty-five or forty-five people. You'd go there at 11.30; dinner would start at midnight—with waffles and fried chicken. [*There's an upward tone as if to say, 'Could you get better than that'*]

The upstairs room at Wells' was exclusive—the destination of the true music lover. Ran would arrive early to get a table at the front. The atmosphere was "sedate" compared to the liveliness below. The tables were small, and—between sets—customers were served adaptations of the food offered downstairs. The lower floor was open from late afternoon. The atmosphere there was one of "barely suppressed boisterousness"[5]; patrons were dressed for a night out. Here, Joe Wells mingled in the crowd—greeting regulars, welcoming newcomers, finding tables, beckoning waiters. His easy manner made people feel relaxed as they ordered drinks (and the fried chicken and waffles for which the club was renowned).

> Mr. Wells would meet me at the door personally, and I felt there were three distinct characteristics to Mr. Wells.

The first characteristic Ran noticed was that Joe Wells was an affable, charismatic club owner who was very warm and solicitous to the patrons.

The second characteristic was something undefinable, but it nevertheless left Ran feeling a little uneasy. Although he was disposed to liking the man, he sensed a certain caginess that caused him to ponder whether there might have been some "underground gambling or other spice available."[6] For underneath the geniality—muted by the smoke, the sound of people talking, glasses clinking, and the delicious smell of the chicken—was the taut awareness of a businessman, preoccupied with the smooth running of his club (which included attending to the needs of his musicians).

And this was the third quality Ran observed in Joe Wells: "an attention to musicians." For musicians, often neglected in the rush to care for patrons, this must have been very welcome.

However, Ran also remembers that Joe Wells "struck a hard bargain" and "never gave many discounts." Even when Ran took a lot of people there, he never got as much as a free drink, although Joe Wells would often bring extra portions of chicken and waffles:

One night, he realized I spent a lot of money, and he said, 'Ran, my car will take you home.' I was put into an outrageous car—one that an undertaker might drive. There were all various types of people who were going to different addresses—I heard Italian and Portuguese [spoken].
Joe Wells: W-e-l-l-s—don't add an 'e' like in Orson. 'Joe Wells.'
I got to be a rather frequent customer. And it must have been after I had resigned as a waiter at The Jazz Gallery—there was a year that I was seen there very often. I would often spend Saturday nights there. And on spring nights, I could walk home—I knew enough to walk down the main Avenue, turn to my right at 125th, and go down Amsterdam where, at 119th, I would pass a Vietnamese restaurant, which was very popular with Bob Labaree's[7] family—particularly his wife—but I didn't know them then.

Up the block from Joe Wells' Supper Club was "the elegant bar" that "bears the name of Count Basie" (on 132nd Street). It was a popular place for jam sessions. The newly renovated bar opened in early 1958:

Harlem was great. You walked a block or two after the Apollo—up 7th Avenue—and Count Basie had a club, and I remember Shirley—the organ player. Jimmy Smith was the famous one, and then Shirley—Shirley Scott.

Other clubs Ran frequented were Smalls' Paradise—a large basement club in Harlem, just over the road from Joe Wells'. When Ed Smalls opened his club in 1925, it had a huge capacity (for 1500 people); there were big bands, grand floor shows, and dancing waiters. But it was more expensive than the average Harlem local could afford. It was open all night, with jam sessions starting around 2 am. (In the 1960s, when Ran was there, the club had been bought by basketball hero Wilt Chamberlain.)

I went to Smalls' Paradise—the original one. They were playing pool inside [...] I heard Ted Curson and Charles Mingus at the Half Note. [Here] the performers played in the middle of a large room—they were elevated. And there was Ray Charles at the Apollo.[8]

The Half Note, operating in what was then a dreary location in the West Village,[9] was where Ran took Martha to see Charles Mingus; the Village Vanguard was where they saw Chris Connor. The Vanguard launched many careers, including Thelonious Monk's. (It billed itself as "the showcase for new talent.") During 1960, the Modern Jazz Quartet played many Sunday 4 pm matinees, and Ran remembers seeing Aretha Franklin when she debuted there. With its superb acoustics, the Vanguard has been the venue for many seminal live jazz albums, recorded there throughout its history.[10] As evidenced in its mural and posters, the club's ethos has always been a mix of jazz and social justice.

It was this combination—of jazz and social justice—that characterized Ran's early New York experiences. He was tapping into the energy and lifeblood of a whole movement. The overlay of music, protest, and cultural diversity in the parts of New York City that Ran frequented had awakened a spirit of freedom; jazz musicians were carrying their message to the world. At the Jazz Gallery, Max Roach and Abbey Lincoln played their newly recorded, *We Insist! Freedom Now Suite*[11] to appreciative audiences. Sidney Poitier and James Baldwin were there to support—and Ran was serving drinks to all of them. It was typical of the New York jazz scene in the early sixties. Ran "found it vibrant."

5

Nica de Koenigswarter

*There are two means of refuge from the miseries
of life: music and cats.*

Widely attributed to Albert Schweitzer

Ran came to New York ready for new experiences. In his case, these radiated from the tight central core of the city's jazz scene:

> And of course, it wasn't just jazz—I went to Carnegie Hall, to the Greek and Hispanic neighborhoods, to Gospel churches and the rhythm and blues clubs in Harlem, as well as the philharmonic orchestra.

His enthusiasm was contagious, and many were drawn into his orbit. Some were to become life-long friends. One such friend (and mentor, albeit at a distance) was the Baroness Pannonica de Koenigswarter.

The baroness (Nica to her friends, but always "Baroness" to Ran) was well known in New York jazz circles from the early 1950s till her death in November 1988. She was a friend to many jazz players, including Teddy Wilson, Lionel Hampton, Art Blakey, Horace Silver, Charlie Rouse, Charlie Parker, and especially Thelonious Monk. She was warm and kind and without a hint of prejudice. Generous to a fault, she often hosted jam sessions in her hotel suite and regularly attended gigs at the Five Spot, the Jazz Gallery, the Village Vanguard, Smalls (in Harlem), and Birdland to support jazz artists. She would arrive after midnight in her 1953 Rolls Royce,[1] which she'd nicknamed the 'Silver Pigeon,' often bringing with her a group of musicians who were not working that night.

R: Sometimes she came alone too. She had her own special table at The Jazz Gallery. She was known as the 'jazz baroness' or 'bebop baroness.'

The baroness was an incongruous figure at the jazz clubs of Harlem and the Village. Her fur coat and pearls were carelessly worn, and her fading hair, pinned back from her pale face at the ears and temples, hung loose to her shoulders. She had the soft, dreamy expression of a child, yet she smoked (using a long, long cigarette holder) and drank (pouring her whisky from a teapot into a cracked china cup) with seasoned aplomb. Her voice was very much English upper class with an overlay of gravel. The youngest of four children born to Charles Rothschild (of the Rothschild banking dynasty) and Baroness Rózsika Edle von Wertheimstein of Hungary, Nica (Kathleen Annie Pannonica), spent her early years at various family estates in the bosom of the English countryside.[2] Here she enjoyed every luxury along with strict discipline. Nica's father, a sensitive and gentle man with an interest in nature and natural science,[3] was temperamentally unsuited to the work of the family banking business. The long hours he put in there led to melancholy—and emotional breakdown. He had been attracted to his wife Rózsika, and indeed, to her whole family because of their cheerful manner and uncomplicated approach to life. This was a happy contrast to the restrained and work-driven Rothschilds. Unfortunately, after falling prey to the great flu pandemic in 1918, Charles contracted encephalitis and was left physically and emotionally depleted. He committed suicide in 1923.

Nica was nine years old at the time of her father's death, and while Rózsika shielded her children from the circumstances, the family was nevertheless bereft. Before his illness took hold, Charles had been a loving father, and though his death was not discussed, the horror of it was haunting.

Rózsika moved her family to Tring Park, Hertfordshire, to stay with Charles's mother. Nica's sister, Miriam, remembered how they were ushered into the hall, where their grandmother appeared at the top of the stairs and looked down at them.[4] She would have, of course, been in shock, but this grandmother—Emma— was remote by nature. (In twenty-five years under the same roof, she never hugged or kissed Rózsika, whose spontaneous and joyful nature was smothered as a result.) Rózsika became more and more serious. She took on the organization of the household and family finances and proved to be very proficient—and disciplined—in this respect. Rózsika seemed in control, but she was plagued by anxiety. She developed such a horror of illness[5] that she was compelled to organize the lives of her children so as to keep them from all possible contagion, going so far as to reserve private rail carriages when they traveled. There was also a large staff of people, including nurses, governesses, and tutors whose responsibility it was to keep the children from harm.

Thus, Nica's life, though privileged, lacked warmth and companionship. She became increasingly wild (climbing trees and riding her horse with reckless abandon). She was often alone. She remembered this period as one when she had no friends—apart from her horses. For someone who, in later life, was friend to so many (and who obviously craved friendship), it would have been very restricting. Nica was eager to get away. She didn't fit in. Her only solace was art; she had always loved painting. Music also consoled her. Somewhere in her memory echoed the sound of the music her father had played on his gramophone. She was unable to identify it; she only knew that it wasn't classical. But it was one of the few memories she had of him, and it was precious. At the same time, her brother was fascinated by American jazz. In the early 1930s, he let her sit in on a couple of lessons he managed to arrange for himself with Teddy Wilson.[6] The seeds were sown for a lifestyle change, but first, Nica followed expectations. In 1935 she married French diplomat Baron Jules de Koenigswarter. They lived in a chateau in the northwest of France.

However, war intervened, putting an end to domesticity and changing everything. The baron was called into the army, and Pannonica, with two children, a stepson, and several nurses, was forced to flee to London, then to America, where she left the children (with their nanny) in the care of Harry and Alicia Guggenheim at their Falaise estate on Long Island.[7] Pannonica was determined to rejoin her husband in the Congo. In December 1940, she volunteered "to ferry eight tons of medical supplies onboard an old Norwegian cargo [ship] to the Free French Forces."[8] Working with the Free French Army, she demonstrated great courage and determination, driving ambulances and army vehicles on the battlefields of North Africa, and later, Europe. The baron, also with the Free French, distinguished himself and was decorated with la Croix de la Libération and la Croix de la Légion d'honneur. Nica, who by the end of the war had reached Berlin with the Free French Forces, was awarded the Médaille de la France Libre. Between 1940 and 1945, Pannonica, "worried about her children's health and wanting to be by their side, sailed across the Atlantic four times despite serious bouts of malaria and narrowly missing being torpedoed twice by U-boats."[9]

For his war effort, Baron de Koenigswarter was rewarded with a diplomatic position that took him to Norway and then to Mexico City. But things could not go back to the way they were. Pannonica had witnessed first-hand the horrors of war; she had come to understand the fragile and transitory nature of life. As well, she'd tasted freedom and independence; it became increasingly difficult for her to settle into her new life as a diplomat's wife. She began making trips to New York (from Mexico City), and it was here that her fascination with the jazz world grew. On one such visit in the late 1940s, Teddy Wilson introduced her to "Round Midnight." It was a significant moment and one that changed the course of her life. She listened to it twenty times straight—and missed her plane back to Mexico.

Eventually, the spirit of the jazz world—its spontaneity and freedom—won out. In the early 1950s, just prior to the baron's appointment as French Ambassador to the United States and Canada, the couple, "though they cared for each other dearly,"[10] agreed to separate. In jazz, Nica had found something that marriage, position, and wealth could not offer her: "It's a desire for freedom. And in all my life, I've never known any people who warmed me as much by their friendship as the jazz musicians I've come to know."[11]

Her decision brought her unwanted attention, and many seemed threatened by her lifestyle. Her association with black musicians and her courage in challenging racism made Pannonica a target for narrow-minded resentment and criticism. When Charlie Parker died in her suite at the Stanhope Hotel on upper 5th Avenue on March 12, 1955, she was the subject of speculation. In 1958 she made headlines when police in Wilmington, Delaware picked her up, driving Thelonious Monk and Charlie Rouse to an engagement in Baltimore, Maryland. The police alleged that they found marijuana in the boot of the car, and Nica, to protect Monk, told them it was hers. She faced a prison term and deportation. On the eve of her trial, she wrote to Mary Lou Williams: "This is the day upon which my entire future may well depend."[12] She was sentenced to three years in prison, which she immediately appealed, and after much legal wrangling, the conviction was overturned on a technicality. Nica sheltered Thelonious and his wife, Nellie, from much of the anxiety she suffered as a result of this drawn-out affair, feeling they had enough worries of their own. Despite any criticism she received in the press, she remained generous and understanding—and extremely kind.

RAN FIRST HEARD of the baroness during his studies with Ralph Ellison at Bard College. He'd taken Ellison's course on American literature. It was only for one semester, but it made a great impression. Ellison "talked about an amazing lady—the Baroness Koenigswarter de Rothschild—she and Ralph were friends." Ellison promised to get Ran an introduction.

> I called her up, but at that point, I was a waiter at the Jazz Gallery—so I must have waited on table to her first... [*The sequence of events is hazy and intrigues him.*] We had Monday night off; it must have been a Monday night that I went out there and at 63...that's an important number because Mary Lou Williams lived at 63 Hamilton Terrace in Sugar Hill, Harlem, and Baroness Nica de Koenigswarter lived at 63 Kingswood Avenue in Weehawken, and I remember calling her. I said, 'I've never heard of that Wee waa... ' She said, 'Hawk, as in hawk,' instead of saying the bird I knew—Coleman Hawkins!

So during that winter of '60/'61, Ran waited tables at The Jazz Gallery, while Abbey Lincoln, Max Roach, and their group performed six nights a week. And each time they launched into the *Freedom Now Suite*, the atmosphere in the club was charged with emotion. Patrons responded to the cry for tolerance, and those who cared about the movement (for racial equality) kept coming back for more.

Prominent writers, actors, and thinkers would also be in the audience. Sidney Poitier sat at a table with James Baldwin—Ran, as will be seen, has cause to remember this—and, of course, the Baroness Pannonica de Koenigswarter often came to see Thelonious Monk. As always, she stood out—her nationality, her bearing, her title, her pearls, her Bentley, not to mention her reputation. Her actions were bold and decisive yet overlaid with charming eccentricity. She had rejected the prestige associated with her wealthy upbringing—her house at Weehawken was filled with cats. Apart from her car (Ran remembers her cats were not allowed in the garage nor in the car), she had no interest in possessions. Her kitchen cupboards were full of cat food—there were no ingredients or recipe books as she had never attempted to learn how to cook. Nevertheless, the cats needed to be fed:

> All these cats were coming. They were all over; her bed was very wide. She would get up at 5.30 or 6 [pm], and it looked like Lobster Newberg that she had [for them], but I was told it was not. And you know, she goes to bed 9.30 or 10 in the morning because the sessions get over 8.30 or 9, and she then has a wee bonnie scotch—the Chivas Regal with no ice... and me, I love ice.

Ran arranged that an old friend, Barbara Belgrave,[13] should take care of the meat for Nica's thirty-five or forty cats:

They said she had three hundred and six cats over a twenty-year period, which is amazing. I don't know if Barbara Belgrave was really 'Le Boucher,'[14] but she would bring big quantities from the New York markets and go out and see Nica. She had a key and would go out every week with piles of meat for the animals.

L: Did you get along well with Nica?

R: Yes, I did.... You know, The Jazz Gallery had to fire me because I dropped the coffee on James Baldwin and Sidney Poitier, and every time Monk played, I stumbled, but I remembered... [people's preferences.] 'You wanted a bourbon, you wanted a...' and once Monk said, 'Ran, make me that rice dish'—fried rice—and they said it was so good that I got a job in the kitchen, and then one night, I set the stove on fire, and they said I could leave!

But then, a month later, I got a call that Nica had hired me as her private waiter. And when I came back, I made a mistake—I put a piece of ice in her scotch! She said, 'Never ice—do you remember?' And I never got a tip, and then, on New Year's Eve, I got a hundred dollars, and my parents couldn't get over it when they saw the check from Nica. I'm a 26-year-old kid from Connecticut. I didn't know a thing, except I loved Monk's music. I didn't know about the Rothschild family. I didn't know that she was from one of the most famous, illustrious Jewish families in Europe—Rothschild. They helped people escape Europe. I didn't know about the Rothschild family, but my parents did. My parents called people up—it was just like the Eleanor Roosevelt [invitation]. Suddenly, they just could not get over it!

We framed the check—we've lost it now—but to be given a hundred dollars...[15]

L: What year was that?

R: '61 or '62.

L: So that would have been a lot of money?

R: Yup. When you think that I paid for my apartment in New York a hundred and ten dollars for a bedroom, a guest room, a studio, a living room, a kitchenette—the kitchen wasn't good—and a bath and a small gallery for my paintings: one hundred and ten dollars!

Ran remembers visiting the baroness "only three or two times in life," but she was a life-long friend. It was only natural that it should be so. Ran and the baroness had the same generosity of spirit, the same childlike trust and sense of wonder. Like Ran, she was a lover of animals—particularly cats—and her cats feature in the letters that Ran received from her over many years. These letters are joyful and original. The notepaper she painted for herself is a combination of bold strokes and whimsical design. An assortment of cats—black cats, tabby cats, ginger and white—all beautifully drawn, parade around the edge of the paper; the address in bold red print announces: "The Cat House N.J." The main text is written in thick, blue ink, with words meant to be emphasized printed in red or circled by a curly red cloud. Charming as it was, the baroness never considered her artwork to be good. In 1958, at a dare from Thelonious, she contributed to a group exhibition in New York. She was surprised that her work was taken seriously and shrugged off subsequent interest in how she mixed her colors as her "secret formula." Later, she confessed to using such strange additives as scotch or milk—even perfume.

Nica had an eye for visual composition. Her photographs, many of which appear in her book, *Three Wishes*, are spontaneous and full of character. In July 1986, she wrote to Ran: "This is just a Polaroid I took of Boo Boo,[16] so I don't know if it will be good enough, but I DO [in red!] dig it, don't you???" (Of the three question marks, the middle one is red.) Ran *did* love the photo; it features on the cover of his *Short Life of Barbara Monk* album, which was recorded with Ricky Ford (tenor saxophone), Ed Felson (bass), and Jon Hazilla (drums) two years after Barbara Monk's death.

Nica appreciated Ran as a loyal friend—thoughtful and supportive. She did not hesitate to show this appreciation. In 1971 she sent him a card (complete with extravagant punctuation):

"You could have knocked me down with a feather (??!??) when I opened your letter !!! ~ you REALLY ARE TOO MUCH! (The words are underlined several times in thick strokes of blue and navy.)

She goes on to add that "It couldn't have come at a better moment!"

A letter written in April '82 begins: "Thank you so much for your letter which touched me more than I can say…"

In July '82, she wrote: "Your tape was a GAS (in red) ~ thank you VERY (again, in red) much indeed for it!"

THE BARONESS HAD many compositions dedicated to her, including "Pannonica" by Thelonious Monk, "Nica's Dream" by Horace Silver, "Tonica" by Kenny Dorham, "Blues for Nica" by Kenny Drew, "Nica Steps Out" by Freddie Redd "Nica's Tempo" by Gigi Gryce…

> L: Did you write one, Ran?
> R: I'm in the process of doing one—I think it's going to be some type of a waltz.
> L: Sing us a little line of the melody.
> R: Dum-dar-dum-dar…[*He sings a snatch.*]

L: Well, that sounded good—give us more.
R: No, I can't because it keeps disappearing. I started to work on this, and I got distracted by so many other things—so that's all I'll treat you to in my elegant voice.
L: What key do you reckon it will be in?
R: I don't know.
L: What key do you reckon describes the baroness?
R: I like the key 'E' a lot; I'm tired of the flat keys.
L: Well, you're changing! When we first met, you would have been very much a 'G flat' or an 'A flat' kind of person.
R: Well, maybe in the winter of my life, it changes.
L: You're getting a bit brighter?

6

Mostly Monk

*All these links—all these people linked together.
The Monks—I might have been a footnote to
them, but they were really my New York family
to me.*

RAN BLAKE

At the time when Nica was becoming increasingly devoted to Monk's music—traveling back and forth between New York and her home in Mexico City, before finally moving permanently to New York[1]—Ran Blake, in Suffield Connecticut, had also discovered Monk. In 1952/53, when he first heard "Smoke Gets in Your Eyes" on Hartford radio, he said, "This is amazing!" He'd known the Jerome Kern piece from the 1935 movie, *Roberta*, but he'd never heard it played quite like this before:

> I said, 'Who IS that? This person's out of their mind—and it's SO wonderful! At that time, Monk hadn't joined Riverside, and he was on Prestige—[he had released] two Blue Notes: 1510 and 1511.[2] A few years later, I was working at the Witkowers bookstore in West Hartford, Connecticut, selling records, when I heard the piece 'Criss Cross'—that was 1509.[3] It was on the end of a Milt Jackson LP, and I liked Milt, but I didn't go bonkers, so I just couldn't get over it [this piece].

Like the baroness, Ran would listen to Monk's records "over and over and over and over again."

He started going to see Monk at The Five Spot. By 1957 Harry Colomby[4] (with the assistance of Nica de Koenigswarter) had got Monk's cabaret card restored. (Colomby also arranged for Monk to play at the Five Spot, starting on July 4—a residency that was to become one of the most celebrated in jazz history.)[5] Ran was still at Bard and trying to complete a jazz major—with no assigned jazz teacher. Enterprisingly, he approached Monk and asked for a lesson as part of his study and—as Ran recalls—Monk said:

> 'Sure, you can have a lesson,' and then he winked at his sideman [*Ran mimics the wink*] 'and I'll send your report card.'

Ran took no offense.

> L: Did you ever get that lesson with Monk?
> R: No! [*emphatically*] He even denied... he didn't even remember [about the lesson] when I came back two weeks later to The Five Spot, and then I was too shy to speak to him [about it] again.

On June 14, 1960, Monk opened at the Termini brothers' new club, The Jazz Gallery. He was relaxed; he felt he was among friends. The gig ran for four months and was highly successful—so much so that the Terminis re-signed him on November 15, for a seven-week period, which took them to New Year's Eve.[6]

By this time, the young Ran Blake, newly arrived in New York, had found himself a job as waiter at The Jazz Gallery and was delighted to be able to hear Monk play every night. (In fact, he had to be reminded that his job was to wait tables!) He was working on New Year's Eve; the mood was happy. Ran had brought Nica her Chivas Regal—with no ice—and received a generous tip for his attention. The gig was going very well. Nica and Nellie Monk were there to celebrate—there was no better way to welcome in 1961. Ran had, over the past six weeks, attempted to approach Monk in the hope of private lessons; Monk had, up till then, avoided the subject. However, the mood was special on that New Year's Eve—everyone was feeling good—and somehow Ran was invited to the Monk apartment at 243 West 63rd Street.

JANUARY 1961 WAS cold—very cold—with record snowfalls. From January 19 to February 4, New Yorkers endured sixteen consecutive days of sub-freezing temperatures. February 2 was the coldest day of the year. It was followed by two days of raging blizzard, which brought copious snow and winds of eighty miles per hour. The wind had dropped by February 5, and though still bitterly cold, with snow piled high all around, Ran ventured out to visit Monk.

Unbeknown to him, the previous twenty-four hours had been devastating for the Monk family. A fire caused by faulty electrical wiring had broken out late in the evening on February 4. The fire had begun in a closet, and though the Fire Department were able to contain the flames, much of the apartment and all of the family's belongings (including Monk's rented piano) were ruined by the combined onslaught of fire, smoke, and water. When Ran arrived on the evening of the 5th, the family were back at the apartment, surveying the damage and trying to salvage whatever they could.

From the outside, it was not apparent that there had been a fire, but when no one answered the bell, Ran, sensing something was wrong, pushed the door open and walked in. A scene of devastation greeted him:

> I thought they might be surprised to see me because of the snow, but I had no idea there had been a fire. I just remember opening the door, and all four [Monk, Nellie, Toot, and Boo Boo] were sitting on the bed… [they were] fully clothed—shivering.

Ran, who would prove to be very practical in a crisis, swung immediately into action. He rang Nica, who gave him a list of contacts who could help. He then went out to get dinner for the family—for he could see that the children were unsettled and hungry—before busying himself, contacting other musicians and friends to gather whatever he could in the way of clothes, blankets, and the like. Perhaps, however, his greatest assistance was the time he put into caring for the Monk children, Toot and Boo Boo.[7] For the following four months, Ran devoted himself to their care.

> I think Nellie was so devastated by the fire that she was pleased of the help.

It was a busy period. Contractors were repairing the Monk apartment, and Nellie liked to go there, "cleaning, sweeping the floor."[8] Ran kept the children occupied, happy to be of assistance to his "favorite pianist in the whole world."

> I went there three or four times a week for six weeks. I took the children shopping. I never had a key to their apartment—I probably just barged in. The kids liked it, and I would take them for hamburg-

ers. It was just great. They liked my Jewish landlady. She had them for gefilte fish lunch—they didn't use pepper; they used more seasoning. So, when Miss Lehrfeld came ninety-one, she started having T.S. Monk and Barbara Monk over for afternoon ice cream, and the Monk kids were sliding down the banister at her building and Miss Lehrfeld... DID she love Toots and Boo Boo! She said, 'I feel like a grandmother.'

Greg Flowers[9] had a cute little sister who came to Miss Lehrfeld's once. Miss Lehrfeld loved the little sister, and I just remember her on the phone when her niece Myra invited her to Yonkers, and Miss Lehrfeld said, 'Oh, I can't come—the Monk family are coming!'

And Myra said, 'Oh, he is famous in bebop—why are they coming to see YOU?'

But it's funny; I never took them to see Nica—I went to Nica on my own. I would ask Monk himself to come up to see Miss Lehrfeld, and [I'd ask] Nellie, but they never did. Monk didn't want to meet people.

On Wednesday night, February 22, just over two weeks after the fire, Monk was present at the Nola Studios when Abbey Lincoln, along with Max Roach and the rest of the band,[10] recorded *Straight Ahead*. Lincoln had written lyrics to Monk's "Blue Monk" and obviously wanted his approval. Ran, there for the recording, felt elated by the whole experience. He remembers Monk was thrilled with Abbey's singing. It was at this session, also, that Ran met Mait Edey; Orrin Keepnews[11] was sitting close-by. Simply being present at such a significant recording event was amazing enough, but connections were forming between Ran's own life and the world of New York jazz that were exhilarating.

With Buz Gummere's help, Ran managed to secure a scholarship for the Monk children to attend the Windsor Mountain Summer School. Activities on offer included music, theater, wilderness, and adventure. In the meantime, he helped Toot and Boo Boo select "nice new clothes for the Spring." (Nica had given him $100 to buy children's clothes.) He also continued to take the children to visit his landlady, Amelia Lehrfeld. And if Miss Lehrfeld felt she had a family, so did Ran. Art Lange quotes him as saying:

> They became sort of family. They were my family—I was not their family. There was still a detachment, and I would just be there, half-servial [sic], half-hanging on, probably Monk would say, 'I wish this blue-eyed cat would get out of the house and leave me alone.' But I did run errands; he loved his fried rice.[12]

Monk appreciated Ran's flair for flavor:

> I put in onions, garlic; I brought some spice—Miss Lehrfeld later began to get spice after George Russell visited her—and different herbs and things. So, I created more and more special dishes for Monk with chopped-up shrimp and other things. I got my rice recipe from the Uncle Ben's rice they had at The Jazz Gallery, and I bought Arborio Italian rice and special little packets of herbs. Nellie ate healthy organic cakes; she may have taken one spoonful of rice. I may have cooked at Monk's place five times in all those months, but seems to me I did it fourteen times, but I'm sure it was only five times.
> L: I'll meet you in the middle and say ten times.
> R: Okay. [*readily*]

Five, ten, or fourteen times, Ran was very much at the heart of the family during those visits:

> One time the light went out. Monk was in his room, and I remember getting some kind of a ladder, and I started to change it, and he grabbed me—his arm was tough, and he was tall—and he said, 'That's not your thing, Boy... that's not your karma.' He took a little time before he called me Ran. And to this day, I've never changed... [a light bulb.] I never get above the piano.
> And I remember hearing George Russell on the radio—THAT I'm vivid about. WP New Jersey radio was playing George Russell's first Riverside record, and Thelonious Monk said, 'Now this I like! This is the future wave. This could be the future.'
> George Russell was so happy when I told him that because Thelonious DID NOT know George very well.

It had always been Ran's wish to introduce Monk and George Russell: "I wanted those two giants brought together." But though Ran remembers that Monk "finally got to call me Ran" (while Ran himself maintained the polite "Mr. Monk"), he is uncertain about whether they ever did go to hear George together:

> You know, George came to Columbia [University][13] to hear me play, and I took him [George] out to hear Chris Connor in Boston, but I don't think Monk ever... I would go to where Monk was, and it never occurred to me to bring George. I mean, I felt George knew Monk—he spoke about him politely, and, of course, he recorded 'Round Midnight' with Eric Dolphy, but I don't think George Russell went 'gaga' for Monk, although he knew my obsession.

By summer, the Monk family, though still not back into their apartment on West 63rd Street, felt comfortably "at home" with Nellie's sister,

Skippy. (Nica's home at Weehawken had become Monk's second home.) Things were getting back on track, and by May or June, Ran was seeing them less:

> I did see the children at their aunt's house—do you know the piece called "Skippy" by Monk? It's one of the hardest pieces you've ever done, and Skippy lived right behind Jeanne Lee's parents.[14] Nellie's brother had a daughter called Jackie, and she was one of my closer friends—I've lost touch with her now—Jackie Bonneau.[15] And of course, Thelonious wrote a piece called 'Jacki-ing,' and that's on one of his Riverside's... pah pah pah pah pah pah [*He starts singing*] ... that tritone 'dah-pah,' and it's one of the delightful, easier pieces of Monk.

RAN NOW FELT very much at home in New York City, and his career was going places. He was rehearsing with Jeanne Lee, and by the end of 1961, they had experienced some success at the Apollo, as well as having recorded *The Newest Sound Around*. This was followed in 1962 by a performance at the Monterey Jazz Festival and then their first European tour in 1963.

> But you know I moved to Boston in '67. I went with Jeanne Lee to Europe in '66. Years went quickly; like, I'm getting to know the Monk family in '61/62; I go to Europe in '63 and again in '66/'67; I come back, and I know I take Barbara Monk to a thanksgiving dinner...

The '60s were an important period in Monk's life. He was very popular—the name on everyone's lips. In Europe, he received critical acclaim and was swamped by fans at airports. He signed with Columbia in 1962, and on February 28, 1964, his face looked out from a striking red background on the cover of *Time Magazine*. Fame, however, brought media speculation about the nature of Monk's sometimes eccentric and seemingly detached behavior. *Time Magazine* referred to him as "the loneliest Monk." But Ran knew a different man:

> Monk was nobody's fool—he was very sharp. And I think that he did not suffer fools. He liked to be mysterious... and dancing. He knew the media would heat up.

After moving to Boston, Ran would catch up with the Monk family a couple of times a year when he visited New York. Monk had been touring and playing extensively, but his health was suffering and the relationship with Columbia souring. Nellie, concerned for his health, researched juices and restorative foods:

> In the '70s and '80s, Nellie ran a juice bar on Broadway—frozen carrot juice. Nellie appreciated me coming as a customer, and I would buy the Gummere family a lot of that frozen juice. For years I had a key to Richard Gummere's apartment at 325 Riverside Drive, and of course, Barbara Belgrave was [near] there, and many of my connections would go up to that apartment, and I would bring them juice.
> The juice came in plastic—you could see right through it—it was a big square. I know Nellie ran the store. She had one assistant. I think they lived ten blocks below Gunther, but I know Marjorie Schuller came to love their carrot juice […], and they would fill my bag with fruit sometimes. I don't think the kids were at the store much, and I never saw Mr. Monk there.

By early 1969, Ran was in Boston, working at New England Conservatory:

> I would beg him [Monk] to come to the Conservatory. He wouldn't come. They were always warm—particularly Nellie—when I ran into them.

On one occasion, he saw Nellie and Thelonious at the Parker House Hotel.[16]

> They were playing out of a very good venue. And to stay at Parker House… The Parker House was then the 'Ritz' of prestigious hotels. I think sometime in the early '60s, it was $12 for an egg and a cup of coffee—that was really high money. And I remember Nellie giving me a whole pile of twenty-dollar bills—about two hundred dollars—and [were they] FAMOUS! They'd heard about me in Greece. Nellie said, 'You have been very good to us.'
> And then, by '69 or '70, it [all the fame] had passed, and then around '71, Columbia drops him. Then in about '73, he begins to become a recluse, and I was at his last concert in Carnegie Hall,[17] and he appeared once at Bradley's Bar; I don't think I was there. And then I'm reminded, he moved to the baroness's house in New Jersey.

Ran would also see Monk when he came up to play at the Jazz Workshop (in '69 and '70) and at Lennie's-on-the-Turnpike[18] in 1972 (known, at the time, for its roast beef on pumpernickel sandwiches).

> Monk would be appearing a lot at Lennie's-on-the-Turnpike. You'd have to go north of Boston for twenty miles, and I would go there and hear Chris Connor and Monk and a lot of other people.
> Monk seemed to talk to me more at Lennie's. He wouldn't come up to my table, but I would go in the dressing room if there was one, and he wouldn't ask about school, [he] would just ask, 'How are you doing?'

Monk battled with illness for ten years before his death on February 17, 1982. Ran flew down for the funeral. Barbara Monk's death, from cancer, followed her father's by less than two years. This was too much for Ran to bear. He remembered her as a little girl, sliding down Miss Lehrfeld's banisters or ice-skating in Central Park.

> I started to fly down for Barbara's funeral and got sick at Logan Airport...

Barbara died on January 10, 1984. The memorial service at Riverside Church was on January 17. Her cousin Jackie contacted Ran soon after via a little note dated 2/13/84:

> Dear Ran
> Just a note to say, 'Hello.' I'm fine. Nellie and Toot are holding on as best they can. Enclosed is a copy of Boo Boo's services. I thought you might like to have a copy.
> Take care. Love Always,
> [and it's signed] Jackie and Family

In 1986 Ran released his album, *Short Life of Barbara Monk*, on Soul Note. Here, he plays in a quartet made up of his former NEC students (bassist Ed Felson, drummer Jon Hazilla, and tenor saxophonist Ricky Ford.[19]) The album cover photo was taken by Nica de Koenigswarter.

Two years later, there was a big tribute to Monk staged at the Lincoln Square Amphitheater:

> I saw Nellie two or three times after Monk's death and told her how sorry I was—and then there was Barbara's funeral at Riverside. I phoned Nellie occasionally, but it would be only every other year. It was so great seeing her at that big Lincoln Center dedication.[20] The Lincoln Center was packed. All the people came from North Carolina. There were people dressed in white—choirs; church people

from Rocky Hill... I remember so many people came up from Rocky Mount, North Carolina, where Monk was born, and I met nieces from there, and they knew Monk played piano, but they really didn't know; they had no conception... They knew the Lincoln Center was like the White House of New York City, so they knew it was something pretty important, but I didn't sense they knew [just how big he was].
And after that, Nellie had me back to their very new modern apartment—almost at the deluxe end of the street.

Some months after this tribute, Ran wrote to Nellie at her West 85th Street apartment. (January 6, 1989)

Nellie,
You have been such a strength of support throughout your life for others.
If I ask you to think of yourself, I may never win the argument.
So my latest idea for 1989 is that you consider recreating those delicious vegetable drinks you produced in the '70s. Maybe you should not be burdened with managing your own store, but it would be wonderful if you could find a couple of partners and bring back your carrot cocktail, plus invent a green vegetable drink and perhaps a tart fruit one.
My love to you, Nellie

THE LINK BETWEEN Ran and the Monk family is still strong, as is Ran's admiration for Monk as a musician. After more than fifty years, Ran can say, "Monk, still, is most unique." On April 15, 2011, T.S. Monk was performing at Scullers Jazz Club in Cambridge. John Campopiano,[21] who accompanied Ran to the gig, was touched when T.S., spotting Ran, introduced him to the audience. T.S. emphasized the fact that not just "anyone" could be admitted to the inner Monk family circle. "Ran was a special case." In the break, Ran and T.S. talked of New York in the '60s (and friends there), of carrot juice and "peeling pounds and pounds of carrots for days and days." They talked about the fire, and T.S. told Ran, "My father would be so proud of what you've done." For John "Campo," the highlight of the night was when T.S. invited his son over to meet Ran: "Hearing T.S. say to his son, 'This is Ran Blake. He was a friend of your grandfather's,' was very touching." As John saw it: "Generations of stories and memories were coalescing."

7

TEACHERS

Dear Ran,
In any school, in any city, in any country, in any world, there is <u>no-one</u> quite like you. God love and keep you going forever.
My love, always – Margaret Chaloff, '76[1]

The New York Ran remembers when he moved there in 1960 was vibrant and colorful. Throbbing with humanity, it was a meeting place of cultures and ideas. For Ran, its beating heart was jazz, and from his experience at the Lenox School, he knew who he needed to meet and what he wanted to achieve there. He immersed himself in all that the city had to offer while, at the same time, assiduously pursuing his musical formation—for he had an undeniable capacity for self-direction.

The teachers from whom he took lessons in New York were central to his experience of that great city—they would have a profound influence on his musical development and, indeed, his own teaching. Getting to these lessons were high-points of excitement and anticipation—each step of the way was savored. They remain as markers in an intricate memory map of this period. Ran has created his own 'List of Teachers,' arranged into various time periods, and this chapter will keep to his list.

Lenox Teachers

Oscar Peterson

The Music Inn at Lenox had, for Ran, "atmosphere and an unbelievable faculty"[2] which included Gunther Schuller, George Russell, Kenny Dorham, Max Roach, Dizzy Gillespie, John Lewis, Percy Heath, Jimmy Giuffre, Bill Russo, Bill Evans, Willis Laurence James, and Oscar Peterson. Ran recalls that he took studio with Oscar Peterson during the first two years of Lenox. He fondly remembers Peterson's enthusiasm and how encouraging he was. Peterson also gave Ran three lessons during Ran's period of work experience at Atlantic Records.[3]

Gunther Schuller[4]

> Gunther had me study the Beethoven symphonies, but I still can be fooled. He said, 'Mozart's a lost game for you Ran, you'll never have the patience.'
> There was an opera by Ravel[5] [and the] *Rite of Spring*.[6] There were about four or five records, but we never quite... we always had so many plans, and we ran out of time. I played a lot of piano, and he'd say, 'Why are you wandering off course?'
> And I said, 'Well Cecil Taylor once said that it's good to extend pieces, and Gunther didn't answer; he went like that [*Ran purses his lips to demonstrate*] because he also admired Cecil Taylor. So, I don't know what he felt. I know that I had to have that ability not to censure every minute because that would corrupt my performance. He said it was a very worthwhile experience to write something and learn how to edit it. He said, 'You have to edit, but don't over-scrutinize. And you have to be aware if you are going away from the frame.'
> So much of the lessons were on me gaining a sense of form. He felt because of the nature of the orchestra or the sounds, that form was very important, that you should go right to the target. Then he would put on *Pastoral Symphony* and get me to listen to that... and to listen to what Bartok did in *Suite for Celesta*.[7]

Harlem Teachers

LaVerne Powell and Hugh Porter

I remember walking through Morningside Park on 116th Street—walking through Spanish Harlem. Or I could do my favorite route, walking down 123rd by a Vietnamese restaurant on 123rd and Amsterdam, and then I would make a right-hand turn to Sweet Daddy Grace's church, and diagonally across the street was the Apollo Theater. If I was hungry, there was chicken and waffles at Joe Wells' Supper Club, and then I would walk further down, and if you could see *The Pawnbroker*...[8] [that's what it was like.]

Then you go down to Park Avenue—which was elegant in the '90s—and I got to know that block. And one [either Powell or Porter] was on the second floor, and one was on the third floor—walk-up—and they had little signs outside the window—Gospel Piano, Jass: j-a-s-s [*He spells it.*] Piano. And I've never forgotten that.

Miss Powell really slapped me once in Harlem—she could be quite critical. But it was really the happiest six years. Jeanne Lee would come down to Miss Lehrfeld's every Sunday, and Jeanne Lee became quite a teacher, moving through Billie Holiday. And she taught me "One Mint Julep"—Ray Charles recorded it.

Mary Lou Williams

Ran first saw Mary Lou Williams play when his parents took him to the Composer's Lounge, where she was playing alternate sets with the Billy Taylor Trio (which included Earl May and Ed Thigpen). John Mehegan was the opening act:

> We came early to see the cocktail set which John Mehegan was playing. He was my teacher at the Juilliard extension program. He had many books published on jazz piano; he had records out too. He would be the opening act, and [then] Mary Lou would go on.

Mary Lou Williams, by this time, was a veteran performer, having made her debut with a band at the age of twelve (in 1922).[9] A child prodigy, she'd cut her first solo record by the time she was twenty. With the emergence of bebop, she moved to New York City and got to know many of that style's principal innovators. She had first met Thelonious Monk in Kansas City in 1935; in New York, they became close friends.[10] In 1943, Mary Lou had a regular engagement at the Cafe Society and from there moved to the Uptown Cafe on 59th Street. Then, Bop City opened (where The Hurricane used to be), and Mary Lou worked there.[11] She had an apartment on Hamilton Terrace, and everyone who was "anyone in the jazz world" would be drawn there to talk, listen to music, and try out new compositions.[12] Monk, who had begun to write more and to see himself as a composer, "trusted Mary Lou's ear and her frank opinions,"[13] and, as he was "something of a big brother and mentor to [Bud] Powell,"[14] he introduced him to these gatherings as well.[15]

But Mary Lou's interests extended beyond playing and discussing music. In 1958 (after converting to Catholicism in 1954), she established the Bel Canto Foundation. It aimed to help needy musicians and was funded, in part, by a thrift shop on Amsterdam Avenue.[16]

> [...] on 2nd or 3rd Avenue near East 56th Street and not far from the Bellevue Hospital. In Dahl's book,[17] she mentions that this foundation was further uptown, and perhaps the main corridors were, but I distinctly remember a storefront shop where people donated clothing and other necessities for people with great needs. You know, all these people had shops—Nellie Monk was in frozen carrot juice and green juice; Mary Lou was clothing. I tried to raise money for the Bel Canto Foundation—I don't think I brought in $10.

Ran made his first personal contact with Mary Lou Williams at Bel Canto:

> [I asked her if I could take some lessons from her] I think she said, 'Come and meet me at Bel Canto.' She wanted to look me over and all that.
> And so I came to New York a couple of times, and she so kindly arranged that I stay [overnight] with a friend of hers, named Kurt, who had a wonderful modest support apartment on far East 57th Street—which must be a very elegant area these days.

Ran also saw Mary Lou Williams perform at Lenox in 1958 when, along with Joe Turner and Pete Johnson, she appeared at The Music Barn. (In his third year there, she was visiting faculty.) Ran remembers that, after the evening's program, Mary Lou and Anita O'Day did a "short, impromptu concert at the Inn, in a lounge area adjacent to the large dining room."[18]

He says that she was a "divine accompanist" and hastens to add that she was just as important as Anita and wasn't just "cocktail accompaniment." The pair did "What's Your Story Morning Glory," "Night in Tunisia," "Body and Soul," and "I Can't Get Started." Ran remembers "how beautifully Mary Lou caressed the keyboard."

When Ran moved to New York City, he recalls he had lessons with Mary Lou at her home on Hamilton Terrace in Sugar Hill in Harlem.

> [I had] five lessons in life [with Mary Lou Williams]. I went up to Sugar Hill in Harlem. I would walk down 125th Street, west towards 8th Avenue and take a subway to Sugar Hill—this was in '58/'59/'62. I think she lived at 63 Hamilton Terrace. It was Number 63 because I remember Nica Koenigswarter lived at 63 Kingswood Road, Weehawken... the baroness was not my teacher, but she taught me life!

Everything about these lessons with Mary Lou Williams was memorable:

> She had high cheekbones and beautiful black hair—majesty! She dressed beautifully—I think she didn't try to overdress—she looked beautiful. I remember walking through the door, and then I made a right-hand turn in the building, so it might have been a first-floor apartment. When I walked in, a Counsel upright piano was on my left, and straight ahead was a sofa. There was another room, and there must have been a kitchen. There was a rug, and I want to say a bay window on my right... this is amazing, but I think I'm right! You know, I can't describe Mal Waldron's house, and I was there more often in Queens. I can't even remember Bill Russo's, but I think on some of the points, [about Mary Lou's] I'm right.
>
> There were three pauses where she reached for her rosary beads—she had become Catholic. So, we would pray; then, I would play piano. She was basically very reserved on her feelings about my music, though she did feel I had talent,[19] and she said, 'Where's your pulse? Can we have this correct?' And she had—not a ruler—but by hand, she beat on my hand, and I was so proud—I had a little red spot! And the next day, I went back to Connecticut, and I said, 'Mary Lou Williams did this!' And the postman said, 'Who's that?' and I said, 'The Queen of Jazz Piano.' And then, [*resuming story*] we would move to chairs in that same room and pray again... I don't remember being on my knees.

Then there would be more music, and she would say, 'Hold on, I think we need another kind of nourishment,' and the plate of divine fried chicken came out. She said, 'Will you have some fire-water?' and I got a nice scotch on the rocks with water. I thought, 'Gee, can I have more ice?' but I thought that was my Connecticut foibles. I got there at four—thank God I made no plans for a couple of nights—at seven or eight o'clock, I'm still there! And we go back to the rosary…
L: And what did you think, Ran, when she asked you to pray? That would seem really weird! How did you respond to it?
R: Well, in so many ways, I was naive; I just took it. I'd heard about it from Russo. She really felt that God helped her. She really gave me something to think about—both spiritual and a feeling for the blues and the past. She really did help me rhythmically. Mary Lou was something!

Looking back on those lessons, Ran can see the various elements of Mary Lou Williams' teaching style:

the meditation, concrete piano work, and then…there wasn't always food or wine, but the small talk at the end [which] would be [about] how was I doing, how were my studies; there would always be…not a real hug but a warm pat on the back.

It was later, in the 1970s, that Ran would again experience this warm and genuine support. As he recalls:

Mary Lou had a residency at the Cookery, a very brightly lit, rather noisy club on a corner on 8th Street, near 5th Avenue. Although I have an ego, I'm sure friends will attest to the fact that I don't often go up and play at someone else's gig. However, one night, Ms. Williams invited me to sit next to her at the piano and do a couple of pieces with her. There was a smattering of applause, but Barney Josephson—the manager—was furious. How could I do this to a jazz legend?
Mary Lou neither exonerated me nor criticized me. She gave me an earthy smile as [if to say] 'if this was all I had to worry about in life… [I'd be okay].' In an earlier encounter, we had talked about my being humble but also gaining confidence, and I thought this might be a test. Her eyes never wavered.[20]

NEW YORK CITY TEACHERS

Bill Russo

I did one hundred and twenty—or was it one hundred, or ninety—written lessons with Bill Russo,[21] which included elements of Paul Hindemith,[22] counterpoint, writing a jazz score and preparing it. There was reading of Mozart sonatinas for two pianos, which I think now, in retrospect, he wanted to practice himself. I didn't play with Bill that much, so his lessons were really getting ready to do things I hadn't done so thoroughly at Bard College. I feel I worked with him from 1960, and there was one point that Bill said he would not take me for any more lessons unless I worked solely with him, so I had to stop with Gunther. In one way, that was good—to focus on Bill—but when I came back to Gunther, he never had the time that he used to. By '63/'64, Gunther was incredibly busy, every minute he was jumping.

Russo, I would pay twenty-five dollars for two lessons a week (one and a half hours each), and I think I told you I took the Broadway local subway to the next to last stop—the stop south of Van Cortlandt Park. Broadway was gentile-shabby, but it was very safe. Then I'd either walk to his house or, if it was raining, bus [there]. His address was Blackstone Avenue in Riverdale, New York—that's the West Bronx. That's where George Avakian lived, too—you look at the Hudson, and they are beautiful homes. I met a shoe man that made these beautiful black bags, and I bought my bag there—the bag that appears on my records.[23]

Then Jeremy [Jeremy Warburg—Russo's wife at the time] would often give me a little lunch. I really scored a lot of meals with the Russos, Mal Waldron, [and] Mary Lou Williams.... But Bill Russo was awfully important to me, and Hankus[24] feels that he is one of my great influences—where I got all of my chords—from just hearing his music with the ear.

Mal Waldron

L: Was it because you saw Mal Waldron at the Jazz Gallery playing with Max Roach and Abbey Lincoln that you got lessons?
R: No, I knew his music before. But seeing him every night, I said, 'I've got to study with him. He's fabulous.' And, at first, he said, 'No,' and I said, 'Oh please, Mr. Waldron.' Now, he's probably only two years older than me, but I'm from Connecticut—it's very formal—we say, 'Mr.' 'Mother Carter,' 'Bishop Jefferson.'
I would take a subway to Queens, get off at St. Albans, and I worked on "With a Song in my Heart" and a piece he wrote for Gene Ammons called "Ammon Joy." Those would be evening lessons, and quite often, they would be on Monday—his evening off from the Jazz Gallery. It took about an hour to get there. His wife was Elaine, and they had a two-floor house, and lessons would be an hour and a half. I'm dreaming they had two pianos, but I can't remember. So, a lot of it would be hands-on—exchanging twos and fours. He must have sat next to me on the piano; we would trade hands. There was not much homework—it was really ensemble work. There would be a few pieces to learn—one was called "Straight Ahead," which he co-wrote for the Abbey Lincoln album.

Martin Williams

We should look and see when The Jazz Tradition was published.[25] A great many of our lessons—and there may have been eight or nine formal ones—were things he was writing about. And I studied with him two times when I was at Atlantic Records. I had to know the chorus plans. (There was no piano work, and I really don't think there was much writing.) I had to critique what I was listening to. He found that I had a marvelous breadth to my listening […] that I was going so many places: from Greek Bouzouki bars to the Deutsch Village on East 86th Street to Jelly Roll Morton's "Grandpa Spells"—I couldn't sing the melody for you. We skipped Lester Young—he said I wasn't ready. I flipped over [Horace] Silver and then Monk, and I think for once I might have gotten ahead there.
Lessons started in 1958 January—boy, is that so long ago.

Max Roach

I met Max Roach at Lenox in the summer of '57 and only had one real private lesson with him when we talked about voicing on the piano. He knew all about it; he was very thorough. He said on the next lesson, we could play duets—he would get his drums out, and we could play. But that was the one year that my parents paid for me, and I wasn't earning my keep, so I couldn't run over my budget as each lesson might have been sixty or seventy dollars then.

BERKLEE CLASSES

Richard Appleman, Yakov Gubanov, Ken Pullig, and Herb Pomeroy

These were not private teachers—these were classes I took.
Ken Pullig's class on Mingus was one of the greatest courses. I got up every Friday morning to be there at school at nine o'clock. I didn't pay. Students would wander in late. I was just fascinated the way he would discuss Mingus. He had a breadth of vision and notational ability, and it inspired me to get back to Mingus, so he was such a fascinating teacher.
Yakov Gubanov I just worked with two years ago at Berklee on the history of Shostakovich.[26] It was an undergraduate level [class]. There was not a great deal of delving in[to] it, but it covered wonderful things. I got to know Shostakovich as a politician, a man of fear.
Richard Appleman—of the Fringe—gave a course on the history of bass players—this was the 1990s.

NEC Classes

Peter Row

Peter Row gave me a lot of thinking exercises, so I would call him a mentor; I probably shouldn't call him a teacher. But he told me to think in the future and to think of goals and to do steps backward, so I thought he was avant-garde, and a lot of the knowledge and structural organization I got might be a jigger in my large glass of water, so I would say he was a thinking influence.

Alan Chase

L: You take a lot of classes and often not in your comfort zone. You did the Chase course with me, and there was a lot of transcription, and I know written notation is not your strength, but you will submit yourself to that. Whereas others would feel pressure to be at their best in front of students, you are the first to reveal your own weaknesses! Where did that come from?
R: I think I get a pressure to teach well.

IN BOSTON, RAN came into contact with a legendary piano teacher. Known to her students as "Madame Chaloff," she taught many great jazz pianists including Chick Corea, Herbie Hancock, Mulgrew Miller, Keith Jarrett, and Kenny Werner. Despite being known in the jazz piano world, there was a certain underground "mystique" that preceded her.

Many of her students studied at NEC. Her emphasis was touch—concentrating on the breath to help achieve a weightlessness in the arms. She would not allow students to progress until they had managed to make a single note "sing."[27]

> I studied with Mme. Chaloff—I said, 'I'm here for technique and your pearly wisdom.'

I had to repeat one number over and over again with touch, pedal... she was AMAZING!

Ran is passionate about his teaching. He knows that to be a good teacher, he must be a co-learner—there must be an emotional bond with students. For Ran—whose own education was punctuated by see-sawing emotions: the heightened thrill of multiple viewings of *Spiral Staircase* balanced by quiet reflection in the Mulberry Street Cemetery—education is an emotional as well as an intellectual adventure. As a teacher, it is an adventure he re-lives in the company of his students.

8

GEORGE RUSSELL

L: So, with George Russell—and don't yell at me if you've already said this—when did you first meet, and then how many times did you see him in New York?
R: [*sitting resigned, head in hands—his tone long-suffering*] I met George Russell for the first time in the Year of Our Lord, the Savior[1] 1957... when His Majesty, John Lewis, the director of the School of Jazz at Lenox—L-E-N-O-X [*he spells it loudly*] invited George Russell to look him up for a lecture. The lecture took place in the front hall of Wheatleigh, the latest piece of property that Stephanie and Philip Barber had acquired. George had JUST released his RCA Victor album, which I'd heard part of... So, I called up everybody and his brother to come! I was thrilled to be there for this evening.

WHEN GEORGE RUSSELL came on stage at Wheatleigh Hall, Lenox, that memorable summer of 1957[2] and gave his "customary" bow (with his "little wink at the audience"), Ran could scarcely contain his excitement. He knew Russell as "the king of the New York underground."[3] George Russell inhabited a world that Ran longed to know. At that moment, when the immaculately groomed and poised Russell began to address the assembly, the twelve years' difference in age and experience seemed enormous.

Yet, the two men had much in common. In both of them, a catholic appreciation of music (with early exposure to classical, gospel, and, of course, jazz) had helped form a completely original musical conception. Informed by the past but not defined by it, both men would remain true to their artistic voice with a sense of dogged perseverance to honor their talent—for they were both gifted with the type of talent that brings insight (both would eventually receive MacArthur Foundation fellowships[4]). It was probably inevitable that they would become great friends.

On that day at Lenox, as Russell launched straight into the discussion of his Lydian Chromatic Concept of Tonal Organization, Ran Blake hung off every word. John Lewis, minutes earlier, had introduced him as having, as Ran recalls, "a unique design for the future of tomorrow's music."[5]

Russell's insight into the interrelatedness of linear and harmonic musical elements is profound and far-reaching. According to his book,[6] his concept does not privilege a particular type of music but encompasses all music. As Russell states: "It's only for those who can think big. It is huge. It covers all of music." And so the book has Coltrane in it, but it also has Bach, and it also has Ravel. "What I did is a ladder of fifths and built up to this magnificent all-in-one scale. All scales are within the Lydian Chromatic Scale."[7]

It was a mammoth task and a significant contribution to musical scholarship. George's wife, Alice, sees it as the fulfillment of a life's work of which she feels privileged to have been a part—a "beautiful book"[8] that will continue to inform musical composition and analysis in the 21st century.

Ran remembers George Russell's appearance at the 1957 Lenox School of Jazz as the highlight of his 1957 summer. Later at Bard, Ran played and re-played Russell's *The Jazz Workshop*[9] until he'd worn it out. He was a "major fan." In 1958, George Russell joined the faculty at Lenox, and he and his then-wife, Juanita,[10] moved to the school for three weeks; Ran asked him if he would come to the Bard Jazz Festival:

> And it's my feeling that he came up for one of the panel discussions: 'Is there a Future for Jazz?'

Ran also had a few lessons at George's apartment, at 121 Bank Street, in the "very far west of Greenwich Village."

> It was not a long contract like it was with Gunther Schuller or Bill Russo, but I went down there. Unbeknownst to me, I guess Juanita and George had broken up. I was very naive of relationships—I just cared about music and [film] noir.

When Ran moved to New York in September 1960, he got into the habit of dropping in to see George at Bank Street after rehearsing with Jeanne Lee at her neighboring apartment.[11] In their discussions, George expressed an "appreciation of harmonic innovation, but he also often felt harmony inflicted tyranny on solo artists. He mentioned that he felt that a lot of his writing might inspire young improvisers to explore modal directions."[12]

He was one of a handful of people I knew in the whole of the city.

So when Miss Lehrfeld, Ran's landlady, gave him permission to have a small gathering in the apartment on 113th Street, Ran invited George Russell. And George, with his natural charm, had no difficulty winning the straightlaced Miss Lehrfeld's approval. (And, the approval of her nephew, once George had introduced Miss Lehrfeld to his special "grape juice.")

> He came up to see me all of five times [at Miss Lehrfeld's]. I used to use a whirring blender, and I made a drink called [The] George Russell and another drink called [The] Thelonious Monk Mist—George liked that better than the drink I made for him.

George, who had worked in a soda shop and as a fast-food cook when he first moved to New York, was, as Ran will attest, a good cook who made a "delectable jambalaya."

Ran frequented George's gigs; he heard him six nights in a row at Birdland. George took an interest in Ran's music also. He came to hear him play at Columbia University, and, in return, Ran took him to hear Chris Connor in Boston. It was Ran's great wish to bring the two giants—as he called Russell and Monk—together. However, Ran felt that Monk did not want to meet people, so the introduction did not go ahead. Ran does recall, however, a time in Monk's apartment when Monk commented on Russell's music—Ran can still clap his hands in delight at the memory:

> The radio—WP New Jersey radio—was playing George Russell's first Riverside record, and Thelonious Monk said, 'Now this I like—this is the future wave. This could be the future.' George Russell was so HAPPY when I told him that because Thelonious did NOT know George very well.

Later, in 1961, when RCA/Victor discontinued Russell's *The Jazz Workshop*, Ran took it upon himself to collect signatures to petition RCA for its re-release. The petition gathered many influential signatures.[13]

George understood Ran's enthusiasm: for people, for music, for New York life. As a young man, he had embraced New York too. When he first came to the city in his early twenties, he'd immersed himself in the music scene there. It was a special time—one he'd talked about with his wife Alice, who can recount:

> When he was young, in The Village, he and Bill Evans and Miles, Bobby Brookmeyer and Gerry Mulligan, and John Lewis used to meet in the basement of Bill's apartment, and they would go up to Juilliard to hear the orchestras being rehearsed—Stravinsky, Debussy (that's the first classical musician George ever turned to, in Cincinnati when he was a kid).

After meeting Ran, George also visited Ran's parents in Suffield, Connecticut:

> George Russell had drinks with my parents. He and my father got along well, and he fell in love with my mother. He called her the 'apple dumpling'—he LOVED her. On one of his visits, he met I.L. Jefferson and Hubert Powell of the Church of God in Christ, and he met my 'stepmother,' Sarah Carter, you know, they're stricter than the Catholic Church—there you don't eat meat on Fridays, but at the Church of God in Christ, you couldn't go to movies... no gambling [and] no wine. I said no problem to gambling [and] wine. I said I'd go to the church, but [*shaking his head*] I COULD NOT give up film noir. They made me a part-time...I couldn't become a full-time member of the church, but I got saved there.
> But [*returning to the topic*] George was so impressed with Hubert Powell's writing that he spoke to Gunther, and we arranged to have the church come up to appear in Jordan Hall, and there's a tape of that in the library and a review by Richard Dyer.
> And until four years ago,[14] George had the best memory. He would know what my mother served... I know they had a pecan pie with crème brûlée... ah, crème fraîche and probably my mother's spiced tomatoes; her cooking got better and better when she knew my New York taste.

Russell toured Europe with his sextet in 1964 and remained there. He lived in Scandinavia for five years, working mainly in Norway and Sweden, where he had the opportunity to expand his writing for larger ensembles. (He had already written the suite *All About Rosie* in 1957.)

George and Ran met up again in 1966 in Oslo, Norway (where George was living). It was not long into Ran's second European tour. The days were short with winter approaching, but it was a pleasant little sojourn during which Ran heard part of *Othello*, a ballet suite that George had produced and composed.[15] All the Norwegian engagements in this early part of the tour were "courtesy of George" and their mutual friend, Marit Jerstad, who, Ran recalls, "paid the plane." Ran would return to Norway following a disastrous experience in Greece in 1967.[16] George was very supportive then; however, their friendship—and life paths—were destined to become even closer. This came about through Gunther Schuller.

Gunther Schuller had met George Russell through their mutual friend John Lewis in 1948.[17] They had subsequently worked together on the Brandeis Creative Arts Festival in June of 1957.[18] Schuller had commissioned Russell and four other musicians to each write a piece for a special concert at the culmination of the festival. Schuller himself would also contribute a work.[19] Schuller felt that what was achieved in this concert and the associated recording was a first "in the history of music" and "more clearly and firmly clarified what the third-stream concept meant."[20] Thus, when he was looking to formalize the jazz studies program at New England Conservatory in September of 1969, he turned to George Russell. It was natural that he would want the unique talents of George Russell—as a musician, theorist, and composer—as a foundation member of his new department. Ran was delighted to have his friend, who he regarded as "a master of all music," as a colleague:

> It's '69, so by then, George is in Cambridge—living on Martin Street, I believe—a few blocks north of Harvard Square. For a while—before he got the apartment—a college friend, Carroll (and her husband Steve Moshier), rented him a small suite in their apartment in North Cambridge. And I may have that wrong; maybe George stayed in New York and only came a day or two a week. But then he met Alice,[21] and they moved here when he became full-time.

George found the task of promoting jazz studies a difficult one. Among the "old guard" of classical faculty, there was a significant number who resisted the inclusion of a jazz program. They simply did not take jazz seriously.

Alice recognized this difficulty; for her, there is still an underlying hurt:

> So, coming to NEC... it gave George a base salary and some benefits, and he felt an allegiance to it for that reason—he was grateful for whatever support he was getting. [*she smiles*] He also wasn't a fool about it. He realized how little he was getting paid compared to the other faculty. He demanded a raise—which he got. And at a certain point, everything turned, and George was their golden boy—he couldn't do anything wrong. Neither of us bought into that—we knew why...[22]

Both George and Ran worked very hard, promoting the school. As Alice explains:

> Ran worked hard to build up the credibility, the curriculum, and the veracity of the third-stream because, at first, everybody thought it was a depository for people who really couldn't do… you know, 'real music' very well, and now it has become the thing that the university mentions in all their PR. Ran and the third-stream—He persevered.

Even though George Russell hated recruiting (he was a musician, not a businessman), he sought to promote the jazz and third-stream programs at NEC in whatever ways he could. It was, in fact, through a recruiting visit to The Community Music School in St Louis in 1976 that George met Alice (who was, at that time, the director of the St. Louis school). The school—a non-profit organization where tuition rates were set according to the student's income—sought to give everyone a chance to learn from the very best musicians. As part of a longstanding relationship, the St Louis school hosted yearly auditions for the New England Conservatory, and faculty from NEC would travel to St Louis to conduct auditions.

From 1977 till his death in July 2009, Alice was very much part of George Russell's life work. She remembers his dedication to his work at the conservatory and to his musical theory and the book he had written (and continued to revise):

> I don't think he came to like being classified as a teacher, but he was so dedicated to his work—he didn't miss a class unless he was ill. Even in his later years, he would get up out of bed after no sleep and insist on going. Also, he was very conscientious because, as a kid, he'd learned to be. He was dedicated to his aim, and his aim continued till the end of his life.

In this dedication, George and Ran were of one mind.

> L: So, George… did he like what you were doing musically?
> R: He said he did. He obtained some of my records. He was very good about getting to a lot of my concerts, which many faculty members did NOT do. And I went to everything he did—he must have done thirty to thirty-five Jordan Hall concerts.… Does that bother you when I put my hand over my eye? I'm just looking at his face on Jordan Hall stage! He was quite a dancer and a conductor. When it was time to go home, he would dance down the stage and do "So What" by Miles Davis. [*There is a long pause—Ran has his hand back to his eye. Eventually, in a little muffled voice, he adds*] I think he felt under-appreciated.
> L: Do you think he felt under-appreciated within the jazz department or within the conservatory as a whole?

R: I think both—but I guess in the conservatory as a whole. I know, my first years, I went to a number of concerts…. You know, it takes time to support other people—to do a good job when you've students and [need] to prepare for your classes. Many people… ah, you know… a lot of faculty only come up a couple of days a week and then go back to New York, so there isn't a campus; there really isn't a very warm relationship. I think George felt that a lot of people registered for the Lydian Concept were not committed to [the] long-term study [of it].

When it came to performing, George was unequaled, and Ran's vision of George on the Jordan Hall stage reveals something of his friend's energy and charisma. Alice also pays tribute to George, the performer and conductor:

> He was a Cancer, so he could be very introverted and quiet, but when he was on stage in front of the band, he… was great! I must say, his concerts, as far as the jazz concerts go at NEC, were the best ever; you couldn't top them. I don't think they ever will be [topped] because they were exciting, you know. He was a great conductor who wrote great music and had a lot of energy. And to see him in front of the band in Jordan Hall, shaking his booty…[*She smiles broadly at the memory.*]
> R: [*in agreement*] You should have seen it, Janet!

George's charisma also appealed to Dorothy Wallace, the great patron of jazz and third-stream at New England Conservatory. Ran had introduced them, soon after George came to Boston, and explains:

> It was at a big party, and I think she [Dorothy] said he was the most handsome man she'd ever seen. He would say, 'Hello, Madame.' He liked his own music, but he would do a little bit of "Mood Indigo" and "I Get a Kick Out of You" for her. He knew how to tantalize. They both liked the cocktails.
> When Dorothy Wallace said, 'Who would you like [to invite] for dinner?' I said, 'What about George Russell?'
> Dorothy would put on a party, and George brought so many faculty over with him. And Dorothy served champagne, three cheeses, and desserts, and then the party moved outside on the lawn. Alice wore an evening gown, and the music lasted till midnight. Finally, Dorothy Wallace said, 'Come on now. I've got to have "I get a Kick Out of You." 'No more free jazz,' she said. 'Three hours is enough!' And then he went to the kitchen, and he helped cook the dinner— It was a great relationship.

> I think George had been to my apartment...well, he's come to pick me up a lot, but I don't think he's had ten evenings here since 1980... ah, it's so small to entertain. But he's been fifteen to twenty times at Dorothy Wallace's house. She presented a whole big evening in honor of him when he got the MacArthur, and many times they would have supper together—and drinks.

George was always welcome at the Wallace home, and Ran was delighted to see his friend so appreciated—it was important to him. Alice is able to give, first-hand, an insight into the friendship between George and Ran. She states it simply:

> It was love.... It was love.

It was a friendship—a love—built over a very long period of time. As Alice recalls, it glittered with fun and spontaneity:

> One time, when George was in his seventies, and he came home after taking his bike out, he had a mischievous look on his face, and I said, 'What?' and he said, 'I thought I might go over and surprise Ran.'

Ran remembers this visit:

> I said, 'What is in that bag?'
> He said, 'Ran, it's not a bottle of milk.'

In his latter years, George suffered from Alzheimer's disease, but the friendship between the two men survived. As Alice Russell remembers:

> George loved him very much and thought he was an extraordinary musician and human being. I was so taken with his [Ran's] kindness, his concern, and his generosity, and we became very, very fast friends. And when George was ill, Ran came to the hospital—he was there; he was present—he was wonderful with George, and it meant SO much! George recognized him, which he didn't do with a lot of people.
> There is no one like Ran—he is a total individual. The fact that he is studying algebra—he boggles my mind. I mean, I didn't get it [algebra] when I was sixteen! He's endlessly curious, endlessly embracing, and has a huge sense of justice, never wavering from that.

Ran remembers his friend as:

A very vital, energetic man. I think later, in the '80s and '90s...he slowed down a little bit in the '90s and knew he had to write his book and compose—we get older. [*It's said philosophically.*]

In his "Brief Remembrance of George Russell," written on August 7, 2009, Ran says:

> I consider George's most important contribution in music as that of a composer. There are sounds that he gets from the orchestra and small ensemble that no one else achieves. His music is as identifiable as that of Messiaen and Strayhorn.

George Russell died on July 27, 2009, aged 86 years.

9

THE APOLLO

The night we won, we couldn't believe it. I don't think champagne came our way. We thought it was a dream.

RAN BLAKE

Of all the clubs and venues of New York City, the one most significant for Ran as an aspiring young performer was the Apollo Theater. The Apollo Theater at 253 W 125th Street, one block east of Amsterdam Avenue, had had a long history of entertainment. Hurtig & Seamon's Burlesque Theater—a "whites only" establishment—occupied the site from 1914. It closed down, along with other burlesque houses, in the early 1930s, following a campaign by the puritanical Fiorello La Guardia (who later became Mayor of New York). But Sidney Cohen reopened the theater in January 1934 as a place offering live entertainment for black audiences. The opening show, Jazz à la Carte, was a huge success. The theater was slick and stylish; the cast and crew were the best available, and the sound was terrific. There were fantastic sets built on-site by the theater's carpenters, who also constructed the floating bandstand, which appeared to glide across the stage on its hidden tracks.

But the shows that followed Jazz à la Carte struggled to fill the theater. To address this, Ralph Cooper[1] proposed an amateur night to give the local talent an opportunity to perform. (He believed there *must* be talent in Harlem based on the high attendance at gospel church.) His hunch paid off—the locals loved to sing. By the end of 1934, the Wednesday night amateur shows, hosted enthusiastically by Cooper himself, were in full swing, and many a jazz great got their start there.

With seating capacity for around 1500,[2] and radio broadcasts from 11 pm over the radio WMCA network, the Apollo was a great performance opportunity. If an artist could win-over the in-house Apollo audience—who were encouraged to vocalize their approval or disapproval—they probably had what it took to make a success of their musical career. In addition, the amateur night attracted the sort of people a hopeful young musician needed to know: record company talent scouts, managers, and agents.

Ran was quite familiar with the Apollo. He'd often gone to see Moms Mabley,[3] who he found hilarious, if "a little naughty."

> The Apollo—what smart dressers. Women full of colors, and even the casual wear of the men in bright shirts, some speaking in Haitian accents. And you'd see a torn tee-shirt every now and then—some of the poorer dressers being the whites from Columbia [University]. There was a balcony. There would be a movie first and then the stage act. There probably was a take-out counter of light food... popcorn. Harlem talk can be as lightweight as others, but the color and the characteristics of the sentence structure—the cadence of the voice! I probably sat near the back; later, I was to know there was a live backstage area. There were smart-looking couples, gangs of older teenage people; there was a very aristocratic crowd of older black folks in their fifties/sixties.

Ran knew about the amateur hour. He knew that many big names in jazz had got a start there—Ella Fitzgerald had won, as had Sarah Vaughan. Both he and Jeanne Lee felt they had a chance:

> We had worked every Sunday at the Lehrfeld boarding house practicing, so we knew our stuff, not that we didn't have limitations— I was fresh from Hartford. Black power was percolating in the late '50s, but it really began getting very big in the early '60s, and I must have been not very self-conscious when I went to the Apollo as a patron. Harlem was great, though. We could walk—after the Apollo—go up 7th Avenue to Count Basie's club.

Thus, in 1961,[4] with a great deal of excitement and trepidation, Ran Blake and Jeanne Lee arrived at the Apollo to try their luck with the sometimes fickle audience of "judges."

> We knew you had to get there 7 or 7.30, and you don't go on till 9.30 or 10. Jeanne Lee lived quite a ride away. But it really... As you get

older, time is precious, but even we—who were carefree: young—
didn't want to get there at 6.30 and wait and be ticketed to go through.

Arriving at the backstage entrance on 126th Street to take their place in the greenroom —where, for nearly thirty years, so many hopefuls had sat watching the monitors and awaiting their turn—they must have wondered how their sort of music—the newest sound around—would go down with the crowd. As with any other artist, a lot of formation had gone into the particular style that they brought to the Apollo that night. And as with any artist, public reaction is personal.

> If you won four weeks [in a row], you would get a week's booking and a little cash prize. We won, we lost, we came in second, we won, we lost—we never got four weeks where we won. The audience could be supportive; they could be… [unsupportive.] The people on stage could be victims. I think I got a healthy boo walking out; I was scared. And we had a Portuguese bass player—Wil, one 'l,' de Sola. So we had Latin, white, and black, but let's not make that the title of the book.

When they were eventually called, it seemed appropriate that access to the stage from the greenroom was via a spiral staircase.

> Honi Coles was a well-known dancer—tap. He was the amateur night leader. He liked us a lot, particularly Jeanne Lee.
> I know that if you lost (but the audience didn't hate you), you just didn't get much applause [*He demonstrates barely-polite, sporadic clapping*]. But if they really hated you, the clown would come up—you didn't get really beat up, but… […]
> We were there four or five times in all, and I'm thinking it was five times, and we won three, and one we didn't make it at all, and one time we might have tied second—if there was a second prize—and one of the few times I took a solo, I got my own applause, whether it was worth it…[I'm not sure.]

To win, even one night, was exhilarating. Ran can easily call back the emotions of that first night he and Jeanne performed at the Apollo.

> L: Ran, so you won the first time you went on?
> R: Yes.
> L: Was that a great feeling?
> R: Yes. We couldn't believe it! [*It's said in a tone of awe.*]
> L: Describe it for us.

R: Well, it was jubilation because Jeanne and I were at Notre Dame in April '62.[5] She got a prize, but they didn't like me. People in Harlem much preferred Jeanne, but I was somewhat accepted. And we hadn't any other work in New York other than one night—a benefit—at Jazz Gallery; never had we won a prize. After the win [first win at Apollo], we stayed till about 10.30 or 11. I don't think champagne came our way; we thought it was a dream. I probably walked with Jeanne to the subway and then went home myself, and she went directly uptown with her family to the Bronx. But it was so exciting walking back. Jeanne Lee's parents were thrilled. They were there that first time. They didn't go all the time—they might have gone once or twice. I think the father only went once because he had to get up early—he was the mailman, and he had to be on route 5.30 or 6 in the morning. They were wonderful people. I would call the father 'Daddy Lee' and call the mother Madeleine. But I still remember going home that night, and I think I might have called Miss Lehrfeld to have something cold—something fizzy—for me to drink.... She had gone to bed.

Miss Lehrfeld had got past the stage where she fretted if Ran was out too late at night. She even allowed him to have a drink or two, and, having met George Russell, she knew that it "wasn't grape juice." On the night of that first win, though, everyone was elated; there is no doubt that Miss Lehrfeld would have got up to share in the celebration when Ran got home:

I was very high for a few days, and my parents were ecstatic! Jeanne Lee's parents, my parents; they told everyone. My father worked in Brightwood, Mass.; my mother had a cousin in Longmeadow—it got all over. When I walked into the Church of God in Christ in Hartford, two or three weeks later, they said, 'Our very own has made an identity.' Now, there is nobody to be witness—Mr. Hubert Powell was in knee pants—[but] Bishop I.L. Jefferson announced me from the pulpit, and Mother Carter was in the front... but, you know, are these the exact words they used? No.

And though certain particulars of their win may have faded with the passage of time, the significance of what it meant has not diminished, nor has the music they played on those nights at the Apollo left Ran. It remains for him now, clear and strong, a portal to another time. On their first time at the Apollo, Jeanne and Ran did "Evil Blues," which would appear on *The Newest Sound Around*. At a subsequent appearance, they did "Laura":

> And of course, we hoped it would happen for a second time, and I think we did get first prize one other time—but way later—six weeks later. By then, we'd already lost, and we'd also got second prize. We knew we couldn't be there four weeks in a row, so it was great being re-acclaimed and having the audience liking us, and I think that 'Lover Man' was that one that won later—we did different repertoire each time.
> I met the composer [of 'Lover Man']. His name was Ram Ramirez.
> I met him in '58 at Atlantic Records. He said, 'Do you know who I am?'
> I said, 'I'm sorry, I don't.'
> He said, 'Have you ever heard "Lover Man"?'
> I said, 'I LOVE that piece—it's so great… Billie Holiday on Decca records.'
> He said, 'I'm the composer. I didn't write lyrics, but I composed the piece.'
> I've never forgotten that.

Though Ran and Jeanne may not have won Amateur Night the four consecutive weeks necessary to secure a booking at the Apollo, other opportunities came from the exposure. On one night they appeared, Joachim Berendt, a jazz disc jockey and music journalist from Baden-Baden, Germany, was in the audience. The single engagement in Germany he proposed would serve as the catalyst for the duo's first European tour. It was a milestone. From that one booking for Baden-Baden, the tour steadily gained momentum. Word spread about this new duo and before long there were four months of bookings, all over Europe. Artistically, the tour was a success.

> L: I can just imagine how good you would have felt because I know when I was in New York—you're just trying to make it, and no-one knows you, and you've got all this passion for the music, and then [in your case] you would have really felt like 'okay, things are really starting to move for me.' Was that the way it felt?
> R: Yes, and maybe even more—emotionally and spiritually. I don't mean like religious prayer—I DID thank God—but it meant 'maybe we had some talent! Somebody liked us.'

10

First European Tour

All this is charming material for a story.

George Avakian

For Ran and Jeanne, the Apollo win (and the subsequent invitation from Joachim Berendt to come to Baden-Baden) was a turning point. Although they had had very little work in the United States prior to the win, there was "generally high praise"[1] for their RCA Victor LP *The Newest Sound Around* following its release in 1962;[2] they had every reason to feel optimistic

Furthermore, George Avakian, their album producer, believed in them. He had written to Jimmy Lyons, founder and manager of the Monterey Jazz Festival, on April 30, 1962. After some general comment about the festival and the possibility that Sonny Rollins might be there that year, he urged Lyons to consider including this new duo, who were just at the beginning of their career and, as yet, had no reputation—except among a small number of musicians who felt that they were likely to be "the next Thing." (He typed it with a capital "T".) Avakian went on to say that he had signed them because they were "extremely good" and "unlike anything else." He also admitted that in signing them, he had violated his own principle: avoid trying to "break the ice" with a new act and wait until they had made a start—which he claimed had "worked marvelously with Brubeck, Garner, and Miles Davis, among others." However, Ran and Jeanne were different. In Avakian's words: "they were too good and too unique to resist." He planned on "publicizing them as the newest sound around." With this strategy, he hoped that they would have made some impact before the

Monterey festival and thus be a "sleeper attraction of high artistic merit that will reflect creditably on the Festival."

> L: So, he obviously thought that you guys could be... well, obviously he felt you were as good as Miles and Brubeck and Erroll Garner, and he obviously thought you'd be as commercially viable. Why do you think it didn't work out that way?
> R: Maybe neither Jeanne nor I were pushing? I know Max Gordon—when he saw us at the Village Vanguard—maybe felt... I think he said it was awkward the way I 'kept staring at Jeanne.' But I don't think that would... Maybe because we were black and white, but that wasn't a problem in Europe. In Europe, we had an enthusiastic reception. We did well on the television in Rome and Stockholm; in Paris, we were controversial... so I really... George Avakian did seem to think we were going to make it, and I wonder why... [we didn't.] Maybe George [Avakian] and Gunther thought that more people had harmonic appreciation [than was, in fact, the case.] I don't know. I really don't know why we never made it. With all these records, I don't even make 45 on the *DownBeat* poll, if that's a measure. It really has so little impact now—the music.

But the pair *was* being talked about in 1962, and John Lewis *did* invite them to perform at the Monterey Jazz Festival in September of that year. (They appear on the official program as an "Entr'acte. In keeping with the Monterey Jazz Festival's policy of introducing new talent."[3] They shared a program with the likes of Louis Armstrong and his All-Stars, Dizzy Gillespie Quintet, Carmen McRae, Dave Brubeck, Gerry Mulligan Quartet, Stan Getz Quartet, and Quincy Jones and the Monterey Jazz Festival Orchestra. It was dizzying stuff for the two young musicians. Ran's excitement was intense. The flight to California was his first plane trip. Iola Brubeck was a fellow passenger that day[4] (Ran claims that Dave and Iola Brubeck never traveled on the same plane), and the trip was rough—very rough. As Ran recalls, "the airplane was going up and down." But he still remembers Iola's kind and soothing words:

> 'Ran, stay calm. Stay calm, Jeanne Lee. Try this liquid...' And she took out some liquid, and we stayed calm.

Despite the exciting build-up, the appearance at Monterey was a letdown. Ran puts it simply: "We bombed at Monterey." However, according to George Avakian, this was most likely due to the festival presentation. He obviously felt that they had not been given a fair hearing and was scathing that they were put on "during intermission if you please" and that "stagehands worked on setting up for the Stan Kenton Orchestra[5] behind Jeanne and Ran as they were performing." This had, Avakian stated, caused a "small scandal" in the press afterward, "as well it should have."[6]

It was disappointing for Jeanne and Ran, but they still had the prospect of the visit to Baden-Baden the following April. Although it was their only booking at that stage, with the optimism of youth, they decided to press ahead. And prior to leaving, Joachim Berendt and Horst Lippmann came through with concerts in Fulda and Bremen.

JANUARY 1963 WAS (for Europe at that time) one of the coldest on record.[7] Indeed, the cold weather persisted into March and April. Ran and Jeanne flew into Frankfurt on April 19 and stayed that first night at the Continental Hotel, run by Horst Lippmann's father, who kept saying, "You kids are lucky—one month ago it was the coldest weather." After a concert in Fulda[8] the following day (which thereafter became Ran's favorite German city), they traveled to Baden-Baden[9] on the 21st for their rendezvous with Joachim Berendt.[10] They worked two days straight at the Südwestfunk TV studios,[11] being assured daily that they were lucky to be in Baden-Baden and not Italy, "where the weather was so terrible." Ran noted in his diary:

> Mr. Kieser[12] had created an effect of mystery for "Vanguard"—with maybe just a touch of the macabre—using mobiles, shadows, and the right proportion of gloom. As we performed our two duo numbers, we both realized how perfectly every minute detail of the setting and lighting fitted our music and mood. Appropriately, the staging was less in evidence during Jeanne's solo.

During breaks in recording, Ran and Jeanne wandered through Baden-Baden's narrow streets, admiring the historic buildings and manicured gardens. They discovered a little café, which served snacks of crunchy rolls piled high with cheese and ham that they washed down with refreshing Johannisbeer Schorle.[13]

> We discovered a drink made of currants—Johannisbeer. It was straight blackcurrant [sic] juice—the wine was above our budget unless you wanted a very sweet German wine.

By the 26th, Ran and Jeanne were able to preview the whole program recorded at Südwestfunk, which included the Mitchell-Ruff-Harris trio.[14]

Ran was excited to see Jeanne's performance and couldn't help noticing just how much she had matured as a singer.

By now, Horst Lippmann,[15] who had got them the tour of Germany, had managed to secure further bookings—a radio show in Baden-Baden and a concert in Bremen,[16] which was very well received. And so it was with high hopes that they returned to Frankfurt and flew on to Rome to meet with Francisco DeCrescenzo, who, Ran says, "was affiliated with RCA and RAI—a television company that was very good to us in Rome."[17] It was the last day of April. The weather was finally improving; Rome was bathed in warm sunshine.

On May 4, Francisco collected them at their hotel, The Victoria:

> The second most expensive hotel in the city! And Knife and I, two years ago in 2012, went to the same restaurant Jeanne and I went to forty-five to fifty years ago.

Francisco took them to the RAI studios to film a show called "Smash," that, Ran notes wryly, "was *not* directed by Fellini." "Smash" was the antithesis of effortless styling, and Ran recalls that the costumes and sets were more in keeping with a "modern-day Booth Tarkington novel."[18] Jeanne and Ran both had to wear large sparkling buttons advertising "Smash," and Ran confessed in his diary that he didn't have "the slightest idea whether it is a detergent, a deodorant, or a soft drink."

The gig was a musician's nightmare. Ran is quoted as saying:

> The script called for people in the cast to be milling around us as we worked. The set looked like a high school gym.[19]

Needless to say, Ran and Jeanne's music "failed to make a dent."[20]

Through Bill Smith,[21] George Avakian was able to arrange a two-week booking at the Italian Jazz Festival. This followed on directly from the German gigs. Then George Prutting of the RCA International Department got them on RAI-TV's top variety show.[22]

According to Ran, the duo "bombed in Rome." But this was in stark contrast with their concert in Caserta, a little town in southern Italy (just north of Naples), three days later. Though the piano was "very bad" (Jeanne Lee was forced to sing several numbers solo), there was nevertheless great appreciation among the audience of twenty-five to thirty, who had crowded into the small hall. For the first time, Ran and Jeanne realized the "intense interest" the members of the Italian Jazz Federation[23] had in their music.

The small recital they had intended to give ended up as a full concert—carried along by the enthusiasm of the audience.

Over the following ten days, there were concerts at Perugia, Pistoia, and then Ravenna, where they performed at the Sala Dantesca (Dante's Hall)—a venue usually reserved for classical chamber music. They took a small plane to Sicily and performed in Palermo Conservatory's Scarlatti Hall. The concert was spellbinding. L'Ora, Palermo's daily newspaper, summed it up:

> The atmosphere we had last night, with the hall entirely in darkness, with a single spotlight on the stage, and Jeanne Lee sitting on a high stool, composed, immobile as Bessie Smith used to be, offered us a taste of the fascinating atmosphere of the Vanguard in Greenwich Village.[24]

Under the banner "Jazz Recital in Scarlatti Hall at the Conservatory," L'Ora correspondent hailed Jeanne Lee as "successor to Billie Holiday," noting particularly her "instrumental voice, warm and soft like Coleman Hawkins' sax" and her "dramatic interpretation in the French tradition," while acknowledging the influence of "Mahalia Jackson's gospel singing."

Ran Blake was seen as a "pianist of sure academic training" who gave Lee "all possible assistance by accompanying her attentively and displaying in his solo passages his formal intention of fusion with the classical." The writer concluded he was an "intellectual American committed to his motives for protest."[25]

It was hardly a fair summation of Ran's talent, but ever altruistic, he was delighted to see Jeanne's talent acknowledged:

> I know in Sicily they called Jeanne Lee 'heir of Billie Holiday,' and later when Jeanne and I split, she was more in Europe than I was, and I was always puzzled that they never had her back to Sicily... and Scarlatti Hall came on fire a few years later—it burned down.

THE EUROPEAN TOUR now had its own momentum, and more dates were confirmed as the word spread about the young duo from America until Ran and Jeanne had bookings for a full four months all over Europe. On May 21, they moved to Paris, where they stayed at the Belmont Hotel on Rue de Bassano, just off the Champs Elysées. Le Belmont, built in 1900, was typically Parisian. Made of cream-colored limestone, it had dark green awnings and little balconies that looked down onto the narrow cobbled street below. Ran and Jeanne stayed in the old servants' quarters on the sixth floor. Their tiny rooms had sloping ceilings, a view over rooftops, and a "bath down the hall." Ran remembers the neighborhood as being "elegant chic."

> Now I know subsequent to that, I stayed at the hotel where Thelonious Monk played, and at one time, I had five keys to different apartment houses in Paris—the French can be very warm.

There was nothing planned for the first couple of days of that first trip to Paris—except for a meeting with jazz critic Pierre Lattes—but those days stirred the beginnings of a life-long love of Paris:

> I remember, after maybe one day, going to the most plain cafe, getting a salad—regular salad with maybe a little meat—and taking it to a table, cafeteria-style. It was a green salad, and suddenly a beautiful cooked egg split in half and nourished the greens. Jeanne Lee and I gasped. It was five-minute cooked, so not over runny—those little touches you've never got anywhere else in the world.

With the exception of this "sensation of a salad," Ran was not enjoying his meals; some were memorable for the wrong reasons:

> One night we had terrible food—it might have been horse meat.

But Paris was at its most beautiful in the temperate spring weather. Parisians were out on the streets, walking by the canal or relaxing with a book and a bottle of wine in the parks and gardens. Terrace cafes were crowded with patrons enjoying the sunshine, conversation, a cool drink. Ran discovered *Citron pressé*, a mainstay of these cafés on a warm day:

> They squeezed a lemon, and, if you want, they will put sugar, but I would just drink the lemon juice with a little cold water.

Street stalls were a mass of spring blooms, and vendors sold small bouquets of the beautiful *Le Muguet de mai*—the Lily of the Valley.[26] Ran and Jeanne were drawn out into the streets to explore all the sights:

> A tower called Eiffel—although I didn't go up—Jeanne did, and the Châtelet, which I was later to play in.[27] I'm sure I went to a museum—I would not remember. But it was mostly loving the metro. Jeanne rested at the hotel, and I wanted to know all my metro [stops]; I loved the metro.

L: Why did you love it?
R: Well, it was quiet—rubber tires. I don't know, Leo, if you remember the Boston subway, particularly when you go to the Boylston Street [station], there's a screech—it's louder here. [*He covers his ears.*] In Paris, you could get off the subway; you could connect with it later and stop at a wine shop that would be cheaper than upstairs because they wanted to get more people on the metro. I used to know all the stops, and we found an inexpensive Israeli restaurant, and Jeanne wore her beautiful scarf and her shawl, and I carried the black bag. Jeanne Lee got her hair all done different in Paris; It was just quite wonderful.

Auditions were sought at various clubs, and though most were already fully booked, they did manage one appearance:

Mme. Michel's Club St Germain[28] graciously invited us to perform on the 29th for the French Press.

The duo made a quick trip to London to check out several clubs and returned to Paris on May 29 for the Club St Germain appearance—for which there was a mixed reception:

We created controversy because some people liked us, and some didn't. We packed the club that night, [but] we didn't get paid a cent.
[On re-reading the chapter, Ran is quick to add:
She never promised that we would. Mme. Michel said, 'It is going to cost me money to get all the critics there. This is going to help you or break you.']
[But] they gave us a good dinner and elegant wine, and we thought it was very worthwhile. Jeanne Lee ABSOLUTELY looked sensational—with a special dress. We met the young critic, Barbara Belgrave; I remember her review. She talks only about Jeanne Lee, and her first sentence was '*Elle est là*,' and my father, who had been a student at the Sorbonne, flipped—she is there!
There was a man who ran the Blue Note—Mr. Benjamin—He wanted me to perform without Jeanne—usually, it was the other way round. Jeanne said, 'Go ahead and do it.' I didn't do it because I loved being with Jeanne, and she had refused gigs… there were four or five offers for her to sing without me. She was the hit. The only club I made it—as a solo—was a few years later in Whisky Jazz Club in Madrid. I would say, though, decidedly, we were NOT a hit in Paris. There were some good reviews, but the negative… [outweighed the positive.]

But Jeanne and Ran were not too disappointed. They had an upcoming gig at the Hotel Neptun in Bergen. This had come at the invitation of Dr. Arne Welhaven,[29] whom Ran had got to know in Hartford, CT:

> [...] at a time when I didn't feel very happy. He was a very kind man—very tall—almost like the Vikings, and he wanted me to have a lot of vegetables and fresh food. I remember him saying it is better to give your body no liquor for three or four days and then once a month you can have one drink too many, and I had to have green, green, green vegetables. He felt that was the important thing. And he would have me walk. He didn't have me do [*he demonstrates exercises—hands on head and shoulders in rapid succession*], and he thought it was very important to dig in the family past, but I forgot to do it. I've learned more about my great grandfather from you, Janet.
> Dr. Welhaven was wonderful. He was aware of the tour to Germany on the basis of the Apollo win and suggested a tour of Norway—his family were a well-known artistic Norwegian family. So, he suggested that Jeanne and I go and play for Gunnar Holm, who was the manager of the Neptun Hotel in Bergen, right near the fjords. Jeanne loved the fjords.

And so, Jeanne and Ran arrived in Bergen, Norway,[30] on June 3, for a three-week stay. They were immediately captivated by the beauty of the place. Boats were moored in the pristine water; summer sunlight bounced off colorfully painted wooden buildings along the wharf.

> We took bus trips to see the beautiful parts of Norway. From the Neptun Hotel, we would take a bus that would take us to Grieg's home.[31] We would go out to see the fjords—Jeanne loved nature. I would walk to where she was, but then I would take the bus back to the hotel. I wouldn't want to walk back—it would be two miles. I think the sun would set at 11.30 [pm] to 1[am].

The lounge of the Hotel Neptun held about one hundred people, and Jeanne and Ran found the audience, which included a lot of high school students, to be "polite—though mostly talking among themselves."

Their big success was to be a couple of weeks later at the newly opened Golden Circle in Stockholm. (This was where Ornette Coleman was to make his two-volume album in 1965.) The Golden Circle—*Gyllene Cirkelnhad*—strived to present good jazz in a restaurant setting. It had good acoustics, a good PA, an excellent piano, and a "marvelous director of music—Abbe Johansson." The experience catapulted the Golden Circle into the league of the Joe Wells Supper Club in New York as one of Ran's "two favorite clubs."

> Stockholm. The Golden Circle came right after Norway. It was our biggest success. It was a holiday, maybe the longest night of the year, and we stayed at a little hotel near the Golden Circle—where Ornette Coleman recorded legendary records—and you could have heard a pin drop. And, of course, Jeanne would respond to a chord, and we'd hear people gasping with delight. And there were headlines in the two leading Stockholm papers, and I know they loved what we did with 'Jada,' and we did 'Laura' and other pieces, and there we met a Dr. Kjell Samuelson[32]—you have to choke to say it [*He demonstrates the pronunciation on a choking in-breath.*], and he produced another record with Jeanne and me where we were doing Beatles and Strayhorn.
>
> I don't remember much about Antibes—whether we got good reviews—but the Golden Circle was probably our best gig in Europe. We had an audience of maybe thirty people. DON'T [*with emphasis*] ask me why it was a big success. I think it was getting close to summer-night—June 21, when it's ALL light—but the newspapers loved it. It was just a three-day gig; we got the best reviews.

The reviews were certainly positive. Hans Fridlund wrote in *Aftonbladet*:

> A brave booking by the Golden Circle management! And a beautiful surprise.[33]

Svante Foerster in *Stockholms-Tidningen*:

> Opening night became a complete success for singer Jeanne Lee and pianist Ran Blake! And for the audience, the evening was rich with 'different' experiences—and also contained quite a concept of how modern jazz singing 'can' or 'may' or 'should' sound. […] throughout ran this feeling of beauty within the music.[34]

Rolf Dahlgren in the Swedish magazine *Estrad*:

> The duo Blake-Lee is definitely one of the absolute top attractions the Circle has ever offered.[35]

'Thelonia' in the Swedish Jazz Magazine *Orkester Journalen*:

> Ran feeds the changes: complicated, brilliant, shocking. Jeanne, dressed in black, sings with a 'fog-coated' voice; with a hair-fine pre-

cision, she builds on Ran's chord structures [...] the improvisations grow like living things. This delicate atmosphere transforms the listener; our musical sense of appreciation is heightened.

Thelonia also notes Ran's delight on hearing feedback on his performance:

> 'A pianistic Thelonious Monk,' says the owner of the Neptun. Ran Blake's usually very serious face lights up with a grin. 'A thousand thanks! Monk's a genius, in my opinion.'[36]

George Avakian wrote to Martin Williams on October 14, 1963. He was ecstatic about the reviews the duo had received at the Golden Circle, having never seen, he said, "such reviews for one jazz performance."[37] (He was pressing Williams for the coverage of the tour in *DownBeat*.)

But despite the good press, Ran, looking back, says with a degree of bemusement, "but we never got re-hired" there. This contradicts George Avakian's impression. In a letter written to "Bob" on July 27, Avakian claimed that the Golden Circle was anxious to have them back and that they had "turned people away in droves the day after the opening, thanks to the daily papers and word-of-mouth." He believed that they were keeping open dates for them in the fall, noting that: "lavish praise like this is so rare." This letter of Avakian's also acknowledged that Ran and Jeanne had been an "artistic success" in Europe. He lamented that they were "dreadful correspondents" and that he had received no reviews until, finally, a batch had come from Sweden. He enclosed copies with his letter, stating:

> I don't think I have ever read reviews like this on unknown artists. It's like a press agent wrote them.[38]

George was frustrated at that stage that the "conservative attitudes of U.S. night club and concert entrepreneurs" had meant that the duo had had to go to Europe to be "given a chance, heard properly, and be appreciated."

He was also frustrated by the lack of correspondence from his two young protégés:

> They are dreadful correspondents. Jeanne never writes. Ran writes once in a while, but in incomplete sentences and as though Western Union were charging five dollars a word and the hounds were right behind him on the nearest ice floe. For example, their present manager got a note yesterday from Paris saying merely 'TV Show Tomorrow.' Who knows which, what kind, etc. My last letter from Ran said, 'can contact us in Stockholm next two weeks.' It came in

> the envelope of an Italian hotel, was mailed in Copenhagen and to this day we haven't the slightest idea where in Stockholm they were! All this is charming material for a story, but also gives you an idea of why we don't have more European reviews, etc.[39]

Ran says that Stockholm was the "artistic highlight," and they got invitations from there. They appeared at the two leading Copenhagen clubs—Viengartan and Montmartre—and on radio and television there.

> They said we couldn't be [at] whatever the club was because we didn't use a rhythm section. (In New York, it was because we were one black and one white, but in Copenhagen, you had to be the bass and drums!) The club was called the Cafe Montmartre[40]—as in France. They were perfectly okay to us, but they said, 'We'll hire you if you play with our bass and drums.'

On July 10, Ran also did a radio show with Dr. Samuelson and Hans Fridlund, presenting the music of George Russell and Chris Connor:

> Then we went to Amsterdam and played at the Club Femina. We bombed, and they were rude; they were cold. We gagged on the food. The landlady at Amsterdam was so terrible—if I tried to go to my hotel room with wine, she would say, 'I'm going to ask you to leave tomorrow.'

One of the last gigs in Europe (during the final week of July) was at the Antibes Jazz Festival on the Riviera, which Ran recalls was:

> Extremely well organized. We were put on either the late afternoon or the early evening, and there was a picture of the two of us in this festival—Jeanne's hair blowing—and this photo [the one they used for the festival] was taken in Bergen.

Sarah Vaughan sang that year, and Miles Davis was performing along with the Harlem Beggars. (Ran noted that drummer Tony Williams and bassist Ron Carter were "particularly impressive with Miles.")

> Later we were to meet the Countess Florence de Lannoy—and you've seen her photographs; you should keep a chapter for her in the book, Janet. We went twenty or thirty times (years and years) to her home in Belgium and her castle in France, but that's a later story.

According to Ran, they did well at Antibes:

We didn't do spectacularly—like at the Circle—but they liked us better than Paris, and we had a nice round of applause and an encore. At least we were treated better than we were in California [at Monterey]. On our way back from Antibes, we started to get on the wrong train, and a young French guy came and brought us our luggage, and I wrote him a letter to thank him, and he found the letter three years ago. He contacted me through a website—isn't that amazing. His mother sold the house, and it's amazing that he finds the letter forty years or fifty years afterward. It's so amazing![41]

BUT THE TOUR was coming to an end. August was spent in Zurich, Berlin, Brussels, Amsterdam, and a week in London—at Ronnie Scott's old Soho Club, where the piano was inferior, and the audiences were largely disinterested. There was, however, a broadcast, which Max Harrison[42] classed as "memorable [...] a brief glimpse of the duo's exciting potential."

When this first European tour ended in late August, Ran and Jeanne had been traveling for four and a half months. It was, for Ran, the first of many European tours he would make during his career. The tours that stand out, though, are the first and second. The first for its magic and the second for its trauma.

11

FLORENCE DE LANNOY

> *Le vent tournait dans tous les sens,*
> *En swing, en rock ou en romance,*
> *Musique étrange, dans le vent,*
> *Tout là-haut, sur le Morvan.*
>
> MARIE-DOROTHÉE DE CROŸ (PRINCESSE MIMI)[1] ÉTRANGE MUSIQUE

"Dear Ran
What a very nice and faithful friend you are…"

There is no address, no date—just the generous scrawl across a plain white sheet of best quality linen paper. The hand is open, the words tumble across the page in their haste to make connection… and they carry with them an intelligence, energy, and a spontaneous warmth that is almost palpable. It is typical of the surviving letters of a correspondence—spanning nearly fifty years—between Ran and his dear friend and mentor, the Countess Florence de Lannoy.

∼

THE FRIENDSHIP BEGAN in 1963. Ran and Jeanne were on their first tour of Europe, and the Antibes Jazz Festival,[2] running from July 23 to 31 that year, was on their itinerary.

It was high Summer. Antibes and the neighboring town of Juan-les-Pins were crowded for the festival. Since the first big Jazz Festival there in

1960—when Charles Mingus, Eric Dolphy, and Bud Powell set the benchmark—this section of the Côte d'Azur had become a mecca for jazz devotees. By day, Juan-les-Pins was the perfect holiday resort—sun-bleached Art Deco style buildings, sparkling blue bay, white sands, jaunty beach umbrellas. But on mid-summer evenings, when the sun went down, and the waters of the bay turned inky, a little magic happened. Jazz lovers gathered in their thousands at the open-air theater overlooking the bay. Here, under parasol pines,[3] they could relax and breathe in the sweet-smelling air while enjoying the best jazz in the world. The atmosphere was intoxicating. Miles Davis and Sarah Vaughan were wooing the crowds in 1963, so Ran and Jeanne were exhilarated when they were well received and, later, invited to the press party, hosted by the Countess Florence de Lannoy. It was the first of many evenings hosted by the countess, and for Ran, it was the beginning of a friendship that would last a lifetime. Ran largely credits Florence with "discovering" him and Jeanne in Europe.

Florence de Lannoy was just the sort of person who would discover new talent. She was energetic; she could make things happen. She came from a long line of people who could act decisively and bring about real change in the world around them. One need not delve far into family history to find examples of this. Florence's father, Léopold, along with her Uncle Reginald and her Aunt Marie, received seventeen medals of honor between them for feats of bravery during World War I—Léopold in the army and Reginald and Marie for bravery in the resistance movement. These medals included the Croix de guerre avec palmes and the Légion d'honneur. Léopold was awarded the Military Cross—the only foreigner to receive it—from the King of England (George V). It is reported that Léopold was particularly tickled by the fact that, during the presentation ceremony, the King turned to his aide-de-camp and asked whether Léopold spoke English. "As well as you do, Sire," was the aide's droll response.[4]

Florence staged a resistance of her own during World War II. As a popular student at her boarding school in Boulogne-Billancourt, she had some influence over the forty students in her class. On Sundays, the students, monitored by a nun, would walk three to a row for exercise in the woods. To amuse herself and her classmates, Florence introduced a game of "Follow the Leader," saying, "1-2-3, do what I do," and all her classmates obeyed. Often, they would come across the occupying German officers, who were riding on horseback through the woods. At each encounter, Florence boldly said "1-2-3" and turned her head away to the other side… and the whole class followed suit. The nun in charge was helpless to stop them and no doubt shook inwardly, fearing reprisals for this obvious affront to the German Officers.[5]

Florence had always had a passion for music. As a young girl, she spent many hours practicing piano, her home study bolstered by interludes at the Academy of Vienna (Austria). She believed in getting things done—her motto was *"plus tard, c'est maintenant"* (later is now).[6] She was energetic, full of plans, always creative. After her marriage to Léopold[7] in 1955, she wasted no time decorating their new home in Brussels, with grace and style. But it was not enough to satisfy her hunger for the aesthetic. Before long, she was inviting artists and musicians for private exhibitions and concerts. Her taste was eclectic, and her beautiful home and its garden served as backdrop for concerts by artists ranging from Keith Jarrett to members of l'Opéra de Pékin, from Marion Williams and her "Stars of Faith" to Latin-American tango artists, and, of course, Ran Blake, who was a regular and much-loved guest:

> And if you got my album *Realization of a Dream*, it would give that address right on that record. There's a piece for Florence on that album, and the house was right in a beautiful park outside Brussels. Later she moved to other houses, but Léopold would still drive me there—wherever else they were living—because that's the house that I knew best.

In addition to the piece for Florence on the *Realization of a Dream* album ("Florence de Lannoy"), there is a track entitled "Brindle," which Ran wrote for the countess's dog:

> This is a delightful dog—Brindle—that lived in Avenue du Vivier d'Oie in Belgium. One time she crawled up on Jeanne Lee's evening dress when Jeanne was about to sing a song. This dog also partook—they had beautiful meals there—of my plate. The countess would say, 'Ran, you're hungry tonight—you're having...' she would never use the word 'another' [serving], and I looked to the right of me, and here was this dog wolfing down Roquefort cheese. I hear she was half pig [*sic*][8]—she was not beautiful, but she was a riot. And she could be very nice. A few nights, she would jump up on my bed—her snout would be right near, and I could smell a little delinquent... [breath]—she loved her drink too. She made a special kind of a whine. And then her son was called Vandale, who I guess vandalized some of the farmhouse. But "Brindle" was the toast of Europe, and people who LIKE my music think that's one of the worst things I've ever written; [they say it] sounds like a bad nursery rhyme.

The countess was busy in her traditional role as wife and mother, with added duties associated with her position and her estate, but she always had a great thirst for knowledge in the fields of music and the arts. Writing to Ran in October 1972, Florence apologizes for not responding sooner to the album he had sent her in the summer.[9]

> I did not write then, being very absorbed in the children's [10] holidays… ten or fifteen people for meals every day; horses; riding lessons; swimming; market; etc. were more than I could do.

She goes on to say she was interested in Ran's musical news but that, unfortunately, she didn't know most of the people he mentioned (Eliot Carter, Milton Babbitt, etc.). She continues:

> It seems that in the United States, you show more imagination, more inventiveness, and revolutionary way of thinking than in Europe. Concerning the future of human beings all this interests me very much. If I manage to come to the U. States, would you be able to introduce me in the 'milieu' of modern jazz, modern literature? I am not terribly interested in modern music. […] It is so painful for the nerves![11]

On subsequent tours of Europe, Ran stayed with Léopold and Florence at various addresses in Belgium and France:

> There were so many different homes—some extremely simple. And she had the most amazing castle which I don't think had much running water in it, but it was in…wherever they make Sancerre wine—right in the center of France, in Nièvre.[12] And I would go to Paris and say, 'I've been to Nièvre,' and people would say, 'I've heard of it but never gone there,'—like people would say of Pocatello, Idaho (which I think is a delightful city).
> But this is a castle. Once a year, there'd be a party. I went there, and they invited all the hunters, and they brought all the French horns, and you'd sit out with wonderful farmers, and people would be bringing different vegetables and dandelion salads. It's one of the great nights of my life; I only regret Jeanne Lee wasn't there.

Count Léopold, it seems, was away also, for Ran wrote to him on August 22, 1983:

> So sorry not to have seen you this summer when I was at Saint-Benin-d'Azy. I loved the celebration of the Hunt. […] Have a wonderful year and hope to see you in May.[13]

The Count had obviously been missed. While he left correspondence with Ran to Florence, he was still very much present in the "we" of her invitations—and very much part of the special spirit Ran experienced in their home.[14] Ran remembers Léopold's kindness and "concern and sensitivity" when he was most in need of comfort. He refers to him as "the kindest man." *Florence and Léopold's daughter Rose, on reading this chapter, wrote to say how much she liked the reference to her father. She explained:*

> He was a pillar for all of us, discreet, open to so many things, and kind. Not appearing on the forefront, he was nevertheless making things possible.[15]

IN SEPTEMBER 1974, Florence wrote to Ran. The family had recently moved to Overijse, Belgium, so that the children could enjoy the country, the space, and have their horses. Florence reported they were "beaming with happiness." She described their new house as a "sort of 'Jeremiah Johnson'[16] house—no other house around, pheasants, rabbits, and only a half an hour from Brussels."

But Florence had more things on her mind than country life:

> I am founding a sort of club/center of encounters for music, debates, artists, journalists, philosophers, etc.
> It will be downtown, somewhere near the old square of the Sablon, near the museum of art. It is a lot of work to get it 'on wheels,' and we don't have very much money yet, but someone is going to lend us a house, and several people will help benevolently. You will be able to come and play!

The club was to be called the Jacques le Fataliste Café.

Jacques le Fataliste was the invention of 18th-century French philosopher and writer Denis Diderot. His 1773 novel, *Jacques le Fataliste et son maître*, was a story of fate and how it interacts with individual choice and free will. It is the dialogue of this book—the interpersonal exchange between Jacques and his master—which seems to have inspired Florence's choice of name. In the flyer announcing its opening, the cafe is billed as "a meeting place for the interchange of ideas and information." It goes on to say, "We have imagined it as a workshop designed to awaken the initiative of each individual and offer a variety of entertainment: revues and catalogues, théâtre, films, exhibitions, music, debates, dance, and creations of every kind."

And if Diderot demanded the active participation of his reader with his questions and authorial intrusions, Florence, too, was expecting people to do more than sit back and sip a drink. She was inviting people to come and "discuss and question fate…" and to "question our way of living and the sacred norms of mass consumption" in the premises on Rue de Villers—all for an annual membership of twenty-five francs.

It was during this period, when the Jacques le Fataliste Café was operating, that Ran says he got to know the countess's "many, many moods."

> L: What do you mean by her many, many moods, Ran?
> R: [*clarifying quickly*] She was always kind, but she could be, at times, a little more direct… or sometimes in a trance. She was so interesting to watch at these times, and then I would get in a trance [also] watching her, and she would say, 'Wake up!' [*He claps his hands in time with the words.*]
> There were times she didn't want people around—when she was introspective. She was busy running this club[17] and my attic… my sleeping bed was right there [possibly in the way]. She'd put me up for a couple of weeks. I think she definitely had to get her business done, and I could get lost for a while.

The club, unfortunately, did not last long. In a letter to Ran on February 19, 1976 (posted in a printed Jacques le Fataliste envelope), Florence apologizes for not having had more time when he came, stating she was:

> […] quite worried about the future of Jacques le Fataliste. Finally, I decided to close on the 9th of January as we were not guaranteed a long-term lease for the house, and there were still too many expenses to be made for safety matters, etc.[18]

She went on to say how sad it was to have to close "just when people were getting to know the place."

Ran has vivid memories of the club:

> I would go to those discussions—I couldn't understand because they were in French… and a little Dutch. And there would be a man over there [*He gestures across his room as if he has conjured the scene from the past.*], arguing across the room with a woman, and then somebody would bring a tray with these refined drinks, and then the argument, and the people. And artists would show paintings and drawings. This was the 'club of clubs' in my life. I loved Joe Wells',

but that was music—this was... [*He breaks off, unable to find a suitable word.*]
The whole cafe was about the size of this room.[19] There were six... [*He points out divisions as he speaks.*] There was the conversation room, the library, the administrative office, a room for people to put coats in. This cafe was intriguing, and I don't know any place like it now. I wish I could have understood French—I never [before] saw such exciting people.

Despite the closing of Jacques le Fataliste, Florence remained active in her devotion to music and the arts. In a letter to Ran dated September 10, 1980, she says, "Now and then we have concerts at home—I arranged a music room containing about seventy chairs in the attic of our new house!"[20]

Ran subsequently performed in this room. In 1981, Florence put on a "soirée" to invite musicians and radio people to hear Ran playing. Florence's daughter Rose recalls the excitement of concerts taking place, the discovery of new music, and perhaps most of all, for the young girl she was then, "the thrill of invitations at home for extraordinary receptions." The memory, she says, makes her smile.[21]

Through Ran, Florence developed an interest in Gospel music. On February 23, 1984, she wrote:

> I will be going to New York to see Constance,[22] who will be working for a year or two at the City Bank. [...] Would there be any chance of your coming to N.York when I am there? I would love to go and listen to some gospel with you!
> Best wishes, Best love, Florence.

This letter had an afterthought—added sideways in the space between the date and the greeting:

> Answering your questions about your concert here: I don't have a programme—but I noticed several times that the audience prefers your interpretations [of the] great "classics" if I may say, than your compositions which might seem too "brainy" for the average...
> R: [*Amused and thrilled, he interrupts the reading of the chapter.*] Yeah, that's her! I think I was a little 'out' for her [musically], but she remained a staunch friend.

Ran replied to this letter on March 16, 1984:

> I am delighted to hear that Constance will be moving to New York. [...] When are you arriving in New York? Your letter does not say. I would love to come down to see you. September is the hardest month

for me to leave; however, gospel music is best in Hartford. Maybe we could stop there on the way to Boston, which you must visit, even if for 48 hours. In New York, there is much jazz, and I think I am finally getting an idea of the kind you like.

R: [*interrupting at this point to clarify*] I don't think I met her in New York. It must have been the first day of class, but Constance DID live here; she lived here for a year.[23]

It is difficult to know how much of the correspondence between Florence and Ran has survived, but the letters that remain do show a very warm and relaxed relationship, unhindered by formality. Not long after the letter of March 16, Ran wrote:

> Dear Florence,
> Can we lunch together June 2nd? I can come to your home near the French and Belgium border.[24]
> Best, Ran

This letter, typed on "Third Stream Associates" letterhead and dated May 8, 1984, was answered in generous scrawl across the customary plain white quality paper, dated Brussels, May 15.

> Dear Ran, just received your letter: We will be delighted to see you on June 2nd. [...] We will come and fetch you at Aulnoye Station, 15km from our house.
> [...] Best love, Florence

Florence wrote again on June 27, 1984, hoping—wishing "if only"—Ran might come that September to play at the Moulin d'Azy in Saint-Benin-d'Azy, Nièvre, France. The letter was sent from Brussels, but the family was leaving for Saint-Benin-d'Azy the following week for a two or three-month stay.

Looking back, Ran can say:

> I would say that Florence de Lannoy is the person who really discovered Jeanne Lee and me in Europe. Through the Antibes Festival and the night press party she held, we got to know many people, including those from the BRT Jazz Orchestra, Belgium.[25] She is one of the very important people in my life—oh, what an incredible lady. I'll never forget her.

12

READY, WILLING ... WAITING

We came back; we thought the world would be ours.

RAN BLAKE

When Ran and Jeanne returned from their first European tour at the end of August 1963, they had every reason to be optimistic. On the whole, they'd been well received right across Europe. They'd gained a great deal of experience and had had, at venues like Golden Circle, Stockholm, dizzying reviews and approval. Later, in Caserta, in Southern Italy, they'd seen the "intense interest" members of the Italian jazz fraternity had in their music.

But European approval did not translate into increased interest back home, and Ran and Jeanne struggled to secure gigs, even though news of their success overseas was filtering back.

This must have disappointed George Avakian, who had made his expectations for the duo clear. In a letter to Martin Williams[1] soon after Ran and Jeanne returned from Europe, he wrote of their European success and the need for them now to get "a decent break at an agency." It was his fear that, despite their success overseas, they would "drift just as they did before." He planned to use the good reviews from Europe to capture the interest of "the best managers I know." However, his main purpose in writing to Williams was to secure his help with an article:

> Needless to say, an article about their trip would help arouse interest also, but apart from the help it would give them if you write about

> them, I think there is a valid piece in this whole surprising situation in which a couple of unknowns, ignored in the U.S., parlayed one left-field engagement into a long summer's work and perceptive recognition in Europe. Best regards, George.

> R: [*on hearing these words again*] How lucky we were to have George!

But despite Martin Williams' feature article "With Blake and Lee in Europe,"[2] and a recommendation and demo-tape sent by Gunther Schuller to Max Gordon of the Village Vanguard in June 1965, Ran and Jeanne secured very few engagements.

> L: When you were in New York, in the time between your European tours, did you do many concerts?
> R: I did one or two [solo] at Columbia University… and some gigs with Jeanne Lee at Slugs'. There was a concert Jeanne Lee and I did opposite John Coltrane—he was the star, and we were the smaller… [3]

It is unclear when the gigs at Slugs' took place, but the venue was decidedly sketchy. Slugs' Saloon opened in 1964 at 242 East 3rd Street; by 1965, the club was featuring live jazz. At that time, it was something of a "musician's bar," drawing a crowd of free jazz enthusiasts, even though it was located in a very run-down area on Manhattan's Lower East Side.[4] Jerry Schultz (co-owner) remembers the East Village in 1964 as "a terrible place […] stark [with] tenement houses, five storeys high—one flat on top of another." The streets were dirty and dangerous, and drugs dictated what went on there.[5] Bill Cherry, a bartender who filled in at the club on occasions, is quoted as saying that there was a waitress at Slugs' who walked around with a boa constrictor around her neck while she was serving people.[6]

Ran's friend John D'Agostino[7] painted a vivid picture of the club as he remembered it:

> Slugs' Saloon[8] was a neighborhood bar, full of junkies and prostitutes and wise guys, and they decided to run jazz there, and I recall one evening we went to see Jackie McLean, who could not perform in a nightclub in New York City, having had his cabaret card taken away. I remember Miles Davis coming in buying everyone drinks—only trouble was, with the drinks, you had to keep your hand over them because the cockroaches would fall from the ceiling into your drink. It really had atmosphere with sawdust on the floor. It was a great romantic tradition in New York—people came to the temple, and you

could still see Monk and Sonny Rollins... Cecil Taylor—it was the hotbed for new music.

The club had initially opened as a neighborhood bar until Jackie McLean proposed a Sunday matinee to the club's owners (Robert Schoenholt and Jerry Schultz). The jazz reputation of the club was born, and the Sunday sessions continued. Ran remembers gigs with Jeanne on Sundays at noon.

BUT ANY HOPE Ran and Jeanne may have had of building on these gigs had not taken their changing circumstances into account. Ran had introduced Jeanne to experimental sound poet David Hazelton (at Monterey in 1962), and soon after the European tour, she had moved west to be with him. Before long, she was married with a baby girl called Naima.

It would have been a challenging time for Ran. In Europe, a door had opened just a fraction, and endless possibilities had beckoned. But these possibilities had been for the Blake/Lee duo, and Ran had, for many years, believed his future was in New York:

> In 1960 I was bound and determined to go to New York, and if I'd stayed in Connecticut, lived at the house, worked at the factory, I think my music would never have had any notice.

For Ran, New York represented the music he loved; it was home to the musical heroes whose records he'd collected from an early age. He could not give it up.

So Ran remained in New York, and Jeanne followed her heart to California and became active in the art scene there, collaborating with her husband and composing for other sound poets. She also taught educational psychology. Jeanne's priorities had shifted, and with this, the nature of the friendship she shared with Ran had changed.

With the duo now on hold, Ran looked to advance his career in New York. Of the few concerts he managed to organize, his Town Hall solo concert debut stands out his memory—for the wrong reasons:

> The audience liked me, but the critics said terrible things. Have you read the reviews for that? They were awful!" The *Herald Tribune*[9] was one of the worst reviews I've ever had in my life. So I actually believed that, without Jeanne, I would be a failure.

On December 7, 1964, Ran wrote to Christian Abry.[10] The letter, which was postmarked Suffield, states that he might be in Paris "for a week during Christmas 1965 NEXT [his capitals] year." He adds:

> Jeanne is in California, married, and a mother and teaching... Her husband hates N.Y., so it looks as if we won't be together unless something good happens...

The letter concludes with a confession, of sorts:

> After a terrible, unhappy year, I finally gathered the courage for Town Hall. This time the audience liked it, but the critics said terrible things. Will you ever come to America? This would be great. Best, Ran.

But after the excitement of Europe—with its changing scenery, different clubs every night, and the many, many new friends[11]—even New York seemed to have lost a little of its gloss. Making a living there was just as hard as it had ever been, and Ran struggled to re-adjust:

> I think I got behind; I was a little short. I only paid about eighteen or twenty dollars to live and sixty dollars rent. Jessie Powers[12] would hand me a little money, and I would use that to buy hamburgers—it wasn't to live on... and my father gave me presents too. But it was really hard getting back to the reality of New York—having to make a living.

Ran did not take his family's support for granted. He was aware of the costs involved in living in New York, and he lived simply:

> I didn't run up the bills at restaurants; a luxurious hamburger joint was a big deal—and there was a cheap seven-dollar steakhouse: T-bone steak, a baked potato, a salad, and a glass of iced tea.

But even if his parents were willing to subsidize his cost of living, Ran knew that it was on him to fund costs involved in seeing live music or taking lessons:

> I think where I probably DID spend money was going into clubs, and even if sometimes people let me in free...[it was still a big expense.] And then there was studying with Gunther.

Ran set about finding employment. He was willing to try anything and everything.

I even took a test to become a policeman. That's the first time I ever got an "A" in a test. I never took the physical. Then, about a year later, Miss Lehrfeld died, and I had little jobs... A lot of my jobs in New York were menial, but they gave me a lot of opportunity to experience, to tour.

As has been mentioned, prior to leaving for Europe, Ran was working at the King's Crown Hotel on West 116th Street and at the hotel on West 58th Street. Some of this work continued after his return from Europe, but soon he needed to look elsewhere. Another job at this time was that of "humble pin pricker" for the traffic engineering firm Wilbur S. Smith and Associates on 41st and Lexington Avenue. This job occupied the year 1965/66—just before his second European tour. It was low-paid—$83 a week hardly stretched to pay the rent—but it suited Ran as it left him free to go to jazz clubs in the evening. New York City was in the process of re-designing its entire traffic flow, and there was plenty of work to be had, even if it involved sitting for endless hours counting traffic through traffic lights at intersections throughout Brooklyn and Queens. The overall plan was complex and difficult to follow—Ran remembers that the office walls displayed aerial graphs of streets. Once he was assigned a section, he simply had to go out—"for example, to Madison Avenue and 45th Street—to see how many cars would go up out of a green light." On one occasion, he was sent to Brooklyn where:

> I heard a wailing clarinet player, and I asked the guy there who did they think this could be, and he said, 'It's the pride of the neighborhood. His name is Joseph Maneri.'[13]
> I may have met him years before through Mait Edey at the Abbey Lincoln recording session. But then, when I was counting the cars, this clarinet... Oh... [*He shakes his head in amazement, for he and Joe were destined to share many years teaching together at New England Conservatory.*]
> He's good at saxophone and all that, but when Joe was on clarinet—Ohhhh, it was fabulous. He was just wonderful. I even called one of the engineers and said, 'There's something wrong with the stoplight... oh, and bring your tape recorder.' And Mr. Bill Mason came out, and even he was impressed, and he's not a musician.
> L: And can I ask, was Joe doing his microtonal stuff back then?
> R: If it was—he had the wail—it had the singer's voice of the Middle East. There was microtonality, but what I liked was that it sounded like he knew the music—not just intellectually with microtones— [He knew] the roll of the singers [*Ar-r-r-r he sings an example with*

> *a rolling "r" sound*]. [So his application of microtonality] was so natural and not contrived. Some people just don't have intonation, and they say, 'Oh, I'm being microtonal.'
> L: I know, I hate that.
> R: I hate it.

There were a lot of people working at Wilbur S. Smith and Associates, and, as usual, Ran formed some lasting friendships:

> The reception guy was Phil Garcia, and his cousins became my closest friends in Paris. I stayed with them on my next trip: the Ballé family—Catherine and Freddy—and I recorded a piece for their son, Miguel.
> Gerard Menckhoff from Switzerland also became a friend. There were people from Lima—engineers: I had to bring coffee and donuts to them in the morning—so I knew what it was like to wait on people.

One of Ran's bosses at Wilbur S. Smith's was Keith Stonecipher. His name has been immortalized in Ran's composition "Stoneciphering," a name that echoes the seemingly incomprehensible discussions that bounced off the office walls as Ran delivered coffee and donuts.

> Mr. Stonecipher had a powerful voice. I would hear his voice booming as he walked around the circular offices of the Wilbur Smith traffic engineering firm. He could talk around circles.

At Wilbur Smith's, Ran met Ricardo Gautreau from the Dominican Republic:

> He was sixteen or seventeen at the time. Ricardo carried blueprints and did other chores for a company adjacent in the area. He is a wonderful singer, composer, guitarist, and teacher.

While Ran was working at Wilbur Smith's, Jeanne accepted, on the duo's behalf, a booking for a second European tour. Commencing in September 1966, it lasted for ten months, with Jeanne's husband and daughter joining her on the road. Although both Ran and Jeanne were deeply committed to their duo and its music, their professional priorities were no longer the same. Over the course of the tour, they were both pursuing other performance opportunities and expanding their professional networks. For Ran, an offer to perform a series of solo concerts in Greece seemed a godsend, and he readily accepted. The decision was to prove a fateful one; he would be caught up in the 1967 military junta. The Greek experience had a devastating effect, bringing him close to break-down and leaving a legacy of dreams and nightmares. Looking back, it was a turning point in Ran's life: one that was instrumental in bringing him to Boston and New England Conservatory.

13

A Cat Called Ludwig

Ran's second European tour with Jeanne Lee saw them performing in nearly a dozen countries over the ten-month period.[1] It was a tour destined to make an indelible mark on Ran's consciousness; the last two months away were marred by trauma—he was caught up in the Greek Military Junta of 1967. The experience would shape the rest of his life. Indeed, it was responsible for his leaving New York for Boston later that same year.

But at the beginning of the tour, there were no such shadows on the horizon. Ran, along with Jeanne and her family, were in high spirits as they caught their flight from Kennedy airport. Ran sat across the aisle from Jeanne; her husband, David; and their daughter, Naima. There was a stopover in Iceland, where Ran recalls:

> We were told you could get a drink of whiskey or wine, but beer was forbidden. You could have marijuana—it was legalized—but you could not have beer.

They arrived in Luxembourg the next day—September 16. It was the end of the summer season, and the weather was still pleasantly warm and dry. Jeanne and her family headed for Brussels, where the duo had their first booking. Ran caught a bus to Paris to see his new friends (and cousins of Phil Garcia), the Ballés. He had dined with them several times in New York, where they were living for a time in an apartment on 3rd Avenue. Here, Ran remembers, "Catherine made me the best shish-kebob I ever had." Catherine herself has fond memories of that time as well:

We met many of his other friends, and we were introduced to gospel music and jazz. Even more, we had the feeling to have known him forever. [...] Ran opened many doors—friendship, music, southern recipes.[2]

It was a four-hour journey to Paris; the fact that the bus broke down could not dampen Ran's enthusiasm. He quickly got to know the other passengers—an interesting collection which included an anarchist, a Russian countess, an American (who was on her way to become a Yugoslavian citizen), and a Spanish merchant. In Paris, Ran was made very welcome at Catherine and Freddy Ballé's apartment at 27 rue de l'Echiquier—an apartment Catherine had inherited from a great aunt.[3] The apartment building was shabby, but as Catherine remembers:

> The street and the district were quite special—just at the back of the Grand Boulevards and the corner of Rue Saint-Denis. At that time, the district was a mix of warehouses, working-class apartments, markets, shops, and prostitution, as well as porn theaters. During our trip to the States, a friend of ours came to live in the apartment and redecorated the main room with a different color on each wall and an ethnic tapestry from New Caledonia, which added to the strangeness of the place, considering the shabbiness of the building.[4]

Ran remembers the area as:

> Elegant. Not particularly picturesque but filled with markets. (It was quite busy around there.) It was a Bohemian atmosphere. Ruth Waddy, the painter and activist, was also a guest.[5] She opened the door [to me]. She had a big broom on the floor; She was a friend of Ann Noriega, and I said, 'Hello,' and she said, 'The Ballés are out; you're welcome,' and the next thing it was morning—I'd gone to sleep and slept twenty hours on the couch in the living room.

It was a lively place to be, with guests dropping in. The conversation covered music, art, politics; Ran wondered later whether he'd overstayed:

> They gave me their bed, and they slept in the smaller room with their son.

After a very stimulating two days, Ran took the train to Brussels, where he was to make his home base. There were gigs lined up at the Blue Note: an after-hours club in the Gallerie du Roi area, where nothing ever happened till after 10 pm. Jacques Bekaert, the Belgium-born composer and musicologist, had written and invited him to stay. His flat had no hot water and was, as Ran recalls:

> Near a house of prostitution… and that's where I lived, and I think Florence de Lannoy was shocked. But I had a free place, and I would go to the Lannoy family on the weekend.

While staying in Brussels, Ran discovered—and got to like—retsina because he couldn't afford anything else.

> It's a wine that tastes like turpentine. You have to have it with lamb, and rice, and little artichokes and feta cheese, and I used to hate it, but then the owner would give me a bottle, and I got to like it. And now it's a big treat (it's expensive) but [then,] it was the cheapest thing.

The Lannoy family was a great support to Ran at this time. In between gigs, they cared for him. His diary for September and October is peppered with lunch and dinner engagements at their home; he even visited their holiday cottage at Nieuwpoort:

> [It was] a typical Flemish cottage, with fishing and recorded music of Archie Shepp—that's one of the best records that Jeanne Lee ever made, [the one] with Archie Shepp. The countess was wonderful. Her parties were fabulous.

October was a busy month. Ran and Jeanne performed twice on live radio shows for BRT, which Elias Gistelinck produced. Then Elias and his wife, Lucy, drove Ran to Hamburg for the premiere of Gunther Schuller's opera *The Visitation*. It was a five-hour journey, traveling northeast and passing through Duisburg and Bremen *en route*.

> It was such a joyous day, and Gunther's work evoked the greatest ovation I can ever remember.

Several days later, Ran parted from Elias and Lucy Gistelinck and traveled six hours south to Stuttgart, where he and Jeanne performed. Cecil Taylor was performing on the same bill, and Ran noted in his diary:

> Never have I heard C.T. perform more brilliantly! His left hand seethed with angry pulsating rhythms.

Then, after a quick visit to Baden-Baden, it was back to the home of Count Léopold de Lannoy to perform at a private party. It was the pattern of the months to follow—filled with people, luncheons, meetings. On the last day of October, Ran and Jeanne flew to Stockholm with the Charles Lloyd Quartet and George Avakian. The following day, they had lunch with Dr. Kjell Samuelson before meeting George Russell (now an Oslo resident) for dinner. All the Norwegian engagements were courtesy of George.

In Sweden, Ran found the Golden Circle "disappointing" compared to the last tour, where he and Jeanne had been "flabbergasted by the enthusiasm." Still, it was a nice little interlude, especially seeing George Russell again.

They had been touring for six weeks, but already it was obvious that the magic of the first tour was missing. Jeanne and her family returned to Holland and Ran to Paris. She would call him and say, "Come over. I have a little concert for you." But as Ran remembers, the reviews were bad. He readily admits:

> R: Things were not going well. David Hazelton was a little sad.
> J: Did you get on okay with David Hazelton?
> R: Not horribly, but I probably resented that he took Jeanne away to California. I think he was getting very depressed. I thought it was against me, but he really was getting not very well. Jeanne was very private. I don't know—she never told me. Jeanne had met Gunter Hempel[6] and was already musically involved. Jeanne and I had very little work in France—I guess Belgium was our big thing. There were nice reviews in Spain and Italy, but I don't think anything phenomenal. I don't think Avakian was interested in us [anymore].[7] So I can remember a lot of friends I met, and there must have been enough money to keep me there for nine months; we came back on 4th July—with nothing.
> L: I don't know, maybe I'm imposing my situation on it, but when you are playing with a singer, it is a very intimate thing [*Ran nods*], even though there is no actual romantic thing—it is just so intimate…
> R: It is.
> L: I always feel a bit awkward—in case her partner doesn't like that… [*Ran is smiling.*]
> R: Intimacy, yes.
> L: When you went the first time with Jeanne, she didn't have David. Do you think he resented that intimacy?
> R: I think so, and I don't…
> L: [*continuing*] And do you think your performances were more business-like… [as a result].
> R: Yes. And I know we lived in different countries, so that was not good economically. But the countess was wonderful—she would let me take bits of food home. Paris and Belgium were my homes.

During his time exploring Brussels, Ran had come across a number of "eerie Greek cafes," which sparked an interest in Greek music. On October 8, Ran wrote in his diary:

> Discovered Thermopyles, 156 Rue de Brabant, where I listened to some of the most exciting music I have ever heard. Admittedly much of it falls into the category of dance music, but what rhythm, what precision—such an excellent bouzouki player.

The seeds were sown for his fateful visit to Greece in April of 1967. But in the meantime, Ran had agreed to act as caretaker for Henri de Seynes' Paris apartment—and his cat, Ludwig.

> I solemnly swore not to let the cat out under any conditions.

Unfortunately, Henri did not obtain other undertakings from Ran as regards the care of his cat, and Ran, it seems, "played it by ear":

> R: I made him beautiful curry of beef with baked potatoes and hot peppers—and had a lovely salad.
> L: [*incredulous*] You made this for the cat?
> R: Yup! [*before reconsidering*] Well, no… I had a couple of guests over, as well as Monsieur Herns Duplan,[8] who taught me "Merci bon Dieu." We set a small table with a small cushion for the cat, Ludwig, and then we left ice cream on the table and went out for a walk, and all the ice cream was gone when we came back. Ludwig was on the dining room table, and did he come over and hug me—he hadn't liked me at first. He came in my bed that night—hopped up—and I thought, 'Oh, he's loving me!'

The next day was busy. Ran had a meeting with jazz trumpeter Ted Curson and, after that, with writer Charles Delaunay,[9] as well as a tour of Barclay Records at 143 Avenue de Neuilly (now, Avenue Charles de Gaulle).[10] With these frequent absences, Ludwig was getting peeved! On December 1, after meeting Francis Paudras,[11] who reminisced on Bud Powell[12] and plied Ran with "wonderful Paudran cognac and other goodies." Ran returned to the apartment late at night; as he opened the door, Ludwig dashed out. Ran's frantic search alerted many of the neighbors, and as he recorded in his diary:

The adventures that ensued would be a short story in itself. Suffice to say that most of the occupants of this elite apartment house, the police, and, finally, Ludwig met at 4 am, and daylight appeared, finding us all in the highest of spirits.

Ludwig's adventure brought together neighbors who had never before met, and in the camaraderie following his re-discovery, Ran was glad that his father had insisted on a grasp of the French language. Ludwig basked in the attention lavished on him. Later, when Ran caught the overnight train to Madrid, the lingering glow of the bonhomie traveled with him. He "awoke to find a change of scenery: huge cacti and welcome warmth."

THE NEXT THREE months were a whirl of countries (France, Spain, Netherlands, Italy) and new faces—meeting with an astounding assortment of musicians, painters, sculptors, composers, critics, producers, architects, and photographers.[13] An appearance in Utrecht at the Persepolis Club was memorable because, as Ran reported in his diary, "not only was the piano out of tune, but it all but fell apart." Ran was delighted, however, in the "rave reviews" for Jeanne Lee. He noted, in particular, one by "Mr. Schouten of the Amsterdam *Algemeen Handelsblad*," who described Jeanne Lee as "rhythmically staggering" and "the most original and best jazz singer of her generation."

Meanwhile, Ran had not forgotten Ludwig. He included a picture of himself with Ludwig on the program cover for a performance in Barcelona. The concert was billed as "something new in modern jazz."

> R: And because of that photograph of Ludwig, I got another concert in Spain, right outside Madrid, because they felt I liked cats.
> L: Really? [*sounding doubtful*]
> R: They thought my music was okay, but they LOVED the cat, and they got pretty angry that I didn't have Ludwig [with me].

When Ran arrived in Madrid for a solo engagement at Jean-Pierre Bourbon's Whiskey Jazz Club,[14] Spain was rumbling. There was labor unrest, and miners were striking for higher wages. A police crackdown on workers elicited a protest by students in Madrid, who were soon joined by those in Barcelona and Valencia. Universities were closed in an attempt to stop these demonstrations. Ran's first appearance at the Whiskey Jazz Club was February 2, the eve of the shut-down. In his diary on February 3, he noted:

Generalissimo Francisco Franco closed the University of Madrid because of student demonstrations.

The music scene, however, was not affected. Ran continued to play each night, relishing the experience of a regular club gig. In an interview with Jose Antonio Luera, Ran admitted that the gig at the Whiskey Jazz was the first time he had played in a club for an extended period.

> And it is one of my greatest satisfactions! In New York, they told me that no club would hire me. It was a challenge for me, and thanks to the generous help that Jean-Pierre Bourbon has given me, I have met it. I am impatient to return to New York and see the expression on certain people's faces when I tell them I played in the Whiskey Jazz Club in Madrid.[15]

Ran said of his reception at the club:

> I am truly thrilled with the audience at Whiskey Jazz because although it is true that the large majority has not responded to my music, nevertheless they have respected it. In brief, they have listened to me, and for this, I thank them very much.[16]

Ran spent three and a half weeks in Spain, staying with Don Strange and his two roommates. Their apartment was on Calle de Luis Cabrera in a predominantly blue-collar section of the city, and Don noted that while Ran did not take an active role in protests, his "rebel spirit" was certainly with the students. Don further marveled at how Ran was able to spend his days meeting the local people and forming friendships "without speaking the language."

After Spain, Ran joined Jeanne for a concert in Amsterdam and then a television program in Brussels before moving onto Paris. Here, Ran caught up with Barbara Belgrave, who introduced him to Georges Arvanitas and Art Farmer.[17] It was late March. Ran flew to Brussels with Barbara, who was sitting-in at Pol's Club on Rue de Stassart. (She created such a sensation; Ran remembers that she was promptly signed for the club's annual jazz festival.) From Brussels, Ran went to Italy, where there were many more people to meet.[18] In Venice, he visited the Modern Gallery and saw "interesting works of sculpture" and "superb paintings," including works of Kandinsky ("Zig Zag Bianco") and Paul Klee.

But it was earlier, in Brussels, that Ran had received an invitation from Jani Christou[19] to perform in the Hellenic Music Festival in Athens—an invitation he accepted.

14

1967—ATHENS COUP

> *I didn't know who Andreas Papandreou[1] was then. I had no social conscience concerning other countries. My only concern was racism, and the way minorities are treated in America.*
>
> RAN BLAKE[2]

Jeanne had declined the Christou invitation to the Hellenic Music Festival for personal reasons, but even though she was preoccupied with her own situation, she worried for Ran. She advised him against going to Greece—the visit that was to affect him so profoundly. When she saw him off at the airport near Stuttgart (where they had earlier played opposite Cecil Taylor), Ran remembers that she said:

> 'Ran, I advise you against going to Greece.' [*He hesitates and clarifies.*] Or maybe Jeanne said, 'Why go to Greece? Ran. It's so far away!' She was more aware than I was.

Ran had been promised a "few thousand dollars" for the engagement. It seemed such a huge amount of money, and he marveled that he would "really have a nest egg." It did puzzle him as to why they would pay him such a sum when he was unknown in Greece:

> But maybe in Greece in '67, having even a secondary American pianist would be quite dramatic, whereas in Paris from the '20s, or from when Copland was studying with Boulanger...[3] I mean, everybody went to Paris. [But] for once, I had two or three hundred dollars extra.

> [*He breaks off, thinking, and then adds philosophically*] You know, if I hadn't gone, I wouldn't be in Boston and meeting you both.

Ran arrived in Athens on April 16, 1967, and settled into a small room on Patroou Street near the Plaka.[4] Wasting no time, he attended a jam session and "heard the best jazz of my ten-month tour." He had a plan to "maybe" get to know Theodorakis and to study some Israeli music.

The next day he met Mme. Pia Hadjinikou,[5] a promotor of foreign musical talent, who had contracted him to do "a big tour of Greece." (There were six concerts lined up through the PIA agency—confirmed while he was in Frankfurt.) Mme. Hadjinikou only spoke French and Greek; Ran's French was again put to the test:

> I signed the contract, and it probably would have been nice if I'd run and got a traveler's check and sent it to my father. Probably I spent money taking people out… a lot. I was thinking, 'Oh, I'm going to really get paid well.' And I was going to try to study Greek music. I heard Manos Hadjidarkis;[6] everybody was playing 'Never on Sunday' … now you know my *Blue Potato* album? 'Vradiazei' and 'Never on Sunday' are on it.

On the way to the PIA agency, located at 8 rue [*sic*] Alexandrou Soutsou, Ran "marveled at the wonderful sights of Athens as any tourist would." He ran into a couple who were at the jazz session the evening before. They expressed much interest in the Rolling Stones, soon to perform in Athens. He visited a painter whom he referred to in his journal as "Georgios." Ran was impressed by his use of color, which he found "vibrant and ominous," describing Georgios' technique as a type of "visual rhythm." Ran kept a journal during this first Greek trip that was subsequently confiscated by the military when he was taken in for questioning. Luckily some of his impressions of Athens at this time survived:

> <u>Monday, April 17, 1967</u>: Early afternoon was spent walking through streets of Athens. Doing surprisingly well with English and broken French. The older Greeks were anticipating Easter, but the younger men talked mostly about the governmental elections to take place two weeks later. I met Maria Adamos, whose second book of poetry was to have been published shortly, and the respected composer, Jani Christou.
> <u>Tuesday, April 18</u>: Outside of a trip to Piraeus,[7] I decided there was so much to see that I wouldn't try to see any of the surrounding countryside before my Saturday concert appearance. Spent the morning wandering through parks—speaking with students primarily. It was

a lovely day. I could hear the sound of a clarinetist with his strange, cascading middle eastern scales. Joined Maria Adamos to attend the ninth annual Panhellenic Art Exhibition. Upon returning to Patroou Street, I was conscious of a dark car prowling slowly through the streets, obviously on the lookout for someone.

Wednesday, April 19: Another wonderful day for me. What people—of such diverse interests! Their enthusiasm ranged from excitement over the premiere of Gunther Schuller's opera *The Visitation* to [enjoyment of] a cartoon being created in Milan. People expressed delight in works ranging from those of Thelonious Monk to Otis Redding. And the constantly repeated question was, 'Why are the Americans at war with the North Vietnamese?' This topic is now forbidden in Greece... I met artists Paris Prekas and Dimitris Poulianos in a group of conservatively dressed communists and a hippy capitalist—all on the best of terms. There seemed to be complete freedom of speech. How many Greeks realized that this was to be their last non-totalitarian evening? What was so surprising was that not more of the politically aware artists I met refrained from voicing the apprehension I'm sure some felt as the storm clouds began to accelerate.

The next day would be Ran's 32nd birthday.

Thursday, April 20: Even now, in retrospect, I find this day to be an unbelievable nightmare. It started routinely enough as I moved from Patroou Street to the Hotel Carolina on Kolokotroni Street. I lunched with Maria Adamos on the Plaka (where I heard the Greek folk tune, 'Vradiazei' being played—it appears in about seven of my records). Later, upon leaving the hotel, a police car stopped me, questioned me in Greek without much success, and then suddenly took off. Still not too alarmed, I visited the artist Marina Karella[8] and her husband, Prince Michael, cousin of King Constantine. Just after leaving their home on Avenue Queen Sophie, I was intercepted by two men who got out of a large car into which I was forced, and I was then searched from head to toe. Later, I learned why my heels were of such fascination—[they are] a favorite hiding place for films. They confiscated my journal, which had so many notes invaluable to me. Next, I was ushered into a somber building, thrust into a small room, and questioned by a third man who knew some English. Eventually, they seemed satisfied that I wasn't a political enemy to what amounted to a governmental takeover. My notes on Greece in my journal must have convinced them of that. This compilation of addresses and names of friends, artists, and innumerable recollections was never returned to me, but I was told I wouldn't be detained much longer.

Since I noticed the door was left unlocked, my immediate escape was probably only dramatic to me…

Afterward, in somewhat of a daze, I do recall the contrast between my mental state of confusion-mixed-with-fear and that of the serene countryside. As I walked toward the home of Georgios (the artist), the crickets chirped as usual, and the olive tree leaves glistened in the moonlight. Georgios and his mother provided much-needed brandy and lentil soup, and I blurted out my story. Later, we were joined by a non-English speaking Greek friend, who showed me some of Georgios's paintings in an upstairs studio.

While there, we heard the door open abruptly. From a landing on the stairway, we saw two men seize Georgios. One of them threw something at a provocative painting—a portrait of a member of the royal family. (This figure had eight hands—symbolic of a greed for power and wealth.) Before we realized what was happening, Georgios was seized and dragged off, leaving his mother wailing. It was the last any of us heard of Georgios. The family friend stayed on while I somehow got to the hotel without further tragedy to anyone. I do remember seeing a military tank hidden behind bushes. When I mentioned this ominous sight to tourists back at the hotel, I found out how politically naïve they still were… and I include myself.

Ran's sleep that night was disturbed. The events of the day—his birthday (he had not given a thought to his birthday)—played on his mind. His dreams were vivid and chaotic, re-living what had happened and reflecting his fear:

> Suddenly, out of nowhere, I saw a tank approaching me. I rubbed my eyes and returned to the hotel. I told a desk clerk. Perhaps he didn't understand my English, for he laughed.

BY THE NEXT day, the coup, led by a group of right-wing army officers, was a reality. Tanks had been placed strategically and, in the surprise and confusion that surrounded the move, the colonels had seized power. At 6 am, Colonel Papadopoulos announced the suspension of certain articles of the Greek constitution. It seemed that now, anyone could be arrested without warrant and brought before a military court.

Friday, April 21: Dashed to lobby. Had (arranged) to see an artist. At the lobby, I was told, 'For your information, we are under martial law. Stay near the hotel.'

1967—Athens Coup

'I better cancel my appointment. May I use the telephone?' I said.

'There are no telephones working today.'

Black horror! We were cut off from the rest of the world. I walked out to the street. Omonia Square was closed off—no buses, no subway, no taxis, stores closed. Three youths were stopped and put into an ominous black car.

Suddenly I realized how alone I was in a strange country. It was a case of being incommunicado with my few contacts. I returned to my hotel room. I heard shots. At seven [that evening], I went to the lobby. The doors were locked into the street.

'My dear, this cheese sandwich isn't fresh,' complained a large lady from Florida. Her companion snickered and said, 'Dearie, I told you so.' I moved on. Two English people were playing travel scrabble. I watched for a while.

Later, Ran wrote that he had never before felt so isolated, though he admitted that his misfortune was minor compared to the lot of the Greeks—being an American was an advantage. The next time he ventured out and was approached by the police, he had his passport ready. This time, he was treated in a friendly fashion and told, "President Johnson very good. America our friend." It was in stark contrast to the treatment of his artist friends.

RAN HAD BEEN depending on his advertised concerts for funds—and he had no hope now of cashing personal checks or any way of getting in touch with his agent. Also, a lot of money—$1000 in two money belts—had been lost. All the concerts that had been lined up were canceled. The following Monday (April 24), "somehow, maybe I borrowed money," he returned to Rome where someone handed him a Paris edition of the *New York Herald Tribune* (The *International Herald Tribune*), and he was able to read, for the first time, about the military coup.

IN ROME, RAN stayed with Floriano Hettner, who "took pity" on him and gave him a room above a pensione for a week. A group of architects organized a concert at Fondazione Rui:[9]

> Apparently, they were in sympathy with the Greek cause, believed in my music, and wanted to help restore my unrealized funds so that I could meet my next engagement in Oslo. I can never forget how hard these people worked selling tickets, publicizing, arranging for a good

piano, etc. The fact that the concert was both an artistic and financial success (the small theater was sold out) was due to the energy of my Italian friends.

The funds that they were able to raise helped Ran secure a ticket to Norway, where there was a concert booked. In Oslo, Ran "missed the warmth of the Mediterranean audiences," but at the Key Club, he was "glad" that Karlheinz Stockhausen[10] was in the audience. He noted that Stockhausen was:

> [...] very impressed with Jeanne Lee's singing and felt my piano reminiscent of Schoenberg.[11]

And so the tour continued, but Ran was simply going through the motions. He traveled to England, Scotland, and Ireland. In Dublin, he visited the Fox Inn,[12] which, he claimed, was his "favorite European club with the possible exception of the Whiskey Jazz Club." In Paris once more, he met up with his friends, the Ballés. Catherine recalled:

> Ran had a terrible experience in Greece, witnessing the Colonels' coup in Athens. He tried to communicate what he saw, but for us, at the time, it did not mean much.[13]

While the rest of the world seemed largely untouched, Ran's experience in Greece dominated his thoughts:

> My stay in Greece may have been short, but my sympathy is very strong and lasting for Georgios and all the fine Greek people I met of whose fate I still am unaware.

THE 1967 TRIP to Greece was to have a lasting effect on Ran's life—with the rumble of the tanks and the strains of "Vradaizi" reverberating into his future. There were to be other trips to Greece, but these have melded together:

> The memories of the third and fourth trips—I thought they were one trip. I can remember being woken up in the middle of the night… I told you this about Sun Ra[14] who, when they said, 'Are you American?' he said, 'I come from a different planet where they only speak in broken English… other people have [a passport]. I don't need a passport—they don't have one on Mars.' [*Ran breaks off here to pon-*

der.] Or was it Mercury? Or was it Jupiter? Or was it the Moon? I don't know. I was asleep in my Greek bed on the third or fourth floor of the hotel. I was called downstairs, and there was Sun Ra in the lobby. He had a little dome on—that golden dome [*he shapes a small cap on top of his head with his hands*]—and he said, ah… he never called me brother. I don't think he knew my name—or didn't wish to. He said, 'Tell them who I am.' And, of course, I had to then say, 'He comes from all interplanetary disciplines,' but then I said [*he lowers his voice slightly and holds his left hand up to shield his mouth*], 'He IS American.'
L: Laughs.
R: I mean, isn't that interesting that three times Greece paid for me to come, but all I talk about is the bad time.
But can we think of it as pivotal in my life—like moving to Boston; working for Gunther?

THOUGH COLORFUL, NONE of the subsequent trips to Greece had the impact of the first one. The memory of "this terrible event" was to leave life-long scars, and the emotional repercussions were instrumental in Ran's re-location to New England Conservatory in September 1967.

> I don't think I ever got over that experience. Every April was a nightmare because of what happened. I came back to America on the 4th of July, but with the exception of a week in Paris years later, I have never, since this experience, known full happiness… but maybe few of us adults do?

POSTSCRIPT

There was a break from performing after Greece. Then in November 1975, pianist Michael Smith arranged a European concert tour with Paul Bley and Andrew Hill and invited Ran along. During the tour, Bley asked Ran to record for his Improvising Artists Label. The result was *Breakthru*. Prior to this, Ran hadn't recorded in six years. It was on this tour also that Ran met Jean-Jacques Pussiau, the founder of OWL records, who would produce *Wende*—the second album to result from the tour.

15

Aftermath

I think in 1967, back from Greece, I had sanity. I knew who the President was; I knew what a chair was; I knew I wasn't Napoleon, but I don't think I had any kind of linear, internal realization that this was a pivotal moment in my life.

RAN BLAKE

"Return to USA on 4th July."

The brief, flat entry in Ran's diary gives no indication of the emotion he felt. Though there was no longer a physical threat to his safety, he could not rid his mind of all he had witnessed—he couldn't stop the flashbacks. "I kept having nightmares—screaming." His sleeping pattern became erratic, and the energy that had always directed his daily activities was missing:

> And the pin-pricker job I had in New York—I couldn't be counted on going…
> When I went to Greece, of course, I lost all the money from the tour, all the savings, and my father said, 'We insist you leave New York City,' because they had to subsidize me a little bit. I had a couple of months back in New York, and I couldn't work… my hair was long… I was a mess.

Aftermath 315

The experience in Greece had shattered Ran. After escaping—"it felt like escape"—to Rome, he used subsequent concerts on the tour to raise awareness of what he had witnessed in Greece. But he still couldn't comprehend what had happened—or why. When he returned home, he met supporters of Melina Mercouri and Jules Dassin[1] in their New York office on 8th Avenue and started working for the American Council for Greek Freedom:[2]

> I volunteered a day or two a week. I don't think I really worked formally.

Here, Ran began to understand the seriousness of the coup, as well as something of its political background. Under the coup, any art, literature, music, or film that was believed to have political leanings was heavily censored. Ran had first-hand experience of how artists, who might be critical of the military regime, were targeted. (He had heard the rumors of torture, and when being questioned, he thought he'd heard screaming from another room.) He was very much aware of the need to support *and* protect artistic endeavor; his aim was to arouse public consciousness of this need through artistic expression

But if Ran was going to support a cause, he first needed to be in a position to support himself, and though he might have felt, in those first weeks back from Greece, that he was being subsidized by his parents and was "unable to work," he was, in fact, actively seeking employment. On August 3, 1967, he received a response from Arnold de Mille, director of the Recruitment and Community Programs of the City of New York Civil Service Commission. It explained that the city did not have "many employment opportunities in the cultural affairs field" but suggested that Ran contact the administration at Recreation and Cultural Affairs. It is evident from the penciled scribblings of a name (Mrs. Doris Freedman), a phone number, and an address in the margins of this letter, that Ran wasted no time in following this up, for on August 11, 1967, he received a letter from Doris Freedman at the Recreational and Cultural Affairs Office of New York City's Department of Parks. She thanked him for his resumé, letters, and reference and noted that she would like to "utilize your background in the area of public service." There were, however, as she informed him, "no openings on the staff of the Office of Cultural Affairs [...] at this juncture."

Ran's parents were concerned about the situation in general. They felt he would not be able to continue in New York City, the way things were:

> My parents came to New York City, and it was advised that I leave. The sight of a police car on the street sent me running back to my apartment building. I was so upset, and I wouldn't answer the phone. Then Gunther—through George Avakian—said, 'We have a position for Ran in Boston.'

It was an offer out of the blue, and Ran's parents saw it as a godsend. New England Conservatory was recognized as a leader among music schools, both at home and overseas. It was the oldest independent school of music in the United States.[3] The nature of Ran's job there did not matter to them; the conservatory seemed to be a place where their son could be safe and happy. They personally supervised the move.

And at NEC, Ran was able to voice his concern for Greek artists. He helped form the Boston Committee for Freedom in Greece, and on Sunday, January 14, 1968, they organized an "International evening for Greek artists" in Jordan Hall to publicize the plight of Greek artists during the junta. There was music by Ricardo Gautreau; Stratis Haviaras[4] read from his publication *Night of the Stiltwalker* and was accompanied by Ran at the piano. Most of the evening was devoted to Gospel performers:

> The black church community of Roxbury opened their hearts to the plight of Greek musicians.[5] They contributed 80% of the music for this occasion. There was also Joe Hardin and Jon Wulp.
> Many Greeks rejected participating in this event because they had families in Greece and feared reprisals.

THE EVENING WAS a precursor of many, many concerts promoted or produced by Ran at the conservatory. Epitomizing the "third-stream" ideal, these concerts continue to this day. Of staggering breadth and vision, they celebrate Ran's students and friends, his inspirations and passions. Whatever the occasion, each concert is marked by a certain warmth—the humanitarian essence that runs through Ran Blake.

Family & Childhood

Above: Ran's Great-Grandfather, Lewis J. Powers—Mayor of Springfield, MA. (Photo in public domain.)
Right: Ran's father, Philip Blake—drafted in 1918, age 18. (Family photo[1])

---

[1] All family photos courtesy of Jen Hoenscheid, Joanna Carpenter, and Wende Reynolds
[2] NEC archive photos with thanks to NEC. Reference: NECA 19.3. "Ran Blake Papers", New England Conservatory Archives, Boston, MA.

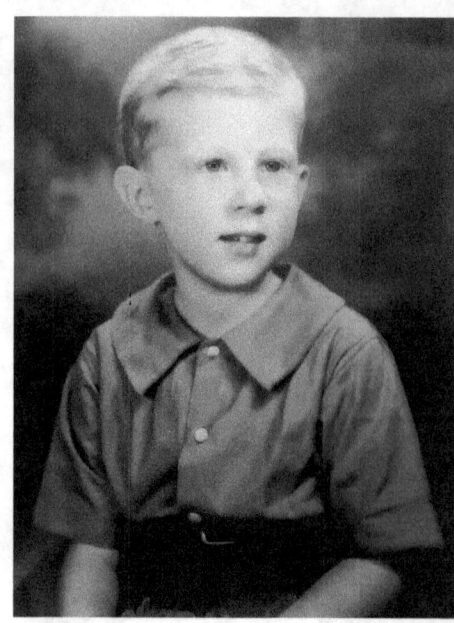

Left: Grandparents Philip and Jessie Powers and baby cousin Joanna (family photo)
Above: Young Ran (family photo)
Below: Summer holidays at Lake Sunapee (from L.) Biscuit, the dog; cousins Wende and Joey, and Ran. The fence was built to prevent the young ones from wandering into the lake beyond. (family photo)

The Blake family home in Suffield, CT, where Ran and Gil Ahrens hosted jazz sessions. (photo Gil Ahrens Sr.)

Ran's sister, Marte, with parents Philip and Alison Blake (family photo)

Marte and cousins Susie and Andy Clapp with Ran (family photo)

Susie, Marte, Ran, and Andy singing carols. (family photo)

Ran and Marte, 2013 (photo: Clare McFadden)

From Bard to New York

Ran Blake and Ricardo Gautreau
(photo supplied by Ran Blake)

Ran as a young man. (photo: NEC archive[2])

Ran Blake and Jeanne Lee (photo supplied by Ran Blake)

Ran Blake with (from L.) Thelonious Monk, Harry Colomby, and young T.S. Monk—Amiri Baraka is obscured by camera. (photo supplied by Ran Blake)

Friends and Mentors

Above Left: Mother Carter (photo supplied by Ran Blake); Above Right: Countess Florence de Lannoy (photo supplied by the family de Lannoy); Below: Dorothy Wallace—or DCW as she liked to refer to herself. (photo: Anne Elvins Grace)

Touring

While on tour in July 2006, Ran and David "Knife" Fabris visit a tiny restaurant on the outskirts of Paris once frequented by Django Reinhardt. (Photo courtesy of David "Knife" Fabris.)

Ran travelling from Caen to Strasbourg in France in May 2017 (photo: Lukas Papenfusscline)

Ran with Luciano Linzi in Italy during 1980 tour. (photo supplied by Ran Blake)

New England Conservatory

Jeanne Lee as guest at Ran's class (photo: NEC archive)

Teaching (and listening)—Both "Golden Arts" (photo: Clare McFadden)

Ran and students L to R: Jerome Harris, Richard Eisenstein, Eric Thomas, Ran Blake, Hankus Netsky, Eleni Odoni, Jan Forney (photo: NEC archive)

Above: Ran, flanked by Hankus Netsky and Dominique Eade at the awarding of his honorary doctorate at NEC (photo: Jeff Thiebauth)

Right: Ran at the piano. (Symphony Hall, Boston)

Below: Gunther addresses the assembled NEC community as part of commencement exercises. Cecil Taylor and Ran Blake are to his left. (photo: NEC archive)

Gunther Schuller: Ran's Mentor and Friend

Ran and Gunther (photo: NEC archive)

Gunther's birthday (photo courtesy of Lee Eiseman)

Two Great Loves: Film Noir & Music

Ran at South Station, Boston, 2002, posing as a film noir character in a coat loaned by Justin Freed for the purpose. (photo: Justin Freed)

Ran playing at Dorothy Wallace's home.

Brookline: The Hub

Dek-Tor posing with portrait by Eliza Graff. (photo: Amanda Ekery)

A sunny spot for reading the news. (photo: Clare McFadden)

Ran and Dek-Tor
(photo: Clare McFadden)

Food: A Celebration

Leo McFadden and Ran Blake consulting the menu at a local Brookline restaurant in June 2017. (photo: Clare McFadden)

Ran's beans—cooked the Julia Child way.
August 2017 (photo: Clare McFadden)

Keepsakes

Snippet of letter from Dorothy Wallace to Philip and Alison Blake, New Year 1981

Critic and writer Martin William's 1958 response to a letter from Ran, discussing some of the questions facing jazz at the time. (supplied by Ran Blake)

Above: Letter from Pannonica de Koenigswarter to Ran—1986. (supplied by Ran Blake courtesy Shaun Koenigswarter)

Right: Spanish concert poster— 1967—featuring Ludwig, the cat. (supplied by Ran Blake)

Part III

Boston

1

CROSSROADS—THE MOVE TO BOSTON

*Life must be understood backwards. But it must
be lived forwards.*

SOREN KIERKEGAARD, *PAPERS AND JOURNALS*

"Here's a question, Ran," Leo said. "Is there any point in your life that was a crossroads—you chose the path that you took, and it has led to here? Was there any other path you might just as easily have taken which would have taken your life to different places?"

They had been circling around Kierkegaard's idea that life makes sense only backward, but it has to be lived forward and had wondered whether there was a vantage place in life—a pivotal or defining point—from which one could look back on childhood and see it with new understanding, but also, considering what has since followed, think, "okay, that moment was the catalyst for what happened." It was the end of September 2009. Ran was preoccupied with the big George Russell memorial to be held that coming Friday, but he was captivated by the question:

> So, have I learned anything from my four trips to Greece? Have I learned anything about Gunther's nurture and care for me, and do I put that with [sic] my students? I certainly look back at my life and see things that don't make sense. I see childhood—walking through the cemetery; then that became the precursor for *Spiral Staircase* and film noir. But this question can be much more philosophical... about the different thinking processes, not just of getting old but really about the changes that it makes in your direction. I guess we can start with action, but what about thinking, and will I remember... [*His*

hands cover his face in an attempt to slow down the rush of ideas.]
But this is such a WONDERFUL question!
[*He rests there for a moment longer—his hands covering his face—before resuming.*] I still think my answer's: 'I don't know.' Do you feel that every mature adult, having undergone experiences, been in and out of love—which I'm not much [*There's a reflective pause before he continues.*]—having studied with people, having witnessed death in the street, and I can't compare [myself] to the news reporters and people in... I'm very, very protected. But would... [*He tries to start again.*] We know... [*He takes a breath for another fresh start.*] As a child, we're told, 'Don't put your hand in the fireplace.'
So, do you think most people do this? Do they look at their future with the information of the past? Should I actually change my thinking and not see so many shadows in life? But we don't know when crossing a street if a car will come out and start shooting—or bring people from the past and other dreams...

And at last, when they'd examined this question from every angle, with all its implications and permutations, Leo posed his question: "Is there any point in your life that was a crossroads." Ran's answer was simple, direct, and unequivocal:

Yes, when Gunther offered me the job in Boston.

The complexity of the choice he had faced then was reflected in the words that followed:

I could have said, 'I'll stay in New York.' I think my parents said they would not give me financial aid if I did. I'd lost all my money in Greece, but I had some minor reputation in New York; [I had] that five-room apartment for $110. I guess I could have rented it out. I like to live alone, but I could have—probably—until I got myself on my feet. I could have rented out part of the apartment. I might have had more time to compose. Would my music have become better? I don't know. There were other offers to go back to Europe, but I don't think I went there for three or four years after I moved.

LOOKING BACK, THE choice was clear; even in 1967, Ran did not entertain other possibilities for very long: "I'm sort of desperate," he'd told Gunther.

Gunther's job offer came at the right time. The experience in Greece had deeply affected Ran. It tainted his memory of the second European tour—a tour that did have its high points, even if it lacked the magic of the first. On their first tour, Ran and Jeanne had been full of youthful optimism, a shared camaraderie. They were in love with Europe, and Europe was in love with them—they had so many dreams. On the second tour, circumstances had changed. Jeanne now traveled with her partner and small child; they stayed in different lodgings, sometimes in different countries. Arranging times to rehearse together was a challenge. However, despite all this, the hopes and dreams for a bright future for their music were still intact—until the 1967 Greek coup when, for Ran, everything came crashing down.

THERE WAS NEVER any doubt that leaving New York City would be a wrench. Leaving the apartment on West 113th Street was even more distressing. Ran's parents had paid the rent to retain the apartment during the whole ten months[1] of the European tour (1966–1967). Leaving the apartment, with all its memories, seemed so final.

> So, I found I loved Miss Lehrfeld's boarding house. I LOVED One Thirteenth Street. I LOVED the subways.

Ran's father had come with a friend, Lowell Henry, to pick him up; they drove back to Suffield where:

> The people came hugging me. There was such a feeling of fellowship. Later, I would go home on weekends when the school let me, and I found… There were very beautiful things [said and done], and [I found] even the more remote people were somewhat caring underneath.

After a short break in Suffield, his parents drove him on to Boston, which proved to be a huge adjustment after New York:

> It was so awful that period—leaving Greece, then giving up that apartment in New York City that had been leased to me for life [was hard]. So for me, then, New York was 'softer,' and my first months at the conservatory [were hard], having to take orders from the people— 'Do this!'
> 'I want my coffee black!'
> 'Bring the newspapers here.'
> 'Why are you late today?'

—that was the awful part. It was no dream position.

And ah, now, I *do* like to go to bed (I'll be ready to go to bed in three hours), but to think that all bars closed in Boston at 10.30 or 11.00! Now, of course, I didn't know there was an underground. There were all night things that pretended to be... closed, but I didn't know this. And there were the clubs where you'd hear music, and there were clubs that had little pianos. [*It's said with wonder.*] But it was so provincial, and I thought, 'Oh my God, at least Hartford I know. This is the worst place: Boston.'

Ran had a choice of accommodation to start his life in Boston. There was the YMCA on Huntington Avenue—it was right next door to New England Conservatory, so this was very convenient. He could get a room there for the weekdays and go home on weekends. Alternatively, he could stay at Lechmere Square with Andy Sexton and his friends.

> Dad urged me not to rent in Boston. He didn't know how long I'd stay, and he didn't want me to rent an apartment. We didn't know what 'condo' meant [at that time]. Gunther knew I was in bad shape. I know my mother was always worried I might end up in some kind of a home with no money.

THE CHANGE OF city changed Ran, too. He'd had a very wide circle of friends in New York. He'd taken them to clubs and parties. He'd even introduced them to his favorite church, Sweet Daddy Grace's in Harlem. There was a big gap to fill:

> I got much more introverted [in Boston]. I still probably liked to introduce people to each other, and of course, the new friends that I did [introduce] were of Greek heritage... But you know, as winter came... I'm really a loner with colder weather. (And Boston's much colder than Suffield.) So, with the cold, just having that small room at the 'Y.'

During this lonely time, music was a constant companion—and consolation:

> I had a key to the conservatory—I could just walk in. And I had a special key to Gunther's office on the second floor. There was a piano there, and I often spent the night there. I played the piano all hours of the night. And that's where Gunther said I developed the sound. I

Crossroads—The Move to Boston

did the best practice I ever did in my life. One time I invited a young lady—Laura Jane—and Gunther said, 'Ran, if I see you with a woman or guy... This is only for you—this office.'

And I spent so many nights going to movies, for the theater was near to the conservatory then, and [afterward] going [back] to that office, playing night after night.

I got an awful lot of piano work done because I didn't go out and party—Boston was nothing like New York—so it did my style... [a lot of good] because I went back and reviewed what Kate Wolf said, so maybe it was a blessing.

But I would have nightmares about Greece. And I know that Chester Williams, who was the President before Gunther, would hear me calling out at night, and he said (he'd heard about my case) he said, 'Ran has to emit it from his body.'

L: So you were very traumatized, obviously, by the experience. How long did it take you to fully...?

[*The answer comes quickly and very quietly—almost as a whisper.*]

R: I don't think I ever... [did.]

RAN ARRIVED AT the Conservatory in September/October of 1967. Russell Sherman, Jon Wulp, Donald Harris, Harvey Phillips, and John Heiss[2] were also new at the time, but Ran's job was less grand than theirs were—his was to deliver coffee and mail.

> I started right at the bottom of the ladder at NEC. I was dusting and helping move pianos and running the postal service. When the mail came, I had to get it into all the various offices.[3]
>
> Mr. Cogan—Bob Cogan, the Musicology guy—wanted his mail at a certain time, and I had to be there! But he wasn't as strict as other people. And we have to pick up our own mail now. [*He pauses, contemplating this, before adding*:] I was allowed forty-eight minutes [*the preciseness is deliberate*] for lunch.

Ran's supervisor was unforgiving:

> He would look at his watch if I came in five minutes late. I had to be there from quarter to nine in the morning to five o'clock. Bob Cogan invited me to lunch one day. Gunther said, 'Yes, Come,' and I remember this guy saying, 'Do you want to use your powers as a friend of Gunther's?' And he looked right in my face.

> I had to get special [permission in] writing to leave Friday afternoons, once a month, to go back to Suffield. Gunther said, 'Ran, I'd like to [allow it], but you can't be the president's pet. You have to ask your superintendent if you may leave this Friday to go home and visit your parents.'

Gradually things started to fall into place; the new city was not quite so new; the faces no longer those of strangers. During the time he was delivering mail and coffee, Ran really got to know the ways of the conservatory.

> I knew the bowels at Jordan Hall—those files underneath. I got to know a whole lot of the staff. But to have no friends... [*He leaves the sentence hanging for a moment, on a downward note, before continuing:*] I wasn't old enough for the faculty, and I was too old for the students.

At night, he befriended the security guards and began to learn something of the city itself:

> Often, I'd bring them a sandwich, and I heard the stories about what it was like in the '30s and '40s. I know that's an awful long [time ago] to remember stories that I was told at midnight, but I remember [they said] there were people that would serve high tea in the '40s. It was the end of an era.
> From Gunther's office, you'd look right out and see Huntington Avenue, and there was an automat right across where Burger King was, and I remember a waitress called Ruthie who got run over, January of that year, crossing Huntington Avenue.
> L: What's an automat? [*Leo has not registered the fate of poor Ruthie.*]
> R: You put in thirty or forty cents, and out a little package comes—a pie or a chicken pie, and [other] hot foods would come out. Now, there would be people hidden there behind, but we never saw the people. They [automats] were 'round Grand Central Station and Times Square in New York, though it was practically dying out [during] my time in New York. I came at the end of an era in New York. It was probably better than some fast food now.[4] Now, I wouldn't be surprised if this one [on Huntington Avenue] may not have been a real automat. There was one in Hartford—one of a chain. But here, I said there was a waitress called Ruthie. I wonder if the police have a record of that accident? I think there were real people there on Huntington Avenue and Gainsborough Street.
> L: So how big was it?
> R: Bigger than Burger King.

One of the men who started at New England Conservatory at the same time as Ran was Jon Wulp. He was ten years younger than Ran, and because of their shared status as "new boys," the pair became friends. Jon was a graduate of Williams College, and Ran recalls:

> My father was so happy that I could hang with a Williams graduate 'cause I'd only made the waiting list—it was my Dad's college.

Philip Blake was indeed happy that Ran had a new friend in Boston. After the worry he'd been through following his son's traumatic experience in Greece, Philip would have welcomed any new friend—Williams' graduate or otherwise; he encouraged the friendship, treating the two young men to lunch once a month at Cafe Amalfi. "He said we could have whatever we wanted to eat," Ran marvels at the memory.

Cafe Amalfi—more restaurant than cafe—was located at 8–10 Westland Avenue, over the road from Symphony Hall: "so close to Symphony Hall you can almost hear the music!"[5] (as ran the catchline used in advertisements in the local papers). This proximity made it a favorite haunt of the BSO players, and going to the Amalfi before and after the Symphony was a tradition for them.[6] It was also the ideal place for a quick lunch during rehearsals. The restaurant was stylishly Italian. It had discreet dining spaces accessed by stairs and through archways. Cast iron handrails, ornamental columns, natural wood paneling, and bold checkered floors sentimentally referenced the Amalfi coast. It all made for a wonderful experience. A taste of Italy served up with (according to Ran) "the best American espresso—with lemon."

> To me, the height of decadence was to go to the Amalfi on Westland Avenue with Jon Wulp for lunch. You'd have a beautiful lunch for $6. They had pasta and spumoni[7] and all these Southern Italian desserts with claret sauce. And we'd be in these private booths, and we'd hear the talk of Leinsdorf[8] and the different conductors of Boston Symphony. And to see different cellists—half the names I didn't know—but just to be there. You couldn't eat there at night—it was very expensive.

Instead, Ran recalls that at night he and Jon would find a meal at one of the little bars on Massachusetts Avenue, close to where Jon lived. And as they chatted and enjoyed the food and drink, the haunting images from Greece retreated just a little:

> L: Can you remember what you ate there?

R: Fish and chips and Ballantine India Ale;[9] sweetbreads—we're talking about basic... Then we'd go to Central Square [Cambridge], and we'd have those four-dollar T-bone steaks with yesterday's baked potato, a piece of bread, iceberg lettuce with mayonnaise and apple pie for dessert and chug it down with Gallo wine.[10] One time they asked Jon and me to leave—we were refused coffee after a few drinks. 'You've had enough, gentlemen,' they said.

Then I'd go back to St. Stephen Street,[11] but I could spend a lot of the nights in Gunther's office playing the piano again and again—with the lights off.

OTHER STAFF MEMBERS also reached out to Ran at this time:

So this lady, Anne Davis, was so wonderful when I delivered mail to the second floor. She had been at the conservatory for years—first as President Williams' secretary and then as Gunther's. She was very loyal to both of them. Anne told me how to dress— it's too bad it didn't last—but I remember there was a stylish place on Huntington Avenue near Northeastern [University]. She helped me buy my first suit so I could dress for my new job. I had a blazing black shirt with little white polka dots, a blue or green tie, a grey coat, and light tan trousers. I paid for it, and Gunther said, 'You look different.'

Anne and her husband (who was a strict Christian Scientist) invited Ran to their home in Quincy for a meal at Thanksgiving:

Anne said, 'Ran, would you come with me to the kitchen?' And her husband winked at me. 'I know what that means' [he said]. And I was given a small daiquiri with rum. His wife was allowed to have a little liquor, but no liquor was served in the front room.

Ran also remembers another "wonderful lady"—Beatrice—who brought coffee.

She wore a uniform and was from the old school. She left in 1968.

'Beatrice.' The mere mention of her name conjures many other memories from that time:

Adelheid Dahl Hestnes[12] from Norway (whose mother and father discovered Marian Anderson in Bergen, Norway) ran the dormitory at NEC. She had a real nurse—Caroline Strovink—and Sr. Noelle, a

Catholic psychiatrist, to help her. There was no Campus Rep. then. Every person had to sign out and sign in.

Harvey Phillips—he and Donald Harris were the two Vice Presidents; the remarkable Russell Sherman who did Franz Liszt so beautifully and John Heiss…It was a very, very exciting place, the New England Conservatory.

Ran has compiled a list of all the people he met at NEC.[13] However, during his first year in Boston, Gunther Schuller was Ran's mainstay.

THERE IS NO doubt that moving to Boston was a turning point for Ran. The life he'd once loved in New York had become increasingly difficult. The warmth of his home base at West 113th Street had diminished with the death of Miss Lehrfeld. Added to this was the memory of the whole experience in Greece and the resultant nightmares and insecurities. And woven through it all was the diminishing of the close artistic collaboration and friendship he'd shared with Jeanne Lee.

For Ran, 1967 was a year of extremes. It opened on the world stage, climaxed in the drama of a military coup in Greece, and was resolved in the safe and peaceful harbor of Boston.

For the nation, also, it was a year of contrasts. It was a year of conflict and of love. Across the seas, the Vietnam War was raging while "back home" opposition to America's participation was growing. On April 4, 1967, Martin Luther King Jr. delivered his speech, "Beyond Vietnam," speaking strongly against the US role in the war.[14] It cost him a lot of white support. Added to this, many blacks felt he should confine himself to civil rights. King, however, felt the Vietnam question was of utmost importance, saying he felt the campaign would "poison the soul of our nation."[15] In an interview on NBC News on May 8, 1967, he admitted his dream for equality had become something of a nightmare; the reality was, there was a long way to go. He stated that any country obsessed with war loses its social perspective.[16] Though King could see that black Americans continued to be victims of discrimination and inequality,[17] he still firmly believed in a peaceful solution. However, he also knew that he was no longer the undisputed voice of the Civil Rights Movement. A younger generation was questioning his insistence on non-violence. Stokely Carmichael, one-time leader of the Student Nonviolent Coordinating Committee (SNCC), talked of "black power" and the need for black people to fight for their rights by "any means necessary."[18]

And yet, 1967 was a year when anything seemed possible. "People power" was intoxicating. Hippies, mainly white and young, gathered in San Francisco for a "summer of love," their senses stretched by the whole experience and by LSD and cannabis, which was widely used. When the Beatles' new—and to some, shocking—LP *Sgt. Pepper's Lonely Hearts Club Band* hit the streets in June, it was dubbed the soundtrack to the "summer of love."[19]

All these things were recorded and reported by an increasingly dominant mass media and brought, with varying interpretations and nuances, into just about every home in America. People couldn't get enough.[20] Moreover, they were being asked to form opinions on matters that would not normally have touched them. It was all highly stimulating and also highly pressurized.

In Boston, Ran was somewhat shielded from the media hype; nevertheless, he had his own demons to face. The loneliness and isolation were daunting; there would have been moments when he questioned his decision to accept Gunther's offer.

> Should I have stayed [in New York]? What might have happened? But how would we know? Then, in my second year, Dorothy Wallace comes in. So… my gosh! If I hadn't moved to Boston—even if I hadn't moved till three years later—who's to tell if Dorothy Wallace… Would she have gotten my name three years later? Maybe not? [*The question is left hanging. Such a possibility is unthinkable.*]

And so it was that the journey made in dejection and the loneliness endured stoically had a serendipitous outcome. For soon after coming to Boston, Ran met his "great patron"—the guardian his grandmother had promised. The decision to move, made out of necessity, seemed to have brought its own blessings. Life, for both Dorothy Wallace and Ran Blake, would never be the same thereafter:

> Now, it seems to me, the conservatory probably was [the] crossroads. I know Gunther once said, 'Ran, with your teaching, don't you want to try to go to New York City and get in a bigger school now that departments are… [opening up?]
> First, at this point, I love this apartment… [so I wouldn't leave it.] Maybe Dorothy Wallace was a comfort zone. And who knows, with winter coming up, it's very tough—the whole world is very tough. I guess people would have liked—a minority [would have liked]—my music, and maybe I would have found little village clubs to play in;

It's hard to say. Would more records have come out… [of moving back to New York]?

In 1968, within twelve months of Ran's coming to Boston to take up a role of mail (and coffee) runner (and occasional chauffeur) at New England Conservatory, Gunther told Ran, without preamble, that he had a "more interesting job" for him. He wanted Ran to co-chair a community services program. The idea of community service (or outreach) programs in 1968 Boston was new. New England Conservatory was "among the first"[21] to consider such a program. It was a concept that appealed to Ran, and he immediately threw himself into plans and preparation. There was plenty of scope, and Ran, who had always had a highly developed sense of community, was perfect for the job. It was, however, not the only innovation Gunther was considering. Gunther was moving fast; the whole of the New England Conservatory was undergoing rapid change under his leadership.

2

GUNTHER—A PERSONAL LOOK

*While sweeping the floor at Atlantic records, I
met a man who would change my life—
that man was Gunther Schuller.*[1]

RAN BLAKE

When Ran, sweeping the floors at Atlantic Records in 1958, encountered Gunther Schuller, it was not really a "meeting" in the true sense, more a passing in the corridor, an exchanged glance. But it was enough to intrigue Gunther, and soon after, when he asked Ran to play something, several things fascinated him: the fusion of jazz and classical; the original composition; and the fact that this composition was not committed to paper and was, in effect, a "constantly reinvented improvisation."[2] As far as first encounters go, it was a promising one.

Ran got to know Gunther a little better during the summers of '59 and '60 at Lenox. At this time, Ran was in his mid-twenties. Artistically, it was a difficult time for him; he knew he had talent but could see no way of promoting or developing it.

> I began to realize in '59 or '60 that maybe I had something. But no musicians called me. I played in a rock group and liked gospel music, but I really didn't feel comfortable. I just didn't think I fitted in.

Gunther Schuller, less than ten years Ran's senior, was already well established in his career. In fact, by his mid-twenties, he already had an impressive list of achievements to his name. In 1943, at the age of seventeen, he won the position of principal horn in the Cincinnati Symphony Orchestra. Two years later, he made a "dual professional debut" with the same orchestra as soloist and composer of his horn concerto.³ He left Cincinnati shortly after to take up the position of principal horn in one of America's finest ensembles, the New York Metropolitan Opera Orchestra. At twenty-four, he ventured into jazz, playing on sessions that would become part of the seminal *Birth of the Cool* album of Miles Davis.⁴ During this time, Schuller served on the faculty of the prestigious Manhattan School of Music. He was also busy raising a young family with his wife, Marjorie, whom he'd met while working in Cincinnati.

His precocious achievements, however, did not make him impatient with the progress of others; he was generous in his support of Ran, right from the start:

> What I heard in that first get-together with Ran was the most interesting free form extemporizing that I had ever heard, especially since it was stylistically, harmonically, rhythmically expressed in a fusion of two distinct musical languages, jazz and classical.⁵

Despite such enthusiastic praise, Gunther also recognized a "lack of control of overall form" in the young pianist's work at this time; nevertheless, he was so taken with his "basic talent" that he:

> [...] decided to help him with this problem by coaching him; in effect taking him on as a student.⁶

It was the beginning of a life-long friendship and working relationship.

RAN WAS GUNTHER'S student "sporadically" at first, due to his commitments at Bard College, then, during the summers of '59 and '60 at Lenox, and later, in New York, during the period from 1960 to 1967.

> Lessons were all-encompassing. I discovered the value of self-scrutiny; use of [a] tape recorder; listening to others (a familiar activity but with added alertness); concentration during performance.⁷

In New York, Ran was involved with friends; he remembers there were times when he was "kicked out" of Gunther's lessons for a couple of weeks because he hadn't done enough work.⁸

> I was not a very functional worker in my study with Gunther during the first year in New York, and later, he ran out of time to teach; this

was a real regret [for me]. New York had such delicious, glorious distractions, and her diversity was overwhelming and still is. Gunther was flexible up to a point, but he knew how to impose pressure when necessary. It was![9]

Ran credits Gunther with teaching him how to organize his time and commitments, as well as a new sort of "conscious" listening:

> He taught me to listen. He also taught me to listen to myself—when I would wander off. I wasn't a very good student at the beginning because I was in love with New York City, but he taught me to have confidence, to go back to some of the European music.[10]

As has been mentioned, Gunther had noted "a certain formlessness"[11] in Ran's improvisations and was striving to address this:

> I made him listen to a lot of well-constructed music, from Beethoven to Stravinsky and Schönberg and Bartók, with an emphasis on how these great masters dealt with form, with logic and proportionality, with continuity and the development of ideas. I wanted him to hear and realize how with the greatest composers nothing in a piece is ever too long or too short [...] Everything is always perfectly balanced in its proportions.[12]

It was a perfect counterpoint of musical personalities—Blake the impressionist and Schuller the formalist. Gunther recorded Ran on a reel-to-reel tape recorder for subsequent commentary and analysis—all with a view to fostering a more acute conceptual awareness in his student. He was a great teacher, and Ran regrets that he did not keep logs:

> [...] there would be the listening to Bach, Mozart, Stravinsky. Often, I would play, but a great deal of each lesson was epistemology. We didn't use these words, but I would have to oscillate between the conscious and the unconscious. If I was too strict, Gunther would say my music was well organized but banal, and if I went the other direction, where I could be innovative and all that, I would be [Gunther said] out of control and structurally not sound. [That's when] he introduced tape recorders; they were reel-to-reel. A few of the lessons would be two to three hours—they were the greatest moments of my life. We never discussed conducting; we did jazz. But a lot was me playing and not holding things together.
> L: What do you mean?

R: Well, because I'm sure I lost my place. My mind would wander. Now that I have made storyboarding a big part of my life, I also have been more... [focused.]

Gunther, when he was all there in a lesson, it was like the best kind of mind control. And then he would say, 'Break away from me and do your own thing.' But when we had regular lessons, he would say, 'Why didn't you do these measures as I asked?' He could be very finicky. He did say, 'Stay with me,' so he had some positive [feedback], but he could be awfully critical. Gunther so often understood my music better than I myself did and was among a handful who could tolerate [it] and demonstrate belief in it.

At the time, this "handful" of supporters included:

Willis Lawrence James (the field cry specialist) and Mary Lou Williams, and Mingus at times. Also, William Russo, Peri and Bill Evans,[13] and Oscar Peterson. There were many lukewarm responses from members of the music community, such as MJQ, and outright negative feedback from Stan Kenton.[14] The only peer support I received was from Jeanne Lee.[15]

BUT GUNTHER'S SUPPORT was pivotal; the lessons and discussions provided Ran an opportunity to identify and hone ideas he was trying to express. Gunther understood Ran; he believed in him, and he took every opportunity to promote his music:

L: Do you think people's perception of you is the real you?
R: I don't know. I'm a man who likes Claude Chabrol and Hitchcock, and Abbey, and Chris Connor; this is psychoanalysis—let me slide on the couch!
L: Ran, be serious!
R: [*without pausing*] Gunther has had a great deal of belief. Hankus has been a great friend ...and Dominique Eade.
L: What do you think about Gunther? Does he have an understanding that most people don't have? Because it seems like before you were acknowledged... It seemed as if it needed Gunther to acknowledge you to have other people acknowledge you.
R: Gunther knows me better than I know myself.
L: Elaborate.
R: Well, he says I have talents that I'm not aware of. He could detect things I did on piano. I think I mean musically, but it could be other

ways. I feel he caught things that I don't know about my piano playing. It's so obvious the things that I DON'T do—some piano players play quicker; some people—everybody—reads better. So, these are tangible things. Maybe I don't want to know them because I don't want to be TOO conscious of what I do, but maybe now at seventy... [*he thinks about it before adding*] four next month, I want to be a little more conscious than I was. But that's about... I don't think I could expand on it.

Of course, I know about myself. I go to the past and go to the cemetery, but there were things that Gunther said—some pedal or echo; something of tone that I do. I don't know how I do it; I just go to the piano and get in the mood.

Gunther has a view of me that nobody else has, and he is quite aware of my foibles; I mean, he's quite aware that he wouldn't use me in a symphony. He said he would not trust me with his will—he thinks I'd be honest but that I would lose it. And he's been known to say I've seen too many movies in my life, and I'd better see more scores.[16]

Right from the beginning, Gunther was kind and understanding towards a young man making his way in New York City. He invited him home, included him in his family:

I knew them in West End Avenue, in New York. I'm sure I called Marjorie 'Mrs. Schuller' at the beginning—she was very warm. Gunther needed a lot of coffee, and then, later, it was Coca-Cola. He could be [an] egoist in the greatest sense, but then when he talked about... The way he looked at Marjorie and the sons—and, occasionally, me—he would be all ears.

At such times, Gunther was a father figure. Ran was drawn into the bosom of the Schuller family, and Gunther's interest in Ran and his playing was more than an epistemological one. It was a special time—to be savored slowly on the walk home.

I could walk home. When I went for a lesson, I was afraid of being late, [so] I would take the subway down to 96th Street. But often, I wanted to save the dollar, or cents, or whatever it cost; then, I could buy a draught beer. And I thought nothing—unless it was a blizzard, or pouring rain, or storms à la Brisbane—I thought nothing of walking home.

Gunther's belief in Ran and his music was evidenced by his bringing him to NEC, where, in 1972, he made Ran Blake head of the newly created Third-Stream Department. For Gunther, Ran was perfect for the role.

His music was the embodiment of third-stream, where "the worlds of jazz, popular music, and advanced 'classical' music intersect, overlap, blend and fuse in an unpredictable array of patterns,"[17] Moreover, Ran Blake's music was not merely a collection of derivative influences; as Schuller noted, the thing that distinguished it from most other attempts in the same direction was "its integrity":[18]

> It is not glib and superficial eclecticism. It springs from the deepest essences of those musical roots which inform his music, and it is probably incorruptible. For Ran has been playing in this way since the mid-fifties. Ran is one of the few successful impressionists and mood painters left in music. His is an improvised music, deeply felt and newly re-interpreted in each performance.[19]

When he first arrived in Boston, Ran was not fully aware of Gunther's plans for him. He struggled with his first job—delivering mail within the university:

> One time, I dropped the postal bag on the marble stairway, and I was so embarrassed as Gunther was showing visitors the school at the time. Gunther said, 'This is one of my protégés, but he's not very good at handling paper,' and they [the visitors] winked at me as they walked by.

Gunther continued to care for Ran. During these early days in Boston, Ran got to know the whole Schuller family more closely:

> I remember a Thanksgiving—my first in Boston—and a Christmas with a red sweater from Marjorie.
> Marjorie and Gunther loved going out. They had various babysitters—Ed and George were young boys; I often… [babysat for them.] There would be food waiting for me—Marjorie would put a lot of dill on the food. I'd sometimes eat in the kitchen with the sons, but I had an adult [meal] with a big glass of wine.
> As it turns out, I was at the house a lot more than a lot of people. Gunther's father, Arthur was often there; he would always be at celebrations.
> Around this time, I started bringing choirs and gospel people to the conservatory; Gunther subsidized it. He kept saying, 'I have plans for you, Ran.' And later, Gunther invited the members of the church on Russell Street to perform at Jordan Hall—this happened on two different occasions.

Gunther was appointed to the faculty at Tanglewood in 1963. (He was Artistic Director from 1970 to 1984.)[20] Ran had more contact with the Schullers there, particularly during the summer of 1968 when he became Gunther's chauffeur. He was, once again, part of the family:

> Marjorie made my lunch and Gunther's every day at Tanglewood. They lived in the old mill house in West Stockbridge.[21] At the end of every day, I would bring Gunther home, and there would be a hot meal waiting for me in the kitchen; they would have me for a cocktail, but then they would go and eat in the front room, in the parlor. But for me to be able to dine on Marjorie's rib-sticking food with dill [*upward inflection of appreciation.*][22] They had me stay at a boarding house; they arranged for me to pay fifteen to twenty dollars a week, and every day, I got up and drove Gunther. I was a very good driver until I drove the car to Boston, and it cracked up, but that's another story for another time, but within Tanglewood, I'm a wonderful driver.
> L: Could Gunther drive?
> R: No, he had one eye that did not have good vision.[23]
> I had my music in the mornings; there was so much... [going on.] Milton Babbitt[24] would drop by; Leinsdorf[25] lived right across the street—he was conducting the BSO at the time; there were friends of the Bernsteins... [dropping in.] So, in this white house—I would be there often—Marjorie got up at dawn, maybe somedays Gunther made coffee and then she did.
> Marjorie just never seemed to get fatigued. She did not ever want an award, or ever be a public person, but her kindness... [*He breaks off, remembering.*]
> I was Gunther's chauffeur for the whole summer of '68 at Tanglewood, and then, when we returned to Boston for the Fall semester, Marjorie let me borrow her car once a week to drive to Wellesley, where we had an extension prep, and I can say this about Marjorie: for years I would say, 'Could I take you to lunch?' and she said she never had time, but as I would stand saying goodbye, we would talk thirty or forty minutes.
> And Gunther visited my parents; the repartee was wonderful!
> L: So, was Gunther teaching you at that stage?
> R: Yes, we did meet regularly, but by then, that was once a month. He got busier and busier. I got out my wallet to pay him, and he said, 'For the pennies you get, I'm not accepting your money anymore as a teacher, but if you could arrange for me to have a martini when Dorothy Wallace comes...' He said, 'I wouldn't mind that—to have a little martini.'[26]

And then, the lessons got more and more erratic; he would say, 'Don't you keep logs or notes of lessons? What did we do last time?

DURING HIS PRESIDENCY of New England Conservatory (between 1967 and 1977), Gunther re-defined the concept of that institution—notably by introducing the first jazz studies[27] course in a "traditional" conservatory in the United States and by bringing in working musicians as faculty.

> It was amazing what happened. [*Ran interjects, shaking his head in wonder.*] May the New England Conservatory last for eternity!
> L: It's very special—because of Gunther probably. I remember Lyle Davidson telling me once that when Gunther was President, if you had a good hand for writing out parts, you didn't want to… [admit it.] The moment Gunther found out, you'd get a call from him at 2 am, and he would say, 'Come to my house. I need this piece copied out.'
> R: [*in delight*] How wonderful! Will you use that in the book?
> L: We could, yeah. He said there'd be a whole heap of faculty there, writing up parts for Gunther's symphony or something.

Ran had many important teachers during the formative years of his twenties and thirties; however, Gunther, more than anyone, understood the overarching aspects of his style. It was almost as if Gunther could see where he was heading before he even knew himself. Such omniscience would have been evident to Ran, who looked to Gunther more and more as his mentor and ultimate counsel in all things musical:

> I would dart to gospel lessons, field cry lessons, even an unhappy semester in the Electronic Lab at Columbia with Ussachevsky and Davidovsky,[28] but I always returned to Gunther for the skills he would enable me to achieve. Plus, he knew me better than I knew myself.[29]

It is a phrase he often repeats—and ponders. While Gunther acknowledged Ran's talent, he also recognized that talent could not be realized without discipline.

> L: I was going to ask you.… You were talking about storyboarding; what did Gunther say [about that] when you were his student? Was he encouraging?
> R: Of course I didn't use that term [at the time], and it's actually one that Alfred Hitchcock uses—but it's not one used in music.… I think

Gunther would say, 'Get back to reality, Ran. Wake up! [*Ran claps to demonstrate urgency.*]³⁰
L: That's what I thought. That's why I asked the question.
R: Yeah, Gunther could be tough.
L: I remember once you told me that Gunther played you something in an odd meter—like seven or something—and you didn't know what it was…
R: [*interrupts*] I probably wouldn't know now.
L: [*without acknowledging the interruption*] and you played along with it to the end, and he said, 'That's why you annoy me Ran Blake because you played that perfectly and this is in 11/16, and so you can play this stuff, you just don't want to!' Now you told me that once.
R: Yes, that's true, but I doubt if I played it perfectly, though. If it's 11/16, I don't think I could play that.
L: You know what I mean. Gunther's very meticulous in the labeling, and yet you have a different labeling system. It is more like a labeling system of spices and flavors, and interesting pictures, and storylines.
R: But Gunther may have some of that too, and I loved working with Gunther because sometimes I needed some discipline.
L: Well, obviously, he realized your talent because he took you on as a student and writes so highly about you in his books and things, but what I'm trying to get at is how did that go? I mean, it's fitting that you are friends because just from the little that I know about him, it seems that you're coming at music from almost polar opposite places.
R: Except that he uses ears as well. I think he's right, though. I think I need to learn how to read a little bit more, so that's very important.

There is no doubt that Gunther was much loved—not only by Ran but also by the many, many musicians he has helped and guided.

AMONG RAN'S PAPERS, there is a photocopied document written by him and typed on NEC stationery. Dated June 28, 1990, it recommends that Gunther should receive the MacArthur Award, and is a fitting tribute to his teacher and mentor:

> Conductor, lecturer, composer, musician, educator, critic, head of a record company, publisher of so much music by living composers, Gunther Schuller wears many hats and is very well known for all of the above.
> Less publicized are three other aspects of his career. First and foremost, Gunther Schuller is a listener of an extremely wide range of

music, including the most contemporary, and is among the least self-obsessed musicians of his caliber.

His two other remarkable traits are less easily separated. He is a visionary and a man of incredible compassion for other men and women within the various communities in which he is involved. As former president of New England Conservatory, he was responsible for creating a Department of Community Services, opening our door to the various communities within Boston and not only sharing our music with them, but also extending a warm welcome and hosting many varieties of ethnic and street music, and exposing our students to the riches of their culture. Our extended musical family also visited the incarcerated and handicapped. There are many examples of the humanitarian Gunther Schuller.

As a visionary, he has an amazingly uncanny ability to predict the role in which artists can best grow, mature, and be of service to others. Often Gunther Schuller is a sort of hidden orchestrator.

If Gunther Schuller could decrease his many conducting demands, he would have time to complete his third book on jazz [...]

GM Records—his record company—has recorded CDs of more than 30 artists. Margun Music publishes the works of more than one hundred living American composers from ragtime to the new music of today.

I can think of no other musician in America who is more worthy of the prestigious MacArthur Award today.

Gunther Schuller was awarded the MacArthur Foundation "genius" fellowship in 1991. Throughout his lifetime, he accumulated a long-list of awards, including the William Schuman Award in 1989 from Columbia University; the Pulitzer Prize in 1994 (for his *Of Reminiscences and Reflections*—a work in memory of his wife, Marjorie); a Jazz Masters Fellowship (for advocacy) from the National Endowment for the Arts in 2008; and a lifetime achievement medal from the MacDowell Colony in 2015. The composer Augusta Read Thomas—chairwoman of the selection committee for the MacDowell medal—said on the occasion of the award, "As a composer and teacher, he has inspired generations of students, setting an example of discovery and experimentation."

Gunther Schuller's death on June 21, 2015, affected Ran deeply. He was *en route* from New York to Boston (after a party that Christine Correa had organized for him with all of his New York friends), when the phone calls started coming through.

Ran had just announced that it had been one of the best days of his life and Aaron Hartley, who took the calls, skillfully disguised their tenor. As

Aaron said later, "How do you tell him something like this after he says something like that?"

After Aaron got him home and was able to break the news, Ran said bleakly, "The last person of my generation is gone. There's no one left."[31]

3

Mentors and Father Figures

Gunther was one of a handful of people to influence Ran's life in a profound way. To Ran, these people are "family," and he refers to them as mentors and father figures. These terms he applies somewhat interchangeably. Gunther, in particular, was seen as both mentor and father figure—though he was perhaps more a "big brother" than a "father," being only ten years Ran's senior. Buz Gummere, whose expert advice and guidance regarding Ran's course of study at Bard was invaluable, was above all a "father figure," providing care and emotional support.

> Now, I may have had… I mean, there have been other people, but Willis Laurence James, Gunther, Buz Gummere, and Bishop I.L Jefferson were my four father figures.

Though Ran insists that there were other people, these were the four names that kept coming up in interviews. Fathers have many roles, and Ran's "father figures" had a wide range of life skills and knowledge to impart.

Bishop I.L. Jefferson of the Church of God in Christ, Hartford, was the first of these "fathers." Ran believes he met him as early as 1951 or '52. Bishop Jefferson was warm and demonstrative—with a "wonderful hug." He was also very much the performer. His sermons had a great sense of theater—starting off calmly and swelling to a dramatically shouted "Hallelujah." Ran has described him as "the Big Sid Catlett[1] of the Gospel church field—a unique rhythmical attack!" His brimstone lectures were tempered by a sensible earthiness—it was, he said, alright for people to spend a little money on clothes and a good meal, and Ran remembers, there was one week when they didn't have to do penance. There were celebrations, too—with sweet potato pie and "the best lemonade and cold tea." Bishop Jefferson had a lot to teach about living a good life; he provided robust spiritual direction.

The next father figure—Buz Gummere—gave much-needed emotional support for a young man on the cusp of adult independence. Richard (Buz) Gummere was Director of Admissions at Bard College[2] when Ran was a student there. For Ran, who had already faced up against intractable figures of authority (notably in the music department at Suffield), meeting Buz Gummere was a revelation—and a relief. Buz was patient, kind, encouraging, supportive—a family man who opened his heart and home to the young Ran Blake.

Ran first got to know Buz Gummere in the Spring of 1956. He had been wondering how best to organize his course, and he took the opportunity to meet the director of admissions to find out if he could be a jazz major at Bard. Buz Gummere assured him he would speak to Jim Case.[3] Ran was overjoyed and hastened to explain that his favorite musicians were Thelonious Monk, Mahalia Jackson, and Chris Connor. Buz was an educational administrator, not a musician, but he had recently seen *The Benny Goodman Story* and good-naturedly referred to this movie, saying how much he liked the music. As Ran now looks back on his long association with Buz Gummere, his wife, Peg, and their children Duff,[4] Lish (Elisha,) John, and Christine[5] and their importance in his life, he can state unequivocally:

> In more than fifty-five years, this was the only thing I disagreed with him about.

Ran vividly remembers his first visit to the Gummere home in Barrytown[6] in 1957. He also remembers the food served—corn pudding and "a delicious casserole." The tranquility of the home impressed Ran: Peg was painting when he arrived—with Duff looking on. Buz was there, whistling "All About Ronnie" as Lish played it on his trumpet.[7]

Ran must have impressed the Gummeres, too, for a few Sundays after this, they took him to their Quaker meeting. It was the beginning of a long and special friendship.

According to Ran, he had his "third drink in life" at the Gummere home. Buz cautioned him how dreadful blended whiskey could be and gave him the advice, "Always drink it straight, Ran." The family often included Ran in their social engagements—dinners with the Walsh's, Clair Leonard, Kate Wolff. Ran was delighted. He and Jeanne Lee were invited for "a fancy plate of appetizers" with Carroll Moshier. On one occasion, one of Ran's "few student friends," the Frenchman Henri de Seynes, brought a bottle of wine with him to the Gummere home. (Henri was dating John and Christine's babysitter at the time.) Ran was impressed by the gesture. "This was a tradition I tried to uphold," he recalls.

At the Walsh's, he dined with Barry Ulanov[8] and Philip and Stephanie Barber, who ran the School of Jazz in Lenox (and no doubt ignited his enthusiasm for that school.) On another occasion, at dinner, Buz encouraged Muriel DeGré[9] to offer Ran a job at the *Dutchess County Journal*, the local newspaper.[10] (Ran remembers reviewing an Oscar Peterson record.)

The Gummeres provided a much-needed support base. Ran still remembers the night when, after a confrontation with Paul Nordoff (composer, music therapist, and professor of music at Bard from 1948–1959), he turned up at the Gummere home with "suppressed tears." Buz counseled him and advised him to speak to Mrs. Borick:

> So that [confrontation] was because I wanted to be a major in jazz. Mrs. Borick was a widow in a little town outside of Poughkeepsie, and if I had a map, I could see it. And Emil Hauser was also [there]. He was in the Budapest Quartet; he was quite well known. He, Mr. Leonard, Mr. Nordoff, and Kate Wolf were the music faculty.

Buz Gummere's fatherly advice was exactly what Ran needed at the time. Buz treated Ran as another son, even giving him a key to his office. Later, Buz and Peg were to give Ran the key to their New York apartment.

> And of course, at one time, I had eight keys; I could stay in Paris in the Champs-Élysées district. I was given more keys in my life... [than you can imagine].
> L: That's nice, Ran.
> R: It is nice. Anyway, I did have a lot of keys. Everything's interconnected, isn't it?

Buz helped Ran establish the Bard College Jazz Lab. (Lish was a founding member.) He also helped him set up a hospitality committee to welcome guests playing in the Bard Jazz Festival (which Ran had instigated) and sell tickets to those attending. As well, he gave Ran a budget to bring the Church of God in Christ from North Hartford to the festival.

> And Janet, hear this, I was given money to invite the WHOLE church's [choir]. Four busloads came up!

Bishop I.L. Jefferson and Hubert Powell were among the group. Buz gave the kick-off speech in the Bard College chapel, and Ran remembers that "three or four students were saved that night." Ran must have been an astute manager of the budget he'd been allocated as he recalls:

> We served Lobster Newberg for them—they had never had this dish. And then the Bard College cooks made creole rice and salads, and this became a tradition!
> Buz Gummere [*It's said on a new note, rounding the conversation back to his role as a "father figure"*], I asked him could I be a jazz major—that I liked Thelonious Monk... and now I'm doing a lick... [*He interrupts the dialogue, suddenly aware of its construction, before continuing with the musicians he liked.*] and Oscar Petersen...
> Okay [*abruptly closing the conversation*], shall we go in for a culinary... Janet, we're about to offer your hard-working son a very good sandwich. I might say, the best that's made in Brookline.
> L: [*Laughing*] And on that note, signing off, Ran Blake.

Ran's friendship with the Gummeres continued after Bard. When it came time for him to move to Boston:

> They gave me a departure [send-off] and sent me to Roxbury church [Boston], which was quite different from the Church of God in Christ. It was on whatever that big square is—the main place in Roxbury where the Mass. Avenue bus goes... [*For a brief moment, he is there—his eyes have a far-away look—before he deliberately re-focusses.*] Oh, my mind wanders!

They invited him to Duxbury for mussel digging outings:

> Peg loved Duxbury—I can see her in the water.[11]

And during these times, there were dinners with the "outspoken but divinely lovely" Dorothy Wallace.

When Ran re-visited New York, they housed him, fed him, and gave him "elegant midnight drinks." They often put him up in the small room by the kitchen and, in the morning, served "coffee with steamed milk." Later, Ran persuaded his students to read Buz's book *How to Survive Education* but admits it was never as inspirational as hearing Buz himself speak.

Ran was very touched that Buz and Peg made the five-hour trip to be present at his 70th birthday celebrations in 2005. Buz was in his nineties, and Peg her late eighties, at the time. When Buz died, the community journal of the Dutchess and Columbia counties, *About Town,* printed the following tribute:

> Buz always said that people should never give up searching for the work that gives them joy. He was a man of grace, intelligence, and humor with an unflagging interest in people. He asked that he be remembered as 'a gentleman, a scholar, and a judge of good whiskey.' His last clear word was marvelous.[12]

ANOTHER "FATHER FIGURE" for Ran was Willis Laurence James—violinist, academic, and collector of folklore and folksongs[13] (particularly from along the levees of the Mississippi). He was one of Ran's favorite teachers at the Lenox school:

> And I can still hear his field cries. We would walk on the Housatonic River and amble over to the Hawthorne House.[14] One day he literally broke into a field cry, and the birds seemed to answer. I wish Messiaen had been present. He sang—or moaned—these cries. I've never heard anything like it. He would tell stories of his father, who was a slave. He was a faculty member at Morehouse and Spelman College. And I had hoped to see him when, in 1968, I flew down to Atlanta to perform music in support of Maynard Jackson, but it was too late.[15] My first song on *Wende*,[16] "Field Cry," is dedicated to him.

James's research focused on cries and calls. He saw them as the "powerful urge" to express and communicate life's emotions.[17] He collected field cries, transcribing them by ear. As well, he collected the calls that people used—their selling calls. (He mentions, in particular, the call of the tobacco auctioneer—a call Ran would have known from his boyhood, living, as he did, in a tobacco-producing area.) He also referred to the religious cries of the "Negro preacher" as he delivered his "'gravy' type of sermon." These sermons, though fiery, had a musical use of voice that, according to James, defied description. They built to an "oratorical cadenza," which was answered with "vocal 'shouts' among the congregation."[18] The description conjures up the shouts of "Hallelujah" from the church at Hartford. It is little wonder, then, that James's teachings resonated so deeply with Ran.

James had, up to 1943, done most of his recording without a machine. Instead, he chose "to live with the people and learn to sing the songs just as they do."[19] Once learned, he could transcribe the songs himself. The approach required humility and a lot of hard work—an approach he modeled for Ran.

As well as his "father figures," Ran had two wonderful women who were his mentors and "mothers." The first of these was Mother Sarah Carter.

> R: [*interrupting in excitement*] Mother Carter, whose picture is in the hallway! You've seen my stepmother? She was Bishop I.L. Jefferson's 'star assistant.'

Mother Carter was an active lifetime member of Holy Trinity Church of God in Christ (and the Latter Rain Christian Fellowship, as it became). Ran recalls going to the church "in '50/'51—but maybe earlier, maybe later." For years, Mother Carter "reigned supreme." She was the choral director, and Ran has written of her influence:

> The musical growth of the Church of God in Christ might have been impossible without Mother Carter, who served as a catalyst in a way similar to Duke [Ellington] in the forties.[20]

He remembers Sarah Carter with great fondness:

> I was twenty when she was fifty. We said we'd have her to Suffield, but how would she get there? She was at the church five nights a week! I was told that once, as a child, she might have had a little elderberry wine when she was twelve. But basically, she never tasted a drop of Satan's liquor—she led a holy life. And I've seen people like her in other churches where they get very pious, and do you know François Mauriac who has a person called Brigitte Pian who went to church every day but was not kind?[21] Mother Carter was kind. I did see her one day—one guy was chewing—she went like that. [*He demonstrates—as if to slap his own cheek.*] She deliberately missed his face. She said, 'I'll take that'; she had a little napkin. 'Out, out,' she said. Oh, it was like Kim Novak.... She would be there at the back. And later, of course, there was Sr. Tee, when we get to Harlem and Sweet Daddy Grace's, who led the brass band.
> Mother Carter was something, not maybe as important as Dorothy Wallace, but she WAS something!

4

D.C.W—Mentor, Patron, and True Friend

You have turned for me my mourning into dancing.

Psalm 30:11

The demons that had haunted Ran after his return from Greece followed him to Boston and persisted there, as fleeting shadows, dimming the edges of each new experience. There was none of the happy anticipation that he had felt seven years before when he'd moved to New York, and Boston, in sharp contrast to that city, had no welcoming home base of the kind provided by Miss Amelia Lehrfeld.

Nights were often lonely and filled with bad dreams about Greece. Occasionally, Ran went home to Suffield for the weekend, where he would be drawn, briefly, into the warmth, love, and security of his family... and the Gospel Church. And though both tried to dispel the ghosts, there was only so much they could do—his life was now in Boston.

> I think my parents paid for me to take the train back [to Suffield] some weekends, but usually, I stayed right where I was. I did not have the social life of New York. Basically, I got much more introverted. The piece "Vradiazei" haunted me every night. It's very innocent; it's not even political, but it was being played in the Plaka on the night of the coup.

It would have worried Ran's family to see him this way. He was distressed, and they were powerless to do anything about it. But Ran's grandmother, Jessie, had foretold that there would be someone for him. She had always promised he would meet "an important person" who would protect him and guide him through difficult times.

> She said there would be a lady; she'd be very, very special.
> J: Was she psychic, Ran? She told you that in great detail.
> R: My grandmother? Yes! But she wouldn't give the names of people. She would look in the water and would take a pair of dice... look at hands, and then she knew things.

It is impossible to know what, exactly, Jessie envisaged when she made this prediction. She would have hoped, as a grandmother, for someone who loved Ran as dearly as she did, probably imagining someone who was warm, caring, understanding, and encouraging—a bit like herself. It was a tall order, but Ran did meet someone with these qualities and more: someone who, with a combination of boundless energy and deep concern, was always able to make good things happen. Ran called her his mentor, his great patron. Her name was Dorothy Wallace, and she and Ran were to become very dear friends. She had the happy knack of meeting difficulties head-on while promoting peace... and stillness.

IT WAS INEVITABLE that Ran and Dorothy Wallace would meet (putting aside Jessie Powers' prediction), for, in addition to supporting many charities and causes, Dorothy was a great promoter of young musicians—and of the arts in general. They met in 1968 when Ran was still relatively new to Boston:

> through a man called Timothy Marquand, who I met through a guy called 'Cracker.' He [Cracker] was born on 4th July. [*It's added matter-of-factly.*] His [real] name was James Piladon, and he was the night security guy at the YMCA in Cambridge. Timothy Marquand was the son of John Marquand,[1] who wrote an insightful, witty novel called *The Late George Apley*.[2] It was made into a movie starring Ronald Colman. The Marquand and the Wallace families were old friends, and so Dorothy invited me to lunch. She came and picked me up—I was staying at the YMCA.

Ran, in his usual eagerness to "connect" people, invited the daughter of the head of the extension prep school, Eve Bernard, to come along with him:

> I raved about the spinach. She [Dorothy] said, 'Next week come [again] and this time bring seven people—we weren't expecting you, Miss Bernard, today.'³

Anne Elvins Grace, Dorothy Wallace's daughter, also recalls this meeting, though in slightly different detail. She remembers it was a Greek student from MIT who introduced Ran to her mother:

> Somehow Mother met a Greek student from MIT named Stelios Argyros. Stelios suggested that Mother should meet a young jazz pianist named Ran Blake. As Mother told me, she was to pick Ran up outside the New England Conservatory and take him back home to 11 Chestnut Place in Brookline for lunch. She made him creamed spinach for that first meal, and because of it, they instantly became fast friends.⁴

So, although details of this first meeting differ, there is no doubt about the spinach. And whoever it was who brought Dorothy and Ran together can take credit for planting the seed of a wonderful friendship—a friendship that was to last for thirty-two years, until Dorothy's death at age eighty-seven in the year 2000. While Dorothy was perhaps Ran's closest friend, the friendship was by no means one-sided. Anne Elvins Grace puts it simply, "I do know that Ran changed my mother's life, and I am forever grateful to him."

Dorothy came from Rockford, Illinois: Her father was an inventor—Howard Colman:

> And there's no "e" in Colman.⁵ One of her father's inventions was to press a button and have the garage door open. Dorothy and her husband, Richard Wallace, a surgeon, settled on High Street, Brookline.⁶ [It was] an exclusive area right next to Whiskey Point. The subway stop would be Brookline Hills.

Dorothy and Richard (always known as Dick) married in 1935 in Munich, where her father's business associate Herbert Speidel⁷ arranged the beautiful wedding, complete with a white coach drawn by horses. Dick's work as a surgeon at the Massachusetts General Hospital brought the couple back to Boston after the wedding. Here, they had social position and financial security. They brought five children into the world, "each with their own unique spin on life."⁸ And things seemed good. They had been married twenty years when Dick succumbed to cancer.

Anne Elvins Grace recalls the early years before Ran came into their lives:

Mother was a very powerful woman. She had many friends, and they were tremendously important to her. My father was a surgeon, and while he was alive, my mother's social life was pretty much restricted to a group of doctors and their wives—a group we later called 'the old guard.' Mother was forty-six when my father died, and she soon turned to making new friends. Interestingly enough, Mother's new friends were often a generation younger than she, but almost all these friends remained friends for life.

Dorothy Wallace certainly had courage and resilience. It took character to face life without her husband—guiding five children into adulthood on her own. But Dorothy Wallace had "character" in every sense of the word. She was larger than life—energetic, gregarious, strong, and resolute. As Ran's grandmother had predicted, she came into his life when he needed her most—and changed it for the better.

RAN WILL READILY admit, he was not in good shape during the first year in Boston. The reasons for this were personal but also reflected a wider social disquiet. When Dorothy came into his life, she provided a whole new perspective. Dorothy was philanthropic by nature. Ran's work in community outreach interested her greatly; not surprisingly, she threw herself wholeheartedly into supporting him in this field. She was also a huge supporter of Ran on a personal level—and of his music.

She used her contacts and influence to make opportunities for him:

> There would be restaurants [where they'd say], 'There is no bill for you, Monsieur.' Suddenly I'm at Chicago with Warne Marsh[9] as the headliner, and Dorothy walks in with people from the Barber-Colman company, and when Dorothy went out to use the facilities, I heard one lady say, 'The food's good here at least. Why did we have to come to hear this pipsqueak?'... meaning me.
> L: [*interrupting*] You were playing with Warne Marsh?
> R: Not with him. He was with his quartet, and I was [the] intermission pianist. We don't know who arranged it. Did Dorothy? Did Art Lange from *DownBeat*? But I got booked there, and she walked in.
> L: What did Warne Marsh think?
> R: If he'd hated me, I would remember. If he'd liked me... [*He breaks off without offering any possible indication of such approval. Instead, he summarizes*] So I would say: benign neglect. I can't remember the year, but this was years after I met Dorothy.

FROM THEIR FIRST meeting, Dorothy's support for Ran (and for his projects) never wavered. Her home was open to him at all hours. He even felt free to invite friends there. He was able to rely on her in the same way that you could expect to rely on a very close family member—quite possibly in the same way that he used to rely on his beloved grandmother, Jessie.

> I introduced her to people from work, and she was able to get closer to them than I was. She provided a hotel for my friends, and she subsidized a great deal of things that happened in Boston.

Some abused her hospitality, causing Ran to reflect with embarrassment:

> My friends took over the house—can you imagine—before Dorothy put her foot [down]. One person walked in and took the sixty-five-dollar bottle of burgundy—and that would be two hundred dollars now—and started drinking it!
> And Dorothy bought a saxophone for a struggling student at school, and he called up the next day and said, 'Is this Dorothy Wallace? I can call you Dorothy? Thanks for the baritone sax; could you bring me two more?'
> And some of the people—there were Daughters of the American Revolution, Black Panthers—three or four tramp friends came; they were smoking grass. She said, 'You know I'm liberal, but I can't…'
> And somebody said, 'Hi, Dotty.' And she *hated* that word! I mean, her son and daughter felt… [*He does not continue, but one imagines they would surely have felt affronted—even alienated—by this invasion of their home-space.*]

These uncomfortable moments were, as Ran explains later, at the very beginning of their friendship—probably when parameters were being tested and set. Dorothy very quickly made her position clear:

> She did say would I kindly not give open invitations to everybody I met. She said that this included people from 'inside'[10] as well as… Ah… I think I was mad. [*It's said with resignation.*]

But these uncomfortable moments quickly faded—eclipsed by wonderful ones. From 1974, once the third-stream department was underway, the house was regularly filled with people, and music, and good food, and Dorothy Wallace became famous for the concerts, soirées, and dinner parties she hosted.

Anne Elvins Grace remembers:

> In a trice, Mother was inviting all kinds of fascinating people [suggested by Ran] to dinners and soirées—featuring Ran and his jazz musicians—at Chestnut Place. Mother was in her element—meeting new friends, having parties, and quietly supporting jazz musicians and others who needed help. This became her life until shortly before she died.

The house, at 11 Chestnut Place, was eminently suited to entertaining. Eileen Murphy, long-time personal assistant to Dorothy Wallace, recalls it was:

> A grand old house with many, many rooms, a fireplace, and cute, little terraces. It was really something—an amazing 1850 Italianate.

By the time Eileen arrived at Chestnut Place in 1984, the friendship between Ran and Dorothy was well established—and so were the parties. These were held every two or three weeks, and Eileen was able to observe them close at hand, for she lived in the carriage house on the property. She recalls:

> Dorothy Wallace was always the mistress of ceremonies, and there were many different occasions which provided excuses to have parties [in] this beautiful home—a very, very, special, magical place in itself.

From the moment Dorothy appeared on the stairway to greet her guests; from the moment the musicians broke into "I Get a Kick out of You" (which became her anthem—alternating with "Mood Indigo" or "Night and Day") in answer to her greeting,[11] Dorothy was effortlessly in charge. There was a certain protocol of introductions to be followed, and then Dorothy would take up a microphone and announce, "Ladies and Gentlemen... " and direct people to the food, the cheese, the wines. Dorothy enjoyed this showmanship.

> Dorothy Wallace was not Mother Teresa. She still wanted people to do 'I get a Kick out of You' when she would go down the stairway, so she had a little ego. She'd say—after we'd done Ornette and all that—she'd say, 'Please end with my anthem.' She loved to have

flowers presented to her. That's why it was so great for other people—because she enjoyed herself.

Birthdays were an obvious occasion for celebration and, as Dorothy had a large family and so many friends, there were many, many birthdays. Ran, and various "third-stream" groups, would come over to entertain. But birthdays were not the only occasion. Maxine Dolle, a neighbor, remembers that when she and her husband moved into Brookline, it wasn't long before Dorothy visited, proposing a welcome party for them. Dorothy loved meeting new people—she also loved putting on a party. As Maxine fondly recalls, "She would have a party simply because the wisteria came out."[12] These parties were lavish affairs, meticulously prepared. They conjured up another age—both gracious and generous. They usually took place in the dining room or, as Maxine likes to remember it, "the grand music room" that looked out over the garden.

It was a very beautiful room. The 1913 Steinway Grand had pride of place in the window bay, where light flooded through floor-to-ceiling mullioned windows. If it was dark or cold outside, the brocade curtains (light gold to match the tones in the Persian rug) could be drawn, but usually, they were left open to make the most of the view. The garden, from this aspect, was particularly beautiful. Following the lines of an ancient esker, it was softly verdant and framed by a stand of conifers... magical. More than an acre in size, the gardens were a haven for squirrels, raccoons, and chipmunks; they often came into the house as well! Ran recalls:

> There was a jungle walk. There was a forest. It was a miracle.

And the miracle was that, through Dorothy's generosity, this beautiful place, as well as her home at Cohasset, could be shared with so many.

DINNER PARTIES WERE always preceded—or followed—by musical items. For a recital, Dorothy would remove the elegant timber dining table and bring in little gold-colored chairs. She would set out as many as thirty chairs (concert-fashion) facing the piano. Prior to a concert, guests would congregate in the living room on the second floor for cocktails, hors d'oeuvres, and lively conversation. Dorothy was an excellent hostess, skilled in introducing different people—finding something they had in common to encourage discussion. Maxine Dolle remembers:

> She had a large cross-section of acquaintances. There were neighbors, a group of her husband's friends, peers, friends of her children, and then people she had met (because she knew so many in the arts). She knew people who had restaurants; when they opened up, she would go along to patronize.
>
> And she had grand parties! I recall her parties were time-specific. It would be a brunch—lots of brunches. There were lots of cocktails—the cocktail hour. And when there was going to be a performance, it would be first cocktails, then performance, and I know there were some dinners along the line. She would have hors d'oeuvres, cocktails, and then a performance. And sometimes it wasn't necessarily thirty or forty people—it could have been smaller. It was a really glorious time—I felt it was like the *Great Gatsby*.[13]

Maxine also remembers that when Dorothy introduced Ran to the audience, it was always a "grand introduction" in which she stated how talented he was and the importance of his work in the Third-Stream department.[14]

RAN HAS HIS OWN memories of these events:

> The younger students in the department were always given opportunities to perform—that would be in the earlier part of the evening. There were a few rules—don't wear sneakers at dinner—she didn't want ultra-formal, but she was critical of me if I wore a red shirt with the wrong… [*He fades out, leaving this past fashion indiscretion unspoken.*] She befriended Rocky Birigwa—a prince from Uganda; she was a friend of Mait Edey, who I met on the Abbey Lincoln recording. There were negotiations to bring Ornette, but he was getting too big. She loved Ella, Sarah, Cole Porter, Gershwin. Later she liked a little Coltrane. She got to like Chris Connor in the end. I wrote "Indian Winter"[15] for her. Peter Row[16] played there. And Gunther, George Russell,[17] Jimmy Giuffre [would come]. Adelheid Dahl Hestnes, who ran the dormitory, would bring over Scandinavian food. And the dog was Brünnhilde, from the Wagner…[opera.][18]

Ran would usually plan the guest appearances, having them fit into the theme of the concert. No two concerts were alike. Then, one time, Dorothy made the announcement that there was to be a special guest; Ran wondered who it could be. He was quite overcome when Jeanne Lee came out and started singing.

Every March 1st was Dorothy's birthday. One of her birthday parties, Dorothy said, we have a special guest. I thought it might be Jon Wulp or a student. And she loved Hankus… or maybe Dominique or even Gunther. And then, Jeanne Lee walked out in the room! And the capacity of this room is ninety-two people, and she did her scatting right there in Wallace Hall. I just flipped—people brought out water for me—I mean, to have Jeanne Lee… [*He breaks off with an upward tone of incredulity.*]

THERE IS SOMETHING quite miraculous about the story. Jeanne Lee, whose life had taken such a different path, was suddenly there—right in the middle of Ran's new world—singing, and Ran's old life and his new were stitched together with her song. It says a lot for Dorothy's sensitivity and generosity, for it is certain she would have invited Jeanne (on the occasion of her own birthday) simply to please Ran.

Dorothy was unstinting in her support and care. Maxine Dolle observed:

> It was clear there was a close relationship between her and Ran—that she adored him and thought of him very much as a son. There was a great deal of respect and love between the two of them.[19]

Eileen Murphy saw this also:

> There was almost a maternal aspect to her relationship.[20]

And like a mother, Dorothy was not backward in offering Ran her advice and admonishments. Again, according to Eileen:

> Dorothy always said he didn't know how to take a bow properly—because he was so humble and awkward about taking any praise. Just the way he would take a bow on stage, you could see how uncomfortable he was—he was always taking an opportunity to promote other people's music.
> Dorothy also would correct him sometimes and berate him or take him to task for certain things—often that his shirt was not tucked in, or his tie was not right, or she couldn't believe that he wore that red tee-shirt again! And that's just the way she would say it—AGAIN! and look right at him.

The tee-shirt rings true. Ran, in his eighties, still instinctively adds a dash of color to everyday outfits—a red tee-shirt, a colorful scarf, bright green sox. Like some sort of mnemonic, they focus the eye and help create an instant memory snapshot of the occasion. Dorothy Wallace had a similar understanding of color—a red carnation in the buttonhole of a black blouse, a vase of bright blooms at the center of a formal dining table—little things to catch the eye. But it is the people, the music, and day-to-day rhythms that have sustained the memory of eleven Chestnut place. Ran is more than happy to guide us through:

> I know you're very interested, Janet, in the interior. You walked in, and there would be the foyer with the fireplace—gins and vodkas and Jack Daniel's would be there, and there would be Bible readings—Dorothy felt it was not incongruous.
> I said, 'You mean we can have firewater and the Bible?'
> She said, 'Who do you think I am? We can do whatever we want here.'
> This foyer[21] had a portrait of [Dorothy's] two daughters—never would there be a picture of Dorothy [*It's said gravely*]—painted by a very famous portrait painter, Mr. Polonsky, and it's not spelled like the Polish director.[22] Dorothy also commissioned the first book of the Bible, Genesis, to be done by a Hungarian artist, Lajos Szalay.[23]
> Then you would descend one or two steps into a dining room. This was a large room that was just a little smaller than the park across the street (probably half the size), which she made into a theatre concert hall. [*He pauses for a moment and then adds upon reflection*] More like one-third the park... Dorothy bought my mother and father's antique dining room table that could get big or small.[24] Then there was a large kitchen with a Walter Colman stove [*sic*][25] and a new icebox, and then, behind that, was a laundry and [a supply of] wood.

The tour continues to the "forbidden quarters" upstairs—Dorothy's suite. And then there was the "tunnel" that took her directly to the swimming pool:

> So she could go into her house—she didn't want people to see her in bathing clothes. She would not swim after 9.30 am.

There's a sense of mystery about the statement, which Ran recognizes:

> I think tunnel is not... It's not *Lord of the Rings*. I think it's not really a rabbit tunnel [either].

Tunnels aside, the house did have much of the magic of Alice's wonderland—with perhaps a little of the mystery of Tolkien's Middle Earth.

The house was a wonderful place for entertaining, but it was also a refuge. Eileen Murphy remembers that Ran—for many years—would go there for a vacation, even though it was only "a mile or something" from his apartment—"He would go there as a retreat."

> And [*Ran quickly adds,*] there was also a library upstairs, a parlor—You don't say living room—[you say] parlor.

The house and gardens were ordered, restful, still. There were no distractions—no noise. Dorothy was aware of the importance of stillness: "You cannot hear music and noise at the same time."[26] She was also mindful that the bustle and clutter of everyday life could take over a person—deprive them of the things of beauty. She wrote on February 8, 1957:

> Debauched and worn-out senses require the vibrations of an instrument to excite them. One would think from the critics that music is intermittent as a spring in the desert—depending on some Paganini or Mozart—but music is perpetual, and only hearing is intermittent.[27]

She saw to it that there was every opportunity for rest and renewal: when the senses could be trained solely on the music, when worries could quietly fade.

In his one-week retreat at the house, Ran stayed on the top floor:

> Dorothy would be out of the house. I was allowed house wine. I was allowed only three or four calls a day—I was quite a social butterfly then. I could have a few guests, and I was also told what I could serve them; certain rooms were forbidden. To be there in that house for one week a year [*Ran's tone is one of wonder*]. And how much I loved Dorothy, but to be alone...
> The first night or two, I partied with people; they couldn't get over a house like that. But to be at the piano hours at night—the grand piano. Squirrels and chipmunks came in... I was quite a good cook for Brunhilda [*sic*], Dorothy's adopted daughter—a bi-racial spaniel that sang. She was brown and white. She was very attractive and very warm. I felt great at Chestnut Place. That's the happiest I've ever been, [being] in that house—and certainly, ever since Greece.

In a letter to Dorothy, dated August 14, 1973, Ran wrote of these times:

> I cherish very highly the moments alone in the house with its deep silences.

Ran also had the opportunity to visit Dorothy Wallace's summer house on a "beautiful little cove" in Hobart Lane, Cohasset. Cohasset—tranquil, small—is perched on the rocky shores where Boston Harbor meets Massachusetts Bay, about twenty miles south of Boston. It is an idyllic spot with secluded beaches, deep water mooring for boating and fishing, and, because it is a peninsula, the opportunity to see both sunrise and sunset over water. In the summer, Dorothy would commute to Boston for appointments. It was an easy forty-minute drive, hugging the coastline.

The house at Cohasset was a peaceful place—comfortably part of its environment. It was old, rendered in stucco, and built, as Maxine Dolle remembers:

> in the style of Frank Lloyd Wright—very elegant but old. There were twenty-two beds—we counted them.[28]

Dorothy's generosity had no sense of *noblesse oblige*. Her love of people, her capacity for friendship, and an apparent selflessness allowed her to go further than simply supporting artists and causes. She was quite happy to share her home and her life with others. Taki and Akemi Masuko, both students at the conservatory, lived at one time on the top floor at Chestnut Place in return for cooking meals a few nights a week. Akemi was a classical pianist, and Taki was a percussionist in Ran's Third-Stream Department, so the house was always full of music. They also kept the large kitchen "meticulously clean." This would have been no mean feat when considering Eileen Murphy's fond memory of Dorothy in the kitchen:

> Oh, she was a fabulous cook—just a whirlwind in the kitchen. She made a huge mess with everything she cooked, and she was accustomed to having other people who could then clean up. But she loved to bake cookies and biscuits and things like that and be dusted with flour from head to toe—as well as her glasses and everything else that was in reach! So I feel blessed that when the *Joy of Cooking* cookbook came out (it was a new edition), she gave me her old *Joy of Cooking*. And I have it, which is, you know, *covered* [*Eileen gives the word appropriate emphasis.*] with buttery fingerprints and blobs of cookie dough.
>
> So yes, really, she was a great cook. She loved to cook and still did, up till the very end of her life. She would cook a small dinner for her friends (one or two people) but anything more than that...Well, before she moved out of Chestnut Place into a much smaller place,[29] she had people on staff—I was across the driveway in the carriage house,

Taki and Akemi were upstairs; she had handymen, and groundsmen, and pool people, and everything else.

Ran, reading through the first draft of this book, added his own memory:

> She made a spicy steak dish called 'Steak Blake,' and she gave me a pepper mill to take to school because they didn't have pepper. She had shad roe. Oh, you should have been here for the food. [*It's said rapturously.*]
> Curtis ate at Dorothy Wallace's—wild duck and shad roe.[30] It's fancy, and every spring, Dorothy Wallace would serve it.
> And, of course, she and Eileen were the concierges of the swimming pool, so every hour after 9.30 [when Dorothy had had her swim], anyone could go there if they signed the ledger.
> L: Did you swim there?
> R: Yes, but one time I got there late! She said, 'You've lost your place; you can come back next season. Don't be late.' [*Demonstrating, he wags an admonishing finger.*] She said she would not have it [the pool] grossly hot. 'If you want it warmer, take a martini.'

Dorothy Wallace's heart was big, and her friendship circles were wide. She brought together people from all walks of life. She had many different charities with which she was involved. She shared "the breadth of herself"[31] with others. But despite the demands of her busy life and her many commitments, her friendship with Ran was special. Anne Elvins Grace recalls that Ran and Dorothy chatted on the phone every morning at seven. She also remembers that her mother did not hesitate to advise, direct, organize, or admonish Ran:

> Mother had a way of getting really angry at her very closest friends. One morning when I happened to be in the house, I heard Mother say, "NOW, RAN!" [*Using upper case, underlining, and exclamation mark, Anne's letter conveys a very exasperated tone.*][32]

Whatever Ran had said to warrant this stern response is unknown, but these morning phone calls from Dorothy Wallace were part of the loving support that helped him through the difficult times he experienced:

> At 7.30 every morning, Dorothy Wallace called me. I loved that. We talked about the events of the day—I was supposed to have read the *New York Times* before she called so I could be questioned about things. We'd talk of the international, the national, the local [news], polite gossip—never evil gossip. I could sleep late on Saturdays; Sunday, I had to get up early.

Eileen Murphy remembers Dorothy's occasional irritation toward Ran:

> He [Ran] used to refer to it as 'the vinegar' when Dorothy corrected him in some way. I remember after she died—he'd never seen her give *me* 'the vinegar'—and he asked me one time, 'Did Dorothy ever give you the vinegar?' He was aware of that side of their relationship. It was particular to her relationship with Ran.

Ran wrote of this relationship and the things he valued in a letter to Dorothy:

> You are also unpredictable and complex in your warmth, compassion, humanitarianism—these are always spiced with a drop of vinegar—or perhaps something else.[33]

But it was in the sweet and the sharp—in the little, day-to-day things—that the friendship was forged and tested. Dorothy threw herself wholeheartedly into Ran's projects at New England Conservatory. She was his "rock." She loved his music and was a founding member of the Third-Stream Foundation,[34] which supported his work and the work of his department. Her enthusiasm for this foundation knew no bounds:

> Oh, she had so many plans. She wanted to endow the department. She had many plans to help people in life.

Dorothy, though, was never reckless with her support. She well understood her responsibilities and realized that her ability to give continued support relied on her own astute stewardship of the resources she had. She expected Ran to do likewise. Eileen Murphy remembers:

> Dorothy couldn't believe at times what a genius he [Ran] was, [and yet, she felt] he sometimes lacked common sense. I remember once she became irritated because she always thought he was spending too much money taking students out to dinner and that he should be saving. She worried a lot about what was going to become of Ran in his old age. She used to bring food to him all the time (care packages), especially if he wasn't feeling well. She had me deliver things all the time (and she did that for other people too), but she always had Ran on her mind; she was just there for him in a lot of very difficult times and was his biggest supporter, I would say. She sent Ran away once, and while he was away, she had her architect friend[35] come in and design him a studio, and she bought him a piano, and when he came back, it was all installed.[36]

Ran, reading this, is eager to add details of how the apartment renovation was accomplished:

> Dorothy said, 'Cole Porter said, "Get Out of Town." I'm asking you to get out of town.'
> I said, 'What? Did I do something wrong?'
> She said, 'I've found a place for you to stay—you're not to go to Coolidge Corner. You're allowed to be in South Brookline and go to Boston for the movies, but not Coolidge Corner... and we have ways of checking up on you!' [*Again, he holds up a cautionary finger.*]
> It used to be two little rooms here. Dorothy said, 'Jeez, these rooms are too small.' And then I saw her and Greg Silberman,[37] and they stopped talking when I came near. Then she said, 'Somebody's coming. We want to pack you and send you on a trip.'
> I said, 'Dorothy, where are you sending me... to Europe?'
> She said, 'Just down the street. Get out of town!'
> L: And did you have any idea what was going to happen?
> R: [*Shakes his head in a solemn negation.*]
> L: How did you feel when you came back and saw it?
> R: Oh! [*He is lost for words.*] I think Dorothy was outside the window, watching, and I just moaned and moaned. I could NOT get over it. These people that made the Falcone piano...[38] Years before, she once said, 'What sort of piano do you like?' and I said, 'German Steinway,' and she said, 'Only kings have that.'
> So we had one of the ten pianos they [Falcone] made—and now they've gone into the white chocolate business...
> But when I came back and saw this room and windows... the whole thing was different. And this is the same man who did her swimming pool, Ron Freilich. And the pool's considered one of the best pools in New England.
> L: Well, I've always loved that room that you're sitting in now.
> R: Just wonderful.

Sadly, the largesse central to Dorothy's lifestyle had to be somewhat curtailed just after 1985, when she was embezzled. The musical evenings Ran loved so much were reduced to six a year.

> I had a waiting list of forty-five people to get to one of her dinners—it was hard to get them on the list. I can't tell you enough, Janet and Leo, about those evenings. Larry Lesser[39] never came, but many [did]... Christine Correa—Dorothy loved her.[40]
> One of the first appearances of Dominique Eade[41] was with Gary Joynes.[42] Hankus Netsky played there, Jimmy Giuffre, George Russell, Ricky Ford...[43]

Eventually, she had to move from her beautiful home to a modest place, a few blocks from Harvard Square.

Here, no matter who was performing, no matter how good those parties were, it was a very difficult time for Dorothy. She felt she'd lost face with her friends, though she never complained. Her only regret would have been that she wasn't able to fulfill her philanthropic plans—in particular, endowing the Third-Stream Department, as well as many churches and charities. She continued with her active life. She made trips to Suffield (and then to Florida) to see Ran's parents. She kept up with Ran's friends. At times, Ran accompanied her to her church (the Trinity Church at Copley Square), where he felt the minister was "more spiritual and more informed than Dr. Gilkey."

> But she did say she liked the music of Hubert Powell, "There's been a Change." I took her to the Hartford Church; she got so excited, and a nurse came over with a thing for her head. She said she'd never heard Christ being talked about in that way. They said, 'Oh Madame,' and they put water on her head, and they said they took Jesus to the well with Dorothy Wallace, and then they said, 'Have you drunk…' and she said, 'You don't want to hear what my drink is, but I love the Bible.' One boy said he'd had one drink when he was young—Satan had given him a Jack Daniel [sic].
> But oh! You should have seen Dorothy—religious, with a dash of naughty, elegant humor. She was something!

Later, Ran was able to reflect quietly on her life and the quality of their friendship… and the inspiration she was.

DOROTHY WALLACE:
REFLECTION ON A LIFE OF FRIENDSHIP

> *Life is no brief candle for me. It is a sort of splendid torch which I have got hold of for the moment, and I want to make it burn as brightly as possible before handing it on to future generations.*
>
> GEORGE BERNARD SHAW

DOROTHY WALLACE HAD an extraordinary capacity for life; she embraced it with exuberance. She also had a great understanding of friendship and what it meant. To maintain so many friendships, she needed to be organized. She shared some of her methods with Ran and advised him to single out one person each day for a prayer or a toast.

Eileen Murphy once described Dorothy as an "active friend maker," saying:

> She was a person—and Ran is like this too—who was truly interested in other people's lives. She was a very, very good friend to many, many people, and she often said to me that one of Ran's best qualities was his capacity for friendship and his caring of other people.[44]
> R: [*interrupting hurriedly*] But she was better.

Dorothy spent a lot of time actively nurturing her friendships. She initiated contacts and followed up on ideas. As Eileen Murphy can attest:

> In her foyer, she had a fireplace with a stone mantel, and she had this sculpture, which was metal, above it. She called it 'the fence,' and she would line up her outgoing letters, and she would have me count them—before the postman came to pick them up, she would have me count the outgoing pieces of mail—and there were days when there were dozens. It was as if she was showing me that she was working hard—while I was sleeping probably—and had done her work before I arrived.[45]

Dorothy had given a lot of thought to friendship and to what constitutes a good friendship. In July 1979, she wrote:

> A friend is a person for whom one has a continual and sustained affection; for whose feelings one is always concerned; to whose aid one would always wish to come; to whom one would never knowingly cause pain.[46]

The friendships that Dorothy Wallace shared with Ran and with her assistant, Eileen Murphy, were very special; over the years, they had become, in effect, "family."

Eileen Murphy hints at this:

> I never thought of her as my friend while she was alive. She once said I was her guardian angel, and I said, 'Well, if I'm your guardian angel, you're my fairy godmother'—because she really gave such meaning to my life. The first time I met her, I really had no idea how it was going to change my life. And she was the most important teacher I've had in my life... and I think Ran feels the same way.

> Dorothy Wallace was a very, very good friend to Ran. When Dorothy Wallace died, Ran and I—she was a mentor to both of us—I felt, at that time, we were kind of like orphans.
> [*Ran nods firmly.*]
> And I felt Ran and I became much closer friends and have gotten to know each other much more personally since her death.
> Ran expresses himself so deeply in his music, but he's such an amazing friend—and that's how I have come to know him.
> I'm telling you—we were so blessed.
> And Ran... it's so difficult for him that she's gone—along with so many of his contemporaries. To both of us, it was a huge blow.
> For me—I spent more time with her than anyone— it was a different kind of relationship I had with her. And I found this letter to me, written just months before she died.
> She died April 5, 2000, and on February 12, 2000, she wrote to me.[47]

Though Eileen does not reveal the nature of the letter, it is apparent that she is moved by the fact that Dorothy was thinking of her at this time.

It was hard for Dorothy Wallace's family (and for Eileen and Ran) to see this great lady deteriorating in her last year. She had been such a life-force, such an inspiration. But though her body failed her, her spirit was indomitable. She had always had great energy and interest in life, and she maintained this interest right to the end. Eileen Murphy recalls her last years:

> She had a Russian lesson on the telephone every morning (with a Russian tutor) [for] the entire many, many years I worked for her. And when I came through the door, that was what she was usually doing. And she would have sat with her Russian dictionary and listened to national public radio, select the news of the day, and then she would make notes on the news in Russian so that when her tutor called, she would have a conversation prepared.
> And when she was about eighty-six years old (about a year before she died), one morning, when I came into work, she said, 'Sit down, Eileen. I've made a decision I want to tell you about,' and I thought, 'Oh bother, what has happened here?' She could be very formal, and sometimes you would think something was really up and nothing was. But she said (when I sat down with her), 'I've decided to stop my Russian lessons,' and I said, 'Mrs. Wallace, how do you feel about that?' and she said, 'If I knew it was going to feel this good, I would have done it years ago!'

When she died, her mind was very active. She knew all the scores of the Red Sox—they hooked up a television set in hospital for her to see the game—and that night, she died.

When Dorothy Wallace died (April 5, 2000), her funeral at Trinity Church was "full to overflowing."[48] The make-up of the crowd emphasized the breadth of her friendship ties. People from different faiths, people from different nations, people with widely varied musical interests—they were all there. Someone ran into Hankus Netsky and said, "Hankus, what are you doing here?" Hankus replied to the effect that Dorothy Wallace was instrumental in the survival of Klezmer music at NEC.[49]

For Ran, the funeral was a huge challenge:

> I just don't remember much of what happened. I had to be carried out of the funeral—not literally—I remember somebody walking me out. I don't know how I got home, and I missed the reception for Dorothy. Curtis Faire from Texas, whom she had supported [was there];[50] the people from Greece—there were twenty people from Greece [who] were Dorothy's friends...

Though the funeral was a blur, Ran was later able to reflect quietly on her life. There was a lot of material to guide his thoughts. Dorothy left behind her an impressive paper trail. She was a prolific letter writer, and many of these had survived. A letter to Ran in 1997 attempted to outline the things that interested her:

> Dear Ran,
> You asked me last night what I'm interested in—a big question. I'd like to make another attempt to answer it. I'm interested in Christianity—the relationship of man to God; our spiritual responsibility—why are we here dancing in the dark?[51] I'm interested in the terrible, incomprehensible questions of the injustices of fate and our gratitude to God and, in many cases, the lack of it—one sin I do not commit. I thank God every day for the inestimable blessings he has bestowed upon me—but how about the Rwanda refugees?
> I'm interested in nature—my love of nature is closely bound up with my religious awareness—in conservation; in history; in historical preservation; in poetry; in art and in my own small but treasured art collection;[52] in personal relationships which are, to me, the most important element in life—except for health and religious experience—actually, even more important than health. I'm interested in your kind of music... I'm also interested in the English language, which I love and respect; in food; wine; the art of interior design; death.[53]

Another letter (undated) is breezy—full of color, warmth, and care at a time when Ran was unwell:

> Greg drove Carroll Moshier and me to Sandi Peaslee's birthday party, as I'm sure you've heard. I was glad we went. Sandi was radiant. I met some congenial people, and in spite of the fact that there were about fifty guests, I managed to get a seat on a big, comfortable sofa in front of a roaring fire. The food was abundant, elaborate, and superb. David and two of Sandi's friends worked steadily for three days to prepare it. I do hope Sandi has brought some of the duck pâté and salmon mousse to you—if any morsels of these particular delicacies escaped the hungry mob.
>
> This one time, I will allow myself the intimation of a comparison, and that's to say that no big birthday party could EVER outdo the one you gave for me here in this house in 1974. Never!
>
> [*The letter continues with news of people they both know, before concluding*]
>
> Must say goodbye now and set off through the freezing, bitter cold for my last class in Cambridge. I pray that you are feeling better. Connie and I are leaving on the 20th—a week from Friday. Don't feel obligated to call me before we go. I understand.
>
> Much love
> Dorothy

Ran, hearing this letter once again, is overcome and remarks quietly, "That's wonderful to have that letter." The letter glitters with the spontaneity—the improvisation—that was part and parcel of how Dorothy communicated. In his book *Primacy of the Ear*, Ran discusses improvisation and its link to story-telling—how the story must have its core content or "spine" to which each rendition can then add its own variation and color. He cites Dorothy Wallace as one of his favorite storytellers—the master of many nuances. But he goes further to state that her written letters "are often superb as well," and she is thus a composer and an improviser.

This combination of skills, adept in planning but always ready to improvise, was central to Dorothy's life approach. And when things didn't go to plan, she was always able to identify the crux of the problem and creatively work out a way through. Ran well remembers the period when he was struggling to finish *Primacy of the Ear*. Feeling overburdened, he began to withdraw. He was ignoring telephone calls ("I began to hate telephones") and shunning contacts. So Dorothy concocted an original solution:

She locked me in at the Hotel de Charles and told them to disconnect my phone, and I had to write a chapter a day of my book.
L: *Primacy of the Ear*?
R: Yes—and that's how it got started. Three times a day, the phone was connected, and she said, 'Where are you now?' And I hear she was patrolling the hallway! And that's the hotel, right on the Charles River—Marriot Hotel—you can check that; I have witnesses. It was about '75/'76; her whole family knew [about] it. I was allowed wine my third night when I could come home. There was no drink until I produced. It was martial law!

Alice Russell remembers Dorothy as:

> An extraordinary woman—they broke the mold when they made her—she was kind, and warm-hearted, and generous, and intelligent, and literate… I don't know; she was just unique—the kind of 'old dame' that you don't see much anymore. And she championed all the musicians and took them in. But she was nobody's fool, and that's what I really liked about her.
> Her funeral was so wonderful—with the bagpipes and the eulogies—the church was packed.
> And she always used to send little notes, even when you were her guest, and you thanked *her*—she would send a note thanking *you*! I saved all of them because all of them were just adorable—sweet and funny and just the right tone about everything.

Eileen Murphy was perhaps in the best position to observe Dorothy's habit of jotting down her thoughts and advice. Some were scribbled urgently on any available scrap of paper; others were more deliberate projects—set out with careful purpose:

> She was a great one for making lists. At one time, she made a list of all the people who were dear to her—dear friends who she'd met through Ran. And it was a very, very, long list of people who'd become very, very close to her. And of course, she was the type of person who every year, around January 1, made a list of all the friends she'd made in the previous year—so she was an 'active friend maker.' I've also found a list of 'Manners,' and this was a hand-written list, which was on the back of a pottery invoice from Mexico. It says:
> Rules of good manners.
> 1. Do not denigrate the town, area, or college of your companion.
> 2. Do not complain repeatedly—once is enough—about unsatisfactory arrangements.
> 3. Do not act surprised by other people's accomplishments.

4. Do not comment on other people's appetite or eating habits.
5. Be careful how you hold your knife. Do not gesticulate with it.
6. NEVER CHEW GUM (*in capital letters*).[54]

Gunther Schuller, writing about "Dorothy—just 'Dorothy'—as we all knew her," after her death, remembered her as:

> [...] both kind and tough, generous and demanding, direct (mincing no words) and solicitous. They just don't make people like that anymore.

And he added, "And boy, did she know how to make one hell of a great martini!"[55]

RAN IS QUICK to acknowledge his great fortune in meeting Dorothy Wallace. For him, she was the answer to a prayer, the fulfillment of a promise. She taught, protected, supported, and admonished him. She found brightness in the darkest shadow. She was always there when needed. When she died, it was a wrench, but she bequeathed to her family and friends a sense of purpose, hope that is open-ended, and a solid grasp on friendship. Dorothy was always larger-than-life; such a vital force can never be extinguished. As Ran confides, "Dorothy Wallace keeps herself very busy in heaven."

5

COMMUNITY SERVICES

*A thousand fibres connect you with your
fellow-men.*

REV. HENRY MELVILL, THE GOLDEN LECTURES[1]

New England Conservatory had been struggling when Gunther arrived in 1967. There were only two hundred and fifteen students enrolled, while the capacity was seven hundred and fifteen.[2] The century-old school was on the brink of closure; they needed to attract more students. The new president envisaged expansion on a broad scale—through community involvement, as well as through courses offered. He was thirty-eight, full of energy and ideas, and eager to tackle the problems he could see before him; there were so many problems that a less active man may have been overwhelmed. Rather than waiting on procedure, Gunther often took matters into his own hands—to the extent of mopping a corridor that needed attention or donating a considerable sum of his own money to get things started at a funding meeting.[3] Nevertheless, many of his proposals met with resistance.[4]

One such proposal was introducing a course for jazz. Gunther had been devoted to jazz since the age of fourteen when he'd heard a radio broadcast of Duke Ellington at the Cotton Club.[5] At first, it had been the "basic compositions with all their originality and innovativeness" that had caught his attention. To him, jazz was a "musical language" that he had no trouble "understanding" or "feeling."[6] For him, this "language" was in every way "art music"—equal to that of the western classical tradition he had grown up with. Bringing the same academic rigor that accompanied his study of classical music to his study of jazz, Gunther realized jazz was a music that was eminently teachable. Moreover, the rich opportunities that jazz presented to the fields of musicology and music pedagogy were largely untapped. To a brilliant visionary like Schuller, it seemed natural that this most American of art forms be studied at an American conservatory—that the likes of Louis Armstrong, Charlie Parker, and Thelonious Monk be held up alongside the pantheon of the western art music tradition. He was determined to start jazz studies at the conservatory. But, at a time when NEC was struggling for its very existence, the proposal was not greeted with enthusiasm. "Almost everyone" on the board was against starting up a jazz department. At that time, it was widely believed that jazz was impossible to "teach," that doing so would make it "stiff and unspontaneous."[7]

Gunther was not to be dissuaded. While lamenting the fact that it was necessary for him, as late as 1967, to be pleading for a place for the "one home grown music" of America, he pushed ahead with plans. It would take him two years to organize both the finances and the structure for a jazz department.[8]

When Carl Atkins was recruited by Gunther Schuller to join the faculty at New England Conservatory, he was, as an African American, very much in the minority. He appeared first as part of the Faculty for Orchestral Instruments (saxophone),[9] but there's little doubt that Gunther was thinking ahead to the "Department of African-American Music and Jazz Studies"[10] that he was planning. At New England Conservatory, Atkins initially found himself thrust into another new venture: co-chairing the community services program with Ran Blake.

The program came at a significant time in Boston's history. The city had been experiencing periods of unrest for some years. These stemmed from inequality in welfare, housing, and education—a problem exacerbated by urban renewal programs that had begun in Boston in the 1950s and reached Roxbury and North Dorchester in 1964/65. In their wake, "large population losses" and "economic decline" became evident.[11] (Funds injected into both public and commercial projects in the heart of the city had eliminated cheap housing and thus displaced the poor, who were forced into ghettos—often based on race.[12]) As a consequence, by 1965, de-facto segregation was in place with black children attending the schools in the black neighborhoods of Mattapan, Roxbury, and parts of Dorchester, while white children attended schools in the predominantly white communities of South Boston, Charlestown, and East Boston.[13] In April 1965, Martin Luther King Jr.[14] addressed a vast crowd on Boston Common after leading a mile-long march for freedom through the city's streets. He called for the desegregation of housing and schools.

New England Conservatory, in the Fenway section of Boston's Back Bay, was situated in Boston's cultural and educational heart, occupying the block bounded by Huntington Avenue, St. Botolph Street, and Gainsborough Street, and rubbing shoulders with Symphony Hall, as well as Northeastern University. Thus, NEC's landmark buildings,[15] notably the acoustically excellent Jordan Hall,[16] were never in danger of being earmarked for urban renewal. But renewal was needed if the school was to avoid closing, and part of that renewal needed to be in looking outwards and recognizing the needs on its doorstep. Roxbury, only four miles or so south of NEC's campus, was seething. Mothers for Adequate Welfare, who had come together to address the shortcomings they could see in the process of welfare distribution, had been organizing sit-ins since April 1965. These had been peaceful (and thus largely ignored by authorities) until June 1967, when Boston witnessed three days of rioting, which many attributed to the police handling of the sit-in[17] at the welfare office in Roxbury. Rioting raged along fifteen blocks of Blue Hill Avenue from June 2-4, 1967.

This period of so-called welfare riots coincided with Gunther Schuller's arrival at NEC as President. Less than a year later, on April 4, 1968, riots broke out in African American neighborhoods across the country following the assassination of Martin Luther King Jr. In Boston, the rioting took place once more in Roxbury, as well as in North Dorchester and the South End. Earlier that day, Ran had been visiting Dorothy Wallace, who'd invited him to meet Curtis Faire, a young African American. As soon as the dreadful news of the assassination broke, Ran, shocked and shaken, took his leave and headed home. While on his way, he was caught up on the edge of the riots on Massachusetts Avenue:

> The police were more than the people. You could see the people were seething—they were so angry.

One of the rioters approached Ran:

> I think he was just going to insult me. I don't think he was going to hurt me.

Police armed with clubs appeared, and at that moment, a car drove up. Curtis Faire opened the door and said, "Hop in!"

> Curtis Faire—I'd seen him earlier that evening: he was a student Dorothy Wallace was trying to get through medical school—everything

goes through the Wallace house. [*He makes a spiraling, circular movement with his hand.*] Anyway, he said, 'Hop in,' and he drove me just two or three blocks away. I feel he saved me.

I retreated to Gunther's office. The Jordan Hall memorial was to follow. Russell Sherman participated.[18] The student body was electrified and stayed electrified. And of course, these events formed my recording—my protest record—*Blue Potato and Other Outrages*.

Gunther Schuller was fully aware of the racial unrest and the underlying problems that had long been ignored. He was passionate about the issue. He also realized that, through music, the conservatory could build bridges and provide opportunities. Addressing the graduating class of 1969, he spoke in part of "these times of turbulent change." He acknowledged that the students would have no difficulty remembering that during their time at the conservatory, "two of our great Americans were cruelly and senselessly destroyed"[19] but went on to beg them "to remember too that in those dark days we also dedicated ourselves anew to do, through music and music education, all that we are intellectually, financially, spiritually and physically capable of to restore some of the accumulated debt owed our brothers of all colors."[20] Gunther had a staunch supporter in Ran Blake, who equally recognized the "debt owed" and was desperate to redress it.

By 1969, a program that linked the pedagogical formation of conservatory students with an outreach arm to bring the best possible musical experiences to individuals (and groups) of limited means was underway. New England Conservatory students and alumni were able to go out—initially into Greater Boston schools— to either start a music program in a school or supplement an existing one. They were able to train teachers and present small performances. It was a beginning.

Right from the start, Dorothy Wallace was vitally interested in the outreach arm of this project. She was a humanitarian. She was also practical; she could see the need, and she wanted to help. As well as giving financial assistance, she began teaching in the black community in Roxbury. She was a great supporter of Ran in the work he was doing.

All the while, the idea for a jazz studies department at New England Conservatory had been simmering away, and in September 1969, the school, having received approval from the National Association of Schools of Music, became the first major conservatory with a fully accredited jazz studies program. Carl Atkins was appointed as the first department chair.[21] At that time, the idea of jazz at the core of a tertiary studies music program was still considered to be, at best, novel. Hoping to address lingering worries that there was no existing pedagogical method for teaching such a course, Gunther Schuller immediately recruited George Russell to the fledgling department. Russell's *Lydian Chromatic Concept of Tonal Organization* provided a theoretical basis for the course. To complement this appointment, Schuller also employed pianist-saxophonist, arranger, and composer Jaki Byard with a view to strengthening the program's improvisational offering.[22] Further, he brought in—as visiting professors—friends and associates from the jazz world. These were working musicians who were touring and traveling. Sometimes Gunther could only hire them for a few days, but they gave vibrant energy to the course.

> And we also had Jimmy Giuffre—he [be]came permanent, the same year as George Russell—it was AMAZING. Gunther got... he brought these classical people in—Russell Sherman, John Heiss... it was fabulous. It was so exciting, Janet!

By 1969, the conservatory was a very different place from the one that Gunther had inherited two years earlier. The new faculty who had joined the jazz department had changed the racial make-up of the college. As well, there was a "Black Student Committee," and while its primary aim was to address the problems that affected black students and improve their existing conditions, it was also committed to improving "the conservatory community as a whole."[23]

Before long, the scope of both community services and the jazz department began to widen. Joe Maneri[24] joined the jazz department in 1970—though his interest was microtonal composition.[25] Ran was also asked to join the department and teach "Extension of Vision," initially to children in the afternoons.[26] He was already teaching Extension Prep: offering lessons for young students of any level, including beginners, as well as being director of the music education division of the community services program.

With Carl Atkins' move to jazz studies, Calvin Hicks was appointed to the outreach program—by this time known as the community services program.[27] In 1971, Helen Harrington was appointed as registrar director of the program.[28] She brought, Ran remembers, "this dynamo," Kay Nurse with her. Kay was a skilled organizer with a "warm, kind, and generous spirit"[29] who had many contacts through her work and varied interests. She succeeded in putting the community services program "on the map" and in making fresh inroads into the Boston public school system.[30] Ran loved working with her.

The program had rooms allocated below Brown Hall. People could come there for free lessons. There was also a summer school.

> The 'prep.' school took over Saturday—we had classes at night because the prep. students wanted to have the building until four… So, a lot of working men came at night, and we would find that after eight weeks, some people wouldn't continue studying, and I began to be quite an authority in dealing with all kinds of social problems.
> L: What do you mean?
> R: People had financial problems—some couldn't pay the rent. People had medical problems; some had… maybe drug… they never said; I could see they weren't well. Some felt racism. There were also poor white students and Italians—there were a lot of white students, and they felt the white 'superior' students looked down on them. And the buses from Roxbury—It was terrible. People would come late because Harvard Square and all the white areas had way better transportation [than Roxbury], and even a taxicab often, in those days, would not pick up a black customer—even if they had a little money and they were running late. It was just terrible getting to the school.

Ran was paid a token salary[31] and had a part-time assistant. He was expected to supplement his salary with his own gigs,[32] but community services took up most of his time. He even took classes at his home at 25 St. Stephen Street, a short walk from the Conservatory. These would take place in the daytime, allowing mothers to come. On top of all this, Ran managed to find time to go to concerts to support faculty and students—a habit that became a lifetime commitment; however, his interest in their work was, he felt, sometimes not reciprocated.

> I often wondered why faculty didn't return the favor by coming out more to community service events.

There would have been no shortage of chances for them to do so. Ran was tireless in his search for performance opportunities for participants of the program. Perhaps the faculty were still coming to terms with this new direction the conservatory was taking and saw the community services program as non-essential. Nevertheless, it was a difficult time for Ran, who has confessed to feeling "ostracized by the faculty."

> R: It would never occur to them to invite me for…
> L: Why do you think that was?
> R: I don't know. [*The tone is mystified—almost a whisper.*]

It is possible that Ran was never "still" long enough to engage with other faculty; however, Alice Russell is not under any delusions regarding the perceived exclusion. When she arrived in Boston in 1977, she felt that the "old guard" of the conservatory did not take jazz—or George—seriously. And of course, George would have discussed *his* feelings with her:

> NEC at the beginning (because of the nature of the university in those days)—having the majority of the faculty and the admin. take jazz seriously was a huge problem. The majority of the so-called 'classical' faculty—particularly old guard in that period—they felt: 'This isn't anything to be taken seriously.'[33]

She adds ruefully:

> George was not treated with any respect until he started getting awards—if you got an award, they gave you a raise in salary and used your name every chance they could get. [34]

However, even if many on the faculty tried to ignore its existence, the area devoted to the community services program below Brown Hall buzzed with life and commanded Ran's full attention. As he recalls, "It was the hippie part of the school."

This would have been quite literally true. The youth counterculture, nourished on ideals of love and peace and a total and liberating free expression during the Summer of Love in San Francisco, 1967, had dispersed to spread its message. In July 1968, hippies were camping on Boston Common. They brought with them a sense of optimism—again, anything seemed possible.

When the rock musical *Hair* opened on Broadway on April 29, 1968, many Americans were confronted by its strong anti-war message[35] and angered by scenes of drug-taking and nudity. But the production was timely, echoing the hippie ethos and a plea for change—from war to peace, from hate to love. Major cultural and political shift was palpable.

But if the hope for a better future was to be realized, there was urgent need for action. So much needed to be done to redress past wrongs and tackle inequality. Ran was swept along in the never-ending demands of his community services program. Focusing his energies on securing students for the program, he left the administration side to Kay Nurse while he went out into Boston's streets and clubs looking for people who might benefit from the program:

> Everywhere I went, I talked about community services, and I got people—there were no auditions.
> [You] would have found me in pool rooms; I went all over soliciting students—all the bars in Mass. Avenue. There were Asian and Irish

bars. The bartenders knew I was hustling for the department, and at one time, we had eighty to one hundred students.

And I may not have been the most thoughtful teacher; I was all over the map. People would ring my doorbell at 12.01 in the morning, and I was reminded that I used to have open house on Friday nights at the Hotel on 58th Street [New York]. I had almost open house on St. Stephen Street. People dropped by; money was stolen… I kept a pot full of money for people to take, and sometimes… one time, I woke up with a hundred-dollar bill, so somebody gave back. Ah [*He considers this for a moment*], I accused Dorothy Wallace of the gift; she said, 'I don't creep into bachelors' houses at one in the morning—get another victim,' and she abruptly left.

Things were getting out of hand, though. If by day Ran appeared to be positive, enthusiastic, and energetic, there remained a deep sadness that surfaced at night, in the form of bad dreams and tortured memories of Greece. Without the steadying home base that Dorothy Wallace provided, Ran may not have coped. Even so, he stretched the friendship:

> It really got all-consuming. I mean, I brought everybody… [to Dorothy Wallace's home]. She walked in, and there were people raiding her icebox.

Gunther also registered the untenable nature of the situation:

> He said, 'Come on, Ran. There's "community," and [then there's] your practice. You haven't been in my office recently [to practice the piano].'

Additionally, some of the students Ran recruited were possibly unsuitable or disinterested:

> I remember the vice president interviewing a guy, and he said, 'What do you play?' and the guy said, 'I play pool,' and Mr. Harris mentioned this in a trustee meeting—he was trying to do a power thing with Gunther. So I guess it got bad—it got laughed at—and I would never collect money, and the accounts were wrong. Kay Nurse said, 'Come on, Ran, you're not going to teach school here and just get people off the street [with] their funny tasting cigarettes—we have to establish, you know…'
> L: Protocol?
> R: [*Nodding in agreement*] for the trustees, so it was great that Kay kindly reined me in. She said, 'Ran, let people pay a little bit.' So we charged twenty-five dollars a semester—twenty-five dollars! [*His*

tone is incredulous.]—and they had to buy a couple of tapes and a textbook. They came to the conservatory—we couldn't start teaching till six at night.

There were, among these students, notable success stories. One of the most impressive of these was Ricky Ford:

> Some became great, and Ricky Ford's the prize. He got a full scholarship.
> L: Where did you find him?
> R: Through a guy who ran a place called The Huntington[36]—or something—right across from the school.[37] They had terrible sandwiches; I just spoke to the kitchen staff—I had no shyness [*He says it with an upward lilt, marveling*]. I asked them, 'Say, does anybody play music? Would you like a free education?' and somebody said, 'I know somebody who knows Ricky Ford.' Then I met Webster Lewis[38] at a bar and recruited him. I met Tony, an organ player who also became [an] administrative assistant at Yelena's Bridal Shop—he was the son of Italian immigrants; I met Maxine Major at a sewing school.
> L: How about Ricky? What sort of standard was he when he entered the program—musically?
> R: Phenomenal ears—terrific tenor saxophone. I mean, he had a lot to learn, but I knew he had soul and talent.[39]

Ran credits Carl Atkins with the idea of taking community services out to the aged and the homeless, but on his own initiative, Ran went to the North End or "Little Italy," where the Italian community lived, and to the ethnically diverse JP (Jamaica Plain). Later, around 1972/'73, it was Ran's idea, also, to go to the prisons:

> We did Alderson Prison[40] for women and a men's prison that was more psychiatric—Walpole.[41] I did all the contacts—calling the prison—and let me tell you, there was red tape getting there. People were searched as they came in.
> Walpole was the big success. I called prisoners by their name, and we sent cards, and Dorothy Wallace sent a hamper of food—it had to go through security and all that.
> I produced a couple of concerts there [at the prison], and they cried one night—the prisoners—when I played for them.
> I know there're people that played at Attica.[42] I know Johnny Cash did something for Folsom.[43] I know there have been great audiences. I know the prisoners of war [heard] Messiaen's *Quartet for the End of Time*.[44]
> L: Did all this receive any acknowledgment in the press?

> R: I think I said, 'No.' [*momentarily impatient with the question*] A rock critic from the *Globe* did do one review; I know that I knew Kay Bourne from the *Bay State Banner* at that time. Later, I began to be the white columnist writing for that paper.[45]

As it wasn't always possible to arrange concerts in the communities where he was working, Ran also put on community service concerts at the conservatory, thus giving people the opportunity to hear a concert in the excellent acoustics and beautiful setting of Jordan Hall:

> R: We couldn't get the people out of Walpole prison.
> L: You mean they wouldn't release the prisoners?
> R: For a concert in Jordan Hall! [*with an upward lilt as if to say, 'Can you believe that?'*]
> L: Well, yeah, I mean, you can probably... I mean, it would have been nice to bring them out... [*there is a 'but' that is left unsaid.*]

Ran knew the prisoners by name. Their crime did not matter to him.

> I think that Dorothy Wallace put in piles of money that I don't even know about. She had a secretary at her house who would make phone calls for the prisons. Kay Nurse and Dorothy would meet; Dorothy Wallace subsidized that program. After a while, I didn't go [to finance meetings]. I set up all the teaching. Dorothy Wallace gave the conservatory money for students' tuition and for the prisons' program. Also, I got a little extra money—a special phone put in. My office was right below Williams Hall; I would be there all hours of the night.
> Gunther did credit me for the good teaching, but I was so available and accessible. Nobody had to pay me for lessons, so nobody would choose me at the college when they could get me free, and when I joined the faculty, it was still 'community,' and oh boy, I had an exhausting life!

In 1972, Gunther created the third-stream department.[46] Third-stream was a term he'd previously coined to describe a synthesis of classical and jazz musics in the work of contemporary composers and improvisers. The initial concept was later broadened to include world music and to accommodate the changing perception of musical boundaries. The atmosphere was unique, encouraging students to develop their skills in a different way—without restrictions and with the freedom to experiment. Ran was appointed its first chair. But before he could devote himself fully to the new venture, there was a transition period in which he was still affiliated with community services. It was a stressful time for Ran:

> I remember one time coming back—I think it was my first trip to Europe after the Greek one—where Dorothy was there to meet me, and I had been awake for hours. I was taken to Westland Avenue—this is like a gothic mystery—to a basement room at a restaurant called Amalfi, and Gunther came, and he said, 'Ran, we're going to have to let Helen Harrington and Kay Nurse go.'
> I never knew the reason why.
> Then Gunther said, 'Your new boss is Webster—you discovered him at a bar years ago,' and Webster and I shook hands.

Webster Lewis was director of community services from 1972 to 1978.[47] Ran took up his role as chair of third-stream in 1974—the two years prior to this were difficult. The community services program was his "baby." He had nurtured it right from the beginning. Webster Lewis was younger than Ran. Indeed, he was a newly graduated student, and Ran had been instrumental in getting him a scholarship through community services. But Webster needed to make a mark in his new position, too. Inevitably, there were differences of opinion. Things came to a head when Ran tried to enroll a young girl Dorothy Wallace had recommended. Webster felt there were more needy students and confronted Ran about this. Words were exchanged:

> There's a hidden stairway above Jordan Hall—in front of Brown Hall. I think it's all different now [...]. One night he [Webster] came to me [there], and I said something to upset him; he really was upset [...]. He tried to have me fired, and that's when I fainted above the spiral stairway, three floors above Brown Hall—because he said white people shouldn't improvise. But he said, [later], he never said that to me, and I know that I could have exaggerated. I think that was his intent, though—we played games. But I hadn't recovered from Greece.

The exchange between the two men reflected wider unrest. The past decade had been stormy.[48] Though there had been some advancement in race relations through legislation, socio-economic equality seemed unattainable, and racial discrimination remained deep-seated.

Ralph Ellison, Ran's teacher—and mentor—at Bard, had seen music as central to understanding race in America;[49] indeed, he saw it as a means of cultural exchange. Ran had been inspired by this ideal. But outside the college, there was disagreement as to the essential nature of jazz. It was seen by some solely as an expression of black experience and culture.[50] America had had a long history of white domination of minority groups. Ran was painfully aware of this and of his white, middle-class upbringing and the dominance of white middle-class culture. He was deeply disturbed that African Americans needed to struggle for basic civil rights. He also knew that no matter how much he loved the music and culture of the African American people, and no matter how deeply he cared or desired to make a positive difference in the world around him, he could never change the fact that he was a white kid from Connecticut whose life was privileged. Ran's general sense of disaffection with his own music and the way things were going in the world at the time (including the situation in Greece) combined to unsettle him:

> I was so, so depressed. I didn't want to exist as a white musician in '69.

So when Webster confronted him, his uncertainties re-surfaced. He was deeply unhappy about aspects of his job in the community services program and the "games" that he and Webster Lewis played there. A tide of conflicting emotions threatened to overwhelm a young man whose love of people and music sprung from a pure spirit and a unique blend of innocence and empathy—with an overriding zeal for justice. It was fortunate that Dorothy Wallace was there to provide safe harbor.

Ran came to Boston at the end of an era. Third-stream studies, as introduced by Gunther Schuller, raised the curtain on a new direction for the conservatory. It opened minds (and ears) to a musical diversity that remains a hallmark of NEC's jazz and improvised music programs today. Ran's early work in the community services program ensured that a music education was available to anyone, regardless of ethnicity or social-economic standing.

Postscript: An email from Ricky Ford

I met Ran in the late '60s. I was introduced to him in the Community Services department. My best friend told me about the department and Ran. Ran gave me an appointment to have a lesson with him, and the first song I learned was "Breakthru." Ran was very dedicated to sound—he insulated his studio in the basement of the New England Conservatory with egg cartons. They were there for a couple of years until the fire department—during a routine inspection of the building—told him it was a fire hazard.

Ran introduced me to the faculty, administrative staff, students, and Gunther Schuller. Ran changed my life at that time, and I have many fond memories of my academic commitments as they developed. And about a few years later, I received a four-year scholarship to study at the conservatory in their jazz department.

Ran was a guest at the 2012 Toucy Jazz Festival with my group of eighteen musicians, the Ze Big Band, for a retrospective of the concert we did at Brandeis University in the late eighties.

We recorded at least five CDs and, in 1991, Ran participated in an interview for my documentary *Encore*.

Ricky still remembers the sessions for their records for Universal Impulse—one dedicated to Claude Chabrol and the other to Chris Connor. Geographic distance precluded any rehearsal in the formative stages, so these projects were etched out gradually—through correspondence and the exchange of music, recordings, films—before the two men finally came together for the sessions themselves, which took place in Brussels, July 2012. Ricky was booked for two sessions, starting at 4 pm and finishing by 7.30 pm on consecutive days. As he recalls:

> These two dates are incredible. I will never forget that energy and the level of communication that Ran and I had.

RICKY FORD, AUGUST 31, 2014

6

THE THIRD-STREAM

> *Music is the only art form that has been systematically taught by the wrong sense perception (in Europe and most of the Americas).*
>
> RAN BLAKE [1]

In the Third-Stream Department, Ran was starting to hit his stride. Away from the churning activity and demands of community outreach, he was able to immerse himself in the diversity of musical influences that made up his own unique style. Moreover, the department provided the luxury of structured time. It gave Ran the space to seek out and follow his dreams and the scope to interpret them to inspire his students. Right from the outset, the department was close to Ran's heart. It was something he had been thinking about for some time:

> Gunther Schuller and I spoke about the dream of a department such as this during the sixties. We wanted a haven where individuals with musical diversity could study—expand their musical horizons and hunger, through the assimilation of a broad but focused repertoire, learned through the ear and afterwards, feel free to recompose this material—reflecting their own emotions. Musicians must experience the practice of absorbing music directly through their own ears and replicating essential elements of melody, harmony, rhythms and develop appreciations for mood, timbre, dynamics without visual aids.[2]

The beauty of the program's approach was its flexibility. Also, it focused on the ear (privileging aural learning over visual), which was unusual for a college-level syllabus at that time. Over the years, there were distinct phases when the department seemed to concentrate on a particular style—rock music, klezmer, or American folk music. Before long, the original idea of a fusion of jazz and classical was only one of many combinations being explored.

But the combinations themselves were not important—the department's main aim was to develop a "complete musician"[3] based on an improvisational ability formed by an intensive ear training program. This "practical" training was coupled with a more philosophical investigation of the student's musical style, looking to the musical influences which lay at the heart of the student's reason for playing music and then charting a course of study from these, toward their synthesis in the student's own style.

In 1976, Ran summarized the course, as it was evolving, in the *Music Educators Journal*:[4]

> An incoming freshman pursues courses in theory, music literature, and a foreign language, or humanities, as well as one half-hour a week of private instrumental study; one half-hour a week of improvisation; and the Third Stream seminar.
> The ear training given to freshmen is very specific. Students first must memorize at least thirty melodies, many of them taken from the Afro-American heritage. The art of memorizing is itself very important—especially for those who have been overexposed to the written page. Students must first sing or whistle these melodies before playing them on their instruments. Omitting this step can be unsatisfactory. Too often, immediately performing a melody upon an instrument is a poor shortcut because fingering and visualizing the notes can act as a crutch that, in the long run, hinders aural retention. The students must be able to duplicate and retain at least five melodies a week before moving on.
> Students are also encouraged to keep a log of studies outside the department as well as of departmental work and outside activities.
> The biggest goal of the program is to help students begin to develop a personal style in improvising and composing.

This process of finding a personal style reflected Ran's own experience. Improvisation was a central tenet of the course, and this, Ran stressed, had to be approached through the "primacy of the ear." After having studied a broad repertoire in this way, the student's long-term aural memory would be sufficiently developed to begin a process that Ran termed "recomposition."[5] This involved the use of an existing musical work (almost always in its recorded form) as a point of departure for the student's own creative exploration (both improvised and strictly composed) of the musical "essence" of that work. For Ran, this was imperative in the development of the student's personal style.

Significantly, third-stream was coming into focus when world and home events were forcing a more outward-looking attitude. Airfares were becoming affordable, and people were traveling and experiencing different cultures and music. The student population was also more diverse; by the early 1980s, the department had grown in both enrollment and status. It had several faculty members, including Hankus Netsky, who started as a teaching assistant in third-stream after graduating as a composition major in 1976.[6]

THE DEPARTMENT ALSO offered performance opportunities. These gave students the chance to perform in programs featuring an eclectic selection of guest artists. Many of the guests reflected Ran's passions. Hubert Powell and the "Heavenly Choir" from the Holy Trinity Church of God in Christ, Hartford, Connecticut, appeared in a Jordan Hall concert on April 14, 1976. Powell played the organ with Natalie Arter as soloist. They presented "There's been a Change in My Life."

By 1986, the department was annually producing three major concerts in Jordan Hall.[7] One of these concerts, in collaboration with the New England Conservatory Symphony Orchestra (and Larry Livingstone as conductor), resulted in the recording and release of the album, *The Portfolio of Doktor Mabuse*.[8]

Ran was tireless in his promotion of the third-stream program, which in introductory letters to various universities and student groups, he presented as "the only program of its kind in the world." In April 1976, soon after the Third-Stream Department had been formed, he took a trip to Texas, New Mexico, and Arizona in the hope of recruiting students. When Ran arrived in Houston, he phoned the station manager at Radio KPFT and asked him to announce that he was accepting inquiries on behalf of the third-stream program at the New England Conservatory. Giving his hotel phone and extension number, he adjourned to the lobby to make some personal calls from the payphone there (keeping the other line free for calls from prospective students). Here, he was accosted by an elderly woman who had heard he was in town searching for "this third-stream river." She pointed out there was enough water in the east for bottling, and when Ran tried to explain, she refused to let him finish—"I smell a gimmick," she said.[9]

His mission indeed appeared unusual. An article in Houston's *Music Monthly* stated that Ran Blake of the New England Conservatory was in Houston looking for students and street musicians to join his third-stream music program and that applicants need not even read music.[10] The third-stream approach did not deny the important role that notation had played (and could continue to play) in music education; however, it did seek to redress a bias whereby an art form for which the principal mode of reception is by way of the ear, was often learned and executed by way of the eye. It must also be noted that, for Ran, 'the ear' was not simply the physical instrument for receiving sound, but also the cognitive elements of the brain which allowed for its processing (in a musical sense). The goal, therefore, was to create, through specially conceived exercises, as immediate a relationship as possible between these two 'aspects' of the ear. Once seamless integration was achieved, the student could more readily absorb the emotional and spiritual aspects of the music—elements which could, in time, be used in the student's own music and as a vehicle in the discovery of a personal voice.

The task Ran had set himself (promoting his third-stream program) was not an easy one. While some may have been persuaded, some were skeptical, and others were simply disinterested. Ran recalls ruefully that on April 22 at Rice University, he gave a brief lecture about third-stream music but felt the students were bored and that the sunshine and activities outside were too much of a distraction.

Ran spent the Fall of 1979 recruiting in Winnipeg, Quebec City, Wisconsin, Cincinnati, Iowa, and Chicago. His dedication to the department saw no limits. He threw himself wholeheartedly into its promotion and, for many years, bore the expenses of administrative help out of his own pocket—to the extent that he had accumulated "a sizeable five-figure debt."[11]

Ran's exceptional dedication to his music and to the Third-Stream Department over which he presided was recognized in 1988 when he was awarded a MacArthur Fellowship. According to the foundation's website, recipients of the award must show "exceptional merit and promise." The considerable sum attached to the award is viewed as an investment in the recipient's "originality, insight, and potential."[12] Ran, writing to the conservatory soon after, was able to quote this recognition:

> The fact that the Third Stream concept, and my work in particular, has been singled out for the most prestigious award in the Arts and

Humanities ought to indicate how highly, at least in some circles, Third Stream music-making is regarded.[13]

Behind the words, there is a hint of the hurt he felt when his work seemed to go unrecognized by certain faculty at NEC. The letter goes on to urge the conservatory to "exploit my good fortune in receiving a MacArthur Foundation award and use my name in a rigorous recruiting effort."[14]

In 1991 there was a setback when, because of falling undergraduate numbers, the decision was reached at an administrative level to "phase out" the undergraduate division of third-stream studies. Ran was devastated; such a prospect shattered his dream of a comprehensive third-stream program.

In an effort to raise the department's profile and to garner for it much needed funds, Gunther Schuller set up the Third-Stream Foundation. Dorothy Wallace and Ran Blake were named as the foundation's directors, while Schuller himself was to be its president. The foundation sought to achieve its goals through hosting lectures, workshops, and commissioning research (on the aural reception of music) as well as subsidizing concerts, recordings, and tours. At the meeting on July 14, 1992, Gunther pointed to the irony that 98% of music was taught visually (via notation—European style) while globally, 98% of music was accessed aurally. He also highlighted the fact that (at that time) there had still been no study into how humans acquire musical skills (in contrast to the studies done on how people acquire verbal skills).[15]

But by June 7, 1995, Gunther had written to Ran admitting that he was "not at all optimistic" about the future of the foundation. He acknowledged having failed to come up with concrete ideas which could "propel the foundation forward" and concluded that the concept of third-stream had "lost its novelty, its potential impact," adding, "not its validity, mind you, but rather just its urgency." He pointed out that "World Music" had taken its place. "There is no way that you and I and a few other interested folks can buck this trend." He felt that third-stream was ahead of its time and largely misunderstood. Gunther, aware that his letter would be a difficult one for Ran to receive, attempted to soften the blow:

> Your deriving from the Third Stream concept, an educational process based on the primacy of the ear, is absolutely on the mark—and you shouldn't ever be modest, apologetic, or hesitant about it. It is a totally valid concept (teaching/learning tool) in principle, but the education world is still not ready for it except, as I said earlier, spottily here and there.[16]

So Ran continued to work to attract students. After Third-Stream changed its name to Contemporary Improvisation, he approached his friend Jean Plumez, an advertising specialist, for help with its promotion. Plumez suggested "professional literature" to promote this "unique concept."

Schuller was to be proved right. The general musical community at large was not ready for third-stream; the movement, which had at one time looked poised to change the face of music forever, gradually faded into insignificance.[17] But for the students of the third-stream program at NEC,[18] the educational offering was beyond what any academic review or course description could convey. What was on offer was a generous gift of self, born of a whole-hearted life investment by its founding professor, Ran Blake.

In early 1999 in a memo to Bob Freeman,[19] Ran named the following "pre-1968" events which he said helped form the Third-Stream Department (already known as Contemporary Improvisation at time of writing.):

'46: *Spiral Staircase* and the film noir movement;
'52: Hubert Powell: Church of God in Christ, North Hartford CT;
'53–'57: being an outsider;
'58: job at Atlantic Records and beginning to study with Gunther Schuller;
'67: Greece coup d'état;
Sept '67: beginning work at NEC;
'68: first Jordan Hall production; Martin Luther King assassination.

To anyone reading this book, these events will by now be familiar. And although they had a profound effect on Ran at the time of their happening, it is in his constant returning to them—as a source of fascination, inspiration, awe, and fear—that these events have shaped him as a man, musician, and educator.

Part IV

Man, Musician, Educator:
A Distillation

1

Mainly Music

Who in the world am I? Ah, THAT'S the great puzzle!

Lewis Carroll, *Alice in Wonderland*

Critics have tried to categorize Ran's music with varying degrees of success. There can be no denying, however, that it is steeped in narrative. "What he is doing is telling stories at the piano—that is the essence of his style."[1]

But of course, it is the way in which these stories are told that is important, and Ran has the charisma of a master storyteller. The tone of the telling: "the subconscious expressing an influence that it picked up somewhere,"[2] and the sense of narrative timing is what makes it unique.

Nini Gambaré is one of the many critics who has tried to define Ran Blake and his music. Gambaré's description comes tantalizingly close to teasing out the puzzle:

> Ran Blake is a refined and sensitive pianist, a master of the keyboard, and a prolific composer. His highly personal style, his watchful choice of notes, and his manner of producing them, require attentive listening in order to fully seize the carefully thought-out value of each shading. The silences, the pauses, the suspensions, which reveal improvised tension, are more eloquent than the sounds themselves and are dense with emotions: they are the outpourings of a soul. He pours into his music the content of the innermost folds of his self, the existential conflicts, the contradictions of the world around him, his own longing for freedom, justice, mysticism, but also his anguish at

iniquity and the fear of death. From this, springs a universe of sound that releases the silvery refractions of a complex individuality and can be read as the autobiography and the self-analysis of a man gifted with superior introspective faculties and a fervid imagination.[3]

Ran Blake's "autobiography," as told through his music, is a search for meaning at both a conscious and subconscious level. It is complex: springing from formative influences that have been contemplated in solitude then distilled in the dream world. It is a story that not many are ready to hear; it is confronting in its honesty. The outpouring of thoughts, dreams, hopes, fears; and the cry for freedom and justice—all this can be challenging. It is the manifestation of the human spirit, laid bare in all its simple beauty and complex aspiration.

It all began in Springfield, MA., with his parents providing a home that had harmony, contemplative space, and inspiration. Here, he could dream and think—though, for him, the boundaries between contemplation and the dream world were often blurred. Here, he became aware of the power of music to touch people; to communicate emotions. And here, he discovered the Robert Siodmak film *The Spiral Staircase*, with its brilliant cinematography by Nicolas Musicara and sinister moments in the music of Roy Webb.[4] And so it was here, in Springfield, that his life-long devotion to film noir commenced. From this young age, music and film became inextricably entwined:

> L: Was music a bigger love for you, or was it film?
> R: How could I separate them? I was IN a film! When my parents went out, a young lady came to be in charge. She was dressed in black, and I thought it [sic] was a policewoman, and I went into the [piano] room, and she said, 'What nonsense are you playing?' She said, 'We won't have more of that!' She had white gloves... And we had no cell phones, so I tried to dial out of the house; she almost caught me. I dreamt about it the next night. It became one of my movies—to replay in my head. Remember, I'm a product of every movie I saw. I walk in and out of life, and dreams, and reality.

The second great influence was the Gospel Church, discovered by accident during the Springfield years.[5] Ran later described the music of the Gospel Church as "both earthy and sanctified." The music of Eunice Glover and Edith Powell of the Hartford Gospel Church created a lasting impression that would lead Ran to Mahalia Jackson, Ray Charles, Marion Williams, Claude Jeter.[6]

Ran's music, of course, is more than an expression of his feelings and emotions or a reference to his experiences; it is laced with attitude—a social awareness and desire for change, which also had its beginnings in Springfield. His parents had traveled to experience cultural diversity and had witnessed inequality in some of the places they visited. His mother told him about her trips to Asia and how she had been shocked that people were called "coolies" and other "awful terms."

His babysitter, Mary Garvey,[7] wove ideas of Irish oppression into the stories she told him. Later, as a schoolboy, he would walk to the Gospel church to hear the music. There, the contrast between poor and rich, black and white, was immediately apparent in the drab surrounds and spartan structures of a neighborhood that was only blocks from his own.

And underscoring all these incidental experiences were his parents' direct assessments:

> Okay, so my father talked about injustice in the Charles Dickens novels. He would talk about Victor Hugo's *Les Miserables*—the miserable—you know that one? He said how terrible [it was for] Jean Valjean; he [talked of the] injustice in prison.

It was part of a wide-reaching formation, made all the more meaningful and cohesive because of the fact that it was unhurried. There was time to think, to dream, to soak it all in.[8] Expression was encouraged, whether it be at the piano or in written form, and, by the time Ran left for Bard, the idea of musically interpreting emotions and attitudes was as necessary to him as breathing. Bard provided the structural base from which he could branch out and acquire the technical skills needed for his expression. It gave him the opportunity to immerse himself in music—to compose, to play, to listen, and to pursue the ideas and leads available to him at a vibrant liberal arts college. Ran has often voiced his disappointment that the modern university precludes contemplation. Because there are so many demands on time, so many deadlines to be met, there is no time for soul-searching—a skill that's lost in a tide of practicality:

> A lot of people don't have the time to do what I've done in life.

Ran spent the time he was given wisely, developing strong foundations for a musical career. His mind was occupied with composers—from Bartok and Messiaen to Monk. It was the foundation of a distinct piano style. It wasn't a conscious development. Rather, it came from:

> [...] darkness, films, dreams. I mean, of course, I knew Bartok, and Monk appealed to me more than Gilbert and Sullivan, but no, it just came to me. And when I studied with Hankus for a year, I wanted to un-noir for a bit, so when I do the beginning of "Vilna," I try to do it straight, but the noir won't go out.... [*He raises his voice dramatically.*] It is in me. [*He scoops his hands inwards to his heart.*]
> People mention my keyboard sound, which does not include a lot of right-hand speed, but instead deals with the sounds of the orchestra and "ghost tones."[9] Early teachers in keyboard included Kate Wolff of the Berlin Philharmonic, who taught me at Bard College, and Ray Cassarino, who introduced me to a lot of the 1950s standards. When in Boston, I spent incredible weeks with Madame Margaret Chaloff.[10] My most important New York keyboard teachers were Mal Waldron and Mary Lou Williams. Mal helped me considerably in the field of mood study, and Mary Lou gave me education in Catholicism, the blues, and encouragement in pseudo-noir stride.[11]

Though Ran does not claim to be analytical, he does admit to three components of his piano style:

> R: I think it has music of noir, early 20th century—no twelve-tone[12] but definitely classical—and some gospel. Now [at first] I hadn't known Aretha[13] or [Willis] James, so it didn't have the real beat, but I'm more into it now, and I think now, people would say I *do* play jazz—and I sometimes do—but, you know, when someone said I HAD to play jazz, ah... it didn't sound like it 'cause my ears were on the Russian music and the gospel and then noir, noir, noir, and Bernard Herrmann[14] and stuff, so it was like my ears were different—I picked up chords.
> My music has hints of Mississippi Blues; it has nothing of the bebop, the salsa, or all that, and I think just the mystery of decay and yesterday... and footsteps in the night. Darkness—not of real Frankenstein, or a horror person coming out, but an image I see going into the kitchen—a white sheet around somebody, or did I dream it? [*He finishes on a quavering upward inflection.*]

Dreams, mystery, dark shadows—they are repetitive themes, and though Ran goes on to state that Charles Ives,[15] Anton Webern,[16] Thelonious Sphere Monk, and Edgar Allan Poe[17] were also influences on his music, it is the complexity of life and the reality of injustice that compel him:

> [...] the street, the dream world, racism, and, especially, the exhaustion of long-suppressed anger.[18]

The meaning of life in all its complexity and the emotion evoked by injustice were a challenge for Ran. Gathering these threads together, assimilating them, and giving them form has been his life's work. The manifestation of such work can be complex—too complex for many.

> R: Most people don't like my music—a few people like it, but my records don't sell.
> L: Steve Lacy at the "Con"[19] was saying about Monk that in his experience, it took people fifty years to catch on to what they were doing with Monk, and I think that might be the same with your music.
> R: Well, that means I'll be dead when they catch on. I don't know whether people will, as people don't look backwards.

And perhaps it is true that people, in general, do not look backwards—or inwards. They prefer to remain unburdened. Because to engage with the concerns that inspire Ran Blake's music *can* be confronting. Joe Milazzo, writing in 2001, said that, in some ways, Ran Blake's music "extends to us [...] the freedom to contemplate."[20] The question is posed—it is left up to the listener as to how they engage with it.

> L: What is the relationship between the emotion that inspires the music and the emotion that stirs the concerns?
> R: [*He is impatient with the question.*] I think I've already answered that—through my music! All my stuff is political or film noir, and everything has a story, a plot, a scenario, and camera movements—whether you want a deep focus like Orson Welles... So, for me, I do that. So, I'm acknowledging that emotion, and all this goes for Mahler, Messiaen, Monk, Mingus, not just Ran Blake.
> L: That was a good answer. You can answer them when you want to.

Without Gunther, who was a stalwart supporter right from the first, Ran's own self-belief could well have been shaken. Gunther saw in Ran's music something that went beyond the general perception. He has referred to Ran as "one of the most remarkable and original pianist-improvisers in the last half-century." He recognized something "purely instinctual"[21] in Ran's work.

> L: So, Gunther seems one of those people who can identify something special in you that not many other people can see. There seem to be only a few people who are able to understand you on a musical or a personal level—beyond the superficial.
> R: Is that my understanding?
> L: That's my understanding.

R: Yes, I agree.
L: And what I want to know is, why is that?
R: I don't want to evade this for a moment, but do you think truly I have the answer?

THERE IS SOMETHING at once miraculous and mysterious about Ran Blake's music. Aaron Hartley has coined the term "ghost notes" to describe the unique meeting of harmonic, timbral, and registral elements in the music of Ran Blake. The term is apt, conjuring up shadows and darkness, an other-worldliness—the supernatural. But these elusive whispers are achieved through a very down-to-earth dedication to technique, and in particular, to the development of a pedaling style.[22]

> Ran's genius is such that, through what can only have been years of weird experimentation at the piano, he has managed to gain secure, expressive control over the unwanted upper partials that can occur during pedaling. Sounds signaling an accident in the otherwise homogenous tone of a well-trained classical pianist are skillfully extracted to evoke ghosts and shimmers—sounds I never knew the piano could make before I heard Ran Blake and his awe-inspiring pedal precision.

Despite this pedal precision, Ran is quick to find shortcomings in his own technical style. He points out that he doesn't notate and thus doesn't see himself as a real academic musician. He laments his own lack of theory, but Leo is quick to dismiss any such regret:

> Look at the substance; it really doesn't matter how you get to it.

It would not be possible to bring together the diverse experiences and emotions—and their inspiration, in the dreamworld and films that are the substance of Ran Blake's work—without a high degree of musicianship. This is the foundation he builds upon. It's a hard-earned skill, honed over a lifetime.

EVERYONE HAS A quest. For most people, the engagement with that quest is intermittent and episodic. For Ran, the quest is enacted daily. Music provides a space where he can explore the great questions of his life, of the world, of the spirit. These questions perhaps don't have answers in this world, but they are vitally important for the survival of culture—and in our "search for meaning."[23]

2

MORE MUSIC—ESSENCE AND PROCESS

> *Without culture, and the relative freedom it implies, society, even when perfect, is but a jungle. This is why any authentic creation is a gift to the future.*
>
> ALBERT CAMUS[1] *THE ARTIST AND HIS TIME*

The task of the musician, and indeed of any creative artist, is to observe the society in which they find themselves, assimilate it and, through some process of their own, give it form—for the benefit of the future.

Ran's gift to the world through music is significant. It is evidenced in his huge body of recorded work and his commitment to future generations of musicians through his teaching[2]—the offering of a unique pedagogical perspective, continually refined and developed over a long career as an educator and now distilled (with equal measures of cutting insight and warm good humor) in his book, *Primacy of the Ear.* Though he may be drawn to shadows (he writes about death and maintains that sadness is the "other side" of all life's celebrations), though he claims that "the color of joy" is not evident in his music, Ran's gift to the world is uplifting. It is an affirmation of life in all its complexity—its sadness as well as its moments of joy. As Francis Davis puts it: "It's a tribute to Blake's complexity as a composer and performer that the tone is so doggedly life-affirming—in the manner of all great music."[3]

The celebration of life has always been a part of Ran Blake, though its form may have changed over time. Maturity brings a knowledge of "what not to say" in music. Maturity has also seen him develop his control of form on a larger scale—a skill that has allowed him to pursue an expansive approach to performance (and recording). And though this "formal control" (or "unit control" as Ran likes to call it) may not be exactly what his mentor Gunther Schuller had in mind (when he suggested that Ran focus on this aspect of his music), he would have no doubt been pleased to see the directions in which Ran took his advice. Each Ran Blake performance (and recording) is an offering of music, film, experience, and reflection that has been meticulously planned to honor friends, past and present (there is no distinction between the living and the dead); to give opportunities to students; to capture a mood; to explore a theme; to link to a memory; to tell a story. It is multi-layered yet seamless. For Ran, composition, preparation, practice and performance are all interrelated. The resulting art, however, relies still on a commitment on the part of the listener to make it complete.

> R: I do think it is such an interesting thing to try to see the audience and see if they make a commitment, but there may be members of the audience that have had a bad day.
> L: Do you prefer live performance or recording?
> R: Recordings! And a wonderful young lady who is studying with me from Turkey says this about Chris Connor—when Chris Connor makes a recording, it's a sanctuary, but when she does a live performance, it's a battlefield—I think that's so incredible and if you hear Chris Connor *Live at the Village Vanguard* and you hear what she does with 'Angel Eyes,' it's so different. They're both on Atlantic Records. It's *Live at the Village Vanguard*, and the studio version is on the album *He Loves Me, He Loves Me Not*.

Walter Benjamin has questioned whether you can capture the essence of something when it comes to recording and asks whether its essence is lost forever in the process.[4] But whether or not an essence can be captured, there is something un-repeatable about a live performance—something that speaks of primal connection and communication.

> L: Yeah, when I got to NEC, on my first day there, you played (in Williams Hall, I think), and it was just so amazing for me to hear because those dynamics you play on the piano and those sounds… they can't be captured on a recording and it sounded so much better in the flesh—so it was really great for me to hear. And I was prepared for the possibility that you might not be a nice person—because, you know, just because you like someone's music doesn't mean he won't be an arrogant person… or proud. But you and other people were just so enthusiastic and kind to me.

> R: [*with self-deprecation*] Well, you didn't know me on Thursdays when I was arrogant.

Through performance, the artist seeks to make an authentic connection with their audience, to reveal to them the true nature of each piece. For Ran, preparing for any performance involves a great deal of soul-searching—sifting through memories, thoughts, dreams, and aspirations—seeking this essence. And when the piece is not his own, there still needs to be an "ownership." It is hard work.

> R: [*interrupting*] I do agree. I do soul searching every time I have to perform in public, and even when I have to prepare for my big rehearsals. For a week (with the lights off), there's a little glass of wine, cheese, and then espresso iced coffee with added cream and a small [serving of] orange marmalade—Spanish style—on an English muffin. And I do one little [part] of the prayer of Mary Lou Williams, the Catholic... And I don't do this for my twenty minutes in the morning—when I'm just warming up—no! I'm talking about when the lights are off at night. And I do this four nights a week; one night, I just have wine and go to bed, watch television, but yes, it's very, very important to do this.

The discussion turns naturally to time—the lack of it—and the impact of this on the nature of performance:

> R: Everything's on YouTube now. First-year students—seventeen years old—[have] six things on YouTube. And the parents ask me have I watched it.
> L: I know what you mean! And that was a good thing about the technology of the past—you weren't able to just release something—a lot of money and preparation had to go into it. And now, because you can just do it [on YouTube], no one gives anything any thought, and there's so much music out there; you're inundated. And if you want to be a musician, you have to spend some time in silence.
> R: Oh, it's so important! I know Dorothy Wallace would say she would go up to her room with the bible and an Agatha Christie, with a glass of Jack Daniels with ONE ice cube. [*He holds up a very definite pointer finger.*] I liked two; she said ONE! [*another definite pointer*] She would read the *Book of Job*, and then, at eleven o'clock, Agatha Christie for a little bit, and then a final prayer. She always did that as a nightly ritual.
> L: [*returning to the theme*] Maybe you feel you like recording better, but I think the audience gets more of the essence of Ran Blake in a live performance.

> R: I think you're right; maybe twenty years ago, they might have listened to LPs, but nobody has time [now]. They will make time for a concert, but I don't know if they even hear CDs twice—I don't hear everything twice. I have piles. [*He stretches his hand way above his head to indicate the height.*] They're coming by truckloads!
>
> L: I know exactly what you mean; it's gone nuts. Like, I'm glad that I grew up before this technology ruined everything because when I was around eighteen/seventeen, discovering jazz, and you'd go into the record store in the city, and the guy knew me by then, and he'd say, 'Oh we've got this in,' and they had little listening booths. And you'd say, 'Oh, I hear there is this new Ella Fitzgerald, Joe Pass re-issue. Can you get it in?'
>
> And he'd say, 'Yes, it'll take three weeks to arrive from the States,' and you'd be like, 'Ah yeah,' and you'd pay a lot of money for it because it was really a boutique sort of thing. But now, it's all on the internet, and people don't hear a whole album—they hear one track while they're checking email—so too much aural cocktail and not enough listening to an album.
>
> R: Exactly, Leo!

And so, the conversation swings back to time and its impact on performance—and preparation for performance:

> R: To prepare a piece for a concert [...], I have to have ten or eleven months really owning the piece before I'm ready to perform it; it's a process. Now, that doesn't mean that if your sister had a birthday and wanted three bars of some national anthem, I mean, I'm not going to say 'no' to that, but basically, I prepare. There really needs to be an ownership, but it's not about getting to your own psyche, your own 'me, me, me.' [It's] Do you really know the piece to the extent that you can deconstruct the bridge, you can drop the bridge, you can put the bridge in early? If there are words, do you know them? Do you disagree with the words? And now, that doesn't mean you're always going to play it great, though.
>
> L: Right.
>
> R: So, I don't want that as a concrete guidepost—you know, a + b + …algebraic b + a can be a negative number.
>
> L: [*laughs*]
>
> R: There's a whole long process. You have to have the essence; essence is a cocktail—the spirit, the soul…

After consideration, he adds:

Or maybe I should just say the 'craft of the essence' so that I don't make it all spiritual passion.

But reading this back at a later date, Ran is still not happy with his definition of essence:

> No! essence is the George Russell terminology of something.[5] And craft is sort of a vulgar word in this context anyway; gee, isn't it also the taste of the listener? I mean, it sounds a little self-affirmative, Leo, my tone, I must say. I don't think I appreciate it—doesn't it sound a little professorial?
> L: I don't know. I think it sounds… well, it's exactly what you said.
> R: Well, if I did, I must have had a liquid…
> L: [*laughs*]
> R: But it's a little exaggerated—I think it's a little bit absolute, Leo. Essence is a very private thing.
> L: Okay.
> R: I still haven't gotten to first base over essence, really. George Russell's 'Ezz-thetic' I've been playing since I was twenty-five or so, and there's one thing I still trip on, but I own the essence—I was told I did by George Russell—I really own the piece.

Ran himself likes to get "right in the atmosphere" when he is learning a piece:

> Right now, I'm spending a little bit of time on Olivier Messiaen. I'm being asked to do it, so I'm planning—and there's still learning for me to do as well. For instance, I bought a tape of birds singing, so I want to get right in the atmosphere, and if you're doing a hundred things a week, you can't do that.
> It should be… playing should be like a composer—a composition. I want to make last-minute thoughts in chords, and so it's really the role of recomposition…. [*He breaks off on a sudden thought.*] Do we want to be specific [regarding] which book of birds I have on the tape?
> L: Please!
> R: Well, let me go to the other room and get it. [*In a delighted, excited tone as he springs from his chair*]…just a minute now, and it's probably going to be the first of many books. It's called *The Singing Life of Birds* by Donald Kroodsma, and it's probably good we're doing this—*The Singing Life of Birds*. He [Kroodsma] came to New England Conservatory in Spring 2008. It's very important to put year dates, I notice.[6] You know, we may still be working on this—if you're still interested—in three years…

L: I think quite possibly we will be.
R: I think so too, Leo.[7]

It is through his steady commitment to 'owning' a piece—living in its world; making links between it and the wider catalog of its creator; investigating the context surrounding it; and building a complex web of connections between people, places, flavors, films, books, political movements, and many other things—that Ran is able to recompose. Recomposition is a term that is specific to Ran's own methodology; it forms an integral part of his concert preparation.

Gunther Schuller makes the point:

> Like Monk and Gil Evans, Ran Blake is an ingenious 're-composer' to be distinguished from an arranger.[8]

OVER THE PAST twenty years, Ran has developed the idea of an "aural cocktail"—to be taken at bedtime and while he sleeps. It's yet another example of the lengths to which he will go in order to enter the world of the music that he plans to perform. These "cocktails"—an eclectic mix of music and styles—are prepared (following Ran's instructions) by his young assistants and set to play after Ran is in bed (with a late-night drink or even dessert as a nightcap). The lights are dimmed, and the assistant gets ready to leave. There is a note on the door—a last-minute checklist:

> [*Ran agrees.*] Yes! 'Reconnect aural cocktail,' It must be on at eleven o'clock at night, and [then] I have to press buttons on the computer [to activate it]. So that should be on the door, [along with] lock the door, water for Dek-Tor, and a couple of other things.

The cocktail varies, depending on what work Ran is preparing, but though the ingredients differ, the method is basically the same:

> R: Aaron's doing a loop tape tonight—called the 'Aural Collage Cocktail'—and so, tonight, I'm going to hear Chris Connor's great version, with Stan Kenton, of 'If I Should Lose You,' arranged by Bill Russo. She's twenty-seven years old. She's at Birdland. I have a 1953 bootleg [copy].[9] And then, we're going to hear two Herbie Nichols [tracks], Bill Evans' 'Love for Sale,' and I have five... [others.] 'Malindy Sings,' [*sic*] by Abbey Lincoln... So today at three or four in the morning, [I'll be in] my bed, the little recording will be above

me, and it's going to play it all through the night—these different versions. And then, I wake up at nine o'clock tomorrow morning, and I oralize them—I turn off the tape, and I see what I remember. Last night, I had Chris Connor doing 'Night Bird' and Sarah Vaughan doing 'Autumn in New York' because I'm working on an 'Autumn in New York' piece for George Russell.[10]

Janet, do you have an aural cocktail for tonight? You could have a paragraph by John Steinbeck, Agatha Christie, your favorite psalm from the *Book of Psalms* in the bible and maybe a little bit of Edgar Allan Poe, and Leo will give you one of my pieces to listen to—and maybe a little Sara Serpa and one piece by himself.

L&J: Sounds wonderful!

THE AURAL COCKTAIL is a seemingly painless way to listen when compared to more active listening. Active listening is an art—one that takes time to acquire. But the art of listening is vital to understanding Ran Blake. Listening is a conduit to the heart of the music, but it's also, through the contemplation of the music on the part of the listener, that each listener discovers their own innermost spirit. Ray Cassarino from Wethersfield first encouraged Ran to forget about comparing himself with others but rather examine his own direction and formation through listening to records. But it was in New York that Ran seriously began to explore the art of listening:

> I became fascinated by New York, but even more so by the chance to listen and listen.[11]

Gunther went further and taught him to listen to himself. Ran became so attuned to listening that it canceled out everything else:

> I know when I hear certain strains, I forget what's being said at restaurants—even if it's a hammy version of 'Laura.' The sound, the pictures, and the placement of the beat, and then, the re-occurring walking beat—it's so essential. And for me, the sound of the drum and the voice of the song is more essential than conversation.

Such focused listening is both compelling and exhausting. Ran claims he can maintain focus for fifteen to twenty minutes, though for someone he knows well (Chris Connor or Abbey Lincoln), he can do more. So, it does depend on the music. However, as Ran is at pains to point out:

> No matter how good you are listening to a particular style of music, the art of listening to music is exhausting; that should be underlined. And we can't absorb a lot of things if we are under stress, or haven't gotten enough sleep, or...
> [*He makes a new start.*]
> SO, the art of listening to music is exhausting, depending on the level [at which] you are trying to listen to that music. And then, it's also exhausting because it brings back memories—to hear Jeanne Lee, who's not here anymore....
> [*The pause is deep and significant.*]
> Also—another thing—are you hearing as part of a community or alone? When I put on a movie, and there are three or four people [present], people sit and watch it and sip their drink... When I put on a CD, they're quiet for the first four minutes. [*It's said with a perplexed tone.*]

Listening requires genuine connection, whether it is listening to recorded music or to a live performance. When Ran attends concerts, the performing artist has his full attention. He finds it difficult to understand anyone giving any less. He has always taken the need to support fellow musicians seriously. In *Primacy of the Ear*, he calls this "an act of good citizenship, something that keeps our music community alive."[12] Up until his early seventies, he was attending five concerts a week. He would arrive early and choose a seat where he could be best connected with the performance. And at any performance Ran attends, the intensity of his listening is evident:

> L: Ever since I've known you, every time you listen, you get, you know, a troubled look on your face, and sometimes you bury your head in your hands. And then—other times—you are like doing thumbs up to the other audience members. You're probably not so aware of this, but I've noticed it.
> R: [Surprised] So I sometimes nod to other audience members?
> L: Yeah, you'll be like, 'YES!'
> R: I know sometimes I can have my head in my arms—which doesn't mean I'm putting it down, and sometimes I'm bored...
> L: I think that YOU, more than most people, go through the full gamut of emotion.
> [*Ran agrees.*]

The emotional content of a musical piece is a very real preoccupation for Ran Blake, both as a listener and a performer. Whereas many musicians judge musical complexity on purely technical grounds (whether these relate to compositional elements or to their musical execution), for Ran, technique, style, and sentiment all contribute to a work's complexity. Ran is full of praise for performers who manage to master such subtle artistic nuances:

> Like Giovanna Daffini—who sings "Bella Ciao"—that [piece] is so simple, but you have to get the gorgonzola note for it—the brie cheese. And the brie is French, not Italian. Sometimes something simple can be deviously complex.
> So, it really is determined by the content and the sound of the performers. And then, are you just trying to do a blueprint or really trying to get into the performer's soul with your own? So there's so much… [to consider.] Which sip of the cocktail are you satisfied with? It's multi-layered—fifth dimension.

This other universe is accessed by dedicated listening—stillness. It requires discipline and maintained concentration. Listening to music, absorbing it, is indeed so complex and demanding that Ran feels the necessity to allow his ears to rest:

> [for] three hours a day in order to focus when I am hearing music. [There must be] No background—not even street drilling—absolute silence.[13]

There is one exception to this discipline, however. Even when he is preparing a concert, Ran allows himself some time to watch movies:

> I will see certain films because they relax me. I'll go to the piano and have Marilyn Monroe there as a babysitter in *Don't Bother to Knock* with Richard Widmark. And I'll try to incorporate that.[14]

These movie breaks help with the creation of mood. Ran has said that he is "more interested in creating moods than anything else."[15]

Once mood is established, then comes the plot—explored through storyboarding:

> I hear a piece of music over and over again, and then I storyboard it with a plot, and then I listen to it back, quietly. I don't sing much, but I hear it, and then I go to the piano. I make sure the lights are off, and then I do a plot. It takes a week or two for the recipe to work. It's not, you know, inst…[fast] food. It takes a long while.

Ran's plotting has a strong visual element:

Usually, it takes place at night, outside a dark house… near trees. At times it helps if there's a spiral staircase, or a mountain, or a man called Doktor Mabuse—M-A-B-U-S-E. Do you know him? He lives in Germany—Fritz Lang discovered him. There's a song about Doktor Mabuse—I could play it on the piano.
[*Leo starts humming, and Ran claps, delighted.*]
L: Yes, I don't think many musicians do that, do they? I've never met anyone else who storyboards.
R: Yup—you see, that helps me also get the fundamentals of the piece. [But] I can't only use fantasy. I have to go back and hear it again, and again, and again—like distilling a good gin cocktail with Charles Mingus.

While the plotting is pictorially based, Ran is adamant, as he states in *Primacy of the Ear*, that "putting the ear at the center of your musical learning, rather than the fingers (technique) or the brain (theory) is the key to forming a truly personal style."[16]

His commitment to listening is total. The musical score is incapable of communicating the subtle nuances that exist in a live performance, but these can be preserved (to a high degree of accuracy) on the recorded medium. The recording thus provides for Ran a means of internalizing elements that, in days gone by, would have been inseparable from the fleeting moment in which they were created during a performance:

> There is no more important activity in influencing one's style than hearing the same record—four songs of Horace Silver, Jack Teagarden, Bartok, or whatever it may be—for an hour a night for a week or three.[17]

Personal style reflects identity. In Ran's case, it is the story of a boy who found his way to the church on Hancock Street, who became obsessed with *Spiral Staircase*, who liked to dream in the Mulberry Street cemetery. It is the story of a young man who doggedly, despite cautions, stuck to his plan to visit Athens at the time of the military coup.[18] It is a story that continues on his return home, where, more attuned than ever to suffering and injustice, he endeavors to make a small difference in the way he knows best—through his music. This life story told through music has been a long time in the making:

> L: Too many people are obsessed with being new—would you agree?
> R: Yes—but they're not—they're not very original. To be original, you have to have a drink of the past. You have to drink history and re-combine it. Perhaps in 1961, there could be a new timbre—I'm

sure Cage[19] was new, the 12 tones, Schoenberg—but perhaps the only brand-new thing [nowadays] would be the drumming of Africa, which is so complex I don't think our western ears could hear it. But I don't think there is anything called 'new' anymore. There may be new ways of making the cocktail: 20% Aretha; 40%... There are new combinations, but you've got to personalize it.

Ran has spoken of the need to have something of the personality of the artist in a work of art. If it does, the work will express "something of creative importance," even if it fails on other measures.[20]

THE EVENTS OF Ran's life provide the program for his music. His personal style is the medium through which he tells his stories—and their message. It also conveys ghostly whispers, otherwise inaccessible, from deep within his subconscious and assimilates these into his narrative. Thus all these elements are integrated into one cohesive form, and while there may have been a program to this form, the music "completely transcends its original programmatic aims.."[21]

It is in this transcending that the gift to the future lies. It is somewhere at the balance point of emotion and intellect—of feeling, experiences, attitudes, and the methodology necessary to express them. Here at this point—a 5th dimension presented and communicated through performance—here is the essence. George Russell understood this:

> The reason I write music is that I feel it's a vehicle or channel which leads to your true self, your essence.[22]

But the channel is more than just a personal connection. At its core, music is a means of communication—one that transcends language and is capable of expressing the innermost yearnings of the spirit. Ran, when questioned (in Spain in 1967) as to what his music meant to him, answered:

> [It means] so much that when I am playing, that is the only time of day in which I believe I exist.[23]

Further into the interview, Ran said that if he wasn't a pianist, nothing "could have filled my emptiness."[24]

> L: Ran, is this still true?
> R: Yes, I suppose... I'd hate to have no DVD player... but yes.

The essence of Ran Blake's gift to the world goes deeper than the music he played. It is something that spans the conscious and unconscious; the spiritual and the temporal; the past, present, and future across a vast emptiness to a higher level of existence. It is probably impossible to define. It must be carried forward in the collective memory of students and concertgoers.

3

Performance

> *I really always have Gunther, Dorothy Wallace,
> Thelonious Monk, and Florence de Lannoy on
> my mind when performing.*
>
> Ran Blake[1]

The quest for authenticity is at the heart of artistic pursuit. While self-expression through the medium of art is fundamental to our human nature, making an artistic statement that resonates with others remains elusive. Getting to the point where one can publicly express something of themselves—their experiences, reflections, memories, desires—is a significant achievement. It requires that all extraneous elements (such as technique, language, style, etc.) are integrated by the artist to the point where they cease to exist. To express oneself in this way, without falling back on technique or pre-learned material, is where true artistry lies. It is the point at which "intellect has to surrender to instinct."[2]

Ran Blake has sure instincts; however, performing before an audience will always involve an element of trust. It assumes the audience will be receptive to such a profoundly personal offering. It leaves the artist extremely vulnerable.

> I don't want to be there where I'm going to be… what is it when somebody is rejected? I'm tired of my music being rejected, even though I have a little cult following.

The artist seeks connectedness—a lack of response is hard to take. It is something Ran has experienced personally:

> I direct my music to the community of man—a community which so often is uninterested in artists who reach out for new forms.[3]

Though such words disclose a pragmatic awareness of the real-world truth, Ran has not given in to cynicism. He is unwavering in his quest and unstinting in his invitation to his audience to join him as he explores uncharted musical landscapes. When Ran plays a concert, he visits a world of dreams—sometimes nightmares; he accompanies the movie of his life. He plays with lights dimmed, as if "to take the focus off himself, as he's offering all of himself to the audience."[4]

> My existence is there in so many movies going around me—the future, the past, the present—real movies, then movies of life.

Re-visiting the narrative of his existence is emotionally draining.

> L: So, when you play, do you see the narrative? Do you see it visually as you would a movie, or is it vaguer than this?
> R: What time of day? It depends on the time of day. Am I in Jordan Hall, or am I in that room with [the] methodology... [class].
> L: Okay, maybe I'll read out the next question, and you can incorporate both. You have said, in the past, you are sometimes a 'producer' putting on a show. How important is the audience to this show? Could you do without them? Do you try to challenge them and demand that they take...
> R: Hold! [*in a wail*] My memory's not too good...
> L: [*shortly and dismissively*] Your memory's fine. [*then, continuing without pause*] Do you try to challenge them, e.g., demand that they take more responsibility for their enjoyment of the performance? Once you start playing, do you feel the audience's presence, or are you unaware of them?
> R: [*eager now to answer*] When I'm playing solo, or with Knife?
> L: Do both.
> R: When I do solo—and let's say, the people are on my side—the first five minutes, I'm very aware of the room... and the expectation. Have I been mislabeled as jazz [for example]? But [after that]—even small noises of drinks being poured—I don't notice a thing.

Jose Antonio Luera once asked Ran why he did not acknowledge the audience after each piece. And Ran replied, "But I cannot do this. While I am playing, I concentrate tremendously on my music. If I greeted the audience after each number, it would break this concentration."[5]

Lapses can, however, happen. Joseph Brenna asked Ran how he dealt with these. Ran's answer was simple:

I just have them—and I may cut a piece short. Maybe I do rely on some structure more; you still have some skeletal idea.

There are just some times I don't play well. I do try to have the right amount of wine before; I think of films or books I've read; it's like the way I plan my dreams at night—I used to keep a dream log—I do try to put myself in a mood for a concert.

I rarely have an evening where it's all bad; also, I rarely have an evening where everything works.[6]

Each artist has their own way of accessing that part of themselves that enables them to perform. And while Ran's style may be labeled as avant-garde or esoteric, his process is simple—born of his love for cinema, interwoven through the narrative of his life:

"I don't approach it intellectually; I don't even approach it particularly trying to stream or integrate. I approach it programmatically and emotionally."[7]

L: And so, are certain songs hard for you to perform?
R: 'Never on Sunday' is—it's emotionally hard. Then there's one 'Reincarnation of a Love Bird,'[8] which can be physically and aurally challenging (and I was reminded I played that in Brown Hall a few years ago).[9] So, of course, I'm seeing the reincarnation of Mingus; I'm reading all the things about coming back to the earth, but then I have to remember how to pivot a scale of F sharp minor, so I have two realities—I can't separate them—and when I modulate, sometimes I do it without realizing it. So sometimes, I am not in control; the plot takes over. I'm the object, and instead of the ego —when I'm performing to play solo—the music takes a hold of me! I try to do storyboarding; I try to say to people that this piece will begin pleasantly before the storm, but occasionally... Oh, I think this is true of many improvisers. I mean, after a while, does it speak to the audience? So maybe I'm now giving you too long an answer, Leo, because you didn't ask about the quality of playing, but yeah, I find it very mixed emotions. If I worry about playing correctly, I take all my vinegar and horseradish out.
L: Is that why, when I've seen you play, you can't really talk to people afterward?
R: Yeah.
L: Is that to do with that you can't really exit out of that world very easily?
R: Yes, it's tough.
L: In programming...

R: [*interrupting*] Some people think that's the best part of my concerts—they love the programs.
L: Yeah, well, when you're performing for other people, I know you do it purely out of theatrical concerns—you're like a director for those Jordan Hall concerts—and you do it purely because of what needs to come next.
R: Sequence.
L: Yeah, exactly! When you're performing yourself, do you ever compromise on that for the sake of yourself? Like, do you ever let yourself down gently towards the end? So you're ready to enter reality sooner than you would…
R: Well, I think I did. I was going to close next week's concert with 'Never on Sunday,' and I decided I will go a little bit back to a [favorite] Dorothy Wallace piece called 'Dancing in the Dark'—I wanted to make it easier for the audience… once in a while it doesn't work. And of course—a new subject—nobody can tell me what the piano's like. [So] do I want to end with a happy bar song so that I can go and say [*he puts on a light, bright voice*], 'Oh, there's Janet and Peter McFadden!' Sometimes the concert has to end with a 'PARM!' [*He brings his hands together in a clap to demonstrate.*] But it's… ah… so have I answered that satisfactorily, Leo?
L: That's a good answer.

Whether performing solo or collaborating with others (most often in duo), Ran's concerts prefer to draw audiences in rather than project out to them. Dimmed lighting is essential in creating the world in which Ran will tell his stories; stories told, for the most part, without recourse to spoken word or explanation—such things that would diminish the dramatic element at the heart of his creative process. And although there will inevitably be moments of levity, his performances are, for the most part, somber affairs—an exploration of the shadows that dwell just beyond the periphery of consciousness. Ran programs meticulously, devoting weeks to the sequencing of the pieces. Sometimes he makes a diagram; often, he allows his dreams to dictate the order of songs:

L: How does the dream world dictate?
R: I have my little Armagnac—my favorite liqueur—and then I control my dreams. As I'm sleeping, I keep thinking, [what song] should it start with?

∽

L: [*Later. Listening to the interview being transcribed.*] That's the thing I love about Ran—the program has an arc—a listening arc. He really puts a lot of thought into how it's going to flow as a whole story and not just one song after another. He plans for an overall climax in the programmatic narrative—like a film.

And just as, after viewing a film, there is that fleeting moment of unreality as one steps from the cinema into the real world outside, there is, after each performance, a moment of awakening, when reality is viewed with detachment.

R: Now, there's a short piano piece about awakening in the morning and trying to recall dreams. Isn't that on my *Doktor Mabuse Portfolio* [*sic*] that I did with the New England Conservatory Symphony? I collaborated with Larry Livingstone—he was the Vice President after Gunther.
I do find awakening a very interesting time of day—when your mind is floating, and you have to get back to reality—it's like walking out after a concert.
It's *Vertigo*... noir, and people come up and say, 'You played well; you remember me?'
I say... [*He shakes his head solemnly to demonstrate his answer.*] And I don't [even] remember myself, but I remember Dorothy Wallace, Gunther, Chris Conner, Mary Lou Williams, Thelonious Monk, President Obama. But [even though], maybe, I've had a TINY Jack Daniels, or a wine—I'm stone sober... but I'm not. [*His tone is full of amazement.*] I feel it after physical therapy, too—I'm drunk. And believe me, I haven't had a drink.

The process has come full circle.

R: So, a lot of the conceiving takes place in my bedroom. And then I go to the piano—and again, it feels like an orchestra. The range below middle C is the trombone section of Kenton, and then, I try to capture Abbey, Mahalia, Ray Charles, Chris Connor with my right hand... and the Messiaen and the Catholicism of the very top right [hand register], and then, over the bottom would be the Pentecostal Church. So I feel I have a whole orchestra, right on my piano. And different registers bring different meanings to me. And then sometimes I do a prayer. I'm not kneeling—it's not particularly denominational—it's any religion. And then I'm daydreaming of film noir... and then I go to the piano.

L: That's really fascinating—the way you divide up the piano and the different parts are different instrument groups. I find that very interesting.
R: I don't think I've told anybody this before.
L: No—I've never heard it before—so I loved to hear it!

4

Pluperfect Flashbacks

It's a poor sort of memory that only works backwards.

Lewis Carroll, *Alice Through the Looking-Glass*

Ran is fascinated by time and where he dwells in it. His memories give him access to a place where borders merge and histories blend. Here, the accumulated experiences of the Blakes and the Powers; of Mary Garvey, Amelia Lehrfeld, Mother Carter; of Dorothy Wallace, Gunther, and Jeanne Lee combine with so many other histories to form one tantalizingly rich unconscious. Here, in dreams and flashbacks, images and feelings, patterns and sound, lies the inspiration for Ran's music. His unconscious mind allows him to roam vast landscapes and cross time barriers. These memories, cocooned in the past, become very much alive in the "present" of his playing. Here, the focus can change from performance to performance, allowing different elements of each memory to be revealed.

Memory is not confined to linear time; rather, it holds associations and experiences that, used as a base for imagination, can just as easily be projected into the future—a future, for example, where Dorothy Wallace, vibrant as ever, welcoming as she always was, is entertaining her friends with a glass of "Jack" in "Hotel Heaven." Though Ran's visions of the future are not always so convivial:

> Sometimes—whether there's heaven or not—I'm in the future, and there's death. And what's going to happen to the world? And there's a lot of nightmares.[1]

It is an experience that Leo has observed in him:

> He turns around in his memories and sees something he didn't see there before. He's revisiting rather than recreating. It's scary because sometimes he sees things he hasn't experienced yet. He sees the future there! And sometimes, I think he sees the future distorted by the past, and that can be horrifying.[2]

Throughout his life, Ran has been absorbed by the endless possibilities of his "dream world" and stimulated by the creativity it inspires. And all the while, he has been exhorted by others—starting with his father and then his teachers, who felt he was spending too much time with his dreams—to join the "real world." Gunther added to the chorus, entreating Ran to get out of his spell a little bit. Ran was aware of their concerns; there have been times when he has consciously tried to limit the time travel that is behind his music.

> Yes, I was very interested in the tenses—the pluperfect and the future tense—and I gave myself exercises to live in the present for ten minutes of practice.

He notes that he had to stay in the present when he played with Jaki Byad:[3]

> I found that rigorous to do. I played that (my piece "Present Tense") at a concert in Paris.[4] I don't know if it was Jeanne on the program—I tried not to think about Édith Piaf,[5] Mahalia... any background. I stayed in the present. I would look at the people, and I would practice it in the mornings, and probably, I would practice it at the studio in Paris and get on the stage—it was probably three minutes long, and it was probably bad free improvisation. But just no memories. I wanted to hear the notes that I played on the piano, but without memory and without the premonition of the future. It was one of the hardest things I ever did.

Hard for anyone to step aside, even for a short time, from the inner thoughts that shape their being; well-nigh impossible for Ran, who cultivates memories. Colors, tastes, sounds, places, moods are all present where memory meets the dreamworld. All can serve as the point of departure for creative exploration:

> I have so many of my own memories constantly with me.

Although Ran's memories provide him with an abundant source of inspiration, they are far from passive elements in his creative process. They wield enormous power and must be accessed judiciously:

> Back to spirituality and emotionality—I really go in trances. I wouldn't DARE practice an hour before I have to go to the conservatory—what if I forgot to leave the house!
> When I am REALLY relaxed, I am transported, and I am really hearing things. I know I see the oboe, but it might be in the shape of a donkey going up the hill, and it's so...
> In one number at Brooklyn, I saw visions, but they're not Jesus, Mary, and the shepherds—they WERE once or twice. [*He muses, remembering.*] But they're often Kim Novak and the Tower in San Francisco[6] and Leo House[7] WITH the crucifix.
> I don't get it when I'm with a rhythm section [*starts tapping definite urgent beat*], and I know, 'BOY, I've gotta pay attention.'

Memory also plays a key role in Ran's pedagogical process. He asserts that developing a long-term musical memory is essential for the development of a personal style.[8] The artist needs to understand their musical heritage (i.e., the music that has been important to them in their life) if they are to create anything of worth. A well-developed long-term musical memory is crucial to understanding one's musical heritage *and* using it as a point of departure for genuine creative expression.

> Most improvisers have at some time felt a surprise influence jump out during a solo—something not practiced, whether it be a lick, or a tone color, or a rhythm. This is the subconscious expressing an influence that it picked up somewhere. And all musical hearing is based on what has been gathered by long-term memory and the subconscious.[9]

Memories can be so vivid that they present as a re-experiencing of a past event—a flashback—that suddenly takes control of consciousness. Flashbacks are a big part of Ran's teaching: "My whole life is a flashback." He would love for his students to have a "history"—a library of flashbacks—but admits that it takes time.[10]

> You can be creative on something new, but for me, it cannot be integrated without long-term memory.

There is a great deal of effort involved in nurturing long-term memory: the past into the "perfect past"—the pluperfect. In his teaching, Ran promotes a "type of introspection" that requires the student to:

> Examine things that are already a part of you—the style that is already your own, your feeling of heritage or nationality, a passion for a certain historical time period or geographical region, an intellectual bent, and/or an emotional need to express. It could be your sense of fashion or a deep commitment to a social/political movement. It can be as specific as one color you like to wear and as broad as your sense of reality or view of life.[11]

The words seem to go beyond personal experience as they delve into uncharted awareness of history and heritage. As such, they touch on the idea of a collective unconscious—the "great memory" that renews the world and men's thoughts age after age.[12]

But out of all these memories, this great collective unconscious of waking and sleeping experience, there are certain memories that are special. The very personalized memory—nostalgia—which "links compositions, performance, and improvisation to films, politics, street life, friendships, and other facets of daily life. The fun begins when we interweave these through our musical experience to form their own tapestry."[13]

A lot of Ran's memories—both those looking back and those projected forward—are woven in and out of the movies he loves. Movies have a predominantly visual narrative, and Ran often plays them with the sound turned off. For him, the original score can be too pervasive, vying with the visual elements of the narrative and his own musical interpretation of them.[14]

Memories for Ran have a visual beat also; one which echoes the music and sounds that originally accompanied them. These include memories of Amelia Lehrfeld, tapping her foot or her stick to the music that he, Jeanne Lee, and George Russell were playing in her apartment; memories of piano lessons with Mary Lou Williams with a chant measured on rosary beads and the tempo marked by her hand beating on his.

Memory is a reconstruction of past experiences which uses associations for retrieval. It is not static—it is dynamic and changing. And so, seemingly mundane experiences can take on enormous significance at a later stage.

5

A Catalog of Dreams

*And when I sleep, let me dream all the time so
that not one little piece of living is ever lost.*

BETTY SMITH, *A TREE GROWS IN BROOKLYN*

Sleep is essential for optimal memory function, as it is during sleep that events of the day are reorganized and transferred into long-term memory. Experiences that may have gone unnoticed during the day can appear in a dream and indeed play a part in producing that dream.[1] Dreams allow the brain to sort through its conscious experiences to make sense of them, to revisit them in a different dimension. For Ran, dreams have become a way of life.

> I think, perhaps, had Hitchcock, Dizzy, and riveting church services been everyday occurrences, the memories would not be so vivid. I needed time where my daily activities were not so all-consuming in order to comprehend what I had seen on the weekend.
> These events, these services, these film outings—not just running to a film, but the repeated viewing of a specific genre of films and of specific films—were external to me at first, but they filled internal needs and became so integrated into my subconscious that I now identify them as parts of myself.[2]

Dreams incorporate the present and the past, as well as possible future scenarios. Often, they bring with them unexpected or forgotten emotions:

> R: It's very sad, going back to childhood... and the dreams I've had in the last few weeks, where I'm one age and my parents are my age, and I don't know where my home is.
> L: Do you write your dreams down?
> R: I used to.
> L: Do you have any of the records?
> R: Who can find anything here? [*His tone is quizzically challenging.*]

Dorothy Wallace first encouraged Ran to record his dreams. She would ring him at a quarter to seven/seven o'clock each morning to check what he had written. (Unfortunately, this dream diary has since been lost.)

> And memory is a mood, and the memory CAN include some light and ah... It's just sometimes you can't leave sadness out because so many of my favorite people are in the country called 'Heaven,' and it's hard to get there—there's no return trip. I would like to be able... So that's why my dreams are important because I feel that the passport [to the dream world] is easier—there's no airplane security. But those re-occurring moments are amazing... and to be in two worlds at once! Just as last week, I went to Jordan Hall to rehearse and to travel around the building—which I DON'T go to often—and to SUDDENLY switch back to 1968—oh, it's amazing! So in a film of my life, the concept of memory would be extremely important. We're carrying on the noir tradition of flashbacks, and I'd say about an hour and a half of my day is a flashback.

DREAMS REMAIN A significant part of Ran's life. Talk of his past can bring them about. In the proof-reading stages of this book, he would often say:

> Oh, this is wonderful—I will have good dreams tonight.

During January 2014, when his sister, Marte, was gravely ill, Ran's dreams brought him comfort and hope. He reported to Leo that he had seen Marte in a dream, where she had been with Leo and quite able to speak, "though she did have a crutch."

The night of January 6, 2014, was cold and frosty—North America and Canada were experiencing a polar vortex. Ran messaged the following day:

> Hi Janet. So many dreams last night. I dreamt I was going to the Conservatory and there was a meeting just behind the Jordan Hall

stage—Leo will describe that hall—and suddenly, there was a visit by Dorothy Wallace. It was not a big concert—twenty people in the audience—and Dorothy was a trustee, and she was going to meet Hankus Netsky. And when she got on stage, she was so limber; she danced a little bit of the Charleston, and the students burst into applause.

I also, two nights ago, had a long talk with Amelia Lehrfeld in my dream; I wish I'd written it down. But that's my update. You're on your way to bed—you're probably already asleep! I'll speak to you tonight, bye-bye.

Ran loves to hear other people's dreams as well:

R: [*He's addressing Clare.*] Do you remember your dream?
C: Not from last night.
L: Tell him about the diamond hand—it's pretty noir.
C: I don't know…it's a bit gruesome, but I had this dream the night before last that there was a lady who had lost her hand in an accident…
R: Ohhh [*enthralled as well as horrified.*]
C: I know, it's terrible, and it sort of gets worse because when she lost her hand, she said she wanted to get a replacement hand made in diamonds.
R: Ohh, oh, I LOVE that.
C: It cost her 700,000 dollars…
L: [*interrupting*] which I thought was quite reasonable—for a diamond hand.
C: [*continuing*] So whenever she was working on the computer at night, it was sort of gleaming—with all the diamonds.

Ran is delighted by the diamond hand. Diamonds have featured in Ran's own dreams too:

I had Chris Connor doing "Night Bird," and Sarah Vaughan doing "Autumn in New York" on my "aural cocktail" because I'm working on an "Autumn in New York" piece for George Russell, and I had the most vivid dream that I was in New York City and that George Russell died that terrible day where the twin… [*he can't say it*], and ah, Alice Russell was in a big square—Now, this is a dream—Nobody else was there, and she said, 'I've never felt more alone in the world,' and her hands went up [*He demonstrates with his arms outstretched.*] and it was like there was a movie camera. And then, she cried a little bit, and the tears became diamonds on the street.

And then, we see Alice walking back, and then all the dead leaves coming in, and then I woke up like that. [*This is said with a dramatic rush of words as he clutches at his hair and pulls it up on end.*] It was 5.30 this morning, so I went to the piano, and I was afraid I'd hear a knock [of complaint], so I played quietly, and I played here in the morning.

So, the vivid dreams, and then going right to your instrument and putting them down. Because Alice Russell wasn't in New York on that day in 2001 and George Russell did NOT die that day, and her tears don't become diamonds, but they did in my dream… and in my heart. That Alice Russell, she's fabulous. [*He shakes his head in wonder.*]

When it comes to dreams, Ran is discriminating. He even goes so far as to try to program them.

L: Okay, you've mentioned that you program dreams. How do you program dreams?
R: And I'm not always successful. But I would go and read *Five Little Pigs* by Agatha Christie because I'd like my dreams to take place in late Victorian England where there could be a body or two—but nobody you care about [*He hastens to add.*]—and have the mystery and all that.
So, I succeeded, and I did get back to an earlier place, and then it turned out that one of the bodies that died was Chris Connor, and I woke up screaming.

Ran applies his dreams creatively; he draws upon the insights they give him. He uses his dreams to inspire him when he is producing a concert. (When planning the order of the pieces, he lets his dream world dictate.)

Always conscious of setting, Ran has an unerring eye for detail. He has served a long—if unofficial—apprenticeship with the great movie directors and knows instinctively how each concert should be produced and presented. It is not surprising that, for Ran, the dream world of the cinema, the world of dreams, and "real life" are so often intertwined:

I'm a fantasy person. I go out to see stars and musicians, but, you know, I am always going home alone. I worship people from afar and go home and dream. That's one of my favorite activities—the dreams.

And when the world of the movies, very briefly, stepped into Ran's "real" life, when he played "Laura" for Gene Tierney at a cocktail party in West Hartford in 1955 or '56, the whole experience took on a dream-like quality.

> R: And I don't know what I was even doing there in that house at that time, one little day on a gray afternoon.
> L: But it's great! You could write a song about it.
> R: Yes, I could. I just worshipped some of her performances like *Whirlpool*—the film noir—and *Laura* and ah... I played the song. She gave me a very, very, brief kiss and she said, 'Thank you for "Laura."'

In January 2017, Ran visited Gene Tierney's grave in Houston.

IN RAN'S DREAM world, people from his past visit his present, giving glimpses of a future that is full of dancing and delight:

> I've been having dreams, and last night I was with Nica, and she was having a martini with Dorothy Wallace, and in the dream, the priest was serving the martinis. Nica is Jewish and Dorothy Episcopalian, but in the movie last night—the movie of my dreams—they were in a Catholic church.
>
> Oh, these dreams I am having! [*He holds his head as if to contain them all.*] Last night, I was with Florence de Lannoy, and she was dancing, and suddenly Dorothy Wallace walked in the room—and in real life, they hadn't met! And then, Gunther was there, composing, and it was so great—being in this house. And I don't know where it was—could it have been Brisbane? They're so amazing these dreams. Anne Elvins sang in Florence's apartment, but Dorothy and Florence never met. But they *did* last night—in my dreams. [*His face lights up in a delighted smile.*] But [*with a sudden change of direction*] I'm just really a loner, and I think also, we have quite enough about dreaming! You could add a few more, but I DO hope people know I played the piano and used to run a department, and not just sit on my bed with dreams.

6

Film Noir

*We are such stuff as dreams are made on, and our little life is
rounded with a sleep.*

WILLIAM SHAKESPEARE, *The Tempest*[1]

Film noir has been an extraordinary part of Ran Blake's life. He has an exhaustive knowledge of the genre and familiarity with all the films—many of which he has watched over and over again. Indeed, he has become so fully immersed in them that he can describe his life as "living in a film."

Film noir and Ran Blake grew up together. Film noir had its beginnings in a distinct historical period that coincided with Ran's childhood and youth. The classic period of film noir—during and just after World War II, the time of Ran's childhood—was, in truth, a time of anxiety, upheaval, and grieving. So many lives had been lost; families were shattered. In America, it seemed that the war, despite bringing prosperity and an end to the Depression, was also responsible for a loss of innocence—opening a pandora's box of fear, and threat, and mistrust.[2] Classic film noir captured this mood. The tone of the movies reflected tensions of the period and provided a needed counterbalance to the unbridled optimism of the Hollywood musicals of the time.

It was the French film critics who first noticed a trend towards "dark" (or "noir") themes in many of the American detective films released in France after the war. These films have a bleak tone and a sense of foreboding. Cynical, "hard-boiled," and disillusioned anti-heroes are the main male characters. Bit by bit, often in flashback, reasons for their disillusionment are revealed. Techniques chosen to represent these reasons unveil a gloomy and forbidding place where heartlessness is prominent. Female characters are either dutiful and loving or mysterious and predatory femmes fatales. To reinforce the overall tone, these movies are shot in grays, as much as in blacks and whites. Shadows are emphasized, with lighting effects and camera angles serving to heighten the uneasy feeling that prevails. The mood is brooding—a dream world (or perhaps nightmare) vantage from which to discern reality.

At first glance, there are tantalizing similarities between Ran Blake's home in Brookline and the visual world of the "noir" film style. His basement apartment could well be a noir film set. The lights are often dimmed—"It's too damn bright"—and the windows, high up on the wall, create a certain disorientation by allowing a skewed view of strangers' feet as they walk along the street above. Dek-Tor, the cat, has the necessary combination of mystery and detachment; he is the master of the chilly stare. Very often, flickering silently on a large screen overhead, a favorite noir movie provides a degree of mystery and enchantment. [*Ran adds at this point that Dek-Tor's favorite film is* Cat People.]

But though visual elements of film noir are there, the atmosphere in the apartment is quite the opposite, for it is cozy and welcoming. And while conversation in the Brookline basement (as dialogue in any good noir) is razor-sharp—if somewhat convoluted—the themes are warm and positive.

Ran's fascination with film noir had its beginnings with the Robert Siodmak film *Spiral Staircase*. Many noir devotees would exclude this film from the style because of its "homely" setting. However, it was this very homeliness that allowed a young eleven-year-old boy to enter the world of noir. This world would have appeared as a shadowland, existing in chiaroscuro, just beyond his understanding had it not been for Ethel Barrymore's Mrs. Warren, in whom he was able to catch a captivating glimpse of his grandmother. The word even escaped his lips, "Grandmother!"

> Right in the theater [*Ran interrupts in excitement*], and the sailor behind me said, 'Will you shut up!'

Ran became obsessed with *Spiral Staircase*:

> The visual characteristics of this film haunted my day and night dreams for years. Mirrors, staircases (each one had its own personality), shadows, lighting, tracking shots, stark black and white.[3]

The film had a huge impact, and Ran says that it is a film:

> [...] that perhaps I overrate, but one that changed my life when I watched it for the first time at age eleven.[4]

Afterward, Ran was able to venture into the more hard-boiled scenarios of the style. This allowed him to find narrative coherence—to "follow the plot," as it were, of a sometimes conflicting and puzzling world. In the noir style, he found concrete expression for the world of his dreams and subconscious fears. Film, and film noir in particular, became an alternate world for him—a world that played out some of his childhood worries.

> Here are some of the films that remind me of the terrors and doubts of childhood—the uncertainty.[5] They probably do not fit into the classical definition of noir—a tough-guy Bogart in a trench coat in a seedy Los Angeles office—but here they are:
> *Les Abysses; Belle de jour; Le Boucher; Juste avant la nuit; Bunny Lake is Missing; Laura; Whirlpool; The Cabinet of Doctor Caligari; Twins; Sisters; Gas Light; Cry Wolf*—it's certainly noir, but it's an awful film. It's more confusing than my conversation! The first thirty minutes are good, and then it goes down, down, down; *Spiral Staircase* [*He resumes his list without warning.*]; *Pursued*[6] (a western which has the feel of noir); *Vertigo.*[7]
> I've got eighty others.
> L: Are there many parts of your childhood that you tried to escape from as a boy—parts you didn't want to acknowledge?
> R: Maybe the reality of school—why would I go to the cemetery so much? I think that the movies and the church, with damnation and hell, and the gospel music... and again, the film noir music style. And maybe when my grandparents died... I didn't want to—now I'm speculating—I didn't want to see death, and all these people going, and then the pain. I had to go back to trying to creep into the movies and not be seen—scavenging for a little bit of change—that was more important. Was it an escape from reality? Yes!

Spiral Staircase had opened the door on another world, from which "plots, scenes, melodic-harmonic surfaces intermingled—obtruding into my day life as well as dreams."[8] It was followed by *Red House, Laura, Kind Lady, Cat People,* and other Jacques Tourneur films and then Alfred Hitchcock's *Shadow of a Doubt* and *Vertigo.*

> This special selectivity of films, later defined as film noir, had great impact on my music and its solitude, and this inspired me to investigate Stravinsky, Prokofiev's *Scythian Suite,* and Stan Kenton's *City of Glass,* and the work of Bill Russo. The mood and emotion that music

produced fascinated me, and the constant viewing of films encouraged me to listen to records and to wear out many 78's by repeated listening.⁹

Ran is very susceptible to atmosphere—particularly when there are gothic undertones:

> The artist in me cries out for a dark mood—one that is vague, full of shadows, of twilight [...]. Of course, there are enough of these in the real world and inside all of us (for those of us who wish to recognize this) without relying exclusively on cinema.¹⁰

Ran applies visual images of cinema—shadows, twilight, a cemetery—when conjuring a dark mood. There is often a visual presence in his apartment—a flickering film, minus the soundtrack—which underlines the importance of the visual aspect of these movies. Ran loves to improvise to films. One of his classes on film music at NEC required students to respond (in real-time, using their instruments) to a muted sequence in one of Ran's favorite films.

> My fascination for film does not lie with the bulk of the music which is scored for films. Although I admire some moments of the composer Bernard Herrmann, who Hitchcock relied on for the music of *Psycho* and *Vertigo* [*Ran adds on reading: 'and Pierre Jansen who did all the Chabrol movies'*], it is purely the visual connection on the screen itself which fascinates me. It is the interrelation of the characters, not only with each other but, especially, within themselves, which trigger certain ambiance and atmospheres that inspire my music.¹¹

And so, it is through movies that the collective menace of death, defeat, pessimism, and suspicion can be brought out of the shadows and seen for what it is. This menace is present in the films he loves the most—films that he is always keen to discuss.

Ran has an extensive collection of DVDs—they have been his passion for many years. He owns every Claude Chabrol film available on DVD.

> And also every Hitchcock! I have enough to last a lifetime. When I go through my collection, I have to start again to pick up on things I don't pick up on [*the previous viewing*]. I have *flipped* over Claude Chabrol's films since the mid-'60s. Three of them, *This Man Must Die*, *Le Boucher*, and *La Rupture*, are fabulous, and the first two are particularly real classics.
> François Truffaut is a big influence after Chabrol and Hitchcock. (It took me until later in life to appreciate him.)

TRUFFAUT AND CHABROL were both, like Ran, devoted to film from an early age. Truffaut was obsessed from the age of eight. He played truant from school, sneaking into movie theaters because he did not have the money to pay for admission. Expelled from several different schools, he decided, at age fourteen, to take his own education in hand and resolved to watch three movies a day and read three books a week.[12]

Chabrol, who was expected to follow his father and grandfather into pharmacy, also developed a fascination for cinema at an early age. At age twelve, he ran a film club in a barn in the remote village of Sardent, where he had been evacuated during World War II.

Hitchcock's formation was different. He is said to have had a lonely, sheltered childhood; he only became interested in film when, at age fifteen, he got his first job as a draftsman and designer of advertising material. His interest in design and photography developed after designing the title cards for silent movies at the Islington studio of Famous Players-Lasky. (Later, the studio became Paramount, and later still, when sold to producer Michael Balcon and his associates, Gainsborough Pictures.) In a remarkably short time, Hitchcock moved on to an initial role of screenwriter and assistant director on a series of five films for Balcon and then onto directing in his own right. *The Lodger*, his first thriller (1927), was also his first commercial success.

Hitchcock worked with meticulous care; he planned scripts down to the smallest detail. Notes on costumes were so precise that specific colors, silhouettes, and details on accessories were written into his scripts. But Hitchcock, it seems, could be persuaded to make changes. In *Dial M for Murder*, he wanted actress Grace Kelly to wear a velvet robe—he was seeking the particular effect of light and shade on velvet fabric—when she answered the plot's crucial late-night telephone call. Kelly, however, insisted on a pale blue and white lace nightgown, saying that her character would not put on the velvet robe just to answer the phone, particularly when she knew there was no one else in the apartment.[13]

Alfred Hitchcock was a significant influence on Truffaut. When Truffaut arrived in New York to do press interviews for the release of *Jules and Jim*, he was shocked that Hitchcock was not recognized there. So Truffaut wrote to him, proposing a series of interviews that would explore his filmmaking—he wanted to look at all the films of his whole career. He concluded his letter of proposal by saying that if the cinema ever had to revert to silent films, many directors would be out of work; however, Alfred Hitchcock would survive. Then, people would, at last, realize that he was "the greatest film director in the world."[14] (Hitchcock replied, saying that the letter had brought tears to his eyes and that he was very grateful to receive such a tribute from Truffaut.)

At the AFI Life Achievement Award for Alfred Hitchcock, Truffaut referred to the series of interviews, and the ensuing book, as a cookbook full of recipes for making films.[15]

The ingredients for making a Hitchcock film are certainly evident in his surviving storyboards. Hitchcock planned entire films through a montage of individual frames, each representing one particular shot within a scene. Each shot included camera angle, instructions for cast and crew, color filters, and lighting. Indeed, the complexity of some of his scenes meant that storyboarding would have been the only way to explain them adequately to other members of the production team.[16]

Storyboarding was part of a process, but Hitchcock's storyboards were more than just technical documents. In a 2018 documentary, one of Hitchcock's storyboard artists, Harold Michelson, recalls the director's multi-faceted integration of storyboards across all stages of the filmmaking process. Perhaps most of all, however, Hitchcock used storyboards as a way to organize his thoughts, outlining and refining a film's formal structure before the start of filming and thus anticipating and solving problems that may have otherwise gone unnoticed once production was underway. Michelson believed that, by the first day of filming, each movie existed in its entirety in Hitchcock's head. Thus, as he saw it, the final production "is like a symphony—is like music—it builds up, goes down, you're the composer, you have complete control over the music and the emotions that it gives forth."[17]

If Alfred Hitchcock saw storyboarding as an opportunity to consider a movie's structure on such a macro—overarching—level, for Ran, specifically, it is:

> […] a useful tool in composing or recomposing a piece as I prepare it for performance. It is a way to move beyond the spine of a piece without simply abandoning it, and it is a creative alternative to a sketch based simply on theory or abstract motivic development.[18]

For the most part, the storyboards that inspire Ran's music take form in his head, but in recent years he and longtime friend Gardiner Hartmann have been working on a book, *Storyboarding Noir*. Here storyboarding finds itself at the juncture of film and music in the creative process of Ran

Blake. The book grew out of the many, many hours that Ran and Gardiner have spent watching (and re-watching) favorite film noir movies. As Gardiner explains, apart from being a record of their favorite films, the book discusses:

> The creative process in music and how storyboarding, a filmmaking technique, can help inspire student and professional musicians to create original and distinctive work.[19]

Prior to this, Blair Dutra was responsible for the "Blair list," which set about summarizing each film, frame by frame, as well as noting any anomalies or problems in continuity.[20] Such an approach exemplifies Ran's relationship to art and is manifest in his own creative process—an "honoring of—and focus on—the fundamental elements, rather than the instantaneous pleasure of its whole."[21]

These fundamental elements are central to deep understanding. They are what Truffaut was looking for in his interviews with Hitchcock—the building blocks for creative endeavor. At NEC, students are given the opportunity to gain an understanding of the fundamental elements of film noir in a course devised by Ran. Through lectures, discussions, and a comprehensive viewing program, students explore the possibilities of music creation inspired by film. It is Ran's hope that students leave the course equipped to use the themes and emotions discussed as a creative stimulus for their own musical expression.

> R: [*on reading this paragraph*] Excellent! Some people take the course and do well and forget it, but some people remember storyboarding, and they bring aspects of their life and their friendship to music—so that's one goal—and then, they appreciate older movies. This year, we're doing 1955 to '60, and then next Fall, we'll do the early period. This is the fourth year [of a cycle]. It's been going since 1993, but the cycle repeats every five years. This year, we are doing three Hitchcock films: *The Wrong Man, Vertigo* and *Psycho*, and then, later, we'll do *Marnie*, and the next to last film, which people don't like [*he gives thumbs down*], is called *Topaz*. It's got a great scene in Harlem, but some of it's not very good—the scenes in the Washington area—very second-rate Hitchcock, and we end with Olivia de Havilland's *Lady in the Cage*.

Matt Delligatti, a former student and teaching assistant of Ran's film noir course, explains the process:

> Each year in 'Film Noir,' a director is chosen as a focal point. The class views the director's films, learns excerpts from the film scores, and practices weaving these into improvisations and recompositions that can either accompany scenes from the film or serve to recall a scene's emotional content as a stand-alone performance. Ran employs a method of storyboarding his improvisations that is not unlike the way a writer or a director might storyboard a scene. Watching him talk down a storyboarded improvisation, or even better yet, watching him improvise completely off the cuff along with one of his favorite scenes, is truly inspiring and educational.[22]

Ran can reference the events of his life through film noir movies. He has a book with details about his favorites—when each was released and what he was doing at the time. Movies punctuate his life: "They're what I live for."

In one of their discussions, Leo asked, "When did *Vertigo* come out?" Ran's response was immediate and full of excitement:

> R: Well, let me look at it right now! Why do you think I have this book here? I knew you'd ask me. I can tell you a lot [*the excitement rises*]. Oh my gosh, *Vertigo*!

The locations in San Francisco where *Vertigo* was filmed have become attractions for fans of this film. Many visit the sites that remain; Ran is no exception.

> You know, there's a movie of me in San Francisco—*Ran Blake's Vertigo Tour*. It's a twelve-minute film [1970] made by Ashley James. Now that's a guy's name—he was a filmmaker. The film shows me going into the flower shop[23] and on to the cemetery, but a lot of places had closed.
> I tried to make reservations at the McKittrick Hotel. It's not there anymore.[24] Dolores Mission is there, but I asked, 'Where is Carlotto Valda's grave?' and the man said, 'There is no Carlotta here.' So then I went to the museum[25] and said, 'Where is the portrait of Carlotta?' People didn't know what to make of me. And then, an older man came. He said that this was the biggest day of his life!

The man, it transpired, had had a small role in *Vertigo*.

> He says three words in the movie. He was thrilled to meet me; we spoke and spoke and spoke. He said, 'Ran, it was the greatest day of my life when I worked for Hitchcock.'
> I said, 'Can I come back next week?'

and he said, 'This is my last day—I'm an old fossil; they're having me leave today. And they gave me a beautiful watch, but I'll never forget the day Alfred Hitchcock came to the museum.'
That's the biggest day in this man's life, and I forget his name; Paramount can't remember; my notes got lost. But to have met that man on his last day, his last week...
L: He actually worked there? He wasn't an actor?
R: Yes, he was in the archive department. And his mother fixed up his tie that day to be with Alfred Hitchcock, and he's never forgotten it.[26]

Later, Ran went to Ernie's Restaurant:

And I sat at the same bar as James Stewart. They said, 'Would you like dinner, sir?' and when I thought 'thirty dollars'—and this was 1970—well that... [was expensive.] So I couldn't. I said, 'I'll have a drink,' and... I don't like soda water with scotch, but I got it! And I asked this gentleman could I sit in this chair, and he said, 'Well, I'll accommodate,' and it's the same chair where James Stewart watched Kim Novak. And I sipped that soda water and scotch—I just had the bar scotch. I saw the menu—thirty dollars for an hors d'oeuvre... for two people! But they brought a tiny, little biscuit with a little food, and I had that, and then, I went out to an Irish bar where I had corned beef and cabbage—where I could EAT! [*It's said with emphasis. Then he pauses and adds, musingly*] It's always in my dreams—*Vertigo*.
L: Did you try to jump from roof to roof?
R: [*shaking his head and smiling*] I have no courage. But here's an interesting relationship. *Vertigo* was released in 1958; I would have been a sophomore junior at Bard College. So that explains why I went to Red Hook movie theater a lot, and I began flunking in class— It was all Hitchcock's fault!

Ran has spent a lot of time in movie theaters.[27]

The Red Hook movie theater [The Lyceum]; along with the Capitol at Springfield; the Art Theatre;[28] Loew's Poli Theatre; Paramount Theatre; the Arcade Theatre... I knew all the Springfield theaters, and... what was the name of the theater at Hartford? [*He answers himself promptly*] the Loew's Poli Palace Theater with its huge chandelier, painted ceiling, and ornate sculpture; and its sister theater, the Loew's Poli, next door on Main Street.[29] Hartford theaters all hold fond memories.

Ran also frequented New York theaters. The New Yorker, on 88th Street and Broadway, had had a couple of identities—as the Adelphi and the Yorktown—before rebranding itself as an art-house cinema in 1960.[30] It introduced French new wave movies, including those of Truffaut and Chabrol, as well as contemporary German cinema to its audiences. It was also at the forefront in distributing political films and documentaries. The theater was frequented by movie enthusiasts, directors, and critics. (Woody Allen used its lobby to shoot the Marshall McLuhan[31] scene in *Annie Hall*.)[32]

The Thalia, a basement theater on West 95th street, was a brisk twenty-minute walk from Ran's apartment on 113th Street. Purpose-built in 1931, the Thalia's dish-shaped sloping floor gave patrons a uniform view of the screen; its lighting, seating, and projection method also guaranteed the best possible cinema experience.[33] It is not clear when the Thalia became a revival house. It is more than likely that it began showing old films during World War II when first-run films were not readily available. In the late 1990s, this theater was "gutted and reconfigured as a multi-purpose performance venue."[34]

When Ran first came to Boston, one of the things he missed most was the New York cinemas. However, in time he discovered that the Brattle Theatre and the Coolidge Corner Theatre showed the sort of movies he liked.

The Brattle in Cambridge had been operating as an art-house theater since the 1950s. Located on the first floor of the beautiful and historic Brattle Hall,[35] this theater is one of the few remaining movie theaters using a rear-projection system (where the projector is located behind the screen).

The Coolidge Corner Theatre, Brookline, was easier to access from NEC and so became a favorite. Originally a Universalist church, the building was turned into an art deco movie theater in 1933. When Ran began going there in 1969, it was a revival theater, showing "classic" or older films of enduring merit. Movie enthusiast Justin Freed owned the theater from 1977 to 1989. It was a golden period, which saw the Coolidge host international art films, retrospectives, documentaries, and independent films. (It was also possible to watch a whole program of vintage Hollywood trailers!)!)[36]

Speaking at Ran's Lifetime Achievement Award presentation, longtime WGBH-Boston presenter Steve Schwartz recalled:

> Justin Freed would give his friends a season's pass, and there was never a time when I would be sitting in the balcony at the Coolidge when I didn't look over my right shoulder and see Ran Blake up in the top row. It could be a Japanese film; it could be Buster Keaton; it could be film noir; it could be a jazz film festival.[37]

> R: And he called it the Doktor Mabuse Seat—right next to the projection room—I had a special chair there. And Justin Freed took the photo on the cover of *Suffield Gothic*—he went to my hometown.

Ran's preference for the Coolidge may have come about as a result of his reception there:

> After being thirty cents short one day, the manager came and allowed me in. He said, 'You have to make this up.' [*Ran repeats this with a wry smile.*]
> Justin had incredible taste—he made the most fabulous programs. Usually, Monday or Thursday nights were noir. There would be festivals for Hitchcock and other directors—none of them [*It's said with regret.*] were for Chabrol. Coolidge was so supreme in those days.
> [*On hearing this read back, Ran exclaims*] Oh, I practically lived there! I said, can I sleep there? Fabulous!

But by the early '80s, Freed was noticing the in-roads of video sales and the changing preferences of his student audiences. For them, seeing old movies was no longer the "thing to do."[38] In 1987, he was forced to sell. Fortunately, a non-profit organization, the Coolidge Corner Theatre Foundation, was awarded a ninety-nine-year lease of the property, ensuring its importance as a venue for independent films for generations to come.

> But it's dwindled though. [*Ran interrupts the reading.*] They're showing the new Woody Allen film, [but] you can see it at five other theaters—it's really not the same. It's a nice theater, but it's not the same.

Film noir permeates every aspect of Ran's life. The annual Halloween concert in Jordan Hall, presented by the Contemporary Improvisation Department, is a unique celebration of the genre through his eyes. The concept was launched casually in 2004, but by 2006, growing interest among students necessitated increased pre-production; invitations needed to be sent out:

> Greetings
> Am planning our Halloween concert, which will take place at Jordan Hall the 30th of October. The title of the concert is *Cat People,* and it's to be dedicated to Jacques Tourneur and Claude Chabrol.[39]

After inviting students to compose a "five or six-note snippet, which may be incorporated into this quilt of cats," Ran's invitation went on to say that he would be on campus after class in "a room yet to be determined," where presumably they could discuss the project. There was, he warned, "a definite exception"—October 3, "when I dash back to Coolidge Corner to hear a small lecture by Clea Simon, who writes mystery novels with a cat detective."[40]

The concert has, over the years, become a much-anticipated annual event, timetabled for late October/early November—around the celebration of Halloween. Each year is themed around a particular film noir movie, and current and former students, along with faculty and other special guests, join in the performance. It's a multi-dimensional production, combining music, film, poetry, and narration (and Ran's comprehensive program notes and production storyboard) in a concert that blends excerpts from films with live musical performance.

Ran's love of film noir is apparent in his recorded output. Some of his albums include:

Film Noir (1980)
Portfolio of Doktor Mabuse (1982)
Vertigo (1985)
Duo en noir— with Enrico Rava—(1999)
Cinema Chatelet (2006)
Camera Obscura—with Sara Serpa—(2010)
Whirlpool—with Dominique Eade—(2011)
Vilnius Noir—with David "Knife" Fabris—(2012)
Kitano Noir—with Sara Serpa—(2015)
Chabrol Noir (2016)
Northern Noir— with Andrew Rathbun—(2020)

7

THE GOLDEN ART

You think—at the time—he's taught you nothing, and looking back, you realize he taught you everything.

LEO McFADDEN, 2007

THE DISCUSSION HAD started with a question:

L: You have achieved at the very highest level as a performer, composer, and educator. For most people, achieving in any one of these areas would usually mean the other areas are underdeveloped or neglected. How do you see these different aspects of your talent? Are they interwoven or quite separate; do you consciously allocate time to each, or does that happen naturally; and is there, in your opinion, a hierarchy of importance in the way that these go?
R: Now that's five questions.
[*He says it, with matter-of-fact detachment before meandering into a stream-of-consciousness offering that flows from notation—or the lack of it—to storyboarding, to 'alone time' watching DVDs, to producing. At last, he returns to the question.*]
R: I would say that teaching is a separate compartment. Performance preparation—which includes composition—[is] not separate from a performance…so, I would say there are two activities: the teaching, where there is a LITTLE bit of connection with the other—that's one thing… [then] the piano and performing, and composition and storyboarding are all together, even though there are small components that are separate. So that's the mini question 'number one,' I think.
L: Okay, is there a hierarchy of importance?

> R: [*without hesitation and most definitely*] Teaching! Teaching... it's a really worthy...
> [*It's said reverently, in a hushed tone. He pauses, searching for an explanation, but words elude him, and he tries again.*]
> Teaching is very... you're transmitting knowledge. To me, that's a very important thing for my life and should be for all teachers. It is one of the most important roles. It's a real commitment, Leo. Teaching is a VERY important thing. It's a Golden Art.

The words resonate, rich in meaning. He has not chosen them lightly. In teaching, "golden" principles have been realized, over time, by dedicated practice that has been re-applied and passed down. Ran comes from a long line of teachers—from parents whose love of nature, art, literature was the knowledge they passed on to their students... and their own children. For Ran, teaching is a way of life; it encompasses all parts of life. His instinct for reflection and contemplation—his retreat to the dream world—has allowed him to integrate, or even fuse, his music and emotions; it is this primary integration that informs his teaching. Ran, the teacher, addresses more than just the music, as Leo observes:

> Ran taught me to embrace the cultural aspect of music. It's not just about the music as an abstract thing; it's about the food, and the people, and the history of the place. Ran, he's close to the heart of it.

It is a discovery that many students make—sometimes many years after having finished their studies. Ran's method of teaching is not always apparent for a beginning college student:

> R: Of course, I DON'T want to look in the book[1] [and observe] that *only* I have the answers—that if you ONLY do what Ran Blake [says]—the singing and playing—then... [you will succeed.] There are still other things to learn in music.
> L: Yes, it's struck me that the older I get—and I'm sounding like an old-timer here...
> R: [*laughs.*]
> L: the older I get, the more silly I realize that I was—particularly with some of my teachers, of whom you were one. I just was too young and too stupid to realize some things, but...
> R: I wish you'd put that in the book because, you know, some of the... well that's another—a different subject, but... we have people going to school too young.... But go on, finish, you were too stupid, you said?

L: Yes, because I listen back—at LEAST I recorded them—because I listen back, and I cringe at what I said... and did.

R: [*laughs out loud*]

L: And you know, I remember there was this one thing where we were playing, 'I Wish that I Could Talk to You Baby' and you were playing with me, and I NOW listen back to it and think, 'Oh my God, that's so hip,'—what you were doing—but at the time, I stopped because you'd gone so far out of key. Now that I've studied a lot more, I can hear how very much related to the piece [it was], but at the time I stopped, and you said to me, 'Look, if I put a bit of spice in, you don't want to let that throw you off—I'm just spicing it up a bit.'

R: [*enthusiastically endorsing this*] Yeah, yeah.

Ran has a comprehensive understanding of the learning process. He offers freedom and encouragement so that students can feel confident to step away from their preconceptions.

> On visiting Ran's classes, I am always struck by what a gifted teacher he is. He draws all students in—making certain everyone contributes yet never putting anyone on the spot. He tells them, 'There's no such thing as wrong here, so just have fun.' He states that an emotional response is the most important thing in music and begs his students not to worry about intonation or correctness. Over and over, he tells them that there's no such thing as a mistake in his class. He tailors the learning so it is just right for every individual. Ran is thinking all the time about what each student needs.[2]

Ran's approach to teaching is a slow absorption method, and there is much to absorb. Contemporary Improvisation students must study composition, performance, and improvisation as well as developing their ear and a personal style. However, those who embrace the slow approach, those who resolve to understand music on a deeper level (than that which is required to pass an assessment or to play gigs in a hotel lobby), these people will, in time, discover that they hold the key to travel to the heart of the music. Here, they will also discover themselves. Memory is an integral part of the process. In memorizing a piece of music, one is required (through the repeated listening that this process entails) to connect with the work on a more profound level. In doing so, the music becomes part of one's own cultural context. It exits the realm of abstraction (to which music is all too often confined in the western-art tradition), taking on meaning that is at once personal and communal—intimately linked to the emotions and memories that the individual associates with it, while at the same time, providing a point of access for the individual to a wider community of people, living and dead, whose own histories are also linked to this same music.

Ran seeks this emotional connection with music. He wants each student to know music on a deeper level, to explore their own heart. In his efforts to show them the way, he makes himself vulnerable—exposing his own heart and his memories as, sitting at the piano in a darkened classroom, he takes the students, step by step, through a piece that has significance for him.

> He doesn't just tell his students a version of his past but revisits it in front of them—I saw this unfold in the version of "Vradiazi," the Greek piece he played for the class. He wasn't just playing the music; he was returning to the memory that held the music.[3]

Ran, in encouraging students to develop their own memories, is broadening the scope of his class to the point where it is almost unworkable. It must be navigated carefully, both on a personal and a musical level.

> L: As someone who has taught these students for so many years—looking for a personal style, how do you deal with all this fusion? You have to be very careful, don't you, because if you muck around too much, you lose something of the essence. How do you counter that as a teacher? How do you make sure that you don't lose what's real about the music?
>
> R: I often don't succeed. [*It's said humbly, regretfully.*] First of all, the student has to have the curiosity to go back in history—to go to the primary colors. [For example] field music—Willis Laurence James. And if we want to say twelve-tone Gunther Schuller, [then] Schoenberg is a source.
>
> Then it's number two—ears: the ability to listen, long-term memory; number three—timbre: the essence you can convey on the instrument; THEN [emphasized] number four would be technical apparatus with your piano... [*He pauses, unhappy with his analysis.*] You see, another problem, Leo, is so many of us are a product of television—the best-selling movies. Also, half the students I know are deaf—they have to have it loud because they've hurt their ears. They can't hear Debussy—they absolutely CAN'T with the distortion so many of them have grown up with. They may revolt against Barbra Streisand, but then, so many like the Rolling Stones. I mean, people have such conventional tastes [in] what they are listening to. I don't know if you can teach taste. [*He shakes his head sadly.*] And people are performing so much and not listening. They all want to get up and perform, and I'm guilty of that too—because I get students... [to perform.]

So, I think going back to the past is number one and developing a curiosity; then, can you hear it? And can you retain some of it?

Time, or the lack of it, is a subject that worries Ran. He sees it as central to the changes he has noted in his students over the years. For him, it seems that listening habits have changed. With the plethora of information available on the internet, people have become used to skimming the surface to select what they need:

> There's so much information, and it's very hard to keep up, and people don't really have time to go to the past.
> I think [now] they're very concerned about gigs and being exposed, and they are less historically [oriented]... So I find the students are interested in films; they will go out and support each other at a concert, but I don't think they hear CDs—I don't think they go back. They do if they have a paper [to write], and [then] they hear Coltrane and Alan Copeland, but they're not collecting—they're not CD/LP collectors like they used to be. And they don't read critical information. Everybody can do their own blog—why bother to read the critics?
> L: So do you think they have different priorities, these students?
> R: Yes. Mostly being heard themselves.

Ran's teaching approach is based on true praxis. It is the embodiment of a lifelong devotion to music and search for its essence, a genuine commitment to—and respect for—students, and a flexibility of application. It is creative—tested in dreams, in the noir world, and in deep, deep listening. It is simple and harmonious. It addresses what Ran sees as the particular set of characteristics that make up a "good" musician:

> 1. Curiosity
> 2. Imagination—if we can define that [*he adds quickly*]
> 3. A sense of history
> 4. A good ear
> 5. A timbre on your instrument, with your voice. To have your own DNA.
> [*He's pleased with the way his list is going and adds*]
> This is good. Now, I might ask you to send this back to me for my...
> [*He trails off, abruptly returning to the task.*]
> 6. Composition. There has to be a sequence—a plot flow. To be able to know when you're repeating a story, to embellish it differently. There's creativity and discipline but a sense of composition—not necessarily symmetrical. If you're composing or improvising, you

should have a sense of composition, but that is less important maybe than vitality.

This vitality—this life force—is a crucial part of the individual's creative energy and is closely linked to personality. As an educator, Ran sees each student as an individual with a unique personality. Respecting individuality and nurturing it in a musical style is paramount. Ran has reflected deeply on the best way to guide his students by way of constructive criticism. For him, criticism must be broached:

> [...] so that you DON'T offend and yet are not so worried about offending that you're too indirect. There's a whole psychological dimension [to feedback or criticism].

There are so many demands on the modern-day teacher and so many expectations. The sheer volume of work to be covered and the perceived need for quantifiable assessment can lead to a "best practices," "outcomes-based" approach. Ran has consistently resisted this trend:

> In a culture dominated by marketplace values, in which musical conformity is rewarded, and individuality shunned, we respect and defend the sanctity of the individual and his or her right, indeed, if he or she is being honest, NEED, to create a music true to the uniqueness of his or her personality.[4]

Authentic art is always true to the personality of the artist. Ran works with each student to nurture the link between personality and artistic expression. The process can be slow—there are no shortcuts. What each student needs to learn will vary, but Ran can attest, from personal experience, that the learning never really stops. Rather, it becomes more personalized as the boundaries between style and technique merge. At this point, true artistry is evident.

To this end, Ran can be quite specific in his demands, and the advice he gives does depend on the student. He might recommend "special attention" to a particular CD collection or the commitment of forty minutes a day to "selectively listen to a movement... a rondo; the cry of a cornet player; or the moan of a gospel singer." Within each recommendation, there is another level of specificity, for example, going to the second chorus of a given song to see how the singer sings a particular word. Such fine detail requires resolute commitment:

> The guidance of a mentor, who is both supportive but discriminating in praise, is invaluable, and this tradition is being lost today because of youth's thirst for teacher-hopping, grants, and internet prowess.[5]

In a world of instant gratification, such a slow approach is challenging. Often students are inattentive and uncomprehending:

> In fact, my class is really not considered very important [by many of my students]. People sleep and do texting in my class.
> [*He spits out the words—there's a trace of hurt—before adding*] I really feel my teaching has flaws. I don't think I'm inspirational like Hankus. I suffer from a lack of organization, and sometimes, I can't stand my music. I don't want to hear Ran Blake—it's a big bore.[6]

But this perception of his teaching is not shared by his students. Claire Ritter's words sum up a general sentiment:

> Ran gives to his students the rare gift of sincerity. [...] Ran has brought to my music—and composing specifically—a mystical enlightenment like no other teacher has ever done before.[7]

Often, the validity of Ran's unique approach doesn't become clear till years later. Leo reflects that it took "years of distance" before he was able, gradually, to "see this tapestry, where his [Ran's] methods are woven into the person you've become... the teacher I've become."

> R: You know "Vradiazi" was the forbidden song of Greece. Didn't I make you learn that, Leo?
> L: No, unfortunately.
> R: Because you resisted. We could have gone faster.
> L: It was too early for me, Ran.
> R: [*Musingly*] I resisted...Gunther was early for me.

It seems that neither Ran nor his teaching is entirely definable—the more you discover, the more there seems left to learn. As he cautions:

> It isn't easy; there are no shortcuts. Work hard, be prepared, persevere, listen until you can hear it, sing it before you try to play it, and, above all, go out and listen to others. Take it all in, and, someday, when you're ready, it will be your turn to play. And you, too, won't sound like anyone else.[8]

8

A Sense of Wonder

Ran's ability to awaken in students a new level of awareness—of giftedness—is born of his capacity for wonder and his willingness to embrace silence. Beyond the senses, there is another dimension, a deep-seated center of peace. It is far beyond the "tyranny of noise and distraction"[1] that has gained supremacy in a modern society driven by technology. It is a place of unhurried contemplation—close to the essence of being. It is a place of wonder. It is a place that is entered through silence.

Ran is conscious of the importance of silence in his life. He avoids noise and saves his ears "for music that is important to me:"[2]

> As a musician, I experience ear fatigue after sitting in an office with background music, riding elevators, shopping, or being kept on hold on the telephone. Music is now everywhere, and I often return home not only aurally disquieted and disgusted but also exhausted, unable to compose or perform with any energy whatsoever. I recommend most people regularly get away, not only from music and crowded rehearsals but from as much sound as possible, so as to give the ears much-needed rest.[3]

He sees this as the only way that a musician's own "projects" can be realized and feels that silence is essential for the "inner self" to tune in to "what is coming from within."[4] Here, deep in the unconscious—where dreams are made—, there's peace.

Visiting his dream world is a habit Ran formed long ago in the solitude and silence of the Mulberry Street Cemetery. More than anything else, these periods of quiet contemplation allowed him to acquaint his "inner self" with the mystery and wonder available there.

Ran's capacity for wonder is multidimensional. It springs out of love—for people, animals, and nature; for music, story, and film. It is seen in his appreciation of food and flavor, his fascination with shadows and dreams, and his quest for knowledge. It doesn't discriminate, allowing seemingly insignificant things to be viewed with new interest.

Ran's quest for knowledge has never diminished. As a young boy captivated by the stars of *Spiral Staircase*, he took upon himself the task of finding out about them—to make contact with them. The project was a huge undertaking, spanning several years, and the only response he got was one from Carlton, the bulldog.

But Ran enjoys a challenge. When asked to consider Kierkegaard's idea—that life makes sense backward, but it has to be lived forward—and apply it to his own life, he was delighted with such a "wonderful question":

> I think that is going to be a great assignment for me.

Assignments are a big part of his life—he sets them for himself regularly. Beginning in his seventies, he took up studying algebra; he has persevered with it since. There is a real sense of commitment:

> Quadratic algebra takes a lot of time. I promised my parents I would go back to some of that stuff—because you can't tell ghost stories with algebra.

There are echoes of Dorothy Wallace and her Russian lessons, but unlike Dorothy, Ran has shown no inclination to abandon this interest.

> R: Leo, how are you with exponents and their functions and algebra?
> L: Awful!
> R: Do a chapter, Janet, called "The Algebra Days of 2013."
> R: Now they want to put me with fourth graders in an arithmetic class, and I have to go very fast. [It's in] the arcade right behind Khao Sarn—remember that restaurant? And when I go there, they won't go, '2 + 2 is 4' but '4 times 8, times 12 square, 17 exponent is the square root...' [*and he claps urgently.*] Do it quickly! They want me to be quicker, so things are cracking.
> I [really] haven't done enough algebra... it really is medicine—it helps me so much.

Ran was taking lessons from a tutor, Yoshino, at this stage and admitted joyfully one July evening: "I had the best lesson!"

Another of Ran's assignments involves taking notes on the news—which he has pre-recorded. (With this task, he is running three years behind "real-time.") He "sits in" on courses at New England Conservatory. He has even studied the Beatles' music by correspondence.

> R: And Leo, did you know I took a course on Beatles… from correspondence?
> L: Wow, I'm impressed.
> R: They're good composers. Do you like their voices? [*The tone implies that you surely can't!*]
> L: But in the same way, it would be silly to compare Ella Fitzgerald with Pavarotti because someone who loved opera would say Pavarotti was a much better singer, but that wouldn't be 100% correct because he can't phrase like Ella Fitzgerald, so…
> R: Well, they are both way better than Ringo.

In recent years, Ran has become interested in "basic emotional rhythm" (as first described by Abby Whiteside).[5] Whiteside encouraged pianists to coordinate all of the muscles in the body from the center to the periphery because, as she states in her book on piano playing, "Nothing less than the entire body can furnish the control for a real rhythm, for the most delicate gradations in the use of dynamics, for the most powerful climaxes."[6]

Sophia Rosoff, who has carried on Whiteside's legacy as President of the Abby Whiteside Foundation, has been instrumental in helping Ran recover from playing-related injuries.

> She's 91 years old and fabulous. I was ready to take the bus this morning, alone, to New York—just 'cause she's so good. She tells you what NOT to do on the piano.

He also looked into the Dorothy Taubman[7] method and its focus on re-training movements to address injuries in pianists.

> I injured my hand doing Stevie Wonder—"Sir Duke" or "Se Tu Ragazza Mia" [*He sings a little bit*]… do you know that ending? It's hard to play, and I did it with double octave—oh my God! [*He hides his face in his hands.*]

Ran also sets himself projects to do on holidays and long winter evenings.

> I've seen all the [film] versions of *Crime and Punishment*, I've just got through Dostoyevsky—I was entranced by that novel—so I'm

A Sense of Wonder 463

not only [limited to] film noir. Of course, that [book] is on a great high plane of moral punishment and redemption.

And when the rest of Boston was bunkered-down in a series of snowstorms, Ran: "weathered the Blizzard of January 2015 fine—using the two days of downtime to catch up on reading (mystery novels by Clea Simon), studying math, reviewing several films (including both versions of *Gaslight*, *Doktor Mabuse* and *Night of the Hunter*), and hanging out with his cat, Dek-Tor."[8]

He is always ready to offer recommendations for others as well.

> L: What are five movies that I should try and watch over the holidays?
> R: *The Window*! [promptly]; *Belle de jour*; and I think you should see the *Portrait of Jennie*; and let's see... *The Leopard Man*, which is a chilling mystery; and have you seen *Laura*? Why don't you put *Laura* and *Whirlpool*—*Whirlpool* is even more important. It's about Doktor Mabuse's grandson in Los Angeles, 'David Korvo,' and that's *Whirlpool*...

The suggestions are given with eager enthusiasm as he anticipates the pleasure to be had in these viewings.

RAN HAS A great energy and appetite for everything he does:

> R: I guess I have an appetite for life—even though I'm [often] thinking of the sad part.

Despite sad memories and partings, Ran's appetite for life is indomitable. It is fueled by his sense of wonder and runs on high-twitch energy, an energy that Ran says is embedded in his psyche.

> R: I think to have energy, you really have to have interests.
> L: And I think that in terms of internal energy and optimism, I've NEVER seen you... I'd be very worried, Ran, the day I saw you with no internal optimism. You know, sometimes you'll be a bit frustrated; sometimes you can be a bit short and grumpy, but you've never lost that spark, and I think if you'd lost that, I'd know that it was a dire day because you'd be on the way out, you know...
> R: So, Leo, do you think I have optimism in my music? [*It's said with a challenging eye-to-eye look down the camera.*] People say I'm the saddest pianist. Of course, I can be...

L: [*animated*] YES, YES! You have melancholy in your music; you have a sense of nostalgia in your music, so it's usually hued constantly by sadness; that's true. But that's one level of it because there's a beautiful kind of tenderness about it [*At this point, Ran flings his face into his hand, as if trying to escape such an observation.*], and I think that's why people who are not musicians can relate to it. [*Ran resurfaces to listen more closely.*] I think that's really the litmus test, you know. You couldn't [for example] go down to the Brookline nursing home and say, 'We've got Cecil Taylor to perform for you.' They probably wouldn't like it, even though he'd be playing at an amazingly high caliber—and really great music. But YOU, who appeals to the same audience [as Taylor], I mean, that's really your niche group [*Ran is nodding*], you could go down there and play the music that you play on your records, and they would love it.

R: But... [*Getting straight back on topic*] but I think the energy... the deeper thing, is that most nights—sometimes I flop in bed—but [most nights] I TRY to give myself a sense of renewal; I try to orchestrate what the [next] day's going to be. I go in bed, and I have my Bordeaux, and I think of the next day or two, and I make a little movie [in my head] of what is to happen. I do this five nights a week; I dream of this, and then, I have the ice and coffee in the morning... and I run through the day and what my favorite part will be—what student, what person is going to [come]... I like to network. [For example], if Janet comes here to Boston, who should she meet first? Should she meet Aaron Hartley? Would it be appropriate over a Bourbon, hot tea, or iced tea? Would the scene be Dalia's; would it be Khao Sarn?[9] What's going to happen? Would there be a third or fourth person there for this meeting? Should Peter go to the home of David Ryder to talk about his new interest in making guitars... and there's a string place in Harvard Square. How do I locate it? What restaurants are there? Oh [*as if just remembering*] the Blue Moon Restaurant—I can't afford to take five people there (it's too much), — so can we arrange it at lunchtime when things are half price? Oh, and there's a buffet on Thursday, so are David Ryder and Peter McFadden free that Thursday for the discount lunch? Will there be enough New Orleans coffee that morning for me to energize? Can I say, 'Goodbye Peter and David, I have to leave and go back and practice, but can I leave you both in the restaurant to talk about guitars? Now, David, I know you're very busy—you're not looking for guitars now, but you know another person who is opening a store [selling] guitars for ten thousand or twelve—could they have a meeting? [*He dramatically shakes his hand to dismiss this notion.*] Don't embarrass him. Maybe he can't buy any of them... and maybe Peter will have retired then and is going into a gardening business?[10]

The plans are complex and cover every eventuality. They are filled with wonderful possibilities—and they do require energy. Ran is certain that this energy comes from:

- Number One: The double N espresso. [*A blend of coffee he recommends—New Orleans and Napoli.*]
- Number Two: The anticipation—the interest of who's to connect.
- Number Three: Booking quiet time with a book. (Film is not so quiet.)
- Number Four: What musicians can we get together—I think a lot ahead, and then, Leo, what keeps me going is the review of the day—but we all do that, don't we? We have a drink at night, and we say, 'Was it a good or a bad day?'

A LOT OF the things that interest Ran in his quest for knowledge are solitary pursuits:

> I'm quite a loner. Even as a child, I would just replay dark films in my imagination, and now, even though I have web pages and all that, I'm really a recluse. I'm really very solitary.

Solitary could spell sadness—but it would be far from the truth where Ran is concerned. Ran does, however, have categories—'mode categories,' as he calls them—for his music and favorite films:

> 'Fear'—(*Spiral Staircase*);
> 'Anger'—*Touch of Evil*; "Driva Man" (Max Roach and Abbey Lincoln)
> 'Joy'—I sort of overlooked 'joy,' but 'Sadness' and 'Terror'...those are the big ones...
> [So it's really] 'Rage,' 'Anger,' 'Physical Fright.' and then the 'Fear'—who's behind the curtain? And the unknown—when do we die; who's there waiting? All kinds of fear.
> And then the 'Tragedy'—Dorothy Wallace, Jeanne Lee... my mother, my father—so many people dying.
> L: All those categories you mention, they are all categories of bad things, and fear, and terror, and pain. And you said you didn't really have a category for joy. Now why, when you're such a giving

person—you're one of the most generous people I've ever met, and you're not preoccupied with pain [physically], but your thoughts often are—now why is that?
R: I keep a good shield over myself... by the way [*it's added inconsequentially*], I want to recommend a good film—*The Chant of Jimmy Blacksmith*. But I mean, I might be happy at the moment I'm with you, but then...
Now right now, I thought I would do a little reading—*Little Dorrit*, by Charles Dickens. I don't think I will set it to music, but I wanted a book that would keep the sad mood but would have moments of happiness. By the way, do you have my album, *Realization of a Dream*? There's a piece called 'Brindle,'[11] and that's happy. You know, don't listen to too much Ran Blake—it's all going to blur.
L: Can music fill you with joy, Ran?
R: Hearing the *Hallelujah* brings me joy. [*The answer comes quickly, definitely, positively.*] Ah, but really... [only] once in a while. I don't know about joy. I don't know if I experience that emotion very much, and that may be one color that's limited in my music.

But joy and sorrow, hope and grief are deeply intertwined; if joy, for Ran, seems ephemeral, it is always there just under the surface—stitched into the tapestry of love, support, understanding, inspiration, and friendship that is the backdrop to his life experiences. And if Ran sees joy as lacking from his music, it is not how others see it. His music has been described as "doggedly life-affirming"[12] and having "so many moments of pure grace."[13]

These moments of grace reflect Ran's attitude to life, which is full of joy, wonder, and enthusiasm. Thus, Leo was quick to challenge the idea that joy was a "color" missing from Ran's music:

L: Yeah, but it might have different shades—I think it's important to isolate specifically what yours are. What are the sources of light? I mean, I know you're very noir—you live in a noir world—but I wouldn't say you were a dark person; you're not dark to be around.
R: Well, I think the joys come from introducing people—but I'd rather do that in absentia—I don't have to be here every night. [However] I do know that every time I go to the movies and the theater darkens, I'm thinking of my first time seeing *Spiral Staircase*—so EVERY time I go to the movie theater is a moment of light, and I can't wait to be at the movie theater.
And then there's memory. Memory is a mood, and the memory CAN include some light, but ah... But look at that sweet mammal! [*The*

young assistant who has just arrived—Amanda—has a small white dog with her; Ran's face is a picture of joy.]

Ran may feel that joy is just out of reach, but it *is* there. It is *always* there when those other mammals, his "brother" dogs and cats, are present. Joy is there in the moments when he is able to bring two people together, introduce them and watch their friendship blossom. It is present in a wonderland of dreams and memories of those who have supported him and sought to promote his creative impulse. It is in the yearning that fuels his curiosity and search for purpose.

In the silence of his inner life, Ran delves into the pluperfect, the present, and the imagined future, the conscious and unconscious, and adds a good sprinkle of mystery—enough to keep his search for meaning alive and vital.

Saul Bellow laments the "great noise now threatening the sanity of civilized nations." He laments that the world can no longer marvel at works of literature, art, and music and believes that the only hope for the "restoration or re-creation of culture" is the recovery of an individual's "significant space."[14] This is a space—a quiet space—where outside events can be received and contemplated. This is the space where Ran retreats in his search for wonder and joy.

9

Food and Music—"The Master of Spice"

*Ran Blake was always in a giving mood,
whether it was food, money... He had an ear,
and he was always listening for people.*

John E. D'Agostino[1]

For Ran, the senses have a fluid inter-connectedness. While for many of us, smell and taste can trigger memories (in which people, places, and meals shared are inextricably entwined), Ran's appreciation of food goes further than this. Food is a story; it is colorful and cultural. It involves characters, setting, atmosphere, and it also has a style. Ran has a predilection for the exotic—the spicy. This stylistic preference extends to all of Ran's life-passions: his film noir, his music, his books.

From a very early age, Ran had a discriminating palate. Definite in his likes and dislikes, he defied Grandmother Blake, who had instructed him to "never put cinnamon on apples." He rebelled against Mary Garvey's mashed potato and boiled carrots, though he loved the seaweed her parents sent over from Ireland! Eunice Bell introduced him to pecan southern pie, while at the Colony Club, after church, there was peppermint stick ice cream and macaroons. His grandfather Powers tempted him with mango chutney and shrimp and "all kinds of relishes and pickles, sharp cheeses, all kinds of olives, and elaborate hors d'oeuvres." As a young lad, working over the summer as a messenger at the Union Trust Bank, he took himself, once a week, to the second floor of the Forbes and Wallace Department store and ordered a "Waldorf salad and a little iced tea." Later, in New York, Miss Lehrfeld served gefilte fish and matzah ball soup (to which she later added a little curry or Sister Tee's hot Louisiana sauce). In fact, New York in the sixties was a carnival of tastes. Vietnamese restaurants served "elegant, almost raw stuff," and right next to where he lived (on 113th and Amsterdam), V&T Pizza[2] served delicious pizzas at bargain prices. Then, there was the soul food—chicken and waffles and collard greens at Joe Wells' club:

> Abbey Lincoln and many other people would be there, and they would serve chicken with waffles and collard greens. That was S-O-U-L—soul food. The syrup of Joe Wells' was not maple; it was made with hot Spanish peppers. It [Joe Wells' Club] would open at eleven at night those days, and I was young and hungry.

Ran was hungry for life, and food was at the center of the celebration—a celebration of people and their cultures. A lot of Ran's memories have a "signature dish." In Boston, his friendship with Dorothy Wallace began over a meal of creamed spinach; in Bordeaux, he met ("four times for ten minutes") a man who made his own cheese:

> I went to one restaurant, and I said 'Oh!' [*He says it covering his mouth and closing his eyes at the gustatory memory.*] It was a creamy cheese, and I said, 'No dessert!' And then I came back for lunch, and I said, 'I will pay full price for the cheese and a spoon, with a little wine—that's all I need.' This was in Bordeaux, so he must have looked me up in Paris [as he came to hear my music there], and he said, 'I so much appreciate you, but oh, my ears, they ache!' [*Ran covers his ears to demonstrate before admitting*] This might be a little exaggerated, but there was Brie cheese that was so fresh and new that it was like a chocolate sundae with spices… savory, savory.

In addition to the savory and spicy, Ran looks for the visual and the "sometimes surprising" in all experiences. In the small "plain" cafe on his first day in Paris in 1963, he and Jeanne Lee "gasped" in admiration when a golden egg yolk split open on his plate and "nourished" the salad greens. [*Ran interrupts at this point of the reading.*]

> It was fabulous! We never had it in Suffield. Jeanne flipped. All the waiters kept coming, and she said, 'It's fab-u-lous.' She sang, 'fab-ulous,' and they wanted us to get up and dance. She sang, 'It's wonderful, *c'est* beautiful,' and she raised the salad on high, and the staff clapped. Oh, they loved her in France.

Ran has a knack for finding places that have good food—even when traveling:

> If you're going to have interesting food, one of the best meals is twenty-eight cents 'white pizza,' which you get in the streets of Milano. It's made white, and they chop it off for school children and the homeless, and maybe it's thirty-two cents now, but it's VERY cheap. You get a big slice, but there's no cheese or tomatoes on it. It's one of the great foods. There's nothing compared to the French and Italian food—West France, Bordeaux, and Hungarian food that comes through from the Magyars and the Italia. The freshness, the herbs, the spices, the exciting taste, the way the wines embellish the food and the foods embellish the wines… and the conversation—you must hear comfortable words and have plenty of legroom. And it's very important that a meal has an ending. An hour and a half is perfect, but sometimes, in Spain, it is three hours, and I want to go home—I want to play the piano. Everything—act one, act two, act three—it has to have timing: adventure in the middle; [a] happy …or sad ending with tartness of lemon soufflé. And it has to stop at one time—like the way Hitchcock WRAPS it up at the end.

Meals, like music and movies—introductions even—need planning. And while, like movies, Ran may have a fondness for certain foods, he delights in the adventure of tasting something for the first time; he values each introduction to the food of a specific culture or region. Time spent abroad is a precious opportunity to connect more deeply with a place—its people and their culture—and what better way than through the cuisine! While in Norway on his first European tour, Ran visited Bergen's Hotel Neptun, where he was impressed by a fusion of flavors and cultures integrated into a menu that retained a distinctly Scandinavian theme. Despite this spirit of culinary adventure, however, Ran has his limits. Of Copenhagen's Noma restaurant, with its specialty of "beef tartar with sour ants," he voiced his apprehension with a droll comment—"now that's too third-stream."

IT WASN'T ALWAYS necessary to travel to find interesting food; over the years, Ran has developed close relationships with the owners and wait staff of his local restaurants. One of his notebooks from his New York days details a number of restaurants that were there at the time, as well as the fare on offer. In Boston, too, Ran has his favorite restaurants; he is ever keen to acknowledge: "there are several amazing restaurants in this town."

But it is not only restaurants that Ran appreciates. He brings a certain elan to his appreciation of all food. He is attuned to each nuance in taste, smell, texture; the sensory perceptions associated with food form a vital part of the way he distinguishes—and describes—music and film:

> R: You have to say the Roy Webb[3] music is at its best when the sinister is going to happen because otherwise, there's a part of the music that is mashed potato. It's gotta be in the second half of the movie—when the murder takes place—otherwise, it [the music] has its potato moments... maybe a baked potato—that's not as bad as mashed.
> L: In general, do you think, though, you need the potatoes to appreciate the spice?
> R: Yes, but only a baked potato... not the mashed. French fries and baked potato are okay. [*smiling*]
> L: But about mashed potato. In Paris, I once had this duck, and there was mashed potato on the side, and it was mashed potato to perfection—it had a little bit of butter and asparagus...
> R: I know [*sweeping his hands down in a dismissive gesture*]. And everybody HAS to have me to dinner saying, 'I'll make carrots that aren't mushy,' and 'here is mashed potato with cheese'... I'm tired of it [*and he sweeps the thought away again with the same gesture*].

Ran has a horror of mashed potato. He prefers unusual ingredients from far-away places. Even breakfast has a touch of the exotic:

> Now, I like to start, 7.30 in the morning, with a big glass of grapefruit juice; a small "NN" espresso coffee (New Orleans and Napoli—the two great coffees—you mix them together); an English muffin with a little curried mayonnaise and deviled egg. Then, at 9 o'clock, I like somebody knocking at the door. [There will be] over twenty-two emails [waiting], and I like them to go to the park [with me] and do them [there].

Ran's young assistants are in and out—doing emails, shopping, preparing meals for him. They do their work with youthful enthusiasm. (They keep him young.)

> Jessica: [*returning from a shopping trip*] I got the raspberries and the green garlic. I couldn't find...
> R: And it's so late. Do you want to get the meal now?
> J: How much fish will I do? I got a lavender plant, and I'm going to put lavender in the fish.
> R: I'm going to be hungry later—I didn't have breakfast. Jonah will be hungry...

> J: I've got quinoa that is already ready—the quinoa from the other night.
> R: You're going to give directions to Jonah and me on how to do the dinner tonight?
> J: I'll do it, and I'll just leave it.
> R: You'll have to tell us how long…
> J: I will.
> R: [*enthusiastically*] I think this is going to be a good meal. It's good you're here, Jonah and Leo. We're going to have some nice, special bluefin tuna, made by Jessica, with crunchy flatbread and French baguette over a special salad with strawberries and yellow vegetables… do you drink wine—retsina?
> L: I don't think so. Hang on. How do you spell it?
> R: R-E-T-S-I-N-A. Real snobbish wine connoisseurs don't like it because they think it tastes like resin—you know, you coat paintings with resin. But if you eat lamb, a lamb that's not cooked too much… not lamb *à l'anglaise*—English lamb, with cooked carrots and peas that have been cooked for two hours—but a rare lamb with… do you like oregano?
> L: Yeah.

And the conversation continues. The meal is a mix of cultures and flavors: Greece, Italy, France. There are herbs and spices, berries, and ancient grains.

Ran's appetite for foreign places and different customs is tangible, and as he speaks enthusiastically about his culinary experiences, both at home and abroad, he's equally eager to discover what is as yet unknown to him. His animated questions now touch on the food in Australia before he detours mid-sentence to China. (He's heard it is hard to get iced tea there.) But even against this backdrop of travel and adventure, there's a recognition of the turning of time:

> My parents retreated to their garden clubs. And now, I'm retreating to a basement apartment with a calendar, a chair, a television, a grand piano—I'm not living in the world of 'street' [anymore]. I'm near Khao Sarn restaurant; I use Dalia's, so I wouldn't say I'm exactly deprived.

The thought bothers him:

> R: Many people live in elegant houses, and then, they go on Friday afternoons with the Red Cross, delivering hampers of food to poor people. And then, they go back to the safety of their neighborhood,

> so everybody seems to make some posture, don't they... wanting to help the poor?
> L: Some don't even bother making the posture—you actually DO care...
> R: [*breaking in*] I DO—but I still use my credit card to go to Khao Sarn.
> L: But you can't...The point is... I mean, you're very generous with those people who you *can* help, and you don't... [discriminate]. When you met me, you didn't ask how rich or how poor I was.
> R: Oh no!
> L: [*continuing*] you just say, 'Let's go to Khao Sarn'... [and it was] the most wonderful steak of my life, by the way... [when you bought me lunch at Dalia's.]
> R: What? Oh, you say that still?

For Ran, food goes far beyond sustenance. It is a tribute to diversity, to generosity, to friendship. It is the makings of memories. It is also very important from the point of view of his own artistic expression. It guides him in forming a vocabulary for the sounds that he plays at the piano, relating them back to food—to taste, to texture, and to color.

In an interview one day, when Leo and Ran were discussing (only as a matter of interest) the phenomenon of synesthesia, some of Ran's intriguing connections between food and musical appreciation came up.

> L: When you see colors, do you hear music? Do certain colors consistently evoke the same sort of music, or do certain colors evoke particular notes?
> R: Oh, I want to be relaxed [*jokingly implying that he is undergoing psychoanalysis*]. Yes, green makes me think of jealousy—isn't that original... *All About Eve*. Red for apple... and I see a banana there, so for banana, I think of an A-flat: a rich, beautiful...
> L: [*Interrupting*] You really do?
> R: I don't know [*irritated*].
> L: I know you categorize keys because when I brought in one of my compositions for the first time, you commented that the key wasn't good for...
> R: I felt that it was too...
> L: So you wanted it changed, so I said...
> R: But it wasn't just register—it was a thin...
> L: Yes, it was in E-flat, and you asked what other key could we do it in.
> R: Why not A-flat or D?

L: Well, I remember I thought F 'cause it was close by, and you said, 'Awff [*derisive*], it's like mashed potato—it's so boring!'
R: [*agreeing with himself*] It IS a boring key.
L: And you said E was a bit better than F...
R: Oh, much better—it's much more interesting.
L: Much more shimmering.
R: Yeah. And D's not bad if you have to be vanilla. So, I do think B is somber; E minor is very sad—I think of Poland and Ireland.
L: C major—what do you think about C major?
R: Oh, that's even worse than F.
L: It's the worst of the worst?
R: I don't know—F is pretty bad.
L: What do you think of C minor?
R: It's like something when you want a little dessert. It's nice—imperfect.
L: Please elaborate
R: Okay, doctor [*still alluding to being analyzed*], C minor... [*musing*]. C minor makes me think of Ridgewood Place, near where I was born.
L: Why?
R: Oh my gosh! Because it's Halloween time, and I can hear... and now I'm thinking of the movie *The Snake Pit* about a nervous breakdown of Olivia de Havilland. So, C minor is moving to the richness and the *crème caramel* of Aflat major. It's not quite there—it's minor—but it's getting down to the dark path. Now Aflat major is much more rich than Fsharp... or even Gflat. Aflat—it's so... it's heavy gorgonzola [*said with a heavy tone*], whereas E minor is like one of Jessica's salads with strawberries, yellow vegetables, a little bit of mint... it's... [But] Aflat minor—what a wonderful key!
L: What about Aflat minor?
R: I think that's Jessica's salad with even more spice.
L: Try and be a little more specific.
R: So, Aflat [major] is heavy pasta... [it] still can be crisp with gorgonzola, oregano...
B minor is like vinegar, mung beans.
F minor's rich! [*It's said on an uplifted note.*] It's not the gorgonzola Aflat, but it's thick—brandy before you go to bed. I have a feeling though I would say that about two other keys, so I've improvised....
[*He ponders for a moment.*]
But I think that part of the time you could give me a test—I can be a half-step off, but usually, I know if the key's white or black. So have I got a name for every note—NO! I mean, I think D major is not that

far out—it's near C. G major is pleasant—there's a little movement… it's a wonderful key for blues.

L: Do you think there's a difference between Fsharp and Gflat?

R: Fsharp? Yup—because sharp does mean sharper taste… though Gsharp major—that's Aflat major, so that's consistent. But Fsharp and Gflat? I feel that's not awfully original; I'm sure everybody has a mood. I think Eflat major's a bore. It makes me think of Juilliard on a Saturday afternoon, where all those people are doing little scales. Dflat… Eflat minor's nice. I like D major, and that only has two sharps, so don't think I'm anti-white. I think G major is great with one sharp.

L: Gives me a little yin and yang.

R: E major—how beautiful!

L: Yes, it is very beautiful. Nice and shimmering.

R: B minor's wonderful; that goes with D.

L: Do you ever think of F-Sharp as something?

R: I like its relationship to C.

L: Are there certain intervals that evoke certain things? I mean, you've spent so much time with intervals.

R: Yup, tritones and major sevenths have a spicy Indian, Mexican theme; the minor ninth—D with an Eflat an octave up—it's spicy vindaloo that you can't eat! It's straight grappa à la Giacomo,[4] where it's so hot that you can't… it's too strong.

The minor seventh is very respectable, but on 'Stratusphunk,'[5] it's got a little clash—it's like a ride back from the airport: you've gotten off the plane, and things are now still, but it's not dull.

L: I can relate to that. What about major sevenths?

R: I've already answered that—I said that and tritones—they're wonderful; they're delightful—I like them melodically, whereas major seconds—just a 'do dah' [*he sings*]—apply it together; as long as it's not 'Chopsticks,' you're great.

Thirds and sixths, I have a little problem with—they're like old milk or cold peanut butter. Fifths and fourths are great—sort of Gregorian—remind me of the Catholic church that I attended once at Hartford, and I was told by the choir director that they were out of key that day, but I thought it was great—I loved it. I think about fourths as upside-down fifths.

L: Really? You don't think it's a different quality?

R: No. [*definite*]

L: Really? I definitely think of them as different.

R: Great! Now let me take the microphone: what do you think people are thinking about you thinking about fourths and fifths?

L: [*laughs*] Okay, I'll move on.

Food is evocative. Taste, smell, texture conjure memory—mental flashes—the more unusual the food, the deeper the impression. Food connects with people, and each connection has its own story—its own memory. Past, present, and future are combined in a multi-sensory total experience.

> I had a flashback the other morning, and I said, 'Mother and Dad, how are you? And they were eating Gardiner Hartman's baking powder biscuits. It's an old New England recipe.

Ran sees food as energizing—both for body and spirit; his culinary preferences fall in line with his spirit of adventure and his sense of wonder. His sound-world on the piano draws heavily on his "spicy chords," and Ran revels in the music of composers—from Bartok to Thelonious Monk—whose distinct musical voices incorporate their own 'special sauce.' The assignments he sets his students are often aimed at opening their ears to these qualities in the music of others so that they might feel confident to venture from mundane, well-trodden paths and add a touch of spice to their own music. Leo recounts such a moment of discovery where, while studying with Ran, he was required to learn "Wish that I Could Talk to You Baby" by '70s R&B/Soul group, The Sylvers:

> The verse of the song features a minor/major 7th chord at the end of each six-measure phrase. Such a chord is little 'left of center' for a pop song, as it has more 'clash' in it than one would expect to find in the standard Top 40 fare. (The six-measure phrase-length is also a departure from established norms of four or eight.) Ran had told me to learn whatever track it was on the compilation CD that he'd made me. No further explanation was given. That's his method: you're expected to learn the material by ear. Quite early into the learning process, I noticed the 'spice' of the minor/major 7th chord. What had initially sounded like a dated disco hit now revealed its own distinct nuance. I could see why Ran had assigned the song; I started to really enjoy listening to it too. In my version, instead of putting the 'spice' chord at the end of every six-measure-phrase-group of the verse, I decided I would 'save' it for the time leading into the chorus—that way when the spice came, it might have more of an impact (the song is about a love lost, and I wanted to express that in my version). When I went to play it for Ran the following lesson, he stopped me at the point where the first occurrence of this 'spice' would have been. He said, 'Oh, but you've missed something here—a little hot pepper of the southern Californian variety.' (The Sylvers were a group from Watts, Los Angeles.) I rushed to explain that I'd indeed heard the chord to which he was alluding, but that I'd made a decision to play it

'mashed potatoes' the first time, saving the 'sting' of the peppers until just before the chorus (when the protagonist of the song realizes that he is, indeed, left alone). Ran was delighted; he loved this twist. 'I do apologize,' he said theatrically, 'Please, continue!'

10

Brookline—The Hub

The home he had made for himself, the home he had been so happy to get back to after his day's work. And the home had been happy with him, too.

Kenneth Grahame, *The Wind in the Willows*

Ran Blake collects things. His basement flat in Brookline is a treasure-trove of books, DVDs, records, CDs, and papers accumulated over decades. Despite this, the apartment has order, warmth, and charm. A fusion of shabby chic and film noir, it is a welcoming place in any season. In spring, it is particularly joyful when, at the street level front door, a riot of pansies jostles with Dorothy Wallace's Brazilian mint:

> They've dug it up two or three times, but it keeps coming back.

Once inside, a door opens onto a flight of stairs. Posters, flyers, and sketches line the walls of the stairwell; soft lighting from below illuminates a series of framed photographs. Chris Connor, Abbey Lincoln, Thelonious Monk, and Jeanne Lee are there, along with Florence de Lannoy, Mother Carter, Dorothy Wallace …Ran's parents. There's a mask of Alfred Hitchcock above the studio door. The impression is one of heading down into a cavern jazz club or basement cinema.

The apartment owes a lot of its charm to Dorothy Wallace.[1] When Ran first moved in, she was dismayed at the size of the rooms. She felt the two front rooms were much too small and poky. There was no place for a decent piano, and she had her heart set on buying him a Falcone grand.[2] She arranged to have her friend, the architect Ron Freilich, re-design the space, transforming the two small rooms into one beautiful studio. It remains a testimony to Dorothy and Ron's combined vision—a spacious, welcoming room full of memories. The walls are lined with shelves that are filled with music, books, and films. Ran can point out with ease "my bibliography of films—my Chabrol collection, my Hitchcock collection." There are mysteries and novels on the top shelf: James Hadley Chase[3] (whose books, according to Ran, are now regarded as "a little sexist") and Agatha Christie. Sections are allocated to different artists— Shostakovich, Chris Connor, Tristano, Thelonious, Mahalia—arranged roughly in alphabetical order:

> Look at Ray Charles, Betty Carter, Elliot Carter! I love composers that begin with "M"—Messiaen, Mahalia, Miles, Monk...

There are algebra books and notebooks.

> Look, there's my own book, *Primacy*. [*He shortens the title with easy familiarity.*] And Gunther Schuller's... [*His voice rises in pleased recognition. The room is packed with old friends.*]

It is in this room that Ran entertains and teaches, watches movies, and sends cryptic emails.[4] It is a cheery and welcoming space. Sometimes the room is too bright for Ran; often, depending on the time of day, it can seem mysterious. The street-level mullioned windows have a gothic feel, and the light that slants through them searches into dark corners, making soft splashes that are tinged with the green of the trees outside. It is a room where the grand piano presides, in which music and movies jostle for supremacy. Movies often flicker silently in the background—like a moving painting. Guests are sometimes invited to watch selected scenes from one of these old favorites. They are never shown in correct sequence, "so you might watch the denouement first, then the very beginning, then a section one-third of the way in."[5]

Perhaps Dorothy Wallace was thinking of her own grand music room, where the light from the garden flooded through mullioned windows, when she planned this room. Perhaps she anticipated the music that would fill the space. She certainly would have been delighted with how daylight magically finds its way, via the curious interior windows prescribed for the far wall of the studio, into the corridor beyond. Ron Freilich's vision has allowed this once dark interior corridor to become a beautiful space for displaying framed photographs, posters, and pieces of art—just as Dorothy's own foyer displayed portraits and paintings she'd commissioned. Ran's artworks include the carved stone and marble animal figures done by his father; and his mother's dreamy (and slightly ghostly) painting, *Whisper my Tree*.

Just as Dorothy loved to entertain, so too does Ran. There is a space on the second shelf of one of his bookcases devoted to "Menus."

> Janet, when you come here, you'll be given good food; it won't be mashed potatoes and carrots.

The kitchen, directly behind the studio, has plenty of open shelves where jars, spices, and condiments are neatly displayed. There is a small wooden cupboard with a generous assortment of bottles—whisky, gin, wine. The light from the single, high-set window takes on a green-tinge as it filters through the thriving potted herbs on the windowsill. There is order and simplicity and always the possibility of culinary adventure.

If, however, Ran or his assistants don't want to cook, the Brookline apartment is ideally situated, and over the years, some favorite restaurants have been within easy reach. For Ran, proximity is essential. In this way, he can be social; he can celebrate among friends before slipping back to his apartment—often paying for everyone's drinks before he leaves—to enjoy time alone with his films and the piano. However, Ran is never truly alone. Waiting for him at home is his "bi-racial" brother (of Persian–Rhode Island descent), Dek-Tor the cat.

For Ran, atmosphere is important, and so Dek-Tor is the perfect roommate. Dek-Tor has a sense of the theatrical; slightly foppish, with his shaved body and pom-pom at the end of his tail, he knows precisely when to make an appearance—to claim center stage. Ran will drop whatever he is doing to attend to Dek-Tor's demands. He is the ideal companion for late-night screenings of film noir and will usually curl up comfortably close, one lazy eye on the action, one ear alert and twitching—listening.

For the Brookline apartment echoes with voices: the voices of James Stewart and Kim Novak, Gene Tierney, Ethel Barrymore, Marlon Brando, Rod Steiger, John Rowe, Catherine Deneuve, and countless other actors from well-loved and much-watched movies. Over the years, these have blended with the voices of students, of young assistants, and of old friends. They are a companionable mix, adding to the apartment's warm, "lived-in" feeling. Beyond them are other voices—those etched on memory—echoes and whispers from long ago. Sometimes, the voice might be Ran's own, bouncing back to him in the transcripts of interviews he has given; sometimes, it is the words of a critic, whose review has been clipped from a newspaper, read and re-read, and then stored away with all the others in files. Many of these clippings are hopelessly referenced, with few dates or sources. They nevertheless give a fascinating glimpse at the bits of Ran Blake's life that he, himself, felt might be worthy of a second look.

Ran, unsurprisingly, has his own thoughts on critics and musical criticism. Among the papers filed away is a typewritten sheet (no date) with a green post-it note stuck to the front, on which is scrawled "by Ran."

> My concepts of music criticism are varied and, at times, ambivalent. Careers such as those of Ornette Coleman and Michael Tilson-Thomas have been launched by the press and communication media. And yet, as a part-time critic myself, I often feel like a parasite and know that if my writing were to appear in [there is a space left blank] publications, I would harbor guilt over some of my "god image" pronouncements. Did I give the wrong verdict? Is the artist innocent of a borrowed cliché until scrutinized on half a dozen hearings?
>
> The best music criticism should include facets found in journalism: enthusiasm, some PR identification, some more general observations on the artist and a small dose of objective reportage about an orchestra, the structure of a chart, the idiom and possible influences of a solo. But the writer must be able to say far more. S/he must be able to express a critical judgment based on a host of credentials: technical command of the music being discussed, vision with generous boundaries, a perceptive fascination for the history of the style and the artist, and the ability to evaluate. Naturally, literary techniques are important, but I prefer straightforward writing that intensely probes the subject than a more sophisticated, handsomely ornamented, stylized approach with less substance.
>
> The critic must be able to describe aurally the description which straddles between artist personality, journalism, and introspective, subjective judgments. Is this so rarely done because the writer underestimates the public's intelligence, or is the critic unprepared?

Ran goes on to ask whether the critic has the right to "dictate private tastes as the gospel" and whether the writer can "stimulate readers to think, reflect, imagine." He also asks whether they owe the artist "responsibility."

He concludes that "at any rate, it is not happening," as many are working in their "own little territory of thought." He longs to find critics "with more renaissance passions," as he feels that "the right critic can exercise benign power over a given art form and that a concerted effort must be made to rally the support and enthusiasm of the publishers."

Ran's own "renaissance passions"—his spirit of inquiry and wonder; his interests, deep and eclectic— are manifest on the bookshelves of his Brookline apartment. Algebra texts rub shoulders with works of literature; film noir movies jostle jazz and gospel singers. Such breadth of vision has allowed Ran to see the unique artistic potential in each of his students, and the music resulting from thousands of lessons given here now lends the space a palpable energy, even when all is quiet. But most of all, there is a warmth here—a tangible expression of Ran's capacity for friendship, for his Brookline apartment is full of the warmth of friends and friendships from all parts of the world.

11

Spiral Revisited

> *They are the episodes of that cyclic poem written by Time upon the memories of men. The Past, like an inspired rhapsodist, fills the theatre of everlasting generations with their harmony.*
>
> Percy Bysshe Shelley *A Defence of Poetry*

Ran's grandmother Jessie Powers predicted that certain people would come into his life to guide him. She also discerned the life-long influence his encounter with the movie *Spiral Staircase* would have:

> R: Jessie Powers foretold there would be people in my life—a composer—and, of course, that would be Gunther, and then, she said there would be a lady who would be very, very special—who would be only five or ten years younger than her—and that was to be Dorothy Wallace. (She said she'd be a very important person that would protect me.)
> J: Was she psychic, Ran? She told you that in great detail.
> R: My grandmother? Yes! But she wouldn't give the names of people—she would look in the water and would take a pair of dice or look at your hands, and she knew things. She said, 'You will never forget *Spiral Staircase* in your whole life.' She said, 'Catholicism will come back in the family.' She said there would be a lot of sadness too.

While she acknowledged there would be sadness, her approach to life exemplified joy.

Ran has lived this joy. He has lived it in his teaching, in his friendships, in his celebration of food and culture, and in his great love of music, of film, and of the animals he regards as brothers. These are the motifs that form the pattern of his life. While he still describes his music as "mystery, anger, outrage, and dark solitude," this same music is itself a source of life, bringing new perspective to the sadness that is there, just below the surface. For Ran, music and film noir have offered a precious means of integration. Looking back there is coherence.

L: Okay, now let me... to return to our discussion of Kierkegaard's view, there is a sense that, depending on your perspective, life is a coherent narrative. In any narrative, there is a compression of time and place and an integration of seemingly random and inconsequential details; if you were the director of a film of your life:
1. What are the sources of integration in your life? And,
2. What would be the key motifs in the film?

R: Well, it's clever of you and your mother to put it in the idea of a film because I know more about that than biography, and looking at my life and then, some of the sources we've talked about—the Afro-American Church, Pentecostal [church], the interest in film noir, how political events have determined changes in my life and then—I would say the motifs would be (you're going to probably say I haven't answered the first part thoroughly), but the motifs would be fear, anger, sadness [*He puts his hands over his eyes at this point, before removing them to add*], but that wouldn't be unique to Ran Blake. Wouldn't possibly Gunther Schuller or Anthony Braxton, or Billie Holiday have all these? Wouldn't they experience these moods?

RAN DOES SPEND a lot of time looking back, and that can be "very punishing." When pressed, though, he admits there is not much he would have changed:

And it doesn't really matter what people think anymore. I must go back now and re-study Monk. Instead of being worried what other people feel—that I sound too much like Monk—I am not so worried what other people feel now. It does begin to matter less, and really, the person that I have to impress most is my conscience.

IF LIFE ONLY makes sense looking backward, one thing is certain—it takes courage to step forward and tackle it head-on with generosity and love. On this score, Ran can have no regrets. The years have brought serenity. His Brookline retreat has everything he, and his "half-brother," Dek-Tor, could ever need. He has the time to think, to dream, and to re-visit the past. It is very satisfying—and liberating:

> Now that I'm spending more nights alone, I do this thinking, and I DO have more power.

And though he considers there is still much to be done—for people like Ran Blake, there will always be much to do—he is now more philosophical about the possibility of achieving it all.

> I guess there are a lot of CDs here [*he gestures with a wide sweeping arm*] and things that I'm never going to review, but the important decisions are really what I practice. How can I tell people I care about them? I cannot be out six nights a week with people as I was in my younger days. If I were, I couldn't keep up with my music and thinking, and I'm doing a lot of thinking on the piano.

He is happy, instead, to re-examine the strands of his life experience—to allow the anxieties to unravel so they may be drawn together in some sort of resolution:

> So how do we review the past? I look upon my childhood, and I really feel how little I understood—so much of life I did not understand.

Ran has embraced (and committed to memory) the myriad experiences of a young boy whose insatiable curiosity compelled him to look beyond the bounds of his own upbringing to find a larger sense of self. Understood through film noir and interpreted in music, this precious time of discovery remains the creative wellspring of the man, now in his eighties. And though the innocence of childhood itself may be fleeting, the unbridled joy of that initial encounter is still present, a living truth in an uncertain world. And so Ran can now endorse his grandmother's prediction:

> Every time I go to the movies and the theater darkens, I'm thinking of my first time seeing *Spiral Staircase*, so EVERY time I go to the movie theater is a moment of light.

This moment of light is a central theme in Ran's life story:

You can repeat a few things in the book because it is so important—the Gospel Church and this *Spiral*. Really, when my parents were getting older, they said, 'We know we'll leave you with your friend the *Spiral Staircase*' (because of videos).

At the end of *Spiral Staircase*, when the multiple menaces of threat and fear, of shadows and storm, have been resolved, there's a point of stillness when Helen realizes she is at last free. She has regained her voice; she has overcome all odds. And as the camera moves away, her figure is suffused in light as she looks forward, in wonder.

Postscript

Ran often invites people to watch a favorite movie with him in his Brookline basement apartment. It is a way of sharing something precious—a moment of light. It is a way of showing he cares. Sometimes the movie will be *Spiral Staircase*, and as the beginning credits roll, there are probably not too many of his guests who realize that Ran has flashed away momentarily, to the Capitol Theatre in Springfield Massachusetts. He has entered his dream world:

> ... in *Spiral Staircase*. I know every time that movie creaks differently; I know that film! Seeing it again and again and again—that was life.

But when he has guests, he doesn't stay long in his dreams. Always keen that his friends may gain as much pleasure from seeing the movie as he does, he returns to guide them through the experience. John Campopiano, a frequent viewer of movies in the "Basement Theater," has shared "the experience":

> Watching a film in Ran's studio apartment isn't a casual affair— certainly not one to be taken lightly. For Ran, watching a film is an all encompassing experience—one that triggers a flood of emotions: nostalgia, excitement, sometimes anxiety, always enjoyment. Having a cocktail is typical and having the lights down is a must. They're both pieces of a larger puzzle I like to think of as 'the experience.'
> In his music, Ran likes to paint landscapes, set moods, and engulf himself and his listeners in a color-sonic ride of the senses.
> Watching a film with Ran is no exception to this. He's shouting back at characters on the screen, laughing alongside them, or—if it's a film he's intimately familiar with—hinting at what's to come are all things

that take place in any given screening, Ran becomes part of the film and if you're lucky enough to be present with him, so do you.

One part of watching films with Ran that can be frustrating is how he tends to fragment the viewings. Likely as a way of extending the joy of the viewing experience in general, Ran will often stop before a pivotal scene, leaving the viewer in sweet anticipation for what comes next. Almost always with a slight grin, he'll glance over to the viewer(s) and ask if they'll be up for watching some more at another time. It can be frustrating but in a fun way!

Viewing with Ran is like stepping into a noir state-of-mind that, I think, Ran perpetually walks in. Films are transformative for Ran. They're escapism in the most literal sense. During these events you take the ride with Ran and learn many things—from cinematic history, to less technical, more humanistic qualities such as sympathy—even for the devil, sometimes. Ran is the first person to come to the defense of someone committing a wrong—in real life and cinema. In his tendency to try and see the fuller picture, he's taught me—as a film viewer—to seek greater context in the characters I see on the screen, to ask questions that are not the obvious, to dig deeper.

Watching films with Ran isn't just fun and unpredictable at times—like many other experiences with Ran, it's an education.[i]

---

[i] Submitted via email, 16 October, 2014.

Appendices

I

Discography

This discography is ordered chronologically according to the album's initial release. (In some cases, the recording itself was made many years earlier). Certain albums (or tracks from albums) have been reissued multiple times and/or on different labels. These details are not included here. Although every attempt has been made to locate the primary source (the album liner notes), where this was not possible, we have relied on correlating information from Ran Blake's website with that found on existing online discographies; upon notification, we will be happy to correct any inconsistencies in future editions of this book.

The Newest Sound Around

| 1962 | Jeanne Lee (vocals) and Ran Blake (piano) with George Duvivier (double bass on 5 & 8) | RCA-Victor (LSP2500) | Producer: George Avakian | Recorded at RCA Victor's Studio A, NYC, NY—Nov/Dec 1961. Engineers: Ed Begley; Lew Layton | Liner notes: Gunther Schuller

Ran Blake Plays Solo Piano

| 1965 | Ran Blake (piano) | ESP Disk (ESP1011) | Recorded at Bell Sound Studios, NYC, NY—May 1965. Engineer: Art Crist | Liner notes: Gunther Schuller; Poem: Bob Marius; Art direction: Paul Frick; Design: Jonathan Granoff; Cover design: Saul Stollman; Photography: George Klabin

The Blue Potato and Other Outrages...

| 1969 | Ran Blake (piano) | Milestone (MSP 9021) | Producer: Mait Edey (supervised by Dick Katz & Orrin Keepnews) | Recorded at Stereo Sound Studios, NYC, NY—1969 | Liner notes: Mait Edey

Breakthru

| 1976 | Ran Blake (piano) | Improvising Artists (IAI 373842) | Producer: Paul Bley Coordinator: Richard Seidel | Recorded at Arne Bendiksen Studio, Oslo, Norway—1975. Engineer: David Baker | Artwork: Carol Goss

Wende

| 1976 | Ran Blake (piano) | Owl Records (OWL 05) | Producer: Jean-Jacques Pussiau; Management: Pascal Bod; Artistic Production (USA): Gregg Lunsford | Recorded at Dimension Sound Studios, Boston, MA—August 1976. Engineer: Thom Foley | Liner notes: Alain Gerber; Portrait illustration: Valérie Lancaster; Art design: Bernard Amiard

Crystal Trip

| 1977 | Ran Blake (piano) | Horo Records (HZ06) | Producers: Aldo Sinesio; Gianni Gualberto | Recorded in Italy—June 1977. Engineer: Raimondo Caruana | Liner notes: Gianni Gualberto; Art direction: Antonio Ortolan; Cover design: Maria Teresa Tannozzini; Photography: Isio Saba

Open City

| 1977 | Ran Blake (piano) | Horo Records (HDP 7-8) | Producer: Aldo Sinesio; Asst. Producer: Gianni Gualberto | Recorded in Italy— June 1977. Engineer: Raimondo Caruana | Liner notes: Gianni Gualberto; Art direction: Antonio Ortolan; Cover design: Maria Teresa Tannozzini; Photography: Isio Saba

Third Stream—The Second Chapter: 1977– 1979

| 1977 | Ran Blake with Dominique Eade (vocals) and Eleni Odoni (vocals) | NEC (NEC–123)

Take One—Third Stream

| 1978 | Ran Blake (piano) | Golden Crest Records, Inc. (CRS 4176) | Liner notes: Bob Blumenthal

Take Two—Third Stream

| 1978 | Ran Blake (piano) | Golden Crest Records, Inc. (CRS 4177)

Realization of a Dream

| 1978 | Ran Blake (piano) | Owl Records (OWL 012) | Producer: Jean Jacques Pussiau | Recorded at Studio Comedie des Champs Elysses, Paris, France— June 1977. Engineer: Jean-Pierre Pélissier | Cover photo: Jean Jacques Pussiau; Cover concept: Bernard Amiand

Rapport

| 1978 | Ran Blake with Ricky Ford (tenor sax: 1,4,7,8,11), Anthony Braxton (alto sax: 2), Rufus Reid (bass: 4,5), Jerome Thomas (guitar: 5), Chris Connor (vocals: 5), and Eleni Odoni (vocals: 9) | Arista Novus Records Inc. (AN3006) | Producer: Michael Cuscuna | "Vradiazi" recorded at Century Three Studios, Boston, MA—Apr. 1978. Engineer: Michael Green. All others tracks recorded at CI Recording Studios, NYC—Apr/May 1978. Recording engineers: Dave Achelis; Elvin Campbell; Chuck Irwin; Mixing engineer: Elvin Campbell | Creative director: Steve Backer; Photography: Thomas Zimmerman/F.P.G (front); Mark Sherman (back); Art direction: Katrinka Blickie

Third Stream Today

| 1979 | Ran Blake (piano) with a large number of young guest artists, as well as the choir of the Holy Trinity Church of God in Christ (Natalie Arter—soloist: "There's Been a Change in my Life") | Golden Crest Records Inc. | (NEC116) | Recorded at Jordan Hall, NEC, Boston, MA—1973, 1975–1977 | Liner notes: David Noble; Design: Barbara Burg

Film Noir

| 1980 | Ran Blake (piano) with Daryl Lowery (alto sax: 6,11; sop. sax: 8; tenor sax: 9), Ed Jackson (alto sax: 7,9), George Schuller (drums: 10), Jon Hazilla (drums: 1,4,5,6,7,8), Paul Meyers (electric guitar: 1,6; electric bass: 4,5,7,8), Christopher Brooks (electric guitar: 7), John Heiss (flute: 5), Hankus Netsky (oboe: 1 flute: 5), Pat Hollenbeck (percussion: 7,9), Norman McWilliams (trombone: 9), Chris Pasin (trumpet: 7,9), Frank London (trumpet: 7), Ingrid Monson (trumpet: 7), Spencer Macleish (trumpet: 7,9), Ted Curson (trumpet, 2) | Arista Novus (AN3019) | Producers: Michael Cuscuna; Greg Silberman; Series director: Steve Baker | Recorded at Dimension Sound, Jamaica Plain—Jan. 1980. Engineer: John Nagy |

Liner notes: Andrew Sarris; Ran Blake; Art direction and design: Howard Fritzson

Improvisations

| 1982 | Ran Blake (piano) and Jaki Byard (piano) | Soul Note (SN1022) | Producer: Giovanni Bonandrini | Recorded at Barigozzi Studio, Milan, Italy—May 1981. Engineer: Giancarlo Barigozzi | Liner notes: Lee Jeske; Artwork and design: Pick Up Studios; Photography: Elena Carminati (back)

Third Stream Recompositions

| 1979 | Ran Blake (piano) | Owl Records (OWL 017) | Producer: Jean-Jacques Pussiau; Co-producer: Guy Van Minden | Recorded at Comédie des Champs-Elysées, Paris, France—June 1977. Engineer: Jean-Pierre Pélissier | Liner notes: Jaki Byard; Photography: Jean-Jacques Pussiau; Art direction and design: Bernard Amiard

Portfolio of Doktor Mabuse

| 1982 | Ran Blake with NEC Symphony Orchestra conducted by Larry Livingstone | Owl Records (OWL 029) | Producers: Guy Van Minden; Jean-Jacques Pussiau | Recorded live at NEC, Jordan Hall, Boston—May 1979 | Liner notes: Max Harrison

Duke Dreams—"The Legacy of Strayhorn-Ellington"

| 1981 | Ran Blake (piano) | Soul Note (SN1027) | Producer: Giovanni Bonandrini | Recorded at Barigozzi Studio, Milano, Italy—May, June 1981. Engineer: Giancarlo Barigozzi | Liner notes: Gary Giddins; Photography: Renzo Chiesa; Roberto Polillo (liner); Cover art: Pick Up Studios

Suffield Gothic

| 1984 | Ran Blake (piano) with Houston Person (tenor sax: 1,4,7,9) | Soul Note (SN1077) | Producer: Giovanni Bonandrini; Greg Silberman (asst.) | Recorded at Vanguard Studios New York, NY—Sept. 1983. Engineers: David Baker; Rebecca Everett (asst.); Mastering: Gennaro Caroneat, PolyGram, Tribiano | Liner notes: Bob Blumenthal; J.R. Taylor; Photography: Justin Freed

Vertigo

| 1985 | Ran Blake (piano) | Owl Records (OWL 041) | Producer: Jean-Jacques Pussiau | Recorded live at the Brattle Theatre, Cambridge, MA—Nov. 1984. Engineers: Eric O'Brien; Sam Negri | Liner notes: Stephen Schiff; Design: Bernard Amiard

Short Life of Barbara Monk

| 1986 | Ran Blake Quartet: Ran Blake (piano); Ricky Ford (sax); Ed Felson (bass); Jon Hazilla (drums and percussion) | Soul Note SN1127 | Exec. producer: Giovanni Bonandrini; Producer: Greg Silberman | Recorded at Blue Jay Recording Studios, Carlisle, MA—Aug. 1986. Engineers: Gennaro Carone; Gragg Lunsford; Mark Wessel; Rob Feaster; Mastering: Dr Toby Mountain | Liner notes: Francis Davis; Photography: Nica de Koenigswarter (cover photo)

Painted Rhythms: The Compleat Ran Blake Vol. I

| 1987 | Ran Blake (piano) | GM Recordings (GM3007CD) | Producer: Gunther Schuller; Timothy Geller | Recorded at Houghton Chapel, Wellesley College, Wellesley, MA and North Shore Music Theatre, Beverley, MA—1985. Engineer: John Searle; Mastering and manufacturing: Laser Video Inc. | Liner notes: Edward Fuente; Cover photography: Justin Freed; Booklet design: Akiko Iriyama; Art direction: Timothy Geller; Editing: Amelia Rogers; Timothy Geller

The Legendary Duets

(Re-Issue of *The Newest Sound Around* with new tracks 11,12,13,14 added)

| 1987 | Ran Blake (piano) and Jeanne Lee (vocals) with George Duvivier (bass: 5,7) | Bluebird (6461-2) | Producer (Original album): George Avakian; Exec. producer: Steve Backer; Re-Issue producer: Ed Michel | Recorded at RCA Studio A, New York City, NY—Nov./Dec. 1961. Engineer: Ed Begley; Lewis Layton; Digital transfer: Ray Hall | Liner notes: Michael Ullman | Art direction: J.J. Steimach; Cover illustration: Daniel Maffia

Painted Rhythms: The Compleat Ran Blake Vol. II

| 1988 | Ran Blake (piano) | GM Recordings (GM3008CD) | Producer: Gunther Schuller; Supervised by A.G. Merrill Hurlbut | Recorded at Houghton Chapel, Wellesley College, Wellesley, MA and North Shore Music Theatre, Beverley, MA— Dec. 1985. Engineers: John Newton; John Searle | Liner

notes: Edward Fuente; Photography: Justin Freed; Design: Akiko Iriyama; Digital editing: Timothy Geller; Amelia Rogers

You Stepped Out of a Cloud

| 1989 | Ran Blake (piano) and Jeanne Lee (vocals) | Owl Records (R2-79238) | Producers: François Lemaire; Jean-Jacques Pussiau; Preparation for release: Pascal Bod | Recorded at Jordan Hall, NEC—Aug. 1989. Engineer and post-production: Henk Kooistra; Asst. engineer: Ruth Campbell | Liner notes: Alain Gerber with adaptation by Patrick Saunders; Cover concept, art, and design: Bernard Amiard; Edited by: Henk Kooistra; Portraits: Mephisto

That Certain Feeling (George Gershwin Song Book)

| 1991 | Ran Blake (piano), Steve Lacy (soprano sax), Ricky Ford (tenor sax) | Hat Hut Records (Hat ART CD 6077) | Producers: Pia and Werner X. Uehlinger; Special thanks to Art Lange and Charles Pfeiffer. | Recorded at Radio DRS, Zürich, Switzerland—July 1990. Engineer: Peter Pfister | Liner notes: Art Lange; Cover art: Daniel Gaemperie; Photos: Peter Pfister and Werner X. Uehlinger; Design: Walter Bosshardt; Cover photo (re-issue): Luca Buti; Special thanks to Willy Bischof

Epistrophy

| 1992 | Ran Blake (piano) | Soul Note (121177-2) | Producer: Giovanni Bonandrini with Art Lange and Charles Pfeiffer | Recorded at Barigozzi Studio, Milano, Italy—April 1991. Engineer: Giancarlo Barigozzi; Mastering: Gennaro Carone; PhonoComp, Tribiano, Milano | Liner notes: Art Lange; Paintings: John D'Agostino

Roundabout

| 1994 | Ran Blake (piano) and Christine Correa (vocals) | Music and Arts Programs of America Inc. (CD807) | Producer: Frank Carlberg | Recorded Dec. 1992 and Sept. 1993. | Photography: Joshua Lavine

Masters from Different Worlds

| 1994 | Ran Blake (piano) and Clifford Jordan (tenor & soprano sax), and featuring Julian Priester (trombone) with Alfredo Mojica (congas), Steve Williams (drums), the Windmill Saxophone Quartet (Clayton Englar, Jesse Meman, Ken Plant, Tom Monroe), and Claudia Polley (vocals) | Mapleshade (o1732) | Producers: Fred Kaplan & Pierre Sprey | Recorded at

Mapleshade Studio, USA—Dec.1989; Engineer: Pierre Sprey (live mastering); Glass master: Nimbus; Digital mastering: Digital Domain | Liner notes: Fred Kaplan; Art direction: Daniel Vong; Photographer: Michael Wilderman

Free Standards: Stockholm 1966

| 1995 | Ran Blake (piano) and Jeanne Lee (vocals) | Columbia (COL481383 2) | Producer: Kjell Samuelson; Exec. producer: Henri Renaud | Recorded in Borgarskolan Studio, Stockholm, Sweden—Nov. 1966 (previously unissued); Engineer: Erik Lundberg | Liner notes: Kjell Samuelson; Photography: Christer Landergren; Graphics: F.A. Warzala

Unmarked Van: A Tribute to Sarah Vaughan

| 1997 | Ran Blake (piano) with Tiziano Tononi (drums: 10) | Soul Note (121227-2) | Recorded at Mu Rec Studio, Milano, Italy—Dec. 1994. Engineer: Paolo Falascone; Mastering: Aldo Borrelli | Cover photo: Justin Freed; Cover art: Maria Bonandrini

A Memory of Vienna

| 1997 | Ran Blake (piano) and Anthony Braxton (alto sax) | Hat Hut (hatOLOGY 505) | Producers: Pia and Werner X. Uehlinger; Art Lange | Recorded at Haus der Begegnung, Mariahilf, Vienna—Nov. 1988. Mastering: Peter Pfister | Liner notes: Art Lange; Cover photo: Ohner Kraller; Special thanks to Ingrid Karl (Wiener Musik Galerie).

Something to Live For

| 1999 | Ran Blake (piano) with Guillermo Gregorio (clarinet: 4,7,11,14,17) and David "Knife" Fabris (guitar: 2,6,12,15,18) | Hat Hut (hatOLOGY 527) | Producers: Art Lange; Pia and Werner X. Uehlinger | Recorded at: WGBH Studios, Boston, MA—March 1998. Engineer: Antonio Oliart; Mixing/mastering: Peter Pfister | Liner notes: Bob Blumenthal; Andrew Rathbun; Design: fuhrer Vienna; Photography: J.K. Rogers; Written by: Guillermo Gregorio

Duo en noir

|1999 | Ran Blake (piano) and Enrico Rava (trumpet, flugelhorn) | Between the Lines (btl 004) | Recorded at the concert "Between the Lines—Reconnaissance in Chamber Jazz," Südbahnhof, Frankfurt, Germany—1999. Engineer: Gordon Friedrich | Art direction: Franz Koglmann; Cover art:

Jutta Obenhuber; Special thanks: Ilona Tip, David "Knife" Fabris; David Reider; Wolfgang Rüger

Horace is Blue: A Silver Noir

| 2001 | Ran Blake (piano) with David "Knife" Fabris (electric guitar); James Merenda (alto sax) | Hat Hut (hatOLOGY 550) | Exec. Producer: Werner X. Uehlinger; Producer: Art Lange | Recorded at WGBH Studios, Boston, MA—Aug. 1999. Engineer: Antonio Oliart; Mixing/mastering: Peter Pfister | Liner notes: John Litweiler; Design: fuhrer Vienna; Photography: Elio Ciol

Sonic Temples

| 2001 | Ran Blake Trio: Ran Blake (piano); Ed Schuller (bass); George Schuller (drums, bells, whistle) with Nicole Kämpgen Schuller (alto sax: 5,11 on CD1 and 5 on CD2) | GM Recordings (GM 3046 CD) | Producer: Gunther Schuller | Recorded at The Sonic Temple, Roslindale, MA—2000 & 2001. "Laura" recorded at Church of the Redeemer, Chestnut Hill, MA—1998. Engineers: Joel Gordon; Patrick Keating; Dave Locke; Mixing, editing, mastering: Dave Locke | Liner notes: Gunther Schuller; Dedication: Ran Blake; Design: Tracy Kane; Cover: Alison Powers Blake; Photography: Joan Rogers; Kathy Chapman; Scott Menhinick

Indian Winter

| 2005 | Ran Blake (piano) and David Fabris (electric guitar) | Soul Note (121327-2) | Recorded at Mu Recording Studio, Milano, Italy—Nov. 1999. Engineer: Aldo Borrelli; Mastering: Flavio Bonandrini | Liner notes: Art Lange; Artwork: Maria Bonandrini; Cover art: Julio Osende

Cinema Châtelet, July 2006

| 2008 | Sans Bruit (SBR001) | Recorded at Théâtre du Châtelet, Paris France—July 2006. | Photo: Bénédicte Gallois; Layout and editing: Sans Bruit

All That is Tied

| 2006 | Tompkins Square (TSQ1965) | Exec. Producer: Josh Rosenthal; Producers: Jonah Kraut; Ran Blake | Recorded at Rear Window Recording Studio, Brookline, MA. Engineer: Nate Dube; Mastering: A.T. Michael MacDonald | Liner notes: John Medeski; Design: Joel T. Jordan; Photography: Kathy Chapman

Driftwoods

| 2009 | Tompkins Square (TSQ2097) | Producer: Michael Cuscuna; Jonah Kraut | Recorded at Mabuse Studios, Brookline, MA (Ran's apartment)—2008. Engineer: Jonah Kraut; Mastering: Harris Newman | Liner notes: Brian Morton; Ran Blake; Edited by Aaron Hartley; Design: Joel T. Jordan; Photography: Jonah Kraut; Creative director: Steve Backer

Out of the Shadows

| 2010 | Ran Blake (piano) and Christine Correa (vocals) | Red Piano Records (RPR 14599-4404-2) | Producer: Frank Carlberg | Recorded at Rear Window Recording Studio, Brookline, MA—Aug. 2009. Engineers: Nate Dube; Michael Perez-Cisneros; Mixing/mastering: Michael Perez-Cisneros | Cover design: Nicholas Urie; Photography: Katherine Brummett

Camera Obscura

| 2010 | Ran Blake (piano) and Sara Serpa (vocals) | Inner Circle Music (INCM0015) | Produced by: Sara Serpa | Recorded at Rear Window Recording studio, Brookline, MA—Dec. 2009. Engineer: Brett Rautenberg; Mixing: Pete Rende—Jan. 2010; Mastering: Mike Perez-Cisneros—Apr. 2010 | Liner notes: Bernardo Sassetti; Karla Kelsey; Artwork: dseny; Cover photo: Tony Kellers; Sara's photo: João Ornelas

Whirlpool

| 2011 | Ran Blake (piano) and Dominique Eade (vocals) | Jazz Project (JP 3002) | Recorded at Rear Window Recording studio, Brookline, MA—June 2004, Feb. 2008. Engineer: Nate Dube; Asst. Engineer Eric Oligney; Mixing/ mastering: Alan Mattes | Cover: Zimri Yaseen; Design photography: Andrew Hurlbut; Photography: Cercie Miller

Down Here Below: Tribute to Abbey Lincoln, Vol. 1

| 2011 |Ran Blake (piano) and Christine Correa (vocals) | Red Piano Records (RPR 884501686228) | Producers: Frank Carlberg; Aaron Hartley | Recorded at NEC Recording Studio—June 2011. Engineers: Jeremy Sarna, Michael Perez-Cisneros; Mixing/mastering: Michael Perez-Cisneros | Design: Nicholas Urie; Cover photography: Kristoffer Albrecht; Portrait photography: Blake - Esther Cidoncha; Correa - Julio César Audisio

Grey December: Live in Rome

| 2011 | Tompkins Square (TSQ 2592) | Producer: Dave Fabris; Production Manager: Cecilia Guerrieri Paleotti | Recorded at Casa del Jazz, Rome, Italy—Dec. 2010. Mixing/ mastering: The Magic Shop; Engineer: Ascanio Cusella; Sound supervisor: Pasquale Minieri; Technical director: Marcello Fagnani; Mixing/mastering: Warren Russell-Smith | Italian liner notes: Luciano Linzi; Photography: Dave Fabris; Design: Joel T. Jordan

Aurora

| 2012 | Ran Blake (piano) and Sara Serpa (vocals) | Clean Feed (CF 264) | Exec. producer: Trem Azul; Producers: Ran Blake; Sara Serpa | Recorded at Auditório da Culturgest, Lisboa, Portugal—May 2012. Engineer: Luís Delgado; Mixing/ mastering: Luís Delgado | Design: Travassos; Photography: Vera Marmelo

Vilnius Noir

| 2012 | Ran Blake (piano) with David "Knife" Fabris | No Business Records (Germany) (NBLP45) | Producer: Danas Mikailionis; Co Producer: Valerij Anosov | Recorded live at St. Catherine's church, Vilnius, Lithuania—Dec. 2010. Mixing/mastering: Arūnas Zujus MAMA studios, Lithuania | Liner notes: Robert D. Rusch; Marc D. Rusch; Design: Oskaras Anosovas

Annette Stevens featuring Ran Blake

| 2012 | Annette Stevens (voice) and Ran Blake (piano); George Russell (piano) | Marvelous Industries (ML Music01202) | Producer: George Russell | Recorded 1960, New York, NY.

Kaleidoscope

| 2013 | Ran Blake (piano) and Jon Hazilla (drums) | CIMP Records (CIMP 391) | Producer: Robert D. Rusch; Recorded at Rear Window Recording Studio, Brookline, MA—Jan. 2009. Engineer: Marc D. Rusch | Artwork: Kara D. Rusch; Typesetting: Hillary J. Ryan

The Road Keeps Winding: tribute to Abbey Lincoln Vol. 2

| 2015 | Ran Blake (piano) and Christine Correa (voice) | Red Piano Records (RPR-14599-4415-2) | Producers: Frank Carlberg; Aaron Hartley | Recorded at NEC Recording Studio, Boston, MA—June 15 & 27, 2011. Engineers: Jeremy Sarna; Michael Perez-Cisneros; Mixing/mastering: Michael Perez-Cisneros | Photography: Kristoffer Albrecht; Portrait Photog-

raphy: Katherine Brummett; Design: Wideopensource

Lettuce Prey Featuring Ran Blake

| 2014 | David "Knife" Fabris (guitar: 1–6, 8 to 12, 14–17; bass: 1,10,12) and Ran Blake (Hammond organ, tracks 4,5 and piano tracks 2,4,6,9,10,12,15,16) with Gill Aharon (piano track 6); Scott Arunda (trumpet track 16); Mike Caglianone {tenor sax track 16); Steve Chaggaris (drums tracks 1,4,5,6,9,10,12,15,16); Tom Duprey (trumpet track 16); Russell Jewel (trombone track 16); Jeff Luke (trumpet tracks 4,6); John Manning (tuba tracks 4,6); James Merenda (alto sax track 9); Jon Nelson (trumpet tracks 4,6); Blake Newman (electric and acoustic bass tracks 4,5,6,9); Rachel Stern (vocals track 16); Maria Tegzes (vocals tracks 11,12); Ilona Tipp (vocals track 5);Stephen Villane (bass tracks 15,16); Joel Yennior (trombone tracks 4,6) | Great Winds (GW3169) | Engineers: Eric Doberman and Andrew Lypps, Zippah Recording, Brookline MA (tracks 15,16); Brian Kingman, Six String Recording, NYC, NY (recording and mixing tracks 1, 10, 11, 12); Arūnas Zujus, recording live at St Catherine's Church, Vilnius, Lithuania—Oct. 2010 (tracks 2,3,8,14); Dave Locke, Rear Window Recording Studio, Brookline MA (recording and mixing tracks 4 to 7, 9,13,17); Mark Hutchins, Royal Eagle Studio, Brooklyn NY (recording vocals and mixing); Mastering: Dave Locke, JP Masters, Jamaica Plain MA | Cover photo: Robert Kaufman; Back cover: Chris Rossow; Design: Janice Cincotta

Cocktails at Dusk: A Noir Tribute to Chris Connor

| 2014 | Ran Blake (piano) with Laïka Fatien (vocals: 2,5,13) and Ricky Ford (tenor sax: 7,8) | Impulse! (379 318-1) | Exec. Producer: Farida Bachir; Producers: Jean-Phillippe Allard; Ran Blake; Assoc. Producer: Aaron Hartley | Recorded at ICP Recording Studios, Belgium—July 13–15, 2012. Engineer: Jay Newland | Liner notes: Thiérry Quenum; Art direction: Patrice Beauséjour; Artwork: Marielle Costosèque; Design: CB Graphic

Kitano Noir

| 2015 | Ran Blake (piano) and Sara Serpa (vocals) | Sunnyside (SSC1362) | Recorded live at Jazz at Kitano, NYC, NY—June 2014 (Field Cry rec. June, 2013). Engineer: Jimmy Katz; Mixing/mastering: Katsuhiko Naito | Photography: Jorge Colombo; Design: Christopher Drukker

Ghost Tones: Portraits of George Russell

| 2015 | Ran Blake (piano—electric piano: 2,3,12,14), Brad Barrett (bass: 12), Charles Burchell (drums: 3, timpani: 12,14, vibraphone: 14), David Flaherty (drums: 8,14), Eric Lane (piano: 3, electric piano: 12), Luke Moldof electronics: 6), Ryan Dugre (guitar: 8), David "Knife" Fabris (pedal steel guitar: 10,16), Jason Yeager (piano: 12), Doug Pet (tenor sax: 3,14), Aaron Hartley (trombone: 3,5,8,10,12, 14), Peter Kenagy (trumpet: 3,5,8,10,14), Rachel Massey (violin: 10,16) | A-side Records (a0001) | Producers: Aaron Hartley; Art Lange | Recorded at Jordan Hall, New England Conservatory, Boston, MA—August 24 & 26, 2010. Engineer: Jeremy Sarna (recording/mix); Mastering: Peter Pfister | Liner notes: Ran Blake; Design & artwork: Tony Kellers

Chabrol Noir

| 2016 | Ran Blake (piano) with Dominique Eade (vocals track 15), Ricky Ford (tenor sax tracks 4,9,11,12,14,16) | Impulse! (0602547627520) | Exec. producer: Farida Bachir; Producers: Jean-Philippe Allard; Ran Blake; Co producer: Aaron Hartley | Recorded at ICP Recording Studios, Belgium—July 2012. Engineer: Jay Newland; Recording assistant: Paul-Édouard Laurendeau; Mastering: Mark Wilder (Battery Studios, NY) | Liner notes: Philippe Carles; Ran Blake; Design: Patrice Beauséjour; Marielle Costosèque (CB Graphics, Paris); Artwork: Marielle Costosèque

Town and Country

| 2017 | Ran Blake (piano) and Dominique Eade (vocals) with Prudence Steiner (narration on "Thoreau") | Sunnyside (SSC1484) | Recorded at Jordan Hall, NEC—Aug.2015; Jan. 2016. Engineer: Jeremy Sarna; Mastering: Jonathan Wyner (M. Works Mastering, Cambridge, MA) | Liner notes: Ingrid Monson; Notes: Kirk Silsbee; Cover photo: George Eade; Back cover: Erin X. Smithers; Graphic design: Christopher Drukker

The Dorothy Wallace Suite

| 2017 | Ran Blake (piano) and Kresten Osgood (percussion) | ILK Music (ILK274LP) | Recorded in Brookline

Streaming

| 2018 | Ran Blake (piano) and Christine Correa (vocals) | Red Piano Records (RPR 14599-4434) | Producers: Frank Carlberg; Aaron Hartley | Recorded at NEC—May 2015. Engineers: Jeremy Sarna; Michael Perez-Cis-

neros | Photography: Gaia Petrelli Wilmer

Eclipse Orange

| 2019 | Ran Blake (piano) and Claire Ritter (piano) with Kent O'Doherty (sax) | Zoning Recordings (ZR 1013) | Recorded live at Queens University of Charlotte (Concert for Thelonious Monk's 100th birthday, 2017). Engineer: Rick Dior (recording and mastering) | Liner notes: Michael Ullman; Photography: Luke Davis

The Newest Sound You Never Heard: European Recordings 1966/1967

| 2019 | Ran Blake (piano) and Jeanne Lee (vocals) | A-Side Records (a0005) | Radio Producers: Elias Gistelinck; Paul van Dessel; Compilation producer: Aaron Hartley | CD 1 recorded at: Jazzpanorama XVI Studio 1, Vlaamse Radio en Televisieomroeporganisatie (VRT) – (Oct.1966); CD 2 recorded by: Vlaamse Radio en Televisieomroeporganisatie (VRT)—(1967), location unknown | Liner notes: Danilo Pérez; Dominique Eade & Ran Blake; Design, photography and artwork: Tony Kellers

When Soft Rains Fall

| 2020 | Ran Blake (piano) and Christine Correa (vocals) with Frank Carlberg (piano) |Red Piano Records (RPR14599-4443) | Producers: Frank Carlberg; Aaron Hartley | Recorded Jordan Hall, NEC, Boston, MA—July 2018. Engineer: Jeremy Sarna; Mixing/mastering: Michael Perez-Cisneros | Liner Notes: Ran Blake, Christine Correa; Artwork: Hery Paz; Design: Andrew Schiller

Gray Moon

| 2020 | Ran Blake (piano) and Frank Carlberg (piano) | Red Piano Records (RPR 14599-4440) | Producers: Ran Blake; Frank Carlberg | Recorded in Jordan Hall, NEC, Boston, MA—July 2016. Engineer: Jeremy Sarna; Mixing/mastering: Michael Perez-Cisneros | Cover art: Hery Paz; Design: Andrew Schiller; Photography: Gaia Petrilli Wilmer

Northern Noir

| 2020 | Ran Blake (piano) and Andrew Rathbun (tenor sax) | Steeplechase Records, Denmark (SCCD31899) |Producer: Nils Winther; Asst. Producer: Aaron Hartley | Recorded August 2018; Engineer: Aaron Saidizand; Mixing/mastering: Nils Winther | Liner notes: Neil Tesser; Photography: Aaron Hartley

Looking Glass

| 2021 | A-Side Records LLC | Producer: Aaron Hartley; Asst. Producer: Tony Kellers | Recorded Jordan Hall, NEC, Boston, MA—July 2015. Engineer: Jeremy Sarna; Mastering: Patrick Keating | Graphic Design: Tony Kellers

Other albums that contain tracks featuring Ran Blake (original releases)

Orte der Geometrie

| 1990 | Franz Koglmann (arranger/composer/flugelhorn) with guest artist Ran Blake (arranger/composer/piano) playing "In Between" (track 5) and "The Short Life of Barbara Monk" (track 12) | hatART 6018 | Producers: Pia Uehlinger; Werner X. Uehlinger | Recorded Nov. 1988 at Haus der Begegnung Mariahilf, Vienna, Austria. Engineer: Peter Pfister | Liner notes: Art Lange; Photography: Christian Lukow; Cover art: Helmut Federie

River of Joy (Solo Portraits)

| 2001 | Claire Ritter with Ran Blake (track 6) and Steve Swallow (track 4) | Zoning Records (Zoning Records #1007) | Recorded at Acoustic Barn Studios, Charlotte NC and Blue Jay Recording Studio, Carlisle MA—Jan. and March 2000. Engineers: Rick Dior; Mark Tanzer; Mastering: Rick Diork

Art-i-Facts: Great Performances from 40 years of Jazz at NEC

| 2009/10 | Various artists— Ran Blake plays track 13 "Round Midnight" | Producer: Ken Schaphorst | Track 13 recorded by NEC Audio Visual Services, NEC, Boston MA—Nov. 2004

II

Dorothy Wallace's Creamed Spinach

with thanks to Anne Elvins Grace

- 10 oz. bag of fresh spinach, washed, cooked, and chopped (or 1 box chopped frozen spinach, cooked)
- 2 tablespoon butter
- 1/2 onion, chopped
- 1 tablespoon lemon juice
- 1 tablespoon flour
- salt and pepper
- 1/3 cup heavy cream

Drain the spinach well and squeeze out the extra water with a spoon. Cook the chopped onion in the butter until translucent. Sprinkle with flour and stir well. Add the heavy cream and stir until thickened. Add spinach, lemon juice, and seasonings and stir.

This recipe appeared, using frozen spinach and two teaspoons of onion salt, rather than real onion, in a cookbook, called *Family Secrets*, edited by Dorothy Wallace, my mother, and Anita Smith, for the benefit of the Shady Hill School in 1952. My siblings and I all grew up on these recipes, as Mother had to test them at home. I use fresh spinach and real onion, and I omit the flour, cooking the onion and heavy cream a few minutes longer until the cream itself reduces a bit and thickens.

III

Gardiner Hartmann's Baking Powder Biscuits

with thanks to Gardiner Hartmann

- 2 cups all-purpose flour
- 1 teaspoon salt
- 4 teaspoons baking powder
- 2 tablespoons shortening (butter or lard[i] or half of each).
- 2/3 cup milk

Sift dry ingredients into mixing bowl. Using fingertips, lightly work in shortening. Quickly stir in milk with a knife. Gradually add more milk until dough is light and soft – but not sticky. ("Flours differ so much that it is impossible to tell the exact amount you will need," says Fannie Farmer.[ii])

Turn onto floured board. Pat down and press lightly to 3/4 inch thick. Cut into diamond-shapes with a knife. Place on ungreased baking sheet and prick with fork. Bake 12 to 15 minutes at 450F. Makes 12 to 15.

This recipe is adapted from Gardiner Hartmann's mother's ancient copy of *The Boston Cooking-School Cookbook* by Fannie Farmer.

---

i   Lard makes very flaky biscuits. For richer biscuits, double the shortening, or use cream.

ii   Fannie Farmer, *The New Fannie Farmer Boston Cooking-School Cookbook*, 9th ed. (Boston: Little, Brown, and Company, 1951), 91.

IV

Ten Favorite DVDs

L: What are your ten favorite DVDs?
R: [*launching immediately into an impromptu list*] So, *Dr. Mabuse*; then Hitchcock's *The Lodger*; and *Blackmail*; and if you send me an email, we'll send you this list [*But—he continues nevertheless*]; *M* by Fritz Lang; *Sabotage*; then, *Shadow of a Doubt*; *Curse of the Cat People*; *Hangover Square*; *Spiral Staircase*; *I Confess* [*he curves his hand as if tracing a tiny mound*]. It's medium. It's about... you saw that...
L: I loved it!
R: [*ignoring the interruption*] about the priest; *Whirlpool* with Gene Tierney; *Mirage* is super, but it's more fun; *Pawnbroker*; *Bunny Lake is Missing*—Oh, I should have put *The Green Room*. I have nothing by Truffaut [*he stretches for a pencil to scribble this down*]—*The Green Room*; *Vertigo*; *Topaz*—which gets VERY bad reviews—It's not one of my ten, but the scenes in Harlem and in Cuba are terrific. This is Hitchcock's third from last film; then Chabrol's *This Man Must Die*; *Le Boucher*; and *Rapture*; *Stage Fright*; now I don't... I'm not... I'm putting them there because I studied it. *Belle de jour* by Luis Buñuel; *Woman of the Dunes*, which is a Japanese film with Takemitsu's music. Every now and then, I add more. I mean, Part II *Godfather* is good; ar, *Sisters* by—why didn't I put *Sisters*? —Brian de Palma. You know, I'm very interested in twins.
L: Why is that? Why are you interested in twins?
R: [*surprised*] I don't know. I think my parents took me to see *The Dark Mirror*. I think there were twins in different parts of my life—never close friends. And I used to think one of the twins would be a murderess (and that often happens in noir movies). Do you know many twins?

L: Some. Are you left-handed?

R: No, but I've been told to start writing with my left hand—that would change my personality. Why? Have I been using my left hand a lot?

L: No, it's just because, you know... that's your left hand right there. [*It has been supporting his chin in the style of Rodin's The Thinker.*]

R: Who told you about the left hand?

L: Oh, there's a sort of old wives' tale about the left-handed. If you are left-handed, it's thought that you may have had a twin and that they were lost in the early stages of a pregnancy.

R: Oh, you've got wonderful folk legends in Brisbane. Would Brisbane be good for a murder mystery... with noir... late at night?

[*Leo and Ran entertain this possibility for a moment or two until Ran returns, without preamble, to the list of films.*]

The 400 Blows B-L-O-W-S. It's the first feature film by François Truffaut. He did *Jules and Jim; Shoot the Piano Player...*

L: Let's talk about him for a minute—is he a big influence on you?

R: I'd say so—after Chabrol and Hitchcock. It took me later in life to appreciate him because I wouldn't call him... [strictly noir]. Out of twenty works, there might be four or five that are noir. But so many deal... like *The Green Room*, which I'd recommend. It is ABSOLUTELY [*he stresses it*] fantastic. [It's a] depiction of death, of a man, and the people who were alive in his mind but may not be on the earth. It's a man who honors and remembers the dead and one who... [erects a shrine to his dead wife]. And it really is, very much, the dreams of my youth, *The Green Room*. Well, I guess I was a little older than a youth. I was in my early teens when my grandfather died; he died on a very bright, clear winter day, and in my dreams, I'd... it mesmerized me. And later I knew Ethel Barrymore died, and I saw other people—animals that I knew and loved—either had an accident or out of old age died, and I just...

I mean, I can't believe there are going to be people like Dorothy Wallace and Gunther [who] I'll keep meeting. I mean, I don't pray every night—like *Green Room*—but I'm constantly dreaming. I'd say there hasn't been a week in the last month that I haven't had two hours a day of Gunther. Now I'm not making out that he's speaking to me from heaven. Some of it's dream, some of it is what he did for me, and some of it is his writing. I'm thinking of his *Of Remembrances and Reflections* that he wrote for Marjorie, and I'm just spending every day thirty minutes on a minute and a half [of it] to get in my ear. I will recognize it till I die. It's so dense; it's so special.

So, these dreams and images feed me so much more than, say, a conversation. Well, I love my students, and I love people—you say

I'm a good host—but this is very much [love] in absentia. Last night, I had a happy dream where Dorothy Wallace introduced Monk to her dry 'Gunther Schuller' martini. He said, 'Very interesting. Why did I never have this?' and then Dorothy Wallace said, 'You know, Thelonious, it's legal.' And then I told this to somebody, and they said that in heaven you don't get drinks, but I want to pretend that it does [happen].

Once, at Leo House in New York, I saw a priest. When I used to go there, I'd feel I should go to chapel because they'd given me a discount. So I got up at 6.30, and this wonderful priest said, 'Well, you know, when somebody is having a happy death, and they have a good mind, please tell them to send a sign from heaven.'

And I had only one candidate, and by the time I got to her, it was too late. She had said, 'I'm Jewish, will I be allowed in Catholic heaven?' and I said, 'You're so wonderful, you'll be allowed everywhere.'

I'm not sure if she registered—she was supposed to call me back. Anyway, Janet, when I go, I promise to write you. I don't know if they have email there?

[*He thinks for a moment or two.*] It's alright once in a while to consider the scientific—that there's no heaven—but I want 80% of me to believe there is. I want heaven to be a little bit supernatural but fully natural; I think it's such a beautiful belief.

V

TEN FAVORITE PIECES

L: Okay, choosing from all music genres—and don't scoff at this question, it's my mother's, and I think it's valid—could you name your top ten pieces and why?
R: Genres?
L: No, your top ten pieces.
R: Well, I thought your mother wanted it by genres, so I was about to say the Chris Connor, Stan Kenton, Bernard Herrmann school, so that's… in other words, that's not from authentic blues; it's not from Russian Shostakovich; it's not from 12-tone, and it's not from Charlie Parker bebop—so then you want ten pieces from that genre?
L: No, ten pieces from all different genres.
R: Oh well, first I'd better… then I would say "Vertigo" by Herrmann; Chris Connor singing "If I Should Lose You," from her Birdland date with Stan Kenton and that—if I have to have [only] ten—that would have Bill Russo, my teacher, and the conductor Stan Kenton.
I would say… Charles Ives: 4th movement of the 2nd symphony; I'm not sure I could pick a conductor; the 13th string quartet by Dmitri Shostakovich; "Fables of Faubus" by Charles Mingus—the studio version on Columbia; Abbey Lincoln, singing "Straight Ahead"—Candid records… Um, I'm not sure now. I think "Ezz-thetic" is a great George Russell… I'm not sure I would think it's the best performance, but George Russell… maybe "You Are My Sunshine" with Sheila Jordan; Mahalia Jackson doing "Elijah Rock" and "I'm Gonna Tell God"… a lot of these things are listed on my CD *Driftwoods*; Chris Connor's "Driftwood"—but I probably shouldn't give the same singer twice…
ar, I would say Miles Davis—maybe the theme song for *Elevator to the Gallows*; Ornette Coleman—"Space Church."

At this point, the phone rings, and Ran complains:

R: That really interrupted the flow—having the phone ring.

A: [*Aaron is helping Ran that day.*] Yes, I couldn't prevent that. We should really go soon, though, cause they're going to close.

R: Okay. Yeah, the drugstore's going to close.

L: Okay, Ran.

R: I mean, there would be Gunther Schuller—the piece he did...

L: Hey Ran, nice talking to you.

R: Leo, so nice to talk to you. [*And then, as he's hurried away*] Would you send me the rest of the questions?

VI

Ran: The Master Weaver of Friendships

Ran's capacity for friendship is something recognized by all those who know him. It is a source of great joy. For someone who claims to be a "loner," Ran has managed to gather a collection of friends from all over the world. His secret may be that he maintains contact with people—often "out of the blue." The shelves of his Brookline apartment contain contact details of people he has met, both overseas and at home. Correspondence is also filed away. "Ran invests a lot into physical things that either trigger memories for him, or that represent a part of his life which he holds dear."[i] This correspondence provides a record of—and a recipe for—friendship building.

The letters and memos that exist often express a similar sentiment[ii]:

> Thank you so much for your letter which touched me more than I can say.
>
> Baroness Nica de Koenigswarter, April 1982

••••••••••••••••••••••

---

i   John Campopiano, Ran's assistant for five and a half years from August 2008.

ii   With the exception of the letter from Dorothy Wallace (which was read aloud by Eileen Murphy) during an interview, all of the letters cited in this section were sourced from Ran Blake's personal archive. Dates (to the extent that these exist) have been provided in the text introducing each piece of correspondence.

What a very nice and faithful friend you are.

FLORENCE DE LANNOY, MARCH 1987

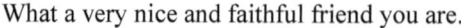

One of Ran's best qualities is his capacity for friendship and caring of other people.

DOROTHY WALLACE[iii]

They usually come in response to initiation on Ran's part. Communication is key to the way Ran maintains friendships. He has a habit of dashing off a letter or a voice mail to someone, just as a sign that he is thinking of them. On January 6, 1989, he wrote to Nellie Monk urging her to think of herself, telling her she had been "such a strength of support" [for others] throughout her life, suggesting that now was the time for her to "bring back your carrot cocktail plus invent a green vegetable drink and perhaps a tart fruit one." He envisaged a store that "a couple of partners" could run.

At other times he wrote, promoting his friends. On March 20, 1997, he wrote to President Freeman, New England Conservatory. The letter was a brief outline of Dorothy Wallace and the support she gave to musicians. The letter was unexpected, and the president, obviously puzzled, returned it, with a note scribbled on the bottom:

> Ran, was there an attachment for this? What should I most appropriately do to meet Ms. Wallace? Lunch with you and her?
> [*As the chapter is read to him, Ran is grinning mischievously.*]
> R: Yeah, I wanted to get her an honorary degree.

Ran loves to promote people and to introduce them.

> R: I love to make a lot of people meet. [*He brings his two hands together, fingertips to fingertips.*] Like I loved Leo meeting the bartender Noon at the Khao Sarn restaurant; Clare met Yoshi—I like to connect.

---

iii   Letter read aloud. Eileen Murphy, Reflections on Dorothy Wallace and Ran Blake, interview by Janet McFadden, Telephone, April 8, 2011.

Connections are often unexpected. On December 22, 1990, he wrote to Yoshiaki and Eiko Masuko in Nara-City, Japan. It was a simple gesture of friendship towards two people who, at that stage, he didn't know. (They were the parents of the young musicians who lived with Dorothy Wallace.) As with all Ran's letters, the letter to Yoshiaki and Eiko is short, to the point, and very sincere.

> Dear Yoshiaki and Eiko
> It's such a pleasure to have Taki and Akemi in Brookline. Dorothy Wallace, myself, and everyone else at the Wallace residence treasure their company. Happy New Year!
>
> LOVE, RAN BLAKE

•••••••••••••••••••••••

Often, the inspiration for contacting people was found in newspapers. Ran scoured the newspapers daily, always keen to follow up on any books or music reviewed. On May 30, 1990, he wrote to Ahmet Ertegun, whom he had worked for at Atlantic Records, thirty years before:

> Dear Ahmet,
> You may not remember me, but several years ago, January 1958 to be precise, Nesuhi kindly hired me for a six-week internship from Bard College. Among my duties was to help Tom Dowd and his assistants. It was one of three experiences that changed my life. I could write three pages on this. The big musical revelation was Ray Charles, who I had only heard superficially before.
> I'm leading a Ray Charles seminar June 18-22 at New England Conservatory. How I'd wish you could drop by for a day. I don't suppose you have other business in Boston, do you?
> I would, however, like to call you and discuss how Jerry Wexler and you persuaded Ray into creating his wonderful music; how he left the influences of Charlie Brown and Nat King Cole and developed his own sound. Also the role of Jesse Stone.
> Meanwhile am searching for the new book out about you.
> My very best regards, Ahmet.
>
> RAN BLAKE, CHAIR, DEPT. OF THIRD-STREAM STUDIES.[iv]

•••••••••••••••••••••••

Ran always acted upon thoughts that came to mind. In mid-1989, he wrote to Benson Ford Jr. at Grosse Pointe Shores, Michigan.

[iv] Whether or not Ahmet responded is unknown.

> R: Near Detroit. [*Ran interrupts the reading eagerly.*] His father made the automobile. They got me on the private plane so I could visit Aretha Franklin's father.

The letter was posted twenty years after their first and only meeting. It said, simply:

> Benson,
> I'll never forget my 1969 trip to Detroit on your plane. Hope everything is well with you.
>
> BEST REGARDS, RAN BLAKE

....

In May 2001, he wrote to bassist Eugene Wright[v]:

> It was wonderful reading Dave Brubeck's biography and seeing your name in print again. You may vaguely remember me as a semi-depressed student at the Lenox School of Jazz in the late 1950s. I feel that you, Willis Laurence James, and Gunther Schuller saved my life.
>
> RAN BLAKE

....

And then there were the responses. On May 7, 1993, a letter from Bill Russo, scrawled in bold, black marker on music manuscript, thanking Ran for his kindness and expressing regret at not seeing more of him, adding "but I think of you often—and fondly." The letter finishes with a snatch of music notation.

Another letter on music manuscript on June 1, 1966, is from "J. Giuffre." It also is written in bold black marker—two pages of notes and playing suggestions for his song "Cry Want" and a quick scribble at the bottom: "To Ran, Thank you for asking for my piece from *Fusion*." It's signed "Good luck, Jimmy Giuffre."

An undated letter from Doris Leete[vi] reads:

---

v   Wright worked with (among others) Dave Brubeck as part of his Quartet. His playing features on the seminal 1959 album *Time Out*.

vi   The neighbor who lived two doors down from the Blakes on North Main Street in Suffield and who featured in Ran's boyhood memories of Halloween.

Dear Ran,
You were a dear to send me that beautiful vase—and a get-well card--and that very flattering mailgram! I was completely cured after such a lovely surprise!

FONDLY, DORIS LEETE.

••••••••••••••••••••••••

A bulky letter from Br. Alphonzo E. L. Thomas, Gospel singer, has a nostalgic theme. In five pages of large, loping cursive Br. Alphonzo tells Ran he is thinking of him. He remembers when Ran gave him the opportunity to play at Jordan Hall in 1968 and recalls he opened with "Meeting Tonight." He also remembers going with Ran to the prisons and wonders if Ran still hears from any of "those folk from that time" now. He finishes by saying: "Well, I want you to know others might not ever appreciate what you done, but always remember Alphonzo still is grateful to you for allowing me that opportunity just to be on your program."

[*Ran interrupts to add*]
I love that he spoke about himself in the third person. You should have seen him. He had phosphorescent fingernails that showed up in the light, a big wig—lopsided [*He demonstrates the angle.*]— and he walked on stage with a white gown, and people said, 'My God!' They knew it wasn't Mozart. Many memories... [*shaking his head with a smile*]

VII

Four Perspectives on "the Rhythms of Ran"[1]

The past is forever.

Ricardo Gautreau

David "Knife" Fabris

David "Knife" Fabris is a guitarist and educator who, in an association spanning three decades, has been Ran's student, assistant, manager, and tour coordinator. He has collaborated with Ran on six albums and produced another, and they have performed together in numerous concerts across Europe, the United States, and Canada. He describes Ran as his "mentor and dear friend." Knife's memories of his time on tour shed some light on how this special bond was formed.

November 17, 1999 (my first international trip with Ran):
Why did I do it?! Why did I even mention the *Cambio* booth at the train station—Atocha in Madrid? Ran had about four or five bucks in Portuguese change that was burning a hole in his pocket, so he stood in line to exchange it, despite the fact that no one changes coins. I give him a hundred-dollar bill to change while I attend to our luggage on a cart a few feet away. Ran puts his briefcase containing his passport, plane ticket, and loose cash (American, French, Greek—we're not even going to Greece) on the floor against the booth. As he advances in line to the window, his briefcase stays behind a few feet. Two guys

come very close to us, and one gets in line behind Ran while the other walks past me asking, "¿Dónde está taxicab?" In the second it took for me to respond to him, the man in line grabs Ran's briefcase off the floor and slips away. I could have run after the man who distracted me, but the luggage (and my guitar) would have been left with Ran, who, by now, was starting to panic.
We had been played.
I spent the next hour trying to fill out a police report in what little Spanish I could remember from high school until we made it to the hotel bar, where I calmed Ran with a nice brandy.
The police found the case and the passport later that afternoon, but everything else was gone, including several letters from Dorothy Wallace. (She would send mail to Ran at the hotels while Ran was on tour—to welcome him to each different city.) That upset Ran the most.
I must admit here that I made the situation worse the next day by forgetting I had taken his newly retrieved passport and locked it in the safe in my room at the hotel. I yelled at him for losing his passport while I had it all along.... Life on tour can be trying![ii]

Knife has a wealth of memories from his many tours with Ran, but despite the trials that are inevitable with any overseas travel, he is able to conclude that:

Throughout it all, what was always a joy for me was to experience his genuine curiosity about all the people we met and the places we visited. Before every trip, he would have lists of countless people to contact in almost every city we traveled. At first, I was annoyed that I had the extra duty of keeping these lists and contacting these people for him, but I came to really enjoy this aspect of my job. I realized how deeply Ran touched so many people, some of whom I am now fortunate to consider my friends. His memory for specific details about people astonishes me (a signature dish someone cooks, a favorite movie...). Ran's curiosity about the places he visits is infectious and is something his hosts usually are happy to indulge. [...] I really learned how to travel from Ran—having a true curiosity about the local culture can lead to the most magical experiences.[iii]

---

ii   Knife notes that the piece "Incident at Atocha," from the *Indian Winter* album, is Ran's musical take on the robbery. Dave "Knife" Fabris, "Ran Gets Knifed," May 21, 2013, 4.
iii   Fabris, "Ran Gets Knifed."

John Campopiano

John Campopiano is a filmmaker, archivist, and digital records manager. He worked as Ran's assistant from 2008–2013 and generously responded to any questions that arose in the research of this book.

FIVE AND A half years working with Ran:

> I began working for Ran in August 2008. I had graduated that May from Wheaton College in Norton, Massachusetts, with a Bachelor of Arts in Ethnomusicology. It was a very rough time for anyone to be graduating, as the job market was tanking.
> One day in August, just as my aspirations of finding work in Boston were dwindling, I saw what I believed was a one-sentence job description on Craigslist that read, "Coolidge Corner pianist looking for personal assistance." Though cryptic and even a little odd for a job posting, I was desperate to find ANYTHING related to music, and so I sent in my resume. I was hired that following week, and, as they say, the rest is history. Five years later, I'm still working for Ran (though in a very limited capacity these days) and have trained numerous other employees for him over the years. (Nowadays, our job ads for Ran are a bit more descriptive!)
> Working for Ran was rewarding, entertaining, stimulating, challenging, and illuminating all at once. [...] No set of texts can adequately prepare one for the "rhythms of Ran." Like his music, working with Ran can be intense and scattered and then quickly calm, relaxed, focused.
> But above the day-to-day lessons gleaned from the employee-employer relationship, I learned a deeper sense of compassion, loyalty, and friendship by working for, and knowing, Ran. [...]
> I think the most valuable lesson Ran has taught me is to be fair. Ran could be sitting down with a saint or a sinner; he will strive to find the good and give each and every person a fair shot. He finds the good in everyone and places high value on balance.[iv]

[iv] John Campopiano, "Ran Blake Book," November 26, 2013.

Four Perspectives on "the Rhythms of Ran"

Lukas Papenfusscline

Lukas met Ran in 2012 while an NEC student. In 2014, they worked with Ran as his teaching assistant. Over time, the teacher/student dynamic shifted, giving way to an enduring friendship and a fruitful artistic collaboration. In May 2017, Lukas accompanied Ran on a tour of France. During this time, they sent regular email updates for Ran's friends "at home," giving an insight into life on tour. Here is an excerpt from one of them:

> Tuesday, Ran led a masterclass with students in the jazz department of the conservatoire of Caen. […] There were two solo pianists and a trio (of piano, bass, drums), each of which picked one of Ran's tunes ("*Barbara Monk*" or "*Memphis*") to work on for the afternoon. Ran included some discussion of his methodology and inspirations (we played some favorite tunes—"*Silent Night,*" as sung by Mahalia; "*All or Nothing at All,*" as sung by Chris Connor; "*Canti Partigiani,*" [as sung] by Daffini; and Monk's [version of] "*I Should Care,*" and the students seemed generally blown away by Ran and his insightful comments for their playing and learning music. Toward the end of the class, Ran mentioned Normandy Cider about four times, so Antoine[v] and I made sure to have one cooling in the fridge for day's end.
> After delicious "*crêpes d'Antoine*" and a quick screening of *LAURA*, Ran crashed in preparation for his concert the following night. […] The piano [for his performance] was the best on the tour, and the space (a concert hall at the conservatory) […] a beautiful, cavernous room for Ran's playing to grow and reverberate. The audience was smitten, we sold many CDs, and Ran went home in a great mood.[vi]

---

[v] Antoine Polin is a French musician and filmmaker. A graduate of Berklee College of Music, he has authored four books on learning guitar for the French division of the "Dummies" series. His documentary film on Ran Blake, *Living with Imperfection*, was part of the official selection of the 43rd international Cinéma du réel festival of 2021 (Pompidou, Paris).

[vi] Lukas Papenfusscline, "Final France Update #3," May 19, 2017.

RICARDO GAUTREAU

Singer, songwriter, and guitarist Ricardo Gautreau first met Ran while Ran was working as a pin-pricker at Wilbur S. Smith's. (Ricardo worked close by.) According to Ran, Ricardo made "the best" Dominican Republic iced coffee.

Ricardo recently wrote the following email in response to Ran's inquiry as to how they first met in 1966.*

> Subject: The past is forever
> Hey, Mammal,[vii]
> So nice to hear from you. Hope you're doing well. Your letter brought back so many memories! I remember the day we met at Wilbur Smith. I don't know if you remember, but the floor below Smith was vacant, so the echo was incredible. I discovered it by mistake one day when I got out at the wrong floor; after that, I would always go and sing, 'cause the echo made it sound great. You heard me singing and came down to meet me!
> If you think about how these things happen, you wonder whether they're "coincidences" or whether they're meant to be. For example, I had a job that a friend got me, and the place I worked for happened to do business with Wilbur Smith. You happened to be there and be a musician; we had so much in common aside from our love for music. So there are so many variables that align to make certain things happen.
> Certain memories never die. It's like an alternate reality or something. When something is meaningful to you, you think back and remember—relive again. Sometimes it's words… or music, or people, or images of some kind that will trigger the memories. Then, you can travel back in time, as it were. That's why we invented nostalgia—'cause it's something everyone experiences at one time or another.
> I even remember the people that used to work with you; they used to always come to your concerts; I can't remember their names, but I remember their faces.
> Take care, my dear friend, and best of luck. Hope we'll be able to see each other soon.
> Your friend always, Ricardo[viii]

[vii] Ran often calls friends Mammal; a greeting Ricardo has returned.
[viii] Ricardo Gautreau to Ran Blake, "The Past Is Forever," July 30, 2018.

* Ricardo is evidently a master of deciphering. The email from Ran that prompted this response was typed on Ran's iPad.[ix] It is an excellent example of his self-confessed "horrible typing."

> I am widering how we meantyou made deliveries to Wilbur
> S smith traffic enginnreeringbatv325 Lexington son. That summer66-thrn I would Leave Belgium puld injeeta thst October
>
>
> P
> Nmaybe iolxLl
> Ppppuitie
>
>
> Butvrudnybi jewnbyoubbeforevtgwt

. . . .

> *'Twas brillig, and the slithy toves*
> *Did gyre and gimble in the wabe;*
> *All mimsy were the borogoves,*
> *And the mome raths outgrabe.*
>
> LEWIS CARROLL "JABBERWOCKY," *THROUGH THE LOOKING-GLASS*

[ix] Ran Blake to Ricardo Gautreau, July 29, 2018.

Endnotes

The Early Years

Chapter 1: That Spiral Staircase Boy

[1] There is a lot of argument as to whether *Spiral Staircase* fits into the film noir style. However, the comprehensive compilation *Film Noir: The Encyclopedia* claims that while the film may challenge traditional concepts of film noir—being set in a home and not being "hardboiled"—it is nevertheless a good example of a noir style film which was aimed at a female audience. According to the compilation's authors, "until women's film noirs are properly recognized, a comprehensive history and balanced analysis of film noir will be, by definition, impossible." Alain Silver et al., *Film Noir: The Encyclopedia* (London: Gerald Duckworth & Co Ltd, 2010), 276.

[2] This book conforms to US spelling and grammatical norms. However, proper nouns and historical references remain faithful to their original spelling. Thus, "theater" is spelled "theatre" on numerous occasions. This includes some old US movie "theatres," which adhered to British spelling conventions. Similarly, when titles appear in French, these are written using the French convention of capitalizing the first-word letter and, where applicable, the first important word letter. German references also follow local conventions (all nouns capitalized).

[3] Ran's edit: "Now we have to say that the Capitol was my favorite, but the Paramount showed those Bing Crosby movies, and the MGM (movies) were at Loew's Poli. So there were three or four other big theaters; Loew's was maybe the biggest."

[4] See also: Dr. Russ Durocher, "Capitol Theatre in Springfield, MA," Cinema Treasures, accessed February 3, 2021, http://cinematreasures.org/theaters/3717.

[5] "But don't give away the murderer!" Ran interrupts anxiously on a first-draft reading.

[6] Bosley Crowther, "The Spiral Staircase," *The New York Times*, February 7, 1946, sec. The Screen in Review.

[7] Springfield loved Ethel Barrymore—especially since her live appearance at the Court Square Theater in April 1943, where she played Miss Moffat in Emlyn Williams' *The Corn is Green*.

[8] The name "Helen" has remained a favorite female name of Ran's. While he points out that Chabrol's use of "Helen" has influenced this—and that Gene Tierney (in the later discoveries of *Laura* and *Whirlpool*) was more beautiful than Dorothy McGuire—he concedes that "Dorothy McGuire was something!"

[9] *Murder My Sweet,* the Edward Dmytryk film adapted from the 1940 novel *Farewell my Lovely* by Raymond Chandler, was released in late 1944. It is considered early noir, locating, as it does, the detective story into the noir style.

10 *Shadow of a Doubt* was a 1943 American thriller directed by Alfred Hitchcock. Though filmed in sunny California, it does have noir themes and plenty of shadows.

11 *The Thirty-Nine Steps*, directed by Hitchcock, is a 1935 British thriller based on John Buchan's adventure novel of the same name.

12 *Frankenstein* and *Dracula* were horror films of the early 1930s; *The Wolfman* was a horror film of 1941. *The Public Enemy* was a 1931 gangster movie, and the drama *Big City* came out in 1937. While all preceded *Murder My Sweet*, the comparison is being made retrospectively. Ran's parents were, according to Martha, considered quite daring to have taken their children to *Murder My Sweet*, but they would not have exposed them to horror.

13 Mary Garvey was a young Irish girl, hired initially as a live-in babysitter for Ran's young sister, Martha (Marte).

14 Ran became an expert at finding back roads. He worked out a similar "back road" to get home from the Gospel Church on Hancock Street that he began secretly attending as a boy.

15 Ran developed, from an early age, a horror of mashed potatoes and carrots, which he associated with Mary Garvey but which were probably typical of 1940s cooking in general. WWII rationing was in place until 1947; carrots and potatoes were not rationed.

16 Until his move to Brookline, Ran kept this paw-print "safely on my wardrobe."

17 Ran Blake, "Filed Document," July 21, 1999, 3, Ran Blake's private archive.

18 *The Spiral* Staircase is used in the class to guide students in the art of improvising to the visual stimulus of a film.

Chapter 2: Springfield, Mass.

1 "Springfield, Massachusetts," Community Guide 360, accessed February 3, 2021, http://www.communityguide360.com/location/ma/springfield.html. And as evidenced in many postcards of the early 20th century. Springfield has also been called the "City of Firsts" (because of the list of innovations coming from the city) and the "City of Homes" (in view of its varied architecture).

2 Springfield Technical Community College, "Springfield, MA," Our Plural History, 2009, http://ourpluralhistory.stcc.edu/industrial/armory.html.

3 James O'Connell C., ed., It's Time for Springfield: Rebirth of Downtown (Massachusetts USA: City of Springfield, Massachusetts and Springfield central, Inc., 1978), https://archive.org/details/itstimeforspring00spri/page/n1/mode/2up.

4 Massachusetts Historical Commission, "Reconnaissance Survey Report: Springfield" (Boston, MA, March 1982), https://www.sec.state.ma.us/mhc/mhcpdf/townreports/CT-Valley/spr.pdf.

5 This title, "City of Homes," dated from the 1880s.

⁶ Springfield was listed as a "manufacturing town" by census records as early as 1820. At this time, 58% of its population was employed in manufacturing industries, ranging from iron castings to buttons and paper goods.

Massachusetts Historical Commission, "Reconnaissance Survey Report: Springfield."

⁷ The Milton Bradley Company, manufacturer of board games, had been established in Springfield in 1860. It had, however, struggled during the Depression, and during WWII, it began producing a universal joint for use in the landing gear of fighter planes, as well as gunstocks. But game kits for soldiers maintained the company's board game tradition. After the war, the company returned to teaching aids and to games, and later, to games based on television shows.

Jay P. Pederson, ed., *International Directory of Company Histories* (Michigan: St. James Press, 2001).

⁸ Lewis Powers, son of George W. Powers (who was involved in the trucking business in Springfield) and Miriam Pierce.

⁹ Lucius was later to become chief of the Springfield Fire Department.

¹⁰ Lewis H. Everts, History of the Connecticut Valley in Massachusetts, with Illustrations and Biographical Sketches of Some of Its Prominent Men and Pioneers, vol. II (Philadelphia: J.B. Lippincott & Co., 1879), 888.

¹¹ Massasoit House opened in 1843. Being next to the railway depot, it attracted many guests, including Charles Dickens as well as Presidents Franklin Pierce, Ulysses S. Grant, and Andrew Johnson.

¹² Everts, History of the Connecticut Valley in Massachusetts, with Illustrations and Biographical Sketches of Some of Its Prominent Men and Pioneers, II:888–89.

¹³ At twenty, on borrowed money and the small capital he had accrued himself, Lewis bought a third interest in his employer's business. (Around this time, he briefly formed a partnership with his brother—L.J. Powers and Bro—but four years later, he was the sole owner. By the time he was twenty-eight, he had bought into several paper mills and consolidated his interests in this area of the paper business under the name "Powers and Brown Paper Company." In 1870, he built (in company with the Agawam National Bank) the northern part of the building known as the Agawam Bank building. In 1875, when the previous building became too small, he built "a fine brick building fifty by one hundred feet, seven stories high, with a factory in the rear," in Lyman Street, Holyoke, for his paper goods company, the "Powers Paper Company." [Everts, II:889.]

Another source states that the building was "four stories high above a fine basement." This same source also provides an illustration of the building that seems to support this statement. In the illustration, one can clearly make out the small basement windows at the level of the sidewalk, in addition to larger windows, a little above street level, and above these are four additional floors of windows.

Moses King, ed., *King's Handbook of Springfield Massachusetts: A Series of Monographs* (Springfield, Massachusetts: James D. Gill, 1884), 326.

By this time, Powers products were being sold throughout America and into

Canada, with annual sales of nearly a million dollars. The company gave employment to three to four hundred people.

William Richard Cutter, ed., *Encyclopedia of Massachusetts-Biographical/Genealogical*, vol. 12 (New York: American Historical Society, 1916), 160.

See also: Amos H. Powers, *The Powers Family: A Genealogical and Historical Record of Walter Power (and Some of His Descendants to the Ninth Generation.)* (Chicago: Fergus Printing Company, 1884).

[14] Everts, History of the Connecticut Valley in Massachusetts, with Illustrations and Biographical Sketches of Some of Its Prominent Men and Pioneers.

[15] Everts.

[16] Even as early as 1855, this connection would have brought a certain amount of prestige. Forefathers Day in 1799 was one of the first recorded celebrations of the Pilgrims by their descendants.

By 1905 the Rev. Albert Parker Fitch was speaking of the 'high ancestry' and the 'spirit, vision and ideal' inherited.

For further ref: https://www.massmayflower.org/index.php/38-about/history

[17] Frank Bangs, Lewis J. 2nd, Philip C, and Walter C.

Cutter, *Encyclopedia of Massachusetts-Biographical/Genealogical*, 12:160.

[18] Leipsic is the old English spelling for the German city of Leipzig. As the article mentions, he went abroad; this would have been the "Leipsic" he visited.

Cutter, 12:160.

[19] Philip Carson Powers was born in 1869, and Walter was born in 1870. Philip attended MIT from 1887–1889 but left without graduating. Walter was in the same class year as his brother but went on to complete his studies, graduating in 1891 with a Bachelor of Science in chemical engineering.

Massachusetts Institute of Technology Cambridge-Register of Former Students, vol. 55, 15 (Cambridge, MA: MIT, 1920), 471.

[20] An article in the *St John Sun*, May 24, 1909, reports on "the largest factory in the world devoted to the manufacture of envelopes is about to be built at Springfield by the Powers Paper Company of Holyoke […]"

"Big Expansion Taking Place- More Industries for New England," *The St. John Sun*, May 24, 1909, Google News Archive.

[21] "Mr. Powers had entertained many distinguished men at his home in Springfield; among whom were:

Hiram Powers, the sculptor and a kinsman; Charles Dickens, Sir Henry Irving, Charles Stewart Parnell, Senator George Frisbie Hoar, Chief Justice Marcus P. Knowlton, Colonel William Edwards,

President William Taft, John Shepard, Samuel Bowles, Honorable Frederick Gillett, Senator Murray Crane, General Leonard Wood, James G. Elaine, General Nelson A. Miles, W. H. Gocher, a Russian Grand Duke, and Governors Robinson and Bulkeley."

Edwin Hill Charles, *The Historical Register– A Record of People Places and*

Events in American History (New York, 1922), 149.

[22] American Bibliophile Society was a scholarly society dedicated to books, magazines, articles, and reviews—one of several clubs/societies to which Lewis belonged.
Cutter, *Encyclopedia of Massachusetts-Biographical/Genealogical.*

[23] Hill, The Historical Register– A Record of People Places and Events in American History, 149.

[24] He "invented many of the mechanical devices used in the making of envelopes, and also perfected other machines which had been in use."
Cutter, *Encyclopedia of Massachusetts-Biographical/Genealogical*, 12:160.

[25] Robert Messenger, "Oz.Typewriter: Why Didn't I Think of That? Weird Ideas in Typewriter History (III)," Oz.Typewriter (blog), August 1, 2011, https://oz-typewriter.blogspot.com/2011/08/why-didnt-i-think-of-that-weird-ideas.html.

[26] Frances was born October 23, 1900; Alison (Allie) was born June 30, 1902; and Josephine was born April 16, 1906.

[27] Josephine's daughter, Wende Reynolds. Wende Reynolds to Janet McFadden, May 8, 2019.

[28] Frannie, the eldest, never married, but the bond with her sisters and their families was very strong. Her great-niece, Jen Hoenscheid, reports that it seemed she just wanted to be near her sisters and "watch over them… The bond was great."

[29] When Philip and Jessie married in January 1925, Allie already had plans of her own. She was issued a passport to travel to France and Italy in February of 1925 and, in March, sailed out of New York on the "Paris." On September 1 of that year, she married John Saeger (the marriage did not last); by 1930, she was living independently in Manhattan and teaching at a private school. She married Philip Blake in Manhattan in 1934, and they lived in New York before moving to Springfield.

[30] As remembered by her niece Wende Reynolds.

[31] According to her grand-daughter, Jen Hoenscheid.

[32] Nieces, Joanna Carpenter, and Wende Reynolds. (Wende credits her aunt with the fact that she, herself, also paints and does needlework.)

[33] Elsie (b.1885), Mabel (b.1887), William (b.1889), Margaret (b.1891), Dorothy (b.1893), George E. (b.1896–and possibly nicknamed "Ted"), Philip R. (b. July 8, 1900), and Richard M. (b.1907).

[34] Joanna Carpenter and Wende Reynolds. (As a child, Wende found her "Uncle Phil" a little remote and could not remember him "interacting with any of us kids beyond cocktail hour niceties.")

Of course, by this time, Phil Blake had left his position at Deerfield Academy and had joined his father-in-law in the paper manufacturing field—a move that, Ran believes, changed him.

Jen Hoenscheid, Phil's granddaughter, saw Phil's reserve in a different light. She saw him as the "calm, steady, and very caring one," who was always there to promote the plans Allie had for them. He would drive the children on all the adventures Allie planned for them. Jen described him as "kind, quiet, and efficient."

[35] The Progress Era in America (1890–1920) was a time of political, social, and economic reform, supported by an urban, educated middle-class.

[36] They both came from well-established New England families. Philip Blake's forefather, James Blake built—in 1661—what is now the oldest surviving house in Boston, Massachusetts. James Blake had a prominent role in Dorchester, and the house he built (using no nails—the house was put together using large wooden spikes or "trunnels") was fitting for a man of his standing. It had many fireplaces and fine architectural features. James Blake married into the Clapp[1] family. The Blake family owned this elegant house till 1825.

"The James Blake House," Dorchester Historical Society, accessed February 13, 2021, https://www.dorchesterhistoricalsociety.org/james-blake-house.

[1] The name "Clapp" is also spelled "Clap" and sometimes "Clappe" in historical documents. I have opted for "Clapp," which is perhaps the most common. It's also the spelling used by Jerry Powers in his email correspondence.

[37] Ran refers to this house as "the Fulton House." (Albert Fulton, treasurer of the Phelps Publishing Company, which published agricultural periodicals and the popular magazine *Good Housekeeping*, did move from his home on Ridgewood Terrace to a home at 372 Union Street in 1924. But whether or not this is the house to which Ran refers to is pure speculation.)

[38] Throughout the book, Ran resorts to "the Year of Our Lord" to indicate that he is bored with the line of questioning.

[39] This interview was recorded in 2007.

[40] Mass Humanities, "Flood Devastates Springfield," Mass Moments, accessed February 7, 2021, https://www.massmoments.org/moment-details/flood-devastates-springfield.html.

[41] With its Armory, Springfield would have been considered a target, and blackouts were customary following the bombing of Pearl Harbor. (*The Springfield Daily News* was advertising blackout procedures from December 1942.) Ran remembers that his father was a blackout warden—and wore a white helmet. (It was not Philip Blake's first time in uniform. At age 18, while still in college, he had been drafted—and photographed in his army uniform. This was 1918, and the war was over in November, so, fortunately, he did not see combat.)

[42] Dudley Wallace and family lived on Ridgewood Terrace, next door to Lew and Betty Powers and their son, Jerry.

[43] This house was at 359 Union Street, Springfield, MA.

In August 2020, Ran received a letter from Wilma Parker. (The Parker family bought the house when the Blakes moved to Suffield in 1951.) Ran had initiated the contact, and Wilma wrote back saying: "For the past 70 years, we have been waiting to hear from you." She is able to tell Ran that: "Your room with adjoining bath is still there." and that, "Hardly a year goes by that we do not mention you." She ends the letter with an invitation to come and visit: "You have been missed all these years, by the house, by us; it will always be a part of you, so please come back. Your letter made our day."

44 Jerry Powers, the son of Lew (L.J. Powers 3rd) and Betty Powers, grew up on Mulberry Street. He is a Block Island artist and teacher.

45 According to Ran's understanding, Albert Bruff was the husband of Claire Bruff—the sister (he believes) of his "grandmother," Jessie (Arnold) Powers.

46 Jen Hoenscheid (daughter of Marte Blake and Michael Koleda) has noted this closeness. "I wonder if the husbands Phil and Dunc liked how the Powers' sisters came in a group of three… Phil and Dunc also worked for the Powers Paper Company, so they were immersed in Powers."

Jen remembers that her grandfather, who she says was "always immaculate—everything was orderly." was the treasurer at the Powers Paper Company. She is certain that the books would have been "very organized."

Her grandmother, Allie, on the other hand, was "the more scattered one. (In a good way.)" She had a more disheveled approach with "hidden treasures in drawers and shoeboxes in her closet." But, Jen is keen to clarify that her grandmother was very organized in the way she planned holidays for her grandchildren. They were crammed full of exciting adventures.

Jen Hoenscheid to Janet McFadden, "Checking In," June 17, 2020; Jen Hoenscheid to Janet McFadden, "Philip R. Blake Part 1," June 27, 2020.

47 Lewis J. Powers 2nd was P.C. Powers' older brother. His son was also Lewis J. (3rd.)

48 Wellesley College, located in Massachusetts, west of Boston, is a private liberal arts college for women. (Chiang Kai-shek was a political and military leader of 20th century China. His wife was Soong Mei-ling, American educated and known there as "Madame Chiang.")

49 It seems that Ran's parents had to deal with Ran's running away more than once—but one episode left his mother in tears.

Ran suddenly remembered the occasion in a flashback on September 2, 2020. The recount came via an email entitled "Winnipesaukee":

"Flash.

I'm at camp, maybe 1945. I actively disobeyed a camp rule, or maybe I was late.

Mr. Park forbade me to touch the piano in a secluded room.

I got more and more anxious. I ran away—hiding in houses… I must have disappeared two days. I found a nice family that let me hide, but a neighbor turned me in. [There] must have been a radio broadcast. I was found and whipped. [My] parents came to get me. Dad upset—my mother in tears."

Ran Blake to Janet McFadden, "Winnipesaukee," September 2, 2020.

50 Aunty Jeanne was one of the four children of Alison Blake's birth mother, Marion Burbank, after she had divorced Philip Powers and married her second cousin, Reginald Burbank. Of these four children (Margaret, Jeanne, Marion, and son Reginald), Jeanne seems to have been the only one to have had a close relationship with the Blake children and their cousins. (Reginald had gone to Westpoint and was killed as a young man.) According to Ran, Jeanne would come and visit often and would take him to school and to church. "She was really

great, and she loved good wine," he recalled.

51 Joanna Carpenter to Janet McFadden, "Re: Fwd.," April 28, 2019.

52 Wende Reynolds to Janet McFadden, May 2, 2019.

53 Carpenter, "Re: Fwd."

54 Forbes and Wallace closed in 1974. According to *The Department Store Museum* website, an auditorium and *Top o' the Town* restaurant were located on the Eighth (top) Floor. The Meridian Snack Bar/Lunch Bar (The Meridian Room) was located in the Basement and was frequented by Classical Junior High students for an after-school snack.

BAK, "Forbes & Wallace, Springfield, Massachusetts," *The Department Store Museum* (blog), accessed February 7, 2021, http://www.thedepartmentstoremuseum.org/2010/09/forbes-wallace-springfield.html.

55 This was where the *Top o' the Town* restaurant was located—Ran's parents took him there as a young child.

56 For details see discography in appendices.

57 The Friendly Ice Cream Corp.—later to become a restaurant chain known as Friendly's—opened in Springfield, MA. in 1935. "Awful Awful" sodas had a squirt of every flavor mixed together. Peppermint stick ice cream is *still* Ran's favorite.

58 Mary Garvey's Catholic Church (Cathedral of St. Michael the Archangel), near Cathedral High.

Chapter 3: Spellbound–The Power of Story

1 Jen Hoenscheid recalls her grandfather was quite a scholar. He was a Phi Beta Kappa at Williams College. This award promotes excellence in the liberal arts and sciences, and recipients must have grades of a very high standard.

This "love of learning" (and respect for it) certainly did guide his life. But he was very humble about his achievements, and when Allie pressed him to talk about them, he would just smile and say, "Oh, I forget."

Hoenscheid, "Philip R. Blake Part 1."

2 The love of French literature was obviously passed on to his daughter, Martha. Martha's daughter Joan recalls that her mother read Balzac's *Le Père Goriot* and then started calling her father "Goriot." The name stuck, and as Joan adds, "In fact, my siblings and I only knew him as 'Goriot.'"

Joan Kade to Janet McFadden, "Re: Questions About My Uncle Ran," September 9, 2019.

3 Ran considers storytelling a vital part of musical styles that draw upon improvisational elements.

See also, Ran Blake, *Primacy of the Ear*, 1st ed. (USA: Third Stream Associates, 2010), 4–5.

⁴ Both Ran and Martha have said that Julia was connected with the Woolworths family.

⁵ When proof-reading this chapter, Ran is at pains to point out: "Do remember I liked *Mary Poppins* a little but liked Edgar Allan Poe and Agatha Christie much more."

⁶ Powers, who was to serve as Springfield's 15th Mayor in 1879 & 1880, was, at the time of Dickens' visit, a member of the Springfield Common Council and undoubtedly met Dickens in this capacity.

Cutter, ed., *Encyclopedia of Massachusetts-Biographical/Genealogical*, 160.

⁷ The performance was to a capacity crowd at the Haynes Opera House and Music Hall on the corner of Main and Pynchon Streets, where Dickens "kept the crowd spellbound, switching his voice to suit the characters of Scrooge, the Cratchit family, Mr. Pickwick, and Sgt. Buzfuz."

Wayne Phaneuf, "Charles Dickens Two Trips to Springfield Mass.," Mass Live, April 2, 2010, https://www.masslive.com/history/2010/04/charles_dickens_trips_to_springfield_mass.html.

⁸ Both Philip and Alison were a little shy. Martha remembered that her father never voluntarily talked; rather, he waited to be drawn out. (He would sing a few Scottish songs if pressed.) Allie, it seems, needed to be drawn out too. Though Jen Hoenscheid remembers her grandmother as the more chatty of the pair and recalls that she was "so much fun," always arranging "a fun schedule" when the grandchildren visited.

Hoenscheid, "Checking in."

⁹ Susan Alima Friar to Janet McFadden, "Pictures and Stories from Ran's and My Early Life.," September 1, 2015.

Chapter 4: A Little Drama

¹ Presumably, it was Miss Rude herself who administered this discipline, as Martha remembered a similar incident with less dramatic consequences. She remembered chanting, with Ran, at the dinner table, "Miss Rude is rude" over and over, while Philip and Alison looked on indulgently.

² Marlon Brando's career commenced in 1944 when he made his debut on Broadway in *I Remember Mama*. Soon after (1946), he was voted Broadway's most promising actor.

³ The plunder could be associated with pirates. Ireland's history, from as early as 400AD, is peppered with stories of pirates and piracy. Some of these stories belong to myths and legends, but they have sprung from history. Pirates have been evident in Ireland for 14 centuries of its recorded history. Viking raids occurred as early as 795AD. It was Vikings who settled in Dublin and also founded Waterford and Wexford. As well, homegrown pirates—of the O'Malley, O'Flaherty, O'Sullivan, and O'Driscoll clans—reigned in the west and southwest of

the country for centuries.

Des Ekin, *Ireland's Pirate Trail: A Quest to Uncover Our Swashbuckling Past* (The O'Brien Press Ltd, 2018).

[4] There are a couple of possible meanings. The magical drink could have been mead—the traditional wine of honey, fruit, and herbs produced from an ancient Irish recipe.

Another possibility would be the traditional Irish distilled beverage, poitín. The first dram from the pot—the pure drop—is renowned for magical healing effects.

[5] The connection between pirates and moonstones is not explained, but the implication is that the moonstones were evidence of pirates having passed through the area.

Chapter 5: Radio

[1] American Telephone and Telegraph Company., "Bell Telephone Quarterly." 13, no. April (1934): 75–97; Steven Schoenherr E., "History of Radio and Television," Recording Technology History, July 14, 2004, http://www.aes-media.org/historical/html/recording.technology.history/radio-television0.html.

[2] *Inner Sanctum* was brought to the public by Colgate Palmolive on Saturdays and Wednesdays, by Carters Little Liver Pills on Sundays, by Mars Candy Bars on Mondays, and by Lipton Tea on Tuesdays. Raymond Johnson was host till 1945.

Old Time Radio Researchers Group, "Inner Sanctum Mysteries," archive.org, January 3, 2020, http://archive.org/details/OTRR_Inner_Sanctum_Mysteries_Singles.

[3] On December 7, 1941, following the attack on Pearl Harbor, programs were interrupted to announce the shocking news, and Franklin D. Roosevelt's war declaration speech attracted ninety million listeners.

Margaret A. Blanchard, ed., *History of the Mass Media in the United States: An Encyclopedia* (Chicago: Routledge, 1998).

[4] Olive Higgons Prouty was an American writer and poet. Educated at Smith College, she was known for her philanthropic work, through which she came to be associated with Sylvia Plath, whom she encouraged and supported financially. She lived in Brookline for most of her life—a block away from Ran's friend and mentor Dorothy Wallace, with whom she was friends. Ran met Prouty when he moved to Boston.

[5] Jack Armstrong had weekly adventures in all parts of the world. He was the embodiment of the "All-American boy," and the series was extremely popular. It was sponsored by Wheaties.

[6] *Forever Amber* was praised by some for its relevance in depicting historical events in 17th century England; others were scandalized by its sexual references, and fourteen US states (incl. Massachusetts) banned it. Nevertheless, it was the

best-selling US novel of the 1940s.

Elaine Showalter, "Emeralds on the Home Front," *The Guardian*, August 10, 2002, http://www.theguardian.com/books/2002/aug/10/featuresreviews.guardianreview19; Lise Jaillant, "Subversive Middlebrow: The Campaigns to Ban Kathleen Winsor's Forever Amber in the US and Canada," *International Journal of Canadian Studies* 48 (January 1, 2014): 33–52, https://doi.org/10.3138/ijcs.48.33; Peter Guttridge, "Kathleen Winsor," *The Independent*, September 26, 2013, online edition, sec. Obituaries, https://www.independent.co.uk/news/obituaries/kathleen-winsor-36575.html.

CHAPTER 6: THE DREAM WORLD

[1] It is still possible to experience something of what the seven-year-old Ran must have felt all those years ago when he lay sobbing in fear—horror even. Many of the *Inner Sanctum* murder mysteries are still available on internet archives. Out-dated though they may seem, they are highly effective.

[2] These included impromptu stories performed at the piano as well as more formal written stories. (Martha recalls that their father was so impressed with some of the stories that he had them typed up and bound into a little book called *Variety Stories*.)

[3] Frances Powers was the eldest daughter of Philip Powers and Marion Burbank. She was Ran's mother's (Alison's) big sister.

[4] Mulberry Street Cemetery—a block from his home on Union Street and very close to his grandparents' home on Ridgewood Place.

[5] The tai chi venue in Brookline called Brookline Tai Chi at 1615 Beacon St Brookline was primarily a tai chi venue but was rented out as a space for music performance.

[6] This interview was recorded on June 20, 2007. Ran had already planned, for the final day of the summer class on Chris Connor in August of that year, to call Connor in New Jersey and have the class interview her. Connor died on August 29, 2009, from cancer; she was eighty-one.

[7] Mother Carter's photo is there.

[8] Andrew Fenlon— Friend and former student of Ran's and one-time personal assistant.

Alonzo Harris—NEC alumnus who has a gospel band, A7, with his brothers.

Giacomo Merega—Italian electric bass player and NEC alumnus who was an assistant of Ran's. He had arranged for earplugs for Ran, with a cord connecting them, which Ran wore draped around his neck. In this way, Ran could easily insert them when the sound levels at the concerts he was attending became bothersome.

FBI special agent Dale Bartholomew Cooper is a fictional character from the ABC television series *Twin Peaks*, which was telecast in 1990/91 and became an instant success and talking point. Cooper was idiosyncratic, with an interest in the mystical. His crime-solving was based on his intuition—and sometimes even on dreams—and Cooper (in monologues) directed messages to his assistant Diane, who was never seen. The show had a certain otherworldliness, which the theme music by Angelo Badalamenti emphasized. *Twin Peaks* was filmed in the vicinity of Seattle.

[9] Jose Antonio Luera, "Untitled Article," trans. Don Strange, *Aria Jazz*, March 1967.

Chapter 7: Church—Its Heart and Soul

[1] Designed by architect William A. Potter, this church in the High Victorian Gothic style is built in the distinctive "reddish" Longmeadow stone (with contrasting features in yellow Ohio stone.)

Joan M. Marter, *The Grove Encyclopedia of American Art*, vol. 1 (Oxford University Press, 2011), 169.

[2] The Powers' family church—the church from which Lewis Jerroldton Powers was buried on September 18, 1915, was the church of the Third Congregational Society of Springfield: the Church of the Unity (207 State Street). This beautiful Gothic structure, designed by Henry Hobson Richardson, was demolished in 1961. The site is now a parking lot.

[3] Rev. Dr. Gordon Gilkey was Pastor at South Congregational Church from 1917 to 1954. He was a graduate of Harvard and Union Theological College. He taught at Amherst College. He was a prolific writer, though many of his books are now out of print.

[4] This interview was dated September 5, 2007.

[5] A photograph of Dr. Gilkey in The Troy Record December 3, 1943, shows a balding man in his early fifties with a lean, intelligent face and a direct look. "Dr. Gilkey To Address Students," *Troy Record*, December 4, 1943, Morning edition, https://newspaperarchive.com/troy-record-dec-0–943-p-8/.

[6] Springfield Technical Community College, "The Springfield Armory," Our Plural History, accessed February 25, 2021, http://ourpluralhistory.stcc.edu/industrial/armory.html.

[7] Wellesley is a liberal arts college for women, founded in 1870 and located just west of Boston. Its aim is to promote women who will "make a difference in the world."

[8] The Colony Club, with all its old-world splendor, was founded in 1915. It was established in the beautiful Wesson Mansion, the former home of Daniel B. Wesson (Smith and Wesson, manufacturers of revolvers). The imposing mansion with its steeply-pitched roof-line, towers, and turrets had twenty rooms, each with a marble fireplace. It was built in the eighteen nineties of Milford pink granite in

The Early Years 535

the French Renaissance (Chateau) style. The building was destroyed by fire on February 19, 1966.

9 Mary's church, near Cathedral High on the other side of State Street, was just a few blocks from Ran's Union Street home. At that time, Cathedral High was still on Elliot Street.

10 Later, Ran went on to study Latin at Classical High, Springfield, MA. and Suffield Academy, Suffield CT.

11 A meditative and repetitive prayer said using beads. Mary Lou Williams later insisted Ran recite this prayer with her prior to lessons.

12 Reference to the song: "Our Fair Cat"—composed by Leo McFadden for the Cat People concert, produced by Ran at NEC in 2006. The song was recorded by Ran and Sara Serpa on their album, *Camera Obscura*.

13 The Jinxey Bar was located at 30–32 Hancock Street. It was a very plain red-brick front/cement structure, which was at that time run by Frankie Jones.

14 Chase Glass and Allied Products has operated since 1934, most recently at 123 Hancock Street.

15 Dalia's Bistro and Wine Bar at 1657 Beacon Street, Brookline (now closed) was a favorite haunt of Ran. It was a 15-minute walk from his Brookline apartment.

16 The Holy Trinity Church of God in Christ at North Hartford CT, which was to have a bigger influence on him.

17 Eunice Bell was a great friend of Joe Hardin. Eunice's daughter, Ethel, and son-in-law, Nathanial Wilson, were members of the Pentecostal Church at North Hartford.

Chapter 8: Celebration—A Perspective on Joy

1 Ran claims that Mary "lived" her stories.

2 *Sisters* was a 1973 horror film directed by Brian De Palma and starring Margot Kidder. De Palma was said to be influenced by Hitchcock.

3 "Digression's my middle name," quips Ran when the chapter is read to him.

4 *Home Sweet Homicide* was a 1946 mystery/romance directed by Lloyd Bacon starring Peggy Ann Garner, Randolph Scott, and a very young Dean Stockwell.

5 Aaron Hartley: trombonist, composer, educator, artist manager, and valued friend to Ran.

6 In Greece, on April 21, 1967, a group of right-wing army officers overthrew the caretaker government just prior to scheduled elections. They established instead the Regime of the Colonels. Any person who might have prevented the coup was arrested the night before. Artists and foreigners were questioned.

7 Leo remembers purposely avoiding Greece at this stage of the interview—he

knew it was a "no-go" area; he knew that if he brought it up, Ran could get very upset and would have to finish for the day. Leo explains: "I was traveling out to his apartment for those early interviews, and when I lived in New York, I continued to catch the Greyhound bus up to Boston. So whether I was living in the Boston area or whether I was coming up from New York at the time of this interview, I was not wanting to put the interview in jeopardy by digging too deeply with a line of questioning about Greece. It was such a sensitive subject…. I did finally get to talk to him about it one day in the small square/ garden directly outside his apartment. It was a lovely day, probably mid-spring as it was unusual for us to be outside, but the weather was so inviting, we'd decided to find a park bench and have the interview there."

[8] Dorothy Wallace, Ran's great patron.

[9] Ran's Grandparents had "three cocker spaniel dogs—three brothers. Biscuit was the eldest, then came Sammy, S-A-M-M-Y, and the third, the youngest, was Cricket. These mammals would be there at Ridgewood Place."

[10] Lyle Davidson (1938–2021) and Frank Carlberg—both on the faculty at New England Conservatory at the time of this interview.

[11] Hearing this chapter, Ran is delighted with the choice of word: "I really insist you keep that word. I am truculent. I don't want people thinking I'm Mother Teresa's uncle. I give through music and helping people, and I used to give people free lessons, but I am truculent."

[12] "Keep that!" Ran shouts out as the chapter is read to him.

[13] First published in 1842 in the literary annual *The Gift: a Christmas and New Year's Present for 1843*. Poe takes the Spanish Inquisition as a starting point for this fictional story and relates a prisoner's torments during imprisonment. He focuses on the senses to create terror and horror.

[14] It is reported that once, after misbehaving as a five-year-old, Alfred Hitchcock (normally a quiet child) was sent, by his father, with a note to hand in at the local police station. The policeman on duty immediately locked him in a cell, telling him that was what happened to people who did bad things—who misbehaved. Though only in the cell for five minutes, the experience had a lasting effect on Hitchcock. He cited this as a reason for his never learning to drive (so as to lessen the chances of being pulled over by the police—of whom he had a phobic fear). The "wrong man" theme in his movies is also attributed to this experience.

[15] The site was originally known as Martha's Dingle—sold by Martha Ferre to raise a dowry.

Chapter 9: A World of Wonder—The Lady of the Lake

[1] Algonquin culture refers to a number of different North American aboriginal tribes who spoke related dialects. The family of languages was spoken by tribes over vast areas from northern Canada to Carolina, including the Pennacook tribe which, had a village near Newbury and many camping places around the lake. In addition, other tribes visited the lake by way of the Connecticut and Sugar rivers.

The Pennacooks belonged to a larger group: the Abenakis (to the north). The fact that different tribes shared a similar language base could explain the different meanings attributed to the word *Sunapee* (e.g., it is also known as "rocky pond" or "rocks in the water" in Pennacook; whereas "wild goose waters" is attributed to Abenaki.)

See also: Myra B. Lord, *A History of the Town of New London, Merrimack County, New Hampshire, 1799-1899.* (Concord, NH.: The Rumford Press, 1899); Chester B. Price, ed., "The Historic Indian Trails of New Hampshire," in *The Indian Heritage of New Hampshire and Northern New England*, Paperback edition (Jefferson, NC.: McFarland & Company, 2008), 173; Paul D. Rheingold, *Lake Sunapee* (New Hampshire: Arcadia Publishing, 2012).

[2] Joanna Carpenter to Janet McFadden, "Re: Sunapee," May 10, 2019.

[3] John Greenwood, "We Remember Newbury: A Collection of Recollections of Lake Sunapee," http://johngreenwood.net/Sunapee-History/Sunapee_Recollections-Memories_w_Pix.pdf.

[4] Kelly Belinsky, who grew up not far from Herrick Cove, had further details to add: "New London Pharmacy is located across from the green in the center of town. The soda fountains were located in the back of the store. Mr. Bob Lovely greeted everyone by name as they came into the store. His son of the same name took over after the Bob you knew, Ran."

Kelly also remembered, "The Poors and Ran's grandparents lived on Herrick Cove. We live 1/2 mile from there and would often walk down for a swim out to the three rocks or the little lighthouse."

[5] On 4 July 1862, the Rev. C.L. Dodgson and Canon Robinson Duckworth rowed the three daughters of Henry Liddell (Vice-Chancellor of Oxford and Dean of Christ Church, Oxford) to a meadow upstream on the Isis River (as the Thames was known in this reach at the time). It was a sunny, summer's day—a 'golden' day—and they stopped for tea in the shade of a newly constructed haystack. It was on this boat journey, and in the shade of this haystack, that Rev. Dodgson (Lewis Carroll) created Alice and first told the story of her "Adventures Underground," as he first called the book.

[6] Goldenrod: a wild, tall, flowering plant of North America, which multiplies by sending out runners so that it tends to grow densely. It belongs to the Aster family.

[7] Poor Road runs off the main road, just south of Herrick Cove Lane, New London, NH.

Edward and Grayce Poor were very important to Ran as they really encouraged his music at a time when, according to Ran, "My family thought my playing a drag."

[8] Carpenter, "Re: Sunapee."

[9] Wende Reynolds to Janet McFadden, "Re: 42 Ridgewood Place," April 29, 2019.

[10] Newbury Historical Society, April 2012 Op. Cit.

Karen Matthews (referring to Blodgett Landing) remembers: "most of the houses back then had at least a stand up [sic] piano, and I remember at least one or two having baby grand pianos."

[11] Reynolds, "Re: 42 Ridgewood Place."

Chapter 10: Suffield, Connecticut—A New Start

[1] "Population of Towns 1800-2010," CT.gov-Connecticut's Official State Website, accessed February 26, 2021, https://portal.ct.gov/SOTS/Register-Manual/Section-VII/Population-of-Towns-18002010.

[2] Alison Blake had a sure eye and a strong appreciation of natural beauty. One of her paintings, "Whisper My Tree"—a beautifully evocative depiction of two trees, their pale branches reaching out in some sort of ghostly *pas de deux*—hangs on the wall of Ran's Brookline apartment.

[3] Hamilton Standard—an aircraft propeller parts supplier. It opened a plant at Windsor Locks, CT. in 1952, the building of which would have coincided with the Blakes' arrival in Suffield, just seven miles away.

[4] The Lion, the Witch and the Wardrobe by CS Lewis © copyright CS Lewis Pte Ltd 1950.
Used with permission.

[5] Ran believed his family had been attempting to limit his radio listening-time, but Martha had no recollection of any such conspiracy.

[6] Commercial production of television equipment was banned from 1942.

[7] Following the end of the war, only 44,000 American homes had TV, but by the end of the decade, there were close to a million sets (and 20 million by 1953). Color television began with a commercial broadcast in late 1953. However, the first all-electronic color set was not placed on the American market until 1954.

[Jacob Clifton, "How Did World War II Affect Television?," How Stuff Works, March 11, 2011, https://people.howstuffworks.com/culture-traditions/tv-and-culture/world-war-ii-affect-television.htm; Tom Genova, "1946-1949," Television History-The First 75 Years, 2013, http://www.tvhistory.tv/1946-1949.htm.]

[8] Robert J. Thompson and Steve Allen, "Television in the United States," in *Encyclopedia Britannica*, accessed February 26, 2021, https://www.britannica.com/art/television-in-the-United-States.

9 Ginger Cruikshank, *Images of America: Springfield*, Illustrated edition, vol. 2 (Charleston, SC: Arcadia Publishing, 2000), 95.

10 Thompson and Allen, "Television in the United States."

11 The *Ed Sullivan Show* was called *Toast of the Town* until 1955.

12 *Perry Mason* made its TV debut in September 1957. Wikipedia contributors, "Perry Mason (1957 TV Series)," in *Wikipedia*, February 25, 2021, https://en.wikipedia.org/w/index.php?title=Perry_Mason_(1957_TV_series)&oldid=1008908717.

13 Della Street was Perry Mason's fictional secretary.

14 The original series of *The Twilight Zone* was produced between 1959 and 1964. The writers often used science fiction to get social commentary past the sponsors and censors. Themes included nuclear war, McCarthyism, and mass hysteria. There was a revival of the series from 1985 to 1989.

15 Classical High School on State Street opened in 1898. Initially known as Central High School, the school changed its name Classical High School in 1934. It was closed in 1986. Ran continued at Classical High School for a little over a year after his family had moved to Suffield.

16 Rather than changing schools when the family moved to Suffield, Ran was initially permitted to stay at Classical High School in Springfield. He was doing well there, both academically and socially. He had just been nominated as Vice President of his class. Ran has described this nomination as "a happy event" and still remembers it with pleasure. It took place in April. The following Fall, his parents thought he should enroll at Suffield Academy. [Ran Blake to Janet McFadden, "A Random Memory," May 31, 2016.]

17 Thompsonville, on the east bank of the Connecticut River, was the urban center of Enfield. It had been established in 1828 as a carpet manufacturing district—an industry which continued till 1971.

18 The Blueways bus company, owned by the Aselton family, was always associated with Springfield. It had a terminal at 90 Worthington Street at this time, so it was likely that this was where Ran caught his bus. (This company lost its bus-line in 1956 and was forced into receivership after 36 years of operation.) The Greyhound bus terminal in Worthington Street was built in 1954—prior to that, their terminal was around the block on Bridge Street.

19 Jack Roosevelt Robinson, born in Georgia in 1919, pioneered racial integration in professional sport in America by playing for the Brooklyn Dodgers baseball team in 1947. He was inducted into the Baseball Hall of Fame in 1962. In 1944, he took a similar stand to the one Rosa Parks would take a decade later by refusing to move to the back of a segregated bus.

20 Joseph Louis Barrow (1914–1981). Born in LaFayette, Alabama, Barrow was boxing heavyweight champion of the world. He had a twelve-year run as heavyweight king.

Biography.com Editors, "Joe Louis," Biography.com, April 2, 2014, https://www.biography.com/athlete/joe-louis.

[21] Gilbert P. Ahrens (June 24, 1938, to June 21, 2017) lived all his life in Suffield.

[22] Ran explains: "Named after Mary and Bernard Ahrens—just like the music companies Margun and GunMar are named after Gunther and Marjorie Schuller."

[23] James de Preist—conductor. He was one of the first African American conductors to gain worldwide acclaim. He was music director of the Oregon Symphony from 1980 to 2003. He was the nephew of the great 20th-century contralto, Marian Anderson.

[24] Sidney Bechet was a jazz saxophonist who was an important early soloist in jazz. His primary instruments were the clarinet and the soprano sax.

[25] Kenton was a significant bandleader of the 1950s. His Progressive Jazz Orchestra (which fused jazz and modern classical) did not necessarily swing. It was full of dissonance and atonality and was more suited to concert halls than to dance floors. Pete Rugolo and Shorty Rogers, who did arrangements for Kenton's bands, later pursued film music careers. It is interesting to note that music in some 1950s noir films is reminiscent of Kenton's music. Both incorporated a "symphonic range of sounds and textures,*" and sought to use existing instrumentation in new and creative ways.

At this time, Duke Ellington was expressing an interest in scoring for film. However, Ellington was black and Kenton white, and this was significant. While jazz was becoming acceptable for 'Hollywood' film music, the idea of a black composer for this type of music was still a bridge too far.

* David Butler, "Touch of Kenton: Jazz in 1950s Film Noir," in *Jazz Noir: Listening to Music from Phantom Lady to The Last Seduction*, 1st ed. (Westport, Conn: Praeger, 2002), 107.

[26] Chris Connor, *Atlantic 1228*. Released in 1956, this album became one of Ran's favorites.

[27] Gretsch Birdland drums epitomized the "great Gretsch sound" endorsed by many jazz players, including Art Blakey, Mel Lewis, and Max Roach. The Gretsch company was founded in 1883 in Brooklyn by a German immigrant, Fredrich Gretsch, who was only twenty-seven at the time. The company grew slowly and surely, but when Frederich died suddenly twelve years later, his young son Fred, then fifteen, took over. Young Fred had "remarkable" business sense, and before long, the company was prospering and expanding. Fred Gretsch began to sell his drums with their name on them. His son, Fred Gretsch Jr., who became president of the company after his father retired in 1942, was also very experienced, having joined the company at ten years of age. Fred Gresch Jr. made a point of going to clubs to find out what drummers actually wanted. New products that featured portability and quick set-up were the result. When Gretsch drums were at their peak, they were promoting "Gretsch Drum Nights" at Birdland. These nights broke all attendance records there for many years. They were the inspiration for a new drum kit—the Gretsch Birdland. Made in a limited edition in the fifties, these drums had a "Cadillac Green" lacquer finish with gold-plated hardware.

"Gretsch Drums," in *Guide to Vintage Drums*, by John Aldridge (Hal Leonard Corporation, 1994), 47–54.

[28] Ahrens, Gil Jr. to Janet McFadden, "Information for Ran Blake Biography," August 31, 2013.

[29] Gil Ahrens to Janet McFadden, "More Information for Ran Blake Biography," September 9, 2013.

[30] *Billboard* reports that out of the eight "name" bands booked during the Compounce season that year, Stan Kenton and Vaughan Munroe were the only ones to draw outstanding crowds.

Kenton also appeared on the Bob Snyder show at Lake Compounce during the 1950s. This would have coincided with the period when Ran was "flipping records" at the Belmont Store—where he first came to love Kenton's music.

Joseph G. Csida, "Compounce Beats 1950 by 25-30%," *The Billboard*, October 27, 1951.

[31] Kay Fisk was the mother of Ran and Marte's friend Sandi.

[32] Suffield Academy had two Principals: Konrad Hahn and Appleton Seaverns (who had been a student of Ran's father at Deerfield and whose wife, Jeanice, according to Ran, "DID like my music").

Jeanice Hodges Seaverns (1919–1987) devoted her life from 1952 to 1972 to Suffield Academy (the years her husband, "Ap"—Appleton—was headmaster). Ran is quoted as saying: "I remember as if yesterday so many talks I had with Jeanice Seaverns and the encouragement she and Ap gave me. I vividly recall a conversation with Jeanice, which took place at the Baptist church, when she exhorted me never to give up my peculiar brand of music. She said, 'You will never experience the deep satisfactions or creativity and accomplishment if you do not begin establishing goals at this time, and you must acquire the courage to continue this work, even without the encouragement and support of your peers.'" (Written in a tribute piece. Source: Ran's papers.)

[33] Byron Coley, "Ran Blake," *The Wire Magazine*, July 2009, https://www.thewire.co.uk/issues/305. (used with permission).

[34] Ran remembers the Episcopal church, where he "was always welcome," as being near the junior high school.

[35] This album was named by the mission's officer at Bard (Buz Gummere).

[36] R: But I think you should both remind me—I should do a record called *Springfield*.

L: You should write some new songs for it. One could be called "Mulberry St Cemetery."

R: Yes, I'd love that.

Chapter 11: Early Teachers and Strange Chords

1. "History of Film," in *Encyclopedia Britannica*, accessed March 15, 2021, https://www.britannica.com/art/history-of-the-motion-picture.

2. *South Pacific* was performed first on Broadway in early 1949, starring (originally) Mary Martin and Ezio Pinza.

3. *Annie Get Your Gun* premiered on Broadway in 1946, with Ethel Merman starred as Annie. She also starred in the 1966 Broadway revival of the show.

4. This was a disc player introduced by the Victor Talking Machine Company. Instead of having the horn outside the cabinet, it was now inside and completely invisible.

5. George Ives, at age seventeen, was a US Army bandleader in the Union army in the American Civil War. Though devoted to music, this path was not approved by his family, and he eventually had to settle for working in a bank. He did, however, greatly influence the musical education of his son, Charles Ives.

Though also not fully recognized in his lifetime, Charles Ives came to be known as an American modernist composer of renown. His music referred to popular tunes, marches, classical music, and to the church music of the "camp meetings" that his father led for Methodist religious festivals. George influenced his son in an open-minded approach to musical theory, encouraging experimentations in bitonal and polytonal harmonizations.

J. Ryan Garber, "The Influence of George Ives on His Son Charles," ryangarber.com, 2008, http://www.ryangarber.com/ives.html.

6. Here, Ran is most probably referring to the second movement of *Three Places in New England*, "Putnam's Camp, Redding, Connecticut" by Charles Ives.

7. Joe Maneri—American jazz composer. He played saxophone and clarinet. He founded the Boston Microtonal Society, which was dedicated to microtonal music and tunings.

8. Janet Wallace's brother, Dudley, had gone to Williams College with Philip Blake.

9. Byron Coley, "Ran Blake Interview Transcript–The Wire," The Wire Magazine, July 2009, https://www.thewire.co.uk/in-writing/interviews/ran-blake-interview-transcript.

10. Coley.

11. 297 Asylum Street. See also: Jane E. Dee, "Once a Hartford Hot Spot, Building's Soon to Be History," *Hartford Courant*, March 26, 1996, online edition, https://www.courant.com/news/connecticut/hc-xpm-1996-03-26-9603260695-story.html.

12. Ray Cassarino died on February 22, 2008, aged 86.

13. See Part II, chapter 7, "Teachers."

Chapter 12: The Church on Russell Street

[1] The Hartford church was the Church on Russell Street which features on the 1962 groundbreaking album, *The Newest Sound Around*. [Lee, Jeanne, and Ran Blake. The Newest Sound Around. Vinyl LP, Album. US: RCA Victor, 1962.]

[2] Eunice's daughter and son-in-law, Ethel and Nathanial Wilson, were members of the Pentecostal church.

[3] Mother Sarah Carter, who Ran regarded as a mentor and mother figure ("I was twenty when she was fifty."), was a lifetime member of the Holy Trinity Church of God in Christ, Hartford (now Latter Rain Christian Fellowship, Hartford). Her photo hangs at the bottom of Ran's entrance stairway. She died on August 4, 2001, at the age of ninety-seven.

[4] Bishop I.L. Jefferson was a father figure, along with Buz Gummere from Bard, Willis Laurence James from Lenox, and, of course, Gunther Schuller. Ran adds to this: "and George Russell. There were four or five very important people—just like, for women, Dorothy Wallace and other people..."

[5] Mother Lula Jefferson was well known and loved in Greater Hartford for her work for the church on a state and international level. She died on March 23, 1998, at the age of ninety-six. Her death notice appeared in the Hartford Courant [http://articles.courant.com/1998-03-23/news/9803230077_1_mother-jefferson-christ-god]

[6] In addition to Ran's "father figure," Bishop I.L. Jefferson, and his mentor, Mother Sarah Carter, Sisters Edith Powell and Eunice Glover were prominent members of the Holy Trinity Church of God in Christ, Hartford, CT.
(Eunice Glover joined Mother Sarah Carter as musical director in 1959. She was a composer. In 1962, she abruptly left the church and the music slowly declined.

[7] Ran has performed "There's Been a Change" throughout his career. He has also recorded it on the following albums: New England Conservatory and Ran Blake, *Third Stream Today*, LP, Album (US: New England Conservatory, 1979); Ran Blake and Houston Person, *Suffield Gothic*, LP, Album (Italy: Soul Note, 1984); Ran Blake, *Driftwoods*, CD Album (US: Tompkins Square, 2009); Ran Blake and Claire Ritter, *Eclipse Orange*, CD Album (US: Zoning Recordings, 2019); Ran Blake and Andrew Rathbun, *Northern Noir*, CD Album (Denmark: SteepleChase, 2020).

[8] Hubert Powell and the Heavenly Choir of the Holy Trinity Church of God in Christ, Hartford, CT. appeared in a Jordan Hall concert on April 14, 1976. According to Ran, this second time "might have been even more exciting musically, but we only brought one busload."

[9] Ran describes her voice as: "rich contralto that cuts even more deeply into this 'blues tonality' [which he feels distinguishes gospel music from the older African American spiritual] than Ray Charles or Bessie Smith. She is altogether a personal singer." Ran describes her tone as "purely held with the vibrato emerging just before its release."

[10] American jazz saxophonist, singer, and composer, recording during the free jazz era of the 1960s.

[11] Ran's papers.

[12] Blake, Ran. notes, no date, unpublished. The structure was as Ran has recorded in his notes as follows:

A Solo

A(i) Piano RIFF

B Choir

A Soloist

Call and response

A/B/drum break/solo break (no rhythm section

A/DB/SB/B/A/B/B/organ piano riff/B/Close

"Sections were shortened as they repeated. Later music by Sister Glover became even more harmonically challenging, and the choir responded so well and with such a high degree of <u>intuitive understanding</u> [These last two words were underlined] that we were constantly amazed. Later I moved to New York and would return to the church a few times and be constantly amazed at Sr. Glover's growing maturity as a composer."

(filed with Ran's papers.)

[13] Joe Hardin– An African American singer and friend of Ran's, who appears on the cover of Suffield Gothic (front, far left-hand side). Hardin "had played and sung with Ellington maybe two weeks of his life."

Ran Blake to Janet McFadden, "Joe Hardin," October 5, 2019.

[14] Ran recalls she slapped him when he playfully pulled the pigtail of the girl sitting in front of him. "I think I was going to use the pigtail to help me stand up—to shout, 'Hallelujah.'" (At this time, Ran would have been around fifteen.)

[15] Reading the chapter, Ran makes a suggestion: "Maybe you should tell the readers that, although she's there in my thoughts, there is also the physical imprint of a wonderful photo… it's sounding very Ran Blake-ish, but maybe that should be a footnote. She and Dorothy, Thelonious Monk, and Mr. Gummere, and Gunther are often… they always say… 'take care of the stairs and remember your ancestors.'"

[16] Written by Ran and filed in his papers.

[17] Ibid.

[18] David (Knife) Fabris: New England Conservatory graduate (1990 BM), guitarist and educator. Frequent collaborator with Ran Blake.

[19] James Alonzo Harris: New England Conservatory graduate (2006 MM. IMPG), singer, pianist and composer.

[20] Gil Ahrens, "Reflections for Ran Blake Biography," June 12, 2016.

[21] Ran Blake, "Filed Document," July 21, 1999, Ran Blake's private archive.

[22] Owen McNally, "Bassist Fred Tinsley Comes Back to UConn to Receive

Award," *Hartford Courant*, April 25, 2010, Online edition, http://www.hartford-info.org/issues/documents/artsandculture/htfd_courant_042510.asp.

[23] The opening minutes of the Robert Siodmak thriller *The Spiral Staircase* confront the audience with the terrifying closeup of a menacing eye, watching a defenseless young woman from behind the clothes in her closet.

[24] Historic Inn in Main Street, Sturbridge, Massachusetts. It was opened in 1771 for the convenience of travelers on the Boston Post Road. It has provided hospitality for travelers ever since.

[25] Scott Allen Sandvik: New England Conservatory graduate (1987 BM. TSTR. 1989 MM. TSTR), guitarist, educator, and former NEC faculty member.

[26] Sandi Peaslee taught choral and theory groups at Lexington High School for 29 years until her retirement in 1993.

Rev. Dr. Wendy von Courter was the Minister who presided at Sandi Peaslee's memorial service at the Unitarian Universalist Church of Marblehead in April 2016

Chapter 13: Jazz Clubs of Hartford, Connecticut

[1] The term "The Golden Age of Jazz" was coined by writer-photographer William Gottlieb and is the title of his book of recollections and photographs of jazz musicians during the late 1930s and throughout the 1940s. [William P. Gottlieb, *The Golden Age of Jazz: Text and Photographs* (Pomegranate, 1995).]

[2] Owen McNally, "Bassist Fred Tinsley Comes Back to UConn to Receive Award," *Hartford Courant*, April 25, 2010, Online edition, http://www.hartford-info.org/issues/documents/artsandculture/htfd_courant_042510.asp.

[3] McNally.

[4] Wooster street ran parallel to Bellevue Street and Canton Street joined the two at their southern end. Bellevue Square Park occupied a large parcel of land between Wooster and Bellevue Streets. These intersections have since been remodeled as part of an urban renewal project.

[5] McNally, "Bassist Fred Tinsley Comes Back to UConn to Receive Award."

[6] M Oakley Stafford, writing in The Hartford Courant (1923–1984), posted an article on June 30, 1950, that placed the Horace Silver Trio at the Club Sundown. On June 1, 1956, Stafford wrote an article informing readers that the club was introducing New York and Las Vegas entertainers and "packing them in." These were articles posted in the newspaper's "society" and "entertainment" columns, and the events at the smaller clubs were largely advertised by word-of-mouth. The Bushnell and The State Theater events were advertised in feature articles and were thus more widely known.

M Oakley Stafford, "Informing You," *Hartford Courant*, June 30, 1950; M Oakley Stafford, "Informing You," *Hartford Courant*, June 1, 1956.

Owen McNally, writing a "Special to the Courant–Pianist Emery Smith To Close

'Baby Grand' Jazz Series" on April 22, 2012, acknowledges the dual purpose of these clubs: "The club scene included not just name artists coming to town from Boston or New York—like Charlie "Bird" Parker ascending at Club Sundown—but also the rich lode of homegrown Hartford players."

Owen McNally, "Pianist Emery Smith To Close 'Baby Grand' Jazz Series," Hartford Courant, April 22, 2012, Online edition, https://www.courant.com/hc-xpm-2012-04-22-hc-emery-smith-0422-20120422-story.html.

[7] See following chapter—*Records, Records, Records*. This happened during Ran's Junior Year at Bard; the job, for him, was part of a work placement requirement for Bard College.

[8] Judy Grisamore to Janet McFadden, "Ran Blake Biography," April 23, 2011.

[9] Judy Grisamore to Janet McFadden, "Ran Blake Biography," February 9, 2012.

[10] Owen McNally, "Hartford Jazz Society: At 25, Silver and Swinging," *Hartford Courant*, October 6, 1985.

[11] The grand Victorian-style Heublein Hotel was torn down in 1965 to make way for Bushnell Towers.

Owen McNally, "Jazz: The Fine Art of Art Fine," Hartford Courant, January 4, 2008.

[12] *The Adajian's* at 297 Asylum Street closed in 1986 after 40 years as a family restaurant. An article (by Jane E. Dee) in the *Hartford Courant* on March 26, 1996 (the day that the historic brick building with its "red mosaic facade" was to be demolished), describes the restaurant and how the Adajian family were hoping to be at the demolition to rescue the charcoal and yellow-colored mosaic that spelled out the family's name.

In the Courant article, former band leader Paul Landerman remembers that the restaurant: "had excellent Armenian food" and a "very high-class clientele." He also remembered the unusual murals (by Thurston Wells Munson) that were "pretty hot stuff in those days" (Art Deco-style murals, featuring the naked "golden woman" of Hartford with her ice-blue eyes.) These murals were particularly memorable, it seems, because they were well lit, while the lounge was kept dark.

Jane E. Dee, "Once a Hartford Hot Spot, Building's Soon to Be History," *Hartford Courant*, March 26, 1996, online edition, https://www.courant.com/news/connecticut/hc-xpm-1996-03-26-9603260695-story.html.

[13] Barbara and Sandi were friends of Ran's sister, Marte.

[14] "According to Byron Coley, this was the club where he had his first "rum and Coke."

Byron Coley, "Ran Blake," *The Wire Magazine*, July 2009, 26.

[15] Earlier, Ran had wondered whether this "first drink" was enjoyed at Elks or at the Jinxey Club in Springfield.

[16] Ernie Wilson was completing his studies at the University of Connecticut, leading to an engineering degree and a job as a Flight Test Engineer.

[17] Ernest Wilson to Janet McFadden, "Ran Blake Biography," August 11, 2013.

[18] Erroll Garner (1923–1977) was an American jazz pianist and composer. His best-known composition was "Misty." Ran first got to know him during his last year at Bard, at the Lenox School of Jazz.
"I hated that his soft drink was 7up instead of ginger ale or Coke. I thought 7up was just liquid sugar. I said, 'Wouldn't you like something stronger?'
He said, 'Horrifying thought—give me a 7up.' I thought he'd want a little nip."

[19] Bellevue Square Park

[20] *Jazz at the Philharmonic: The Ella Fitzgerald Set* was re-issued in 2016 on the Verve Label. Tracks 16 and 17: "Bill," written by Jerome Kern and P.G. Wodehouse, and "Why Don't You Do Right?" written by Joe McCoy, were recorded at Bushnell Memorial Hall, Hartford on September 19, 1953. Tracks 18 to 22 were also (in all probability) recorded there on September 17, 1954.

[21] Vassar—a private college in Poughkeepsie.

[22] *Suffield Gothic* was recorded at the end of September 1983 and released on the Italian label *Soul Note*.

[23] Wil de Sola and his Modern Jazz Trio represented Trinity at the Bard Jazz Festival, held in November 1958.

Chapter 14: Records, Records, Records

[1] The Belmont record store (owned in Ran's time by French Canadian Joe Cyr) was opened on Putnam Street in 1943 but moved to the corner of Park and Washington Streets around 1955. The store gradually switched to country music, which was the owner's preference.
[Andrea Comer, "Belmont Spins into History," *Hartford Courant*, May 21, 1998, online edition, https://www.courant.com/news/connecticut/hc-xpm-1998-05-21-9805210530-story.html.]

[2] Prestige Records (initially called New Jazz) was a jazz label founded in 1949 by Bob Weinstock.

[3] A distance of two to three miles.

[4] S.S. Pierce and Co, general grocers and importers of fine foods, had their beginnings in Boston in 1831 with Pierce and his partner, Eldad Worcester, selling staple provisions to the ships that came to Boston's harbor. Soon they began exchanging the provisions for fine foods from distant places and by 1886 were well known as S.S. Pierce and Co., Importers and Grocers. They were appreciated for their wide variety of exotic goods (including truffles, pâté de pheasant, pickled reindeer tongue, and turtle soup) and also for excellent personal service. They eventually operated eight stores of their own across New England and supplied America through 3,500 distributors and via a mail order service. The

store at Coolidge Corner, Brookline, was opened in 1898. They supplied groceries (including their own label of canned goods); fancy goods, such as wine and cigars; and toiletries (with a remarkable "list of odors.") The stores had their own "cheese counter," which offered a large variety of foreign cheeses, American cheeses as well stocking soft French cheeses which were received fresh "every other morning."

Anthony Sammarco, "S. S. Pierce: A Boston Tradition" (Filmed keynote, Boston Athenæum, September 28, 2015), https://vimeo.com/140696028.

5   Ran would have known of her work at the Human Rights Commission. He had written to her twice before receiving the invitation in 1959.

Eleanor Roosevelt was elected head of the United Nations Human Rights Commission in 1946. Her work there included the drafting of the Declaration of Human Rights. In 1952, she resigned from the United Nations position but was re-appointed by J.F. Kennedy in 1961.

6   The letter of invitation was dated October 12, 1959—for a lunch appointment on November 21. Ran was required to ring closer to the time to find where the lunch would be held, as Mrs. Roosevelt was "in the process of changing address." Hyde Park was the hometown of Franklin D. Roosevelt. It was where the Roosevelt family estate and home, "Springwood," was located, approximately 90 miles north of New York City, in the northwest part of Dutchess County, New York State. Val-kill (Dutch for waterfall and stream) was a part of this estate, set aside by Roosevelt as a retreat for his wife, Eleanor. The second cottage on this estate, Val-kill cottage (which incorporated the furniture factory Eleanor had established in the hope of training locals in skills that could supplement their incomes), became very dear to Eleanor Roosevelt. It was the place where she did much of her work and entertained many dignitaries. It was her permanent home after President Roosevelt's death. Throughout her life, Eleanor Roosevelt was a staunch advocate of the Civil Rights Movement.

7   Kay Bourne was a journalist and educator who devoted her working life to the promotion and integration of African Americans. Through her efforts, African Americans became an important part of Boston Arts. Ran knew her well through his work with the Community Services Department at New England Conservatory, and she knew many of the people in that department, particularly Kay Nurse.

8   Bard College integrated work-experience for students in fields connected with their study. In January 1959, again as part of such a field project, Ran had a six-week placement at Atlantic records. It was during this time that Ran would encounter his future mentor, Gunther Schuller.

9   Many years later (when she was a teacher of gifted minority children in Chicago), Ran came to talk to Judy's students about his music and to urge some of them to try [out] for a scholarship at New England Conservatory.

10   Judy Grisamore to Janet McFadden, "Ran Blake Biography," February 9, 2012; Judy Grisamore to Janet McFadden, "Ran Blake Biography," April 23, 2011.

11   Grisamore to McFadden, "Ran Blake Biography," February 9, 2012.

[12] The transition from school to college was not a smooth one for Ran. It was always expected that he would attend college, but after graduating from Suffield Academy—having completed an extra college preparation year—the path ahead was not clear. The College enrollment boom in the years after World War II had seen the necessity to formalize the College admissions process, and by the mid-1950s, college entrance requirements included high school diplomas and rank, recommendations, personal interviews, and a standardized test which, up to 1957, required students to answer up to 170 verbal questions in under 100 minutes—a daunting task, especially for someone whose handwriting was very difficult to read.

Jillian Kinzie et al., "Fifty Years of College Choice: Social, Political and Institutional Influences on the Decision-Making Process," *Lumina Foundation for Education*, New Agenda Series, 5, no. 3 (January 9, 2004).

CHAPTER 15: CIVIL RIGHTS AND ELEANOR ROOSEVELT

[1] Owen McNally, "Pianist Emery Smith To Close 'Baby Grand' Jazz Series," *Hartford Courant*, April 22, 2012, Online edition, https://www.courant.com/hc-xpm-2012-04-22-hc-emery-smith-0422-20120422-story.html.

[2] Brown v. the Board of Education of Topeka, Kansas, when Rev. Oliver Brown protested the fact that his eight-year-old daughter did not have access to a school (designated 'whites only') which was closer to her home than the one she was obliged to attend.

Juan Williams, *Eyes on the Prize: America's Civil Rights Years, 1954-1965* (New York, NY: Penguin, 2002).

[3] Claudette Colvin was a fifteen-year-old girl who was a member of the National Association for the Advancement of Colored People (NAACP). Her protest preceded Rosa Parks' by nine months, but as she was unmarried, pregnant, and "feisty," it was felt this might jeopardize the outcome of any court challenge to the segregation laws. But Colvin agreed to join other women who had followed her in resisting the segregation policy in Alabama—Aurelia Browder, Susie McDonald, Mary Louise Smith, and Jeanette Reese—as plaintiffs in a federal civil action, which effectively bypassed the Alabama courts. Jeanette Reese dropped out of the case because of intimidation, but in June 1956, the District Court ruled that the segregation on the Montgomery buses violated the constitution. After appeals by the state of Alabama and the city of Montgomery, the Supreme Court upheld the District Court's ruling in November 1956.

[4] Instigated by the Women's Political Council, led by Jo Ann Gibson Robinson, the boycott meant that the black community of Montgomery avoided the buses. As they made up three-quarters of all passengers, this was significant economic pressure for the bus company. The boycott was initially only intended for one day (the day of Rosa Parks' trial), but with Martin Luther King Jr.'s encouragement, the boycott lasted over one year.

[5] Owen McNally, "Bassist Fred Tinsley Comes Back to UConn to Receive Award," *Hartford Courant*, April 25, 2010, Online edition, http://www.hartford-info.org/issues/documents/artsandculture/htfd_courant_042510.asp.

[6] The march on Washington on August 28, 1963, when Martin Luther King Jr. spoke to a crowd of 250,000 civil rights supporters gathered at the Lincoln memorial. It was a critical point in the civil rights movement and illustrated its gathering momentum.

[7] McNally, "Bassist Fred Tinsley Comes Back to UConn to Receive Award."

[8] Byron Coley, "Ran Blake Interview Transcript–The Wire," The Wire Magazine, July 2009, https://www.thewire.co.uk/in-writing/interviews/ran-blake-interview-transcript.

[9] Ran had also written to Eleanor Roosevelt in 1958, inviting her to the 2nd Bard Jazz Festival in November of that year. She answered on April 28, saying that she wished she could attend but regretted that her calendar was "filled for November." She wished him success in the venture and said she appreciated his "thought in writing me."

[10] Eleanor Roosevelt established Val-Kill Industries on the Roosevelt family estate in Hyde Park, New York, in 1927. It was meant to provide supplementary income for local farmers (by making colonial-type crafts and furniture). The business was dissolved in 1938, and Eleanor then used the property as a retreat and a place to entertain guests.

"Val-Kill," Franklin D. Roosevelt Presidential Library and Museum, August 28, 2012, https://fdrlibrary.wordpress.com/tag/val-kill/.

[11] It was, in fact, November 1959.

[12] On October 1, 2020, Ran emailed to ask if he had told me what Eleanor Roosevelt had advised him to do. She had told him that he must "persevere, use caution at times, be brave and bold and LISTEN." (Upper case is Ran's.)

Ran Blake to Janet McFadden, "Eleanor r," October 1, 2020.

[13] See Chapter 8: "Celebration—A Perspective on Joy"

[14] While there is no detail of what was played, it can be noted that Ran and Jeanne Lee had, soon after they met at Bard College, recorded a demonstration tape which included "Jeepers Creepers." around 1956. Around this period, Ran also recorded with Annette Stevens (originally Annette Stefopoulos) from Springfield.

Byron Coley, "Ran Blake," *The Wire Magazine*, July 2009, 28.

[15] At this time, King had been newly elected as leader of the non-violent direct action group, which would eventually be called the Southern Christian Leadership Conference (SCLC).

[16] Martin Luther King Jr., WMAQ Radio Interview, interview by Etta Moten Barnett, March 6, 1957, https://kinginstitute.stanford.edu/king-papers/documents/interview-etta-moten-barnett.

The Early Years

[17] They were guests of Prime Minister Jawaharlal Nehru and discussed Mahatma Gandhi's non-violent resistance.

Martin Luther King Jr., "My Trip to the Land of Gandhi," *Ebony*, 1959, The Martin Luther King, Jr. Research and Education Institute.

[18] On February 1, 1960, four young students from the (all black) North Carolina Agricultural and Technical College commenced a non-violent protest aimed at Woolworths' segregationist policies. Denied service at the lunch counter (the shop was open to all, but the lunch counter was whites only), they stayed in their seats until the store closed and returned the next day with more students to support them. The events were covered on television, and by February 5, 300 students were involved in the sit-in. The sit-ins spread to 55 cities and 13 states, bringing the spotlight onto the segregation that existed in many public facilities at the time. The sit-in in Greensboro led to Woolworths abandoning the policy of racial segregation that had existed in their stores in the southern states.

[19] The Sharpeville massacre (March 21, 1960) occurred when 300 South African police opened fire on a crowd of at least 5000, demonstrating against a law that required blacks to carry passbooks if ever they left their designated areas. One hundred eighty were injured, and 69 were killed. The shootings were followed by world-wide protests and condemnation by the United Nations. Since 1994, the date has been commemorated in South Africa as "Human Rights Day."

The Sharpeville Massacre by Matthew McRae, Canadian Museum for Human Rights

https://humanrights.ca/story/the-sharpeville-massacre

[20] Max Roach, *We Insist! Max Roach's Freedom Now Suite* (US: Candid, 1961).

Chapter 16: Bard College

[1] Williams was founded in 1793, and Bard was founded in 1860.

[2] This would have been greater than the median yearly household income at that time.

[3] Buz Gummere was director of admissions at Bard College 1950–1961. Ran points out that he "was really 'junior.'—Richard Gummere Jr.—His father, Richard Gummere, was director of admissions at Harvard and the grandfather was also the director of admissions at Harvard."

Frances Powers, Ran's aunt, was a graduate of Smith College, Northampton (class of 1923) and became director of Alumnae House and vice-chairman of the Board of Counselors.

[4] David Robison, Avron Soyer, and Ernest Singer, eds., "Interview with Mr. Gummere: Admissions, Reputation, Change...," *Bard Comment*, 1957, 4.

[5] Black Mountain College was a liberal arts college in rural North Carolina. It saw the study of the arts as central to the learning experience while also expect-

ing participation and involvement in the practical running of the college (e.g., through maintenance and work on the college farm). It was progressive and experimental and became renowned for its musicians, performers, visual artists, and writers. It closed in 1957.

"The Artists of Black Mountain College," American Masters, PBS, October 16, 2006, https://www.pbs.org/wnet/americanmasters/artists-black-mountain-college/5719/.

[6] Robison, Soyer, and Singer, "Interview with Mr. Gummere: Admissions, Reputation, Change...," 11.

[7] This was reversed in 1944 when Bard became co-educational.

"Bard College Celebrates 150th Anniversary and President Leon Botstein's 35 Years Of Leadership with Jubilee Gala," Institution webpage, Bard News, November 3, 2010, http://www.bard.edu/news/releases/pr/fstory.php?id=2006.

[8] Werner Wolff (1904–1957) was interested in how the conscious and the subconscious self align. He taught at Bard from 1942 to his death in 1957.

[9] According to the Bardian: "She was a student of Leonid Kreutzer and Walter Braunfels in Munich and soloist with the Berlin Philharmonic orchestra" Donn O'Meara et al., eds., "Guest Soloist," *The Bardian* 11, no. 9 (April 10, 1946): 4.

[10] Scott Pass and Christina Griffith, eds., "Kate Wolff: Reminiscences," *The Bard Observer* 1, no. 7 (November 12, 1984): 9.

[11] Pass and Griffith.

[12] Pass and Griffith.

[13] Pass and Griffith.

[14] Pass and Griffith.

[15] Mrs. Curt-Marie Crane was Assistant Director of Admissions

[16] Nadia Boulanger was a French composer, conductor, and teacher who had a significant influence on 20th-century composers. She was devoted to education and taught for 70 years—right up to her death, aged 92.

[17] Walter Piston was a classical composer and music theorist. He studied composition and counterpoint with Nadia Boulanger. Upon his return to the United States, he taught music at Harvard University for 34 years. Clair Leonard taught music and French at Harvard during this period.

[18] Charles Hollander, ed., "Clair Leonard Dies at 62," *The Bard Observer* 5, no. 7 (March 4, 1963): 1.

[19] Clair Leonard, "Concerning Attitudes and Standards," ed. John Deimel et al., *Bard Week* 1, no. 8 (June 6): 3.

[20] Paul Hindemith was an early 20th-century German composer, musician, teacher, conductor, and musical theorist. He sought to revitalize tonality and opposed the 12-tone school of Schoenberg.

[21] Ralph Ellison, *Invisible Man* (New York, NY: Random House, 1952).

The Early Years

[22] The Brown vs. Board of Education was a landmark civil rights case in Topeka, Kansas, which challenged segregation in public schools and ruled that such segregation was a violation of the 14th amendment and thus unconstitutional.

[23] Emmett Till was a 14-year-old Chicago boy who had been visiting relatives in Money, Mississippi. He was tortured and killed after supposedly speaking in a familiar fashion to a white woman in a local grocery store.

[24] Buz Gummere took on Ran's case and wrote to the President of Bard College for him.

[25] John Hammond was a record producer and talent scout who was responsible for furthering the musical careers of Billie Holiday, Count Basie, Teddy Wilson, Pete Seeger, Aretha Franklin, Bob Dylan, Bruce Springsteen, among many others. He was a crusader for racial integration in the music industry.

[26] Albert McCarthy was the editor of *Jazz Monthly* (later, *Jazz and Blues*) from 1955 to 1972.

[27] The village of Red Hook lies three and a half miles to the southeast of the Campus. The theatre there was the "Lyceum." "The Starr" at Rhinebeck was not far away—together, they operated as the "Lyceum-Starr."

[28] The Hitchcock film, Vertigo was released in the U.S.A. on May 9, 1958.

[29] When Guy Ducornet first contacted us to contribute his memories for this book, it was December 2008, and Guy was working on his recollections of Ralph Ellison. (In 1959-60, when Guy was a Fulbright Scholar who had come to Bard College from the Sorbonne—Ellison was his adviser and teacher.) Later, in 2012, Guy Ducornet published his book *Annandale Blues: A Journey in Ralph Ellison's America.* (Chicago: Charles H. Kerr, 2012). His memories of Ran, as quoted here, also appear in Ch. 19 (pp.153 - 160) of *Annandale Blues.*

[30] Bard Jazz Lab included fellow students K. Walsh, B. Meredith, G. Quimby, C. Maynard, T. Gummere, and O. Nichols. The group played in Bard Hall in 1956 (with the assistance of a dog called Count Basie).

[31] He had been supported by a letter from Buz Gummere to the President of Bard, petitioning, on his behalf, for a Jazz Department.

[32] The first Bard Jazz Festival was held in 1957 and was such a success that Ran organized subsequent festivals in his Junior and Senior years. David R. Moulton, "Jazz Takes Over at Bard for a Day," ed. Naomi Parver, *The Bardian* 1, no. 2 (November 16, 1959): 2. http://www.bard.edu/bardmakesnoise/pdfs/jazz-bardian1959.pdf

Also, Naomi Parver, "Bard Jazz Festival Scores Big Success," *The Bardian* 1, no. 1 (November 26, 1958): 4. http://www.bard.edu/library/archive/newspapers/students/Bardian/1958/BA58_11_26.pdf

[33] Tony Scott was a jazz clarinetist. During the 1950s, he worked with Sarah Vaughan and Billie Holiday, as well as a young Bill Evans. Around the time of the Bard Jazz Festival, he had won the critics poll from *Down Beat* magazine four times (1955, 1957, 1958, 1959.)

34 Parver, "Bard Jazz Festival Scores Big Success."

Chapter 17: Jeanne Lee

1 Bill Coss, "The Agonies of Exploration-Jeanne Lee and Ran Blake," *DownBeat*, September 13, 1962.

2 Art Lange, "Ran Blake's Third Stream," *Downbeat*, February 1980.

3 Matana Roberts, "Ran Blake: From Music to Film and Back Article @ All About Jazz," All About Jazz, January 9, 2004, https://www.allaboutjazz.com/ran-blake-from-music-to-film-and-back-ran-blake-by-aaj-staff.php.

4 Byron Coley, in his article in *The Wire*, says it was $100. [Byron Coley, "Ran Blake," *The Wire*, July 2009.]
Coss, "The Agonies of Exploration-Jeanne Lee and Ran Blake." says the recording was part of a series of audition records/tapes.

5 Coley, "Ran Blake."

6 Coss, "The Agonies of Exploration-Jeanne Lee and Ran Blake.".

7 National Association for the Advancement of Colored People.

8 Naomi Parver, ed., "Ran Blake Plays at Notre Dame Festival," The Bardian 2, no. 3 (March 22, 1960): 1,6.
The Festival Program for March 18–19, 1960, is archived at:
"Collegiate Jazz Festival 1960" (University of Notre Dame, March 18, 1960), Full Text Publications; Student Life, University of Notre Dame Archives, http://archives.nd.edu/ndcjf/dcjf1960.pdf.
Ran's recollection of this event is, however, that he was "highly condemned" and that the "only sympathetic panel member was Bob Share of Berklee, and perhaps Charles Suber of *DownBeat*." (Bob Share was administrator of the Berklee School, Boston, and Charles Suber was publisher of *DownBeat* magazine at the time.)

9 November 15, 16, and December, 7 1961—recorded at RCA Victor's Studio A, New York City
Jeanne Lee and Ran Blake, *The Newest Sound Around,* Vinyl LP, Album (US: RCA Victor, 1962).

10 Edgar Allan Poe lived for a time in Carmine St, overlooking St John's Graveyard (which has since been converted into a small park—James J. Walker Park—between Leroy, Hudson, and Clarkson Streets). It was here, perhaps inspired by the graveyard, that he wrote *The Narrative of Arthur Gordon Pym; The Murders in the Rue Morgue*; and, one of Ran's favorites, *The Gold Bug*.
Henry James was born in Washington Place, and his novel *Washington Square* was inspired by the house at 18 Washington Square North, where his grand-

mother lived.

Mark Twain also lived in Greenwich Village (Fifth Ave.).

"Greenwich Village Historic District Designation Report" (New York: Landmarks Preservation Commission, 1969), http://s-media.nyc.gov/agencies/lpc/lp/0489.pdf.

[11] The first racially integrated nightclub in the United States—Café Society—opened in 1938 at 1 Sheridan Square. It was here, in 1939, that Billie Holiday first performed "Strange Fruit." Sarah Vaughan's career was also launched here. The club also hosted political events and fundraisers in the quest for integration. The club closed (following poor publicity and suspicion of left-wing views) soon after World War II.

[12] Bill Dixon was an American musician, composer, and visual artist who strongly influenced the free jazz movement. He was a professor of music at Bennington College, Vermont, from 1968–1995.

[13] See later chapter: "The Apollo."

[14] Coss, "The Agonies of Exploration-Jeanne Lee and Ran Blake."

[15] They were programmed to appear on the evening of Friday, April 6—the second act after intermission, following the North Texas State University Big Band and under the name of "The Jeanne Lee - Ran Blake Duo, Columbia University." There was a very simple bio: "Ran Blake appeared in CJF '60 as a piano soloist. This year he has added vocalist Jeanne Lee."

"Collegiate Jazz Festival 1962" (University of Notre Dame, July 6, 1962), Full Text Publications; Student Life, University of Notre Dame Archives, http://archives.nd.edu/ndcjf/dcjf1962.pdf.

[16] "Collegiate Jazz Festival 1962."

[17] Coss, "The Agonies of Exploration-Jeanne Lee and Ran Blake."

[18] Coley, "Ran Blake," 28.

[19] Byron Coley, "Ran Blake Interview Transcript-The Wire," The Wire Magazine, July 2009, https://www.thewire.co.uk/in-writing/interviews/ran-blake-interview-transcript.

[20] There were three albums with Jeanne: *The Newest Sound Around* (Later reissued on CD as *The Legendary Duets*); *You Stepped Out of a Cloud* (1989); as well as *Free Standards, Stockholm 1966*. A fourth double album of previously unreleased material (recorded in Europe in 1966 and 1967) was released in 2018 on the a-side records label under the title *The Newest Sound You Never Heard*.

Chapter 18: Those Summers at Lenox

[1] Americans, still grieving from the war, endured further casualties and deaths in the Korean War. There was also a fear of communists, and anti-communism was a widely held sentiment.

[2] The Barbers, both public relations professionals who had a great knowledge and love of music, had purchased the outlying buildings of the Boston Symphony Orchestra's property "Tanglewood" with a view to opening up a place where music could be performed, enjoyed, and discussed. The buildings they bought had included the barn, where they opened their Music Inn in 1950.

[3] Marshall Stearns was an English professor and jazz historian. He is the author of *The Story of Jazz*, Oxford University Press, 1956.

[4] John Lewis—jazz pianist, composer, and arranger—was founder of the Modern Jazz Quartet and assumed a lot of responsibility for its direction (1952–1974 and then again 1981–1997, almost forty years in total).

Gunther Schuller, in his biography, recalls attending a couple of the "Folk and Jazz Roundtable" discussions in 1955, and soon after, John Lewis mentioned to him the possibility of creating the jazz school at Lenox and sought advice as to what form it should take. Gunther advised him to look no further than the neighboring Tanglewood, where the "master-apprentice" concept of bringing master musicians and talented students together was practiced. Schuller refined this basic concept by suggesting that master and "apprentice" should perform together in rehearsals and concerts.

Gunther Schuller, *Gunther Schuller: A Life in Pursuit of Music and Beauty* (Rochester, NY: University of Rochester Press, 2011), 487–88.

*References to Gunther Schuller's book are used with permission from University of Rochester Press, Boydell and Brewer Inc.

[5] Gunther Schuller was convinced of the need for required courses in composition, arranging, and jazz history.

Schuller, 488.

[6] Lenox School of Jazz, Inc., "Detailed Brochure," JazzMF, November 1, 1993, https://jazzmf.com/school-of-jazz-inc-detailed-brochure/.

[7] "Music Inn – The Lenox School of Jazz," lenoxhistory.org, February 11, 2016, https://lenoxhistory.org/lenoxhistorypeopleandplaces/music-inn-lenox-school-jazz/.

[8] George Schuller to Janet McFadden, "Lenox Chapter," February 17, 2020.

[9] "Music Inn – The Lenox School of Jazz."

[10] Wheatleigh was built in 1893 by financier, banker, and real estate tycoon Henry H. Cook to celebrate the wedding of his daughter Georgie to Spanish Count Carlos de Heredia. Though palatial in design, the family referred to Wheatleigh as their "summer cottage."

"About the Hotel - Wheatleigh Hotel," Business, Wheatleigh Hotel, 2020, https://wheatleigh.com/about-the-hotel/.

[11] Tanglewood was the summer home of the Boston Symphony Orchestra.

[12] Lenox Faculty has been listed by Michael Fitzgerald:

Michael Fitzgerald, "The Lenox School of Jazz," JazzMF, November 1, 1993, https://jazzmf.com/the-lenox-school-of-jazz/.

[13] This jazz theory book, written by George Russell, is frequently hailed as the first truly original work of jazz theory. Ran's quote comes from:

"In Memoriam: George Russell 1923-2009," All About Jazz, accessed November 10, 2020, https://www.allaboutjazz.com/in-memoriam-george-russell-1923-2009-george-russell-by-aaj-staff.php.

[14] Students took two private lessons per week. Ran recalls he took studio with Oscar Peterson during the first two years of Lenox.

[15] Stearns taught jazz history from 1957–1959. His lectures gave an overview based on his own collection of recordings. Gunther Schuller taught the History of Jazz Styles in 1959 and 1960. He "took a more musical view and delved into a comparison of styles rather than simply an historical overview."

Fitzgerald, "The Lenox School of Jazz."

[16] Michael Fitzgerald, on his website, also states that Jimmy Giuffre was involved with the composition classes. [Fitzgerald.]

[17] Fitzgerald.

[18] Ran Blake, "Cat People–Concert Programme" (New England Conservatory, October 30, 2006).

Blake.

[19] Benny Goodman's Carnegie Hall Concert of January 16, 1938, had broken new ground. Carnegie Hall had been the home of classical music, and no one knew how a jazz concert would be received there. Phil Schaap, a curator of Jazz at Lincoln Center, concluded that the Goodman concert established that jazz had value "for listening purposes only."

The concert was recorded but not released till 1950 (when it sold over a million copies). The first Newport Jazz festival (1954) photos show concert-style seating.

Tom Vitale, "How Benny Goodman Orchestrated 'The Most Important Concert In Jazz History,'" NPR.org, January 16, 2018, https://www.npr.org/2018/01/16/578312844/how-benny-goodman-orchestrated-the-most-important-concert-in-jazz-history.

[20] Leonard Bernstein and Aaron Copland were regular visitors, and Randy Weston remembered opera singers singing along with his piano.

Jeremy D. Goodwin, "Lenox's Music Inn Was Jazz's Secret Hotspot," *The Boston Globe*, July 8, 2012, https://www.bostonglobe.com/opinion/2012/07/07/lenox-music-inn-was-jazz-secret-hotspot/faPfekeIc40u2VKQ2xkCVN/story.html.

[21] "with some exceptions (there were occasional Tuesday and Wednesday night

concerts during the late 50s), but for the most part, they kept to those three days of the week… Folk and World Music concerts were primarily held on Saturday afternoons. Lots of area camps would attend those concerts. The jazz concerts were generally scheduled on Thursday and Sunday nights."
Schuller to McFadden, "Lenox Chapter," February 17, 2020.

[22] According to the schedule of evening events for 1957, Mahalia Jackson gave a concert in the Music Barn on Thursday, August 15. This schedule, with the embedded outline of the panel discussion, appears on Michael Fitzgerald's excellent website, JazzMF. It is well worth exploring: https://jazzmf.com/lenox-school-of-jazz-1957-evening-event-schedule/

[23] Michael Fitzgerald, "Lenox School of Jazz- 1957 Evening Event Schedule," JazzMF, November 1, 1993, https://jazzmf.com/lenox-school-of-jazz-1957-evening-event-schedule/.

[24] The concert took place in the Music Barn and was called "School of Jazz on Parade." There was a clear focus on featuring the compositions of students and faculty. Several of these have titles which reference the Lenox school itself— Fran Thorne's "Housatonic Huzzy," Jimmy Guiffre's "Blues for the Barn," and Dizzy Gillespie's "Wheatleigh," which, as Michael Fitzgerald observes, is most probably the same composition that Gillespie would go on to record on his *Duets* album, under the title of "Wheatleigh Hall," in December of that same year.
Michael Fitzgerald, "1957 Concert Program," JazzMF, November 1, 1993, https://jazzmf.com/1957-concert-program/.

[25] Coleman's three pieces were "The Sphinx," "Compassion," and "Giggin'."
Michael Fitzgerald, "1959 Concert Program," JazzMF, November 1, 1993, https://jazzmf.com/1959-concert-program/.

[26] Milton R. Bass, "Modern Jazz Quartet, Jazz School Concerts," *The Berkshire Eagle*, August 31, 1959, https://www.newspapers.com/image/531714150/.
Quoted with permission, *The Berkshire Eagle*

[27] In the first year, 19 out of 36 musicians chosen to attend were pianists.
Fitzgerald, "The Lenox School of Jazz."

[28] Blake, "Cat People–Concert Programme."

[29] Blake.

[30] Randy Weston, jazz pianist, and composer. His music encompassed the rhythm and heritage of Africa. The Music Inn made a big impression on him—he embraced the opportunity to talk to people like Dr. Willis James about the African American experience. He returned to Lenox (Avaloch Inn) year after year, and it was there that he wrote "Berkshire Blues."

[31] Now called Apple Tree Inn

[32] In an email, Ran remembers the summer of 1958 when he was a security guard at the Newport Jazz Festival:
"This was the second or third summer I applied for the job. I bugged the hell

out of George Wein and Charlie Bourgeois, his number one ace man. I would be hanging around the back tent. Some well-known musicians did not have identity cards, and I could recognize most. So, with an ungracious sigh, I was told to go backstage and help them."

The Barbers also gave Ran time off to attend the Oakdale Musical Theater at Wallingford, CT:

"There I was special assistant, to be available for Erroll Garner. I would massage his hands and deliver his preferred drink."

Ran Blake to Janet McFadden, "Newport Recollections," January 27, 2018.

[33] At Lake Compounce in the early 1950s. See Chapter 10: Suffield, Connecticut—A New Start "Friendship."

[34] Oscar Peterson (1925–2007). Canadian jazz pianist and composer who released over 200 recordings, won numerous awards, and is considered one of the greatest jazz pianists of all-time. Interestingly, there have been comparisons made to Art Tatum (who was a model for his musical mastery in the 1940s and '50s), but when Peterson, in his early teens, first heard a Tatum recording, he was intimidated. He became disillusioned with his own ability and refused to touch the piano for several weeks. To Ran, who had also had his own doubts and periods of disillusionment (notably after Kenton's perceived criticism), Peterson showed kindness and encouragement towards Ran at Lenox.

[35] Fitzgerald, "The Lenox School of Jazz."

[36] Schuller, *Gunther Schuller*, 494.

In addition to the aforementioned sources, the author wishes to acknowledge Jeremy Yudkin's excellent book on the Lenox School of Jazz, which helped provide context for her research writing this chapter.

Jeremy Yudkin, *The Lenox School of Jazz: A Vital Chapter in the History of American Music and Race Relations*, 1st Edition (South Egremont, MA: Farshaw, 2006).

Chapter 19: Atlantic Records

[1] Nesuhi and Ahmet Ertegun were sons of the Turkish Ambassador to the US. After their father's death, they remained in the United States and, in 1947, Ahmet, along with his friends Herb and Miriam Abramson, founded Atlantic Records. Their aim was to sign a few of the artists whose music they liked. Their first major signing was Ruth Brown in 1949. She had big hits with "Teardrops From My Eyes" (1950) and "Mama, He Treats Your Daughter Mean" (1953). Ray Charles signed to the label in 1952.

In 1953, When Herb Abramson was called up to serve as a dentist in the US army (he had trained as a dentist in a government training scheme), Jerry Wexler (the Billboard journalist) took over his role of producer. In 1955, Nesuhi (who had previously established the Crescent record label and purchased Jazz Man

Records) joined Ahmet and Jerry Wexler at Atlantic. In 1958 Abramson sold his stake in Atlantic to Nesuhi and his (by then) ex-wife, Miriam Bienstock. (Ahmet credited Miriam with keeping the "discipline" at Atlantic, stating that without her in those early days, the label would have folded.)

[2] The talk was part of the evening event scheduled for Saturday, August 24, at 8.30 pm.

Michael Fitzgerald, "Lenox School of Jazz- 1957 Evening Event Schedule," JazzMF, November 1, 1993, https://jazzmf.com/lenox-school-of-jazz-1957-evening-event-schedule/.

[3] Atlantic had started up in 1948 in a two-room suite at the old Hotel Jefferson on Broadway and 56th Street. The recording studio was just around the corner on West 56th Street, above Patsy's restaurant (though Patsy's would move to the adjoining building—its present location—in 1954). In May 1956, with growing success, and a larger administration staff, Atlantic took up new quarters at 157 West 57th Street (while retaining two floors of the old building). In 1959, the studio moved to 11 West 60th Street, where the new space included a large tracking room and control room and was big enough to house the new Amplex eight-track—which was 7 feet (2.1m) tall and weighed 250 lbs (110 kg).

Gary Kramer, "Atlantic and R&B Trend Developed Side by Side," *The Billboard*, January 13, 1958.

Dave Simons, "The Atlantic Story," in *Studio Stories: How the Great New York Records Were Made: From Miles to Madonna, Sinatra to the Ramones* (San Francisco: Backbeat, 2004), 46–56.

[4] Tom Dowd was a young bass player and student of physics from New York. In the days before unlimited tracks, he excelled at mixing "live," that is, as a recording was being made. He was innovative, had exceptional talent, and played an important role in Atlantic's success.

[5] Simons, "The Atlantic Story," 51.

[6] Wexler has been credited for conceiving the term "rhythm and blues."

[7] Simons, "The Atlantic Story." 51.

[8] The first Amplex model 5258 8-track was sold to Les Paul for his home studio. The second was sold to Atlantic in early 1958; they were the first record company to use the model in their studio.

[9] "Atlantic Records Discography: 1957," Jazz Discography Project, 2020, https://www.jazzdisco.org/atlantic-records/discography-1957/.

[10] Ornette Coleman's *The Shape of Jazz to Come* was released on Atlantic in October 1959. It challenged traditional notions of jazz.

[11] The French Renaissance Revival Style building is based on a 16th-century hunting lodge built by Francis I of France. It is listed on the National Register of Historic Places.

New York Landmarks Preservation Commission, *Guide to New York City Land-*

marks, 4th edition (Hoboken, NJ: Wiley, 2008); Norval White, Elliot Willensky, and Fran Leadon, *AIA Guide to New York City*, 5th edition (New York: Oxford University Press, 2010).

[12] Byron Coley, "Ran Blake Interview Transcript–The Wire," The Wire Magazine, July 2009, https://www.thewire.co.uk/in-writing/interviews/ran-blake-interview-transcript.

[13] Coley.

[14] Most of Atlantic's archived tapes were destroyed in February 1978 when a fire swept through the warehouse in New Jersey, where they were stored.

[15] Willie "The Lion" Smith (1893–1973) was an American jazz pianist and composer. A leading exponent of Harlem stride piano, he drew upon a diverse range of musical influences, including klezmer, African American, and European-classical. Smith was a major influence on Duke Ellington, who wrote and dedicated several compositions to him. He also influenced Fats Waller, Thelonious Monk, and Art Tatum. He earned his nickname for his intuition and nerve, serving on the frontline during World War I.

For further information, see: "Willie 'The Lion' Smith: Stride Piano Master," NPR, 11 2008, https://www.npr.org/2008/06/11/91365108/willie-the-lion-smith-stride-piano-master.

[16] *LaVern Baker Sings Bessie Smith* was recorded in January 1958 and released as Atlantic 1281 on October 20, 1958.

"LaVern Baker - Sings Bessie Smith," Discogs, accessed November 17, 2020, https://www.discogs.com/LaVern-Baker-Sings-Bessie-Smith/release/3047089.

[17] Coley, "Ran Blake Interview Transcript–The Wire."

[18] Gunther Schuller, *Gunther Schuller: A Life in Pursuit of Music and Beauty* (Rochester, NY: University of Rochester Press, 2011), 475.

[19] Schuller, 475.

[20] Ran Blake, "Document Examining the Teaching Methodology of Ran Blake" (Unpublished, typed, Brookline, Mass, July 21, 1999), Unpublished documents of Ran Blake.

[21] Professor Alex Bradford directed the Abyssinian Baptist Gospel Choir. He was a composer, singer, and choir director. (He wrote for Ray Charles and LaVern Baker.) In 1961, he performed in and composed music for *Black Nativity*.

[22] See Part 2, Chapter 3: Sweet Daddy Grace's Church.

[23] One day Belkis, a young woman who was a cousin of the Erteguns', came to visit Nesuhi; Ran remembers "walking out to 57th Street and seeing the sunlight on her profile." The occasion was captured in his piece "Belkis on West 57th Street" and, according to Ran's program notes, "This memory (and this piece) is less than a minute."

Ran Blake, "'Noir' Programme Notes" (Center for Improvisational Music, May 17, 2007).

[24] This meeting is covered in the chapter "Gunther."

New York — "The Happy Period"

Chapter 1: Miss Amelia Lehrfeld

¹ "I've heard of him," Ran quips as the author of the quote is revealed to him. "I want that quote in my obituary too."

² A friend, David Robinson, had introduced Ran to his grandmother's good friend, Miss Lehrfeld, who was looking for a boarder.

³ This block has been singled out by Vincent Cannato in his book The Ungovernable City, where he recounts that the blocks bordered by West 110th and 113th Streets, Amsterdam Avenue and Broadway were placed off-limits to Navy midshipmen, training at Columbia during World War II "because of the plethora of prostitutes working out of the buildings." Vincent Cannato, *The Ungovernable City: John Lindsay and His Struggle to Save New York* (New York: Basic Books, 2009), 237.

⁴ Sarah Waxman, "The History of New York City's Upper West Side," ny.com, accessed November 18, 2020, https://www.ny.com/articles/upperwest.html. Nicholas Pileggi, "Renaissance of the Upper West Side," *New York Magazine*, 1969, https://nymag.com/news/features/47182/.

⁵ At the beginning of the 20th century, West 113th Street was at the center of a growing residential district that had sprung up in response to the extension of the IRT subway in 1904. Apartment buildings of six to eight stories were built to accommodate the largely middle-class white community who were able to take up the opportunity. The year 1909 alone saw construction commence on thirty-five new apartment buildings. However, after WWII, many middle-class owners abandoned the area and headed for suburban areas, which were then opening up. During Ran's time living at 113th Street, a few remaining red brick and stone-clad row-houses remained, shoulder to shoulder with the taller apartment buildings.

⁶ In 2020, Sally Bolhower, Amelia Lehrfeld's grandniece, contacted Ran "out of the blue." She was able to tell him that Amelia's family—her mother, Eugenia Bankien Lehrfeld; father, Morris Lehrfeld; five sisters, Ida, Fanny, Mary, Amelia, Selma; and one brother, Abraham—came to New York from Vienna, Austria. They arrived in the mid-1880s and settled on Stanton Street, on The Lower East Side.

"They lived there a couple of years and then moved to The West Bronx, which in those days was a desirable place to live. [...] When she lived on Claremont Avenue and West 113th Street, Aunt Amelia shared both of these apartments with her sister Mary. When my Aunt Fanny became a widow later in life, she moved into 507 West 113th Street with her two sisters, Mary and Amelia. [...] Aunt Mary died in 1954, and Aunt Fanny died a few years before Aunt Mary. Aunt Amelia died in 1962."

[7] (slightly inclining their head with the greeting is implied.)

[8] The Triangle Shirtwaist Factory Fire of March 25, 1911, claimed the lives of one hundred and forty-six of the mostly immigrant female workforce. These workers, ranging in age from fifteen to twenty-three years, worked long hours in poor conditions for very little pay. On the day of the fire, as was the factory's custom, the doors were locked from outside on the pretext of preventing theft.
"Triangle Shirtwaist Company Fire," in *Encyclopedia.Com*, Gilded Age and Progressive Era Reference Library, accessed November 18, 2020, https://www.encyclopedia.com/history/encyclopedias-almanacs-transcripts-and-maps/triangle-shirtwaist-company-fire.

[9] Sally Bolhower recalls that "Ran took Aunt Amelia to Birdland and introduced her to the audience as 'Miss Amelia Lehrfeld.'"

[10] This comparison stems from the embarrassment Ran felt when he took Jeanne Lee home to Suffield in the late 1950s, and they were subjected to racial comments by some locals.

[11] In the December 2012 issue of his monthly newsletter, Ran describes her friends as "mild and elegant." "Ran's Monthly Newsletter," *Ran Blake* (blog), December 1, 2012, https://ranblake.com/newsletters/2012-2/december-2012/.

[12] "Ran's Monthly Newsletter."

[13] "Ran's Monthly Newsletter."

[14] "Ran's Monthly Newsletter."

[15] "Ran's Monthly Newsletter."

[16] Martha Koleda, Telephone Call, interview by Janet McFadden, Telephone recording, January 14, 2010.

[17] Koleda.

[18] After Miss Lehrfeld's death, Ran took over the rent of the apartment for $110 a month.

[19] A fine non-alcoholic wine produced since 1893 by Welch's Grape Juice Company, Westfield, New York, and made from native American Concord grapes. It was highly popular with the Temperance Movement and for church services. [Wikipedia contributors, "Thomas Bramwell Welch," in *Wikipedia*, February 21, 2020, https://en.wikipedia.org/w/index.php?title=Thomas_Bramwell_Welch&oldid=941926042.]

[20] Ran Blake's composition "Amelia Lehrfeld" (1964) was first performed in 1964 in Riverside Church, New York City.
The Boston Area Libraries, *The Boston Composers Project: A Bibliography of Contemporary Music*, ed. Linda I. Solow (Cambridge, Mass: The MIT Press, 1983), 52.

Chapter 2: New Jobs, New Friends, New York

1. Pin pricker is the term Ran used to describe his job—counting vehicles through intersections during green lights—for the traffic engineering firm Wilbur Smith. Ran admits it was a bit of a "come down" after his European tour with Jeanne Lee.

2. Ran Blake, "Lenox School of Jazz," n.d., 2, Ran Blake's private archive.

3. Constructed in 1906/7, it housed, in its early days, the Sesrun Club, a residence for nurses (Sesrun is Nurses spelled backward). Later, it was known as the Hotel Westminster before becoming the King's Crown. It had, however, since the 1930s, at least, been affiliated with Columbia University.

4. Columbia University School of Public Health and Administrative Medicine, "Bulletin of Information: The DeLamar Institute of Public Health" (New York: Columbia University, 1931 1930), http://archive.org/details/columbiauniversi-1930colu.

5. Dan Carlinsky lived at the King's Crown for three of the four years of his undergraduate course.

6. Dan Carlinsky to Janet McFadden, "Ran Blake Book," May 31, 2013.

7. Dan Carlinsky recalled a "lady from Iceland" called Eria.

8. Carlinsky to McFadden, "Ran Blake Book," May 31, 2013.

9. Ran knew him as "Stew" while Dan Carlinsky remembers him as M.P. Stewart.

10. Carlinsky to McFadden, "Ran Blake Book," May 31, 2013.

11. Carlinsky to McFadden.

12. Carlinsky to McFadden.

13. Carlinsky to McFadden.

14. Carlinsky to McFadden.

15. Carlinsky to McFadden.

16. Tennessee Williams—American 20th-century writer whose plays for theater date from the 1930s and have become classics, e.g., *Streetcar Named Desire* and *Cat on a Hot Tin Roof*. His plays reflect the human condition in the setting of the American South.

17. Bruce Rhodenizer, known as Mr. Bruce—according to Dan Carlinsky

18. Ran first met Ann Noriega when he was chauffeuring at the Music Inn. As Ran recounts: "I was told to pick up Ann, and we became friends. She was the daughter of Ermin Noriega, and then he lived at 154th between Amsterdam Avenue and St. Nick's… I want to say 220. She was one of Edythe Dimond's friends—they got me a small stool (for the work at Wilbur Smith's—counting lights)."

[19] Don Strange remembers that: "a very diverse group of 'jazz groupies,' artists, poets, and other assorted characters" would be there. "Barry [Tobin] would sometimes bring in his 8mm projector to show films against the wall, Ricardo Gautreau played guitar and sang, and Steve and Gloria Tropp would recite poetry. On other occasions, we would move on to the West End Bar on Broadway and 114th street."

Don Strange, "Ran Blake in Spain," September 9, 2020.

[20] Wilma Srob Odell, *Phone Conversation*, 2013.

[21] Ran spent some time studying in the music department at Columbia University. Here he met with people at the forefront of electronic music—Vladimir Ussachevsky and Mario Davidovsky. Walter (later Wendy) Carlos popularized early electronic music with the recording *Switched-On Bach.*

[22] (Ran had approached this record company at the suggestion of Martin Williams. ESP-Disk had been established by lawyer Bernard Stollman to promote non-commercial and experimental music. Ran called and was invited to "drop by" Stollman's place on Riverside Drive. He remembers that Donald and Albert Ayler were sitting there; he remembers the little dog, Pico. He was served oatmeal cookies and states, "Bernard treated me well.")

[23] Nahid Mahdavi to Janet McFadden, "Ran Blake Biography," April 11, 2010.

Chapter 3: Sweet Daddy Grace's Church

[1] The church in Harlem was one of the oldest African American Baptist churches in America. Formed in 1808 as a protest against segregated seating at the First Baptist Church of New York, it was a center of African American culture. The music was a rich fusion of many genres, including gospel, spirituals, high anthem, praise, jazz, and hip hop. At the time of writing, tourists—sometimes numbering up to one thousand—still line up outside on a Sunday, hoping to hear the music. (The seating is arranged as in a theater, with the focal point on the pulpit. The choir flanks the pulpit. Sermon and song are obvious priorities.)

[2] Adam Clayton Powell Jr. was pastor of the Abyssinian Baptist Church on West 138th Street from 1937 to 1971. He followed his father, Adam Clayton Powell Sr., who had laced *his* leadership with social activism and was an early member of the NAACP. Adam Clayton Powell Jr. continued in his father's footsteps, and when he was, in 1941, elected to the newly formed New York City Council, and in 1944 to the U.S. Congress (representing the newly formed 22nd District), he encouraged the Abyssinian congregation to engage in boycotts demanding the end of racial discrimination and seeking better healthcare and employment opportunities for African Americans.

In 1965, Rev Dr. Martin Luther King Jr. preached at services to mark the church's 157th anniversary.

"History of The Abyssinian Baptist Church," Organization, Abyssinian Baptist Church, 2015, https://abyssinian.org/about-us/history/.

3 "Prof." Alex Bradford, composer of the hit "Too Close to Heaven," was at this time director of Newark's Abyssinian Baptist Church Choir.

4 Ran Blake, "Gospel (Draft Manuscript).," no date, 4, Unpublished documents of Ran Blake.

5 Bishop Grace died in January 1960. Eventually, "Sweet Daddy" Walter McCollough was elected bishop.
Tad Hendrickson, writing in The Village Voice (May 7, 2002), gives the following account of the church's music: "a 16-piece shout band replaces human voices with brass while maintaining gospel's choral harmonies and dramatic presentation." He goes on to describe *The Thunderbirds*—the name of the group that had been playing at the Harlem Church for over 40 years. Ages of this group range from late teens to mid-eighties, and instruments include seven trombones, one sousaphone (marching tuba), one trumpet, one tenor tuba, drums, cymbals, and tambourines. The volunteer players have had no formal training in music. Elder Edward Babb, trombonist, leads the band. He plays with, according to Hendrickson, "fire and brimstone." Most of the music is composed by Babb. It has no title and is not written down. Tad Hendrickson, "Listings," Magazine, The Village Voice, May 7, 2002, https://www.villagevoice.com/2002/05/07/listings-150/.

6 Morningside Avenue and the intersection of Manhattan Avenue with St. Nicholas Avenue at 124th Street have been passed over without mention.

7 Adam Clayton Powell Jr. Boulevard

8 Malcolm X Boulevard

9 The nearest subway was only one block away on 125th Street, just across St. Nicholas Avenue.

10 Her name was, in fact, Sr Eliza Lowery. She was from Newport News, Virginia. (Gunther Schuller, in liner notes for *Ran Blake Plays Solo Piano*, called her "Eliza Carter"—possibly confusing her with Mother Carter from Hartford.)

11 *Ran Blake Plays Solo Piano*, first released in 1965, was reissued by ESP-Disk in 2013. His composition, "Sister Tee," is track eight of this release.

12 Porgy is the name for small, shallow-water fish with sharp teeth. They are excellent for cooking.

13 The way the light fell on the two women, highlighting some parts and plunging the rest into deep shadow, would have struck Ran immediately. This is a lighting technique of film noir. Visually stunning, it adds to the intrigue and suspense of these films.

14 Though the term had been used from the 1950s when the Civil Rights Movement was gaining momentum, it was the head of the Student Nonviolent Coordinating Committee (SNCC), Stokely Carmichael, who first used the words "Black Power" as a rallying cry. (This was in June 1966 in Greenwood, Mississippi.) The movement instilled a sense of racial pride and self-esteem, but there were those, like Martin Luther King Jr., who felt that the term carried with it violence and a whiff of separatism; he preferred a concept of all the people of multi-racial

America as "partners in power." [Stanford University, "Black Power," Institution webpage, The Martin Luther King, Jr., Research and Education Institute, April 26, 2017, https://kinginstitute.stanford.edu/encyclopedia/black-power.

"Black Power," Encyclopedia.com, October 16, 2020, https://www.encyclopedia.com/social-sciences-and-law/sociology-and-social-reform/social-reform/black-power-movement.]

[15] *Ran Blake Plays Solo Piano*

[16] Gospel singer, known as "the Songbird of the East." She was the wife of Bishop Frederick Douglas Washington, Pentecostal minister of the Church of God in Christ in Brooklyn, New York.

[17] Bishop Walter McCullough (or McCollough) was the church leader in 1967 and was said to bring a "respectable" look to the organization. By the time of his passing on March 15, 1991, McCullough had presided over 3 million church members (in 132 cities) during 31 years of service. (There were 27,500 members in 137 churches in 1965.) Bishop McCullough's eulogy remembered that he had used the church to sponsor feeding programs and housing projects and had encouraged his people to vote. ["Revival," *Washington Daily News*, August 28, 1967; Sherry Sherrod DuPree, "African-American Movements Influenced by African-American Pentecostalism," in *African-American Holiness Pentecostal Movement: An Annotated Bibliography* (New York: Taylor & Francis, 1996), 374.]

[18] Wilma Srob Odell, *Phone Conversation*, 2013.

[19] Pronounced *Weeda*.

[20] Fittingly, Ran's composition "Sister Tee" is in the key of A major.

Chapter 4: Jazz Clubs of New York

[1] Thelonious Monk was engaged at the Five Spot (for what eventually became a six-month gig) on July 4, 1957. The band featured John Coltrane on tenor sax, Wilbur Ware on bass (replaced in early August by Ahmed Abdul-Malik), and Shadow Wilson on drums.

Robin Kelley, *Thelonious Monk: The Life and Times of an American Original*. (New York: Free Press, 2010), 225–36.

[2] Ornette Coleman made his New York debut at the Five Spot on November 17, 1959. His supporting players were: Don Cherry (cornet), Charlie Haden (bass), Billy Higgins (drums). Leonard Bernstein, Miles Davis, and John Coltrane were there for opening night…as well as, it appears, Ran Blake. Coleman's appearance at the Five Spot was soon after The *Berkshire Eagle* had run the article in which they named "pianist Ran Blake and alto saxophonist Ornette Coleman" as best individual performances in the Lenox School of Jazz's 1959 concert.

Lawrence Walker, "The Five Spot," Pure History, May 20, 2014, https://purehistory.org/the-five-spot/.

³ 80 St Mark's Place

⁴ The Jazz Gallery was the Terminis' second club.

⁵ Ran Blake, "Typed Document (No Title)," n.d., 2, Ran Blake's private archive.

⁶ Blake, 8.

⁷ Robert Labaree: Musicologist and faculty emeritus of the New England Conservatory.

⁸ Ran Blake to Janet McFadden, "More," November 26, 2020.

⁹ The Half Note operated from 1957 to 1972 at 289 Hudson Street. It was owned and run by the Canterino family, with Pop and Mama cooking pasta and meatballs and other Italian specialties in the kitchen.

¹⁰ John Coltrane, Sonny Rollins, Stan Getz, Bill Evans, Dizzy Gillespie were among the many artists to record live at the Village Vanguard.

¹¹ Which referenced the Greensboro sit-ins on its dramatic cover. The album itself was significant in that it was explicitly political—with Roach being in the vanguard of artists to address racial and civil-liberties issues.

Chapter 5: Nica de Koenigswarter

¹ She would later switch to a Bentley.

² Her early childhood was divided among the family's homes—Ashton Wold, a Georgian mansion near Oundle in the English countryside of Northamptonshire, and their city base at Kensington Palace Gardens. After her father's death, the family moved to Tring Park, Hertfordshire—her grandmother's estate.

See also: David Kastin, *Nica's Dream: The Life and Legend of the Jazz Baroness* (New York: W. W. Norton & Company, 2011).

³ He was considered one of the pioneers of the modern conservation movement, setting aside the bulk of his property at Ashton Wold as a nature reserve. He also was an expert on fleas, with a collection of 30,000 species. He identified the parasite responsible for the spread of the bubonic plague.

⁴ Hannah Rothschild, *The Baroness: The Search for Nica, the Rebellious Rothschild and Jazz's Secret Muse* (Great Britain: Virago, 2012), 76.

⁵ This was quite understandable considering the circumstances that led to her husband's suicide, as well as the infant mortality rate of the period. Nica was born on December 10, 1913—pre mass childhood immunization. (The great flu pandemic of 1918–1920 infected one-third of the world's population and claimed at least 50 million lives.)

⁶ Teddy Wilson was in England with the Benny Goodman Trio. [Kastin, *Nica's Dream*, 25.]

⁷ Harry and Alicia Guggenheim were the founders/owners of the New York Newsday newspaper.

⁸ Shaun Koenigswarter to Janet McFadden, "Re: Letters from Pannonica de Koenigswarter to Ran Blake," August 12, 2020.

⁹ Koenigswarter to McFadden.

¹⁰ Nadine de Koenigswarter, "Introduction," in *Three Wishes: An Intimate Look at Jazz Greats*, by Nica de Koenigswarter (New York: Abrams Image, 2008), 17.

¹¹ Nat Hentoff, "The Jazz Baroness," *Esquire*, October 1, 1960.

¹² As reported by her great-niece, Hannah Rothschild, in her documentary *The Jazz Baroness*.

Hannah Rothschild, *The Jazz Baroness*, Documentary (British Broadcasting Corporation, 2009).

¹³ Barbara Belgrave was a jazz musician and critic for Jazz Hip in the 1960s. Ran remembers that: "When I was twenty-seven, in Paris with Jeanne, she (Barbara) was so worldly and experienced—I felt like a Connecticut simpleton next to her. (She was five years older than Ran.) She loved the music, but I don't know if she wrote more than ten big articles. She was a friend of the boy I wrote 'Pourquoi Laurent?' for."

Ran included a "30-second tribute" to Barbara on his album with "Christine" (Correa), *Out of the Shadows*. According to Ran, Barbara and Nica became good friends, and "they would be seen together in clubs in the mid'60s."

¹⁴ Here Ran is referencing the 1969 film of the same name by one of his favorite directors, Claude Chabrol.

¹⁵ Ran has in his files a yellow Memo "from the desk of Baroness Koenigswarter." It is dated February 24, '61, and states, "Please cash this cheque [sic] for Mr Ran Blake." This wasn't long after the fire at Monk's apartment on West 63rd Street, and Nica was well aware that Ran had been a great help to the Monk family at this time, particularly in looking after the children, Toot (T.S. Monk) and Boo Boo (Barbara Monk).

¹⁶ Boo Boo was the nickname for Thelonious Monk's daughter, Barbara.

Chapter 6: Mostly Monk

¹ Nica separated from her husband in 1952. With her oldest daughter, Janka, she then moved to Hotel Stanhope in New York. [Nadine de Koenigswarter, "Introduction," in *Three Wishes: An Intimate Look at Jazz Greats*, by Nica de Koenigswarter (New York: Abrams Image, 2008), 17.]

² Blue Note BLP 1510 & 1511, *Thelonious Monk - Genius of Modern Music*, Volumes one and two, respectively. Blue Note Records started the 12" LP era in the mid-1950s with some trad. jazz albums, but then launched the 1500 modern jazz series in which 99 LP records were issued between 1955 and 1958.

"Blue Note Records Catalog: 1500 Series," Jazz Discography Project, accessed November 24, 2020, https://www.jazzdisco.org/blue-note-records/catalog-1500-series/.

³ Blue Note 1509: Milt Jackson—*Milt Jackson and the Thelonious Monk Quintet*

⁴ Harry Colomby was Monk's manager from 1955 onwards. He often referred to Monk's "great dignity."

⁵ By July 16, Monk had a group with Shadow Wilson on drums, John Coltrane, tenor sax, and Wilbur Ware on bass (replaced in August by Ahmed Abdul-Malik). [Robin Kelley, *Thelonious Monk: The Life and Times of an American Original.* (New York: Free Press, 2010), 225–36.]

⁶ Kelley, 294–96.

⁷ Thelonious Sphere Monk III (Toot—now T.S.) would have been just-turned eleven at the time, and Barbara (BooBoo) would have been seven.

⁸ Before the contract work was complete, Ran had offered to get Sister Tee (who had begun helping Miss Lehrfield occasionally) to help with the cleaning, but there is no indication this offer was taken up.

⁹ Toot's friend Gregory Flowers, "a kid from further up the block," was often included in their activities.

¹⁰ Art Davis, Bass; Max Roach, Drums; Mal Waldron, Piano; Eric Dolphy, Reeds; Coleman Hawkins, Walter Benton, Tenor Sax; Julian Priester, Trombone; Booker Little, Trumpet; and Abbey Lincoln, vocals.

¹¹ Orrin Keepnews was a jazz writer and record producer. He co-founded Riverside Records. Keepnews supervised Mait Edey when he produced Ran's album The Blue Potato and Other Outrages on Milestone in 1969.

¹² Art Lange, "Ran Blake's Third Stream," Downbeat, February 1980, 26.

¹³ Ran played a full recital at Columbia and then co-produced a concert series there before being "kicked out."
Ran Blake to Janet McFadden, "Re: Quick Question," January 20, 2021.

¹⁴ In an email sent on July 4, 2020, Ran, reflecting on a Fourth of July of his past, described "an amazing day at the house of the Jeanne Lee family. Skippy of the Monk family joined us in the backyard." Though he also remembers that he "was afraid of fireworks, having been unpleasantly surprised ten years earlier at my grandparents' country home in Sunapee—the lake in New Hampshire."
Ran Blake to Janet McFadden, "Fourth of July," July 4, 2020.

¹⁵ Jackie Smith Bonneau, daughter of Nellie Monk's brother Sonny and sister-in-law Geraldine Smith, died August 19, 2016.

¹⁶ Parker House Hotel is a luxury hotel located along the Freedom Trail near Beacon Hill, Boston, MA.

¹⁷ Barry Harris was booked to perform at this concert—a tribute to Monk's music—by the New York Jazz Repertory Company—on April 6, 1974. Harris called Monk and asked him to play. No one expected he would come, let alone play, but just as the band (including Monk's son, T.S. on drums) was about to start, Monk walked on stage and played the whole concert. T.S. remembered the night as

"absolutely magical."

"Unexpected Thelonious Monk," Organization, Carnegie Hall, January 2019, https://www.carnegiehall.org/Blog/2019/01/Unexpected-Thelonious-Monk.

[18] Lennie's-on-the-Turnpike was a Jazz Club operated from the mid-1950s to 1972. It was located in Peabody, Massachusetts, about twenty miles north of Boston.

The *Jazz Workshop* was a cellar room on Boylston Street, Boston, which closed down in 1978.

[19] Ed Felson Esq. 1984, BM JAZZ; Jon Hazilla, 1980 BM, TSTR.; Ricky Ford (Richard Allen Ford) 1983 BM, JAZZ

[20] "The Thelonious Sphere Monk Music Festival—A Tribute" was an all-day celebration of Monk's music and took place in August 1988 at the Lincoln Square Amphitheater, West 64th Street.Florence Fletched, "A Complete Entertainment Guide for Seven Days Beginning August 24," *New York Magazine*, August 29, 1988.

"The Thelonious Sphere Monk Music Festival—A Tribute," *New York Magazine*, August 29, 1988.

[21] Film-maker, archivist and digital records manager, John was Ran's assistant from 2008–2013.

Chapter 7: Teachers

[1] Written on a card sent by "Madame Chaloff" (the legendary piano teacher) to Ran Blake. The front of the card features the UNICEF peace dove.

[2] Ran Blake, "'Noir' Programme Notes" (Center for Improvisational Music, May 17, 2007).

[3] In a Downbeat article, Ran is quoted as saying, "Oscar never charged me a penny."

Art Lange, "Ran Blake's Third Stream," *Downbeat*, February 1980, 25.

[4] Gunther Schuller played an important role in Ran's life. This is discussed more fully in a later chapter.

According to the Boston Composers Projects, Ran studied with Oscar Peterson in 1958; William J Russo 1960–62; Mary Lou Williams 1960–64; Gunther Schuller 1960–67; Mal Waldron 1962–63

[5] *L'Enfant et les sortilèges*, a one-act opera, written by Maurice Ravel between 1919 and 1925.

[6] *The Rite of Spring*: A ballet by Russian composer Igor Stravinsky. Premiered on May 29, 1913, at the Théâtre des Champs-Élysées, Paris.

[7] Béla Bartók *Music for Strings, Percussion and Celesta*, Sz. 106, BB 114.

[8] 1964 film, directed by Sidney Lumet. The film has an important place for Ran;

New York — "The Happy Period"

he has used it in his teaching and his music.

9 By age ten, she was known as the "little piano girl," performing throughout Pittsburgh. Her professional debut – age twelve – was as substitute pianist for the Buzz and Harris Review. It was a traveling show, and occasionally, over the next four years, she toured – passing through New York and playing with the likes of Jelly Roll Morton, Fats Waller, Willie ("the lion") Smith, and Duke Ellington. The Editors of Encyclopaedia Britannica, "Mary Lou Williams," Encyclopedia Britannica, May 24, 2020, https://www.britannica.com/biography/Mary-Lou-Williams.

10 Robin Kelley, *Thelonious Monk: The Life and Times of an American Original.* (New York: Free Press, 2010), 47.

11 Mary Lou Williams, "Mary Lou Williams Interview," *Melody Maker*, June 1954, https://ratical.org/MaryLouWilliams/MMiview1954.html.

12 Robin Kelley names Tadd Dameron and Kenny Dorham, as well as established performers like Lena Horne and Billy Strayhorn. [Kelley, *Thelonious Monk*, 91.]

13 Kelley, 92.

14 Kelley, 81.

15 "Mary Lou Williams- The First Lady of Jazz Piano and Composition," Pittsburgh Music History, accessed December 30, 2020, https://sites.google.com/site/pittsburghmusichistory/pittsburgh-music-story/jazz/jazz---early-years/mary-lou-williams.

16 She also founded the New Reform Foundation for Gifted Children.

17 Linda Dahl, *Morning Glory: A Biography of Mary Lou Williams* (New York: Pantheon Books, 1999).

18 Ran has written about this in his 2-part series on Mary Lou Williams. [Ran Blake, "Memories of Mary Lou Williams," *Ran Blake* (blog), July 10, 2018, https://ranblake.com/blog/memories-of-mary-lou-williams/.]

19 In an email, Ran reflects: "She was not overenthusiastic about my talent, gave me left-hand exercises, some encouragement, and we spoke a lot about the blues." [Ran Blake to Janet McFadden, "Re: Mary Lou," March 26, 2018.]

20 Ran Blake, "On Mary Lou Williams," official website, *Ran's Reflections* (blog), June 2013, https://ranblake.com/blog/memories-of-mary-lou-williams/.

21 Bill Russo was a composer/arranger and jazz musician. He wrote scores for the Stan Kenton Orchestra. He featured in the trombone section of Kenton's Orchestra.

22 Paul Hindemith (1895–1963) was a German composer, violist, violinist, conductor, and teacher. He emigrated to the USA in 1940, became an American citizen but returned to Europe in 1953.

23 Ran's "black bag" Thelonious.

24 Hankus Netsky is Ran's colleague and friend at New England Conservatory, Boston. Ran has said that Hankus is: "A great friend and an influence—Hankus

studied with me, but more importantly, I studied with him: the klezmer, the Hasidic music, the temple music, the Holocaust, and learnt quite a bit through him and his organization. Hankus had a wonderful relationship with Dorothy Wallace and made her a supervisor of the jazz department—they clicked. He performed at her house many times."

[25] *The Jazz Tradition* by Martin Williams was first published in 1970 by Oxford University Press, New York. It explores the musicians that have defined jazz and its uniquely American sound. In 1958, Williams founded *The Jazz Review* with Nat Hentoff.

[26] Ran is talking in July 2009.

[27] Madame Chaloff studied privately with Russian pianist Isabella Vengerova. "From her Madame Chaloff learned "the Russian method," a way of pressing each piano key so that the key never quite touches its lowest position but still retains its resonance through to the next note. The piano speaks with a singing tone, and this approach to the piano is instantly recognizable […]" Louise Myers, "Commonwealth Avenue's Musical History," ed. Lee Eiseman et al., *The Boston Musical Intelligencer*, April 3, 2020, virtual journal.

Chapter 8: George Russell

[1] Ran resorts to 'the Year of Our Lord' when he is bored with the line of questioning. This time he puts 'the Savior' in for good measure.

[2] Ran consistently recalls this happening in 1957, and indeed, the Evening Event Schedule for 1957 includes: "Wednesday, August 21, 8:30 PM - TECHNIQUES IN JAZZ COMPOSITION - George Russell, assisted by School Faculty." However, George Russell is not listed as faculty this year—he appears on the faculty list for 1958.
Michael Fitzgerald, "Lenox School of Jazz- 1957 Evening Event Schedule," JazzMF, November 1, 1993, https://jazzmf.com/lenox-school-of-jazz-1957-evening-event-schedule/; Michael Fitzgerald, "Lenox School of Jazz Faculty," JazzMF, November 1, 1993, https://jazzmf.com/lenox-school-of-jazz-faculty/.

[3] Ran has often recounted this experience, including in the all-about-jazz, tribute to George Russell, "In Memoriam: George Russell 1923-2009," All About Jazz, accessed November 10, 2020, https://www.allaboutjazz.com/in-memoriam-george-russell-1923-2009-george-russell-by-aaj-staff.php.

[4] Russell, in addition to his 1989 MacArthur Foundation Fellowship, received the National Endowment for the Arts American Jazz Master, 1990; was elected a foreign member of the Royal Swedish Academy; received two Guggenheim Fellowships, the Oscar du Disque de Jazz, the Guardian Award, six NEA Music Fellowships, the American Music Award, and numerous other accolades.

[5] Quoted in Ran Blake, "August, 2009," Artist Website, *Remembering George Russell* (blog), August 2009, https://ranblake.com/newsletters/2009-2/august/.)

6 George Russell, *The Lydian Chromatic Concept of Tonal Organization*, Volume I: The Art and Science of Tonal, 4th ed. (New York: Concept, 2001).

7 George Russell and Alice Russell, George Russell NEA Jazz Master, interview by Bob Daughtry, Digital, May 3, 2004, National Museum of American History, https://americanhistory.si.edu/smithsonian-jazz/collections-and-archives/smithsonian-jazz-oral-history-program#Russell.

8 Russell and Russell.

9 George Russell, *The Jazz Workshop*, LP, Album (USA: RCA Victor, 1957), https://www.discogs.com/fr/George-Russell-The-Jazz-Workshop/release/2934510.

10 George, at the time, was married to Juanita Odjenar, a painter. His 1951 composition "Odjenar" was dedicated to her. It was at the Lenox School that Juanita met Jimmy Guiffre, whom she was to later marry.

11 There were three apartment buildings in a row, including 121 and 119. Bill Dixon lived in one, Jeanne Lee in another, and George Russell in a third and, as recorded in Jeanne Lee chapter, the friends referred to the address as "the Jazz Row" or the "Aristocrat Row."

12 Ran Blake, "Ran Blake's Brief Remembrance of George Russell Draft 5," August 7, 2009, Ran Blake's private archive.

13 When I queried Ran about copyright for reproducing this document, he responded, "Well, it's my possession. I collected it. You don't have to ask Bush, or maybe Obama—not even Dek-Tor" (his cat).

14 This conversation took place in January 2011.

15 *Othello Ballet Suite/Electronic Organ Sonata No. 1* was a studio album by George Russell released in 1968. *Othello* was recorded on November 3, 1967, in Stockholm—at the studios of Radio Sweden—and the Electronic Organ Sonata was recorded on October 1, 1968, at Grorud Church, Oslo (using the grand organ there).

16 Refer to chapter: The First European Tour.

17 Gunther Schuller, *Gunther Schuller: A Life in Pursuit of Music and Beauty* (Rochester, NY: University of Rochester Press, 2011), 198.

18 The annual arts festival, sponsored by Brandeis University, commenced in 1952.

19 It was Gunther's idea to present six new compositions—three by jazz composers and three by classical composers. He chose Charles Mingus, George Russell, and Jimmy Giuffre, as well as Milton Babbitt and Harold Shapero. By common consent, Schuller was asked to be the sixth composer.
Schuller, *Gunther Schuller*, 461.

20 Schuller, 461.

21 In 1976, when George was recruiting for NEC.

22 We had been talking about George's growing fame and the many awards that he had received in the latter part of his life. By that point, many prestigious orga-

nizations were starting to recognize the importance of George Russell's contribution to music and musical scholarship.

Chapter 9: The Apollo

[1] Ralph Cooper—actor, screenwriter, dancer and choreographer—was a headline name in Jazz à la Carte. He went on to establish the amateur night and preside as master of ceremonies.

[2] "The Apollo was certainly smaller than a symphony hall [Boston] …slightly larger than Jordan Hall, maybe five or six hundred people, and maybe three or four hundred were there that night on a weeknight. It probably was half price on a weeknight." (Ran Blake)

[3] Moms Mabley (Loretta Mary Aiken) was a stand-up comedian who appeared as a toothless, old woman in a house dress and ragged hat. Her social satire touched on topics others avoided, such as racism.

[4] This date varies according to sources. Ran, himself, has put the date both as 1961, and 1962/63. The choice of 1961 has been made based on the wording of Bill Coss's article "The Agonies of Exploration – Jeanne Lee and Ran Blake" DownBeat, September 1962, p.18 which states: "In 1961, they [Ran and Jeanne] met each other again. Blake was scheduled to appear at the Apollo for an amateur night. He asked Miss Lee to sing with him there. They won and appeared there again." This sequence of events seems to be indirectly supported in letters from George Avakian to Ran Blake.

[5] Collegiate Jazz Festival at Notre Dame University, Indiana. Jeanne Lee won the award for "Outstanding Vocalist."

Chapter 10: First European Tour

[1] Martin Williams, 'With Blake and Lee in Europe', *Downbeat*, 1964, 14.

[2] Recorded November 15 and 16 and December 7, 1961, in RCA Victor's Studio A in NYC. *The Newest Sound Around* was released in 1962; additional takes were included in the 1987 re-issue.

[3] 'Monterey Jazz Festival Program-1962', Monterey Jazz Festival Collection, 19 February 2020, 6–10, https://exhibits.stanford.edu/mjf/catalog/vg280bx0071.

[4] Dave and Iola's Jazz Musical (Iola was the lyricist) *The Real Ambassadors*, was being performed at Monterey that year. The work (addressing music and the civil rights movement - among other themes) had been developed in collaboration with Louis Armstrong.

A taste of this musical is available at: http://www.youtube.com/watch?v=yUgohNKyxak

5   It would appear that Avakian is mistaken here as Stan Kenton's name does not figure on the Festival Program for 1962. On Sunday evening, September 23, the duo first appeared before *The Real Ambassadors* (an original musical production with music and lyrics by Dave and Iola Brubeck) and then, later, before Louis Armstrong and His All-Stars.

6   George Avakian to 'Bob', 27 July 1963, Ran Blake's private archive.

7   According to Ran, Sonny Rollins said, on the basis of this cold weather, that he could not come back to Europe in the winter.

8   Fulda is a small city in the centre of Germany—about an hour north-east of Frankfurt. It is known for its Baroque architecture and historic churches. The city developed around a Benedictine abbey (founded in 744) and was an important seat of learning in the Middle Ages.

9   Baden-Baden is a spa town built around the river Oos, at the north-western border of the Black Forest mountain range. With its mild climate and therapeutic baths, Baden-Baden acquired something of a resort status during the 19th century, becoming known as the "summer capital" of Europe. Its preserved heritage and picturesque surrounds continue to make it a popular destination.

10 Berendt produced the radio show Jazztime Baden-Baden and the ARD television program "Jazz Heard and Seen." On this occasion Ran and Jeanne also met Werner Bucshard [*sic*] and Günther Kieser.

11 After World War II, Baden-Baden became the headquarters for Germany's public broadcasting station, Südwestfunk. It is now part of Südwestrundfunk.

12 Günther Kieser is one of Germany's most important graphic designers. He is known for his poster designs for the Frankfurt Jazz Festival and jazz and rock in general.

13 The berries, named Johannisbeeran or John's berries (red currants) are said to ripen on St John's Day in mid-Summer. Johannisbeer Schorle is a drink made from a mix of redcurrant syrup and soda water.

14 According to Ran, it was a duo format of the Mitchell-Ruff-Harris trio that performed that day. This contradicts information available on the blog jazzrealities which lists the complete program, along with the personnel: the trio of Dwike Mitchell, piano; Willie Ruff, bass; and Joe Harris, drums. According to the program information listed, this trio was augmented by Albert Mangelsdorff, trombone; and Hans Koller, tenor saxophone, for certain pieces. Program information concerning Lee & Blake's performance is not supplied. The broadcast was episode 33 of the SWR-TV series, *Jazz gehört und gesehen* (*Jazz: Heard and Seen*). The episode was entitled "Kleines Kammerkonzert in Jazz" ("Little Chamber Concert of Jazz"). ['Hans Koller discography, part 3, 1960–1970', *Jazzrealities* (blog), accessed 15 December 2020, https://jazzrealities.blogspot.com/2016/02/hanskoller-strings-60-0220-february-20.html.]

15 Horst Lippmann was a partner in the booking agency of Lippman and Rau. He got them the tour of Germany.

16 Bremen—an industrial city an hour southwest of Hamburg and four hours

north of Frankfurt. According to George Avakian, the gig they got was at the Park Hotel night club.

17 On Ran and Jeanne's last night in Italy, the DeCrecenzos put on a party. Ran noted in his journal that the "RCA brass" was present as well as Alex Bradford of *Black Nativity*. (The De Crecenzos had taken Ran and Jeanne to see *Black Nativity*—which was in the second year of a European tour—the previous week).

18 Booth Tarkington was an American writer and dramatist. Prolific in the early 20th century, he won of two Pulitzer prizes for fiction with: *The Magnificent Ambersons* in 1919, and *Alice Adams* in 1922. He wrote often satirical studies of the American class system and its foibles (Ran describes the film version of *Alice Adams* as a "sort of Cinderella Stella Dallas." *Stella Dallas*, starring Barbara Stanwyck, also highlights class differences and a mother's sacrifice to ensure her daughter has access to a better life.)

The Editors of Encyclopaedia Britannica, 'Booth Tarkington', in *Encyclopedia Britannica*, 25 July 2020, https://www.britannica.com/biography/Booth-Tarkington.

19 Williams, 'With Blake and Lee in Europe', 15.

20 Williams, 15.

21 Bill Smith (jazz clarinetist and composer) His composition Schizophrenic Scherzo was probably one of the earliest works that successfully integrated jazz and classical music. (Bill Smith was known as a classical composer under his full name of William O.–Overton—Smith.) At the time, he was in Italy, where he spent six years (following two years at the Paris Conservatoire), after winning the Prix de Rome in 1957 and two Guggenheim fellowships in 1960. He arranged the Italian tour for Ran and Jeanne.

22 In his letter to Martin Williams on October 14, 1963, George Avakian described this show as "the Ed Sullivan show of Italy!"

23 Federazione Italiana Musica Jazz (FIMJ)

24 'Ran Blake and Jeanne Lee', *L'Ora.*, 18 May 1963.

25 'Ran Blake and Jeanne Lee'.

26 Native to Japan, this delicate bell-like flower had reached Europe by the Middle Ages, where it symbolized Spring and was thought to bring happiness.

27 Théâtre du Châtelet on the Seine at the Place du Châtelet was used for a variety of musical performances during the 20th century. Shirley Horn recorded her live album I Love You, Paris there in 1992.

28 Club Saint Germain on Rue Saint Benôit was in the jazz heartland of Paris. They met Mme. Michel through Kenny Clarke (MJQ), who had relocated to Paris in 1956.

29 Dr Arne Welhaven was a leader in the Bioenegetics Movement—an approach that used the body to heal the mind. It was considered helpful for people who tended to intellectualize.

30 Bergen, the capital of Western Norway, is a coastal harbor town build around

the Pullefjord.

[31] Overlooking a lake south of Bergen, the house is a traditional wooden building, with another wooden building in the grounds where Grieg could work. The house was called Troldhaugen or "Mountain of the Trolls."

'Edvard Grieg Museum Troldhaugen', Organization, Kode, accessed 30 November 2020, https://griegmuseum.no/en/about-troldhaugen.

[32] On the opening night, at the Golden Circle, composer Dr. Kjell Samuelson and many musicians were in the audience. In 1966 Samuelson produced *Free Standards–Stockholm* 1966 which, along with Lennon-McCartney, Billy Strayhorn and others, also included some Samuelson compositions. This was released on Columbia in 1995.

[33] Hans Fridlund, 'Sensation at the Golden Circle', *Aftonbladet*, 18 June 1963. The duo's gig ran for four days only—from 17th to 20th June 1963. Fridlund also gave a plug for Olle Helander's "Jazz under the Stars" radio program broadcast from Skansen when listeners would be able to again hear the Lee/Blake duo.

[34] Svante Foerster, 'Unknown at the Circle–But Exceptional', *Stockholms-Tidningen*, n.d.

[35] Rolf Dahlgren, 'Sensation at the Circle', *Estrad*, n.d.

[36] These reviews, translated into English, appear in Williams, 'With Blake and Lee in Europe', 16–17.

[37] George Avakian, 'Letter to Martin Williams', 14 October 1963, Ran Blake's private archive.

[38] Avakian, 27 July 1963. The "Bob" to whom Avakian was writing is most probably Bob Yorke. Avakian was seeking a story (same as he had for Martin Williams) – this time though he wanted a story about how "artists can be "made" in Europe but ignored in the U.S." He mentions his desire for such a story twice.

[39] Avakian.

[40] Cafe Montmartre was also known as Jazzhus Montmartre. It was an historic jazz venue in Copenhagen where artists such as Dexter Gordon, Ben Webster, Stan Getz, and Kenny Drew played regularly.

[41] This man was Christian Abry, with whom Ran subsequently corresponded for a few years following this discovery.

[42] Max Harrison, 'Over the Hills and Faraway: Further American Avant-Garde Releases Reviewed by Max Harrison', *Jazz Monthly*, 1967.

Chapter 11: Florence de Lannoy

[1] Marie-Dorothée de Croÿ was the sister of Ran's friend and mentor, Florence de Lannoy. Known as Princesse Mimi, Marie-Dorothée was a heroine of WWII, having helped British soldiers escape across Paris. At liberation, she was involved driving ambulances for the rescue of survivors of concentration camps. After the war, she became a breeder of Charolais cattle.

Translation of *Strange Music*:
> The wind turned in every direction,
> In swing, rock, or romance,
> Strange music, in the wind,
> Everything up there on the Morvan.[1]

[1] The Morvan—a mountainous region in Central France, much of which is now preserved as Natural Park—lies to the east of Saint-Benin-d'Azy (where the princess was born) and is easily accessed from there.

[2] Often referred to now as Festival de jazz d'Antibes Juan-les-Pins, or simply Jazz à Juan.

[3] The parasol or umbrella pine—the Stone Pine (Pinus pinea)—is native to the Mediterranean and has a distinctive umbrella shape as it matures. It featured in the paintings of many artists, including Claude Monet (Pine Trees, Cap d'Antibes, 1888) and French Neo-Impressionist painter Paul Signac, who often painted the pine trees at Juan-les-Pins.

[4] As per the family's oral history.
Both Marie and Reginald received the OBE in 1920. (Though many who knew of their bravery would have preferred they received a DBE and KBE, respectively.) Marie also received (it seems, at the insistence of the King) the Royal Red Cross, 2nd class (ARRC) in July 1921.
Jon Cooksey and Jerry Murland, The Retreat from Mons, 1914: North: Casteau to Le Cateau (South Yorkshire: Pen & Sword, 2014), 97.

[5] Marie-Dorothée de Croÿ, 'Florence de Croÿ', Personal website, Marie-Dorothée de Croÿ, accessed 16 July 2021, http://mimi.decroy.free.fr/florence.htm.

[6] de Croÿ.

[7] Léopold, Comte de Lannoy. (The House of Lannoy is an illustrious family of the Belgian nobility. The name comes from the city of Lannoy—originally Flanders, now France—which lies approximately 100km west of Brussels.)

[8] Constance de Lannoy—daughter of Florence and Léopold—recalls that Brindle was a Staffordshire bull terrier.
Constance de Lannoy to Janet McFadden, 'Ran Blake Book', 20 June 2017.

[9] At the time, Ran was manager of the Ugandan-born folksinger and drummer, Birigwa. He had sent across his album, entitled Birigwa.

[10] Her own girls would have been, at the time, thirteen, eleven, and six-year-old

New York — "The Happy Period" 581

twins.

[11] Florence de Lannoy, 'Letter: Florence de Lannoy to Ran Blake', October 1972, Ran Blake's private archive.

[12] In actual fact, the 'official' location for Sancerre wine is not in Nièvre but rather the neighboring *département* of Cher. Le Château d'Azy is situated at the edge of Saint-Benin-d'Azy (a little village in Nièvre which is a region of forests and lakes in the center of France). Construction of this grand, neo-Classical style castle commenced in 1847. It was where Florence was born. After her marriage, Florence brought her own family to the castle for holidays. (The castle belonged to Florence's sister, Catherine de Croÿ, after the death of their mother.) Here, Florence was also close to her sister, Dorothée de Croÿ, the Princesse Mimi, who lived in the beautiful 15th century "Manoir de Valotte," just a few kilometers away. The manor house and working farm (Charolais cattle) were open to the public and advertised as "a charming spot to pass peaceful vacations in a pleasant setting." Within these walls, one could be calm, rest and relax, and visit tourist spots or fish and hunt. It was ideal for artistic creation. Many creative artists responded to Princess Mimi's hospitality and found inspiration in these peaceful surroundings.

In the autumn of 1983, Julian Lennon, with two friends and collaborators, lived at the Valotte Manor and set up an eight-track recording studio in the barn to work on demos for Julian's debut album Valotte.

The castle (Château d'Azy) itself has since been converted into a wedding and functions venue.

[BeatleLinks Fab Forum, 'Julian Remembers the Making of Valotte', 1 October 2004, http://www.beatlelinks.net/forums/showthread.php?t=19350.]

[13] Ran Blake, 'Letter: Ran Blake to Count Léopold', 22 August 1983, Ran Blake's private archive.

[14] Ran's many letters to the countess always include, as he signs off, "special greetings" to Leopold."

[15] Rose de Lannoy to Janet McFadden, 'Ran Blake Book', 3 June 2017.

[16] Jeremiah Johnson was a 1972 American western film (Directed by Sydney Pollack and starring Robert Redford). It tells the story of a Mexican War veteran supporting himself in the Rocky Mountains as a trapper. It had its worldwide release at the Cannes Film Festival of 1972.

[17] On reading the transcript, Constance de Lannoy remarked that 'club' would not be the correct term to describe the Jacques le Fataliste Café and affirms that it would best be described as a "*café littéraire*."

de Lannoy to McFadden, 'Ran Blake Book', 20 June 2017.

[18] Florence de Lannoy, 'Letter: Florence de Lannoy to Ran Blake', 19 February 1976, Ran Blake's private archive.

[19] Ran is referring to his living/teaching room in Brookline, MA—a room approximately 26ft x 14ft (8m x 4.5m)

[20] Rue de Prince Royal in Brussels.

[21] Rose de Lannoy to Janet McFadden, 'Ran Blake Book', 3 June 2017.

[22] Florence and Léopold's daughter.

[23] In the end, Constance spent three years in New York.

[24] This house was an old mill with a water wheel (*moulin à eau*) near the village of Soire le Chateau in the north of France. Aulnoye was the nearest train station. It was surrounded by woods, with a river and a lake. The house had no electricity or heating.

Rose de Lannoy to Ran Blake, 'Re: December 1984', 21 September 2018.

[25] BRT (Belgian Radio and Television) Jazz orchestra was a means of introducing the Belgium public to new music. Produced by Elias Gistelinck (Flemish composer, musician, and radio producer—whose own music mixed classical and jazz as evidenced by titles like "Small Cantata" for Jeanne Lee—1968), the orchestra was directed by Etienne Verschueren.

During their 1966-67 European tour, Ran and Jeanne had a couple of engagements with BRT.

Chapter 12: Ready, Willing ... Waiting

[1] George Avakian, "Letter to Martin Williams," October 14, 1963, Ran Blake's private archive.

[2] It was the lead article in *DownBeat* (May 7, 1964).

[3] This concert was promoted by Joe Pinelli. It was held on Friday night, August 12, 1966, at 8.30 pm at the Village Theatre, 2nd Ave and 6th Street, Manhattan.

The Marion Brown Quintet (with Grachan Moncur III, Dave Burrell, Reggie Johnson, and Andrew Cyrille) opened the concert, followed by the Jeanne Lee–Ran Blake duo and concluding with the John Coltrane Quintet.

Chris DeVito et al., *The John Coltrane Reference*, ed. Lewis Porter (New York: Routledge, 2013), 351.

[4] It was the club where Lee Morgan was shot onstage in 1972.

[5] Quoted with permission from an interview with Jerry Schultz (Gopal Krishna) recorded by Daniel Beban in 2010 in Golden Bay, New Zealand.

[Jerry Schultz (Gopal Krishna), Radio New Zealand Sun Ra Part 3: Abstraction, Politics and Noise, interview by Daniel Beban, Radio broadcast, August 9, 2014, https://www.rnz.co.nz/concert/programmes/sun-ra.]

[6] Frank Mastropolo, "'It Was a Joint': Jazz Musicians Remember Slugs' in the Far East," Bedford + Bowery, September 10, 2014, https://bedfordandbowery.com/2014/09/it-was-a-joint-jazz-musicians-remember-slugs-in-the-far-east/.

[7] John E. D'Agostino and his son—also John, and also an artist—were inspired by John E's father, Vito, who rescued many discarded treasures—paintings, sculptures, rugs, and the like—during the Great Depression. (A significant part

of his collection was some of the favrile glass developed by Louis Tiffany in the late 19th century. Tiffany was using glass to trap light and color. In 1933, when the Tiffany Studios were liquidated, Vito rescued sheets of glass that were being smashed prior to dumping in the East River.)

Ran remembers: "I met him [John E.] when Jeanne Lee took me to Sam Rivers' loft. John was so knowledgeable about jazz and he worked with Tiffany glass." (During the '70s, Sam Rivers—jazz musician and composer—along with his wife, Bea, ran a jazz loft called Studio Rivbea in Bond Street, Lower Manhattan. It was an important place in the development of jazz, giving artists their own performing space.)

[8] The word "Saloon" had to be dropped in accordance with New York City regulations as the name had connections with alcohol.

Mastropolo, "'It Was a Joint.'"

[9] Town Hall is a highly regarded venue to play in New York–many concerts recorded there have later been released as seminal albums. The review Ran is referring to is appeared on September 21, 1964, and is available on the New York Times' archive. It is interesting to read with the benefit of hindsight. The reviewer writes that the concert "left one wondering where all that jazz had gone" before criticizing Ran Blake's interpretations of Ellington, Monk, and Mingus (among others), citing a limited use of musical color.

"Ran Blake, Pianist, Plays Own Works," *The New York Times*, September 21, 1964.

[10] Christian Abry was the young Frenchman Ran had met at the rail station after performing at Antibes in 1963.

[11] Ran kept a notebook of all the new friends they had met in Europe.

[12] Jen Hoenscheid believes that Jessie Powers was still alive in 1963 or 1964. Ran can remember she sent him money while he was "still living at Miss Lehrfeld's," though he cannot pinpoint the year. The actual date of death has been difficult to find. Ran remembers that towards the end of her life, "we had to move her to a little home." (He forgets the street.) She obviously remained vitally interested in his welfare.

[13] Joe Maneri—American born of Italian descent—was a jazz composer, saxophonist, and clarinetist. He entered the faculty of New England Conservatory in 1970, where he taught classes in microtonal composition for the following 37 years. On May 17, 2009, shortly before his death, he was awarded an honorary doctorate from NEC.

Chapter 13: A Cat Called Ludwig

[1] September 1966 to June 1967

[2] Freddy Ballé and Catherine Ballé to Ran Blake, "Ran in Paris," February 10, 2010.

³ The apartment at 27 Rue de l'Echiquier belonged to the SNCF—the French National Railways and had been rented to Catherine's great aunt because, before WWII, Catherine's grandfather had been one of their suppliers.

⁴ Ballé and Ballé to Blake, "Ran in Paris," February 10, 2010.

⁵ (This was the advent of the Black Arts Movement.) Ruth Waddy had, in 1962, founded Art West Associated in an attempt to support African American artists in Los Angeles. Years later, she was presented with a blank sketchbook with an inscription, penned by Evangeline Montgomery: "have your friends fill up this book in 1968 and get us (African American artists) published in '69." The landmark study *Black Artists on Art* was published in 1969.

Austen Bailly, "The Ruth Waddy Sketchbook," Los Angeles County Museum of Art, July 12, 2011, https://unframed.lacma.org/2011/07/12/the-ruth-waddy-sketchbook.

⁶ Gunter Hampel—a German musician (jazz vibraphone, clarinet, saxophone, flute, piano, and composition). Jeanne, who met Gunter in December 1966, did vocals for his albums between 1968 and 1983. She appeared—along with Anthony Braxton, Steve McCall, Willem Breuker, and Arjen Gorter—on his album, *The 8th of July 1969*, which was released on Hampel's own newly formed label, Birth Records. Hampel and Lee later married and had two children together.

⁷ George Avakian was certainly interested at the commencement of this tour. On December 7, 1966, he wrote to Jeanne:

"A prominent DJ in Philadelphia, who has the No. 1 jazz show, has become a Lee-Blake fan and is playing your RCA record now and then. I suggest that if you can make any arrangements to record in Europe, you hold out for yourselves the right to arrange distribution in the U.S. and this man—Joel Dorn is his name—and I will do what we can to make possible a U.S. release."

He continues with more advice, adding:

"to get someone to put up the manufacturing costs is the biggest problem when your market is obviously small. Yet I think this may be possible because of the extremely high quality of what you do."

He finishes:

"My best to David and Ran—why not send this letter on to Ran after you read it? Regards–George."

George Avakian, "Letter to Jeanne Lee," December 7, 1966, Ran Blake's private archive.

⁸ Herns Duplan—singer, dancer, and authority on Haitian folklore and the Voodoo religion— He also performed at the party hosted by Count Léopold de Lannoy.

⁹ Charles Delaunay was a French author and jazz expert. He founded (in 1935) *Jazz Hot*, which is one of the oldest jazz magazines. During World War II, he was a member of the Resistance.

¹⁰ Barclay Records was founded and owned by Eddie Barclay—*le Roi du microsillon* (the vinyl king.)

11   Paudras was the friend and unofficial guardian/manager of Bud Powell from 1962 to 64 in Paris. He got Powell back on his feet at a time when he was suffering both mentally and physically. He wrote of his friendship with Powell in his book *La Danse des Infideles*. The story of his friendship also inspired the director of the film *Round Midnight* (Bertrand Tavernier).

12   Ran had his own memories of Bud Powell from the time (during their first European tour) when he and Jeanne had supported the Bud Powell headline act in Copenhagen. They all (including Bud's wife, Buttercup) had dinner afterward, and Ran remembers that Bud started with chocolate sundae dessert and, after the main meal, finished off with a shrimp cocktail.

13   People Ran met included:
Pierre Barbaud, composer of film scores, notably—for Ran—*Les Abysses*, directed by Nikos Papatakis, and Agnès Varda's film, *La Pointe Courte*; Luis de Pablo, Spanish composer (Ran was very impressed with his orchestral piece, *Tombeau*.); Walter Marchetti, Italian composer; and Juan Hidalgo Codorniu (who together with Ramón Barce had founded the avant-garde musical group, Zaj); Edward Mattos, pianist; Colette Magny, French cabaret singer; Jean-Claude Zylberstein, lawyer, journalist, publisher and lover of jazz; Roger Lafosse, researcher and musician; Andrés Lewin-Richter, composer of electronic music, who, in the 1960s had studied and taught at Columbia Princeton Electronic Music Center in New York with Dr. Vladimir Ussachevsky.

14   A ten-day solo engagement starting on February 2, 1967, at the original club on Calle Marqués de Villamagna. Ran stayed with Don Strange, who was studying in Madrid and who he'd first got to know when working as a night clerk at the hotel on 58th Street.

15   Jose Antonio Luera, "Ran Blake – 'Somewhere in the United States, Whose Name I Don't Want to Remember,'" trans. Don Strange, *Aria Jazz*, March 1967.

16   Luera.

17   Georges Arvanitas was a French jazz pianist and organist. He recorded extensively with many top American jazz musicians. Art Farmer was a leading American jazz trumpeter and flugelhorn player.

18   Some of the people Ran met were:
Italian jazz pianist, composer, and conductor, "Maestro Giorgio Gaslini"; Italian contrabassist, Giorgio Azzolini; Italian composer, Aldo Clementi; and Andriano Mazzolette (journalist and radio producer known for his promotion of jazz in Italy).

19   Giannis Christou (Jani) was a Greek composer who studied in Cambridge, Rome, and Zurich. In 1951 he returned to Alexandria, where he married Theresia Horemi in 1961. He died in 1970 in a car accident in Athens.
[Ran recalls: "For years I thought he was liquidated by the junta."]

Chapter 14: 1967—Athens Coup

[1] Andreas Papandreou was a Harvard-trained academic who served two terms as Prime Minister of Greece in the 1980s and 1990s. During that time, he achieved many progressive reforms, including establishing a national health system and improving workers' rights. In 1964, he was (effectively) assistant prime minister in his father's government (George Papandreou). At the time of the coup in 1967, Andreas Papandreou was put in prison but released (at the intercession of American academics) on the condition that he leave the country. In exile in Paris, he formed the Panhellenic Liberation Movement (an anti-dictatorship organization).

[2] Vernon Frazer, 'Ran Blake: A Profile of the First Third Stream Performer', n.d., 9, Ran Blake's private archive.

[3] Aaron Copland, American composer, writer, and teacher, studied, in the early 1920s, with the French composer, conductor, and teacher, Nadia Boulanger. She inspired in him a broad musical taste. On his return to America, he captured the sound of America—his work, which included Appalachian Spring and Fanfare for the Common Man, appealed to popular taste.

[4] The historic Plaka quarter at the foot of the Acropolis was the heart of Greek New Wave music in the 1960s and 70s. Many Greek singers and musicians introduced this new style of music in tiny bars, such as Giannis Argiris' Espirides and George Zographos' Apanemia. Inspired by music coming out of Italy and France and acknowledging this French influence, these Plaka bars were called "*boîtes*."

Plaka was also famous for its restaurants—many of which still exist, like the Mostrou, the Perivoli ton Theon (Garden of Gods), and Geros tou Moria, which advertises live music and traditional food.

'Plaka of Athens: The Most Beautiful Area of Athens Under the Acropolis', Tourism, Athens Greece Guide, 2011 2003, https://www.athensguide.org/athens-plaka.html.

[5] Pia Hadjinikou-Angelini founded the Promote International Arts (PIA Agency) in 1959, with the aim of bringing the best of international cultural acts—ballet, orchestra, jazz, theater—to Greece. She was responsible for bringing the off-Broadway show Black Nativity (which featured Alex Bradford and Princess Stewart) to Greece. She was passionately interested in educating children about the arts. She died in February 2018 at the age of 97.

[6] The military dictatorship in Greece in 1967 focused on music as a means of building national identity and preserving culture. They promoted military marches and Greek folk music. They suppressed foreign music and its attendant foreign ways. Perversely, there were specific Greek musicians (who had indeed composed music connected with the folk tradition) whose music was regarded with suspicion.

Manos Hadjidakis and Mikis Theodorakis were composers and songwriters of post-WWII Greece. Hadjidakis was responsible for incorporating the earthy strains of Greek folk and popular song into respected art forms, thus elevating its status. (He became famous internationally for his movie soundtracks, particularly *Never on Sunday*.) Theodorakis, a resistance fighter in WWII, wrote several symphonies in the 1950s before returning to Greece to explore the traditional Greek music of his youth. In 1964 he composed the music for the film adaptation of *Zorba the Greek*. (He also wrote "Vradiazei," which appears on Ran's *Blue Potato* album.) The colonels banned the music of Mikis Theodorakis, who, himself, was forced underground after the coup and formed a group to combat the excesses of the new regime. He escaped to France, where he spent four years in exile. During this time, his music was respected around the world as a symbol of resistance to the dictatorship.

7   Port of Athens, where Ran met up with Maria Adamos.

8   Marina Karella studied at the Academy of Fine Arts in Athens and then in Paris. In her teens, she was inspired by Yannis Tsarouchis, who lived nearby. Her work has a dream-like quality and springs from Mediterranean culture.

9   The Rui Foundation manages university colleges throughout Italy, primarily for international students, with an aim to promoting social and cultural integration. It initially committed itself to scholarship projects for students from Third World countries. The university residences were established on the teachings of Josemaria Escrivà—the founder of Opus Dei (canonized in 2002 by Pope John Paul II). Escrivà believed that work and daily circumstances were an opportunity to meet God and serve others.

10   Karlheinz Stockhausen was a German composer. He was a creator of electronic music and influenced avant-garde composers in the latter part of the 20th century.

11   Arnold Schoenberg was an Austrian composer whose new methods of musical composition involved atonality. He was also a prolific theorist, developing analytical and compositional systems that would become widely adopted. Most notably, the "twelve-tone technique," which is synonymous with his name.

12   *The Fox Inn* was run by Jim Riley (an American alto-saxophonist) and his wife, Sheila.

13   Freddy Ballé and Catherine Ballé to Ran Blake, 'Ran in Paris', 10 February 2010.

14   Sun Ra (birth name Herman Poole Blount) was an American jazz musician, composer, and synthesizer player of experimental music. He claimed he was from Saturn and his mission was peace. From the 1950s, he was the leader of a musical collective known as "The Arkestra." In the Spring of 1966, Ran was part of an ESP tour of five colleges with music departments in New York State. The Sun Ra Arkestra was part of this tour along with Burton Greene, Patty Waters, and Giuseppi Logan. The tour was funded by a grant from the New York State Council on the Arts. The Byron Coley article quotes Ran as saying, "It was great being with Sun Ra on the road."

Byron Coley, 'Ran Blake Interview Transcript–The Wire', The Wire Magazine, July 2009, https://www.thewire.co.uk/in-writing/interviews/ran-blake-interview-transcript.

Chapter 15: Aftermath

[1] Jules Dassin was an American director, writer and actor. He directed Melina Mercouri in the award-winning *Never on Sunday*. After their marriage in 1966, they worked together in the struggle against the Greek military junta. Dassin's 1974 film *The Rehearsal* (in which Mercouri starred) depicted how the junta affected university students. Mercouri would later become an elected member of the Hellenic parliament.

[2] At the American Council for Greek Freedom, Ran met George Simeomidis. Obviously, he made an impression as many years later, in 2007, he received a lettercard from Dora Simeomidis, George's mother, which read: "Dear Mr. Blake, I will be in Boston for just one day, the 3rd of September, and I would be very pleased to meet you. It would be very nice if you were free to have dinner with us that same Thursday evening."

[3] New England Conservatory was founded in 1867 by Eben Tourjée and Robert Goldbeck.

[4] Stratis Haviaras—poet and writer of fiction.

[5] In his files, Ran provides some information about those who performed:

The Alpha and Omega Singers. Its members are all active workers of the St John Missionary Church in Roxbury; The Disciple Gospel Singers, which include Joe Sparks (baritone) as manager and Lennie Cox (tenor) on guitar. Les Chanteurs Chorale (19 members) with Mrs. Shirley Johnson, director and pianist;

Mrs. Jennie Cox (soprano) who is a member of the Regent Street Roxbury Church of God in Christ performed, accompanied by Lenny, her son.

Margo Miller, "Article Advertising Concert," *The Boston Globe*, January 8, 1968, Ran Blake's private archive; "Boston Council for Greek Freedom—Notes on Performers and Speakers," February 14, 1968, Ran Blake's private archive.

Boston

Chapter 1: Crossroads—The Move to Boston

¹ September 15, 1966, to July 4, 1967.

² Russell Sherman—classical pianist & artist in residence at NEC; Jon Wulp—graduate of Williams College & Concert Halls Booking Manager at NEC. (Though when he met Ran, he was working on the stage crew and loving it.); Donald Harris—composer—was an administrator and faculty member at NEC from 1967—1977; Harvey Phillips, the tuba soloist, took up the position of Vice President for Financial Affairs at NEC (1967—1971); John Heiss—composer, conductor, flutist and professor at NEC. [New England Conservatory Archives, "Donald Harris," Institution webpage, necmusic.edu, accessed December 12, 2020, https://necmusic.edu/archives/donald-harris; New England Conservatory Archives, "Harvey Phillips," Institution webpage, necmusic.edu, accessed December 12, 2020, https://necmusic.edu/archives/harvey-phillips.]

³ Byron Coley, "Ran Blake," *The Wire*, July 2009.

⁴ Automats were at their peak popularity in the '40s and '50s. Joe Horn and Frank Hardart, who opened their first automat on July 2, 1912, were committed to excellent food and low prices. Their food was prepared at a central location and delivered by truck. Fresh coffee was made at each individual outlet every hour, and it was said to be the best coffee in New York. But the cost of fresh ingredients added to trucking costs eventually became prohibitive, and quality declined. The Editors of Encyclopaedia Britannica, 'Automat', in *Encyclopædia Britannica* (Encyclopædia Britannica, 19 May 2017), https://www.britannica.com/topic/Automat; New York Public Library, "Lunch Hour NYC," Institution, The Automat, January 7, 2020, https://wayback.archive-it.org/11788/20200107230316/http://exhibitions.nypl.org/lunchhour/exhibits/show/lunchhour/automat.

⁵ "Advertisement, Cafe Amalfi" (The Boston Globe, December 10, 1981), Newspapers.com, https://www.newspapers.com/image/?clipping_id=32572152&fcfToken=eyJhbGciOiJIUzI1NiIsInR5cCI6IkpXVCJ9.eyJmcmVlLXZpZXctaWQiOjQzNjg4Mzc3NSwiaWF0IjoxNjA3Nzg3MjI2LCJleHAiOjE2MDc4NzM2MjJ9.xtkm6uQGROVE4a1ygAiHMkUFPqQC_VQxqcCbYgpCbYE.

⁶ Boston Symphony Orchestra, "Boston Symphony Orchestra Concert Programs, 1979-1980," archive.org, September 11, 2012, http://archive.org/details/bostonsymphonysub7980bost.

[7] *Spumone*, as it is known in Italy (plural *spumoni*), is a molded ice cream/dessert with layers of cherry, pistachio, chocolate ice cream. Texture is added between layers from thick whipped cream, with cherries, orange peel, and almonds folded through.

[8] Erich Leinsdorf was appointed director of the Boston Symphony Orchestra in 1962 and served there till 1969. He would have been fifty at the time of his appointment. During a concert on November 22, 1963, it was Leinsdorf's duty to announce the shocking news of President Kennedy's assassination in Dallas. He then conducted the orchestra in the "Funeral March" from Beethoven's *Third Symphony*.

[9] Ballantine Brewing Company is a historic American Brewery founded in 1840 in Newark, New Jersey. The Ballantine India Ale was a pale ale that was aged for about a year in wooden tanks.

[10] The Gallo family winery was founded in 1933 (after Prohibition) in California.

[11] By this time, Ran had taken an apartment at 25 St. Stephen Street, Boston.

[12] Adelheid (Dahl) Hestnes was an opera singer who performed in Europe during the 1920s and 30s. In 1939 she was one of the organizers in Oslo of the First Women's March for Peace. "Obituary for Adelheid Hestnes (Aged 89)," *The Boston Globe*, April 2, 1994.

[13] They inhabit his Notebooks—along with menu options on various tours, film lists, setlists, compositions, and music reference lists. There are also book lists: fiction and non-fiction, mystery writers, and theater lists.

[14] By late 1967 there are nearly half a million US troops in South Vietnam. Philip Gavin, "Vietnam War 1965-1968," The History Place, accessed December 12, 2020, http://www.historyplace.com/unitedstates/vietnam/index-1965.html.

[15] Andrew Franklin K., "King in 1967: My Dream Has 'Turned into a Nightmare,'" The Daily Nightly–NBC News, August 27, 2013, http://www.nbcnews.com/nightly-news/king-1967-my-dream-has-turned-nightmare-flna8C11013179.

[16] Franklin. (Referring to Martin Luther King Jr. interview with NBC News correspondent Sander Vanocur on May 8, 1967.)

[17] In April of 1965, he had led a freedom march through Boston streets to the Boston Common, where he addressed the vast crowd, calling for desegregation of housing and schools.
Friends of the Public Garden, *Boston Common*, ed. Linda Cox et al. (Charleston, SC: Arcadia Publishing, 2005), 118.

[18] On April 20, 1967, on the other side of the world, Ran was taken in for questioning just prior to the military take-over in Greece. When he returned to New York in July 1967, he sensed this subtle shift (particularly outside Sweet Daddy Grace's church). In less than a year (April 4, 1968), Martin Luther King, Jr.

would be assassinated.

[19] On June 1, 1967, when the Beatles' *Sgt Pepper's Lonely Hearts Club Band* was released in Mono and Stereo LPS in Britain, "Army Decree No 13," issued by Greece's military junta, banned the playing or listening to the music of Mikis Theodorakis.

Hannah Blubaugh, "The Soundtrack of the Summer of Love," Origins: Current Events in Historical Perspective, September 2017, https://origins.osu.edu/milestones/september-2017-soundtrack-summer-love; Anna Papaeti, "Folk Music and the Cultural Politics of the Military Junta in Greece (1967–1974)," *Mousikos Logos*, no. 2 (2015): 50–62.

[20] Most news programs expanded from fifteen to thirty minutes in the 1960s, and, with the coming of cable TV, CNN (Cable News Network) was launched in mid-1980, providing 24-hour television news coverage.

Daniel Hallin, "Whatever Happened to the News?," *Media&Values* Spring, no. 50 (1990).

[21] Gordon Talley, "Open to Diversity," *Notes*, no. Spring (1995). At the time, Mr. Talley was Director of Public Relations at NEC.

Chapter 2: Gunther–A Personal Look

[1] Ran Blake, "Filed Document," July 21, 1999, Ran Blake's private archive.

[2] Gunther Schuller, *Gunther Schuller: A Life in Pursuit of Music and Beauty* (Rochester, NY: University of Rochester Press, 2011), 475.

[3] With Eugene Goossens conducting. [Schuller, 163.]

[4] Schuller, 437.

[5] This first "get-together" happened soon after meeting at Atlantic Records in January 1958. As quoted in Schuller, 475.

[6] Schuller, 476.

[7] Blake, "Filed Document."

[8] Ran Blake, Interview 320 for "American Music Series," interview by Larry Ruttman, October 10, 2001, 26.

[9] Blake, "Filed Document," 6–7.

[10] Ran is speaking to Ed Symkus, CNC staff writer.

Ed Symkus, "Pianist-Teacher Performs Free Concert at Conservatory," *Metro West Daily News*, February 7, 2002.

[11] Gunther Schuller, *Gunther Schuller: A Life in Pursuit of Music and Beauty* (Rochester, NY: University of Rochester Press, 2011), 476.

[12] Schuller, 476.

[13] Bill Evans' first long-term romance was with Peri Cousins, for whom "Peri's Scope" was named.

[14] Stan Kenton had been a long-time favorite of Ran's, so the disappointment was severe.

[15] Blake, "Filed Document," 6.
(On reading this chapter back, Ran is keen to add to the names of the people who support his music: Hankus Netsky, Aaron Hartley, Dave "Knife" Fabris. He had also admitted earlier that Oscar Peterson, "who I never thought would like my style," was "surprisingly supportive."
George Schuller adds that, in an interview with him, Ran acknowledged that "Eugene Wright, Dave Brubeck's long-time bassist, was very helpful and generous," particularly during "one of those summers at the School of Jazz when the Brubeck Quartet was in residence." (probably 1959)

[16] This interview took place at a time when Gunther was still working. (2009)

[17] Gunther Schuller: Liner Notes: [Ran Blake, *Ran Blake Plays Solo Piano*, LP, Album (US: ESP-Disk, 1965).] (As reprinted for Ran's Regatta Bar concert in honor of his sister, Martha, February 5, 2014), Schuller, *Gunther Schuller*, 2011, 475.

[18] Blake, *Ran Blake Plays Solo Piano*.

[19] *Ibid*

[20] "Gunther was hired to be on the faculty starting in 1963, becoming head of the composition department by 1964 (taking over from Aaron Copland). By 1965, Gunther took over the contemporary music activities (in addition to continuing to head the composition department), when the Festival of Contemporary Music began (otherwise known as the Fromm Festival, named after Paul Fromm, who sponsored the festival. It took place for one week during the Tanglewood summer season).
In 1970, Gunther became co-artistic director with Seiji Ozawa. However, his duties were to oversee the Berkshire Music Center activities, whereas Seiji was considered director of the festival in general. Leonard Bernstein acted as advisor for a couple of those initial years; however, the Schuller family were spending virtually every summer at Tanglewood from 1963 to 1984.
George Schuller to Janet McFadden, "Corrections to Chapter," January 2, 2020.

[21] George Schuller: We were renting the Old Mill in West Stockbridge, MA (built in 1830) for those two summers (1967 & '68). The Old Mill was eventually bought by Jimmy & Juanita Giuffre (where Juanita still lives).

[22] On the subject of herbs, George Schuller is able to add some delightful color: "I should also add that in 1968, Ran was staying in a house across from the Old Mill, with a wonderful diminutive lady with loads of 'nervous energy' (as Ran described her) and genuine goodwill named Alfreda Joslin, who was the primary

herb-lord (like druglord) of the neighborhood and somewhat an influence to my mother's cooking. Alfreda perhaps made daily deliveries of all of her wonderful herbs from her garden over to Margie, who then put them to good use in her famous salads and meals...thus the 'dill' that Ran talks about all the time."

Schuller to McFadden, "More Reflections on Lenox," December 21, 2019.

[23] George Schuller clarifies that Gunther lost an eye in a childhood accident.

[24] Milton Babbitt: American composer and theorist—influenced by Schoenberg's 12 tone music. He was interested in electronic sound synthesis as well as jazz and musical comedy.

[25] Leinsdorf rented a house on the mountain road from West Stockbridge to Tanglewood. This was on the primary route that Ran used to take when driving Gunther back and forth from the mill.

[26] Ran clarifies, on re-reading, that this would have been a Gibson martini with cocktail onions. He also volunteers that Gunther "adored" canned mandarin oranges... and duck.

[27] Various departments at the New England Conservatory have undergone name changes over the years. In the case of the department currently known as "Jazz Studies," its present name seems to have been arrived at more out of usage and less by way of an official name change. It was, indeed, officially called the "Department of African-American Music and Jazz Studies." Carl Atkins, the department's first chair, explains:

"As I remember it, when this went to the NASM (The National Association of Schools of Music) to request a degree, it was called the 'Afro-American Music and Jazz Studies Department,' and the jazz program was a subset of that, because, I think, again, Gunther's vision (and mine) was that this would become, you know, a full-fledged department that looked into many, many aspects of African American music, which is why that—'Afro-American Music and Jazz Studies'—was appropriate at that point. Now, when it changed, I'm like you, I don't have a clue, but I do remember that we had a Ford Foundation grant, we had a Massachusetts Council of the Arts grant, to bring in speakers to the program to start to move the activities and the curriculum in the area of African American or Afro-American music—not just jazz—and that was a part of the plan: to continue, as we went along, to expand these ideas. Of course, the conservatory, as everybody knows, was starting to run into some financial issues, and [like] a lot of things, this kind of got pushed off to the side while they dealt with the financial crisis that the conservatory was going through in some of those early days, so I'm not sure how it all got mixed up in the discussions and when things started appearing in print that didn't include 'Afro-American Music' as a part of the title for the department. Again, Susan [Calkins] has pulled up in her research, if I remember correctly, some programs and various kinds of documentation that show how things were listed in programs, and sometimes they were listed as 'Jazz Studies,' and sometimes they were listed as 'Afro American Music Studies' and then sometimes 'The Jazz Program,' under the 'Afro American Music and Jazz Department,' so, it all got very, very confused, after a while, for everybody concerned."[1]

[1] African-American Music and Jazz Studies @ NEC, NEC Perspectives Forum, 2020, https://www.youtube.com/watch?v=kYyiVJxcKoc&t=823s.

In its use of lowercase, this book does not assume any official name for the department beyond that of its originally listed name, "Department of Afro-American Music and Jazz Studies." For more information, see the discussion and Susan Calkins' doctoral dissertation.

Susan Lee Calkins, "A History of Jazz Studies at New England Conservatory, 1969-2009: The Legacy of Gunther Schuller" (Doctoral Thesis, Boston, MA, Boston University, 2012), https://open.bu.edu/handle/2144/12306

²⁸ Vladimir Ussachevsky: A hereditary Mongolian prince of Russian descent who fled to California after the Russian Revolution (and subsequent execution of his father, who was outwardly critical of the new Russian government). Ussachevsky then studied music and composition in America. After serving in the US Army Intelligence division during World War II, he joined Columbia University as an instructor. Teaching and experimenting with a newly purchased tape recorder, he created, in the early 1950s, the first electronic music compositions to be played in the United States.

Mario Davidovsky: An Argentine-American composer, who, as a young man, had studied with Aaron Copland and Milton Babbitt at the Berkshire Music Centre, Lenox. Through Babbitt (and others), he developed an interest in electroacoustic music and is best known for his compositions called "*Synchronisms.*" He was appointed Associate Director of the Columbia-Princeton Electronic Music Center soon after settling in New York in 1960.

²⁹ Blake, Interview 320 for "American Music Series."

³⁰ It's a message that echoes Ran's father's pleas when Ran was a child.

³¹ Aaron Hartley, "Telling Ran About Gunther," June 23, 2015.

Chapter 3: Mentors and Father Figures

¹ "Big Sid" Catlett—American jazz drummer whose versatility allowed him to transition from swing to bebop. He was admired for his remarkably steady timekeeping. He had a great sense of form and structure, as well as being a great showman.
"Sidney "Big Sid" Catlett: Busting Open Doors To The Modern Drumming Age," Modern Drummer Magazine, March 22, 2010, https://www.moderndrummer.com/2010/03/sidney-big-sid-catlett/.

² Buz Gummere was also Career Counselor at Columbia University for nineteen years. He was certified to teach the Alexander Technique (which aimed to unity "mind, muscle and spirit") and served as adviser to the Fertman Alexander school in Philadelphia.

³ James Case was President of Bard College July 1950–1960

⁴ Duff—named Richard Mott Gummere III—as was the family tradition.

⁵ Christine Gummere is co-founder (2007) and artistic director of "Sinfonia," New York. She is an accomplished cellist. "Sinfonia" is a period-instrument orchestra, playing works from the baroque and classical periods. Christine remembers Ran's visits to her family's Barrytown home and refers to him as her "dear old friend and bed-time storyteller."

⁶ Barrytown is a hamlet in the town of Red Hook. It is just over two miles to the south of Bard College—a pleasant walk away along peaceful country roads.

7 "All About Ronnie" was written by Joe Greene and recorded by Chris Connor with the Kenton orchestra in 1953. The song would become her signature song.

8 Barry Ulanov, an intellectual who pioneered serious writing about jazz, especially after becoming editor of *Metronome* magazine in 1943. Miles Davis referred to him as the only white critic who ever understood him or Charlie Parker. He championed bebop performers, particularly Dizzy Gillespie and Charlie Parker. He was a supporter of the work of Lennie Tristano, who wrote "Coolin' Off with Ulanov" for him. ["Barnard English Professor Barry Ulanov, Noted Jazz Author and Critic, Is Dead at 82," *The Record–Columbia University* 25, no. 22 (May 5, 2000), http://www.columbia.edu/cu/record/archives/vol25/22/2522_Ulanov_Obit.html.]

9 Muriel DeGré—Bard alumni and editor of a newspaper in Red Hook. As Ran recalls, "her daughter, Rikki Ducornet, is a well-known novelist, poet, essayist—Dorothy Wallace adored her. She was married at one time to Guy Ducornet. Muriel's husband, Gerard, was Ran's sociology teacher at Bard.

10 Ran had already worked in journalism, writing short reviews for Thompsonville press, but the *Dutchess County Journal* offer that resulted from Buz Gummere's suggestion was very limited—"one or two times," according to Ran. Later, he did "five or six" articles for the Morningside Heights paper during his first year or two at New York, and "way later" he worked for the *Bay State Banner* in Roxbury, where he reviewed Newport Festival among other things.

11 Duxbury—a seaside town approximately 35 miles (56km) south-east of Boston—is where Peg Gummere wanted her ashes to be scattered.

12 "Remembering Buzz," *AboutTown: The Community Journal of Dutchess and Columbia Counties*, no. Fall (2007).

13 Ran has a small booklet *The Romance of the Negro Folk Cry in America* signed by Willis Laurence James at the Music Inn 1958.

14 Author Nathanial Hawthorne lived for a couple of years in the mid-19th century in the Little Red House on the Stockbridge-Lenox boundary. During this time, he wrote *The House of Seven Gables*, began *Tanglewood Tales* and was visited by his friend Herman Melville (who was staying in neighboring Pittsfield at Arrowhead Farm, where he wrote *Moby Dick)*. The red farmhouse burned down in 1890. The National Federation of Music Clubs built a replica in 1948 to be used as music practice rooms for Tanglewood.

15 James died December 27, 1966—he was sixty-six years old.

16 Owl Records, 1976

17 Willis Laurence James, "The Romance of the Negro Folk Cry in America," *PHYLON-the Atlanta University Review of Race and Culture*, no. first quarter (1955).

18 James, 19.

[19] Willis Laurence James, "Letter to B.A. Botkin," January 1, 1943, Library of Congress, http://www.loc.gov/.

[20] Ran Blake, "Reflections on Mother Carter," n.d., Ran Blake's private archive.

[21] François Mauriac was a French writer, novelist—winner of the 1952 Nobel Prize for literature. His character, Mme. Brigitte Pian, as she appears in the novel La Pharisienne (A Woman of the Pharisees) is a self-righteous woman who feels compelled to interfere in the lives of others because of the extreme nature of her religious principles.

Chapter 4: D.C.W—Mentor, Patron, and True Friend

[1] John Phillips Marquand was an American writer. Prolific during the first half of the 20th century—now largely out of print. In his serious novels, he addressed the issues of privilege and inequality, but he also wrote a series of popular spy novels. He had many short stories published in the *Saturday Evening Post* between 1921 and 1952.

[2] The *Late George Apley* was a 1937 novel by John Phillips Marquand. A satire of Boston's upper class, it won the Pulitzer Prize in 1938.

[3] It is possible that this may have been an impression Ran had and *not* actually the words of Dorothy Wallace—though she could be very direct. At his lifetime achievement award, Ran told this story slightly differently. He said he told Dorothy Wallace he'd never had spinach as she'd made it, and she said, "You may come again next Sunday with eight friends." Obviously, this suggests a different interpretation. Perhaps the truth is somewhere in the middle.

[4] Dorothy, at that stage, would not have known of Ran's great interest in food, especially food that was out of the ordinary!

[5] He headed the Barber Colman Company. Howard Colman has been called a "humble genius inventor on par with Edison or Ford, but without the fanfare."[1]

He has been credited with more than 149 patented inventions: the first at the age of seventeen was a warp drawing machine for weaving cotton into patterns. Colman's inventions covered a broad spectrum. He has been credited with inventing the "original binary bit technology that led to the modern-day computer."[2]

It is reported that he "genuinely cared for his employees and saw to their welfare by organizing recreational outings, a company band, and sports teams. He also took the steps necessary to ensure they kept their jobs during economic depressions."[3]

[1 & 3:] Ken Fager, 'Barber-Colman Factory', *American Urbex* (blog), 23 December 2010, http://americanurbex.com/wordpress/?p=661.

[2:] Ken Kline, 'Top Inventor - The Master Inventor - History of Overhead Garage Doors Automation of Textile Machines - 140 Patents', HubPages, 23 October 2015, https://discover.hubpages.com/education/INVENTOR-THE-MASTER-INVENTOR.

6   High Street, at this point, was known as High Street Hill or Pill Hill because of the many doctors who lived there.

7   Herbert Speidel ran the Munich office of Barber-Colman, Howard Colman's company.

8   Anne, Richard (dec.), James, Connie (dec.), and Dan.

9   Warne Marsh—Los Angeles born tenor saxophonist; a protégé of Lennie Tristano.

10   At the time, Ran was working in prison outreach.

11   Ran recalls one time when he was a Logan Airport, and Dorothy Wallace was getting off the plane, and "Ricky (Ford) had all the students there to play 'I get a Kick out of You.' There wasn't all the security in 1969, so you could go right there (as she walked down the plankway), and Dorothy Wallace was thrilled. People were there photographing another dignitary, but they were all looking at Dorothy."

12   Maxine and her husband had bought a little barn adjacent to Dorothy Wallace's home on Chestnut Place. This was 1973. [Maxine Dolle, Recollections of Dorothy Wallace, interview by Janet McFadden, Skype call, 6 January 2012.]

13   Dolle.

14   Dolle.

15   The composition "Indian Winter" was first recorded by Blake on his *Suffield Gothic* album (Soul Note,1984–with saxophonist, Houston Person). It subsequently featured on Blake's eponymous album of 2005 (Soul Note) with guitarist David 'Knife' Fabris.

16   Peter Row—Sitarist and ethnomusicologist (1944–2018). He served as dean of academic affairs at NEC from 1983 to 1990 and provost from 1990 to 1996 and 2000 to 2004. He was also a neighbor of Dorothy's, living across the street.

17   Eileen Murphy: "Dorothy Wallace's most famous comment to me was that she thought George Russell was the sexiest man she had ever met."

18   Brunhild or Brunhilda comes from Icelandic and German mythology. She was a strong and beautiful princess who was deceived by her lover. Richard Wagner based his opera *The Ring of the Nibelung* on these legends, with Brünnhilde a central character.

19   Dolle, Recollections of Dorothy Wallace.

20   Eileen Murphy, Reflections on Dorothy Wallace and Ran Blake, interview by Janet McFadden, Telephone, 8 April 2011.

21   Anne Elvins Grace remembers these paintings as hanging in the dining room.

22   Ran has a small print of the portriat of Connie Wallace on his windowsill.

23   Lajos Szalay is known for his expressive monochrome drawings.

24   Dorothy Wallace called on the Blake family in Suffield a couple of times, and then, after Philip and Alison retired to Florida, she called on them there also. Ran recalls they were not "close" friends but that "She called them Phil and Allie, and they called her Dorothy."

25   Walter Colman, Dorothy's brother, had lived in the home of George Roper, founder of Roper Stove Corp. Roper stoves took their inspiration from Art Deco and were made of porcelain and chrome.

26   Dorothy Wallace, 27 April 1954, Eileen Murphy's personal archive.

27   Dorothy Wallace, 8 February 1957, Eileen Murphy's personal archive.

28   Dolle, Recollections of Dorothy Wallace.

29   Dorothy was embezzled, and the resultant change in circumstances meant she had to move.

30   Shad Roe—the egg sac of the female shad, or river herring. It is very seasonal as the fishing season is short. It is prized and considered a delicacy. It looks a bit like liver with a soft, light texture.

31   Murphy, Reflections on Dorothy Wallace and Ran Blake.

32   Anne Elvins Grace to Janet McFadden, 'Ran Blake Biography', 16 March 2011.

33   Ran Blake, 'Letter of Appreciation to Dorothy Wallace', 14 August 1973, Ran Blake's private archive.

34   "The Vice President was a famous psychiatrist from Sri Lanka, and her name was Dr. Shera Samaraweera—she's in heaven now." Ran Blake—while reading the draft copy.

35   The architect Ron Freilich was a very close friend whom she had met when he was attending Harvard. (In fact, he had door-knocked the area looking for a carriage house to live in, in exchange for work while he was studying.) According to Eileen Murphy, "Ron, Ran, and myself were an inner circle of close friends of Dorothy Wallace."

36   Murphy, Reflections on Dorothy Wallace and Ran Blake.

37   Greg Silberman was a student of Madame Chaloff.
Ran: "He lived at the Wallace house—in the garage. He hailed from New Jersey and was my manager in the seventies—and a wonderful young man."

38   The Falcone company started building pianos in earnest in the mid-1980s. (Falcone began building pianos in 1982, producing a small, select number in this early period.) Santi Falcone, originally from Sicily, discovered a disused shoe factory in Haverhill, Massachusetts, near the New Hampshire border. The spot was perfect for his hand-crafted pianos, being close to a good labor pool, major highways (important as he wanted to sell direct to the public), and also close

to the raw materials he needed. (Spruce and maple were close at hand in New Hampshire forests.)

Santi Falcone believed that five or six hundred "man-hours" were needed to craft a piano. When, in 1989, the company's board decided to go for faster production, he resigned. (This was after the production of the first 170 pianos, which was done under his personal supervision.) He withdrew his plans and designs; they are preserved in the Smithsonian Archive. Rick Friedman, 'Widely Acclaimed Pianos Symbolize Old Massachusetts City's Resurgence', *New York Times*, 22 March 1987.; William Harris, Prof. Em. Middlebury College. Biography of Falcone.

[39] Laurence Lesser—Artistic Director of NEC from 1982 to 1983 and President of NEC from 1983 to 1996. He presided over the restoration of Jordan Hall.

[40] Christine Correa—Vocalist & former student of Ran Blake. Together they recorded *Round About* (1994, Music & Arts); *Out of the Shadows* (2010, Red Piano Records) *Down Here Below: Tribute to Abbey Lincoln, Vol 1* (2012, Red Piano Records); *The Road Keeps Winding: tribute to Abbey Lincoln, Vol 2* (2015, Red Piano Records); *Streaming* (2018, Red Piano Records).

[41] Dominique Eade—Jazz singer and composer on faculty at NEC. Together Dominique and Ran recorded: *Whirlpool* (2011, Jazz Project) and *Town and Country* (2017, Sunnyside Records). Dominique also appears as a guest artist on Ran's 2015 Impulse! release, *Chabrol Noir*.

[42] Gary Joynes is a songwriter, composer, producer, keyboardist, saxophonist, and educator. A graduate of NEC, he played on George Russell's The African Game (Blue Note, 1984); he was also featured in "Gil Evans' Monday Night Orchestra."

[43] In 2009, when promoting a concert (Ran Blake: Solo Piano–In Concert), Ran listed some of the musicians who had played at Dorothy Wallace's:

"Several important musicians appeared here: May Arnette, Stelios Argyros, Christine Correa, Dominique Eade, Curtis Faire, Jason Freed, Ricky Ford, Anna Gabrieli, Jimmy Giuffre, Jon Hazilla, Gary Joynes, Jeanne Lee, Maxine Major, Raj Motipara, Hankus Netsky, Orland Patterson, Eleni Odoni, George Russell, Ed and George Schuller, and many others."

[44] Eileen Murphy, Reflections on Dorothy Wallace and Ran Blake, interview by Janet McFadden, Telephone, April 8, 2011.

[45] Murphy.

[46] Murphy. (Letter read aloud by Eileen Murphy.)

[47] Murphy.

[48] Anne Elvins Grace to Janet McFadden, "Ran Blake Biography," March 16, 2011.

[49] Elvins Grace to McFadden.

(Ran endorses this statement: "She [Dorothy] and Peter Row [the Dean of NEC

1983–90] kept the department alive after Gunther had left.")

[50] Curtis Faire appears on the cover of *Suffield Gothic*. See page 387, Community Services chapter.

[51] "Dancing in the Dark," with music written by Arthur Schwartz and lyrics by Howard Dietz, was Dorothy's favorite song. She used to encourage Ran to play it at her concerts. She thought it had the most beautiful lyrics of anything she had heard, particularly the line: "We're waltzing in the wonder of why we're here / Time hurries by, we're here and we're gone."

[52] She commissioned the first book of the bible Genesis to be done by a Hungarian/Argentinian artist Lajos Szalay (1919-1995). There's a museum for Dorothy Wallace at Jamaica Plain.

[53] Murphy, Reflections on Dorothy Wallace and Ran Blake.

[54] Murphy.

[55] Gunther Schuller, January 14, 2001, Ran Blake's private archive.

Chapter 5: Community Services

[1] Henry Melvill, The Golden Lectures, James Paul, 1, Chapter House Court, vol. 3 (London, 1855), 300. Rev. Melvill delivered these lectures at St Margaret's Church, Lothbury 1850–1856, a church built by Sir Christopher Wren.

[2] "Jazz Propelled into Mainstream Conservatory Education: Gunther Schuller at the Helm of NEC," Virtual journal, The Boston Musical Intelligencer, December 9, 2009, https://www.classical-scene.com/2009/12/09/jazz-propelled-into-mainstream-conservatory-education-gunther-schuller-at-the-helm-of-nec/. (Quoted with permission)

It is interesting to note that in the Fall of 1946, there was full enrolment, and the conservatory was out of debt. John W. Bond, "National Historic Landmark Nomination: New England Conservatory of Music" (National Park Service, December 17, 1993), 34, National Register of Historic Places, NP Gallery, https://npgallery.nps.gov/NRHP/GetAsset/NHLS/80000672_text.

[3] Gunther Schuller, speaking in an interview with *The Boston Musical Intelligencer* on December 9, 2009, recounted a Board meeting, where it seems the Board was reluctant to allocate required funds. Gunther, obviously frustrated, admitted, "I just got up in the middle of the meeting and said, '$5000! Here! Here it is!'. ["Jazz Propelled into Mainstream Conservatory Education."]

[4] "Jazz Propelled into Mainstream Conservatory Education."

[5] Schuller points out that the Cotton Club is not the original Cotton Club in Harlem but a new jazz venue on 49th Street and Broadway. Gunther Schuller, *Gunther Schuller: A Life in Pursuit of Music and Beauty* (Rochester, NY: University of Rochester Press, 2011), 57–58.

6 Schuller, 182.

7 "Jazz Propelled into Mainstream Conservatory Education."

8 "Jazz Propelled into Mainstream Conservatory Education."

9 Amalie Tucker, ed., "The 1969 Neume" (The New England Conservatory of Music, 1969), Internet Archive, https://archive.org/details/neume1969newe.

10 By Fall 1969, Atkins had "a curriculum, faculty, students, and NASM accreditation for NEC's Department of Afro-American Music and Jazz Studies." Recently, members of the NEC community, including current and former students, have made the point that a title can influence the direction of a program. Discussion continues around this subject and many other issues, with the intention that the department be a good steward of the music that it teaches, in all the aspects that this entails. (For more information, see footnote 27 of "Gunther—A Personal Look")

Rob Schmieder, "Caravan: 30 Years of Jazz at NEC," *Notes*, 2000, New England Conservatory Archives.

11 Boston Redevelopment Authority, General Neighborhood Renewal Plan Project No. Mass. R-50: Roxbury - North Dorchester Urban Renewal Area, Boston Redevelopment Authority, (Boston, Massachusetts, 1965), 2, http://archive.org/details/generalneighborh00bost.1965

12 Jack Tager, UMass Professor of History, speaking with Mike Miliard, identifies the "bigotry" of landlords" as at least partially responsible for the way different races are separated in neighborhoods. Mike Miliard, "Boston's Days of Rage," The Phoenix.com, March 2, 2001, https://bostonphoenix.com/boston/news_features/other_stories/documents/00644216.htm.

13 In the 1971–72 school year, the public school enrolment was 61% white, 32% black, and 7% other minorities, but 84% of white pupils attended schools which were more than 80% white, and 62% of the black pupils attended schools that were more than 70 percent black.

["Morgan v. Hennigan, 379 F. Supp. 410 (D. Mass. 1974)" (US District Court for the District of Massachusetts, June 21, 1974), Justia US Law, https://law.justia.com/cases/federal/district-courts/FSupp/379/410/1378130/.]

14 Martin Luther King Jr. had personal connections with Boston. In 1951 he arrived there to study theology at Boston University. In the same year, Coretta King commenced her study at NEC. She graduated in June 1954 with a Bachelor of Music in Music Education. She studied voice with Mme. Marie Sundelius and music education under the direction of Mrs. Leta Whitney. She lived in the school's dormitory on Hemenway Street, and it was early 1952 that she met her future husband, who was working on his doctorate in theology. They were married in June 1953.

[Juan Williams, *Eyes on the Prize: America's Civil Rights Years, 1954-1965* (New York, NY: Penguin, 2002).]

[15] Built in the Italian Renaissance Revival style with the intention of referencing an Italian Renaissance Palace.

[16] Jordan Hall (named for the benefactor who provided the funds: Eben D Jordan II of the Jordan Marsh retail store was opened in 1903 to wide acclaim. The principal architect was Edmund Wheelwright. (He had built, in 1901, the Horticultural Hall on the corner of Huntington Avenue and Massachusetts Avenue, in the English Renaissance revival style.) Wheelwright had worked for the firm of architects (McKim, Mead, and White) responsible for Symphony Hall on the adjacent corner of Huntington and Massachusetts Avenues.

Symphony Hall was the first concert hall ever designed on the basis of scientific acoustic principles, with a young assistant physics professor from Harvard, Wallace Clement Sabine, serving as the project's acoustical consultant. (The sabin, which is a unit in sound absorption, is named after him.)

Wheelwright drew upon his experience with Symphony Hall when constructing Jordan Hall, which is said to be near-perfect acoustically.

The Concert Hall, along with the conservatory, was designated to be a National Historic Landmark in 1994.

Wikipedia contributors, "Jordan Hall," in *Wikipedia*, June 14, 2020, https://en.wikipedia.org/w/index.php?title=Jordan_Hall&oldid=962552605; "Wallace C. Sabine," Institution, The Collection of Historical Scientific Instruments: Harvard University, accessed December 22, 2020, http://waywiser.rc.fas.harvard.edu/people/3338/wallace-c-sabine;jsessionid=5129DB6251148B8D661E51D-36C00393A.

[17] Mothers for Adequate Welfare was organized in the Spring of 1965 to address the shortcomings seen in the bureaucratic nature of the welfare officials and offices. Their first sit-in was on April 26, 1965, on Hawkins Street. After promises by officials, they left after two hours. In July 1966, they marched on the state house, demanding, among other things, increases in rental allowances. These demands were ignored, so on May 26, 1967, they staged another sit-in (at the Blue Hill Ave Welfare Centre), which again was ignored. On June 2, 1967, a sit-in (and lock-in) at the Grove Hall welfare center (515 Blue Hill Ave) led to three nights of violent rioting.

[Jack Tager, *Boston Riots: Three Centuries of Social Violence* (Boston: Northeastern University Press, 2019), 178–83, muse.jhu.edu/book/68433.]

[18] Three or four days after the assassination of Martin Luther King Jr., Gunther had an assembly for the conservatory, and Ran played "Birmingham, USA."

[19] Martin Luther King Jr. (civil rights activist, pastor, and humanitarian) was assassinated on April 4, 1968, in Memphis, Tennessee.

Robert Kennedy (Senator for New York from 1965 till his death; brother of John F. Kennedy) was assassinated on June 6, 1968, in Los Angeles, California.

[20] Reprinted in: Tucker, "The 1969 Neume."

[21] Writing in Neume, 1970–71, Carl Atkins, signing himself Chairman, NEC

Jazz Program, wrote:

"Commencing with the academic year 1969–'70, undergraduate Diploma, Bachelor and Master of Music programs in Jazz were inaugurated at the College, thereby becoming the first conservatory in the nation offering such programs in this musical discipline. Admission to the Conservatory Jazz Orchestra and various smaller jazz ensembles is by audition and at the discretion of the Jazz Faculty."

Steve Long, ed., "The 1970/71 Neume" (The New England Conservatory of Music, 1971), 73, New England Conservatory Repository, University of Rochester Libraries, http://ir.flo.org/nec/institutionalPublicationPublicView.action?institutionalItemId=106.

[22] Some of the ideas in this paragraph are also discussed in:

Timothy J. O'Keefe, "40th Anniversary Celebration of Jazz at New England Conservatory in Boston," All About Jazz, October 23, 2009, https://www.allaboutjazz.com/40th-anniversary-celebration-of-jazz-at-new-england-conservatory-in-boston-by-timothy-j-okeefe.php.

[23] Tucker, "The 1969 Neume," 88.

Carl Atkins was the faculty advisor, and there were three officers—Thaodis Gaskin, Danyl Windham, and Gwendolyn Lytle.

[24] Ran already knew Joe. Joe was a friend of Mait Edey, who had produced Ran's album *Blue Potato and Other Outrages*—(though Ran thinks that he may have met Joe earlier at an Abbey Lincoln recording session.) Ran had also—while counting cars through traffic lights—heard Joe playing clarinet in Brooklyn.

[25] Neume 1970/71 has him listed as teaching "Theory."

Long, "The 1970/71 Neume."

[26] Ran adds: "and then they gave me one college course."

[27] Now called Performance Outreach.

[28] Helen Harrington replaced Mildred Collins, who died in June 1971. Long, "The 1970/71 Neume."

Under the supervision of Ran Blake, she (along with Kay Nurse) directed the Department of Music Education—a branch of the Department of Community Services.

[29] Taken from her Obituary. Kay died on August 19, 1982. The funeral service was held at St Cecilia's Catholic Church, Boston. In the booklet, it is noted that Kay had been, during the course of her working life, a high fashion model, a top-ranked amateur golfer, and was one of the country's first female welders.

[30] Ran Blake, "A Gospel Jubilee: A Tribute to Kathleen Nurse" (New England Conservatory, February 10, 1983).

[31] Ran was not listed as Faculty till the 1970-71 publication of Neume when he appeared as a faculty member for jazz and community services. Long, "The

1970/71 Neume."

[32] Though Ran admits he was not performing much at the time: "one or two Sunday afternoons with Jeanne Lee in New York—really nothing."

[33] Alice Russell, Interview for the Ran Blake Biography, skype call, June 1, 2014.

[34] Russell.

[35] This was at the height of the Vietnam War. By late 1967 there are nearly half a million US forces in South Vietnam.
Philip Gavin, "Vietnam War 1965-1968," The History Place, accessed December 12, 2020, http://www.historyplace.com/unitedstates/vietnam/index-1965.html.

[36] Ricky Ford suggests it was Hayes-Bickford, 293 Huntington Avenue, where his friend worked.

[37] See chapter postscript.

[38] Webster Lewis is listed in the 1970/'71 edition of Neume as a graduate of the Master of Music in composition. Long, "The 1970/71 Neume," 45.

[39] "Breakthru" was recorded as a duet with Ricky Ford when he was a student in the third-stream department in Jordan Hall in July 1973. This recording appears on the album *Third Stream Today* (released in 1979 on the New England Conservatory label NEC-116).

[40] The Federal Prison Camp, Alderson, West Virginia, is a minimum-security prison for females that has an emphasis on vocational training and personal growth. Ran's piece "Alderson Penitentiary" (1974) was first performed December 15, 1974, with Bruce Henderson on bass clarinet and Ran Blake on piano.

[41] Massachusetts Correctional Institution, Walpole (or Walpole State Prison) was a maximum-security prison for males.

[42] Attica Correctional Facility—a maximum-security prison located in the town of Attica and operated by New York State.

[43] Folsom State Prison in Folsom, California. In 1968 Johnny Cash recorded a live album there. One of the songs on this album is Folsom Prison Blues, which had previously been recorded in 1955 on the Sun label.

[44] Olivier Messiaen was a French composer, organist, and teacher (and ornithologist—he delighted in birdsong and incorporated transcriptions of this in his music.) He was one of the major composers of the 20th century. His music is distinguished by his devotion to Catholicism as it reflects many theological themes. As a French soldier during World War II (during the German invasion of 1940), he was taken captive and imprisoned at the Stalag VIII, a camp in Görlitz, Germany. While held captive, he wrote most of his Quartet for the End of Time. Then—outdoors and in the rain—on January 15, 1941, with fellow prisoners Étienne Pasquier, cellist; Henri Akoka, clarinetist; and Jean Le Boulaire, violinist, joining Messiaen on piano, the piece was premiered. A sympathetic guard,

Karl-Albert Brüll, who had encouraged the composition, as well as other German officers, were in the front row of the audience of about 300. There was even a program, drawn by a fellow prisoner in Art Nouveau style. (Not long after this, the clarinetist, Akoka, escaped while being transported to another camp in a cattle train. He jumped from a fast-moving car with his clarinet under his arm and happily survived.)
Alex Ross, "Revelations: The Story behind Messiaen's 'Quartet for the End of Time.,'" The New Yorker, March 15, 2004, https://www.newyorker.com/magazine/2004/03/22/revelations-2.

45 This was around 1974. The Bay State Banner was founded in 1965 to serve the African American community in Boston.

46 Now known as "Contemporary Musical Arts."

47 Eight years younger than Ran, Lewis was a jazz keyboardist and was Ran's immediate superior in the outreach program. ["Webster Lewis," Institution, necmusic.edu, August 9, 2016, http://necmusic.edu/faculty/webster-lewis.]

48 As part of a larger countercultural movement, the Civil Rights Movement had fought for justice and equality; there had been some legislative success. The Civil Rights Act of 1964 and the Voting Rights Act of 1965, for example, had given legal protection. But inequality remained. The problems were deep-seated, and there was still much to be done. There was frustration at the rate of progress, and the latter part of the sixties saw upheaval, anger, and rebellion. There were widespread riots in 1964 and '65. Malcolm X was assassinated in 1965. Then Civil Rights activist Martin Luther King Jr. was assassinated on April 4, 1968. This resulted in race riots across America as well as a tremendous outpouring of national grief and a day of national mourning on April 7.

49 Gerald Early, "Jazz and the African American Literary Tradition," Educational, Freedom's Story (National Humanities Center), accessed April 5, 2013, <http://nationalhumanitiescenter.org/tserve/freedom/1917beyond/essays/jazz.htm>.

50 Amiri Baraka (or, as he was at that time, Everett LeRoi Jones) sought to promote an authentic African American style. He is credited with starting the Black Arts Movement soon after the assassination of Malcolm X. It was intended to encourage African Americans to find their own voice through the arts and by setting up their own newspapers, publishing houses, etc. It saw the need to fight intensely for black liberation and was instrumental in giving African Americans a presence in the mass media which led to further involvement on a political and community level.

Chapter 6: The Third-Stream

1 Ran Blake, "Filed Document," July 21, 1999, Ran Blake's private archive.

2   Blake.

3   Hankus Netsky, Contemporary Improvisation at 40 Years, interview by JazzEd Magazine, January 2013, https://www.jazzedmagazine.com/archives/january-2013/contemporary-improvisation-at-40-years/.

4   Ran Blake, "Teaching Third Stream," *Music Educators Journal* 63, no. 4 (1976): 30–33, https://doi.org/10.2307/3395185.

5   It should be noted here that Ran Blake is by no means the only musician in the jazz/ improvised music realm to have used the term recomposition. In citing the term here, we refer specifically to Ran Blake's creative process and to the part of it that he terms "recomposition." It is also quite possible that the "recomposition" of Ran Blake was a concept developed in collaboration with Gunther Schuller.

6   Other members included vocalist Geraldine Martin; guitarists Michael Jackson and Mick Goodrick; ethnomusicologist Peter Row; and then later, vocalist Dominique Eade; pianist Evan Harlan; drummer Jon Hazilla; saxophonist Daryl Lowery; and flutist Abby Rabinovitz.

Mike Thompson, "Introduction to the Third Stream/Contemporary Improvisation Archive" (New England Conservatory, May 26, 2006), New England Conservatory Archives; Hankus Netsky to Janet McFadden, "Ran's Bio," October 17, 2019.

7   Thompson, "Introduction to the Third Stream/Contemporary Improvisation Archive."

8   Ran Blake, New England Conservatory Symphony, and Larry Livingston, *Portfolio of Doktor Mabuse* (France: OWL 029, 1982), https://www.discogs.com/Ran-Blake-The-New-England-Conservatory-Symphony-Orchestra-Conducted-By-Larry-Livingston-Portfolio-Of/release/3867034.

9   Ran Blake, "Publicizing Third Stream Music in the Southwest," n.d., Ran Blake's private archive.

10 Kit Van Cleave, "New England Conservatory Seeks Streetwise Musicians," *The Music Monthly* 1, no. 1 (June 1976): 21 & 28.

11 Ran Blake to Andy Falender, "Letter to Andy Falender and Cc. to L. Lesser and P. Row," October 14, 1988.

12 MacArthur Foundation strategy http://www.macfound.org/programs/fellows/strategy/

The MacArthur Foundation supports creative people as well as institutions committed to building a more just, verdant, and peaceful world. Fellows Program awards fellowships to talented individuals who not only have shown originality and dedication but also the capacity for self-direction. There are no restrictions on becoming a Fellow, except that the nominee must be a resident or citizen of the United States.

13 Blake to Falender, "Letter to Andy Falender and Cc. to L. Lesser and P. Row," October 14, 1988.

14 Blake to Falender.

15 Gunther Schuller et al., "Meeting Minutes," § Third Stream Foundation

(1992), 2. Schuller et al., Meeting minutes.

[16] Gunther Schuller to Ran Blake, June 7, 1995, Ran Blake's private archive.

[17] However, it should be noted many of the movement's key exponents moved on to make significant contributions to other types of music. Schuller had also been correct in his assertion that the pedagogical ideas and theoretical concepts, developed by Ran Blake in the "Third Stream Studies" syllabus, were ahead of their time. Numerous university music programs and conservatories around the world have gradually embraced ear training syllabi that opt for more eclectic repertoire sets, with exercises that aim to foster a more critical musical awareness (and which are not limited to the mere recognition or reproduction of a given set of pitches and/or rhythms, as has been traditionally the case).

[18] Remaining true to Blake and Schuller's vision, this program (and its methodologies) has continued to evolve. Such changes have ensured the program's relevancy in the midst of an increasingly diverse musical landscape. To this end, the program has twice since changed its name: to Contemporary Improvisation (1992–2022), and, recently, to Contemporary Musical Arts.

[19] Ran Blake to Bob Freeman, "Memorandum to Bob Freeman (President of NEC, 1996–1999)," March 2, 1999.

Man, Musician, Educator—A Distillation

Chapter 1: Mainly Music

[1] Leo McFadden (reading the book to Ran) qualifies: "That's a quote from me actually," and Ran, who had been already nodding in agreement, says, "That's a good one."

[2] Ran Blake, *Primacy of the Ear*, 1st ed. (USA: Third Stream Associates, 2010), 33.

[3] Nini Gambaré, "Ran Blake: Piano Player or Doktor Mabuse," Unfortunately, this article is incorrectly referenced in Ran Blake's own archive. The original article is in Italian (but with an English title). The publication in which it appears and the date are unknown.

Gambaré later re-shapes this "fear of death" to a "fascination or anguished hypersensitivity in the face of painful farewells."

[4] This line was originally "the music of Roy Webb," but in a reading of the chapter, Ran held up a hand in alarm: "Now, you have to say, the Roy Webb music *only* when the sinister is going to happen because other times, there's a part in the film that's mashed potato. (He shakes his head sadly.) It's got to be in the second half of the movie when the murder takes place; otherwise, it has its potato moments… maybe a baked potato—that's not as bad as mashed."

Nevertheless, in a paper written by Ran (in his personal files), he admitted that though the musical nuances were occasionally banal and cliched, they were also, to the young boy he was then, "eerie, haunting and unforgettable to my ears."

Ran Blake, "Filed Document," July 21, 1999, 3, Ran Blake's private archive.

[5] At Springfield, the church was "more spiritual." It was at Hartford (and in the music of Mahalia) that the earthiness appeared (Ran's clarification, June 3, 2015).

[6] Claude Jeter (1914–2009) was an African American gospel singer. He received many offers to perform R&B and rock and roll but stayed true to the promise he had made to his mother to only sing for the Lord. A line from one of his renditions of an African American Spiritual inspired Paul Simon's Bridge Over Troubled Water.

David McGee, "The Gospel Set: Reverend Claude Jeter," The Bluegrass Special, February 2009, http://www.thebluegrassspecial.com/archive/2009/february2009/gospelsetfeb09.php.]

[7] Ran quickly adds that there was "Another Irish girl, Kathleen, who would come over and visit Mary, and they would tell these stories of murder and boats."

[8] In Primacy of the Ear, when discussing the development of style and its

communication, Ran stresses: "Make sure to give yourself time to process what you're doing, and to reflect on what in your experiences works and doesn't work for you."

Blake, *Primacy of the Ear*, 33.

[9] A term coined by Aaron Hartley.

[10] Madame Chaloff, who Ran claims had a "phone to Beethoven."

[11] Ran Blake, "Letter to Class Blog Members," *Ran Blake's Long-Term Melodic Memory*, September 24, 2011, https://ltmm2011.wordpress.com/2011/09/.

[12] Here Ran is referring to his own personal style of music. However, it should be noted that Ran is one of the few improvising musicians who has successfully integrated 12-tone elements into performances and recordings, which he has made over his career.

[13] Aretha Franklin

[14] Bernard Herrmann was an American composer, music-dramatist, and conductor who began his professional career at the Columbia Broadcasting System (CBS) in New York in 1933. By 1940, he was Conductor in Chief of the Columbia Symphony Orchestra, where he relished introducing new works to American radio audiences. In 1951, after the CBS orchestra was disbanded, he gravitated to England, where he conducted broadcasts of the London Symphony Orchestra. He was introduced to film music by Orson Welles—*Citizen Kane* was Hermann's first film music assignment. He composed fifty musical scores, orchestrating them himself. One of his notable collaborations was with Alfred Hitchcock, who called upon Hermann to provide music for his 1960 film, *Psycho*.

Edward Johnson, "Bernard Herrmann–A Biographical Sketch," The Bernard Herrmann Society, 2011 1977, http://www.bernardherrmann.org/articles/biographical-sketch/.

[15] Charles Ives: (1874–1954) was an American composer who combined the (American) popular and church music of his youth with European art music, thus anticipating many of the musical trends of the 20th century. His work related to American cultural experience.

[16] Anton Webern—Austrian composer and conductor. His mentor was Arnold Schoenberg. At the time of his death (he was accidentally killed by an American soldier at the end of World War II), his music was not well known, but by the 1950s, Webern came to be recognized as one of the most important composers of his generation.

[17] Edgar Allan Poe (1809–1849) was an American writer and critic. He is remembered for his short stories, which were often macabre and mysterious, and for his poetry. He is also regarded as the "father" of detective fiction.

[18] Quote signed by Ran Blake on NEC letterhead, date obscured.

[19] At a workshop at Queensland, Conservatorium, Griffith University. Brisbane

Australia.

[20] Joe Milazzo, "Ran Blake: Freedom To Contemplate," Jazz & Improvised Music Webzine, One Final Note, April 2001, https://www.onefinalnote.com/features/2001/blake-ran/.

[21] Gunther Schuller, *Gunther Schuller: A Life in Pursuit of Music and Beauty* (Rochester, NY: University of Rochester Press, 2011), 475.

[22] Good classical pedaling strives to capture the "purest sound" by pulling the focus of the sound away from the unwanted upper partials of the harmonic series. It takes years to master. Once mastered, a smooth legato line, akin to a singer or a bowed string instrument, can be evoked. Ran takes this skill further. He can, of course, pedal well in the "traditional" sense, but his mastery extends to the ability to actually control and manipulate the upper partials most pianists seek to avoid. His comprehensive pedal technique thus allows him to create ghost-like whispers in one register of the piano (usually an upper register) whilst continuing a melody with a more standard piano tone in the principal register. Often, all this will be executed on top of the "bed" of a dissonant chord, played in the bass register, which as it decays, opens to reveal a shimmering series of upper-partials, far above the other textures, bringing both extremes of the instrument's sonic range together to create an other-worldly cohesive whole. Leo McFadden

[23] Viktor Frankl was an Austrian neurologist and psychiatrist who survived the Holocaust as an Auschwitz inmate. His 1946 book *Man's Search for Meaning* is an account of his experiences in the concentration camp. It attempts to examine the mindset of his fellow prisoners and outlines his theory that the search for meaning in life is an all-empowering force in humans.

Chapter 2: More Music—Essence and Process

[1] Albert Camus—French (Algerian-born) writer. (He always rejected the descriptor "philosopher," though his works delve into the human condition.) Camus won the Nobel Prize for Literature in 1957. He joined the French Resistance during WWII and edited the clandestine newspaper Combat. Though Camus was writing during very dark times, his vision was hopeful and illuminating.

[2] Ran offers a revelatory experience to a great many students. I think a lot of us don't realize exactly how great an influence he has had on us until many, many years later. He comes into our lives and sets a ripple going that profoundly affects the directions we take. It's not a set of ideas that we abandon once we leave his studio or graduate, or change musical direction (or even change life direction—away from music). I feel that if we've got an open heart, even if we're not ready for all of his 'lessons' at the time, his teaching is something that will continue to subtly inform… seemingly insignificant but with potentially profound implications. Leo McFadden (Student of Ran's at NEC 2005-2007).

[3] Francis Davis, *In the Moment: Jazz in the 1980s* (Oxford University Press, 1986).

4   Walter Benjamin, *The Work of Art in the Age of Mechanical Reproduction* (London: Penguin, 2008).

5   George Russell's album The Essence of George Russell was released on the Norwegian "Sonet" label in 1971. Russell sees "essence" as the "true self." George Russell: "The reason I write music is that I feel it's a vehicle or channel which leads to your true self, your essence."

6   It is worth noting that many of the documents Ran has in his own personal archive at his Brookline apartment are missing dates.

7   This interview took place in 2008; the publication of this present book was still 14 years away.

8   Gunther Schuller: from the original liner notes for *Ran Blake Plays Solo Piano*.

9   Ran was probably referring to a live private taping of The Stan Kenton Orchestra when they appeared at Birdland from April 23 to May 6, 1953. It was the first time the Kenton orchestra had played at the venue.
Iván Santiago Mercado, "Chris Connor Bio-Discography: Concert, Radio & Television Dates," JazzDiscography.com, September 14, 2019, https://jazzdiscography.com/Artists/Connor/Connor_live.php.

10 Ran's dedication album for George Russell Ghost Tones (produced by Art Lange and Aaron Hartley) was recorded in August 2010 at New England Conservatory. It was released in 2015. It features seven of George Russell's songs and five of Ran's, along with several standards, including "Autumn in New York" and "You Are My Sunshine."

11 Ran Blake, "Filed Document," July 21, 1999, Ran Blake's private archive.

12 At this point, Ran adds, "It is an act of citizenship, but it's so important to hear a record over and over again, and that's exhausting too."

13 Ran Blake, Interview 320 for "American Music Series," interview by Larry Ruttman, October 10, 2001, 23.

14 Ed Symkus, "Pianist-Teacher Performs Free Concert at Conservatory," *Metro West Daily News*, February 7, 2002.

15 Bill Coss, "The Agonies of Exploration-Jeanne Lee and Ran Blake," *DownBeat*, September 13, 1962, 18.

16 Ran Blake, *Primacy of the Ear*, 1st ed. (USA: Third Stream Associates, 2010), 2.

17 Blake, 9.

18 At this stage, Ran interrupts: "By the way, I didn't go to Greece deliberately because of the junta. It may sound that I'm so courageous going with my care packages and my white flag."

[19] John Cage (1912–1992) was an American avant-garde composer. His early compositions were written in the 12-tone method of his teacher Schoenberg, but by 1939 he was experimenting with unorthodox and adapted instruments.

[20] Blake, *Primacy of the Ear*, 6.

[21] Mait Edey, the liner notes for The Blue Potato and Other Outrages.
[Ran Blake, The Blue Potato and Other Outrages..., LP, Album (New York: Milestone, 1969).]

[22] George Russell

[23] Jose Antonio Luera, "Ran Blake – 'Somewhere in the United States, Whose Name I Don't Want to Remember,'" trans. Don Strange, *Aria Jazz*, March 1967.

[24] Luera.

Chapter 3 Performance

[1] Ran Blake, "Springfield Streams and Standards: A Tribute to My Sister, Marte Koleda," December 3, 2014.

[2] Kenny Werner, *Effortless Mastery: Liberating the Master Musician Within* (New Albany: Jamey Aebersold Jazz, 1996), 90.

[3] Ran Blake, "Untitled Document. Written on NEC Letterhead," n.d., Ran Blake's private archive.
On reading the manuscript, Ran takes sharp exception to this quote, "Why not man and woman?" he asks.
"Well, it was your quote," I protest. But already, he has his arms outstretched in a saintly pose, looking skywards, "Well, that sounds a little like I'm Jehovah in Adam and Eve's garden."

[4] Clare McFadden, "Can You Teach the Art of Listening? Ran Blake and the Long Term Melodic Memory" (Cambridge, MA, Harvard University, 2012).

[5] Jose Antonio Luera, "Ran Blake – 'Somewhere in the United States, Whose Name I Don't Want to Remember,'" trans. Don Strange, *Aria Jazz*, March 1967.

[6] Ran Blake, An Interview with Ran Blake, interview by Joseph Brenna, Typed Document, April 11, 1984, Ran Blake's private archive.

[7] Blake.

[8] "Reincarnation of a Lovebird"—Charles Mingus

[9] This interview is from 2009.

Chapter 4: Pluperfect Flashbacks

[1] Clare McFadden, "Can You Teach the Art of Listening? Ran Blake and the Long Term Melodic Memory" (Cambridge, MA, Harvard University, 2012).

[2] Leo McFadden quoted in: McFadden.

[3] *Improvisations*—an album of piano duets featuring Ran Blake and Jaki Byard was released on the Italian label, Soul Note in 1981.

[4] "Present Tense," was first performed in January 1981 in Paris, France. Album: *Portfolio of Ran Blake*. Owl Records.
[The Boston Area Libraries, *The Boston Composers Project: A Bibliography of Contemporary Music*, ed. Linda I. Solow (Cambridge, Mass: The MIT Press, 1983), 54.]

[5] Edith Piaf—a French singer known as "La Môme Piaf" (The Little Sparrow), who became a symbol of French passion and tenacity during World War II. Biography.com Editors, "Édith Piaf Biography," Biography.com, June 24, 2020, https://www.biography.com/musician/edith-piaf.

http://www.biography.com/people/edith-piaf-9439893

[6] The tower refers to Alfred Hitchcock's 1958 film Vertigo, in which two towers featured: the landmark Coit Tower, used in the film by Madeleine to locate Scottie's apartment; and the bell tower at the Mission San Juan Bautista, the scene of the movie's compelling final moments. (Interestingly, the bell tower at the mission was removed in 1949 because of rot and termite damage. Hitchcock recreated it for the movie, using a painting for exterior shots and studio shots for the interior.

"Vertigo," reelsf.com, accessed July 30, 2021, http://reelsf.com/vertigo-1958.

[7] *The Leo House* on W 23rd Street, New York, is a Catholic guesthouse for travelers. Established in 1889 by papal certification from Pope Leo XIII, it upholds the spirit of Christian hospitality.

[8] Ran Blake, *Primacy of the Ear*, 1st ed. (USA: Third Stream Associates, 2010), 7.

[9] Ran Blake, *Primacy of the Ear*, 1st ed. (USA: Third Stream Associates, 2010), 33.

[10] Byron Coley, "Ran Blake Interview Transcript–The Wire," The Wire Magazine, July 2009, https://www.thewire.co.uk/in-writing/interviews/ran-blake-interview-transcript.

[11] Blake, *Primacy of the Ear*, 2010, 32.

[12] These ideas are fndamental to Jung's theories of the psychology of the unconscious.

[13] Liner notes, Ran Blake, *Unmarked Van: Tribute To Sarah Vaughan*, CD Al-

bum (Italy: Soul Note, 1997).

[14] Though it must be noted that Ran has watched every film in his collection multiple times with the sound on, too. Indeed, his own musical style owes a lot to the soundtracks of his favorite films.

Chapter 5: A Catalog of Dreams

[1] See also: Calvin S. Hall and Vernon J. Nordby, *A Primer of Jungian Psychology* (New York: Plume, 1999).

[2] Ran Blake, Primacy of the Ear, 1st ed. (USA: Third Stream Associates, 2010), 32.

Chapter 6: Film Noir

[1] In the closing scenes of the John Huston film *The Maltese Falcon,* detective Sam Spade, played by Humphrey Bogart, utters the line: *The uh... stuff that dreams are made of.* It was Humphrey Bogart's suggestion to finish with this line, but in general, the film was based on the book, *The Maltese Falcon* by Dashiell Hammett.

The now-famous Bogart quote refers to Shakespeare:

"We are such stuff as dreams are made on, and our little life is rounded with a sleep." (*The Tempest* - William Shakespeare)

[2] In the US, the Cold War, communism, and the atomic bomb were shadows that haunted the childhoods of children growing up during this period and right on through the fifties.

[3] Blake, "Filed Document," 3.

[4] Ran Blake, "Spiral Staircases (Concert Programme)" (New England Conservatory, October 31, 2007).

[5] Ran Blake, "Jazz Magazine (Paris)," January 20, 1984, Ran Blake's private archive.

[6] This 1947 movie, directed by Raoul Walsh, stars Robert Mitchum and Teresa Wright. It is the tale of a fostered boy who is tormented by the murder of his parents when he was a child.

[7] Blake, "Jazz Magazine (Paris)."

[8] Ran Blake, "Filed Document," July 21, 1999, Ran Blake's private archive.

[9] Blake, 4.

[10] Blake, "Jazz Magazine (Paris)."

11   *Jazz World* Issue No 62, Vol. 14, p6.

12   S. Hitchman and A. McNett, "François Truffaut: French New Wave Director," New Wave Film.com, 2020 2008, http://www.newwavefilm.com/french-new-wave-encyclopedia/francois-truffaut.shtml.

13   Hal Rubenstein, *100 Unforgettable Dresses* (New York: Harper Collins, 2012), 169.

14   Kent Jones and François Truffaut, *The Soft Skin*, Digital (The Criterion Collection, 2015), https://www.criterion.com/films/27640-the-soft-skin.

15   *François Truffaut Salutes Alfred Hitchcock at AFI Life Achievement Award*, YouTube, 2009, https://www.youtube.com/watch?v=mvRryx6yzUQ.

16   While there is some debate as to the extent to which Hitchcock relied on storyboarding, surviving storyboards are evidence of his fastidious attention to detail.
Stephen Mamber, "Hitchcock: The Conceptual and the Pre-Digital," *Stanford Humanities Review* 7, no. 2 (1999): 128–36.

17   Harold Michelson (storyboard artist for "The Birds" and Marnie"), interviewed in: Daniel Raim, *Alfred Hitchcock: Writing with the Camera*, The Criterion Collection, 2018, https://www.youtube.com/watch?v=CQn0MJ8uENQ.

18   Ran Blake, *Primacy of the Ear*, 1st ed. (USA: Third Stream Associates, 2010), 83.

19   Ran Blake and Gardiner Hartmann, *Storyboarding Noir*. (Draft Manuscript, November 15, 2019).

20   Blair Dutra, a young friend and assistant, was also responsible for introducing Dek-Tor into Ran's life.

21   Clare McFadden, "Can You Teach the Art of Listening? Ran Blake and the Long Term Melodic Memory" (Cambridge, MA, Harvard University, 2012), 4.

22   Matt Delligatti to Janet McFadden, "Film Noir," July 18, 2014.

23   This flower shop—Podesta Baldocchi—has since moved.

24   McKittrick Hotel was actually the Portman Mansion, at 1007 Gough Street. It was demolished soon after the film was made.

25   Palace of the Legion of Honour

26   Bert Scully was the museum guard who was paid $500 for his small role—identifying a painting of "Carlotta" and handing a museum catalog to James Stewart's character, "Scottie," in the Alfred Hitchcock film, *Vertigo*.
The Alfred Hitchcock Wiki, "Palace of the Legion of Honor, San Francisco, California," 2003, http://the.hitchcock.zone/wiki/Palace_of_the_Legion_of_Honor,_San_Francisco,_California.

27   As previously noted, I have tried to keep the "re" spelling for theater when

its name has incorporated that spelling. Some (like the Paramount Theatre, 1700 Main Street, Springfield, MA) have been through a few transformations. It was opened in 1929 as the Paramount Theatre, then became the Julia Sanderson Theater, and then the Hippodrome. In 2009, it was renamed the Paramount. It has, in recent times, been referred to as "theater."

Ross Melnick, "Paramount Theatre in Springfield, MA," Cinema Treasures, 2011, http://cinematreasures.org/theaters/1261.

For some beautiful photos of the Paramount, see: https://afterthefinalcurtain.net/2017/10/27/paramount-theatre-springfield-ma/

[28] The Art Theatre was opened in 1908 as *The Nelson*. It was renamed Fox Theatre in 1919, and in 1934, it was renamed again—Art Theatre. It closed in the 1950s.

Dr. Russ Durocher, "Art Theatre in Springfield, MA," Cinema Treasures, accessed January 6, 2021, http://cinematreasures.org/theaters/3721.

[29] Both these theaters were demolished to make way for the Bushnell Towers. Loew's Poli, next door to the Poli-Palace, was also very ornate—in the Beauxarts school style.

Suzanne Mittica and Nancy O. Albert, "Hartford's Motion Picture Palaces," *Hog River Journal* 1, no. 3 (2003): 12–19.

[30] The New Yorker was opened by Daniel and Toby Talbot and very soon became "a mecca for film buffs" and critics. In 1964, the Talbots opened a distribution company called "New Yorker Films," which specialized in independent and foreign movies. The New Yorker theater was demolished in the 1980s.

Jennifer Lee, "The Birth of New York's Art-House Cinema," *City Room* (blog), December 16, 2009, https://cityroom.blogs.nytimes.com/2009/12/16/the-birth-of-new-yorks-art-house-cinema/.

[31] Marshall McLuhan was a Canadian philosopher and pioneer in the field of media theory. His seminal work *Understanding Media: The Extensions of Man* was published in 1964.

[32] Woody Allen gave Marshall McLuhan a cameo appearance in his 1977 movie *Annie Hall*. He produced McLuhan from behind a billboard to score a winning point in an argument his own character was having with an overbearing academic in a movie queue.

[33] Its patented floor design (parabolic reverse) by architect Ben Schlanger was the first of its kind in the country. Dipping in the middle, the floor was conceived to allow an equally good view from any seat.

The theater was located in the old Astor Market building, which had been converted to office and retail space in 1917 but had the first floor given over for a theater—the Symphony Theater—which became the Symphony Space auditorium. The basement space under the Symphony opened as the Thalia Movie Theatre in 1931. It became known as the place to see Hollywood revivals, classics, and foreign films.

"History: Our Story," Symphony Space, accessed January 7, 2021, https://www.symphonyspace.org/about/our-history.

34   Simon Spelling, "Symphony Space," NYMag.com, accessed January 7, 2021, https://nymag.com/listings/attraction/symphony-space/.

35   Brattle Hall, a barn-like structure with its gambrel roof and beautiful red-brick facade, is situated near Harvard Square. It dates from 1889 and was designed by architect Alexander Wadsworth Longfellow Jr, nephew of Henry Wadsworth Longfellow.
Douglas Shand-Tucci, *Harvard University: An Architectural Tour* (New York: Princeton Architectural Press, 2001).

36   Susan Quinn, "History & Mission," Coolidge Corner Theatre, accessed January 7, 2021, http://coolidge.org/about-us/history-mission.

37   Steve Schwartz, *A Life in Music*, Video, Ran Blake Lifetime Achievement Award (Boston MA: New England Conservatory recordings, 2012).

38   Eleanor Blau, "Old-Movie Houses Dwindle and the Die-Hard Buffs Worry," *The New York Times*, August 13, 1987, sec. C.

39   Ran Blake to Students of the CI Dept. NEC, "Cat People Concert," August 2006.

40   Blake to Students of the CI Dept. NEC.

Chapter 7: The Golden Art

1   During the interviews with Ran, over many years, the book you are now holding was very much present and tangible.

2   Clare McFadden, "Can You Teach the Art of Listening? Ran Blake and the Long Term Melodic Memory" (Cambridge, MA, Harvard University, 2012).

3   McFadden.

4   Ran Blake, "The Primacy of the Ear," *MENC Journal*, 1988, 4–5, https://ran-blake.com/pote/essays-and-articles/.

5   Ran Blake, "Filed Document," July 21, 1999, 2, Ran Blake's private archive.

6   On proofreading this part, Leo recounts the following story: "Once, in Brookline, I was playing one of his recordings—of a Scott Joplin piece, I think—from the early 80's on his CD player, and he was like, 'this is great! who is this?' Then, when he found out that it was his recording, he wanted me to turn it off. I argued with him about it (in our way that we always do)—how could it have been 'great' 30 seconds ago and have suddenly become something that had to be turned off—but Ran changed the subject as he loves to do, and that was that.

7   Claire Ritter, "Professional Reference," n.d., Ran Blake's private archive.

[8] Hankus Netsky to Ran Blake, "Speech for Honorary Degree," May 25, 2006. The email contains the text of Hankus's speech on the occasion of Ran receiving an Honorary Degree as Doctor of Music. The event took place in Jordan Hall; the words quoted in the speech are Ran's own.

Chapter 8: A Sense of Wonder

[1] Saul Bellow, "A World Too Much with Us," Critical Inquiry 2, no. 1 (1975): 7. Bellow taught at Bard College during the 1950s. He purchased historic Ham House in 1958 and lived there with his family. Ralph Ellison was a frequent visitor. Bellow donated the house to Bard College in 1964; it became student housing for a period before being sold. It has been fully restored by the present owners.

[2] Ran Blake, *Primacy of the Ear*, 1st ed. (USA: Third Stream Associates, 2010), 11.

[3] Blake, 16.

[4] Blake, 16.

[5] Abby Whiteside (1881–1956) challenged conventional piano pedagogy. Instead of focusing on finger position (as was common in classical teaching), Whiteside proposes a holistic approach in which the arm and torso direct movement inspired by an aural image; rhythm is at the heart of this concept. Thus, according to Whiteside, teaching should have as its central concern the cultivation of a heightened awareness of rhythm. Whiteside saw routine "drills" as a poor substitute for this.

Abby Whiteside, *Abby Whiteside on Piano Playing* (Amadeus Press, 1997).

[6] Whiteside, 6.

[7] Dorothy Taubman (1917–2013) was a piano teacher in New York (Professor at Aaron Copland School of Music, Queens College) who is most known for helping pianists overcome technical problems. Her "Taubman method" concentrated on body alignment—getting all the joints in the right place so that the body could work as it was supposed to, rendering playing easy and pain-free. For proper alignment, the fingers, hand, and forearm must move together. The choreography of these finger/hand/arm movements is governed by principles that ensure economy (and freedom) of movement. She called her technique "coordinate motion." She enjoyed a high rate of success in treating injured players; her legacy continues through the work of the Golansky Institute.

[8] As reported in January 2015, Ran Blake's Newsletter

[9] Dalia's and Khao Sarn" were two local restaurants that Ran liked to frequent. Both have since closed.

[10] Peter McFadden has hand-crafted all of (his son) Leo McFadden's guitars. However, it is "the golden art" of teaching (and neither guitar-making nor gar-

dening) that has claimed his "professional" hours.

¹¹ Brindle was the Staffordshire bull terrier belonging to Florence de Lannoy.

¹² Francis Davis *In the moment: Jazz in the 1980s* Oxford University Press.

¹³ Gilles Gautherin, "Voluntarily Exiled from Stages and Studios (5 Recordings in 15 Years)," *Jazz Hot*, 1977, Ran Blake's private archive.

¹⁴ Bellow, "A World Too Much with Us," 7.

CHAPTER 9: FOOD AND MUSIC—"THE MASTER OF SPICE"

¹ John E. D'Agostino, Interview for the Ran Blake Biography, interview by Janet McFadden, telephone recording, August 9, 2014.

² V&T Pizza was owned by Vincent and Tony Curcurato—local boys who were bakers by trade and opened their first pizza place at the end of WWII.
Thomas Hauser, *Reflections: Conversations, Essays, and Other Writings* (Fayetteville, Ark: University of Arkansas Press, 2014).

³ Roy Webb (1888–1982) was an American film music composer known for noir and horror films (mostly RKO).

⁴ Giacomo Merega: Italian-born musician, NEC alumnus ('07 MM), and one-time assistant to Ran Blake.

⁵ "Stratusphunk" is a composition by George Russell. It first appeared on Russell's 1960 album of the same name. The composition has been recorded numerous times since. Notably by Gil Evans on his 1961 album *Out of the Cool*. Ran himself recorded the composition on his 1965 album, *Ran Blake Plays Solo Piano*.

CHAPTER 10: BROOKLINE—THE HUB

¹ Ran recalls how the purchase of the apartment was effected: "Greg Silberman [*Ran's manager at the time*] found a deal about a basement apartment, and [as] my rent kept going up in Boston, Dorothy gave me three thousand and lent me five, [and] my parents gave me two or three [thousand] and lent me five [thousand], and so I had a mortgage of about twelve thousand left. I've just been so happy here."

² Santi Falcone was a piano technician who began his own company, building grand pianos in the Boston area in the early 1980s. Early Falcones were compared to Steinways.

³ James Hadley Chase (born René Lodge Brabazon Raymond) was an English writer in the crime fiction/mystery/thriller genre. His books were very popular

in France, where Éditions Gallimard published ninety titles in their Série noire range. More than thirty were made into movies.

[4] Ran dictates most of his emails using voice recognition software—with *interesting* results.

[5] Leo McFadden, July 27, 2021.

INDEX

A

Abdul-Malik, Ahmed 226
Abramson, Herb 190
Abramson, Miriam 190
Abry, Christian 296
Abyssinian Baptist Church. See churches
Adajian Armenian Restaurant. See music venues: *clubs, cafes, restaurants*
Adamos, Maria 308–309
Adderley, Cannonball 145
Ahrens, Gil 116, 118, 122, 140, 148
Ahrens (home and family) 116–117, 119, 154
Alderson Prison. See penitentiaries & prisons
Alice in Wonderland 55, 60, 76–77, 102, 111, 407
Amalfi Cafe. See music venues: *clubs, cafes, restaurants*
Ammons, Gene 255
Anderson, Marian 116, 119, 342
Antibes Jazz Festival. See jazz & music festivals
Apollo Theater. See music venues: *theaters, concert halls & performance spaces*
Appleman, Richard 256
Armstrong, Louis 71, 185, 274, 386
Arnold, Jessie M. See Powers, Jessie (grandmother, née Arnold)
Arter, Natalie 400
Arthur, Natalie (Sr.) 143
Arvanitas, Georges 306

Astaire, Fred 126
Atkins, Carl 386, 388–389, 393
Atlantic Records xxxi, 173, 178, 190–196, 204, 211, 217, 249, 255, 272, 346, 403, 415, 513
Avakian, George 180, 193, 254, 273–276, 282–283, 293, 303, 316
Ayler, Albert 137

B

Babbitt, Milton 288, 352
Baden-Baden 180, 275–276
Baker, LaVern 191, 193
Baldwin, James 216, 230, 235–236
Ballé, Catherine 298, 300–301, 312
Ballé family 298
Ballé, Freddy 298, 301
Bangs, Martha E. 48
Barber, Stephanie and Philip 173, 184–187, 189, 259, 359, 366. See also universities, schools, conservatories: Lenox School of Jazz
Bard College. See universities, schools, conservatories; Bard Jazz Festival. See jazz & music festivals
Barrymore, Ethel 40–41, 44, 442, 480, 507
Bartók, Béla 121, 151–152, 170, 249, 409, 423, 476
Basie, Count 118
Bay State Banner. See newspapers & magazines
Beatles, the 149–150, 281, 344, 462
bebop 117, 232, 242, 251, 410, 509
Bechet, Sidney 117

Beethoven, Ludwig van 163, 249, 348
Bekaert, Jacques 301
Bel Canto Foundation 251
Belgrave, Barbara 236, 245, 279, 306
Bell, Eunice 89–90, 135, 158, 468
Bellow, Saul 467
Belmont Record Store 150–151
Benin-d'Azy 288, 292
Benjamin, Walter 415
Berendt, Joachim 272, 273
Bergen, Norway 81, 280–281, 283, 342, 470
Berlin, Irving 126
Bernstein, Leonard 226, 352
Birigwa, Rocky 370
Black Bag, the 214, 254, 279
Black Nativity 217
Black Power 222, 269, 343. See also Civil Rights Movement
Blake, Alison 121, 125–126, 174
Blake, Martha (Marte) 52, 63, 74, 84, 92–93, 96, 107, 109, 116, 129, 146, 148, 156, 173, 204–205, 216, 226, 229, 437
Blake, Philip (Phil) 49, 51–52, 55, 59–60, 73, 76, 82, 106, 112, 114, 119, 125–126, 128, 131, 162–164, 174, 341
Blakey, Art 191, 231
Bley, Paul 173, 313
Bonneau, Jackie (Jackie Smith Bonneau) 244, 246
Boston Symphony Orchestra (BSO) 185, 341–342, 352
Boulanger, Nadia 167, 307
Bourbon, Jean-Pierre 305. See also music venues: *clubs, cafes, restaurants*: Whiskey Jazz Club
Bourne, Kay 155, 394
Bradford, Alex 173, 195, 217
Bradley's Bar. See music venues: *clubs, cafes, restaurants*
Braxton, Anthony 155, 484
Brenna, Joseph 427
Brookmeyer, Bobby 262
Browning, Ed 212
Brown, Ray 135, 186, 188
Brubeck, Dave 273–274, 514

Brubeck, Iola 274
Bushnell Towers 145, 147
Byard, Jaki 433

C

Cafe Montmartre. See music venues
Campopiano, John 247, 511, 516, 518
Capitol Theatre; 39–43, 91, 449
Carlberg, Frank 94
Carlinsky, Dan 211, 212, 215
Carmichael, Stokely 343
Carnegie Hall. See music venues: *theaters, concert halls & performance spaces*
Carter, Eliot 288
Carter, Ron 283
Carter, Sarah (Mother) 80, 90, 135–142, 146, 158, 163, 220, 255, 262, 271, 362–363, 432, 478
Case, Jim 358
Cash, Johnny 393
Cassarino, Ray 114, 131–133, 145, 153, 410, 420
Celebrity Club. See music venues: *clubs, cafes, restaurants*
Chabrol, Claude 349, 397, 444–445, 450, 451–452, 479, 506–507
Chaloff, Margaret 248, 257, 410
Chamberlain, Wilt 229
Charles, Ray 140, 191, 192, 217–218, 229, 250, 408, 430, 479, 513
Chase, Alan 257
Christou, Jani 306–307, 308
Christy, June 152
churches. See also Jefferson, I.L. (Bishop); Abyssinian Baptist Church 195, 217; Church of Christ, North Hartford 89–91, 122, 134–135, 142–144, 177, 359, 403; Sweet Daddy Grace's Church xxxi, 195, 200, 215, 217–224, 227, 250, 338, 362
Civil Rights Movement 157, 160–161, 184, 222, 343, 396. See also Black Power; See also King, Martin Luther Jr. (Rev. Dr.)
Clapp family 53–54, 93

index 623

Classical High. See universities, schools, conservatories
Clooney, Rosemary 151
Cloud, Moe 146
Club Femina. See music venues
Club St. Germain. See music venues
Cogan, Bob 339–340
Coles, Honi 270
Coley, Byron 181
Colman, Howard 365–366
Colomby, Harry 240
Colony Club. See music venues: *clubs, cafes, restaurants*
Coltrane, John 191, 226–227, 260, 294, 370, 457
Columbia Records 217, 244–245, 509
Columbia University. See universities, schools, conservatories
Colvin, Claudette 157
Connor, Chris xxxii, 79, 116–117, 145, 152, 155, 165, 186, 189, 191, 192–193, 205, 229, 243, 246, 261, 283, 349, 358, 370, 397, 415, 419–420, 430, 438–439, 478–479, 509–510, 519
Contemporary Improvisation. See universities, schools, conservatories: New England Conservatory (NEC)
Cooper, Ralph 268–269
Corea, Chick 257
Correa, Christine 355, 377
Coss, Bill 176, 180
Cotton Club. See music venues: *clubs, cafes, restaurants*
Count Basie Club. See music venues: *clubs, cafes, restaurants*
Courter, Wendy von, (Rev.Dr.) 143
Curson, Ted 229, 304

D

Daffini, Giovanna 422, 519
D'Agostino, John 294
D'Agostino, John xii, 468
Dassin, Jules 315
Davidovsky, Mario 353
Davidson, Lyle xxi, 353
Davis, Anne 342
Davis, Francis 414

Davis, Miles 264, 273, 283, 286, 294, 347
Debussy, Claude 151, 262, 456
DeCrescenzo, Francisco 276
Deerfield Academy. See universities, schools, conservatories
Delaney, Lloyd (Dr.) 215
DePalma, Brian 92, 506
DePreist, James (Jimmy) 116, 119, 173
DeSola, Wil 149, 270
Dickens, Charles 48, 61, 126, 409, 466
Diderot, Denis 289
Dimond, Edythe 213
Dixon, Bill 179
Dolle, Maxine xii, 369–371, 374
Dolphy, Eric 243, 286
Domino, Fats 149
Dorham, Kenny 237, 249
Dowd, Tom 190–191, 193, 513
DownBeat. See newspapers & magazines
Doyle, Arthur Conan 121
Drew, Kenny 237
Drew, Nancy 93–94
Ducornet, Guy xii, 171, 178
Duplan, Herns 304
Dutchess County Journal. See newspapers & magazines

E

Eade, Dominique 349, 377, 452
Edey, Mait 242, 297, 370
Elks Clubs. See music venues: *clubs, cafes, restaurants*
Ellington, Duke 118, 139, 151, 362, 385
Ellis, Don 227
Ellison, Ralph 165, 169–170, 235, 395
Ertegun, Ahmet 190–192
Ertegun family xxxii
Ertegun, Nesuhi 173, 190–192
Esperence, John 170
Evans, Bill 249, 262, 349, 419
Evans, Gil 204, 419
"Ezz-thetic" (composition) 418, 509

F

Fabris, David (Knife) xxxv, 140, 276, 427, 452, 516–517
Faire, Curtis 381, 387–388
Farmer, Art 306
Felson, Ed 237, 246
Fenlon, Andrew 80
film noir xxxii, 39–42, 44, 57–60, 72, 81, 90, 97, 142, 163, 262, 335, 403, 408, 411, 441–453, 463, 468, 478, 480, 482, 484, 485
Fisk, Kay 120
Fisk, Sandi 145, 148
Fitzgerald, Ella 147, 152, 269, 370, 417, 462
Five Spot, the. See music venues: *clubs, cafes, restaurants*
Ford, Ricky 237, 246, 377, 393, 396–397
Franklin, Aretha 140, 229, 514
Freed, Justin 451–452
Freedom Now Suite. See *We Insist Freedom Now Suite*
Freeman, Bob (president NEC) 403, 512
Freilich, Ron 377, 479–480

G

Gandhi, Mahatma 161
Garcia, Phil 298, 300
Garner, Erroll 147, 273–274
Garvey, Mary 42, 63–74, 84–86, 91–92, 126, 128, 219, 409, 432, 468
Gatto, Helen 115, 116–117, 150
Gatto Music Center 113, 115
Gautreau, Ricardo 216, 298, 316, 516, 520–521
Gershwin, George 126, 370
Getz, Stan 118, 144, 274
Gilkey, Gordon, (Rev. Dr.) 83, 87–88, 122–123, 378
Gillespie, Dizzy 145, 151, 186, 189, 249, 274
Gistelinck, Elias 302–303
Gistelinck, Lucy 302

Giuffre, Jimmy 187, 191, 249, 370, 377, 389, 514
Glover, Eunice (Sr.) 136–138, 140, 152, 163, 408
Golden Circle, Stockholm. See music venues: *clubs, cafes, restaurants*
Goodman, Benny 117, 118, 358
Gordon, Max 181, 274, 294
Gordon, Sheila 227
Grace, Anne Elvins 365–366, 368, 375, 440, 504
Greek military coup (junta) 57, 79, 93, 298–299, 307–318, 337, 343, 363, 403, 423
Grisamore, Judy 145, 147, 155
Gryce, Gigi 237
Gubanov, Yakov 256
Guggenheim, Alicia 233
Guggenheim Foundation xxxiv
Guggenheim, Harry 233
Gummere family 167–168, 172, 245, 358–360
Gummere, Lish 172, 358
Gummere, Peg 172, 358–361
Gummere, Richard (Buz) 164, 172–173, 242, 245, 357–361
Gunn, Cliff 146

H

Hadjidarkis, Manos 308
Hadjinikou, Pia 308
Half Note, the. See music venues: *clubs, cafes, restaurants*
Halloween 95–98, 452, 474, 514
Hammond, John 170, 193
Hampton, Lionel 231
Hancock, Herbie 257
Hanson, Barbara 145
Hardin, Joe 123, 138, 316
Harlem Beggars 283
Harrington, Helen 389, 395
Harris, Alonzo 80
Harris, Donald 339, 343
Harrison, Max 284
Hartley, Aaron 93, 355, 412, 419, 464, 510
Hart, Lorenz 126

Hartmann, Gardiner 446, 505–506
Hauser, Emil 359
Hawkins, Coleman 145, 185, 235, 277
Hazelton, David 181–182, 295, 303
Hazilla, Jon 237, 246
Heath, Percy 193, 249
Heiss, John 339, 343, 389
Hempel, Gunter 303
Henry, Lowell 337
Herman, Woody 131
Herrmann, Bernard 410, 444, 509
Hestnes, Adelheid Dahl 342, 370
Heublein Hotel. See music venues: *clubs, cafes, restaurants*
Hicks, Calvin 389
Hill, Andrew 313
Hill, Martha 162
Hindemith, Paul 168, 254
Hinton, William 212–213
Hitchcock, Alfred 85, 96, 97, 108, 113, 151, 170, 349, 353, 436, 444–451, 470, 478–479, 506–507
Holiday, Billie xxxiii, 176, 178, 181, 250, 272, 277, 484
Holm, Gunnar 280
Horsey, Arthur 212
Hotel Neptun. See music venues: *clubs, cafes, restaurants*
Hughes, Regina 211
Hugo, Victor 59, 409

I

Inner Sanctum 67, 69, 71, 72, 73–75, 110. See also Radio and radio serials
Islington Studio 445
Ives, Charles 151, 410, 509
Ives, George 127

J

Jackson, Mahalia 140, 151–152, 186, 189, 277, 358, 408, 430, 433, 479, 509, 519
Jackson, Maynard 361
Jackson, Milt 193, 239. See also Milt Jackson Sextet, the
Jackson, Willis 191

Jacques le Fataliste 289–291
James, Willis Lawrence 186, 249, 349, 357, 361–362, 410, 456, 514
Jarrett, Keith 257, 287
Jazz Baroness, the. See Koenigswarter, Baroness Pannonica de
jazz & music festivals; Antibes Jazz Festival 283, 285–286, 292; Bard Jazz Festival 119, 170, 173, 260, 359; Creative Arts Festival 263; Jazz Festival, Notre Dame University, IN. 178, 180, 271; Juan-les-Pins 285; Monterey Jazz Festival 180, 181, 244, 273–275, 284, 295; Newport Jazz Festival 154, 188; Notre Dame University (Jazz Festival) 178, 180, 271
Jefferson, I.L. (Bishop) 80, 90, 122, 135, 140, 143, 158, 163, 165, 255, 262, 271, 357–358, 360, 362
Jerstad, Marit 262
Jeter, Claude 140, 408
Jinxey. See music venues: *clubs, cafes, restaurants*
Joe Wells Supper Club. See Wells, Joe; See also music venues: *clubs, cafes, restaurants*
Johansson, Abbe 280
Johnson, Pete 251
Johnson, Raymond 67
Jones, Frankie 148
Jones, Quincy 191, 274
Jordan Hall. See music venues: *theaters, concert halls & performance spaces*
Jordan, Sheila 509
Joynes, Gary 377
Juan-les-Pins. See jazz & music festivals
Juilliard. See universities, schools, conservatories

K

Karella, Marina 309
Kay, Connie 193
Keepnews, Orrin 242
Kelly, Gene 126
Kelly, Grace 445

Kenton, Stan 117–118, 120–121, 151–152, 188–189, 275, 349, 419, 430, 443, 509
Kern, Jerome 126, 239
Kierkegaard, Soren xxxi, xxxii, 335, 461, 484
King Constantine 309
King, Coretta Scott 161
King, Martin Luther Jr. (Rev. Dr.) 161, 184, 343, 387, 403. See also Civil Rights Movement
King's Crown Hotel 194, 204, 211, 212, 297
Klezmer music 381, 399
Koenigswarter, Jules de (Baron) 233
Koenigswarter, Pannonica (Nica) Baroness (Jazz Baroness) 169, 226, 231–247, 252, 440, 511
Kroodsma, Donald 418

L

Labaree, Bob 229
Lacy, Steve 411
Lange, Art 242, 366
Lannoy, Florence de (Countess) 283, 285–293, 302, 426, 440, 478, 512
Lannoy, Léopold de (Count) 287–289, 302
Lee, Jeanne xxxi, xxxiii, xxxv, 57, 124, 133–135, 149, 160–161, 171, 173–181, 201, 206, 213, 216, 244, 250, 260, 269–271, 274, 276–279, 281, 287, 288, 292, 294–295, 300, 302, 305, 312, 343, 349, 358, 370, 421, 432, 435, 465, 469, 478
Leete, Doris 95–96, 148, 161, 515
Lehrfeld, Amelia 179–180, 199–209, 212, 220–223, 227, 242–243, 246, 250, 261, 269, 271, 297, 337, 343, 363, 432, 435, 438, 468
Lennie's-on-the-Turnpike. See music venues: *clubs, cafes, restaurants*
Lenox School of Jazz. See universities, schools, conservatories
Leonard, Clair 154, 165–166, 167, 358
Lesser, Larry 377

Lewis, John 145, 184–185, 188, 191, 193, 249, 259–260, 262–263, 274
Lewis, Webster 393, 395–397
Lincoln, Abbey 80, 143, 161, 187, 226, 227, 230, 235, 242, 255, 297, 370, 419–420, 465, 469, 478, 509
Lindstrom, Raymond 120–122
Lippmann, Horst 275–276
Livingstone, Larry 400, 430
Lloyd, Charles (Quartet) 303
Louis, Joe 115
Lowery, Eliza, Sr. (Sister Tee) 224
Luera, Jose Antonio 81, 306, 427
Lydian Chromatic Concept 185, 260, 265, 389
Lyons, Jimmy 180, 273

M

Mabley, Moms 269
MacArthur Award (Foundation Fellowship) xxxiv, 260, 266, 354–355, 401–402
Macklin, Norman 146–147
Mahdavi, Nahid 212, 215
Mahler, Gustav 411
Maneri, Joe 127, 297, 389
Marius, Bob 215
Marsh, Warne 366–367
Mason, Perry 110
Masuko, Taki and Akemi 374
May, Earl 250
Mayflower 48, 171
McCarthy, Albert 170
McGuire, Dorothy 39–40, 44, 140
McLean, Jackie 294–295
McNally, Owen 157
McPhatter, Clyde 191
McRae, Carmen 274
Mehegan, John 250
melisma 141
Mercouri, Melina 315
Messiaen, Olivier 170, 186, 267, 361, 393, 409–410, 418, 430, 479
Michelson, Harold 446
microtone 127, 297
Miller, Mulgrew 257
Mills, Bunny 146

index 627

Milt Jackson Sextet, the 191
Mingus, Charles 188, 191, 192, 205, 229, 256, 286, 349, 411, 423, 428, 509
Mitchell-Ruff-Harris (trio) 275
Modern Jazz Quartet (MJQ) 118, 184, 191, 193, 208, 229, 349
Monk, Barbara (Boo Boo) 208, 237, 241–242, 244, 246–247, 519
Monk, Nellie 178, 240–241, 246, 251, 512
Monk, Thelonious xxxii, 118, 143, 145, 151, 166, 168–169, 171, 191, 193, 204, 208, 211, 226–227, 229–230, 234–236, 237–247, 251, 255, 261, 278, 282, 295, 309, 358, 360, 386, 410–411, 419, 426, 430, 476, 478, 479, 484, 508, 519
Monk, T.S. 208, 241–242, 246, 247
Monterey Jazz Festival. See jazz & music festivals
Montgomery bus boycott 157, 184. See also Civil Rights Movement
Morton, Jelly Roll 255
Moshier, Carroll 171, 263, 359, 382
Mozart, Wolfgang Amadeus 249, 254, 348, 373, 515
Mulberry Street Cemetery 52–54, 58, 96–98, 123, 258, 423, 460
Mulligan, Gerry 262, 274
Murphy, Eileen 368, 371–372, 374–376, 379–380, 383, 511–512
Musicara, Nicolas 408
music venues; *clubs, cafes, restaurants*; Adajian Armenian Restaurant 132, 145; Amalfi Cafe 341, 395; Birdland 117–119, 231, 261, 419, 509; Bradley's Bar 245; Cafe Montmartre 283; Celebrity Club 225; Club Femina 283; Club St. Germain 279; Colony Club 84, 468; Cotton Club 145, 385; Count Basie Jazz Club 118, 194, 218, 227–228, 269; Elks Clubs 117, 134, 142, 144, 146–149, 158, 160; Five Spot, the 118, 179, 194, 204, 211, 225–228, 231, 240; Golden Circle, Stockholm 181, 281–283, 293, 303; Half Note, the 179, 205, 229;

Heublein Hotel 145–146, 147; Hotel Neptun 280–282, 470; Jazz Gallery 161, 204–205, 213–214, 227, 229–232, 235–236, 240, 243, 255, 271; Jinxey 88, 117–118, 148; Joe Wells Supper Club 194, 214, 218, 227–229, 250, 281, 469; Lennie's-on-the-Turnpike 246; Pol's Club 306; Scullers Jazz Club 247; Slug's Saloon 179; Smalls' Paradise 205, 229; Village Vanguard 179, 181, 194, 205, 227, 229–230, 274, 277, 294, 415; Whiskey Jazz Club 305, 312
; *theaters, concert halls & performance spaces*; Apollo Theater xxxii, 149, 180, 194–195, 200, 211, 216–219, 227, 229–230, 244, 250, 268–274, 280; Ran and Jeanne xxxii, 149, 180, 244, 269–274, 280; Carnegie Hall 191, 194, 213, 227, 231, 245; Jordan Hall 123, 136, 142, 262, 265–266, 316, 340, 351, 387–388, 394, 395, 400, 403, 427, 429, 437–438, 451, 515; Music Barn 185; Music Inn 184, 189, 249; Potting Shed 185, 187; Tanglewood 185–186, 187, 352–353; Wheatleigh 184, 187–188, 259

N

NAACP 178
Netsky, Hankus 377, 381, 400, 438
New England Conservatory (NEC). See universities, schools, conservatories
Newest Sound Around, The xxxiii, 57, 179–181, 214, 244, 271, 273
Newport Jazz Festival. See jazz & music festivals
newspapers & magazines; Bay State Banner 154, 394; DownBeat 176, 180, 274, 282, 366; Dutchess County Journal 150, 154, 359; Thompsonville Press 152, 153–154
Nichols, Herbie 419
Nola Studios 242
Nordoff, Paul 172, 359
Noriega, Ann 213, 301

Notre Dame University (Jazz Festival). See jazz & music festivals
Novak, Kim 180, 362, 434, 449, 480
Nurse, Kay (Kathleen) 389, 391–392, 392, 394

O

O'Day, Anita 252
Odell, Wilma Srob 215–217, 223
Oscar Peterson Trio, the 186. See also Peterson, Oscar

P

Papadopoulos (Colonel) 310. See also Greek Coup
Papandreou, Andreas 307. See also Greek Coup
Parker, Charlie 51, 87, 151, 231, 234, 386, 509
Parks, Rosa 157, 184. See also Civil Rights Movement
Pass, Joe 417
Paudras, Francis 304
Pearl Harbor 76
Peaslee, Sandi 143, 382
penitentiaries & prisons; Alderson Prison 393; Walpole Prison 394
Person, Houston 119, 146, 148
Peterson, Oscar 135, 154, 188–189, 193, 249, 349, 359–360
Phillips, Harvey 339, 343
PIA agency 308
Piaf, Edith 433
Piston, Walter 167
Platters, the 193
Plumez, Jean 403
Poe, Edgar Allan 94, 121, 410, 420
Poitier, Sidney 230, 235–236
Pol's Club. See music venues: *clubs, cafes, restaurants*
Pomeroy, Herb 256
Porter, Cole 126, 370, 377
Porter, Hugh 205, 250
Potting Shed. See music venues: *theaters, concert halls & performance spaces*

Powell, Adam Clayton 217
Powell, Adam Clayton (Blvd) 218, 227
Powell, Bud 251, 286, 304
Powell, Edith 89, 135–138, 140, 163, 216, 408
Powell family, the 90, 134–139, 140
Powell, Hubert 89, 134–137, 140, 150, 262, 271, 360, 378, 400, 403
Powell, LaVerne 250
Powers, Alison (Blake) 49
Powers family 48, 50, 54, 84, 92, 96, 99, 432
Powers, Frances 54, 73, 162, 163
Powers, Jerry 53–54
Powers, Jessie (grandmother, née Arnold) 40, 44, 49, 53–54, 54–56, 60–61, 93, 97, 100–101, 103, 103–104, 128, 170, 296, 344, 363, 366–367, 442, 483, 485
Powers, Lewis J. (great grandfather) 47, 61
Powers Paper Company 48, 52–53
Powers, P.C. (grandfather) 48, 48–50, 49–50, 53–54, 54–58, 84, 99–102, 103–104, 128, 468, 507
Prokofiev, Sergei 131, 443
Prouty, Olive Higgins 68
Prutting, George 276
Pryor, (Rev.) 122, 135
Pullig, Ken 256
Pussiau, Jean-Jacques 313

R

Radio and radio serials xxxiv, 54, 57, 64, 67–78, 82, 92, 105–110, 128, 153, 161, 202, 239, 243, 261, 269, 276, 283–284, 291, 302, 380, 385, 400
Ramirez, Ram 272
Ravel, Maurice 249, 260
Redd, Freddie 237
Redding, Otis 309
reggae 80
Roach, Max 161, 186–188, 204, 226, 230, 235, 242, 249, 255–256, 465
Robinson, Jackie 115

Rodgers, Ginger 126
Rodgers, Richard 126
Rollins, Sonny 273, 295
Roosevelt, Eleanor 154, 157–159, 236
Roosevelt, Franklin 51
Rose, Cevira 215
Rosoff, Sophia 462
Rothschild family 169, 232, 236
"Round Midnight" 234, 243
Rouse, Charlie 231, 234
Row, Peter 257, 370
Russell, Alice 266, 383, 390, 438
Russell, George 56, 136, 173, 179, 185–186, 202, 206–207, 221, 224, 227, 243–244, 249, 259–267, 271, 283, 303, 335, 370, 377, 389, 418, 420, 424, 435, 438–439, 509. See also Lydian Chromatic Concept
Russo, William (Bill) 121, 186, 189, 205, 227, 249, 252–254, 260, 349, 419, 443, 509, 514

S

Samuelson, Kjell (Dr.) 281, 283, 303
Sandvik, Scott 142
Satie, Eric 171
Schoenholt, Robert 295
Schuller family 227, 350–352
Schuller, Gunther xxxii, xxxiv, 80, 121, 136, 173, 184, 186, 189–190, 193–196, 205, 208, 214, 227–228, 245, 249, 254, 260, 262–263, 274, 294, 296, 302, 309, 313, 316, 335, 336–357, 371, 384, 385–389, 392, 395, 397, 398, 402–403, 411, 415, 419, 420, 426, 430, 432–433, 440, 456, 459, 479, 483–484, 507–510, 514
Schuller, Marjorie 123, 227, 245, 350
Schultz, Jerry 294–295
Schwartz, Steve xxxiv, xxxv, 450
Scott, Ronnie 284
Scott, Shirley 229
Scott, Tony 173
Scullers Jazz Club. See music venues: *clubs, cafes, restaurants*
Scythian Suite 131, 443

Segregation 157, 169, 386–387. See also Civil Rights Movement
Serpa, Sara 420, 452
Sexton, Andy 338
Seynes, Henri de 171, 304, 359
Shepp, Archie 302
Sherman, Russell 339, 343, 388–389, 589
Shostakovich, Dmitri 256, 479, 509
Silberman, Greg 377
Silver, Horace 144, 146, 231, 237, 423
Simon, Clea 452, 463
Siodmak, Robert 39, 408, 442. See also *Spiral Staircase, The* (*Spiral*)
Sister Tee 195, 219–224, 227, 469
Skippy (Nellie Monk's sister) 178, 244
Slug's Saloon. See music venues
Smalls, Ed 229
Small's Paradise. See music venues: *clubs, cafes, restaurants*
Smith, Bessie 193, 277
Smith, Betty 436
Smith, Bill 276
Smith, Jimmy 229
Smith, Michael 313
Smith, Wilbur 211, 213–215, 297–299, 520–521
Smith, Willie "the Lion" 192
SNCC 343
Sola, Wil de 149, 270
Spiral Staircase, The (*Spiral*) xxxi, xxxii, 39–46, 52, 58, 61, 88–95, 103, 113, 128–129, 140–141, 188, 214, 258, 335, 403, 408, 423, 442–443, 461, 465–466, 483, 485, 506
Springfield Armory 46, 83
S.S. Pierce and Co. 153
Stearns, Marshall 184, 186
Steinbeck, John 420
Stewart, James 180, 449, 480
Stewart, Princess 217
Stockhausen, Karlheinz 312
Stonecipher, Keith 298
Stoneman, Lloyd 130–131
Straight Ahead (album) 242

"Straight Ahead" (composition) 255, 509
Strange, Don 306
Stravinsky, Igor 151, 262, 348, 443
Strayhorn, Billy 267, 281
student protest movement, the 210. See also Civil Rights Movement
Suffield Academy. See universities, schools, conservatories
Sunapee 77, 98–105, 108
Sun Ra 312
Sweet Daddy Grace's church. See churches

T

Tanglewood. See music venues: *theaters, concert halls & performance spaces*
Tate, Buddy 225
Tatum, Art 177
Taubman, Dorothy 462
Taylor, Billy 250
Taylor, Cecil 249, 295, 302, 307, 464
Teagarden, Jack 423
television 109–111, 139, 184, 274, 276, 283, 306, 381, 416, 456, 472
Termini, Iggy 225
Termini, Joe 204, 227
Terminis, the 226–227, 240
Theodorakis 308
Thigpen, Ed 250
Third Stream 292, 398–403
Thomas, Alphonzo (Br.) 515
Thompsonville 106, 108, 112, 113, 121, 150, 152
Thompsonville Press. See newspapers & magazines
Tierney, Gene 439, 480, 506
Till, Emmett 169. See also Civil Rights Movement
Tinsley, Fred 146
Tristano, Lennie 186, 193, 479
tritone 168, 244, 475
Truffaut, François 444–446, 450, 506–507
Tunick, Jonathan 173, 178
Turner, Joe 251

Twilight Zone 110. See also television
Twin Peaks 81, 110. See also television

U

Ulanov, Barry 359
universities, schools, conservatories;
Bard College 110, 119, 155, 157, 159, 162–177, 191, 203, 225, 234, 240, 254, 347, 357–360, 409–410, 449, 513; Bard Jazz Lab 172; Brandeis University 397. See also jazz & music festivals: Creative Arts Festival; Classical High 56, 77, 111–112, 113–114, 123; Columbia University 50, 164, 194, 200, 204, 210, 210–211, 215–216, 227, 243, 261, 269, 294, 353, 355; Deerfield Academy 50, 53, 60; Juilliard 162, 163, 201, 218, 250, 262, 475; Lenox School of Jazz xxxi, 133, 173–174, 178, 181–190, 199, 206, 211–212, 215, 226, 248–249, 251, 256, 259–260, 346–347, 359, 361, 514; New England Conservatory (NEC) xxxiii, xxxv, 44, 57, 81, 133, 179, 245, 246, 257, 263–266, 297–298, 313, 316, 338–339, 341, 343, 345, 350, 353, 355, 365, 376, 381, 385–391, 396, 400–403, 415, 418, 430, 444, 447, 450, 462, 512, 513; Contemporary Improvisation xxxiii, 143, 403, 451, 455; Suffield Academy 114–117, 120–122, 140, 148, 152, 163
Ussachevsky, Vladimir 353

V

Val-kill 158–159
"Vanguard" (composition) 187, 275
Vaughan, Sarah 269, 283, 286, 420, 438
Vertigo (film) 170, 444, 447–449, 452
Vietnam War, the 215, 343–344
Village Vanguard. See music venues: *clubs, cafes, restaurants*
Votichenko, Sasha 213
"Vradiazei" 308–309, 363

W

Waddy, Ruth 301
Waldron, Mal 205, 252, 254, 255, 410
Wallace, Dorothy 51, 56, 79, 93, 138, 142, 265, 344–345, 352, 360, 362–386, 387–388, 392–397, 402, 416, 426, 429–430, 432, 437–438, 440, 461, 469, 478–480, 483, 490, 504, 507–508, 511–513, 517
Wallace, Janet 126, 129–131
Walpole Prison. See penitentiaries & prisons
Walsh family 167, 358
Walsh, Kip 171–172
Ware, Wilbur 226
Washington, Ernestine (Sr.) 223
Watson, Janice 170
Webb, Roy 408, 471
Webern, Anton 410
We Insist Freedom Now Suite 161, 230, 235
Welhaven, Arne (Dr.) 280
Welles, Orson 411
Wells, Joe 228–229. See also Joe Wells Supper Club
Wende (album) 186, 313, 361
Werner, Kenny 257
Wertheimstein, Rózsika Edle von (Baroness) 232–233
Weston, Randy 187
Wexler, Jerry 190–191, 192, 513
Wheatleigh. See music venues: *theaters, concert halls & performance spaces*
Whiskey Jazz Club. See music venues: *clubs, cafes, restaurants*
White, Leila 227
Whiteside, Abby 462
Williams, Chester 339, 342
Williams, Joe 118
Williams, Marion 140, 287, 408
Williams, Martin 173, 255, 282, 293–294
Williams, Mary Lou 205, 214, 227, 234–235, 250–254, 349, 410, 416, 430, 435
Williams, Tennessee 213
Williams, Tony 283
Wilson, Ernie 144, 146–147
Wilson, Nathanial 89, 135, 137
Wilson, Shadow 226
Wilson, Teddy 145, 231, 233–234
Winsor, Kathleen 70
Witkowers 145, 155, 239
Wolff, Kate 165–167, 358, 410
Wolff, Werner 165, 166
Wonder, Stevie 462
Woolworths, Greensboro 161. See also Civil Rights Movement
Wright, Eugene 514
Wright, Frank Lloyd 374
Wulp, Jon 316, 339, 341, 371

Y

Young, Eddie 117, 148
Young, Lester 255

www.ingramcontent.com/pod-product-compliance
Lightning Source LLC
Chambersburg PA
CBHW071950290426
44109CB00018B/1979